The Structure of Schooling

THE STRUCTURE OF SCHOOLING
Readings in the Sociology of Education

Richard Arum
Irenee R. Beattie
University of Arizona

Mayfield Publishing Company
Mountain View, California
London • Toronto

Library of Congress Cataloging-in-Publication Data

The structure of schooling : readings in the sociology of education / [compiled by] Richard Arum and Irenee R. Beattie.
    p. cm.

       Includes bibliographical references.
       ISBN 0-7674-1070-X
       1. Educational sociology.   2. Education—Social aspects.
       I. Arum, Richard.   II. Beattie, Irenee R.
       LC189.S87 1999
       306.43—dc21   99-24017
                                            CIP

Manufactured in the United States of America

10   9   8   7   6   5   4   3   2   1

Mayfield Publishing Company
1280 Villa Street
Mountain View, California 94041

Sponsoring editor, Serina Beauparlant; production, Michael Bass & Associates; manuscript editor, Helen Walden; design manager, Susan Breitbard; text and cover designer, Linda M. Robertson; manufacturing manager, Randy Hurst. The text was set in 10/12 Book Antiqua by G&S Typesetters, Inc., and printed on 45# Highland Plus by Malloy Lithographing, Inc.

Cover image: Jacob Lawrence, *The Library*, 1960. National Museum of American Art, Washington, D.C./Art Resource, NY.

Contents

PART VI: THE ORGANIZATIONAL ENVIRONMENT   435

Preface

Our interest in preparing a reader in the sociology of education is a result of our frustration with the lack of resources available to teach this material either at the undergraduate level or as an introductory graduate-level course in a teacher preparation program. Although several readers have previously been published on education and society, these are either now dated—and fail to reflect recent trends in research—or were designed with other target audiences in mind.

We have selected writings that illustrate the fundamental ideas and insights developed by past and current academic research in this area. In the past decade, sociological research on schools has attempted to refocus attention on the discipline's earlier interest in identifying the relationship between schools and communities. This research has progressed in several directions: (1) advances in understanding the significance of the school community—for example, the development and application of the concept of social capital; (2) renewed attention to the effects of racial segregation and resource inequality on student outcomes; (3) a redefinition of what constitutes a school community with particular attention paid to the institutional, as opposed to demographic, characteristics of the environment; and (4) a broadened investigation of both relevant school-level practices and significant individual-level outcomes associated with variation in schooling.

This reader differs from others because we have consciously chosen material that is both accessible and engaging. Rather than relying excessively on the reproduction of articles published in the discipline's top research journals (e.g., *Sociology of Education,* *American Sociological Review,* and *American Journal of Sociology*), we have worked to incorporate more accessible readings—largely free of regression coefficients—but reflective of general mainstream sociological concerns. We thus have purposely avoided a heavy reliance on academic journal articles, which often are written for other researchers rather than for classroom audiences. When possible, we also have included contributions from prominent authors in the field. In choice of subject matter, we have followed a broad, inclusive strategy. Instead of focusing narrowly on only educational achievement outcomes, we present research on a larger set of topics as reflected in the organizational structure of the book.

Acknowledgments

In preparing this book, we are grateful for the assistance of many individuals and institutions. First and foremost, we would like to thank Mayfield Senior Editor Serina Beauparlant for advice, assistance, and guidance in defining the scope and scale of this enterprise. The final realized product would not have been possible without her many useful suggestions. For technical assistance in the production and promotion of the work, we would like to thank Mayfield's April Wells-Hayes, Mary Johnson, Jay Bauer, Susan Breitbard, Brian Pecko, and Jeanne Schreiber. We are also grateful for the critical technical skills provided by Michael Bass, Tobi Giannone, Helen Walden, and Corinne Elworth. In addition, Richard Arum would like to acknowledge the National Academy of Education Spencer Postdoctoral Fellowship Program for providing financial support during the time this book was undertaken and completed.

The book also benefited from the useful suggestions of many colleagues around the country. In particular, we would like to thank the following individuals who devoted time and energy to the task of providing constructive feedback on the project: Amee Adkins, Illinois State University; Robert Fiala, University of New Mexico; Adam Gamoran, University of Wisconsin, Madison; Harriet Hartman, Rowan University; Annette Lareau, Temple University; Chandra Muller, University of Texas at Austin; Yvonne D. Newsome, Agnes Scott College; William Vélez, University of Wisconsin, Milwaukee; and Mary Lou Wylie, James Madison University.

INTRODUCTION
The Structure of Schooling

*At present, concentration of industry and
division of labor have practically eliminated
household and neighborhood occupations—
at least for educational purposes. But it is
useless to bemoan the departure of the good
old days of children's modesty, reverence,
and implicit obedience, if we expect merely
by bemoaning and by exhortation to bring
them back. It is radical conditions which
have changed, and only an equally radical
change in education suffices.*

—JOHN DEWEY[1]

At the turn of the nineteenth century, proponents of educational reform, such as John
Dewey, recognized the social nature of the
significant challenge facing U.S. schools. As
economic production shifted to points far
distant from local farms, shops, and homes,
families no longer were capable of training
and socializing their children for productive roles in society. Once children could not
implicitly learn adult roles through daily
involvement in family economic activities,
"the good old days of children's modesty,
reverence, and implicit obedience" were
forever lost. Schools were established to
assume pedagogical tasks that were formerly carried out by families. With the si-
multaneous advancement of technology and
employment outside the home, parents no
longer had the time or the knowledge necessary to educate their children.

A century later, one can recognize both
how schools have changed to meet the needs
of society and how societal transformations
continue to shift responsibilities from families to schools. When Dewey wrote, only
about 10 percent of individuals age 14 to 17
attended high school. Today, virtually all

children growing up in the United States enter high school and only about 10 percent of
these individuals actually fail to complete
their high school education. In addition, the
length of the school year has dramatically
expanded: elementary and secondary public
schools today are in session for almost twice
as many days per year than at the turn of the
century. Postsecondary education also has
greatly expanded: even in the 1940s, less
than 10 percent of individuals attained a
bachelor's degree; by the end of the century,
almost one-third of young adults were expected to obtain such credentials (*Digest of
Educational Statistics* 1995). Social scientists
have referred to this tremendous growth in
the role of formal education as an *Educational Revolution.*

Recent changes in family structure and
labor force participation will likely continue
or accelerate the trend of schools taking increased responsibility in shaping the lives of
youth. As the twentieth century began, the
employment of men outside the home was
perceived as underlying an erosion of the
family's ability to socialize children. Today,
however, concern often focuses on how children are affected by the decline in number
of two-parent families and the increasing
labor force participation of mothers (see
e.g., Hochschild 1997, McLanahan and Sandefur 1994). Although patriarchal assumptions can underlie how these socioeconomic
changes are understood and addressed, the
role of formal schooling in society will likely
expand even further.

As schools in the twentieth century have
become increasingly central to society, sociologists have directed continuous, concerted
effort toward understanding both their

structure and their effects on individuals. Throughout the twentieth century, sociologists who developed the theoretical framework for the discipline as a whole (e.g., Emile Durkheim, Max Weber, Talcott Parsons, Pierre Bourdieu, James Coleman, and John Meyer) also directly focused and wrote on the role of education in society. Because schools were complex institutions, sociological theorizing was multidimensional and multilayered.

Sociology of education as a field developed two separate levels of analysis. At a macro-level, sociologists worked to identify how various social forces (such as politics, economics, and culture) created variation in schools as organizations. At a more micro-level, researchers sought to identify how variation in school practices led to differences in individual-level student outcomes. In addition to these distinct levels of analysis, researchers further developed separate focuses on various aspects of the functioning of education in society. Some researchers concentrated on economic aspects of education (e.g., how economic forces shaped school practices and how schools determined individual productivity and earnings), while others examined related issues of socialization, allocation, and legitimation. When approaching research in the sociology of education, it is useful to keep these distinctions in mind.

The organizational structure of this reader reflects the multidimensional, multilayered analysis that characterizes the sociology of education field as a whole. We begin by providing selections of major contributions that trace the theoretical development of the sociology of education. We then include work that identifies how stratification of schooling creates inequality in access to education within schools, between schools, and by ascriptive characteristics (such as class, race, and gender). We provide research that demonstrates how schools are settings for the formation of adolescent sub-

cultures and peer relations that often promote outcomes at odds with social conformity and school achievement. We highlight how schools affect a range of life-course outcomes: not only cognitive attainment but also adolescent behavior, delinquency, and adult labor market success. In addition, we show how schools are affected not only by neighborhood context but also by their organizational environment (e.g., the influence of private-school competition, unionization, professionalization, and the politics of school reform).

Theoretical and Historical Perspectives

The reader starts with a section presenting theoretical and historical perspectives on education. We begin with readings highlighting the development of a status attainment perspective with the explicit intent of emphasizing this approach. As a paradigm, status attainment has been extraordinarily influential in shaping recent sociological research on the structure of education.

Status Attainment and Social Mobility

Status attainment has its roots in Weber's conceptualization of status groups, which are formed on the basis of various distinctions such as occupation, class, and ethnicity. Weber argued that the education system had a dual character in modern societies: it could be used to increase meritocratic selection of individuals for privileged occupations, but also could be used as a closure strategy to maintain a status group's monopoly over scarce resources. Building on Weber's work, Pitirim Sorokin suggested that schools played a fundamental role in society. They did not simply train individuals for employment, but more importantly they worked to "sort, sieve, and select" those persons who would be granted access to more desirable occupations. To the extent that its schools facilitated the movement of talented individuals from lower social origins to privileged occupations, a society was considered "open" rather than "closed." When individuals from disadvantaged socioeconomic backgrounds attained privileged occupational positions with associated higher social rewards (such as status, prestige, and income), social mobility occurred. Both Weber and Sorokin understood that schools played a critical role in either blocking or facilitating social mobility.

In subsequent years, sociologists often applied Weber's and Sorokin's ideas by comparing how societies differed in their rates of social mobility. Researchers such as Ralph Turner used cross-national comparisons to explore the possibility that developed capitalist countries had differences in their educational system leading to variation in social mobility. In spite of much research, these scholars found only small differences in rates of social mobility among developed capitalist countries. In the context of these findings, Peter Blau and Otis Dudley Duncan began a body of work that would change the focus of social mobility research. Sociologists began to explore the determinants or causes of social mobility, rather than simply quantifying rates of mobility.

Blau and Duncan's work statistically confirmed Weber's and Sorokin's theoretical propositions about the role of education in society. Blau and Duncan's research clearly established the central, critical role education played in individual occupational attainment. In modern society, the occupations that individuals held as adults were primarily determined by how far they had gone in school. Blau and Duncan also established, however, that social origins remained critical in facilitating or hindering an individual's educational achievement,

and therefore influenced occupational attainment. Schools thus worked to reproduce the structure of social inequality: children from affluent families tended to do better than children from poor families in terms of educational achievement. However, schools also allowed vertical social mobility by "sorting and sieving," thus facilitating higher-than-average attainments for individuals from lower-status groups who showed merit and ability in school performance. If individuals from socioeconomically disadvantaged groups did well in school, social mobility and occupational rewards would follow, although the educational deck was stacked against them. Following Blau and Duncan's research, sociologists quickly identified factors other than social origins that influenced an individual's educational attainment. Individual expectations and aspirations, as well as the influence of significant others (e.g., parents, teachers, and peers), were demonstrated to affect an individual's educational achievement.

Human, Cultural, and Social Capital

Although the status attainment paradigm has been extraordinarily influential in the sociology of education, the approach is not the only source for the development of concepts applied to the study of education. Contemporary research on schooling has also been strongly influenced by thinking about educational processes in terms of human, cultural, and social capital.

Economists in the early 1960s developed the concept of *human capital*. Theodore Schultz, Gary Becker, and others argued that one could invest in the human capital of individuals, just as one invested financial capital in a company. Individuals invested in a business because they expected their investments to yield dividends or returns. Economists maintained that one made similar sets of investments in individuals. The acquisition of education led individuals to increase their knowledge and skills; greater knowledge and skills led to increased labor productivity, which was subsequently rewarded by employers. Individuals who pursued further education incurred significant costs (in terms of tuition and foregone earnings), but they would later more than recoup their investment. Becker demonstrated through a series of calculations that, during the time he was writing, returns to investing in high school education were approximately 28 percent and returns to investment in college education were around 15 percent. People were choosing to invest increasingly more in education because the returns were quite large and considerably greater than those expected from an alternative traditional financial investment. The human capital approach was used to explain the rationale behind why individuals and governments were willing to invest increasing resources in education.

Many sociologists have adopted the concept of human capital to understand how education improves an individual's labor market experiences. In the 1970s and 1980s, however, sociologists supplemented the notion of human capital by developing two related concepts that are distinctly sociological: cultural capital and social capital.

Pierre Bourdieu in the early 1970s began elaborating the concept of *cultural capital*. Bourdieu believed that individuals in society were stratified in such a way that they possessed different levels and types of cultural capital. Individuals from privileged classes were trained from birth to possess cultural dispositions, attitudes, and styles that set them apart from ordinary members of society. Privileged members of society made cultural distinctions that other members of society accepted. These distinctions defined elite forms of culture as being superior and other forms of culture as being less

worthy. Individuals who were raised to appreciate upper-class cultural forms such as opera, classical music, and "good manners" possessed greater cultural capital. Bourdieu argued that individuals whose behavior reflected greater accumulations of cultural capital were rewarded by both school personnel and employers, who coded these individuals as being more worthy and deserving. Differences in cultural capital thus led to inequality in educational achievement and related occupational attainment.

In the early 1980s, James Coleman developed the concept of *social capital*. Coleman believed that a focus on human and cultural capital obscured the fact that one of the greatest resources individuals have is their social relationships. Coleman elaborated a concept of social capital to articulate the differences in the character of social relationships that individuals possessed. Although there are many relevant dimensions of social relationships that affect individuals (for example, the frequency, duration, and character of social interactions), Coleman concentrated on one key aspect of social relationships in his work on education: intergenerational closure. According to Coleman, communities around schools varied by the extent to which the parents of children were in contact with youth and with each other. Communities had greater closure when adults in the community had social relationships that allowed them to develop shared norms and values, to monitor children's behavior, and to enforce proper sets of behavior. When communities around schools did not have intergenerational closure, student behavior was less successfully aligned with adult goals.

Alternative Theoretical Approaches

Many of the concepts underlying contemporary research on education are encompassed in status attainment research and the trinity of human, cultural, and social capitals. However, the theoretical insights from these areas are still an incomplete, theoretical tool-kit for the analysis of education.

Emile Durkheim, for example, provides essential theoretical insights on the structure of education that are not reflected either in status attainment research or in the concepts of human, cultural, and social capital. Durkheim, like Weber, is a theorist who laid the groundwork for modern sociology. Unlike Weber, however, Durkheim focused much greater attention on noneconomic aspects of education. For Durkheim, the key function of the education system was to socialize and integrate individuals into a larger society. According to Durkheim, humans confronted society as an entity "superior to themselves, and upon whom they depend."[2] Schools functioned as one of the most critical socializing instruments of society in fulfilling their task of impressing upon youth an understanding that social institutions possessed unquestionable moral authority and that individual satisfaction was possible only when one willingly submitted to their rule. Schools worked to integrate individuals in society by encouraging students to define their own individual will and interests in terms of the larger needs and interests of society—that is, to internalize external social goals. During the middle of the century, Talcott Parsons (1959) further developed Durkheim's functionalist explanation for the role of education and society.

An alternative functionalist account for the structure of education emerged in the early 1970s. Although they shared a similar logic to Durkheim's earlier work, these theorists adopted a more critical neo-Marxist perspective. Samuel Bowles, Herbert Gintis, Randall Collins, and others argued that schools functioned to integrate individuals into an unjust capitalist society; because society was inequitable, the school's role in socializing individuals to accept their place in the social structure was unjust. Bowles and Gintis advanced a *social reproduction* theory: schools worked to integrate individuals into an inequitable system while simultaneously legitimizing that inequality. Similarly, Randall Collins believed that schools produced social inequality not only by providing individuals with unequal access to skills and training, but also by providing credentials and certificates, which were rewarded in the labor market. In recent decades, writers such as Stanley Aronowitz and Henry Giroux (1985) have further elaborated this critical neo-Marxist view of education.

Other theoretical perspectives, which have developed outside of educational research, have been subsequently imported and applied to the study of schooling. Educational researchers, for example, have applied concepts derived from theoretical approaches as diverse as symbolic interactionism, deconstructionism, and feminism. We have included research based on some of these approaches—see, for example, readings by Mary Metz, John Devine, and Barrie Thorne—but space limitations prevent full discussion and presentation of these alternative theoretical paradigms in our reader.

Our book does, however, examine one additional theoretical perspective: *neo-institutionalism*. Beginning with the work of John Meyer in the late 1970s, researchers increasingly focused attention on institutional factors affecting the structure of schooling. Meyer maintained that schools faced institutional pressures that structured educational practices. The organizational environment around schools provided a context that led schools to accept institutional norms, values, and practices as taken-for-granted assumptions. Institutional isomorphism led schools in a common organizational environment to adopt similar sets of organizational practices that often had little to do with meeting the educational needs of students.

Stratification within and between Schools

The theoretical approaches previously identified have informed research designed to explicate the structure of stratification within and between schools. Sociologists argue that the education system is *stratified* in the sense that student assignment to different schools and different classrooms determines the character and the quality of education that students receive. Implicit in the concept of stratification within and between schools is the notion of inequality—that is, Weber's insight that status groups use schools to gain privileged access to scarce resources.

One fundamental way that schools are stratified in the United States is by sector. Some students come from families and communities that provide opportunities to enroll in private schools. Today, approximately 10 percent of elementary and secondary students attend private schools. In the past, Catholic schools dominated this private school market; in more recent years, as many Catholics became more affluent and moved to the suburbs, the role of Catholic schools has declined. The influence of Catholic schools has been replaced by that of fundamentalist private schools located in the South. As courts forced Southern public schools to racially integrate, private fundamentalist schools became an increasingly attractive haven for white flight. From a sociological perspective, it is worth emphasizing that students attending private schools are exposed to different educational experiences. Private schools can often provide greater educational resources (Cookson and Persell reading 13), alternative curriculum emphasis and instructional strategies (Bryk, Lee, and Holland reading 14), and more effective disciplinary climates. Private schools have fewer disciplinary problems than public schools, not only because they tend to have

greater social capital (Coleman and Hoffer reading 7), but more importantly because they have a greater ability than public schools to expel (or threaten to remove) disruptive students without the threat of legal challenge.

U.S. schools are also profoundly stratified in terms of race and social class. More than four decades after *Brown v. Board of Education,* many African American students still attend schools with few, if any, white students (Orfield reading 18). In the Northeast and Midwest, close to half of African American students attend schools where more than 90 percent of their fellow students are nonwhite. In many of America's largest cities, segregation of nonwhite students is even more pronounced. In New York City, for example, 74 percent of African Americans and 68 percent of Hispanic students attend schools that are more than 90 percent nonwhite; in Los Angeles, 70 percent of African Americans and 69 percent of Hispanics currently attend such profoundly racially segregated schools (Orfield and Monfort 1988). Racial segregation of schools is related to inequality in access to academically oriented peer climates (Coleman et al. reading 15), school environments characterized by productive parental involvement (Lareau reading 26), and governmental provision of adequate educational financing (Kozol reading 17). Variation in schools along these dimensions creates increased obstacles to educational achievement for individuals whose early educational experiences are in settings that are less conducive to learning.

Sociologists of education, however, argue that stratification not only exists between schools, but also that inequality is structured by stratification of students into different curricular tracks within schools. This educational practice, known as *tracking,* can have effects on student educational outcomes that are greater than the differences produced by inequality between schools. Students in the same school often have very different life trajectories because of exposure to a college preparatory, general, or vocational curriculum. Students placed in academic tracks take honors classes and other advanced coursework, have higher rates of growth in standardized test performance, and are subsequently more likely to attend and succeed in college. Students taking vocational coursework in high school, although less likely to attend college, are more likely to have positive early labor market experiences. Unfortunately, in U.S. high schools, many students are exposed to neither college preparatory nor vocational coursework. Instead, students often take a general curriculum, which fails to prepare them for success in either college or the labor force.

Class, Race, and Gender

Because of the variation in backgrounds that students bring to classrooms, schools often serve to reproduce preexisting social inequality. In addition, because of variation between schools, tracking within schools, and differences within classrooms, schools also can serve to generate or increase inequality in society. To identify the role of schools in either reproducing or deepening social inequality, sociologists often have examined the trajectories of categorically defined groups of individuals. Class, race, and gender—because of their salience in affecting life-course outcomes—often have been the focus of attention.

Status attainment research has demonstrated that talented and motivated individuals within socially disadvantaged groups can use schools to achieve upward social mobility. Schools work to promote limited meritocratic selection of individuals within groups. However, status attainment research also demonstrates that schools reproduce and intensify the consequences of socially

disadvantaged group membership. This distinction is essential in understanding how schools affect social inequality. In modern societies, individuals from disadvantaged backgrounds can use schools as vehicles for upward social mobility. Disadvantaged groups as a whole, however, face increased barriers and obstacles in their efforts to obtain success in school.

The effects of social class background on educational achievement have long been a focus of sociological concern. Sociologists have identified persistent patterns of the effects of social class on educational achievement: in virtually all developed capitalist societies, with but a few social-democratic exceptions, disadvantaged social class background remains a significant obstacle to educational attainment (Blossfeld and Shavit reading 23). Researchers such as Paul Willis, Jay Macleod, and Annette Lareau have documented the pervasive effects of class background on a wide range of student and school experiences. Class background not only limits the resources individuals have available to pursue continued education but also affects how students and parents interact with school personnel and how individuals articulate, communicate, and produce understandings about the role of schools in their lives.

Racial differences are also associated with variation in educational achievement. Although some researchers have advanced genetic and cultural explanations for these differences (e.g., Herrnstein and Murray 1994, Fordham and Ogbu reading 27), empirical sociological research has largely discredited these approaches. Genetic and cultural explanations for racial differences in educational achievement are clearly fallacious in that they fail to account for the historic pattern of racial differences in educational attainment. Structural factors such as racial segregation of schools, resource inequality, and social class background provide more credible explanation for racial differences in educational attainment. For example, although African Americans as a whole continue to score lower than whites on standardized tests and have lower rates of college and graduate degree attainment, these gaps are closing. Today, in spite of significant disadvantages in class background, African Americans are almost as likely as whites to finish high school. In addition, African American students have higher educational aspirations than white students. These findings suggest that African Americans often do better than expected—not worse, as many cultural and genetic theorists predict—on many educational indicators. Asian American students also outperform white students on many measures of educational achievement. Hispanic and American Indian students, however, continue to have significantly low rates of educational attainment. Hispanics, who often face language barriers in U.S. schools, are almost three times more likely than whites to drop out of high school.

Gender has also structured patterns of historic differences in individual experiences within the educational system (Tyack and Hansot reading 12). Male students tend to receive greater attention from their teachers than do female students; this attention takes the form of both increased praise and sanction. Boys are more often scolded and labeled bad, but they are also more often praised and evaluated as brilliant. These social–psychological dynamics, in addition to structural factors such as gender differences in labor market opportunities, underlie variation in the pattern of male and female educational achievement. On average, contemporary U.S. women have slightly higher levels of educational achievement than men: they are more likely to finish high school and complete college (Mickelson reading 30). Men, however, are more highly concentrated on both ends of the educational attainment distribution. Whereas men are more likely to

drop out of high school, they are also more likely to receive graduate and professional degrees. Men are also more likely to receive postsecondary training in relatively lucrative fields such as engineering and computer science.

Researchers have also highlighted how schools are settings for gender socialization and employment discrimination. Schools often function to socialize boys and girls into acceptance of traditional gender roles (Thorne reading 31). Children often learn these roles as part of a school's "hidden curriculum"—that is, the taken-for-granted assumptions of the school's institutional culture. For example, the majority of elementary and preschool teachers today are overwhelmingly female and occupations in which women are concentrated tend to have lower pay, less prestige, and little professional autonomy (Apple reading 32). Students implicitly learn these lessons through direct observation of social life within schools.

Student Behavior and Adolescent Subcultures

Since Durkheim's early writings on school discipline, sociologists have focused continued attention on how schools structure youth behavior. In recent decades, as more adolescents attend high schools that concentrate youth in settings segregated from general adult society, distinctive adolescent subcultures and behaviors have appeared. Adolescent behavior in schools often is explicitly rebellious and at times impervious to adult efforts to maintain social control. Researchers such as James Coleman worried that adolescents had formed subcultures in direct opposition to the academic goals promoted by the education system. Sociologists attempted to identify structural causes for this rebellious adolescent behavior. Stinchombe (1966), Ogbu, Metz, and others argued that there was a structural logic underlying youth rebellion. Adolescents were not simply acting out irrationally, but were instead responding to the inequality or injustice inherent in their structural conditions.

Recent research suggests that regardless of the underlying causes of student misbehavior, dangerous and violent consequences often result. U.S. schools today face behavior that is not only disruptive but also violent. Recent social surveys indicate that a third of students feel that "pushing, shoving, grabbing, or slapping" is a major problem in their schools. One of five students report that being "threatened with a knife or gun" is a major school problem. Similarly, approximately the same number of high school students report having carried a weapon on school property (*Digest of Educational Statistics* 1995). Sociologists are currently struggling to understand the character and implication of these changes in adolescent behavior (Devine reading 35).

Educational Effects on the Life Course: Delinquency and Labor Market Experience

Student high school educational experiences serve as a *defining moment* in an individual's life-course trajectory. Adolescence is a time when individuals struggle with issues of cognitive, social, and moral development. It is a period in the life course when individuals often begin the process of adult identity formation. Individuals grapple with resolving the question: Who am I?

It is thus not surprising that educational experiences have lasting effects on life-course outcomes. High school settings and educational experiences determine whether youth develop delinquent behaviors (Wilson and Herrnstein reading 36). High school experiences are also associated with the likelihood of teenage pregnancy and the risk of subsequent adult incarceration (Crane 1991, Arum and Beattie 1999). Schools do more than simply provide skills for individuals—they shape attitudes and dispositions that have long-lasting independent effects on adult life-course outcomes.

Sociological research on schools has focused considerable attention on the links between education and adult labor market position. In modern societies, how well an individual fares in the labor market determines not only an individual's access to economic goods and services but as importantly determines his or her access to other related scarce social resources (such as authority, prestige, and status). Although researchers have debated the specific skills and attitudes that are valued and rewarded by employers (Rosenbaum and Binder reading 37, Reich reading 38), research is unequivocal on one point: educational achievement determines subsequent occupational attainment. How well an individual does in school is one of the best predictors of how well he or she will do as an adult in the labor market (Arum and Hout reading 39). Inequality in access to education, therefore, has clear and profound long-term consequences for an individual's future well-being (Fischer et al. 1996).

The Organizational Environment

While much of the sociology of education has focused on identifying how schools affect students, an equally interesting and productive line of research has concentrated on how social factors structure school organization. Although cultural explanations for variation in school practices are inherently appealing (see e.g., Tobin, Wu, and Davidson reading 40), sociologists have attempted to move beyond these simplistic explanations to uncover the deeper underlying structural causes for school variation.

In the last two decades, neo-institutionalist approaches have dominated sociological efforts in this area. Researchers have argued that schools are not efficiently organized for the production of student cognitive gains. Rather, school officials pursue their own ends, which often involve issues of institutional self-interest, expansion, and survival. Schools as organizations are not simply intent on producing educational outputs and meeting the needs of students; more importantly, as institutions they work to ensure organizational growth and survival in uncertain environments (Arum 1996).

The extent to which the organizational environment of public schools is hostile, unstable, and unpredictable is clear from even a cursory examination of recent educational policy debates. Although public schools are graduating more students with mastery of basic academic skills than at any other time in U.S. history, a sociology of school reform suggests that a variety of political forces have coalesced to challenge the very existence of a public education sector. Conservative politicians in recent decades have increasingly pushed for the full-scale dismantling of public education (Cookson reading 44, Berliner and Biddle reading 45).

We find it ironic that public schools are being attacked at a time when society has grown increasingly dependent on their role in socializing and training youth. Although public school critics often focus attention on the low test scores of disadvantaged students, they often ignore the structural factors underlying this poor performance. Whereas policymakers spend endless hours discussing the merits of school restructuring, national standards, integrating curriculum, and even privatization, they spend too few minutes pondering the effects of social background, racial segregation, resource inequality, gender segregation, and other structural factors responsible for inequality of educational opportunity. Policymakers would do well to remember John Dewey's advice on the matter a century ago:

> We are apt to look at the school from an individualistic standpoint, as something between teacher and pupil, or between teacher and parent. . . . Yet the range of outlook needs to be enlarged. What the best and wisest parent wants for his own child, that must the community want for all of its children. Any other ideal for our schools is narrow and unlovely; acted upon, it destroys our democracy.[3]

Educational reform that simultaneously improves our schools and strengthens our democracy is only possible when reforms explicitly recognize and address the structural factors underlying educational inequality.

REFERENCES

ARONOWITZ, STANLEY AND HENRY GIROUX. 1985. *Education under Siege: The Conservative, Liberal and Radical Debate over Schooling.* South Hadley, MA: Bergin and Garvey.

ARUM, RICHARD. 1996. "Do Private Schools Force Public Schools to Compete?" *American Sociological Review* 61:29–46.

ARUM, RICHARD AND IRENEE R. BEATTIE. 1999. "High School Experience and the Risk of Incarceration." *Criminology* (forthcoming).

CRANE, STEPHEN. 1991. "The Epidemic Theory of Ghettos and Neighborhood Effects on Dropping Out and Teenage Childbearing." *American Journal of Sociology* 96:1226–59.

DEWEY, JOHN. [1899] 1964. "The School and Society," reprinted in R. Archambault, ed. *John Dewey on Education.* Chicago: University of Chicago Press, pp. 295–310.

Digest of Educational Statistics. 1995. Washington, DC: U.S. Government Printing Office.

DURKHEIM, EMILE. [1915] 1965. *The Elementary Forms of the Religious Life.* New York: Free Press.

FISCHER, CLAUDE, MICHAEL HOUT, MARTIN SANCHEZ JANKOWSKI, SAMUEL LUCAS, ANN SWIDLER, KIM VOSS, AND RICHARD ARUM. 1996. "Who Wins? Who Loses?" *Inequality by Design.*

Princeton: Princeton University Press, pp. 70–101.

HERRNSTEIN, RICHARD AND CHARLES MURRAY. 1994. *The Bell Curve: Intelligence and Class Structure in American Life.* New York: Free Press.

HOCHSCHILD, ARLIE. 1997. *The Time Bind: When Work Becomes Home and Home Becomes Work.* New York: Metropolitan Books.

McLANAHAN, SARA AND GARY SANDEFUR. 1994. *Growing Up with a Single Parent.* Cambridge, MA: Harvard University Press.

ORFIELD, GARY AND FRANKLIN MONFORT. 1988. *Racial Change and Desegregation in Large School Districts: Trends through the 1986–1987 School Year.* Alexandria, VA: National School Board Association.

PARSONS, TALCOTT. 1959. "The School Class as a Social System: Some of Its Functions in American Society." *Harvard Educational Review* 29: 297–318.

STINCHOMBE, ARTHUR. 1966. *Rebellion in a High School.* Chicago: Quadrangle Books.

NOTES

1. John Dewey, "The School and Society" (1899), p. 299.
2. Emile Durkheim, *The Elementary Forms of the Religious Life* (1915), p. 237.
3. John Dewey, "The School and Society" (1899), p. 295.

Theoretical and Historical Perspectives

Contemporary sociological research relies on theoretical and historical perspectives to help inform analysis. Theory and history provide the concepts we can use to recognize and understand new issues, processes, and social developments. Researchers use theoretical concepts not only to enrich their own work, but as importantly to facilitate dialog and communication with other researchers in a common intellectual community. Part I of this reader provides an overview of the central theoretical and historical perspectives that have played a key role in the development of the sociology of education. As you read subsequent selections in this book, you should consider whether (and how) the research fits the perspectives outlined next or whether the studies rely on concepts from theoretical paradigms outside this core sociological tradition.

The first section includes readings on status attainment and social mobility. Max Weber, one of the most influential theorists in sociology, begins the readings with the argument that education has a dual character in society. Education is used either to promote selection of individuals for advancement by meritocratic processes or by status groups as a closure strategy to keep outsiders from obtaining access to desirable occupations. Weber's concern over this dual character of education stemmed from his experience in Germany with bureaucracy and the use of civil service exams to place individuals in occupations. In the next reading, Sorokin extends Weber's work by arguing that schools sort and sieve students into occupations, thus allowing for a limited amount of mobility within society. Sorokin contends that the role of education in society

is to determine allocation of scarce resources to individuals.

The third reading in the section is Ralph Turner's classic piece comparing English and American educational systems. He maintains that the English norm of sponsored mobility involves the careful, early selection of recruits for advancement to elite status. In contrast, American mobility is normatively a contest in which all individuals are purported to have an equal chance at attaining elite status at multiple stages in their educational careers. These different structures of mobility have profound implications for the value and content of education in each society. In the final reading in this section, Peter Blau and Otis Dudley Duncan build on the previous research on mobility and provide an early statement of a status attainment perspective. The status attainment tradition recognizes the role of education in mediating the relationship between an individual's social origins and social destination.

The second section of theoretical readings includes three central theoretical concepts in the sociology of education: human capital, cultural capital, and social capital. First, Theodore Schultz, an economist, provides an early articulation of human capital theory. He contends that investment in human capital—such as individual knowledge and skills—leads to economic growth for individuals as well as for businesses and society. Schultz sees that these investment decisions occur as a result of rational calculations.

Next, French sociologist Pierre Bourdieu elaborates the concept of cultural capital. Cultural capital includes a host of linguistic and cultural competencies (generally related to art, literature, music, and theater) that are more easily accessed by people from the middle and upper classes. Bourdieu argues that cultural capital is important for education because these competencies are valued—though never really taught—in schools. Although this writing is somewhat difficult, it identifies how cultural attributes affect the role of schools in social reproduction.

In the final reading on the concept of capital, James Coleman and Thomas Hoffer discuss how social capital affects schools. Social capital is the relationship between people, at both familial and community levels, that emerges from social structures in which people live. Coleman and Hoffer maintain that the absence of social capital among public school families represents a loss of vital resources for students in these settings. Private and Catholic schools exhibit greater closure in social networks of students' families and are able both to generate greater consensus of norms among families and to implement intergenerational transmission of these norms through greater monitoring and enforcement. James Coleman's work intellectually dominated the research in sociology of education for more than three decades. (Additional selections of his work appear in this reader in Parts II and IV.)

The third section focuses on changing theories of education systems. Emile Durkheim, a theorist whose work—like Max Weber's—formed the basis for modern sociology, identified the role of education in integrating individuals into society. Durkheim viewed society as an all-powerful force and argued that schools have a critical role in socializing individuals to accept productive social roles. Through interactions with school authority, students learn self-discipline, which is essential to their attachment to the larger society.

The Willard Waller reading emphasizes that, in addition to developing individual

citizens, schools are part of a larger community. This reading is an early articulation of the importance of neighborhood context and family composition in defining school communities. Schools both affect and are influenced by the communities in which they are situated. Waller demonstrates that schools are not merely islands unto themselves, but that they incorporate moral positions and attitudes reflected in the community at large. This role puts particular pressure on teachers to represent the "ideals in the community." Such a task is difficult when there are conflicting ideals and demands or when ideals place additional constraints on a teacher's personal life. Although it might be tempting to shrug off the community and school policing of teacher behavior as an archaic historic artifact from Waller's 1930s, this practice remains very much alive as seen in recent firings of teachers for the use of "objectionable" reading material or for coming out as gay, lesbian, or bisexual.

Next, Randall Collins provides an explanation for trends in educational expansion. Collins returns to the work of Weber by maintaining that education is used by status groups to monopolize scarce resources. He argues that schools are increasingly important, but not because of their role in imparting socially relevant skills and knowledge. Rather, the increasing significance of schooling is a result of the role of education in providing credentials that serve as exclusionary requirements for privileged occupational positions. Collins's work demonstrates that rising educational requirements for jobs are driven by the expansion of opportunities in schooling rather than through changes in the structure of employment. In his later work, Collins (1979) extends this argument to show that such a trend ultimately serves to devalue educational credentials, making continued expansion of degree attainment inevitable.

The final section in Part I includes historical accounts of the development of the educational system. First, Samuel Bowles and Herbert Gintis argue from a neo-Marxist perspective that schools play a central role in the social reproduction of the class structure. Social reproduction theory, which their analysis advances, purports that schools developed in the United States to serve the interest of a capitalist class. Bowles and Gintis maintain that mass education socializes and controls working-class youth while promoting the illusion of meritocratic selection. This perspective challenges status attainment and human capital theories by conceptualizing schools as a hindrance to social mobility and as producers of surplus workers at the mercy of capitalist employers. Most researchers studying the development of public education are highly critical of Bowles and Gintis's simplistic model of class imposition. Even researchers who share Bowles and Gintis's sympathy with working class interests argue that labor movements, ethnic groups, professional educators, and middle-class reformers were primarily responsible for the historic development of modern educational institutions (e.g., Katznelson and Weir 1985, Reese 1986). This alternative reserach tradition views the working class as an active participant in the development of the education system, rather than simply as a passive group on whom capitalists imposed an inequitable schooling apparatus.

Finally, David Tyack and Elisabeth Hansot analyze the development of coeducation in America in the nineteenth century. These historians take a more pluralistic view of the development of public education. They emphasize a consensus reached by a range of interests, including professional educators, in shaping the current structure of education. Tyack and Hansot demonstrate that early high schools were primarily inhabited by middle-class students and that high schools traditionally performed a different role for male and female students.

REFERENCES

COLLINS, RANDALL. 1979. *The Credential Society: A Historical Sociology of Education and Stratification.* New York: Academic Press.

KATZNELSON, IRA AND MARGARET WEIR. 1985. *Schooling for All.* Berkeley: University of California Press.

REESE, WILLIAM. 1986. *Power and the Promise of School Reform: Grassroots Movements during the Progressive Era.* London: Routledge and Kegan Paul.

Status Attainment and Social Mobility

1

THE "RATIONALIZATION" OF EDUCATION AND TRAINING

Max Weber

We cannot here analyze the far-reaching and general cultural effects that the advance of the rational bureaucratic structure of domination, as such, develops quite independently of the areas in which it takes hold. Naturally, bureaucracy promotes a "rationalist" way of life, but the concept of rationalism allows for widely differing contents. Quite generally, one can only say that the bureaucratization of all domination very strongly furthers the development of "rational matter-of-factness" and the personality type of the professional expert. This has far-reaching ramifications, but only one important element of the process can be briefly indicated here: its effect upon the nature of training and education.

Educational institutions on the European continent, especially the institutions of higher learning—the universities, as well as technical academies, business colleges, gymnasiums, and other middle schools—are dominated and influenced by the need for the kind of "education" that produces a system of special examinations and the

Max Weber, excerpt from "The 'Rationalization' of Education and Training" from *Max Weber: Essays in Sociology*, translated by H. H. Gerth and C. Wright Mills. Copyright © 1946 by Max Weber. Reprinted with the permission of Oxford University Press, Inc.

trained expertness that is increasingly indispensable for modern bureaucracy.

The "special examination," in the present sense, was and is found also outside of bureaucratic structures proper; thus, today it is found in the "free" professions of medicine and law and in the guild-organized trades. Expert examinations are neither indispensable to nor concomitant phenomena of bureaucratization. The French, English, and American bureaucracies have for a long time foregone such examinations entirely or to a large extent, for training and service in party organizations have made up for them.

"Democracy" also takes an ambivalent stand in the face of specialized examinations, as it does in the face of all the phenomena of bureaucracy—although democracy itself promotes these developments. Special examinations, on the one hand, mean or appear to mean a "selection" of those who qualify from all social strata rather than a rule by notables. On the other hand, democracy fears that a merit system and educational certificates will result in a privileged "caste." Hence, democracy fights against the special-examination system.

The special examination is found even in pre-bureaucratic or semi-bureaucratic epochs. Indeed, the regular and earliest locus of special examinations is among prebendally organized dominions. Expectancies of prebends, first of church prebends—as in the Islamite Orient and in the Occidental Middle Ages—then, as was especially the case in China, secular prebends, are the typical prizes for which people study and are examined. These examinations, however, have in truth only a partially specialized and expert character.

The modern development of full bureaucratization brings the system of rational, specialized, and expert examinations irresistibly to the fore. The civil-service reform gradually imports expert training and specialized examinations into the United States. In all other countries this system also advances, stemming from its main breeding place, Germany. The increasing bureaucratization of administration enhances the importance of the specialized examination in England. In China, the attempt to replace the semi-patrimonial and ancient bureaucracy by a modern bureaucracy brought the expert examination; it took the place of a former and quite differently structured system of examinations. The bureaucratization of capitalism, with its demand for expertly trained technicians, clerks, et cetera, carries such examinations all over the world. Above all, the development is greatly furthered by the social prestige of the educational certificates acquired through such specialized examinations. This is all the more the case as the educational patent is turned to economic advantage. Today, the certificate of education becomes what the test for ancestors has been in the past, at least where the nobility has remained powerful: a prerequisite for equality of birth, a qualification for a canonship, and for state office.

The development of the diploma from universities, and business and engineering colleges, and the universal clamor for the creation of educational certificates in all fields make for the formation of a privileged stratum in bureaus and in offices. Such certificates support their holders" claims for intermarriages with notable families (in business offices people naturally hope for preferment with regard to the chief's daughter), claims to be admitted into the circles that adhere to "codes of honor," claims for a "respectable' remuneration rather than remuneration for work done, claims for assured advancement and old-age insurance, and, above all, claims to monopolize socially and economically advantageous positions. When we hear from all sides the demand for an introduction of regular curricula and special examinations, the reason behind it is, of course, not a suddenly awakened "thirst for education" but the desire for restricting the supply for these positions and their monopolization by the owners of educational certificates. Today, the "examination" is the universal means of this monopolization, and therefore examinations irresistibly advance. As the education prerequisite to the acquisition of the educational certificate requires considerable expense and a period of waiting for full remuneration, this striving means a setback for talent (charisma) in favor of property. For the "intellectual" costs of educational certificates are always low, and with the increasing volume of such certificates, their intellectual costs do not increase, but rather decrease.

The requirement of a chivalrous style of life in the old qualification for fiefs in Germany is replaced by the necessity of participating in its present rudimental form as represented by the dueling corps of the universities which also distribute the educational certificates. In Anglo-Saxon countries, athletic and social clubs fulfill the same function. The bureaucracy, on the other hand, strives everywhere for a "right to the office" by the establishment of a regular disciplinary procedure and by removal of the completely arbitrary disposition of the "chief" over the subordinate official. The bureaucracy seeks to secure the official position, the orderly advancement, and the provision for old age. In this, the bureaucracy is supported by the "democratic" sentiment of the governed, which demands that domination be minimized. Those who hold this attitude believe themselves able to discern a weakening of the master's prerogatives in every weakening of the arbitrary disposition of the master over the officials. To this extent, bureaucracy, both in business offices and in public service, is a carrier of a specific "status" development, as have been the quite differently structured officeholders of the past. We have already pointed out that these status characteristics are usually also exploited, and that by their nature they contribute to the technical usefulness of the bureaucracy in fulfilling its specific tasks.

"Democracy" reacts precisely against the unavoidable "status" character of bureaucracy. Democracy seeks to put the election of officials for short terms in the place of appointed officials; it seeks to substitute the removal of officials by election for a regulated procedure of discipline. Thus, democracy seeks to replace the arbitrary disposition of the hierarchically superordinate "master" by the equally arbitrary disposition of the governed and the party chiefs dominating them.

Social prestige based upon the advantage of special education and training as such is by no means specific to bureaucracy. On the contrary! But educational prestige in other structures of domination rests upon substantially different foundations.

Expressed in slogan-like fashion, the "cultivated man," rather than the "specialist," has been the end sought by education and has formed the basis of social esteem in such various systems as the feudal, theocratic, and patrimonial structures of dominion: in the English notable administration, in the old Chinese patrimonial bureaucracy, as well as under the rule of demagogues in the so-called Hellenic democracy.

The term "cultivated man" is used here in a completely value-neutral sense; it is understood to mean solely that the goal of education consists in the quality of a man's bearing in life which was *considered* "cultivated,"

rather than in a specialized training for expertness. The "cultivated" personality formed the educational ideal, which was stamped by the structure of domination and by the social condition for membership in the ruling stratum. Such education aimed at a chivalrous or an ascetic type; or, at a literary type, as in China; a gymnastic-humanist type, as in Hellas; or it aimed at a conventional type, as in the case of the Anglo-Saxon gentleman. The qualification of the ruling stratum as such rested upon the possession of "more" cultural quality (in the absolutely changeable, value-neutral sense in which we use the term here), rather than upon "more" expert knowledge. Special military, theological, and juridical ability was of course intensely practiced; but the point of gravity in Hellenic, in medieval, as well as in Chinese education, has rested upon educational elements that were entirely different from what was "useful" in one's specialty.

Behind all the present discussions of the foundations of the educational system, the struggle of the "specialist type of man" against the older type of "cultivated man" is hidden at some decisive point. This fight is determined by the irresistibly expanding bureaucratization of all public and private relations of authority and by the ever-increasing importance of expert and specialized knowledge. The fight intrudes into all intimate cultural questions.

During its advance, bureaucratic organization has had to overcome those essentially negative obstacles that have stood in the way of the leveling process necessary for bureaucracy. In addition, administrative structures based on different principles intersect with bureaucratic organizations.

. . .

The bureaucratic structure is everywhere a late product of development. The further back we trace our steps, the more typical is the absence of bureaucracy and officialdom in the structure of domination. Bureaucracy has a "rational" character: rules, means, ends, and matter-of-factness dominate its bearing. Everywhere its origin and its diffusion have therefore had "revolutionary" results. . . . This is the same influence which the advance of *rationalism* in general has had. The march of bureaucracy has destroyed structures of domination, which had no rational character, in the special sense of the term. Hence, we may ask: What were these structures?

2

SOCIAL AND CULTURAL MOBILITY

Pitirim Sorokin

Definition

In any society there are a great many people who want to climb up into its upper strata. Since only a few succeed in doing this, and since, under normal conditions, the vertical circulation does not have an anarchical character, it seems that in any society there is a mechanism which controls the process of vertical circulation. This control seems to consist in the first place, in testing individuals with respect to their suitableness for the performance of a definite social function; in the second place, in the selection of individuals for a definite social position;[1] in the third place, in a corresponding distribution of the members of a society among different social strata, in their promotion, or in their degradation. In other words, within a stratified society, there seem to exist not only channels of vertical circulation, but also a kind of a "sieve" within these channels

Pitirim Sorokin, excerpt from "Mechanism of Social Testing, Selection, and Distribution of Individuals within Different Social Strata" from *Social and Cultural Mobility*. Copyright © 1959 by The Free Press. Reprinted with the permission of The Free Press, a division of Simon & Schuster, Inc.

which sifts the individuals and places them within the society. The essential purpose of this control is to distribute the individuals so that each is placed according to his talents and able to perform successfully his social function. Wrongly placed, individuals do their social work poorly; and, as a result, all society suffers and disintegrates. Though there scarcely has existed any society in which the distribution of individuals has been quite perfect, in complete accordance with the rule, "Everybody must be placed according to his ability,"[2] nevertheless, many societies have existed for a long time and this very fact means that their mechanism of social testing, selecting, and distributing their members has not been wholly bad and has performed its function in a more or less satisfactory way. The problems to be discussed now are: What represents this mechanism of selection and distribution of individuals? How and on what bases does it test, select and distribute them?

The first question may be answered in the following way: in any given society this mechanism is composed of all the social institutions and organizations which perform these functions.

As a general rule these institutions are the same as those which function as channels of vertical circulation. These institutions, such as the family, army, church, school, political, professional, and occupational organizations are not only a channel of social circulation, but are at the same time, the "sieves" which test and sift, select and distribute the individuals within different social strata or positions.

Some of them, as the school and family, are the machinery which tests principally the *general qualities* of individuals necessary for a successful performance of a great many functions; such as their general intelligence, health, and social character. Some other institutions, such as many occupational organizations, are the machinary which tests the *specific quality* of individuals necessary for a successful performance of a specific function in a given occupation; the voice of a prospective singer, the oratorical talent of a prospective politician, the physical strength of a future heavyweight champion, and so forth. Turn now to the problem of how these institutions perform these functions and what principal types of testing, selection, and distribution exist in different societies. This will give us a somewhat deeper insight into many institutions, and will show that many of them, quite absurd at first sight, have been, indeed, quite understandable under existing circumstances.

· · ·

The School as a Testing and Selective and Distributive Agency

[A] kind of machinery for testing the abilities of the individuals and determining their social position has been the school. The family is the agency which gives the first test; earlier than any other group, it determines the life career and the prospective social position of the children. But even in the caste-society the family test and influences, to some degree, are retested and reconsidered by other agencies, the educator and the teacher among them; still more true is this of societies of another type, especially of those in which we live.

If at the present time the family status and education outline roughly the life career of its children, the school is the next agency which retests the "decisions" of a family, and very often and very decisively changes them. Up to the last few years, the school was regarded primarily as an educational institution. Its social function was seen in "pouring" into a student a definite amount of knowledge, and, to some extent, in shaping his behavior. The testing, the selective, and the distributive functions of the school were almost completely overlooked, although these functions of the school are scarcely less important than that of "enlightenment" and "education." During the last few years many specialists in different fields have begun to see these functions. At the present moment it is certain that the school, while being a "training and educational" institution, is at the same time, a piece of social machinery, which tests the abilities of the individuals, which sifts them, selects them, and decides their prospective social position. In other words, *the essential social function of the school is not only to find out whether a pupil has learned a definite part of a textbook or not;* but through all its examinations and moral supervision to discover, in the first place, which of the pupils are talented and which are not; what ability every pupil has and in what degree; and which of them are socially and morally fit; in the second place, to eliminate those who do not have the desirable mental and moral qualities; in the third place, through an elimination of the failures to close the doors for their social promotion, at least, within certain definite social fields, and to promote those who happen to be the bright students in the direction of those social positions which correspond to their general and specific abilities. Whether successful or not, these purposes are some of the most important functions of the school. From this standpoint *the school is primarily a testing, selecting, and distributing agency.* In its total the whole school system, with its handicaps, quizzes, examinations, supervision of the students, and their grading, ranking, evaluating, eliminating, and promoting, is a very complicated "sieve," which sifts "the good" from "the bad" future citizens, "the able" from "the dull," "those fitted for the high positions" from those "unfitted." This explains what is meant by the testing, selective, and distributive functions of school machinery.

The intensiveness of this function of the school naturally fluctuates from society to society, from time to time. Among other conditions, it *strongly depends on the extent to which the testing and the sifting of individuals is carried out by other institutions, and especially by the family.* If the family performs this role efficiently, in such a way that only an already selected group of children reaches the doors of the schools and enters them, then the testing and the selecting and sifting role of the school is not so necessary as in the case when the doors of the school are open for all children, when there is no selection and elimination preceding school entrance. Under such conditions, naturally, there are a great many children incapable of progressing further than the first few grades of school; the number of failures is greater than where there is pre-school selection. Therefore, the elimination work of the school becomes much greater and more pitiless. It increases as it proceeds, going from the lower grades to the higher, from the elementary to the secondary school, from the secondary school to the college. As a result, out of the many pupils who enter the door of the elementary school only an insignificant minority reach the stage of university graduation. The great majority (see below for figures) are eliminated, not only from school, but automatically thereby

from climbing up this ladder to high social positions. Part of those eliminated succeed in climbing through another ladder (money making, etc.), but only a small part.[3] The majority of those eliminated from the school through "the school sieve" are doomed to be placed at a relatively lower social position. In this way, in certain societies the school does the work of selection, and bars the social promotion of individuals who have not been barred and selected by the family. This explains the fact that, contrary to the common opinion, universal education and instruction leads not so much to an obliteration of mental and social differences as to their increase. The school, even the most democratic school, open to everybody, if it performs its task properly, is a machinery of the "aristocratization" and stratification of society, not of "leveling" and "democratization." The following representative data show clearly the testing, selective, and eliminating role of the school in the United States of America. According to Doctor Ayres,[4] for every 1,000 children who enter the first grade, we have in the higher grades:

> 723 in the second grade
> 692 in the third grade
> 640 in the fourth grade
> 552 in the fifth grade
> 462 in the sixth grade
> 368 in the seventh grade
> 263 in the eighth grade
> 189 in the first grade of high school
> 123 in the second grade of high school
> 81 in the third grade of high school
> 56 in the fourth grade of high school

Admitting that out of 1,000 children who enter the first grade, there must be, owing to the death and increase of population, in the eighth grade, 871, we see that, in fact, we have instead of this figure only 263. The remaining 608 pupils are eliminated and dropped out of school. A similar conclusion is given by Doctor Thorndike.[5] According to his data, 25 percent of the white children in the United States at the beginning of the twentieth century could reach only the fifth grade. According to Doctor Strayer and Doctor Terman, out of 100 children entering elementary school only about 40 remain to enter the high school and only 10 are graduated from high school.[6]

. . .

NOTES

1. From the text it is clear that the selection here means not a biological selection in the sense of a differential survival but a social sorting of individuals among the different strata or groups: non-admission or rejection of the unsuitable and placement or taking in of suitable individuals.
2. This social placement to everybody according to his talent was known long ago; it is the motto of the Indian, of the Chinese, and of the Greek and the Roman writers. It composes the central idea of Plato's *Justice* in his *Republic;* it is the dominant idea of Confucius, Aristotle, and of the *Sacred Books of India.*
3. Even in the field of money making the majority of the successful money makers have been those who successfully met the school test. Part of those who have not had such a test in no way could be regarded as the school failures. They do not have the degrees simply because they did not have the chance to enter the school. Out of 631 richest men of America, 54 percent hold a college degree; 18.5 percent went to high school; 24.1 went to elementary school, only 3.4 percent had no education except self-education. Sorokin, P., "American Millionaires and Multimillionaires," p. 637.
4. Leonard P. Ayres, *Laggards in Our Schools* (New York Survey Association, 1913), p. 13.
5. E. Thorndike, *The Elimination of Pupils from School*, p. 9.
6. G. D. Strayer, "Age and Grade Census of Schools and Colleges," *United States Bureau of Education*, Bull. No. 451, p. 6; L. Terman, "*The Intelligence of School Children*," pp. 87–89.

3

SPONSORED AND CONTEST MOBILITY AND THE SCHOOL SYSTEM

Ralph H. Turner

This [chapter] suggests a framework for relating certain differences between American and English systems of education to the prevailing norms of upward mobility in each country. Others have noted the tendency of educational systems to support prevailing schemes of stratification, but this discussion concerns specifically the manner in which the *accepted mode of upward mobility* shapes the school system directly and indirectly through its effects on the values which implement social control.

Two ideal-typical normative patterns of upward mobility are described and their ramifications in the general patterns of stratification and social control are suggested. In addition to showing relationships among a number of differences between American and English schooling, the ideal-types have

Ralph Turner, excerpts from "Sponsored and Contest Mobility and the School System" from *American Sociological Review* 25 (December 1960). Copyright © 1960.

broader implications than those developed in this [chapter]: they suggest a major dimension of stratification which might be profitably incorporated into a variety of studies in social class; and they readily can be applied in further comparisons between other countries.

The Nature of Organizing Norms

Many investigators have concerned themselves with rates of upward mobility in specific countries or internationally,[1] and with the manner in which school systems facilitate or impede such mobility.[2] But preoccupation with the *extent* of mobility has precluded equal attention to the predominant *modes* of mobility. The central assumption underlying this [chapter] is that within a formally open class system that provides for mass education the organizing folk norm which defines the accepted mode of upward mobility is a crucial factor in shaping the school system, and may be even more crucial than the extent of upward mobility. In England and the United States there appear to be different organizing folk norms, here termed *sponsored mobility* and *contest mobility,* respectively. *Contest* mobility is a system in which elite[3] status is the prize in an open contest and is taken by the aspirants' own efforts. While the "contest" is governed by some rules of fair play, the contestants have wide latitude in the strategies they may employ. Since the "prize" of successful upward mobility is not in the hands of an established elite to give out, the latter can not determine who shall attain it and who shall not. Under *sponsored* mobility elite recruits are chosen by the established elite or their agents, and elite status is *given* on the basis of some criterion of supposed merit and cannot be *taken* by any amount of effort or strategy. Upward mobility is like entry into a private club where each candidate must be "sponsored" by one or more of the members. Ultimately the members grant or deny upward mobility on the basis of whether they judge the candidate to have those qualities they wish to see in fellow members.

Before elaborating this distinction, it should be noted that these systems of mobility are ideal types designed to clarify observed differences in the predominantly similar English and American systems of stratification and education. But as organizing norms these principles are assumed to be present at least implicitly in people's thinking, guiding their judgments of what is appropriate on many specific matters. Such organizing norms do not correspond perfectly with the objective characteristics of the societies in which they exist, nor are they completely independent of them. From the complex interplay of social and economic conditions and ideologies people in a society develop a highly simplified conception of the way in which events take place. This conception of the "natural" is translated into a norm—the "natural" becomes what "ought" to be—and in turn imposes a strain toward consistency upon relevant aspects of the society. Thus the norm acts back upon the objective conditions to which it refers and has ramifying effects upon directly and indirectly related features of the society.[4]

In brief, the conception of an ideal-typical organizing norm involves the following propositions: (1) The ideal types are not fully exemplified in practice since they are normative systems, and no normative system can be devised so as to cope with all empirical exigencies. (2) Predominant norms usually compete with less ascendant norms engendered by changes and inconsistencies in the underlying social structure. (3) Though not fully explicit, organizing folk norms are reflected in specific value judgments. Those judgments which the relevant people regard as having a convincing ring to them, irrespective of the logic expressed, or which seem to require no extended argumentation may be presumed to reflect the prevailing folk norms. (4) The predominant organizing norms in one segment of society are functionally related to those in other segments.

Two final qualifications concerning the scope of this [chapter]: First, the organizing folk norm of upward mobility affects the school system because one of the latter's functions is the facilitation of mobility. Since this is only one of several social functions of the school, and not the most important function in the societies under examination, only a very partial accounting of the whole set of forces making for similarities and differences in the school systems of United States and England is possible here. Only those differences which directly or indirectly reflect the performance of the mobility function are noted. Second, the concern of this [chapter] is with the current dynamics of the situation in the two countries rather than with their historical development.

Distinctions between the Two Norms

Contest mobility is like a sporting event in which many compete for a few recognized prizes. The contest is judged to be fair only if all the players compete on an equal footing. Victory must be won solely by one's own efforts. The most satisfactory outcome is not necessarily a victory of the most able, but of the most deserving. The tortoise who defeats the hare is a folk-prototype of the deserving sportsman. Enterprise, initiative, perseverance, and craft are admirable qualities if they allow the person who is initially at a disadvantage to triumph. Even clever manipulation of the rules may be admired if it helps the contestant who is smaller or less muscular or less rapid to win. Applied to mobility, the contest norm means that victory by a person of moderate intelligence accomplished through the use of common sense, craft, enterprise, daring, and successful risk

taking[5] is more appreciated than victory by the most intelligent or the best educated.

Sponsored mobility, in contrast, rejects the pattern of the contest and favors a controlled selection process. In this process the elite or their agents, deemed to be best qualified to judge merit, choose individuals for elite status who have the appropriate qualities. Individuals do not win or seize elite status; mobility is rather a process of sponsored induction into the elite.

Pareto had this sort of mobility in mind when he suggested that a governing class might dispose of persons potentially dangerous to it by admitting them to elite membership, provided that the recruits change character by adopting elite attitudes and interests.[6] Danger to the ruling class would seldom be the major criterion for choice of elite recruits. But Pareto assumed that the established elite would select whom they wished to enter their ranks and would inculcate the attitudes and interests of the established elite in the recruits.

The governing objective of contest mobility is to give elite status to those who earn it, while the goal of sponsored mobility is to make the best use of the talents in society by sorting persons into their proper niches. In different societies the conditions of competitive struggle may reward quite different attributes, and sponsored mobility may select individuals on the basis of such diverse qualities as intelligence or visionary capability, but the difference in principle remains the same.[7]

Under the contest system society at large establishes and interprets the criteria of elite status. If one wishes to have his status recognized he must display certain credentials which identify his class to those about him. The credentials must be highly visible and require no special skill for their assessment, since credentials are presented to the masses. Material possession and mass popularity are altogether appropriate credentials in this respect, and any special skill which produces a tangible product and which can easily be assessed by the untrained will do. The nature of sponsored mobility precludes these procedures, but assigns to credentials instead the function of identifying elite members to one another.[8] Accordingly, the ideal credentials are special skills that require the trained discrimination of the elite for their recognition. In this case, intellectual, literary, or artistic excellencies, which can be appraised only by those trained to appreciate them, are fully suitable credentials. Concentration on such skills lessens the likelihood that an interloper will succeed in claiming the right to elite membership on grounds of the popular evaluation of his competence.

In the sporting event there is special admiration for the slow starter who makes a dramatic finish, and many of the rules are designed to insure that the race should not be declared over until it has run its full course. Contest mobility incorporates this disapproval of premature judgments and of anything that gives special advantage to those who are ahead at any point in the race. Under sponsored mobility, fairly early selection of only the number of persons necessary to fill anticipated vacancies in the elite is desirable. Early selection allows time to prepare the recruits for their elite position. Aptitudes, inherent capacities, and spiritual gifts can be assessed fairly early in life by techniques ranging from divination to the most sophisticated psychological test, and the more naive the subjects at the time of selection the less likely are their talents to be blurred by differential learning or conspiracy to defeat the test. Since elitists take the initiative in training recruits, they are more interested in the latters' capabilities than in what they will do with them on their own, and they are concerned that no one else should first have an opportunity to train the recruits' talents in the wrong direction. Contest mobility tends to delay the final award as long as practicable to permit a fair race; sponsored mobility tends to place the time of recruitment as early

in life as practicable to insure control over selection and training.

Systems of sponsored mobility develop most readily in societies with but a single elite or with a recognized elite hierarchy. When multiple elites compete among themselves the mobility process tends to take the contest pattern, since no group is able to command control of recruitment. Sponsored mobility further depends upon a social structure that fosters monopoly of elite credentials. Lack of such monopoly undercuts sponsorship and control of the recruitment process. Monopoly of credentials in turn is typically a product of societies with well entrenched traditional aristocracies employing such credentials as family line and bestowable title which are intrinsically subject to monopoly, or of societies organized on large-scale bureaucratic lines permitting centralized control of upward social movement.

English society has been described as the juxtaposition of two systems of stratification, the urban industrial class system and the surviving aristocratic system. While the sponsored mobility pattern reflects the logic of the latter, our impression is that it pervades popular thinking rather than merely coexisting with the logic of industrial stratification. Patterns imported into an established culture tend to be reshaped, as they are assimilated, into consistency with the established culture. Thus it may be that changes in stratification associated with industrialization have led to alterations in the rates, the specific means, and the rules of mobility, but that these changes have been guided by the but lightly challenged organizing norm of sponsored mobility.

Social Control and the Two Norms

Every society must cope with the problem of maintaining loyalty to its social system and does so in part through norms and values, only some of which vary by class position.

Norms and values especially prevalent within a given class must direct behavior into channels that support the total system, while those that transcend strata must support the general class differential. The way in which upward mobility takes place determines in part the kinds of norms and values that serve the indicated purposes of social control in each class and throughout the society.

The most conspicuous control problem is that of ensuring loyalty in the disadvantaged classes toward a system in which their members receive less than a proportional share of society's goods. In a system of contest mobility this is accomplished by a combination of futuristic orientation, the norm of ambition, and a general sense of fellowship with the elite. Each individual is encouraged to think of himself as competing for an elite position so that loyalty to the system and conventional attitudes are cultivated in the process of preparation for this possibility. It is essential that this futuristic orientation be kept alive by delaying a sense of final irreparable failure to reach elite status until attitudes are well established. By thinking of himself in the successful future the elite aspirant forms considerable identification with elitists, and evidence that they are merely ordinary human beings like himself helps to reinforce this identification as well as to keep alive the conviction that he himself may someday succeed in like manner. To forestall rebellion among the disadvantaged majority, then, a contest system must avoid absolute points of selection for mobility and immobility and must delay clear recognition of the realities of the situation until the individual is too committed to the system to change radically. A futuristic orientation cannot, of course, be inculcated successfully in all members of lower strata, but sufficient internalization of a norm of ambition tends to leave the unambitious as individual deviants and to forestall the latters' formation of a genuine subcultural group able to offer collective threat to the established system. Where this kind of control system operates rather effectively it is notable that organized or gang deviancy is more likely to take the form of an attack upon the conventional or moral order rather than upon the class system itself. Thus the United States has its "beatniks"[9] who repudiate ambition and most worldly values and its delinquent and criminal gangs who try to evade the limitations imposed by conventional means,[10] but very few active revolutionaries.

These social controls are inappropriate in a system of sponsorship since the elite recruits are chosen from above. The principal threat to the system would lie in the existence of a strong group the members of whom sought to *take* elite positions themselves. Control under this system is maintained by training the "masses" to regard themselves as relatively incompetent to manage society, by restricting access to the skills and manners of the elite, and by cultivating belief in the superior competence of the elite. The earlier that selection of the elite recruits is made the sooner others can be taught to accept their inferiority and to make "realistic" rather than phantasy plans. Early selection prevents raising the hopes of large numbers of people who might otherwise become the discontented leaders of a class challenging the sovereignty of the established elite. If it is assumed that the difference in competence between masses and elite is seldom so great as to support the usual differences in the advantages accruing to each,[11] then the differences must be artificially augmented by discouraging acquisition of elite skills by the masses. Thus a sense of mystery about the elite is a common device for supporting in the masses the illusion of a much greater hiatus of competence than in fact exists.

While elitists are unlikely to reject a system that benefits them, they must still be restrained from taking such advantage of their favorable situation as to jeopardize the entire elite. Under the sponsorship system the elite recruits—who are selected early, freed from the strain of competitive struggle, and kept under close superivsion—may be thoroughly indoctrinated in elite culture. A norm of paternalism toward inferiors may be inculcated, a heightened sensitivity to the good opinion of fellow elitists and elite recruits may be cultivated, and the appreciation of the more complex forms of aesthetic, literary, intellectual, and sporting activities may be taught. Norms of courtesy and altruism easily can be maintained under sponsorship since elite recruits are not required to compete for their standing and since the elite may deny high standing to those who strive for position by "unseemly" methods. The system of sponsorship provides an almost perfect setting for the development of an elite culture characterized by a sense of responsibility for "inferiors" and for preservation of the "finer things" of life.

Elite control in the contest system is more difficult since there is no controlled induction and apprenticeship. The principal regulation seems to lie in the insecurity of elite position. In a sense there is no "final arrival" because each person may be displaced by newcomers throughout his life. The limited control of high standing from above prevents the clear delimitation of levels in the class system, so that success itself becomes relative: each success, rather than an accomplishment, serves to qualify the participant for competition at the next higher level.[12] The restraints upon the behavior of a person of high standing, therefore, are principally those applicable to a contestant who must not risk the "ganging up" of other contestants, and who must pay some attention to the masses who are frequently in a position to impose penalties upon him. But any special norm of paternalism is hard to establish since there is no dependable procedure for examining the means by which one achieves elite credentials. While mass esteem is an effective brake

upon over-exploitation of position, it rewards scrupulously ethical and altruistic behavior much less than evidence of fellow-feeling with the masses themselves.

Under both systems, unscrupulous or disreputable persons may become or remain members of the elite, but for different reasons. In contest mobility, popular tolerance of a little craftiness in the successful newcomer, together with the fact that he does not have to undergo the close scrutiny of the old elite, leaves considerable leeway for unscrupulous success. In sponsored mobility, the unpromising recruit reflects unfavorably on the judgments of his sponsors and threatens the myth of elite omniscience; consequently he may be tolerated and others may "cover up" for his deficiencies in order to protect the unified front of the elite to the outer world.

Certain of the general values and norms of any society reflect emulation of elite values by the masses. Under sponsored mobility, a good deal of the protective attitudes toward and interest in classical subjects percolates to the masses. Under contest mobility, however, there is not the same degree of homogeneity of moral, aesthetic, and intellectual values to be emulated, so that the conspicuous attribute of the elite is its high level of material consumption—emulation itself follows this course. There is neither effective incentive nor punishment for the elitist who fails to interest himself in promoting the arts or literary excellence, or who continues to maintain the vulgar manners and mode of speech of his class origin. The elite has relatively less power and the masses relatively more power to punish or reward a man for his adoption or disregard of any special elite culture. The great importance of accent and of grammatical excellence in the attainment of high status in England as contrasted with the twangs and drawls and grammatical ineptitude among American elites is the most striking example of this difference. In a contest system, the class order does not function to support the *quality* of aesthetic, literary, and intellectual activities; only those well versed in such matters are qualified to distinguish authentic products from cheap imitations. Unless those who claim superiority in these areas are forced to submit their credentials to the elite for evaluation, poor quality is often honored equally with high quality and class prestige does not serve to maintain an effective norm of high quality.

This is not to imply that there are no groups in a "contest" society devoted to the protection and fostering of high standards in art, music, literature, and intellectual pursuits, but that such standards lack the support of the class system which is frequently found when sponsored mobility prevails. In California, the selection by official welcoming committees of a torch singer to entertain a visiting king and queen and "can-can" dancers to entertain Mr. Khrushchev illustrates how American elites can assume that high prestige and popular taste go together.

Formal Education

Returning to the conception of an organizing ideal norm, we assume that to the extent to which one such norm of upward mobility is prevalent in a society there are constant strains to shape the educational system into conformity with that norm. These strains operate in two fashions: directly, by blinding people to alternatives and coloring their judgments of successful and unsuccessful solutions to recurring educational problems; indirectly, through the functional interrelationships between school systems and the class structure, systems of social control, and other features of the social sructure which are neglected in this [chapter].

The most obvious application of the distinction between sponsored and contest mobility norms affords a partial explanation for the different policies of student selection

in the English and American secondary schools. Although American high school students follow different courses of study and a few attend specialized schools, a major educational preoccupation has been to avoid any sharp social separation between the superior and inferior students and to keep the channels of movement between courses of study as open as possible. Recent criticisms of the way in which superior students may be thereby held back in their development usually are nevertheless qualified by the insistence that these students must not be withdrawn from the mainstream of student life.[13] Such segregation offends the sense of fairness implicit in the contest norm and also arouses the fear that the elite and future elite will lose their sense of fellowship with the masses. Perhaps the most important point, however, is that schooling is presented as an opportunity, and making use of it depends primarily on the student's own initiative and enterprise.

The English system has undergone a succession of liberalizing changes during this century, but all of them have retained the attempt to sort out early in the educational program the promising from the unpromising so that the former may be segregated and given a special form of training to fit them for higher standing in their adult years. Under the Education Act of 1944, a minority of students has been selected each year by means of a battery of examinations popularly known as "eleven plus," supplemented in varying degrees by grade school records and personal interviews, for admission to grammar schools.[14] The remaining students attend secondary modern or technical schools in which the opportunities to prepare for college or to train for the more prestigeful occupations are minimal. The grammar schools supply what by comparative standards is a high quality of college preparatory education. Of course, such a scheme embodies the logic of sponsorship, with early selection of those destined for middle-class and higher-status occupations, and specialized training to prepare each group for its destined class position. This plan facilitates considerable mobility, and recent research reveals surprisingly little bias against children from manual laboring-class families in the selection for grammar school, when related to measured intelligence.[15] It is altogether possible that adequate comparative study would show a closer correlation of school success with measured intelligence and a lesser correlation between school success and family background in England than in the United States. While selection of superior students for mobility opportunity is probably more efficient under such a system, the obstacles for persons not so selected of "making the grade" on the basis of their own initiative or enterprise are probably correspondingly greater.

That the contrasting effects of the two systems accord with the social control patterns under the two mobility norms is indicated by studies of student ambitions in the United States and in England. Researches in the United States consistently show that the general level of occupational aspiration reported by high school students is quite unrealistic in relation to the actual distribution of job opportunities. Comparative study in England shows much less "phantasy" aspiration, and specifically indicates a reduction in aspirations among students not selected following the "eleven-plus" examination.[16] One of the by-products of the sponsorship system is the fact that at least some students from middle-class families whose parents cannot afford to send them to private schools suffer severe personal adjustment problems when they are assigned to secondary modern schools on the basis of this selection procedure.[17]

This well-known difference between the British sorting at an early age of students into grammar and modern schools and the American comprehensive high school and ju-

nior college is the clearest application of the distinction under discussion. but the organizing norms penetrate more deeply into the school systems than is initially apparent. The most telling observation regarding the direct normative operation of these principles would be evidence to support the author's impression that major critics of educational procedures within each country do not usually transcend the logic of their respective mobility norms. Thus the British debate about the best method for getting people sorted according to ability, without proposing that elite station should be open to whosoever can ascend to it. Although fear of "sputnik" in the United States introduced a flurry of suggestions for sponsored mobility schemes, the long-standing concern of school critics has been the failure to motivate students adequately. Preocccupation with motivation appears to be an intellectual application of the folk idea that people should *win* their station in society by personal enterprise.

The functional operation of a strain toward consistency with the organizing norms of upward mobility may be illustrated by several other features of the school systems in the two countries. First, the value placed upon education itself differs under the two norms. Under sponsored mobility, schooling is valued for its cultivation of elite culture, and those forms of schooling directed toward such cultivation are more highly valued than others. Education of the non-elite is difficult to justify clearly and tends to be half-hearted, while maximum educational resources are concentrated on "those who can benefit most from them"—in practice, this means those who can learn the elite culture. The secondary modern schools in England have regularly suffered from less adequate financial provision, a higher student–teacher ratio, fewer well trained teachers, and a general lack of prestige in comparison with the grammar schools.[18]

Under contest mobility in the United States, education is valued as a means of getting ahead, but the contents of education are not highly valued in their own right. Over a century ago Tocqueville commented on the absence of an hereditary class "by which the labors of the intellect are held in honor." He remarked that consequently a "middling standard is fixed in America for human knowledge."[19] And there persists in some measure the suspicion of the educated man as one who may have gotten ahead without really earning his position. In spite of recent criticisms of lax standards in American schools, it is in keeping with the general mobility pattern that a Gallup Poll taken in April, 1958, reports that school principals are much more likely to make such criticisms than parents. While 90 percent of the principals thought that ". . . our schools today demand too little work from the students," only 51 percent of the parents thought so, with 33 percent saying that the work was about right and six percent that schools demanded too much work.[20]

Second, the logic of preparation for a contest prevails in United States schools, and emphasizes keeping everyone in the running until the final stages. In primary and secondary schools the assumption tends to be made that those who are learning satisfactorily need little special attention while the less successful require help to be sure that they remain in the contest and may compete for the final stakes. As recently as December, 1958, a nationwide Gallup Poll gave evidence that this attitude had not been radically altered by the international situation. When asked whether or not teachers should devote extra time to the bright students, 26 percent of the respondents replied "yes" and 67 percent, "no." But the responses changed to 86 percent "yes" and only nine percent "no" when the question was asked concerning "slow students."[21]

In western states the junior college offers many students a "second chance" to qualify for university, and all state universities have some provision for substandard high school students to earn admission.

The university itself is run like the true contest: standards are set competitively, students are forced to pass a series of trials each semester, and only a minority of the entrants achieve the prize of graduation. This pattern contrasts sharply with the English system in which selection is supposed to be relatively complete before entrance to university, and students may be subject to no testing whatsoever for the first year or more of university study. Although university completion rates have not been estimated accurately in either country, some figures are indicative of the contrast. In American institutions of higher learning in 1957–1958, the ratio of bachelor's and first-professional degrees to the number of first-time degree-credit enrollments in the fall four years earlier was reported to be .610 for men and .488 for women.[22] The indicated 39 and 51 percent drop-out rates are probably underestimates because transfers from two-year junior colleges swell the number of degrees without being included in first-time enrollments. In England, a study of the careers of individual students reports that in University College, London, almost 82 percent of entering students between 1948 and 1951 eventually graduated with a degree. A similar study a few years earlier at the University of Liverpool shows a comparative figure of almost 87 percent.[23] Under contest mobility, the object is to train as many as possible in the skills necessary for elite status so as to give everyone a chance to maintain competition at the highest pitch. Under sponsored mobility, the objective is to indoctrinate elite culture in only those presumably who will enter the elite, lest there grow a dangerous number of "angry young men" who have elite skills without elite station.

Third, systems of mobility significantly affect educational content. Induction into elite culture under sponsored mobility is consistent with an emphasis on school *esprit de corps* which is employed to cultivate norms of intra-class loyalty and elite tastes and manners. Similarly, formal schooling built about highly specialized study in fields wholly of intellectual or aesthetic concern and of no "practical" value serves the purpose of elite culture. Under contest mobility in the United States, in spite of frequent faculty endorsement of "liberal education," schooling tends to be evaluated in terms of its practical benefits and to become, beyond the elementary level, chiefly vocational. Education does not so much provide what is good in itself as those skills, especially vocational skills, presumed to be necessary in the competition for the real prizes of life.

These contrasts are reflected in the different national attitudes toward university students who are gainfully employed while in school. More students in the United States than in Britain are employed part-time, and relatively fewer of the American students receive subsidies toward subsistence and living expenses. The most generous programs of state aid in the United States, except those applying to veterans and other special groups, do not normally cover expenses other than tuition and institutional fees. British maintenance grants are designed to cover full living expenses, taking into account parental ability to pay.[24] Under sponsored mobility, gainful employment serves no apprenticeship or testing function, and is thought merely to prevent students from gaining the full benefit of their schooling. L. J. Parry speaks of the general opposition to student employment and asserts that English university authorities almost unanimously hold that ". . . if a person must work for financial reasons, he should never spend more than four weeks on such work during the whole year."[25]

Under contest mobility, success in school work is not viewed as a sufficient test of practical merit, but must be supplemented by a test in the world of practical affairs. Thus in didactic folk tales the professional engineer also proves himself to be a superior me-

chanic, the business tycoon a skillful behind-the-counter salesman. By "working his way through school" the enterprising student "earns" his education in the fullest sense, keeps in touch with the practical world, and gains an apprenticeship into vocational life. Students are often urged to seek part-time employment, even when there is no financial need, and in some instances schools include paid employment as a requirement for graduation. As one observer describes the typical American view, a student willing to work part-time is a "better bet" than "the equally bright student who receives all of his financial suppport from others."[26]

Finally, training in "social adjustment" is peculiar to the system of contest mobility. The reason for this emphasis is clear when it is understood that adustment training presumably prepares students to cope with situations for which there are no rules of intercourse or for which the rules are unknown, but in which the good opinions of others cannot be wholly ignored. Under sponsored mobility, elite recruits are inducted into a homogeneous stratum within which there is consensus regarding the rules, and within which they succeed socially by mastering these rules. Under contest mobility, the elite aspirant must relate himself both to the established elite and to the masses, who follow different rules, and the elite itself is not sufficiently homogeneous to evolve consensual rules of intercourse. Furthermore, in the contest the rules may vary according to the background of the competitor, so that each aspirant must successfully deal with persons playing the game with slightly different rules. Consequently, adjustment training is increasingly considered to be one of the important skills imparted by the school system.[27] That the emphasis on such training has had genuine popular support is indicated by a 1945 *Fortune* poll in which a national sample of adults was asked to select the one or two things that would be very important for a son of theirs to get out of college. Over 87 percent chose "Ability to get along with and understand people;" and this answer was the most frequently chosen as the *very* most important thing to get out of college.[28] In this respect, British education may provide better preparation for participation in an orderly and controlled world, while American education may prepare students more adequately for a less ordered situation. The reputedly superior ability of "Yankees" to get things done seems to imply such ability.

To this point the discussion has centered on the tax-supported school systems in both countries, but the different place and emphasis of the privately supported secondary schools can also be related to the distinction between sponsored and contest mobility. Since private secondary schools in both countries are principally vehicles for transmitting the marks of high family status, their mobility function is quite tangential. Under contest mobility, the private schools presumably should have little or no mobility function. On the other hand, if there is to be mobility in a sponsored system, the privately controlled school populated largely with the children of elite parents would be the ideal device through which to induct selectees from lower levels into elite status. By means of a scholarship program, promising members of lesser classes could be chosen early for recruitment. The English "public" schools, in fact, have incorporated into their charters provisions to insure that a few boys from lesser classes will enter each year. Getting one's child into a "public" school, or even into one of the less prestigeful private schools, assumes an importance in England relatively unknown in the United States. If the children cannot win scholarships the parents often make extreme financial sacrifices in order to pay the cost of this relatively exclusive education.[29]

How much of a role private secondary schools have played in mobility in either country is difficult to determine. American studies of social mobility usually omit information on private *versus* tax-supported secondary school attendance, and English studies showing the advantage of "public" school attendance generally fail to distinguish between the mobile and the nonmobile in this respect. However, during the nineteenth century the English "public" schools were used by *nouveaux riches* members of the manufacturing classes to enable their sons to achieve unqualified elite status.[30] In one sense, the rise of the manufacturing classes through free enterprise introduced a large measure of contest mobility which threatened to destroy the traditional sponsorship system. But by using the "public" schools in this fashion they bowed to the legitimacy of the traditional system—an implicit acknowledgement that upward mobility was not complete without sponsored induction. Dennis Brogan speaks of the task of the "public" schools in the nineteenth century as "the job of marrying the old English social order to the new."[31]

With respect to mobility, the parallel between the tax-supported grammar schools and the "public" schools in England is of interest. The former in important respects have been patterned after the latter, adopting their view of mobility but making it a much larger part of their total function. Generally the grammar schools are the vehicle for sponsored mobility throughout the middle ranges of the class system, modelled after the pattern of the "public" schools which remain the agencies for sponsored mobility into the elite.

. . .

Conclusion: Suggestions for Research

The foregoing discussion is broadly impressionistic and speculative, reflecting more the general impression of an observer of both countries than a systematic exploration of data. Relevant data of a variety of sorts are cited above, but their use is more illustrative than demonstrative. However, several lines of research are suggested by this tentative analysis. One of these is an exploration of different channels of mobility in both England and the United States in an attempt to discover the extent to which mobility corresponds to the mobility types. Recruitment to the Catholic priesthood, for example, probably strictly follows a sponsorship norm regardless of the dominant contest norm in the United States.

The effect of changes in the major avenues of upward mobility upon the dominant norms requires investigation. The increasing importance of promotion through corporation hierarchies and the declining importance of the entrepreneurial path of upward mobility undoubtedly compromise the ideal pattern of contest mobility. The growing insistence that higher education is a prerequisite to more and more occupations is a similar modification. Yet, there is little evidence of a tendency to follow the logic of sponsorship beyond the bureaucratic selection process. The prospect of a surplus of college-educated persons in relation to jobs requiring college education may tend to restore the contest situation at a higher level, and the further possibility that completion of higher education may be more determined by motivational factors than by capacity suggests that the contest pattern continues within the school.

In England, on the other hand, two developments may weaken the sponsorship system. One is positive response to popular demand to allow more children to secure the grammar school type of training, particularly by including such a program in the secondary modern school. The other is introduction of the comprehensive secondary school, relatively uncommon at present but a major plank in the labour party's educa-

tion platform. It remains to be determined whether the comprehensive school in England will take a distinctive form and serve a distinctive function, which preserves the pattern of sponsorship, or will approximate the present American system.

Finally, the assertion that these types of mobility are embedded in the genuine folk norms requires specific investigation. Here, a combination of direct study of popular attitudes and content analysis of popular responses to crucial issues would be useful. Perhaps the most significant search would be for evidence showing what courses of action require no special justification or explanation because they are altogether "natural" and "right," and what courses of action, whether approved or not, require special justification and explanation. Such evidence, appropriately used, would show the extent to which the patterns described are genuine folk norms rather than mere by-products of particular structural factors. It would also permit determination of the extent to which acceptance of the folk norms is diffused among the different segments of the populations.

NOTES

1. A comprehensive summary of such studies appears in Seymour M. Lipset and Reinhard Bendix, *Social Mobility in Industrial Society*, Berkeley and Los Angeles: University of California Press.
2. Cf. C. A. Anderson, "The Social Status of University Students in Relation to Type of Economy: An International Comparison," *Transactions of the Third World Congress of Sociology*, London, 1956, vol. V, pp. 51–63; J. E. Floud, *Social Class and Educational Opportunity*, London: Heinemann, 1956; W. L. Warner, R. J. Havighurst, and M. B. Loeb, *Who Shall Be Educated?* New York: Harper, 1944.
3. Reference is made throughout the chapter to "elite" and "masses." The generalizations, however, are intended to apply throughout the stratification continuum to relations between members of a given class and the class

or classes above it. Statements about mobility are intended in general to apply to mobility from manual to middle-class levels, lower-middle to upper-middle class, and so on, as well as into the strictly elite groups. The simplified expressions avoid the repeated use of cumbersome and involved statements which might otherwise be required.

4. The normative element in an organizing norm goes beyond Max Weber's *ideal type*, conveying more of the sense of Durkheim's *collective representation;* cf. Ralph H. Turner, "The Normative Coherence of Folk Concepts," *Research Studies of the State College of Washington,* 25 (1957), pp. 127–136. Charles Wagley has developed a similar concept which he calls "ideal pattern" in his as yet unpublished work on Brazilian kinship. See also Howard Becker, "Constructive Typology in the Social Sciences," *American Sociological Review,* 5 (February 1940), pp. 40–55.

5. Geoffrey Gorer remarks on the favorable evaluation of the successful gamble in American culture: "Gambling is also a respected and important component in many business ventures. Conspicuous improvement in a man's financial position is generally attributed to a lucky combination of industry, skill, and gambling, though the successful gambler prefers to refer to his gambling as 'vision.'" *The American People* (New York: Norton, 1948), p. 178.

6. Vilfredo Pareto, *The Mind and Society* (New York: Harcourt, Brace, 1935), vol. 4, p. 1796.

7. Many writers have noted that different kinds of societies facilitate the rise of different kinds of personalities, either in the stratification hierarchy or in other ways. Cf. Jessie Bernard, *American Community Behavior* (New York: Dryden, 1949), p. 205. A particularly interesting statement is Martindale's exploration of "favored personality" types in sacred and secular studies. Don Martindale and Elio Monachesi, *Elements of Sociology* (New York: Harper, 1951), pp. 312–378.

8. At one time in the United States a good many owners of expensive British Jaguar automobiles carried large signs on the cars identifying the make. Such a display would have been unthinkable under a sponsored mobility system since the Jaguar owner would not care for the esteem of persons too uninformed to tell a Jaguar from a less prestigious automobile.

9. See, e.g., Lawrence Lipton, *The Holy Barbarians* (New York: Messner, 1959).

10. Cf. Albert K. Cohen, *Delinquent Boys: The Culture of the Gang* (Glencoe, IL: Free Press, 1955).

11. D. V. Glass, editor, *Social Mobility in Britain* (Glencoe, IL: Free Press, 1954), pp. 144–145, reports studies showing only small variations in intelligence between occupational levels.

12. Gorer, op. cit., pp. 172–187.

13. See, e.g., *Los Angeles Times* (May 4, 1959), p. I, Part 24.

14. The nature and operation of the "eleven-plus" system are fully reviewed in a report by a committee of the British Psychological Society and in a report of extensive research into the adequacy of selection methods. See P. E. Vernon, editor, *Secondary School Selection: A British Psychological Inquiry* (London: Methuen, 1957); and Alfred Yates and D. A. Pidgeon, *Admission to Grammar Schools* (London: Newnes Educational Publishing Co., 1957).

15. J. E. Floud, A. H. Halsey, and F. M. Martin, *Social Class and Educational Opportunity* (London: Heinemann, 1956).

16. Mary D. Wilson documents the reduction in aspirations characterizing students in British secondary modern schools and notes the contrast with American studies revealing much more "unrealistic" aspirations; see "The Vocational Preferences of Secondary Modern School-children," *British Journal of Educational Psychology,* 23 (1953), pp. 97–113. See also Ralph H. Turner, "The Changing Ideology of Success," *Transactions of the Third World Congress of Sociology, 1956,* London, vol. V, esp. p. 37.

17. Pointed out by Hilde Himmelweit in private communication.

18. Less adequate financial provision and a higher student–teacher ratio are mentioned as obstacles to parity of secondary modern schools with grammar schools in *The Times Educational Supplement* (February 22, 1957), p. 241. On difficulties in achieving prestige comparable with grammar schools, see G. Baron, "Secondary Education in Britain: Some Present-Day Trends." *Teachers College Record,* 57 (January 1956), pp. 211–221; and O. Banks, *Parity and Prestige in English Secondary Education* (London: Routledge and Kegan Paul, 1955). See also Vernon, op. cit., pp. 19–22.

19. Alexis de Tocqueville, *Democracy in America* (New York: Knopf, 1945), vol. I, p. 52.

20. An earlier Gallup Poll has disclosed that 62 percent of the parents opposed stiffened college entrance requirements while only 27 percent favored them. Reported in *Time* (April 14, 1958), p. 45.

21. Reported in the *Los Angeles Times* (December 17, 1958), Part I, p. 16.
22. U.S. Department of Health, Education, and Welfare, Office of Education, *Earned Degrees Conferred by Higher Education Institutions, 1957–1958* (Washington, DC: U.S. Government Printing Office, 1959), p. 3.
23. Nicholas Malleson, "Student Performance at University College, London, 1948–1951," *Universities Quarterly,* 12 (May 1958), pp. 288–319.
24. See, e.g., C. A. Quattlebaum, *Federal Aid to Students for Higher Education* (Washington, DC: U.S. Government Printing Office, 1956); and "Grants to Students: University and Training Colleges," *The Times Educational Supplement* (May 6, 1955), p. 446.
25. "Students' Expenses," *The Times Educational Supplement* (May 6, 1955), p. 447.
26. R. H. Eckelberry, "College Jobs for College Students," *Journal of Higher Education,* 27 (March 1956), p. 174.
27. Adjustment training is not a necessary accompaniment of contest mobility. The shift during the last half century toward the increased importance of social acceptability as an elite credential has brought such training into correspondingly greater prominence.
28. Reported in Hadley Cantril, editor, *Public Opinion 1935–1946* (Princeton: Princeton University Press, 1951), p. 186.
29. For one account of the place of "public" schools in the English educational system, see Dennis Brogen, *The English People* (New York: Knopf, 1943), pp. 18–56.
30. A. H. Halsey of Birmingham University has called my attention to the importance of this fact.
31. Op. cit., pp. 24–25.

4

THE PROCESS OF STRATIFICATION

Peter M. Blau • Otis D. Duncan

Peter Michael Blau and Otis Dudley Duncan, excerpt from "The Process of Stratification" from *The American Occupational Structure.* Copyright © 1967 by Peter M. Blau and Otis Dudley Duncan. Reprinted with the permission of The Free Press, a division of Simon & Schuster, Inc.

Stratification systems may be characterized in various ways. Surely one of the most important has to do with the processes by which individuals become located, or locate themselves, in positions in the hierarchy comprising the system. At one extreme we can imagine that the circumstances of a person's birth—including the person's sex and the perfectly predictable sequence of age levels through which he is destined to pass—suffice to assign him unequivocally to a ranked status in a hierarchical system. At the opposite extreme his prospective adult status would be wholly problematic and contingent at the time of birth. Such status would become entirely determinate only as adulthood was reached, and solely as a consequence of his own actions taken freely—that is, in the absence of any constraint deriving from the circumstances of his birth or rearing. Such a pure achievement system is, of course, hypothetical, in much the same way that motion without friction is a purely hypothetical possibility in the physical world. Whenever the stratification system of any moderately large and complex society is described, it is seen to involve both ascriptive and achievement principles.

In a liberal democratic society we think of the more basic principle as being that of achievement. Some ascriptive features of the system may be regarded as vestiges of an earlier epoch, to be extirpated as rapidly as possible. Public policy may emphasize measures designed to enhance or to equalize opportunity—hopefully, to overcome ascriptive obstacles to the full exercise of the achievement principle.

The question of how far a society may realistically aspire to go in this direction is hotly debated, not only in the ideological arena but in the academic forum as well. Our contribution, if any, to the debate will consist largely in submitting measurements and estimates of the strength of ascriptive forces and of the scope of opportunities in a large contemporary society. The problem of the relative importance of the two principles in a given system is ultimately a quantitative one. We have pushed our ingenuity to its limit in seeking to contrive relevant quantifications.

The governing conceptual scheme in the analysis is quite a commonplace one. We think of the individual's life cycle as a sequence in time that can be described, however partially and crudely, by a set of classificatory or quantitative measurements taken at successive stages. Ideally we should like to have under observation a cohort of births, following the individuals who make up the cohort as they pass through life. As a practical matter we resorted to retrospective questions put to a representative sample of several adjacent cohorts so as to ascertain those facts about their life histories that we assumed were both relevant to our problem and accessible by this means of observation.

Given this scheme, the questions we are continually raising in one form or another are: how and to what degree do the circumstances of birth condition subsequent status? and, how does status attained (whether by ascription or achievement) at one stage of the life cycle affect the prospects for a subsequent stage? The questions are neither idle nor idiosyncratic ones. Current policy discussion and action come to a focus in a vaguely explicated notion of the "inheritance of poverty."

Thus a spokesman for the Social Security Administration writes:

> It would be one thing if poverty hit at random and no one group were singled out. It is another thing to realize that some seem destined to poverty almost from birth—by their color or by the economic status or occupation of their parents.[1]

Another officially sanctioned concept is that of the "dropout," the person who fails to graduate from high school. Here the emphasis is not so much on circumstances operative at birth but on the presumed effect of early achievement on subsequent opportunities. Thus the "dropout" is seen as facing "a lifetime of uncertain employment,"[2] probable assignment to jobs of inferior status, reduced earning power, and vulnerability to various forms of social pathology.

In this study we do not have measurements on all the factors implicit in a full-blown conception of the "cycle of poverty" nor all those variables conceivably responding unfavorably to the achievement of "dropout" status. For practical reasons, . . . we were severely limited in the amount of information to be collected. For theoretical reasons, . . . and in conformity with the tradition of studies in social mobility, we chose to emphasize occupation as a measure both of origin status and of status achievement. The present chapter is . . . strictly limited to variables we think can be treated meaningfully as quantitative and therefore are suited to analysis by the regression technique. . . . This limitation, however, is not merely an analytical convenience. We think of the selected quantitative variables as being sufficient to describe the major outlines of status changes in the life cycle of a cohort. Thus a study of the relationships among these variables leads to a formulation of a basic model of the process of stratification. In this chapter we consider also certain extensions of this model. . . .

A Basic Model

To begin with, we examine only five variables. For expository convenience, when it is necessary to resort to symbols, we shall designate them by arbitrary letters but try to remind the reader from time to time of what the letters stand for. These variables are:

V: Father's educational attainment
X: Father's occupational status
U: Respondent's educational attainment
W: Status of respondent's first job
Y: Status of respondent's occupation in 1962

Each of the three occupational statuses is scaled by [an] index . . . ranging from 0 to 96. The two education variables are scored on the following arbitrary scale of values ("rungs" on the "educational ladder") corresponding to specified numbers of years of formal schooling completed:

0: No school
1: Elementary, one to four years
2: Elementary, five to seven years
3: Elementary, eight years
4: High school, one to three years
5: High school, four years
6: College, one to three years
7: College, four years
8: College, five years or more (i.e., one or more years of postgraduate study)

Actually, this scoring system hardly differs from a simple linear transformation, or "coding," of the exact number of years of school completed. In retrospect, . . . we feel that the score implies too great a distance between intervals at the lower end of the scale; but the resultant distortion is minor in view of the very small proportions scored 0 or 1.

A basic assumption in our interpretation of regression statistics—though not in their calculation as such—has to do with the causal or temporal ordering of these variables. In terms of the father's career we should naturally assume precedence of V (education) with respect to X (occupation when his son was 16 years old). We are not concerned with the father's career, however, but only with his statuses that comprised a configuration of background circumstances or origin conditions for the cohorts of sons who were respondents in the OCG study. Hence we generally make no assumption as to the priority of V with respect to X; in effect, we assume the measurements on these variables to be contemporaneous from the son's viewpoint. The respondent's education, U, is supposed to follow in time—and thus to be susceptible to causal influence from—the two measures of father's status. Because we ascertained X as of respondent's age 16, it is true that some respondents may have completed school before the age to which X pertains. Such cases were doubtlessly a small minority and in only a minor proportion of them could the father (or other family head) have changed status radically in the two or three years before the respondent reached 16.

The next step in the sequence is more problematic. We assume that W (first job status) follows U (education). The assumption conforms to the wording of the questionnaire . . . which stipulated "the first full-time job you had after you left school." In the years since the OCG study was designed we have been made aware of a fact that should have been considered more carefully in the design. Many students leave school more or less definitively, only to return, perhaps to a different school, some years later, whereupon they often finish a degree program.[3] The OCG questionnaire contained information relevant to this problem, namely the item on age at first job. Through an oversight no tabulations of this item were made for the present study. Tables prepared for another study[4] using the OCG data, however, suggest that approximately one-eighth of the respondents report a combination of age at first job and education that would be very improbable unless (a) they violated instructions by reporting a part-time or school-vacation job as the first job, or (b) they did, in fact, interrupt their schooling to enter regular employment. (These "inconsistent" responses include men giving 19 as their age at first job and college graduation or more as their education; 17 or 18 with some college or more; 14, 15, or 16 with high-school graduation or more; and under 14 with some high school or more.) When the two variables are studied in combination with occupation of first job, a very clear effect is evident. Men with a given amount of education beginning their first jobs early held lower occupational statuses than those beginning at a normal or advanced age for the specified amount of education.

Despite the strong probability that the U–W sequence is reversed for an appreciable minority of respondents, we have hardly any alternative to the assumption made here. If the bulk of the men who interrupted schooling to take their first jobs were among those ultimately securing relatively advanced education, then our variable W is downwardly biased, no doubt, as a measure of their occupational status immediately after they finally left school for good. In this sense, the correlations between U and W and between W and Y are probably attenuated. Thus, if we had really measured "job after completing education" instead of "first job," the former would in all likelihood have loomed somewhat larger as a variable intervening between education and 1962 occupational status. We do not wish to argue that our respondents erred in their reports on first job. We are inclined to conclude that their reports were realistic enough, and that it was our assumption about the meaning of the responses that proved to be fallible.

The fundamental difficulty here is conceptual. If we insist on *any* uniform sequence of the events involved in accomplishing the transition to independent adult status, we do violence to reality. Completion of schooling, departure from the parental home, entry into the labor market, and contracting of a first marriage are crucial steps in this transition, which all normally occur within a few short years. Yet they occur at no fixed ages nor in any fixed order. As soon as we aggregate individual data for analytical purposes we are forced into the use of simplifying assumptions. Our assumption here is, in effect, that "first job" has a uniform significance for all men in terms of its temporal relationship to educational preparation and subsequent work experience. If this assumption is not strictly correct, we doubt that it could be improved by substituting any other *single* measure of initial occupational status. (In designing the OCG questionnaire, the alternative of "job at the time of first marriage" was entertained briefly, but dropped for the reason, among others, that unmarried men would be excluded thereby.)

One other problem with the U–W transition should be mentioned. Among the younger men in the study, 20 to 24 years old, are many who have yet to finish their schooling or to take up their first jobs or both—not to mention the men in this age group missed by the survey on account of their military service. . . . Unfortunately, an early decision on tabulation plans resulted in the inclusion of the 20 to 24 group with the older men in aggregate tables for men 20 to 64 years old. We have ascertained that this results in only minor distortions by comparing a variety of data for men 20 to 64 and for those 25 to 64 years of age. Once over the U–W hurdle, we see no serious objection to our assumption that both U and W precede Y, except in regard to some fraction of the very young men just mentioned.

In summary, then, we take the somewhat idealized assumption of temporal order to represent an order of priority in a causal or

TABLE 4.1   Simple Correlations for Five Status Variables

	Variable				
Variable	Y	W	U	X	V
Y: 1962 occ. status	—	.541	.596	.405	322
W: First-job status		—	.538	.417	332
U: Education			—	.438	.453
X: Father's occ. status				—	.516
V: Father's education					—

processual sequence, which may be stated diagrammatically as follows:

$$(V, X)—(U)—(W)—(Y).$$

In proposing this sequence we do not overlook the possibility of what Carlsson calls "delayed effects,"[5] meaning that an early variable may affect a later one not only via intervening variables but also directly (or perhaps through variables not measured in the study).

In translating this conceptual framework into quantitative estimates the first task is to establish the pattern of associations between the variables in the sequence. This is accomplished with the correlation coefficient. . . . Table 4.1 supplies the correlation matrix on which much of the subsequent analysis is based. In discussing causal interpretations of these correlations, we shall have to be clear about the distinction between two points of view. On the one hand, the simple correlation—given our assumption as to direction of causation—measures the gross magnitude of the effect of the antecedent upon the consequent variable. Thus, if $r_{VW} = .541$, we can say that an increment of one standard deviation in first job status produces (whether directly or indirectly) an increment of just over half of one standard deviation in 1962 occupational status. From another point of view we are more concerned with net effects. If both first job and 1962 status have a common antecedent cause—say, father's occupation—we may want to state what part of

the effect of W on Y consists in a transmission of the prior influence of X. Or, thinking of X as the initial cause, we may focus on the extent to which its influence on Y is transmitted by way of its prior influence on W.

We may, then, devote a few remarks to the pattern of gross effects before presenting the apparatus that yields estimates of net direct and indirect effects. Since we do not require a causal ordering of father's education with respect to his occupation, we may be content simply to note that $r_{XV} = .516$ is somewhat lower than the corresponding correlation, $r_{YU} = .596$, observed for the respondents themselves. The difference suggests a heightening of the effect of education on occupational status between the fathers' and the sons' generations. Before stressing this interpretation, however, we must remember that the measurements of V and X do not pertain to some actual cohort of men, here designated "fathers." Each "father" is represented in the data in proportion to the number of his sons who were 20 to 64 years old in March 1962.

The first recorded status of the son himself is education (U). We note that r_{UV} is just slightly greater than r_{UX}. Apparently both measures on the father represent factors that may influence the son's education.

In terms of gross effects there is a clear ordering of influences on first job. Thus $r_{WU} > r_{WX} > r_{WV}$. Education is most strongly correlated with first job, followed by father's occupation, and then by father's education.

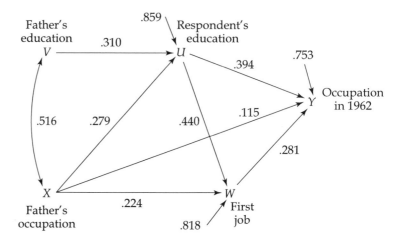

FIGURE 4.1 Path Coefficients in Basic Model of the process of stratification.

Occupational status in 1962 (*Y*) apparently is influenced more strongly by education than by first job; but our earlier discussion of the first-job measure suggests we should not overemphasize the difference between r_{VW} and r_{YU}. Each, however, is substantially greater than r_{YX}, which in turn is rather more impressive than r_{YV}.

Figure 4.1 is a graphic representation of the system of relationships among the five variables that we propose as our basic model. The numbers entered on the diagram, with the exception of r_{VV}, are path coefficients, [suggesting the magnitude of the relationship between the variables]. First we must become familiar with the conventions followed in constructing this kind of diagram. The link between *V* and *X* is shown as a curved line with an arrowhead at both ends. This is to distinguish it from the other lines, which are taken to be paths of influence. In the case of *V* and *X* we may suspect an influence running from the former to the latter. But if the diagram is logical for the respondent's generation, we should have to assume that for the fathers, likewise, education and occupation are correlated not only because one affects the other but also because common causes lie behind both, which we have not measured. The bidirectional arrow merely serves to sum up

all sources of correlation between *V* and *X* and to indicate that the explanation thereof is not part of the problem at hand.

The straight lines running from one measured variable to another represent *direct* (or net) influences. The symbol for the path coefficient, such as p_{YW}, caries a double subscript. The first subscript is the variable at the head of the path, or the effect: the second is the causal variable. (This resembles the convention for regression coefficients, where the first subscript refers to the "dependent" variable, the second to the "independent" variable.)

Finally, we see lines with no source indicated carrying arrows to each of the effect variables. These represent the residual paths, standing for all other influences on the variable in question, including causes not recognized or measured, errors of measurement, and departures of the true relationships from additivity and linearity, properties that are assumed throughout the analysis. . . .

An important feature of this kind of causal scheme is that variables recognized as effects of certain antecedent factors may, in turn, serve as causes for subsequent variables. For example, *U* is caused by *V* and *X*, but it in turn influences *W* and *Y*. The algebraic representation of the scheme is a system of equations, rather than the single equation more often employed in multiple regression analysis. This feature permits a flexible conceptualization of the *modus operandi* of the causal network. Note that Y is shown here as being influenced directly by W, U, and X, but not by V (an assumption that will be justified shortly). But this does not imply that V has no influence on Y. V affects U, which does affect Y both directly and indirectly (via W). Moreover, V is correlated with X, and thus shares in the gross effect of X on Y, which is partly direct and partly indirect. Hence the gross effect of V on Y, previously described in terms of the correlation r_{YV}, is here interpreted as being entirely indirect, in consequence of V's effect on intervening variables and its correlation with another cause of Y.

Path Coefficients

Whether a path diagram, or the causal scheme it represents, is adequate depends on both theoretical and empirical considerations. At a minimum, before constructing the diagram we must know, or be willing to assume, a causal ordering of the observed variables (hence the lengthy discussion of this matter earlier in this chapter). This information is external or *a priori* with respect to the data, which merely describe associations or correlations. Moreover, the causal scheme must be complete, in the sense that all causes are accounted for. Here, as in most problems involving analysis of observational data, we achieve a formal completeness of the scheme by representing unmeasured causes as a residual factor, presumed to be uncorrelated with the remaining factors lying behind the variable in question. If any factor is known or presumed to operate in some other way it must be represented in the diagram in accordance with its causal role, even though it is not measured. Sometimes it is possible to deduce interesting implications from the inclu-

sion of such a variable and to secure useful estimates of certain paths in the absence of measurements on it, but this is not always so. A partial exception to the rule that all causes must be explicitly represented in the diagram is the unmeasured variable that can be assumed to operate strictly as an intervening variable. Its inclusion would enrich our understanding of a causal system without invalidating the causal scheme that omits it. Sociologists have only recently begun to appreciate how stringent are the logical requirements that must be met if discussion of causal processes is to go beyond mere impressionism and vague verbal formulations.[6] We are a long way from being able to make causal inferences with confidence, and schemes of the kind presented here had best be regarded as crude first approximations to adequate causal models.

. . .

Our supposition is that the scheme in Figure 4.1 is most easily subject to modification by introducing additional measures of the same kind as those used here. If indexes relating to socioeconomic background other than V and X are inserted we will almost certainly estimate differently the direct effects of these particular variables. If occupational statuses of the respondent intervening between W and Y were known we should have to modify more or less radically the right-hand portion of the diagram, as will be shown in the next section. Yet we should argue that such modification may amount to an enrichment or extension of the basic model rather than an invalidation of it. The same may be said of other variables that function as intervening causes. In theory, it should be possible to specify these in some detail, and a major part of the research worker's task is properly defined as an attempt at such specification. In the course of such work, to be sure, there is always the possibility of a discovery that would require a fundamental reformulation, making the present model obsolete. Discarding the model would be a cost gladly paid for the prize of such a discovery.

. . .

A final stipulation about the scheme had best be stated, though it is implicit in all the previous discussion. The form of the model itself, but most particularly the numerical estimates accompanying it, are submitted as valid only for the population under study. No claim is made that an equally cogent account of the process of stratification in another society could be rendered in terms of this scheme. For other populations, or even for subpopulations within the United States, the magnitudes would almost certainly be different, although we have some basis for supposing them to have been fairly constant over the last few decades in this country. The technique of path analysis is not a method for discovering causal laws but a procedure for giving a quantitative interpretation to the manifestations of a known or assumed causal system as it operates in a particular population. When the same interpretive structure is appropriate for two or more populations there is something to be learned by comparing their respective path coefficients and correlation patterns. We have not yet reached the stage at which such comparative study of stratification systems is feasible.

. . .

The Concept of a Vicious Circle

. . .

Although the concept of a "cycle of poverty" has a quasi-official sanction in U.S. public policy discussion, it is difficult to locate a systematic explication of the concept. As clear a formulation as any that may be found in academic writing is perhaps the following:[7]

Occupational and social status are to an important extent self-perpetuating. They are associated with many factors which make it difficult for individuals to modify their status. Position in the social structure is usually associated with a certain level of income, education, family structure, community reputation, and so forth. These become part of a vicious circle in which each factor acts on the other in such a way as to preserve the social structure in its present form, as well as the individual family's position in that structure. . . . The cumulation of disadvantages (or of advantages) affects the individual's entry into the labor market as well as his later opportunities for social mobility.

The suspicion arises that the authors in preparing this summary statement were partly captured by their own rhetoric. Only a few pages earlier they had observed that the "widespread variation of educational attainment within classes suggests that one's family background plays an enabling and motivating rather than a determining role."[8] But is an "enabling and motivating role" logically adequate to the function of maintaining a "vicious circle"? In focusing closely on the precise wording of the earlier quotation we are not interested in splitting hairs or in generating a polemic. It merely serves as a convenient point of departure for raising the questions of what is specifically meant by "vicious circle," what are the operational criteria for this concept, and what are the limits of its usefulness.

To begin with, there is the question of fact—or, rather, of how the quantitative facts are to be evaluated. How "difficult" is it, in actuality, "for individuals to modify their status" (presumably reference is to the status of the family of orientation)? We have found that the father–son correlation for occupational status is of the order of .4 (Assuming attenuation by errors of measurement, this should perhaps be revised slightly upward.) Approaching the measurement problem in an entirely different way, we find that the amount of intergenerational mobility between census major occupation groups is no less than seven-eighths as much as would occur if there were no statistical association between the two statuses whatsoever, or five-sixths as much as the difference between the "minimum" mobility involved in the intergenerational shift in occupation distributions and the amount required for "perfect" mobility.[9] Evidently a very considerable amount of "status modification" or occupational mobility does occur. (There is nothing in the data exhibited by Lipset and Bendix to indicate the contrary.) If the existing amount of modification of status is insufficient in terms of some functional or normative criterion implicitly employed, the precise criterion should be made explicit: *How much mobility must occur to contradict the diagnosis of a "vicious circle"?*

Next, take the postulate that occupational status (of origin) is "associated with many factors" and that "each factor acts on the other" so as "to preserve . . . the individual family's position." Here the exposition virtually cries out for an explicit *quantitative* causal model; if not one of the type set forth in the first section of this chapter, then some other model that also takes into account the way in which several variables combine their effects. Taking our own earlier model, for want of a better alternative, as representative of the situation, what do we learn about the "associated factors"? Family "position" is, indeed, "associated with . . . education," and education in turn makes a sizable difference in early and subsequent occupational achievement.

. . .

[A]n accounting of the total variation in respondent's 1962 occupational status (Y), yields these percentages:

(i)	Gross (or total) effect of father's education and occupation	18.06
(ii)	Education of respondent, independent of (i)	24.31
(iii)	All other factors, independent of (i) and (ii)	57.62
	Total	100.00

. . . Here we have imputed to the measures of "family position," X and V, their *total* influence, including such part of this as works through education; the 24 percent contribution of respondent's education refers only to the part of the effect of education that is net of the background factors. Still, education has a greater influence, *independent of these factors,* than they have themselves, operating both directly and indirectly. Overshadowing both these components, of course, is the unexplained variation of nearly 58 percent, which can have nothing to do with "perpetuating status."

Whatever the merit of these observations, they should at least make clear that statistical results do not speak for themselves. Rather, the findings of a statistical analysis must be controlled by an interpretation—one that specifies the form the analysis will take—and be supplemented by further interpretations that (ideally) make explicit the assumptions on which the analyst is proceeding. The form in which our results are presented is dictated by a conception of status achievement as a temporal process in which later statuses depend, in part, on earlier statuses, intervening achievements, and other contingent factors. In such a framework it may not be a meaningful task to evaluate the relative importance of different causal factors. Instead, attention is focused on how the causes combine to produce the end result.

From this point of view we can indicate, first, the gross effect of the measured background factors or origin statuses of a cohort of men on their adult achievement. We can then show how and to what extent this effect is transmitted via measured intervening variables and, finally, to what extent such intervening variables contribute to the outcome, independently of their role in transmission of prior statuses. In a balanced interpretation all these questions should be dealt with explicitly.

Our treatment seems to indicate the advisability of keeping in perspective the magnitude of the gross relationship of background factors and status of origin to subsequent achievement. The relationship is not trivial, nor is it, on the other hand, great enough in itself to justify the conception of a system that insures the "inheritance of poverty" or otherwise renders wholly ineffectual the operation of institutions supposedly based on universalistic principles.

Our model also indicates where the "vicious circle" interpretation is vulnerable. In the passage on the vicious circle quoted there seems to be an assumption that because of the substantial intercorrelations between a number of background factors, each of which has a significant relationship to subsequent achievement, the total effect of origin on achievement is materially enhanced. Here, in other words, the concept of "cumulation" appears to refer to the intercorrelations of a collection of independent variables. But the effect of such intercorrelations is quite opposite to what the writers appear to suppose. They are not alone in arguing from a fallacious assumption that was caustically analyzed by Karl Pearson half a century ago.[10] The crucial point is that if the several determinants are indeed substantially intercorrelated with each other, then their combined effect will consist largely in redundancy, not in "cumulation." This circumstance does not relieve us from the necessity of trying to understand better *how* the effects come about (a point also illustrated in a less fortunate way in Pearson's work). It does imply that a refined estimate of how much effect results from a combination of "associated factors" will not differ greatly from a fairly crude estimate based on the two or three most important ones. Sociologists have too long followed the mirage of "increasing the explained variance."

Let us not fall into the trap of supposing that, had we measured more of the "real" background factors, the outcome would have been greatly different. . . . Either the "real" factors would be associated with the measured ones, or they would not. If the former, they would add little to the "explained variation"—as we illustrated, quite cogently though conjecturally, with two "omitted variables." If, on the other hand, the "real" factors are not associated with our measures of "family position," then they would operate independently thereof and *not* to "perpetuate" family position.

We do not wish to imply that the idea of cumulation of influences, or even the particular form of cumulation describable as a "vicious circle," is without merit. Our aim is to call attention to the necessity of specifying the actual mechanism that is only vaguely suggested by such terms. One legitimate meaning of cumulation is illustrated by the model of a synthetic cohort presented earlier in this chapter. In this case, what is cumulative is the experience of an individual or a cohort of individuals over the life cycle, so that in the latter part of the life cycle achieved status depends heavily on the prior achievements, whatever the factors determining those achievements may have been. The cumulation here consists in large measure of the effects of contingent factors not related to social origins or measured background factors.

The situation of the Negro American, . . . exemplifies mechanisms inviting the label of a vicious circle. What is crucial in this case is not merely that Negroes begin life at a disadvantage and that this initial disadvantage, transmitted by intervening conditions, has adverse effects on later careers. Rather, what happens is that, in addition to the initial handicap, the Negro experiences further handicaps at each stage of the life cycle. When Negroes and whites are equated with respect to socioeconomic circumstances of origin and rearing, Negroes secure inferior education. But if we allow for this educational disadvantage as well as the disadvantage of low social origins, Negroes find their way into first jobs of lower status than whites. Again, allowing for the handicap of inferior career beginnings, the handicap of lower education, and the residual effect of low socioeconomic origins—even with all these allowances—Negroes do not enjoy comparable occupational success in adulthood. Indeed, even though we have not carried our own analysis this far, there is good evidence that Negroes and whites do not have equal incomes even after making allowance for the occupational status difference and the educational handicap of Negroes.[11] Thus there surely are disadvantaged minorities in the United States who suffer from a "vicious circle" that is produced by discrimination. But not all background factors that create occupational handicaps are necessarily indicative of such a vicious circle of *cumulative* disadvantages; the handicaps of the Southern whites, for example, are not cumulative in the same sense. . . . A vicious circle of cumulative impediments is a distinctive phenomenon that should not be confused with any and all forms of differential occupational achievement.

As noted earlier, the issue of equalitarianism is one that has generally been more productive of debate than of cogent reasoning from systematized experience. Without becoming fully involved in such a debate here, we must at least attempt to avoid having our position misunderstood. We have *not* vouchsafed a "functional interpretation" that asserts that somehow American society has just the right amount of stratification and just the appropriate degree of intergenerational status transmission. We *have* indicated that it is easy to exaggerate the latter and, in particular, that it is possible seriously to misconstrue the nature of the causal relationships in the process that characterizes status transmission between generations.

In conclusion, one question of policy may be briefly mentioned, which pertains to the distinction between the plight of the minorities who do suffer disadvantages due to their ascribed status and the influence of ascribed factors on occupational life in general. To help such minorities to break out of the vicious circle resulting from discrimination and poverty is a challenge a democratic society must face, in our opinion. To advocate this policy, however, is not the same as claiming that *all* ascriptive constraints on opportunities and achievements could or should be eliminated. To eliminate all *dis*advantages that flow from membership in a family of orientation—with its particular structure of interpersonal relationships, socioeconomic level, community and regional location, and so on—would by the same token entail eliminating any *advantages* the family can confer or provide. If parents, having achieved a desirable status, can *ipso facto* do nothing to make comparable achievement easier for their offspring, we may have "equal opportunity." But we will no longer have a family system—at least not in the present understanding of the term. (This point has not been misunderstood in radical, particularly Marxist, ideologies.)

We do not contemplate an effortless equilibrium at some optimum condition where the claims of egalitarian values and the forces of family attachment are neatly balanced to the satisfaction of all. A continuing tension between these ultimately incompatible tendencies may, indeed, be a requisite for social progress. We do contend that both equity and effectiveness in the policy realm call for a deeper understanding of the process of stratification than social science and politics yet can claim.

NOTES

1. Mollie Orshansky, "Children of the Poor," *Social Security Bulletin,* 26 (July 1963).
2. Forrest A. Bogan, "Employment of High School Graduates and Dropouts in 1964," *Special Labor Force Report,* no. 54, U.S. Bureau of Labor Statistics (June 1965), p. 643.
3. Bruce K. Eckland, "College Dropouts Who Came Back," *Harvard Educational Review,* 34 (1964), pp. 402–20.
4. Beverly Duncan, *Family Factors and School Dropout: 1920–1960,* U.S. Office of Education, Cooperative Research Project No. 2258 (Ann Arbor: University of Michigan, 1965).
5. Gösta Carlsson, *Social Mobility and Class Structure* (Lund: CWK Gleerup, 1958), p. 124.
6. H. M. Blalock, Jr., *Causal Inferences in Nonexperimental Research* (Chapel Hill: University of North Carolina Press, 1964).
7. Seymour M. Lipset and Reinhard Bendix, *Social Mobility in Industrial Society* (Berkeley: University of California Press, 1959), pp. 198–99.
8. Ibid., p. 190.
9. U.S. Bureau of the Census, "Lifetime Occupational Mobility of Adult Males: March 1962," *Current Population Reports,* series P-23, no. 11 (May 12, 1964), table B.
10. Karl Pearson, "On Certain Errors with Regard to Multiple Correlation Occasionally Made by Those Who Have Not Adequately Studied This Subject," *Biometrika,* 10 (1944), pp. 181–87.
11. See Herman P. Miller, *Rich Man, Poor Man* (New York: Croswell, 1964), pp. 90–96.

Human, Cultural, and Social Capital

5

INVESTMENT IN HUMAN CAPITAL

Theodore W. Schultz

Although it is obvious that people acquire useful skills and knowledge, it is not obvious that these skills and knowledge are a form of capital, that this capital is in substantial part a product of deliberate investment,

Theodore W. Schultz, excerpt from "Investment in Human Capital" from *The American Economic Review* 51 (March 1961). Reprinted with the permission of the publishers.

that it has grown in Western societies at a much faster rate than conventional (nonhuman) capital, and that its growth may well be the most distinctive feature of the economic system. It has been widely observed that increases in national output have been large compared with the increases of land, man-hours, and physical reproducible capital. Investment in human capital is probably the major explanation for this difference.

Much of what we call consumption constitutes investment in human capital. Direct expenditures on education, health, and internal migration to take advantage of better job opportunities are clear examples. Earnings foregone by mature students attending school and by workers acquiring on-the-job training are equally clear examples. Yet nowhere do these enter into our national accounts. The use of leisure time to improve skills and knowledge is widespread and it too is unrecorded. In these and similar ways the *quality* of human effort can be greatly improved and its productivity enhanced. I shall contend that such investment in human capital accounts for most of the impressive rise in the real earnings per worker.

I shall comment, first, on the reasons why economists have shied away from the explicit analysis of investment in human capital, and then, on the capacity of such investment to explain many a puzzle about economic growth. Mainly, however, I shall concentrate on the scope and substance of human capital and its formation. . . .

I. Shying Away from Investment in Man

Economists have long known that people are an important part of the wealth of nations. Measured by what labor contributes to output, the productive capacity of human beings is now vastly larger than all other forms of wealth taken together. What economists have not stressed is the simple truth that people invest in themselves and that these investments are very large. Although economists are seldom timid in entering on abstract analysis and are often proud of being impractical, they have not been bold in coming to grips with this form of investment. Whenever they come even close, they proceed gingerly as if they were stepping into deep water. No doubt there are reasons for being wary. Deep-seated moral and philosophical issues are ever present. Free men are first and foremost the end to be served

by economic endeavor; they are not property or marketable assets. And not least, it has been all too convenient in marginal productivity analysis to treat labor as if it were a unique bundle of innate abilities that are wholly free of capital.

The mere thought of investment in human beings is offensive to some among us. Our values and beliefs inhibit us from looking upon human beings as capital goods, except in slavery, and this we abhor. We are not unaffected by the long struggle to rid society of indentured service and to evolve political and legal institutions to keep men free from bondage. These are achievements that we prize highly. Hence, to treat human beings as wealth that can be augmented by investment runs counter to deeply held values. It seems to reduce man once again to a mere material component, to something akin to property. And for man to look upon himself as a capital good, even if it did not impair his freedom, may seem to debase him. No less a person than J. S. Mill at one time insisted that the people of a country should not be looked upon as wealth because wealth existed only for the sake of people (Mill 1909; Nicholson 1891). But surely Mill was wrong; there is nothing in the concept of human wealth contrary to his idea that it exists only for the advantage of people. By investing in themselves, people can enlarge the range of choice available to them. It is one way free men can enhance their welfare.

Among the few who have looked upon human beings as capital, there are three distinguished names. The philosopher-economist Adam Smith boldly included all of the acquired and useful abilities of all of the inhabitants of a country as a part of capital. So did H. von Thünen, who then went on to argue that the concept of capital applied to man did not degrade him or impair his freedom and dignity, but on the contrary that the failure to apply the concept was especially pernicious in wars; ". . . for here . . . one will sacrifice in a battle a hundred human beings in the prime of their lives without a thought in order to save one gun." The reason is that, "... the purchase of a cannon causes an outlay of public funds, whereas human beings are to be had for nothing by means of a mere conscription decree" (1875). Irving Fisher (1906) also clearly and cogently presented an all-inclusive concept of capital. Yet the main stream of thought has held that it is neither appropriate nor practical to apply the concept of capital to human beings. Marshall (1930), whose great prestige goes far to explain why this view was accepted, held that while human beings are incontestably capital from an abstract and mathematical point of view, it would be out of touch with the market place to treat them as capital in practical analyses. Investment in human beings has accordingly seldom been incorporated in the formal core of economics, even though many economists, including Marshall, have seen its relevance at one point or another in what they have written.

The failure to treat human resources explicitly as a form of capital, as a produced means of production, as the product of investment, has fostered the retention of the classical notion of labor as a capacity to do manual work requiring little knowledge and skill, a capacity with which, according to this notion, laborers are endowed about equally. This notion of labor was wrong in the classical period and it is patently wrong now. Counting individuals who can and want to work and treating such a count as a measure of the quantity of an economic factor is no more meaningful than it would be to count the number of all manner of machines to determine their economic importance either as a stock of capital or as a flow of productive services.

Laborers have become capitalists not from a diffusion of the ownership of corporation stocks, as folklore would have it, but from the acquisition of knowledge and skill that have economic value (Johnson 1960).

This knowledge and skill are in great part the product of investment and, combined with other human investment, predominantly account for the productive superiority of the technically advanced countries. To omit them in studying economic growth is like trying to explain Soviet ideology without Marx.

II. Economic Growth from Human Capital

Many paradoxes and puzzles about our dynamic, growing economy can be resolved once human investment is taken into account. Let me begin by sketching some that are minor though not trivial.

When farm people take nonfarm jobs they earn substantially less than industrial workers of the same race, age, and sex. Similarly nonwhite urban males earn much less than white males even after allowance is made for the effects of differences in unemployment, age, city size and region (Zeman 1955). Because these differentials in earnings correspond closely to corresponding differentials in education, they strongly suggest that the one is a consequence of the other. Negroes who operate farms, whether as tenants or as owners, earn much less than whites on comparable farms. Fortunately, crops and livestock are not vulnerable to the blight of discrimination. The large differences in earnings seem rather to reflect mainly the differences in health and education. Workers in the South on the average earn appreciably less than in the North or West and they also have on the average less education. Most migratory farm workers earn very little indeed by comparison with other workers. Many of them have virtually no schooling, are in poor health, are unskilled, and have little ability to do useful work. To urge that the differences in the amount of human investment may explain these differences in earnings seems elementary. Of more recent vintage are observations showing younger workers at a competitive advantage; for example, young men entering the labor force are said to have an advantage over unemployed older workers in obtaining satisfactory jobs. Most of these young people possess twelve years of school, most of the older workers six years or less. The observed advantage of these younger workers may therefore result not from inflexibilities in social security or in retirement programs, or from sociological preference of employers, but from real differences in productivity connected with one form of human investment, i.e., education. And yet another example, the curve relating income to age tends to be steeper for skilled than for unskilled persons. Investment in on-the-job training seems a likely explanation, as I shall note later.

Economic growth requires much internal migration of workers to adjust to changing job opportunities (Kuznets 1952). Young men and women move more readily than older workers. Surely this makes economic sense when one recognizes that the costs of such migration are a form of human investment. Young people have more years ahead of them than older workers during which they can realize on such an investment. Hence it takes less of a wage differential to make it economically advantageous for them to move, or, to put it differently, young people can expect a higher return on their investment in migration than older people. This differential may explain selective migration without requiring an appeal to sociological differences between young and old people.

The examples so far given are for investment in human beings that yield a return over a long period. This is true equally of investment in education, training, and migration of young people. Not all investments in human beings are of this kind; some are more nearly akin to current inputs as for example

expenditures on food and shelter in some countries where work is mainly the application of brute human force, calling for energy and stamina, and where the intake of food is far from enough to do a full day's work. On the "hungry" steppes and in the teeming valleys of Asia, millions of adult males have so meager a diet that they cannot do more than a few hours of hard work. To call them underemployed does not seem pertinent. Under such circumstances it is certainly meaningful to treat food partly as consumption and partly as a current "producer good," as some Indian economists have done (Brahmanand and Vahil 1956). Let us not forget that Western economists during the early decades of industrialization and even in the time of Marshall and Pigou often connected additional food for workers with increases in labor productivity.

Let me now pass on to three major perplexing questions closely connected with the riddle of economic growth. First, consider the long-period behavior of the capital–income ratio. We were taught that a country which amassed more reproducible capital relative to its land and labor would employ such capital in greater "depth" because of its growing abundance and cheapness. But apparently this is not what happens. On the contrary, the estimates now available show that less of such capital tends to be employed relative to income as economic growth proceeds. Are we to infer that the ratio of capital to income has no relevance in explaining either poverty or opulence? Or that a rise of this ratio is not a prerequisite to economic growth? These questions raise fundamental issues bearing on motives and preferences for holding wealth as well as on the motives for particular investments and the stock of capital thereby accumulated. For my purpose all that needs to be said is that these estimates of capital–income ratios refer to only a part of all capital. They exclude in particular, and most unfortunately, any human capital. Yet human capital has surely been increasing at a rate substantially greater than reproducible (nonhuman) capital. We cannot, therefore, infer from these estimates that the stock of *all* capital has been decreasing relative to income. On the contrary, if we accept the not implausible assumption that the motives and preferences of people, the technical opportunities open to them, and the uncertainty associated with economic growth during particular periods were leading people to maintain roughly a constant ratio between *all* capital and income, the decline in the estimated capital–income ratio is simply a signal that human capital has been increasing relatively not only to conventional capital but also to income.

The bumper crop of estimates that show national income increasing faster than national resources raises a second and not unrelated puzzle. The income of the United States has been increasing at a much higher rate than the combined amount of land, manhours worked and the stock of reproducible capital used to produce the income. Moreover, the discrepancy between the two rates has become larger from one business cycle to the next during recent decades (Fabricant 1959). To call this discrepancy a measure of "resource productivity" gives a name to our ignorance but does not dispel it. If we accept these estimates, the connections between national resources and national income have become loose and tenuous over time. Unless this discrepancy can be resolved, received theory of production applied to inputs and outputs as currently measured is a toy and not a tool for studying economic growth.

Two sets of forces probably account for the discrepancy, if we neglect entirely the index number and aggregation problems that bedevil all estimates of such global aggregates as total output and total input. One is returns to scale; the second, the large improvements in the quality of inputs that have occurred but have been omitted from the input estimates. Our economy has undoubtedly been experiencing increasing returns to scale at some points offset by decreasing returns at others. If we can succeed in identifying and measuring the net gains, they may turn out to have been substantial. The improvements in the quality of inputs that have not been adequately allowed for are no doubt partly in material (nonhuman) capital. My own conception, however, is that both this defect and the omission of economies of scale are minor sources of discrepancy between the rates of growth of inputs and outputs compared to the improvements in human capacity that have been omitted.

A small step takes us from these two puzzles raised by existing estimates to a third which brings us to the heart of the matter, namely the essentially unexplained large increase in real earnings of workers. Can this be a windfall? Or a quasirent pending the adjustment in the supply of labor? Or, a pure rent reflecting the fixed amount of labor? It seems far more reasonable that it represents rather a return to the investment that has been made in human beings. The observed growth in productivity per unit of labor is simply a consequence of holding the unit of labor constant over time although in fact this unit of labor has been increasing as a result of a steadily growing amount of human capital per worker. As I read our record, the human capital component has become very large as a consequence of human investment.

Another aspect of the same basic question, which admits of the same resolution, is the rapid postwar recovery of countries that had suffered severe destruction of plant and equipment during the war. The toll from bombing was all too visible in the factories laid flat, the railroad yards, bridges, and harbors wrecked, and the cities in ruin. Structures, equipment and inventories were all heaps of rubble. Not so visible, yet large, was the toll from the wartime depletion of the physical plant that escaped destruction by bombs. Economists were called upon to assess the implications of these wartime losses for recovery. In retrospect, it is clear that they overestimated the prospective retarding effects of these losses. Having had a small hand in this effort, I have had a special reason for looking back and wondering why the judgments that we formed soon after the war proved to be so far from the mark. The explanation that now is clear is that we gave altogether too much weight to nonhuman capital in making these assessments. We fell into this error, I am convinced, because we did not have a concept of *all* capital and, therefore, failed to take account of human capital and the important part that it plays in production in a modern economy.

Let me close this section with a comment on poor countries, for which there are virtually no solid estimates. I have been impressed by repeatedly expressed judgments, especially by those who have a responsibility in making capital available to poor countries, about the low rate at which these countries can absorb additional capital. New capital from outside can be put to good use, it is said, only when it is added "slowly and gradually." But this experience is at variance with the widely held impression that countries are poor fundamentally because they are starved for capital and that additional capital is truly the key to their more rapid economic growth. The reconciliation is again, I believe, to be found in emphasis on particular forms of capital. The new capital available to these countries from outside as a rule goes into the formation of structures, equipment and sometimes also into inventories. But it is generally not available for additional investment in man. Consequently, human capabilities do not stay abreast of physical capital, and they do become limiting factors in economic growth. It should come as no surprise, therefore, that the absorption rate of capital to augment only particular nonhuman resources is necessarily low. The Horvat (1958)

formulation of the optimum rate of investment which treats knowledge and skill as a critical investment variable in determining the rate of economic growth is both relevant and important.

III. Scope and Substance of These Investments

What are human investments? Can they be distinguished from consumption? Is it at all feasible to identify and measure them? What do they contribute to income? Granted that they seem amorphous compared to brick and mortar, and hard to get at compared to the investment accounts of corporations, they assuredly are not a fragment; they are rather like the contents of Pandora's box, full of difficulties and hope.

Human resources obviously have both quantitative and qualitative dimensions. The number of people, the proportion who enter upon useful work, and hours worked are essentially quantitative characteristics. To make my task tolerably manageable, I shall neglect these and consider only such quality components as skill, knowledge, and similar attributes that affect particular human capabilities to do productive work. In so far as expenditures to enhance such capabilities also increase the value productivity of human effort (labor), they will yield a positive rate of return.[1]

How can we estimate the magnitude of human investment? The practice followed in connection with physical capital goods is to estimate the magnitude of capital formation by expenditures made to produce the capital goods. This practice would suffice also for the formation of human capital. However, for human capital there is an additional problem that is less pressing for physical capital goods: how to distinguish between expenditures for consumption and for investment.

This distinction bristles with both conceptual and practical difficulties. We can think of three classes of expenditures: expenditures that satisfy consumer preferences and in no way enhance the capabilities under discussion—these represent pure consumption; expenditures that enhance capabilities and do not satisfy any preferences underlying consumption—these represent pure investment; and expenditures that have both effects. Most relevant activities clearly are in the third class, partly consumption and partly investment, which is why the task of identifying each component is so formidable and why the measurement of capital formation by expenditures is less useful for human investment than for investment in physical goods. In principle there is an alternative method for estimating human investment, namely by its yield rather than by its cost. While any capability produced by human investment becomes a part of the human agent and hence cannot be sold; it is nevertheless "in touch with the market place" by affecting the wages and salaries the human agent can earn. The resulting increase in earnings is the yield in the investment.[2]

Despite the difficulty of exact measurement at this stage of our understanding of human investment, many insights can be gained by examining some of the more important activities that improve human capabilities. I shall concentrate on five major categories: (1) health facilities and services, broadly conceived to include all expenditures that affect the life expectancy, strength and stamina, and the vigor and vitality of a people; (2) on-the-job training, including old-style apprenticeship organized by firms; (3) formally organized education at the elementary, secondary, and higher levels; (4) study programs for adults that are not organized by firms, including extension programs notably in agriculture; (5) migration of individuals and families to adjust to changing job opportunities. Except for education, not much is known about these activities that is germane here. I shall refrain from commenting on study programs for adults, although in agriculture the extension services of the several states play an important role in transmitting new knowledge and in developing skills of farmers (Schultz 1956). Nor shall I elaborate further on internal migration related to economic growth.

Health activities have both quantity and quality implications. Such speculations as economists have engaged in about the effects of improvements in health has been predominantly in connection with population growth, which is to say with quantity. But surely health measures also enhance the quality of human resources. So also may additional food and better shelter, especially in underdeveloped countries.

The change in the role of food as people become richer sheds light on one of the conceptual problems already referred to. I have pointed out that extra food in some poor countries has the attribute of a "producer good." This attribute of food, however, diminishes as the consumption of food rises, and there comes a point at which any further increase in food becomes pure consumption. Clothing, housing and perhaps medical services may be similar.

My comment about on-the-job training will consist of a conjecture on the amount of such training, a note on the decline of apprenticeship, and then a useful economic theorem on who bears the costs of such training. Surprisingly little is known about on-the-job training in modern industry. About all that can be said is that the expansion of education has not eliminated it. It seems likely, however, that some of the training formerly undertaken by firms has been discontinued and other training programs have been instituted to adjust both to the rise in the education of workers and to changes in the demands for new skills. The amount invested annually in such training can only be a guess. H. F. Clark places it near to equal to the amount spent on formal education. Even if it were only one-half as large, it would represent currently an annual gross investment of about $15 billion. Elsewhere, too, it is thought to be important. For example, some observers have been impressed by the amount of such training under way in plants in the Soviet Union. Meanwhile, apprenticeship has all but disappeared, partly because it is now inefficient and partly because schools now perform many of its functions. Its disappearance has been hastened no doubt by the difficulty of enforcing apprenticeship agreements. Legally they have come to smack of indentured service. The underlying economic factors and behavior are clear enough. The apprentice is prepared to serve during the initial period when his productivity is less than the cost of his keep and of his training. Later, however, unless he is legally restrained, he will seek other employment when his productivity begins to exceed the cost of keep and training, which is the period during which a master would expect to recoup on his earlier outlay.

To study on-the-job training Gary Becker (1960) advances the theorem that in competitive markets employees pay all the costs of their training and none of these costs are ultimately borne by the firm. Becker points out several implications. The notion that expenditures on training by a firm generate external economies for other firms is not consistent with this theorem. The theorem also indicates one force favoring the transfer from on-the-job training to attending school. Since on-the-job training reduces the net earnings of workers at the beginning and raises them later on, this theorem also provides an explanation for the "steeper slope of the curve relating income to age," for skilled than unskilled workers, referred to earlier.[3] What all

this adds up to is that the stage is set to undertake meaningful economic studies of on-the-job training.

Happily we reach firmer ground in regard to education. Investment in education has risen at a rapid rate and by itself may well account for a substantial part of the otherwise unexplained rise in earnings. I shall do no more than summarize some preliminary results about the total costs of education including income foregone by students, the apparent relation of these costs to consumer income and to alternative investments, the rise of the stock of education in the labor force, returns to education, and the contribution that the increase in the stock of education may have made to earnings and to national income.

It is not difficult to estimate the conventional costs of education consisting of the costs of the services of teachers, librarians, administrators, of maintaining and operating the educational plant, and interest on the capital embodied in the educational plant. It is far more difficult to estimate another component of total cost, the income foregone by students. Yet this component should be included and it is far from negligible. In the United States, for example, well over half of the costs of higher education consists of income foregone by students. As early as 1900, this income foregone accounted for about one-fourth of the total costs of elementary, secondary and higher education. by 1956, it represented over two-fifths of all costs. The rising significance of foregone income has been a major factor in the marked upward trend in the total real costs of education which, measured in current prices, increased from $400 million in 1900 to $28.7 billion in 1956 (Schultz 1960). The percentage rise in educational costs was about three and a half times as large as in consumer income, which would imply a high income elasticity of the demand for education, if education were regarded as pure consumption. Educational costs also rose about three and a half times as rapidly as did the gross formation of physical capital in dollars. If we were to treat education as pure investment this result would suggest that the returns to education were relatively more attractve than those to non-human capital.

Much schooling is acquired by persons who are not treated as income earners in most economic analysis, particularly, of course, women. To analyze the effect of growth in schooling on earnings, it is therefore necessary to distinguish between the stock of education in the population and the amount in the labor force. Years of school completed are far from satisfactory as a measure because of the marked increases that have taken place in the number of days of school attendance of enrolled students and because much more of the education of workers consists of high school and higher education than formerly. My preliminary estimates suggest that the stock of education in the labor force rose about eight and a half times between 1900 and 1956, whereas the stock of reproducible capital rose four and a half times, both in 1956 prices. These estimates are, of course, subject to many qualifications. Nevertheless, both the magnitude and the rate of increase of this form of human capital have been such that they could be an important key to the riddle of economic growth.[4]

The exciting work under way is on the return to education. In spite of the flood of high school and college graduates, the return has not become trivial. Even the lower limits of the estimates show that the return to such education has been in the neighborhood of the return to nonhuman capital. This is what most of these estimates show when they treat as costs all of the public and private expenditures on education and also the income foregone while attending school, and when they treat all of these costs as investment, allocating none to consumption. But surely a part of these costs are consumption in the sense that education creates a form of consumer capital, which has the attribute of improving the taste and the quality of consumption of students throughout the rest of their lives. If one were to allocate a substantial fraction of the total costs of this education to consumption, say one-half, this would, of course, double the observed rate of return to what would then become the investment component in education that enhances the productivity of man.

Fortunately, the problem of allocating the costs of education in the labor force between consumption and investment does not arise to plague us when we turn to the contribution that education makes to earnings and to national income because a change in allocation only alters the rate of return, not the total return. I noted at the outset that the unexplained increases in U.S. national income have been especially large in recent decades. On one set of assumptions, the unexplained part amounts to nearly three-fifths of the total increase between 1929 and 1956.[5] How much of this unexplained increase in income represents a return to education in the labor force? A lower limit suggests that about three-tenths of it, and an upper limit does not rule out that more than one-half of it came from this source. These estimates also imply that between 36 and 70 percent of the hitherto unexplained rise in the earnings of labor is explained by returns to the additional education of workers.

. . .

NOTES

1. Even so, our *observed* return can be either negative, zero or positive because our observations are drawn from a world where there is uncertainty and imperfect knowledge and where there are windfall gains and losses and mistakes aplenty.
2. In principle, the value of the investment can be determined by discounting the additional future earnings it yields just as the value of a

physical capital good can be determined by discounting its income stream.

3. Becker has also noted still another implication arising out of the fact that the income and capital investment aspects of on-the-job training are tied together, which gives rise to "permanent" and "transitory" income effects that may have substantial explanatory value.

4. In value terms this stock of education was only 22 percent as large as the stock of reproducible physical capital in 1900, whereas in 1956 it already had become 42 percent as large.

5. Real income doubled, rising from $150 to $302 billion in 1956 prices. Eighty-nine billions of the increase in real income is taken to be unexplained, or about 59 percent of the total increase. The stock of education in the labor force rose by $355 billion of which $69 billion is here allocated to the growth in the labor force to keep the per-worker stock of education constant, and $286 billion represents the increase in the level of this stock. See (Schultz 1961, sec. 6) for an elaboration of the method and the relevant estimates.

REFERENCES

BECKER, G. S. 1960. Preliminary draft of study undertaken for National Bureau of Economic Research, New York.

BRAHMANAND, P. R. AND C. N. VAKIL. 1956. *Planning for an Expanding Economy*. Bombay.

CLARK, H. F. 1959. "Potentialities of Educational Establishments Outside the Conventional Structure of Higher Education." *Financing Higher Education, 1960–70*, edited by D. M. Keezer. New York.

FABRICANT, SOLOMON. 1959. *Basic Facts on Productivity Change*. National Bureau of Economic Research, Occas. Paper 63, Table 5. New York.

FISHER, IRVING. 1906. *The Nature of Capital and Income*. New York.

FRIEDMAN, MILTON AND SIMON KUZNETS. 1945. *Income from Independent Professional Practice*. New York: National Bureau of Economic Research.

HORVAT, B. 1958. "The Optimum Rate of Investment." *Economics Journal* 68: 747–67.

JOHNSON, H. G. 1960. "The Political Economy of Opulence." *Canadian Journal of Economics and Political Science* 26: 552–64.

KUZNETS, SIMON. 1952. *Income and Wealth in the United States*. Cambridge, England. Sec. IV, Distribution by Industrial Origin.

MARSHALL, ALFRED. 1930. *Principles of Economics*, 8th ed. London. App. E, pp. 787–88.

MILL, J. S. 1909. *Principles of Political Economy*, edited by W. J. Ashley. London, p. 8.

MUSHKIN, S. J. 1958. "Toward a Definition of Health Economics." *Public Health Reports* 73: 785–93. U.S. Dept. of Health, Education, and Welfare.

NICHOLSON, J. S. 1891. "The Living Capital of the United Kingdom." *Economics Journal* 1: 95.

SCHULTZ, T. W. 1956. "Agriculture and the Application of Knowledge." Pp. 54–78 in *A Look to the Future*. Battle Creek, MI: W. K. Kellogg Foundation.

———. 1960. "Capital Formation by Education." *Journal of Political Economics* 68: Tables 3–7.

———. 1961. "Education and Economic Growth." In *Social Forces Influencing American Education*, edited by H. G. Richey. Chicago.

VON THÜNEN, H. 1875. *Der isolierte Staat*, 3d ed., vol. 2, pt. 2, pp. 140–52. Translated by B. F. Hoselitz, reproduced by the Comp. Educ. Center, University of Chicago, Chicago, IL.

ZEMAN, MORTON. 1955. *A Quantitative Analysis of White–Nonwhite Income Differentials in the United States*. Unpublished doctoral dissertation, University of Chicago, Chicago, IL.

6

_____

CULTURAL REPRODUCTION AND SOCIAL REPRODUCTION

Pierre Bourdieu

The specific role of the sociology of education is assumed once it has established itself as the science of the relations between cultural reproduction and social reproduction. This occurs when it endeavors to determine the contribution made by the educational system to the reproduction of the structure of power relationships and symbolic relationships between classes, by contributing to the reproduction of the structure of the distribution of cultural capital among these classes. The science of the reproduction of structures, understood as a system of objective relations which impart their relational properties to individuals whom they preexist and survive, has nothing in common with the analytical recording of relations existing within a given population, be it a quesiton of the relations between the academic success of children and the social position of their family or of the relations between the positions filled by children and their parents. The substantialist mode of thought which stops short at directly accessible elements, that is to say individuals, claims a certain fidelity to reality by disregarding the structure of relations whence these elements derive all their sociologically relevant determinations, and thus finds itself having to analyze intra- or inter-generational mobility processes to the detriment of the study of mechanisms which tend to

ensure the reproduction of the structure of relations between classes; it is unaware that the controlled mobility of a limited category of individuals, carefully selected and modified by and for individual ascent, is not incompatible with the permanence of structures, and that it is even capable of contributing to social stability in the only way conceivable in societies based upon democratic ideals and thereby may help to perpetuate the structure of class relations.

Any break with substantialist atomism, even if it does not mean going as far as certain structuralists and seeing agents as the simple "supports" of structures invested with the mysterious power of determining other structures, implies taking as our theme the process of education. This means that our object becomes the production of the habitus, that system of dispositions which acts as a mediation between structures and practice; more specifically, it becomes necessary to study the laws that determine the tendency of structures to reproduce themselves by producing agents endowed with the system of predispositions which is capable of engendering practices adapted to the structures and thereby contributing to the reproduction of the structures. If it is conceived within a theoretical framework such as this, the sociology of educational institutions and, in particular, of institutions of higher education, is capable of making a decisive contribution to the science of the structural dynamics of class relations, which is an often neglected aspect of the sociology of power. Indeed, among all the solutions put forward throughout history to the problem of the transmission of power and privileges, there

_____

Pierre Bourdieu, excerpt from "Cultural Reproduction and Social Reproduction" from Richard Brown (ed.), *Knowledge, Education, and Cultural Change*. Reprinted with the permission of Tavistock Publications and the British Sociological Association.

surely does not exist one that is better concealed, and therefore better adapted to societies which tend to refuse the most patent forms of the hereditary transmission of power and privileges, than that solution which the educational system provides by contributing to the reproduction of the structure of class relations and by concealing, by an apparently neutral attitude, the fact that it fills this function.

The Role of the Educational System in the Reproduction of the Structure of the Distribution of Cultural Capital

By traditionally defining the educational system as the group of institutional or routine mechanisms by means of which is operated what Durkheim calls "the conservation of a culture inherited from the past," i.e., the transmission from generation to generation of accumulated information, classical theories tend to dissociate the function of cultural reproduction proper to all educational systems from their function of social reproduction. Transposing, as they do, the representation of culture and of cultural transmission, commonly accepted by the ethnologists, to the case of societies divided into classes, these theories are based upon the implicit assumption that the different pedagogic actions which are carried out within the framework of the social structure, that is to say, those which are carried out by families from the different social classes as well as that which is practiced by the school, work together in a harmonious way to transmit a cultural heritage which is considered as being the undivided property of the whole society.

In fact the statistics of theater, concert, and, above all, museum attendance (since, in the last case, the effect of economic obstacles is more or less nil) are sufficient reminder that the inheritance of cultural wealth which

has been accumulated and bequeathed by previous generations only really belongs (although it is *theoretically* offered to everyone) to those endowed with the means of appropriating it for themselves. In view of the fact that the apprehension and possession of cultural goods as symbolic goods (along with the symbolic satisfactions which accompany an appropriation of this kind) are possible only for those who hold the code making it possible to decipher them or, in other words, that the appropriation of symbolic goods presupposes the possession of the instruments of appropriation, it is sufficient to give free play to the laws of cultural transmission for cultural capital to be added to cultural capital and for the structure of the distribution of cultural capital between social classes to be thereby reproduced. By this is meant the structure of the distribution of instruments for the appropriation of symbolic wealth socially designated as worthy of being sought and possessed.

. . .

The different classes or sections of a class are organized around three major positions: the lower position, occupied by the agricultural professions, workers, and small tradespeople, which are, in fact, categories excluded from participation in "high" culture; the intermediate position, occupied on the one hand by the heads and employees of industry and business and, on the other hand, by the intermediate office staff (who are just about as removed from the two other categories as these categories are from the lower categories); and, lastly, the higher position, which is occupied by higher office staff and professionals.

. . .

The educational system reproduces all the more perfectly the structure of the distribution of cultural capital among classes (and sections of a class) in that the culture which it transmits is closer to the dominant culture and that the mode of inculcation to which it has recourse is less removed from the mode of inculcation practiced by the family. Inasmuch as it operates in and through a relationship of communication, pedagogic action directed at inculcating the dominant culture can in fact escape (even if it is only in part) the general laws of cultural transmission, according to which the appropriation of the proposed culture (and, consequently, the success of the apprenticeship which is crowned by academic qualifications) depends upon the previous possession of the instruments of appropriation, to the extent and only to the extent that it explicitly and deliberately hands over, in the pedagogic communication itself, those instruments which are indispensable to the success of the communication and which, in a society divided into classes, are very unequally distributed among children from the different social classes. An educational system which puts into practice an implicit pedagogic action, requiring initial familiarity with the dominant culture, and which proceeds by imperceptible familiarization, offers information and training which can be received and acquired only by subjects endowed with the system of predispositions that is the condition for the success of the transmission and of the inculcation of the culture. By doing away with giving explicitly to everyone what it implicitly demands of everyone, the educational system demands of everyone alike that they have what it does not give. This consists mainly of linguistic and cultural competence and that relationship of familiarity with culture which can only be produced by family upbringing when it transmits the dominant culture.

In short, an institution officially entrusted with the transmission of the instruments of appropriation of the dominant culture which neglects methodically to transmit the instruments indispensable to the success of its undertaking is bound to become the monopoly of those social classes capable of

transmitting by their own means, that is to say by that diffuse and implicit continuous educational action which operates within cultured families (often unknown to those responsible for it and to those who are subjected to it), the instruments necessary for the reception of its message, and thereby to confirm their monopoly of the instruments of appropriation of the dominant culture and thus their monopoly of that culture.[1] The closer that educational action gets to that limit, the more the value that the educational system attributes to the products of the educational work carried out by families of the different social classes is directly a function of the value as cultural capital which is attributed, on a market dominated by the products of the educational work of the families of the dominant classes, to the linguistic and cultural competence which the different classes or sections of a class are in a position to transmit, mainly in terms of the culture that they possess and of the time that they are able to devote to its explicit or implicit transmission. That is to say that the transmission of this competence is in direct relation to the distance between the linguistic and cultural competence implicitly demanded by the educational transmission of educational culture (which is itself quite unevenly removed from the dominant culture) and the linguistic and cultural competence inculcated by primary education in the different social classes.

The laws of the educational market may be read in the statistics which establish that, from the moment of entering into secondary education right up to the *grandes écoles,* the hierarchy of the educational establishments and even, within these establishments, the hierarchy of the sections and of the fields of study arranged according to their prestige and to the educational value they impart to their public, correspond exactly to the hierarchy of the institutions . . . according to the social structure of their public, on account of the fact that those classes or sections of a class which are richest in cultural capital become more and more over-represented as there is an increase in the rarity and hence in the educational value and social yield of academic qualifications. If such is the case, the reason is that, by virtue of the small real autonomy of an educational system which is incapable of affirming the specificity of its principles of evaluation and of its own mode of production of cultured dispositions, the relationship between the pedagogic actions carried out by the dominated classes and by the dominant classes may be understood by analogy with the relationship which is set up, in the economic field, between modes of production of different epochs when for example, in a dualist economy, the products of a traditional local craft industry are submitted to the laws of a market dominated by the chain-produced products of a highly developed industry: the symbolic products of the educational work of the different social classes, i.e., apart from knowledge and know-how, styles of being, of speaking, or of doing, have less value on the educational market and, more widely, on the symbolic market (in matrimonial exchanges, for instance) and on the economic market (at least to the extent that its sanctions depend upon academic ratification) in that the mode of symbolic production of which they are the product is more removed from the dominant mode of production or, in other words, from the educational norms of those social classes capable of imposing the domination of criteria of evaluation which are the most favorable to their products. It is in terms of this logic that must be understood the prominent value accorded by the French educational system to such subtle modalities in the relationship to culture and language as affluence, elegance, naturalness, or distinction, all of which are ways of making use of the symbolic products whose role of representing excellence in the field of culture (to the detriment of the dispositions produced by the school and paradoxically devalued,

by the school itself, as being "academic") is due to the fact that they belong only to those who have acquired culture or, at least, the dispositions necessary for the acquisition of academic culture, by means of familiarization, i.e., imperceptible apprenticeships from the family upbringing, which is the mode of acquisition of the instruments of appropriation of the dominant culture of which the dominant classes hold the monopoly.

The sanctions of the academic market owe their specific effectiveness to the fact that they are brought to bear with every appearance of legitimacy: it is, in fact, as though the agents proportioned the investments that are placed in production for the academic market—investments of time and enthusiasm for education on the part of the pupils, investments of time, effort, and money on the part of families—to the profits which they may hope to obtain, over a more or less long term, on this market, as though the price that they attribute to the sanctions of the academic market were in direct relation to the price attributed to them by the sanctions of this market and to the extent to which their economic and symbolic value depends on the value which they are recognized to possess by the academic market. It follows from this that the negative predispositions toward the school which result in the self-elimination of most children from the most culturally unfavored classes and sections of a class—such as self-depreciation, devaluation of the school and its sanctions, or a resigned attitude to failure and exclusion—must be understood as an anticipation, based upon the unconscious estimation of the objective probabilities of success possessed by the whole category, of the sanctions objectively reserved by the school for those classes or sections of a class deprived of cultural capital. Owing to the fact that it is the product of the internalization of value that the academic market (anticipating by its formally neutral sanctions the sanctions of the symbolic or economic market) confers upon the products of the family upbringing of the different social classes, and of the value which, by their objective sanctions, the economic and symbolic markets confer upon the products of educational action according to the social class from which they originate, the system of dispositions toward the school, understood as a propensity to consent to the investments in time, effort, and money necessary to conserve or increase cultural capital, tends to redouble the symbolic and economic effects of the uneven distribution of cultural capital, all the while concealing it and, at the same time, legitimating it. The functionalist sociologists who announce the brave new world when, at the conclusion of a longitudinal study of academic and social careers, they discover that, as though by a pre-established harmony, individuals have hoped for nothing that they have not obtained and obtained nothing that they have not hoped for, are simply the least forgivable victims of the ideological effect which is produced by the school when it cuts off from their social conditions of production all predispositions regarding the school such as "expectations," "aspirations," "inclinations," or "desire," and thus tends to cover up the fact that objective conditions— and in the individual case, the laws of the academic market—determine aspirations by determining the extent to which they can be satisfied.

This is the only one of the mechanisms by which the academic market succeeds in imposing upon those very persons who are its victims recognition of the existence of its sanctions by concealing from them the objective truth of the mechanisms and social motives that determine them. To the extent to which it is enough for it to be allowed to run its own course, that is to say to give free play to the laws of cultural transmission, in order to ensure the reproduction of the structure of distribution of cultural capital, the educational system which merely records immediate or deferred self-elimination (in the form of the self-relegation of children from the underprivileged classes to the lower educational streams) or encourages elimination simply by the effectiveness of a non-existent pedagogical practice (able to conceal behind patently obvious procedures of selection the action of mechanisms tending to ensure in an almost automatic way—that is to say, in a way which conforms to the laws governing all forms of cultural transmission—the exclusion of certain categories of recipients of the pedagogic message), this educational system masks more thoroughly than any other legitimation mechanism (imagine for example what would be the social effects of an arbitrary limitation of the public carried out in the name of ethnic or social criteria) the arbitrary nature of the actual demarcation of its public, thereby imposing more subtly the legitimacy of its products and of its hierarchies.

Cultural Reproduction and Social Reproduction

By making social hierarchies and the reproduction of these hierarchies appear to be based upon the hierarcy of "gifts," merits, or skills established and ratified by its sanctions, or, in a word, by converting social hierarchies into academic hierarchies, the educational system fulfills a function of legitimation which is more and more necessary to the perpetuation of the "social order" as the evolution of the power relationship between classes tends more completely to exclude the imposition of a hierarchy based upon the crude and ruthless affirmation of the power relationship. But does the continual increase, in most highly industrialized societies, in the proportion of the members of the ruling class who have passed through the university system and the best universities lead one to conclude that the transmission of cultural capital is tending to be substituted purely and simply for the transmission of economic capital and ownership of the means of production in the system of mechanisms of reproduction of the structure of class relationships?

Apart from the fact that the increase in the proportion of holders of the most prestigious academic qualifications among the members of the ruling classes may mean only that the need to call upon academic approval in order to legitimate the transmission of power and of privileges is being more and more felt, the effect is as though the cultural and educational mechanisms of transmission had merely strengthened or taken over from the traditional mechanisms such as the hereditary transmissions of economic capital, of a name, or of capital in terms of social relations; it is, in fact, as if the investments placed in the academic career of children had been integrated into *the system of strategies of reproduction*, which strategies are more or less compatible and more or less profitable depending on the type of capital to be transmitted, and by which each generation endeavors to transmit to the following generation the advantages it holds. Considering that, on the one hand, the ruling classes have at their disposal a much larger cultural capital than the other classes, even among those who constitute what are, relatively, the least well-off sections of the ruling classes and who, as has been seen, still practice cultural activities to at least as great an extent as the most favored sections of the middle class, and considering that, on the other hand, they also have at their disposal the means of ensuring for this capital the best academic placing for its investment (that is to say the best establishments and the best departments), their academic investments cannot fail to be extremely profitable, and the segregation that is established right at the beginning of secondary educa-

tion among students from different establishments and different departments cannot help but be reinforced the further one gets into the academic course by reason of the continual increase in the differences resulting from the fact that the most culturally privileged find their way into institutions capable of reinforcing their advantage. Institutions of higher education which ensure or legitimate access to the ruling classes, and, in particular, the *grandes écoles* (among which must be counted the *internat de médecine*) are therefore to all intents and purposes the monopoly of the ruling classes. The objective mechanisms which enable the ruling classes to keep the monopoly of the most prestigious educational establishments, while continually appearing at least to put the chance of possessing that monopoly into the hands of every generation, are concealed beneath the cloak of a perfectly democratic method of selection which takes into account only merit and talent, and these mechanisms are of a kind which converts to the virtues of the system the members of the dominated classes whom they eliminate in the same way as they convert those whom they elect, and which ensures that those who are "miraculously elected" may experience as "miraculous" an exceptional destiny which is the best testimony of academic democracy.

Owing to the fact, first, that the academic market tends to sanction and to reproduce the distribution of cultural capital by proportioning academic success to the amount of cultural capital bequeathed by the family (as is shown, for example, by the fact that, among the pupils of the *grandes écoles*, a very pronounced correlation may be observed between academic success and the family's cultural capital measured by the academic level of the forbears over two generations on both sides of the family), and, second, because the most privileged sections of the dominant classes from the point of view of economic capital and power are not

TABLE 6.1   The Distribution of Cultural Capital among Different Sections of the Dominant Classes

	1	2	3	4	5	6	7
	Teachers	*Public Adminis- tration*	*Profes- sionals*	*Engineers*	*Managers*	*Heads of Industry*	*Heads of Commerce*
Readers of *Le Monde* (penetration index per 1000)	410	235	210	145	151	82	49
Readers of *Le Figaro Littéraire* (ditto)	168	132	131	68	100	64	24
Readers of non-professional books 15 hrs and more per week	21	18	18	16	16	10	10
Theater-goers (at least once every 2 or 3 months)	38	29	29	28	34	16	20
Listeners to classical music	83	89	86	89	89	75	73
Visitors to museums and exhibitions	75	66	68	58	69	47	52
Visitors to art galleries	58	54	57	45	47	37	34
Possessors of FM radio	59	54	57	56	53	48	48
Non-possessors of television	46	30	28	33	28	14	24

necessarily the most well-off in terms of cultural capital, it may be expected that the hierarchy of values attributed by the academic market to the products of the educational work of the families of the different sections will not correspond very closely to the hierarchy of these sections with regard to economic capital and power. Should it be concluded from this that the relative autonomy of the mechanisms of reproduction of the structure of cultural capital in relation to the mechanisms ensuring the reproduction of economic capital is of a kind to cause a profound transformation, if not in the structure of class relationships (despite the fact that the most culturally privileged sections of the middle class such as the sons of primary school and secondary school teachers are able triumphantly to hold their own on the academic market against the least culturally privileged sections of the upper class), at least in the structure of relationships between the sections of the dominant classes?

The structure of the distribution of cultural capital among the different sections of the dominant classes may be constructed on the basis of the collection of convergent indices brought together in the following conspectus (see Table 6.1).[2]

With the exception of a few inversions in which is expressed the action of secondary variables such as place of residence, along with the objective possibilities of cultural practice which are closely linked to it, and income, along with the possibilities which it offers, it can be seen that the different sections are organized according to a single hierarchy with the differentiation of the cultural capital possessed in terms of the kind of training received being shown above all in the fact that engineers give proof of a greater interest in music (and in other leisure activities demanding the application of logical skills, such as bridge and chess) than in literary activities (reading of *Le Figaro Littéraire* or theater-going). If the proportion of individuals who do not possess television (and who are distinguished from the possessors of that instrument by the fact that they go in more often for activities commonly held to be the expression of an authentically "cultured" or refined disposition) varies ac-

TABLE 6.2 Reading Habits, Occupational Categories, and Levels of Education[4]

	Teachers	Top Civil Servants	Profes-sionals	Engineers	Managers	Heads of Industry	Heads of Commerce
Detective novels	25 (6)	29 (1)	27 (4)	28 (3)	29 (1)	27 (4)	25 (6)
Adventure stories	16 (7)	20 (3)	18 (6)	24 (1)	22 (2)	19 (4)	19 (4)
Historical accounts	44 (4)	47 (2)	49 (1)	47 (2)	44 (4)	36 (6)	27 (7)
Art books	28 (2)	20 (3)	31 (1)	19 (5)	20 (3)	17 (6)	14 (7)
Novels	64 (2)	68 (1)	59 (5)	62 (3)	63 (3)	45 (6)	42 (7)
Philosophy	20 (1)	13 (3)	12 (5)	13 (3)	15 (2)	10 (7)	12 (5)
Political essays	15 (1)	12 (2)	9 (4)	7 (5)	10 (3)	5 (6)	4 (7)
Economics	10 (1)	8 (3)	5 (6)	7 (5)	9 (2)	8 (3)	5 (6)
Sciences	15 (3)	14 (4)	18 (2)	21 (1)	9 (7)	10 (6)	11 (5)

	University	Grande École	Secondary	Technical	Primary
Detective novels	28	27	27	32	24
Adventure stories	17	14	22	27	17
Historical accounts	47	49	42	41	25
Art books	25	24	22	18	10
Novels	65	54	62	60	35
Philosophy	19	13	15	11	7
Political essays	16	14	6	6	3
Economics	12	19	5	3	4
Sciences	18	27	11	10	6

cording to the same law, it is because a refusal to indulge in this activity, which is suspected of being "vulgar" by reasons of its wide availability (*divulgation*), is one of the least expensive ways of expressing cultural pretensions (see Table 6.2).[3]

These indicators probably tend to minimize to a large extent the divergences between the different sections of the dominant classes. Indeed, most cultural consumer goods also imply an economic cost, theater-going, for instance, depending not only on the level of education (in a population of executive personnel it ranges from 41 percent to 59 and 68 percent between the primary, secondary, and higher levels) but also on income (i.e., 46 percent for incomes less than 20,000 francs per year against 72 percent for incomes more than 75,000 francs); furthermore, equipment such as FM radio or hi-fi sets may be used in very different ways (e.g.,

to listen to modern music or dance music), and the value accorded to these different utilizations may be just as disparate, by reference to the dominant hierarchy of possible uses, as the different kinds of reading or theater; thus, as is shown in Table 6.2, the position of the different sections, arranged in a hierarchy in terms of the interest they place in the different kinds of reading, tends to draw nearer to their position in the hierarchy set up in terms of wealth in cultural capital the more that it is a question of reading-matter which depends more upon level of education and which is placed higher in the hierarchy of degrees of cultural legitimacy.

. . .

With the exception of the liberal professions, who occupy, in this field too, a high position, the structure of the distribution of economic capital is symmetric and opposite

TABLE 6.3 Distribution of Economic Capital

	Heads of Industry	Heads of Commerce	Profes- sional	Managers	Engineers	Civil Servants	Teachers
Own their own residence	70	70	54	40	44	38	51
Upper-category automobile	33	34	28	22	21	20	12
Holidays in hotel	32	26	23	21	17	17	15
Boat	13	14	14	12	10	8	8
Average income in thousands of francs	33	36	41	37	36	32	33
(Rate of non- declaration)	(24)	(28)	(27)	(13)	(9)	(8)	(6)

to the structure of the distribution of cultural capital—that is to say, in order, heads of industry and of commerce, professionals, managers, engineers, and, lastly, civil servants and teachers (see Table 6.3).

. . .

Those sections which are richest in cultural capital are more inclined to invest in their children's education at the same time as in cultural practices liable to maintain and increase their specific rarity; those sections which are richest in economic capital set aside cultural and educational investments to the benefit of economic investments: it is to be noted, however, that heads of industry and commerce tend to do this much more than do the new "bourgeoisie" of the managers who reveal the same concern for rational investment both in the economic sphere and in the educational sphere.[5] Relatively well provided for with both forms of capital, but not sufficiently integrated into economic life to put their capital to work within it, the professionals (and especially lawyers and doctors) invest in their children's education but also and above all in consumer goods capable of symbolizing the possession of the material and cultural means of conforming to the rules governing the bourgeois style of life and thereby guaranteeing a so-

cial capital or capital of social relationships which will provide, if necessary, useful "supports": a capital of honorability and respectability which is often indispensable if one desires to attract clients in socially important positions, and which may serve as currency, for instance, in a political career.

In fact those sections which are richest in cultural capital have a larger proportion in an educational institution to the extent that the institution is highly placed in the specifically academic hierarchy of educational institutions (measured, for instance, by the index of previous academic success); and this proportion attains its maximum in the institution responsible for ensuring the reproduction of the academic body (École Normale Supérieure) (Table 6.4).[6]

. . .

[T]he educational system tends to reproduce (in the double sense of the word) the structure of relations between the structure of the distribution of cultural capital and the structure of the distribution of economic capital among the sections both in and by the relations of opposition and complementarity which define the system of institutions of higher education. In fact, to the extent that it is the product of the application of two opposed principles of hierarchical ordering,

TABLE 6.4   Cultural Capital and Educational Investment

| | Faculty | | | | Prep.
Class for
Polytech. | ENA | Poly-
tech. | Ulm
Arts | Ulm
Sc. |
	Law	Medicine	Science	Arts					
Proportion of teachers' children	3.2	4.5	4.5	5.2	5.4	9.0	9.9	19.4	17.7
Index of previous academic success	0.4		0.3	0.5	1.2	2.0	2.9	3.1	3.6

ENA: École Nationale d'Administration
Ulm Arts: École Normale Supérieure d'Ulm (Arts)
Ulm Sc.: École Normale Supérieure d'Ulm (Science)

the structure of the system of institutions of higher education may be interpreted in a twofold way: *the dominant hierarchy within the educational institution,* i.e., the hierarchy which orders the institutions in terms of specifically academic criteria and, correlatively, in terms of the proportion of those sections richest in cultural capital figuring in their public, is opposed diametrically to *the dominant hierarchy outside the educational institution,* i.e., the hierarchy which orders the institutions in terms of the proportion in their public of those sections richest in economic capital (and in power) and according to the position in the hierarcy of the economic capital and power of the professions to which they lead. . . .[7]

Analysis of the specifically academic mechanisms according to which apportionment is effected between the different institutions makes it possible to understand one of the most subtle forms of the trick (*ruse*) of social reason according to which the academic system works objectively toward *the reproduction of the structure of relations between the sections of the dominant classes* when it appears to make full use of its own principles of hierarchical ordering.[8] Knowing, first, that academic success is directly dependent on cultural capital and on the in-clination to invest in the academic market (which is itself, as is known, dependent on the objective chances of academic success) and, consequently, that the different sections are recognized and approved by the school system the richer they are in cultural capital and are also, therefore, all the more disposed to invest in work and academic prowess,[9] and knowing, second, that the support accorded by a category to academic sanctions and hierarchies depends not only on the rank the school system grants to it in its hierarchies but also on the extent to which its interests are linked to the school system, or, in other words, on the extent to which its commercial value and its social position depend (in the past as in the future) on academic approval, it is possible to understand why the educational system never succeeds quite so completely in imposing recognition of its value and of the value of its classifications as when its sanctions are brought to bear upon classes or sections of a class which are unable to set against it any rival principle of hierarchical ordering. While those sections which are richest in economic capital authorize and encourage a life-style whose seductions are sufficient to rival the ascetic demands of the academic system and while they ensure or promise guarantees beside which the college's guarantees can only appear both costly and of little value ("academic qualifications don't give you everything"), those sections which are richest in cultural capital have nothing to set against the attraction exercised by the signs of academic approval which make their academic prowess worthwhile to them. In short, the effectiveness of the mechanisms by means of which the educational system ensures its own reproduction encloses within itself its own limitation: although the educational system may make use of its relative autonomy to propose and impose its own hierarchies and the university career which serves as its topmost point, it obtains complete adherence only when it preaches to the converted or to lay brethren, to teachers' sons or children from the working or middle classes who owe everything to it and expect everything of it. Far from diverting for its own profit children from the dominant sections of the dominant classes (as one may be led to believe by a few striking examples which authorize the most conservative sections of the bourgeoisie to denounce the corruption of youth and teachers or the intellectuals to believe in the omnipotence of their ideas), it puts off children from the other sections and classes from claiming the value of their academic investments and from drawing the economic and symbolic profit which the sons of the dominant section of the ruling classes know how to obtain, if necessary, better situated as they are to understand the relative value of academic verdicts.

But would the school system succeed so completely in diverting for its own profit those categories which it recognizes as possessing the greatest value (as is shown, for instance, by the difference in academic quality between students from the ENS and those from the ENA) if the diplomas that it awards were convertible at par on the market of money and power? The limits of the auton-

omy allowed to the school system in the production of its hierarchies coincide exactly with the limits objectively assigned to its power of guaranteeing outside the academic market the economic and symbolic value of the diplomas it awards. The same academic qualifications receive very variable values and functions according to the economic and social capital (particularly the capital of relationships inherited from the family) which those who hold these qualifications have at their disposal and according to the markets in which they use them: it is known, for instance, that the professional success of the former students of the École des hautes études commerciales (recruited, for the most part, among the Parisian business section) varies far more in relation to the way in which they obtained their first professional post (i.e., through family relations or by other ways) than in relation to their position in the college-leaving examination; it is also known that civil servants whose fathers were white-collar workers received in 1962 an average yearly salary of 18,027 francs as against 29,470 francs for civil servants whose fathers were industrialists or wealthy tradespeople (Praderie 1966:346–47). And if, as has been shown by the survey carried out by the Boulloche commission over 600 firms, only 2.4 percent of the 17,000 administrative personnel employed by these firms have degrees or are doctors of science as against 37 percent who have diplomas from an engineering *grande école*, it is because those who possess the most prestigious qualifications also have at their disposal an inherited capital of relationships and skills which enable them to obtain such qualifications; this capital is made up of such things as the practice of the games and sports of high society or the manners and tastes resulting from good breeding, which, in certain careers (not to mention matrimonial exchanges which are opportunities for increasing the social capital or honorability and relationships), constitute the condition, if not the principal factor, of success.[10] The habitus inculcated by upper-class families gives rise to practices which, even if they are without selfish motives, such as cultural activities, are extremely profitable to the extent that they make possible the acquisition of the maximum yield of academic qualifications whenever recruitment or advancement is based upon co-optation or on such diffuse and total criteria as "the right presentation," "general culture," etc.[11]

What this amounts to is that, as in a precapitalist economy in which a guarantee is worth as much as the guarantor, the value of the diploma, outside the specifically academic market, depends on the economic and social values of the person who possesses it, inasmuch as the yield of academic capital (which is a converted form of cultural capital) depends upon the economic and social capital which can be put to its valorization: for the industrialist's son who comes out of HEC, the diploma is only an additional qualification to his legitimately succeeding his father or to his occupying the director's post guaranteed for him by his network of family relations, whereas the white-collar worker's son, whose only way of obtaining the same diploma was by means of academic success, cannot be sure of obtaining a post of commercial attaché in the same firm. In a word, if, as is shown by the analysis of the social and academic characteristics of the individuals mentioned in *Who's Who*, the diploma is all the more indispensable for those from families less favored in economic and social capital, the fact remains that the educational system is less and less in a position to guarantee the value of the qualifications that it awards the further one goes away from the domain that it controls completely, namely, that of its own reproduction; and the reason for this is that the possession of a diploma, as prestigious as it may be, is in any case less and less capable of guarantee-

ing access to the highest positions and is never sufficient to guarantee in itself access to economic power. Inversely, as is shown by the diagram of correlation, access to the dominant classes and, *a fortiori,* to the dominant sections of the dominant classes, is relatively independent of the chances of gaining access to higher education for those individuals from sections closest to economic and politico-administrative power, i.e., top civil servants and heads of industry and commerce. . . . It would appear, therefore, that the further one goes away from the jurisdiction of the school system the more the diploma loses its particular effectiveness as a guarantee of a specific qualification opening into a specific career according to formalized and homogeneous rules, and becomes a simple condition of authorization and a right of access which can be given full value only by the holders of a large capital of social relationships (particularly in the liberal professions) and is, at its extreme limit, when all it does is legitimate heritage, but a kind of optional guarantee.

Thus the relative autonomy enjoyed by the academic market on account of the fact that the structure of distribution of cultural capital is not exactly the same as the structure of economic capital and of power gives the appearance of a justification for meritocratic ideology, according to which academic justice provides a kind of resort or revenge for those who have no other resources than their "intelligence" or their "merit," only if one chooses to ignore, first, that "intelligence" or academic goodwill represents but one particular form of capital which comes to be added, in most cases, to the possession of economic capital and the correlative capital of power and social relationships, and, second, that the holders of economic power have more chances than those who are deprived of it also to possess cultural capital and, in any case, to be able to do without it since academic qualifications are a weak currency and possess all their value only within the limits of the academic market.

NOTES

1. The extremely close relationship that may be observed between museum attendance and level of education, on the one hand, and early attendance at museums, on the other hand, follows the same logic.
2. Sofres, *Le Marché des Cadres Supérieurs Français* (Paris, 1964).
3. A number of indicators suggest that the different sections of the dominant classes can also be distinguished according to the amount of free time at their disposal.
4. The figures in parentheses represent the positions of each section.
5. Managers have a much more "modernistic" style of life than do the traditional "bourgeoisie"—the heads of industry and commerce: they attain positions of power at a younger age; they more often possess university qualifications; they more often belong to larger and more modern businesses; they are the largest group to read the financial newspaper *Les Échos* (penetration index of 126 as opposed to 91 for heads of industry) and weeklies dealing with economics and finance (penetration index of 224 as against 190 for heads of industry); they seem less inclined to invest their capital in real estate; they indulge more often in "modern" leisure activities such as skiing, yachting, etc.
6. The analyses proposed below are based upon a systematic group of surveys, carried out over the last few years by the Centre de Sociologie Européenne, of the faculties of arts, sciences, law, and medicine, and of all the literary and scientific *grandes écoles* and of the preparatory classes for these colleges.
7. The discordance between the two hierarchies and the predominance, within the institution, of the specifically academic hierarchy is at the basis of the meritocratic illusion whose most typical form is the ideology of the "liberating effects of the school" along with the indignation aroused among teaching staff, who are the first victims of this kind of academic ethnocentrism, at the discordance between the social hierarchies and the academic hierarchies.
8. If the role of the system of institutions of higher education in the reproduction of the relations between the sections of the dominant classes often goes unnoticed, it is because surveys of mobility accord more attention to mobility between classes than to mobility within the different classes and, in particular, within the dominant classes.
9. For an analysis of the dialectic of approval and recognition at the final stage of which the school reocgnizes its members, or, in other words, those who recognize the school, see P. Bourdieu & M. de Saint-Martin (1970).
10. The proportion of students who play bridge or practice the "smart" sports increases the nearer one approaches the pole of economic power.
11. Any analysis which tends to consider cultural consumption as simple "conspicuous consumption," neglecting the directly palpable gratifications which always supplement symbolic gratifications, may well cause this fact to be forgotten. The simple ostentation of material prosperity, although it may not have such an obvious legitimating function as cultural ostentation, has at least the effect, in certain sections of the dominant classes, of vouching for success and of attracting confidence, esteem, and respect which, in certain professions, particularly the liberal ones, may serve as an important factor of success.
12. The fact that entrance into the liberal professions presupposes the possession of high academic qualifications should not conceal the fact that access to the highest positions in these professions doubtless depends scarcely any less than it does in the industrial and commercial sector on the possession of economic and social capital, as is shown by the presence of a very high rate of professional heredity, particularly in the elite of the medical profession where can be found veritable dynasties of chief doctors.

REFERENCES

Bourdieu, P. and Darbel, A. 1969. *L'Amour de l'Art: Les Musées d'Art Européens et Leur Public.* Paris: Les Éditions de Minuit.

Bourdieu, P. and De Saint-Martin, M. 1970. L'Excellence Scolaire et les Valeurs du Système d'Enseignement Français. *Annales* I: January–February.

Praderie, M. 1966. Héritage Social et Chances d'Ascension. In Darras, *Le Partage des bénéfices.* Paris: Les Éditions de Minuit.

Sema. n.d. *Le Théâtre et Son Public.*

Sofres. 1964. *Le Marché des Cadres Supérieurs Français.* Paris.

Syndicat National des Éditeurs (National Union of Publishers). 1960. La Lecture et la Livre en France (January–April 1960, survey carried out by the IFOP).

Syndicat National des Éditeurs. 1967. La Clientèle du Livre (July 1967, survey carried out by the IFOP).

7

SCHOOLS, FAMILIES, AND COMMUNITIES

James Coleman • Thomas Hoffer

. . .

Human Capital and Social Capital

Probably the most important and most original development in the economics of education in the past thirty years has been the idea that the concept of physical capital as embodied in tools, machines, and other productive equipment, can be extended to include human capital as well (see Schultz 1961; Becker 1964). Just as physical capital is created by working with materials to create tools that facilitate production, human capital is created by working with persons to produce in them skills and capabilities that make them more productive. Indeed, schools constitute a central institution for the creation of human capital. And just as decisions are made on investment in physical capital based on expected rates of return to these investments, it is useful to conceive of educational decisions as being made on the basis of expected rates of return to investments in human capital (see, for example, Mincer 1974).

There is, however, something quite different and distinct from human capital, yet no less important, which we have called social capital. If physical capital is wholly tangible, being embodied in observable material form, and human capital is less tangible, being embodied in the skills and knowledge acquired by an individual, social capital is less tangible yet, for it exists in the *relations* between persons. Just as physical capital and human capital facilitate productive activity, social capital does as well. For example, trust is a form of social capital. A group within which there is extensive trustworthiness and extensive trust is able to accomplish much more than a comparable group without that trustworthiness and trust. (For example, some economic activities depend greatly upon such trust relations for their very existence. Perhaps the example that shows this best is wholesale diamond markets, in which one merchant will give another possession of a valuable lot of diamonds for inspection, with no formal security whatsoever.)

The distinction between human capital and social capital can be exhibited by the diagrams sometimes used by analysts of social networks. In a diagram like that of Figure 7.1, representing relations between four persons, *A*, *B*, *C*, and *D*, the human capital resides in the nodes, and the social capital resides in the lines connecting the nodes. Social capital and human capital are often complementary. For example, if *B* is a child and *A* is an adult parent of the child, then in order for *A* to be useful for the cognitive development of *B*, there must be capital in both the node and the link, human capital held by *A*, and social capital in the existence of the relation between *A* and *B*.

Furthermore, certain kinds of social capital arise only in networks with a high degree of *closure*. In a network like that of Figure 7.1, the existence of relations between *A*, *B*, *C*, and *D* means that two can discuss a third's behavior and develop consensus about what is proper or appropriate behavior, that is, develop social norms. For example, if *A* and *D* are parents of *B* and *C*, they can develop norms about appropriate behavior for their children. If, in contrast, the network does not exhibit closure, so that *A* and *D*, who have parent–child links to *B* and *C*, respectively, do not have links to one another, then norms to govern and constrain *B*'s and *C*'s actions cannot develop.

Thus, if we are correct, the social capital that we have described earlier as existing in religious communities surrounding a religious school resides at least in part in the norms and sanctions that grow in such communities. These norms and sanctions in turn depend both on social relations and the closure of networks created by these relations.

Social Capital in the Family

Students' families differ in human capital, as, for example, measured in years of parental education. And this research shows, just as has much other research, that outcomes

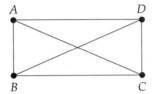

FIGURE 7.1   A Network with Closure.

for children are strongly affected by the human capital possessed by their parents. But this human capital can be irrelevant to outcomes for children if parents are not an important part of their children's lives, if their human capital is employed exclusively at work or elsewhere outside the home. The social capital of the family is the relations between children and parents (and when families include other members, relationships with them as well). That is, if the human capital possessed by parents is not complemented by social capital embodied in family relations, it is irrelevant to the child's educational growth that the parent has a great deal, or a small amount, of human capital.

There are striking examples in the biographies of particular persons that illustrate the importance of social capital in the family. For example, Bertrand Russell once remarked, in response to a comment on his brilliance, that he had no greater endowments than many others; that his grandmother, who engaged him in extensive discussions on intellectual matters when he was a child, is what made the difference. Assuming that his statement contained some truth, it is evident that the major difference between Bertrand Russell's childhood and that of others was not the intellectual resources his grandmother had, but the use of those resources in extended interaction with the boy. John Stuart Mill, who at the age of four had been taught Latin and Greek by his father, James Mill, and later in childhood would discuss critically with his father and with Jeremy Bentham drafts of the father's manuscripts, is another example. John Stuart Mill probably had no extraordinary genetic endowments, and his father's learning, while extensive, was no more so than that of some other men of the time. The central difference was the time and effort spent by the father with the child on intellectual matters.

A third example is from contemporary America. In one public school district where texts for school use were purchased by children's families, school authorities were puzzled to discover that a number of Asian immigrant families purchased two copies of each textbook needed by the child, rather than one. Investigation showed that the second copy was purchased for the mother to study in order to maximally help her child do well in school. Here is a case in which the human capital of the parents, at least as measured traditionally by years of schooling, is low, but the social capital in the family available for the child's education is extremely high.

These three examples contrast greatly with the situation in which many children of well-educated parents find themselves today. The human capital exists in the family, but the social capital does not.

It is the absence of social capital within the family that we have labeled "deficiencies" in the family. What we have labeled as *structural* deficiency is the physical absence of family members. The two elements of structural deficiency that we have used in the analysis are single-parent families and families in which the mother worked before the child entered elementary school. However, the nuclear family itself can be seen as structurally deficient, lacking the social capital which comes with the presence of grandparents or aunts and uncles in or near the household.

What we have labeled *functional* deficiency in the family is the absence of strong relations between children and parents despite their physical presence in the household and opportunity for strong relations.

This may result from the child's embeddedness in a youth community, from the parents' embeddedness in relationships with other adults which do not cross generations, or from other sources. Whatever the source, it means that whatever human capital exists in the parents, the child does not profit from it because the social capital is missing. The resources exist in node *A* of the diagram of Figure 7.1, but the weakness of relation between the parent *A* and the child *B* makes them unavailable to the child.

It is, in fact, precisely the distinction between human capital existing in the family and social capital existing in the family that constitutes the differences between what we have called "traditional disadvantage" of background and what we have called "family deficiencies." . . .What is ordinarily meant by a disadvantaged background is the absence of resources embodied in the parents, primarily represented by parents' education but also represented by a low economic level or racial-ethnic minority status that stand as surrogates for low levels of human capital that is useful for economic success. What we have counterposed to that in identifying "deficient families" is the absence of social capital, the weakness of links between the adult members of the family and the children. If we consider a fourfold table as shown in Figure 7.2, where the two dimensions are human capital and social capital, we can see immediately that there exist families in all four cells of the table. In cell 3 are families in which the parents are of low economic level and low education but with a strong and facilitating set of relations within the family. Poor and uneducated but strong families, such as those often found among immigrants from underdeveloped country to a developed country exemplify this cell. In cell 4 are families that are poor, uneducated, and disorganized, structurally broken or weakened by the personal disorganization of the parent or parents. In cell 1 is the family with both human and social

Social capital (strong vs. deficient families)

		Yes	No
Human capital (traditional advantage of background)	Yes	1	2
	No	3	4

FIGURE 7.2 Families Characterized by Presence of Absence of Human Capital and Social Capital.

capital: The adult members are capable and educated, and relations within the family are strong. The resources of the parents are available to the children to encourage and aid their educational and social development. In cell 2 is the family that is becoming more prevalent today: The adult members are well educated and individually capable, but for a variety of reasons—divorce, involvement with other adults in relations that do not cross generations (as is typical of most work settings), exclusive attention to self-development—the resources of the adults are not available to aid the psychological health and the social and educational development of the children.

By confounding these two dimensions of family resources those concerned with educational policy have targeted their efforts at children from families in cells 3 and 4, and it is those from families in cell 4 that are by far the most deprived. But there has been little attention altogether to children from families in cell 2. Yet . . . students from these families have considerably lower rates of achievement growth and considerably higher rates of dropout than do children from families in cell 1. Perhaps if we could identify sufficiently well children from these four types of families, the children from families in cell 3, that is, disadvantaged but strong families, might have fewer problems in school than those from cell 2, that is, advantaged but deficient families.

Social Capital beyond the Family

Beyond the family is social capital of other kinds that is relevant to the child's development. The most striking instance of that shown in the present research is the social capital provided by the religious community surrounding a Catholic school. The social capital that has value for a young person's development does not reside merely in the set of common values held by parents who choose to send their children to the same private school. It resides in the functional community, the actual social relationships that exist among parents, in the closure exhibited by this structure of relations and in the parents' relations with the institutions of the community. Part of that social capital is the norms that develop in communities with a high degree of closure. If, for example, in Figure 7.1, B and C represent students in school who see each other every day, and A and D are B's and C's parents, respectively, then there is closure if the parents A and D know each other and have some kind of ongoing relation. The importance of this closure for the young persons, B and C, lies in the fact that only if A and D are in some kind of ongoing relation can they establish norms that shape and constrain the actions of B and C. Indeed, in such a structure, there develop relations between one child and the parent of another, as exemplified in Figure 7.1 by the links between A and C, and between D and B.

A social structure that does not exhibit closure is represented by Figure 7.3. If B and C are two students who know and see each other in school, and A and D are the parents of B and C, respectively, then if A's friends and daily contacts are with others outside (E), and D's are also with a different set of others outside (F), A and D are not in a position to discuss their children's activities, to develop common evaluations of these activities, and to exercise sanctions that guide and constrain these activities.

Figure 7.1 represents what we have described as a structure with *intergenerational closure,* while Figure 7.3 represents what we have described as a structure without intergenerational closure. However much closure there may be in the youth community, among *B, C,* and other students in the school, it is the absence of intergenerational closure that prevents the human capital that exists among the adults from playing any role in the lives of the youth. This lack of intergenerational closure constitutes the missing social capital that we have identified earlier as resulting in tangible losses for young persons: lower achievement growth, greater likelihood of dropping out of school. The social capital does exist in some isolated small towns and rural areas where adults' social relations are restricted by geographic distance, and where residential mobility has not destroyed it. It exists in schools based on a religious community, such as the Catholic schools and the few other religious schools in our sample, though the social relations which make up the community are more narrowly focused around a single dimension of social life, a religious institution. In rare circumstances it may exist for private schools without a religious base.

This form of social capital once existed for many public schools, when they served a clientele in which mothers worked in the home, and everyday contacts were largely with neighbors. It may have once existed in elite private schools, when the social elite whose children attended the schools constituted a community with relatively dense interaction. But neither in most modern public schools nor in most nonreligiously based private schools does that intergenerational closure now exist. The evidence presented . . . indicates that the absence of this social capital represents a real resource loss for young persons growing up.

FIGURE 7.3   A Network without Closure.

Social Capital as a Public Good

There is, however, a central fact about social capital that does not exist for physical capital and human capital—and it is this fact which most threatens the social, psychological, and cognitive growth of young persons in the United States and, indeed, throughout Western society. Physical capital is ordinarily a private good, and property rights make it possible for the person who invests in physical capital to capture the benefits it produces. Thus, the incentive to invest in physical capital is not depressed; there is, as an economist might say, not a suboptimal investment in physical capital because those who invest in it are able to capture the benefits of their investments. For human capital also—at least human capital of the sort that is produced in schools—the person who invests the time and resources in building up this capital reaps its benefits, in the form of a higher-paying job, more satisfying or higher work status, or even the pleasure of greater understanding of the surrounding world— in short, all the benefits that schooling brings to a person.

But social capital of the sort that is valuable in the ways we have shown for a young person's education is not like this. The kinds of social structures that make possible social norms and the sanctions that enforce them do not benefit primarily the person or persons whose efforts would be necessary to bring them about, but benefit all those who are part of such a structure. For example, in some schools where there exists a dense set of associations among parents, these are the result of a small number of persons, ordinarily mothers who do not hold a full-time job outside the home. Yet these mothers themselves experience only a subset of the benefits of this social capital surrounding the school. If one of them decides to abandon these activities, for example to take a full-time job, this may be an entirely reasonable action from a personal point of view, and even from the point of view of that household with its children. The benefits of the new activity may far outweigh the losses arising from the decline in associations with other parents whose children are in the school. But the withdrawal of these activities constitutes a loss to all those other parents whose associations and contacts were dependent on them.

Or there are the . . . decisions of parents . . . : The decision to move from a community so that the father, for example, can take a better job, may be entirely correct from the point of view of that family. But because social capital consists of relations between persons, other persons may experience extensive losses by the severence of those relations, a severence over which they had no control. A part of those losses is the weakening of norms and sanctions that aid the school in its task. For each family, the total cost it experiences as a consequence of the decisions it and other families make may outweigh the benefits of those few decisions it has control over. Yet the beneficial consequences of those decisions made by the family itself may far outweigh the minor losses the family experiences from them alone.

Social Capital and the Future for Youth

There are further suggestive implications that this analysis holds for the future of youth and education in modern society. Two sets of facts taken together suggest a future with special problems. One set of facts is the results contained in this analysis . . . that show the importance of social capital within the family and social capital outside the family in the religious community for supporting the involvement of youth in school and their achievement growth. The importance of the social capital outside the family [is] especially apparent in . . . the importance of religious participation generally (not only among Catholics or among students in Catholic schools) in lowering the probability of dropping out of high school, and in research that showed that among the non-Catholic private schools, dropout was least in those which were grounded in a religious body and served a religiously homogeneous set of students.

All these results emphasize the importance of the embeddedness of young persons in the enclaves of adults most proximate to them, first and most prominently the family and second, a surrounding community of adults (exemplified in all these results by the religious community).

But there is a second set of facts as well, not from the data of this study, but observable from social trends. This is the declining embeddedness of youth in these enclaves, that is in families and in intergenerational functional communities. This decline comes from two directions. One is the decreased strength of the institutions themselves, the family and the local community (religiously based, neighborhood-based, or otherwise). We have discussed at length the "modern family deficiencies," and it is apparent that these deficiencies are growing rather rapidly. An example of one is the declining presence of father and mother in the household, through work in settings outside, and organizationally distant from, the household. Much attention has been directed to the recent rise in proportions of women working

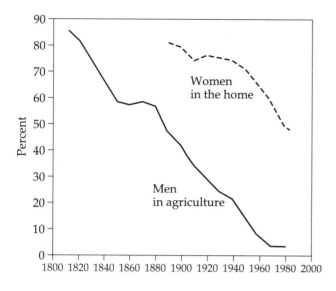

FIGURE 7.4 Percent of Male Labor Force in Agriculture, 1810–1982, and Percent of Women Not Employed in Paid Labor Force, 1890–1982.

outside the household, but what is often forgotten is that this exodus from the household merely follows (by about a hundred years) that of the men. Figure 7.4 shows the proportion of the male labor force engaged in agriculture (used as a proxy for men working in the household, though some nonfarm occupations were, especially in early days, in the household as well) and the proportion of women not in the labor force (that is, in the household).[1] These curves show a nearly parallel pattern, with the men's complete and the women's following the same course. These curves show the household progressively denuded of its adult members.

Other statistics could show different aspects of the loss of social capital in the household. One would be, for example, the declining number of adults in the household of the average American child—a decline that first saw members of the extended family vanish, and now sees one of the parents vanishing. And similar statistics could be presented for the decline of adult social capital available to children in the community outside the family.

But the decreased embeddedness of children and youth in family and community arises from a second source as well. This is the increasing psychic involvement of the youth with the mass media. This involvement is intense only for a fraction of youth; but the fraction may be increasing with the growth of the youth-oriented music industry from radio to television, with MTV (continuous rock video cable TV) its most extreme current expression.[2]

Thus, youth are pushed from psychic involvements in family and community by the reduced substance of those institutions and are pulled by the mass media toward involvements with "persona" of the media. The implications of this movement are many, but one is of special concern here: The former institutions, whatever their failings in specific cases, supported and strengthened the formal educational institution in which children and youth are placed. The latter do not. The implications are that the goals of schools become increasingly difficult to attain, as the social base that supports them comes to be less and less important in the lives of children and youth. The further implication is that something must give, and the most likely direction would appear to be a radical transformation of the institutions into which children are placed, from the schools we now know to something different.

The Inegalitarian Character of Functional Communities

The evidence . . . indicates that functional communities with intergenerational closure constitute social capital that is of widespread value for young persons in high school. Furthermore, the evidence indicates that this social capital is particularly valuable for young persons from families in which the social capital or the human capital of the parents is especially weak. Yet there is a body of research and theory that would predict just the opposite: Students from disadvantaged backgrounds, and perhaps those from deficient families, would do less well in schools surrounded by strong functional communities.

According to this theory and research, higher expectations and standards will be held by teachers for those students from families with high status, while those students from low-status families will be stigmatized with the reputations of their parents, low expectations for their achievement will be held by teachers, and adult members of the community outside the school will treat them differently.

This general thesis has a strong tradition in social psychology and sociology, both in research and in theory. "Expectation theory" or its close relative in sociology, "labeling theory," asserts that persons live up or down to others' expectations of them or to the labels attached to them by others. [See Merton (1968, pp. 475–90), Becker (1973, pp. 177–208), and Rosenthal and Jacobson (1968) for

seminal treatments of the thesis.] This, in conjunction with the fact that it is only where there is a strong functional community that the expectations or labels attached to particular students will be widely held in common by teachers, parents, and other students strengthens the prediction that schools based on a strong functional community will be most effective for students from advantaged backgrounds and may depress performance of students from disadvantaged backgrounds. Where the community extends only to the student body of the school (and nearly all high schools have a community within the student body itself, whatever its attachments to the adult community), these expectations and labels will be shared only among the students and can be expected to be less powerful in their effects on behavior. But where the school is based on a strong adult functional community, it would be predicted to be powerful.

A tradition of research in educational sociology has also held the general thesis of labeling theory and furthermore has used strong functional communities as the site for demonstrating its importance. The best known of these is *Elmtown's Youth* (Hollingshead 1949), based on research in a small Illinois town in 1942. Hollingshead showed the intergenerational inheritance of status in Elmtown and the way this was reinforced through the high school. Although Hollingshead's evidence was suggestive and illustrative rather than conclusive, it provided a graphic portrayal of how a functional community can strengthen the advantages of the already-advantaged and block the opportunities of the disadvantaged.

These theoretical positions, expectation theory and labeling theory, lead to the general prediction that those private schools based on a functional community (Catholic schools in our sample) will confer more benefits on those students from advantaged backgrounds relative to those from disadvantaged backgrounds than is true for public schools, or for those private schools not based on a functional community. In short, they will be internally inegalitarian.

How then can we account for the different findings in this book . . . ? The answer can be only conjectural, due to the lack of direct evidence. However, our conjecture is that a functional community based on the single dimension of religious association is different, in just those respects that relate to inegalitarianism, from a functional community that encompasses all arenas of social and economic life. In part, this is due to the egalitarian ethic of religion itself ("All God's children are equal in His eyes"). In part, it is due to the abstraction of a single arena of activity from the total fabric of social and economic life. This abstraction allows a child to escape a single encompassing evaluation of the family (including its children) based on the totality of its activities. This is an instance of the "role-segmentation" of modern social life, and according to our conjecture, the role-segmentation is important in inhibiting the inheritance by the child of the status of the parent.

. . .

NOTES

1. Data from U.S. Bureau of Census (1975) Table 182–282 for proportion of labor force on farms 1900–1970, and proportion of labor force in agriculture, 1800–1890; and Table D49–62 for proportion of females in labor force 1890–1970.

U.S. Bureau of Census (1984) is used to bring series up to 1982.

2. The question is often raised (ironically, often in the mass media itself) about "the effects of the mass media" (especially television, and the sex and violence on television) on children and youth. A frequent conclusion is that the "effects" are minimal or absent, and that children who have strong psycho-social foundations are impervious to any "undesirable" elements in media contents. But the discussion should make apparent that this misses the point in at least two ways. First, the very attention directed to these media is attention directed away from the adults who have traditionally constituted the social support for education and social development of the youth. Second, if it is the youth with strong psycho-social foundations who are unmoved by these elements, these are precisely the youth who, because of declines of family and community, are decreasing in numbers.

REFERENCES

BECKER, G. S. 1964. *Human Capital*. Chicago: University of Chicago Press.

BECKER, H. S. 1973. *The Outsiders*. New York: Free Press.

HOLLINGSHEAD, A. B. 1949. *Elmtown's Youth*. New York: Wiley.

MERTON, R. K. 1968. "The Self-fulfilling Prophesy." Chap. 13 in R. K. Merton, *Social Theory and Social Structure*. New York: Free Press.

MINCER, J. 1974. *Schooling, Experience and Earnings*. New York: National Bureau of Economic Research.

ROSENTHAL, R. AND L. JACOBSON. 1968. *Pygmalion in the Classroom*. New York: Holt, Rinehart and Winston.

SCHULTZ, T. W. 1961. "Investment in Human Capital." *American Economic Review* 51:1–17.

Changing Theories of Education Systems

8

THE FIRST ELEMENT OF MORALITY
The Spirit of Discipline

Emile Durkheim

. . .

One can distinguish two stages in childhood: the first, taking place almost entirely within the family or the nursery school—a substitute for the family, as its name suggests; the second, in elementary school, when the child, beginning to leave the family circle, is initiated into a larger environment. This we call the second period of childhood; we shall focus on it in discussing moral education. This is indeed the critical moment in the formation of moral character. Before that, the child is still very young; his intellectual development is quite rudimentary and his emotional life is too simple and underdeveloped. He lacks the intellectual foundation necessary for the relatively complex ideas and sentiments that undergird our morality. The limited boundaries of his intellectual horizon at the same time limit his moral conceptions. The only possible training at this stage is a very general one, an elementary introduction to a few simple ideas and sentiments.

On the other hand, if, beyond this second period of childhood—i.e., beyond school age—the foundations of morality have not been laid, they never will be. From this point on, all one can do is to complete the job already begun, refining sensibilities and giving them some intellectual content, i.e., informing them increasingly with intelligence. But the groundwork must have been laid. So we can appropriately fix our attention above all on this stage of development. Moreover, precisely because it is an intermediate stage, what we shall say may be readily applied, *mutatis mutandis,* to the preceding and following stages. On the one hand, in order to show clearly the nature of moral education at this period, we shall be led to indicate how it completes, and carries on from, familial education; on the other hand, to understand what it must later become, it will suffice to project our thinking into the future, taking account of differences in age and situation.

However, this first specification of the problem is not enough. Not only shall I discuss here, at least in principle, only moral education during the second stage of childhood; but I shall limit my subject even more narrowly. I shall deal above all with moral education in this second stage in our public schools because, normally, the public schools are and should be the flywheel of national education. Furthermore, contrary to the all too popular notion that moral education falls chiefly within the jurisdiction of the family, I judge that the task of the school in the moral development of the child can and should be of the greatest importance. There is a whole aspect of the culture, and a most important one, which would otherwise be lost. For if it is the family that can distinctively and effectively evoke and organize those homely sentiments basic to morality and—even more generally—those germane to the simplest personal relationships, it is not the agency so constituted as to train the child in terms of the demands of society. Almost by definition, as it were, it is an inappropriate agency for such a task.

Therefore, focusing our study on the school, we find ourselves precisely at the point that should be regarded as the locus, par excellence, of moral development for children of this age. We have committed ourselves to provide in our schools a completely rational moral education, that is to say, excluding all principles derived from revealed religion. Thus, the problem of moral education is clearly posed for us at this point in history.

I have shown not only that the task to be undertaken is possible but that it is necessary—that it is dictated by all historical development. But at the same time, I have emphasized the complexity of the task. These complications should not discourage us in the least. It is altogether natural that an undertaking of such importance should be difficult; only the mediocre and insignificant tasks are easy. There is, then, nothing to be gained in minimizing the magnitude of the task on which we are working, under pretext of reassuring ourselves.

It is worthier and more profitable to face up to the difficulties, which inevitably accompany such a great change. I have pointed out what these difficulties seem to me to be. In the first place, due to the close bond established historically between morality and religion, we can anticipate—since these are essential elements of morality never expressed

save in religious guise—that if we begin to eliminate everything religious from the traditional system without providing any substitute, we run the risk of also eliminating essential moral ideas and sentiments. In the second place, a rational morality cannot have the same content as one that depends upon some authority other than reason. For the development of rationalism does not come about without a parallel development of individualism and, consequently, without a refinement in moral sensitivity that makes certain social relations—the allocation of rights and obligations, which up to the present has not bothered our consciences—appear unjust. Furthermore, there is not only a parallel development between individualism and rationalism, but the latter reacts upon the former and stimulates it. The characteristic of injustice is that it is not founded in the nature of things; it is not based upon reason. Thus, it is inevitable that we shall become more sensitive to injustice in the measure that we respond to the authority of reason. It is not a trifling matter to stimulate free inquiry, to accord a new authority to reason; for the power thus granted cannot but turn against those traditions that persist only insofar as they are divorced from its influence. In undertaking to organize a rational education, we find ourselves confronted with two kinds, two series of problems, the one as compelling as the other. We must take care lest we impoverish morality in the process of rationalizing it; and we must anticipate the complications that it entails and prepare for them.

To attack the first problem, we must rediscover the moral forces basic to all moral life, that of yesterday as well as that of today, without a priori derogation of the former, even if up to the present that morality has only existed in religious guise. We have to seek out the rational expression of such a morality, that is to say, apprehend such morality in itself, in its genuine nature, stripped of all symbols. Secondly, once these moral forces are known, we have to investigate how they should develop and be oriented under present social conditions. Of these two problems, it is the former that, from all evidence, should first concern us. We must first determine, in their essentials, the basic elements of morality before investigating the changes that may be indicated.

To ask what the elements of morality are is not to undertake a complete listing of all the virtues, or even of the most important. It involves an inquiry into fundamental dispositions, into those mental states at the root of the moral life. To influence the child morally is not to nurture him a particular virtue, followed by another and still another; it is to develop and even to constitute completely, by appropriate methods, those general dispositions that, once created, adapt themselves readily to the particular circumstances of human life. If we are able to push through to their discovery, we shall at once have overcome one of the major obstacles confronting us in the work of our schools. What sometimes creates doubt about the effectiveness of the school in matters pertaining to the moral elements of culture is that these latter apparently involve such a host of ideas, sentiments, and customs that the teacher seems to lack the necessary time, in the few and fleeting moments when the child is under his influence, to awaken and develop them. There is such a diversity of virtues, even if one seeks to fasten on the most important, that if each of them must be at least partially developed, the dissipation of effort over such a large area must necessarily vitiate the enterprise.

To operate effectively, especially since influence can only be exerted during a brief period of time, one must have a definite and clearly specified goal. One must have an *idée fixe,* or a small number of definite ideas that serve as lodestar. Thus, our efforts, pushing always in the same direction, following the same paths, can achieve some results. One must desire strongly whatever he wishes; and few rather than many things. To provide the necessary drive for our educational efforts, we must therefore try to ferret out those basic sentiments that are the foundation of our moral dispositions.

How do we go about it? You are familiar with the way the moralists ordinarily handle this question. They commence with the principle that each of us carries within himself all the elements of morality. Hence, we have only to look inside ourselves with a little care to discover the meaning of morality. So the moralist engages in introspective inquiry and, from amongst the ideas that he has more or less clearly in mind, seizes upon this one or that as seeming to represent the central motions of morality. For some, it is the idea of utility; for others, the notion of perfection; and for still others, it is the conception of human dignity, etc.

I do not wish to discuss at this point whether morality in its entirety resides in each person—whether each individual mind contains in itself all those elements that, simply in their development, constitute morality. Everything that follows leads us to a different conclusion, but we must not anticipate it here. To dispose of this currently fashionable approach I need only point out how subjective and arbitrary it is. After his self-interrogation, all that the moralist can state is his own conception of morality, the conception he has personally contrived. Why is this more objective than the quite unobjective vulgar notions of heat, or light, or electricity? Let us acknowledge that morality may be completely implicit in each mind. Nonetheless, one must know how to get at it. One must still know how to distinguish, amongst all our ideas, those within the province of morality and those that are not. Now, according to what criteria can we make such a distinction? What enables us to say: this is a matter of morality and this is not? Shall we say that that is moral which accords with man's nature? Suppose, then, that we knew quite certainly what man's nature was. What proves that the end of morality is to realize human nature—why might it not have as its function the satisfaction of social needs? Shall we substitute this idea for the other? But first, what justifies us in doing so? And what are the social interests that morality must protect? For such interests are of all sorts—economic, military, scientific, etc. We cannot base practice on such subjective hypotheses as these. We cannot regulate the education that we owe our children on the basis of such purely academic conceptions.

Moreover, this method, to whatever conclusions it may lead, rests throughout on a single premise: that to develop morality empirical analysis is unnecessary. To determine what morality should be, it is apparently thought unnecessary first to inquire what it is or what it has been. People expect to legislate immediately. But whence this privilege? One hears it said today that we can know something of economic, legal, religious, and linguistic matters *only* if we begin by observing facts, analyzing them, comparing them. There is no reason why it should be otherwise with moral facts. On the other hand, one can inquire what morality ought to be only if one has first determined the complex of things that goes under this rubric, what its nature is, what ends it serves. Let us begin, then, by looking at morality as a fact, and let us see what we are actually able to understand by it.

In the first place, there is an aspect common to all behavior that we ordinarily call moral. All such behavior conforms to pre-established rules. To conduct one's self morally is a matter of abiding by a norm, determining what conduct should obtain in a given instance even before one is required to act. This domain of morality is the domain of duty; duty is prescribed behavior. It is not that the moral conscience is free of uncertainties. We know, indeed, that it is often perplexed, hesitating between alternatives.

But then the problem is what is the particular rule that applies to the given situation, and how should it be applied? Since each rule is a general prescription, it cannot be applied exactly and mechanically in identical ways in each particular circumstance. It is up to the person to see how it applies in a given situation. There is always considerable, if limited, leeway left for his initiative. The essentials of conduct are determined by the rule. Furthermore, to the extent that the rule leaves us free, to the extent that it does not prescribe in detail what we ought to do, the action being left to our own judgment, to that extent there is no moral valuation. We are not accountable precisely because of the freedom left us. Just as an action is not a crime in the usual and actual sense of the word when it is not forbidden by an established law, so when it is not contrary to a pre-established norm, it is not immoral. Thus, we can say that morality consists of a system of rules of action that predetermine conduct. They state how one must act in given situations; and to behave properly is to obey conscientiously.

This first statement, which verges on a common-sense observation, suffices nonetheless to highlight an important fact too often misunderstood. Most moralists, indeed, consider morality as entirely contained in a very general, unique formula. It is precisely on this account that they so readily accept the view that morality resides entirely in the individual conscience, and that a simple glance inside ourselves will be enough to reveal it. This formula is expressed in different ways: that of the Kantians is not that of the utilitarians, and each utilitarian moralist has his own. However, in whatever manner it is conceived, everyone assigns it the central position. All the rest of morality consists merely in applying this fundamental principle. This conception expresses the classical distinction between so-called theoretical and applied morality. The aim of the former is to specify the general law of morality; the latter, to investigate how the law thus enunciated should be applied in the major situaions and combinations encountered in life. Thus, specific rules deduced by this method would not in themselves have an independent reality. They would only be extensions or corollaries of the general formula as it was reflected throughout the range of life experiences. Apply the general law of morality to various domestic relations and you will have family morality. Apply it to different political relationships and you will have civic morality, etc. These would not be diverse duties but a single, unique duty running like a guiding thread throughout life. Given the great diversity of situations and relationships, one can see how, from this point of view, the realm of morality seems quite indeterminate.

However, such a conception of morality reverses the real situation. If we see morality as it is, we see that it consists in an infinity of special rules, fixed and specific, which order man's conduct in those different situations in which he finds himself most frequently. Some define the desirable relationships betwen man and wife; others, the way parents should behave with their children; and still others, the relationships between person and property. Certain of these maxims are stated in law and sanctioned in clear-cut fashion; others are etched in the public conscience, expressing themselves in the aphorisms of popular morality, and sanctioned simply by the stigma attaching to their violation rather than by some definite punishment. But whether the one or the other, they have their own existence, their own life. The proof lies in the fact that certain of these rules may be found in a weakened state, while others, on the contrary, are altogether viable. In one country, the rules of familiar morality may provide all the necessary stability, while the rules of civic virtue are weak and ineffective.

Here, then, are phenomena not only real, but also comparatively autonomous, since they can be realized in different ways depending upon the conditions of social life. This is a far cry from seeing here simple aspects of one and the same general principle that would embrace all their meaning and reality. Quite to the contrary, the general rule, however it has been or is conceived, does not constitute the reality but is a simple abstraction. There is no rule, no social prescription that is recognized or gains its sanction from Kant's moral imperative or from the law of utility as formulated by Bentham, Mill, or Spencer. These are the generalizations of philosophers, the hypotheses of theoreticians. What people refer to as the general law of morality is quite simply a more or less exact way of representing approximately and schematically the moral reality; but it is not that reality itself. It is a more or less satisfactory shorthand statement of characteristics common to all moral rules; it is not a real, established, effective rule. It is to moral reality what philosophers' hypotheses, aimed at expressing the unity of nature, are to that nature itself. It is of the order of science, not of the order of life.

Thus, in fact and in practice, it is not according to theoretical insights or general formulae that we guide our conduct, but according to specific rules applying uniquely to the special situation that they govern. In all significant life situations, we do not refer back to the so-called general principle of morality to discover how it applies in a particular case and thus learn what we should do. Instead there are clear-cut and specific ways of acting required of us. When we conform to the rule prescribing chastity and forbidding incest, is it only because we deduce it from some fundamental axiom of morality? Suppose, as fathers, we find ourselves widowers charged with the entire responsibility of our family. We do not have to hark back to the ultimate source of morality, nor even to some abstract notion of paternity to deduce what conduct is implied in these circumstances. Law and the mores prescribe our conduct.

Thus, it is not necessary to represent morality as something very general, made concrete only to the extent it becomes necessary. On the contrary, morality is a totality of definite rules; it is like so many molds with limiting boundaries, into which we must pour our behavior. We do not have to construct these rules at the moment of action by deducing them from some general principles; they already exist, they are already made, they live and operate around us.

Now, this first statement is of primary importance for us. It demonstrates that the function of morality is, in the first place, to determine conduct, to fix it, to eliminate the element of individual arbitrariness. Doubtless the content of moral precepts—that is to say, the nature of the prescribed behavior—also has moral value, and we shall discuss this. However, since all such precepts promote regularity of conduct among men, there is a moral aspect in that these actions—not only in their specific content, but in a general way—are held to be certain regularity. This is why transients and people who cannot hold themselves to specific jobs are always suspect. It is because their moral temperament is fundamentally defective—because it is most uncertain and undependable. Indeed, in refusing to yield to the requirements of regularized conduct, they disdain all customary behavior, they resist limitations or restrictions, they feel some compulsion to remain "free." This indeterminate situation also implies a state of endless instability. Such people are subject to momentary impulses, to the disposition of the moment, to whatever notion is in mind at the moment when they must act, since they lack habits sufficiently strong to prevent present inclinations from prevailing over the past. Doubtless it may happen that a fortunate impulse prompts them to a happy decision; but

it is a situation by no means guaranteed to repeat itself. Morality is basically a constant thing, and so long as we are not considering an excessively long time span, it remains ever the same. A moral act ought to be the same tomorrow as today, whatever the personal predispositions of the actor. Morality thus presupposes a certain capacity for behaving similarly under like circumstances, and consequently it implies a certain ability to develop habits, a certain need for regularity. So close is the connection between custom and moral behavior that all social customs almost inevitably have a moral character. When a mode of behavior has become customary in a group, whatever deviates from it elicits a wave of disapproval very like that evoked by moral transgressions. Customs share in some way the special respect accorded moral behavior. If all social customs are not moral, all moral behavior is customary behavior. Consequently, whoever resists the customary runs the risk of defying morality.

Regularity, however, is only one element of morality. This same conception of the rule when carefully analyzed will disclose another and no less important feature of morality.

To assure regularity, it is only necessary that customs be strongly founded. But customs, by definition, are forces internalized in the person. It is a kind of accumulated experience within us that unfolds itself, activated, as it were, spontaneously. Internalized, it expresses itself externally as an inclination or a preference. Quite to the contrary, a rule is essentially something that is outside the person. We cannot conceive of it save as an order—or at least as binding advice—which originates outside ourselves. Is it a matter of rules of hygiene? They come to us from the science that decrees them, or, more specifically, from the experts representing that science. Does it concern rules of professional practice? They come to us from the tradition of the profession and, more directly, from those among our elders who have passed them on to us and who best exemplify them in our eyes. It is for this reason that, through the centuries, people have seen in the rules of morality directives deriving from God.

A rule is not then a simple matter of habitual behavior; it is a way of acting that we do not feel free to alter according to taste. It is in some measure—and to the same extent that it is a rule—beyond personal preference. There is in it something that resists us, is beyond us. We do not determine its existence or its nature. It is independent of what we are. Rather than expressing us, it dominates us. If it were entirely an internal thing, like a sentiment or a habit, there would be no reason why it should not conform to all the variations and fluctuations of our internal states. Of course, we do set for ourselves a line of conduct, and we say, then, that we have set up rules of conduct of such and such a sort. But the word so used generally lacks its full meaning. A plan of action that we ourselves outline, which depends only upon ourselves and that we can always modify is a project, not a rule. Or, if in fact it is to some extent truly independent of our will, it must rest in the same degree on something other than our will—on something external to us. For example, we adopt a given mode of life because it carries the authority of science; the authority of science legitimates it. It is to the science that we defer, in our behavior, and not to ourselves. It is to science that we bend our will.

Thus, we see in these examples what there is in the conception of rules beyond the notion of regularity: *the idea of authority*. By authority, we must understand that influence which imposes upon us all the moral power that we acknowledge as superior to us. Because of this influence, we act in prescribed ways, not because the required conduct is attractive to us, not because we are so inclined by some predisposition either innate or acquired, but because there is some compelling influence in the authority dictating it. Obedience consists in such acquiescence. What are the mental processes at the bottom of this notion of authority, which create this compelling force to which we submit? This we shall have to investigate presently. For the moment, the question is not germane; it is enough if we have the feeling of the thing and of its reality. There is in every moral force that we feel as above or beyond ourselves something that bends our wills. In one sense, one can say that there is no rule, properly speaking, which does not have this imperative character in some degree, because, once again, every rule commands. It is this that makes us feel that we are not free to do as we wish.

Morality, however, constitutes a category of rules where the idea of authority plays an absolutely preponderant role. Part of the esteem we accord to principles of hygiene or of professional practice or various precepts drawn from folk wisdom doubtless stems from the authority accorded science and experimental research. Such a wealth of knowledge and human experience, by itself, imposes on us a respect that communicates itself to the bearers, just as the deference accorded by the devout to things religious is communicated to priests. But, in all these cases, if we abide by the rule it is not only out of deference to the authority that is its source; it is also because the prescribed behavior may very well have useful consequences, whereas contrary behavior would entail harmful results. If, when we are sick, we take care of ourselves, following the doctor's orders, it is not only out of deference to his authority, but also because we hope thus to recover. There is involved here, therefore, a feeling other than respect for authority. There enter quite utilitarian considerations, which are intrinsic to the nature of the act and to its outcomes, possible or probable.

It is quite otherwise with morality. Without doubt, if we violate rules of morality we risk unhappy consequences: we may be blamed, blacklisted, or materially hurt—either in person or our property. But it is a certain and incontestable fact that an act is not moral, even when it is in substantial agreement with moral rules, if the consideration of adverse consequences has determined it. Here, for the act to be everything it should be, for the rule to be obeyed as it ought to be, it is necessary for us to yield, not in order to avoid disagreeable results or some moral or material punishment, but very simply because we ought to, regardless of the consequences our conduct may have for us. One must obey a moral precept out of respect for it and for this reason alone. All the leverage that it exerts upon our wills derives exclusively from the authority with which it is invested. Thus, in the case of moral rules, authority operates alone; to the extent that any other element enters into conduct, to that extent it loses its moral character. We are saying, then, that while all rules command, the moral rule consists entirely in a commandment and in nothing else. That is why the moral rule speaks to us with such authority—why, when it speaks, all other considerations must be subordinated. It permits no equivocation. When it is a matter of evaluating the ultimate consequences of an act, uncertainty is inevitable—there is always something indeterminate in the outcome. So many diverse combinations of circumstance can produce outcomes we are unable to foresee. But when it is a matter of duty, since all such calculation is forbidden, it is easier to be sure: all problems are simpler. It is not a matter of anticipating a future inevitably obscure and uncertain. It is a matter of knowing what is prescribed. If duty speaks there is nothing to do but obey. As to the source of this extraordinary authority, I shall not inquire for the time being. I shall content myself with pointing out its incontestable existence.

Morality is not, then, simply a system of customary conduct. It is a system of commandments. We were saying, first of all, that irregular behavior is morally incomplete. So it is with the anarchist. (I use the word in its etymological sense, referring to the man so constituted as not to feel the reality of moral imperatives, the man who is affected by a kind of color-blindness, by virtue of which all moral and intellectual forces seem to him of the same order.) Here we confront another aspect of morality: at the root of the moral life there is, besides the preference for regularity, the notion of moral authority. Furthermore, these two aspects of morality are closely linked, their unity deriving from a more complex idea that embraces both of them. This is the concept of discipline. Discipline in effect regularizes conduct. It implies repetitive behavior under determinate conditions. But discipline does not emerge without authority—a regulating authority. Therefore, to summarize this chapter, we can say that the fundamental element of morality is the spirit of discipline.

However, let us be clear about the meaning of this proposition. Ordinarily, discipline appears useful only because it entails behavior that has useful outcomes. Discipline is only a means of specifying and imposing the required behavior, so it derives its *raison d'etre* from the behavior. But if the preceding analysis is correct we must say that discipline derives its *raison d'etre* from itself; it is good that man is disciplined, independent of the acts to which he thus finds himself constrained. Why? It is all the more necessary to consider this problem, since discipline and rules often appear as constraining—necessary, perhaps, but nonetheless deplorable evils that one must know how to bear while reducing them to a minimum. What, then, makes discipline good?

9
_____

THE SCHOOL AND THE COMMUNITY

Willard Waller

One who thinks about the relation of the school to the community which supports it will soon come upon questions of public policy which it would take an Einsteinian grasp of the calculus of felicity to answer. Difficulty arises because the aims of the school and the community are often divergent. It is very well to say that the school should serve the community, but it is difficult to decide what opinion should govern when school and community differ. The lights of the school authorities are often better than those of the community in general. School men have given some study to their own problems, and could reasonably be expected to know more about them than outsiders do. Yet the community is often wiser than the school, because the community is whole and the school is fragmentary. The school, as a fragment of the common life, is a prey to institutionalism. Institutionalism causes the school to forget its purpose; it makes the school give education for education and teaching for teaching, perhaps for teachers; in short, it makes an end of what is logically only a means to an end. This vice the community escapes because the community is whole, because it is not simply a place where teachers teach and children learn. The community is whole because whole men live in it. And the community is sometimes wise with a knowledge of the complete life that surpasses the knowledge of

the schools. It becomes, then, one of the important questions of public policy as to how far the community should determine the policy of the school and how far the school should be self-determining. We have not yet the formula.

A complication of a different order arises from the fact that communities in general, perhaps especially American communities, have chosen to use the schools as repositories for certain ideals. The ideals which are supposed to have their stronghold in the schools are of several different sorts. The belief is abroad that young people ought to be trained to think the world a little more beautiful and much more just than it is, as they ought to think men more honest and women more virtuous than they are. A high-school student must learn that honesty is always the best policy; perhaps his father secretly believes that he knows better; perhaps the boy himself may be learning something quite different in the world of business, but it does the boy no harm to start with that assumption. We can teach him enough honesty to keep him out of jail all his life; later he can make such amendments to our principles as seem necessary to him. All must learn that the United States is the greatest and best of all the nations of history, unequalled in wealth or virtue since time began. Perhaps it does no harm for students to think that the world is getting better and better, though this is a very dangerous doctrine if one thinks about it very long.

Among these ideals are those moral principles which the majority of adults more or less frankly disavow for themselves but want others to practice; they are ideals for the helpless, ideals for children and for teachers. There are other ideals which are nearly out of print, because people do not believe in them any more. Though most adults have left such ideals behind, they are not willing to discard them finally. The school must keep them alive. The school must serve as a museum of virtue.

We have in our culture a highly developed system of idealism for the young. The young have not yet come into contact with a world that might soil them, and we do what we can to keep the young unsullied. There are certain things that are not for the years of the young. There are certain facts about human nature that they must not learn. There are certain bits of reality that they must not touch. There are certain facts of history that we think it best not to teach them. There is an idealized world view that it is thought best to pass on to adolescents. The notion that it is not proper to tell the whole truth is often carried over into college teaching, and it affects materially the point of view of many university professors. There is just enough apparent wisdom in the policy of hiding difficult facts from the young to justify it in the popular mind as a general policy. For it is often argued that character training must begin by the inculcation of an impossible virtue, in order that the individual may have a surplus of virtue to trade upon. The world, of course, is thoroughly committed to the policy of not telling the whole truth to youngsters, to the policy of telling them falsehoods which will make the world more attractive or themselves more tractable and virtuous.

The conventional belief, as we have noted, is that the young must be shielded from contact with the unpleasant and amoral aspects of the universe and that they must be kept in an ultra-conservative environment. These ideals may be justified by the fact that they prevent the demoralization of the young; as to that we have preferred to keep an open mind. But it is certain that the necessity of serving as the repository for these ideals limits the larger utility of the school. For if it is the purpose of education to prepare for life in the world, then the school must give its students that world in order that they may get themselves ready for living in it. Actually it cannot give students the world, but only an imitation or a representation of the world; in any case, it should be an accurate imitation or a faithful representation if the training which the student receives in school is to have any validity. The less the discontinuity between the life of the school and the life of the world outside, the better will be the training for life which the school gives to its students. Any ideal which cuts down the ability of the school to reproduce reality interferes with its real function of preparing students for life. The utility of such ideals may even be disputed from the moral point of view; the argument against them is the good one that the individual upon whom we have foisted off a too idealistic world view will be more readily disorganized by contact with a far from perfect world than will an individual who has already had some experience of the world; it is the old principle of inoculation. In almost any case, if a school man believes in the policy of training young persons to be virtuous by not telling them the truth, he sets very definite limits to his own continuing influence upon those who come in contact with him. There is reason for the bitter jest that a school teacher is a man hired to tell lies to little boys.

Our analysis of the relation between the school and the community has so far been very general. The possibilities of such analysis are limited. We may hope to achieve an analysis which will have greater concreteness by basing it upon the connections which are made between the school and the community by the lives of individuals. If we wish an analysis that will bite into reality we must study the roots which persons involved in school life have in the community at large and attempt to discover the interconnection of their lives within and without the school. Each individual represents a reciprocal channel of influence, an influence of the community upon the school and an influence of the school upon the community. Therefore we must study the relation of the school and the community by studying persons and attempting to learn what burdens they carry as they go back and forth between the community and the school. We turn now to an analysis of this sort.

The place of students as the young of a community we have already noted. Toward young persons the community in general has the conventional attitude of the elders, an attitude of protection mingled with regulation. Children live in glass houses. There is the desire to shield the young from all contaminating contact with the world, and this is one reason for the multitudinous restrictions upon the teacher in the community. Every older person tends to take a paternal interest in the young of the community, whether he has progeny or not. The students in a public school thus have a very definite place in the community, and the community conception of this place materially affects the kind of school which the community maintains.

. . .

Differences of position in the community determine important differences in the school. The child's status as the son of a particular person affects his status in the school and his attitude toward school. The daughter of an influential man in the community does not expect to be treated in the same way as an ordinary child, and yet it is dangerous for a teacher to make exceptions. Thus arise many problems to perplex the teacher. . . .

. . .

The attitudes of students make very clear the cruel distinction between rich and poor.

Many children attain an easy and unhealthy leadership through the use of the economic resources of their parents or merely through their parents' reputations. It is upon the basis of such distinctions that many of the cliques and social clubs of high-school children are formed; the competition is not a healthy one because it is not based upon the merits of the persons competing. Many parents who have the misfortune to be well-to-do or famous have longed to remove their children from this atmosphere. The private school presents a way out of the situation. In Washington it is no distinction to be a Congressman; in a private school it is not usually a distinction to have wealthy parents; competition must therefore ascend to a different plane.

The children of poor and humble parents experience the situation with the opposite emphasis. They are those whom the teachers do not favor; they are the ones excluded from things exclusive. These poorer children frequently drop out of high school because of their inability to sustain themselves in social competition with the children of wealthier parents.[1] Clothes make the student. Teachers sometimes take unusual pains with children who have few cultural advantages and little economic backing at home, and these efforts occasionally have remarkable and heartening results.

Students may likewise stand out as individuals. The high-school athletic hero achieves much distinction in the school, and his prowess is usually bruited about the community as well. Brilliant students may likewise achieve desirable status in the school, with some carryover into the community at large. The girl who becomes implicated in any scandal is singled out for special attention both in the school and the community. Frequently the attention is an attempt to injure her, and it usually succeeds.

Such is the influence of the community upon the school, as mediated through the personalities of students. The opposite process is fully as significant. The school, through its influence upon individuals, exerts a tremendous influence upon the community. This is a process which has often been dwelt upon in the literature, and we need give it here but passing notice. The long-term influence of the school may be very great. Perhaps the school can have but little effect upon the inner make-up of the children who pass through it, but it can have a great effect upon certain specific beliefs. Thus the advocates of temperance strove wisely to get their doctrines incorporated into the curriculum of the schools. Perhaps it seemed futile at the time to show little children pictures of ulcerated stomachs and badly deteriorated livers, but when those children grew old enough to vote, they put prohibition into the Constitution. Likewise the representatives of the public utilities have chosen to make much of their propaganda easily available for teachers in the form of lessons ready planned; some have gone to the extreme of offering to grade the teacher's papers for him. The process of cultural diffusion has sometimes been hastened through the lessons of the schools; a particularly good example of this has been furnished by the rapid spread of the toothbrush in America in the last quarter of a century.

. . .

On occasion, the doctrines of the school and the community come sharply into conflict. The result is that some members of the community attempt to discipline erring members of the faculty. Instances like the following could be multiplied without end.

In studying Caedmon, I asked them to read the Biblical version of the creation story and compare it with his. I especially reminded them that I wanted it read as literature and compared on that basis. I called for the papers the next day. Only three were available. I nonchalantly gave them the same assignment and an additional one. No papers came in. I reminded them of their neglect. Finally, after another day or two, I began to get papers of a distinctly sectarian version of the story. It was not what I wanted and I told them so. It could not be used to the same purpose.

One night after school a rap came at the Assembly room door. There stood three very indignant ladies, one of whom I recognized as the mother of one of my girls. She asked me icily if "The Professor" (everyone called him that) was in. Innocence itself, I took them to his office in my most gracious manner. Miss V and I laughed about how someone surely was going to get their everlasting, for those ladies were mad. Little did I dream! I was thoroughly surprised when, the next day, the superintendent told me what a terrible time he had convincing them that I was not trying to corrupt their daughters' morals. (Autobiographical document, *My First Year of Teaching,* from a twenty-five-year-old woman teacher.)

This incident leads naturally to a consideration of community school relations centering in the personalities of teachers. We may state our two most important generalizations concerning the relation of teachers to the community in this form: That the teacher has a special position as a paid agent of cultural diffusion, and that the teacher's position in the community is much affected by the fact that he is supposed to represent those ideals for which the schools serve as repositories.

Teachers are paid agents of cultural diffusion. They are hired to carry light into dark places. To make sure that teachers have some light, standard qualifications for teachers have been evolved. Not only must the teacher know enough to teach the youngsters in the schools competently according to the standards of the community, but he must, usually, be a little beyond his community. From this it follows that the teacher must always be a little discontented with the community he lives in. The teacher is a martyr to cultural diffusion.

It does not matter where a teacher starts, he must always take just enough training to make him a little dissatisfied with any community he is qualified to serve. And it does not matter much how far he goes, for there is, for most of us, no attainable end. A farmer's daughter decides to teach. It seems to her that a rural school would be just right; she is used to country life and it pleases her well. But she must be a high-school graduate before she is qualified to teach in a rural school. When she has finished her training in the nearby village she is no longer enthusiastic about teaching in a rural school. She goes to a normal school, and learns to live in a cultural center of that level. Then she can teach in the high school of a small town. She goes to a state university, which is a first-rate center of learning. What she learns there makes high-school teaching a little dull and life in the smaller community difficult. University teachers and public-school teachers in the large cities are partial exceptions, but for the rest there is rarely an end to the process. The teacher must always know enough to make his subject matter seem commonplace to him, or he does not know enough to teach it. He must always have received teaching a grade higher than he can give. He must always have adjusted his possibilities to a center of learning one size larger than the one he serves. The teacher must take what consolation he can from the fact, made much of by inspirational writers, that he is a carrier of the cultural values.

This nearly universal maladjustment is not without its effect upon the standards of success in the profession. The successful teacher makes progress; that is, he moves occasionally, and always to a larger community. That is one reason why teachers stubbornly go to school. They hope some time to make tastes and opportunities coincide. But the fact that they rarely succeed accounts in part for the fact that teachers rarely take root in a community. They hold themselves forever ready to obey that law of gravitation which pulls them toward an educational center equivalent to the highest center they have had experience of. That is partly why teachers are maladjusted transients rather than citizens. Although the stair steps of primary groups of children no doubt have more to do with it than the attitudes of teachers, this unadjustment of teachers may help to account for the fact that schools of each level ape the schools of the next higher grade, the grade schools imitating the high school, the high schools pretending to be colleges, and colleges trying to become graduate schools.

. . .

Our second major generalization is that the teacher is supposed to represent certain ideals in the community. These ideals differ somewhat from one community to another, but there is an underlying similarity. The entire set of ideals in their most inclusive form is clearly stated in the contract which teachers in the public schools of a certain southern community are asked to sign. The contract follows:

I promise to take a vital interest in all phases of Sunday-school work, donating of my time, service, and money without stint for the uplift and benefit of the community.

I promise to abstain from all dancing, immodest dressing, and any other conduct unbecoming a teacher and a lady.

I promise not to go out with any young men except in so far as it may be necessary to stimulate Sunday-school work.

I promise not to fall in love, to become engaged or secretly married.

I promise not to encourage or tolerate the least familiarity on the part of any of my boy pupils.

I promise to sleep at least eight hours a night, to eat carefully, and to take every precaution to keep in the best of health and spirits, in order that I may be better able to render efficient service to my pupils.

I promise to remember that I owe a duty to the townspeople who are paying me my wages, that I owe respect to the school board and the superintendent that hired me, and that I shall consider myself at all times the willing servant of the school board and the townspeople.[2]

The contract quoted above is so extreme that it will seem incredible to persons who are not familiar with the moral qualifications which teachers in general are supposed to fulfill. Those a little closer to the facts will be willing to credit its literal truth. In any case, the contract itself is so explicit that comment upon it is unnecessary.

The demands made by the smaller community upon the time and money of the teacher are unremitting. The teacher must be available for church functions, lodge functions, public occasions, lecture courses, and edifying spectacles of all sorts. Not infrequently he is expected to identify himself closely with some particular religious group and to become active in "church work." School executives occupy an even more exposed position than do underlings. Yet some unbelieving superintendents in very small communities have been able to work out compromises that satisfied the community and yet involved no sacrifice of their own convictions. One tactful agnostic declined to attend any church services at any time, but made it a point to be present at all church suppers, "sociables," and other non-religious ceremonies. Such a policy would need to be coupled with a great deal of skill in evasion and putting off if it were to work successfully; the teacher must not only avoid the issue and wear out those who urge church attendance upon him, but he must do it without giving offence or getting himself classed as an adherent of the devil. The teacher is also under considerable pressure to contribute to good causes. The difficulty is that he is not always permitted to judge of the goodness or badness of a cause. Quite aside from any such factor of judgment, the very multiplicity of the good causes to which the teacher is expected to contribute may make them a heavy drain upon his resources.

These demands are often resented, and with reason. But an interesting dilemma presents itself in this connection. A part of the solution of the problems of the teaching profession depends upon the assimilation of teachers to the community. Is not this conscription of teachers for edifying occasions a step in that direction? Where the participation of the teacher is quite unforced, as it sometimes is, it would seem that such demands work out favorably. Yet such participation will never really assimilate the teacher to the community, because it is not the right kind of participation. The teacher participates as a teacher, always formally and *ex officio,* too often unwillingly and by force. What is needed is participation by the teacher as an individual in community groups in which he is interested. If the teacher is ever really to belong, he must join in local groups as John Jones and not as the superintendent of schools.

The moral requirements that go with school teaching are extremely important. A colleague sometimes says, half in jest, that the schools of America are primarily agencies for moral and religious instruction. If anyone accepts the challenge laid down by that proposition, he points out the fact that the most complete ineffectiveness as a teacher does not always constitute a valid ground for dismissing a teacher from his position, whereas detection in any moral dereliction causes a teacher's contract to be broken at once. Undoubtedly the fact that teachers must be models of whatever sort of morality is accepted as orthodox in the community imposes upon the teacher many disqualifications. With regard to sex, the community is often very brutal indeed. It is part of the American credo that school teachers reproduce by budding. In no other walk of life is it regarded as even faintly reprehensible that a young bachelor should look about for a wife, but there are indications that courtship is not exactly good form in the male teacher. The community prefers its male teachers married, but if they are unmarried, it forbids them to go about marrying. With regard to the conduct of women teachers, some communities are unbelievably strict. Youth and beauty are disadvantages. Husband-hunting is the unpardonable sin. The absurdity of this customary attitude, as well as its complete social unsoundness, should be apparent from its mere statement; it becomes all the more significant that, in presenting the subject of sex prejudice against school teachers, one must usually go on to point out that this is a situation almost without parallel in modern life. Women teachers are our Vestal Virgins.

Conduct which would pass unnoticed in a young business woman becomes a matter of moment when the young woman is a teacher. Rarely does an entire community pause to inquire into the affairs of a nineteen-year-old stenographer, but it can, as the following incident shows, become tremendously excited about the affairs of a nineteen-year-old school teacher.

During the summer when Mr. Blank, our superintendent, was on vacation, Miss Jones came to apply for a position. Miss Jones was a very good looking young lady, nineteen years of age, and just graduated from a small sectarian university. She, herself, belonged to the sect. The school board had one fellow sectarian, and, as the principal remarked, two others who were susceptible to good-looking young women. Miss Jones was hired. Mr. Blank had intended to fill her place with a young man.

Miss Jones, being the only member of the high-school faculty belonging to this sect, chose to room alone. From the first it was noticeable that the young men frequented Miss Jones's room in the mornings and noons before school had taken up and after school evenings. That started talk. The story was passed around that Mr. Blank hadn't wanted her in the first place and that she had better be careful. Some of the teachers passing through the hall or otherwise near her classroom reported that she had noisy classes.

Several of the teachers talked to her in order to get her to confide in them. Then the rest of the teachers were informed of what had occurred. She remarked that there wasn't a single man in town that she hadn't dated. Several times she had accepted rides with high-school boys. If she walked up the street with one of the boys at noon this was further cause for gossip. One teacher was reported to have said that she had better leave her gentleman friend alone or she would scratch her eyes out.

One of the mathematics teachers was on hall duty right outside Miss Jones's door and each day she had something to report about Miss Jones.

The first six-weeks examination time came. The examinations were sent to the office to be mimeographed. Miss Jones's questions were considerably revised. Naturally she became bitter. She remarked that she knew that the superintendent and principal were out to oust her. Her conduct was reported as worse and worse. The teacher on hall duty reported that she had heard the principal chase a number of boys out of her room. It was decidedly noticeable that the principal and superintendent were in the hallways a great deal of the time.

Every move she made was watched and catalogued. A teacher told the others that at one of the class parties some boys had come up to her and politely inquired as to how she had enjoyed the party, then turned to Miss Jones and asked her to go riding with a group of them after the party.

Toward the end of the year she started keeping company with a young man reported to be of questionable character. It appears that a member of the school board remonstrated with her, telling her she shouldn't be seen with him. As Miss Jones stated in her own words, she "gave him to understand where he should head in."

By established custom, public dancing was not allowed among the teachers. Miss Jones was seen numerous times at public dances.

Once she told a group of teachers that she was not cut out for a teacher and that she was not coming back.

The school teachers, principal, and superintendent were all brought forcefully to the attention of the public through this unfortunate affair. The town took sides on the question, which disturbed the entire school and the entire community. (Document submitted by a school teacher.)

Miss Jones, perhaps, merits scant concern. But hers is a story that repeats itself every year or every few years in almost every city and village of the nation. In other instances some particular points would stand out more clearly. Cases could easily be found in which much greater injustice was worked upon the individual teacher and a much less charitable attitude taken by the community at large. This community had some cause to be concerned. There were numerous complicating factors, including the young woman's religion, her isolation from the other teachers, and the bad blood between her and them. But this case will serve to show how a storm may descend upon the head of an adolescent girl who is a teacher and who nevertheless behaves as another adolescent girl might behave.

This story calls to mind many others of a similar nature. There is, for example, the not uncommon case of the teacher who is quite efficient in her work and quite discreet in her relations with students, but inclined to lead a somewhat emancipated life outside the school room and the circle of school contacts. The efficient teacher who somehow gets the reputation of being "fast" often becomes a storm center too. Sometimes this reputation is founded upon nothing more tangible than the fact that this teacher prefers to live in a hotel than in a private home, that she does not go to church, that she plays cards, or that she occasionally takes weekend trips. The list of taboos is endless; the president of a certain teacher's college in the south is reputed to look with the utmost disfavor upon any association outside of school between his male and female teachers, though he does not disapprove, apparently, of other arrangements they make in their love life.

. . .

NOTES

1. Cf. The Lynds, *Middletown* (New York: Harcourt Brace and Co., 1929), p. 185.
2. Quoted by T. Minehan, "The Teacher Goes Job-Hunting," *The Nation*, (1927), vol. 124, p. 606. (Reprinted by permission of *The Nation*.)

10

FUNCTIONAL AND CONFLICT THEORIES
OF EDUCATIONAL STRATIFICATION

Randall Collins

Education has become highly important in occupational attainment in modern America, and thus occupies a central place in the analysis of stratification and of social mobility. This [chapter] attempts to assess the adequacy of two theories in accounting for available evidence on the link between education and stratification: a functional theory concerning trends in technical skill requirements in industrial societies; and a conflict theory derived from the approach of Max Weber, stating the determinants of various outcomes in the struggles among status groups. It will be argued that the evidence best supports the conflict theory, although technical requirements have important effects in particular contexts. It will be further argued that the construction of a general theory of the determinants of stratification in its varying forms is best advanced by incorporating elements of the functional analysis of technical requirements of specific jobs at

appropriate points within the conflict model. The conclusion offers an interpretation of historical change in education and stratification in industrial America, and suggests where further evidence is required for more precise tests and for further development of a comprehensive explanatory theory.

The Importance of Education

. . .

Educational requirements for employment have become increasingly widespread, not only in elite occupations but also at the bottom of the occupational hierarchy.... At the same time, educational requirements appear to have become more specialized, with 38% of the organizations in the 1967 survey which required college degrees of managers preferring business administration training, and an additional 15% preferring engineering training; such requirements appear to have been virtually unknown in the 1920s (Pierson 1959:34–54). At the same time, the proportions of the American population attending schools through the completion of high school and advanced levels have risen sharply during the last century.... Careers are thus increasingly shaped within the educational system.

The Technical-Function
Theory of Education

A common explanation of the importance of education in modern society may be termed

Randall Collins, excerpts from "Functional and Conflict Theories of Educational Stratification" from *American Sociological Review* 36 (December 1971). Copyright © 1971 by the American Sociological Association. Reprinted with the permission of the author and the publisher.

I am indebted to Joseph Ben-David, Bennett Berger, Reinhard Bendix, Margaret S. Gordon, Joseph R. Gusfield, Stanford M. Lyman, Martin A. Trow, and Harold L. Wilensky for advice and comment; and to Margaret S. Gordon for making available data collected by the Institute of Industrial Relations of the University of California at Berkeley, under grants from the U.S. Office of Education and U.S. Department of Labor. Their endorsement of the views expressed here is not implied.

the technical-function theory. Its basic propositions, found in a number of sources (see, for example, B. Clark 1962; Kerr et al. 1960), may be stated as follows: (1) the skill requirements of jobs in industrial society constantly increase because of technological change. Two processes are involved: (a) the proportion of jobs requiring low skill decreases and the proportion requiring high skill increases; and (b) the same jobs are upgraded in skill requirements. (2) Formal education provides the training, either in specific skills or in general capacities, necessary for the more highly skilled jobs. (3) Therefore, educational requirements for employment constantly rise, and increasingly larger proportions of the population are required to spend longer and longer periods in school.

The technical-function theory of education may be seen as a particular application of a more general functional approach. The functional theory of stratification (Davis and Moore 1945) rests on the premises (A) that occupational positions require particular kinds of skilled performance; and (B) that positions must be filled with persons who have either the native ability, or who have acquired the training, necessary for the performance of the given occupational role.[1] The technical-function theory of education may be viewed as a subtype of this form of analysis, since it shares the premises that the occupational structure creates demands for particular kinds of performance, and that training is one way of filling these demands. In addition, it includes the more restrictive premises (1 and 2 above) concerning the way in which skill requirements of jobs change with industrialization, and concerning the content of school experiences.

The technical-function theory of education may be tested by reviewing the evidence for each of its propositions (1a, 1b, and 2).[2] As will be seen, these propositions do not adequately account for the evidence. In order to generate a more complete explanation, it will be necessary to examine the evi-

dence for the underlying functional propositions, (A) and (B). This analysis leads to a focus on the processes of stratification—notably group conflict—not expressed in the functional theory, and to the formalization of a conflict theory to account for the evidence.

Proposition (1a): *Educational requirements of jobs in industrial society increase because the proportion of jobs requiring low skill decreases and the proportion requiring high skill increases.* Available evidence suggests that this process accounts for only a minor part of educational upgrading, at least in a society that has passed the point of initial industrialization. Fifteen percent of the increase in education of the U.S. labor force during the twentieth century may be attributed to shifts in the occupational structure—a decrease in the proportion of jobs with low skill requirements and an increase in proportion of jobs with high skill requirements (Folger and Nam 1964). The bulk of educational upgrading (85%) has occurred *within* job categories.

Proposition (1b): *Educational requirements of jobs in industrial society rise because the same jobs are upgraded in skill requirements.* The only available evidence on this point consists of data collected by the U.S. Department of Labor in 1950 and 1960, which indicate the amount of change in skill requirements of specific jobs. Under the most plausible assumptions as to the skills provided by various levels of education, it appears that the educational level of the U.S. labor force has changed in excess of that which is necessary to keep up with skill requirements of jobs (Berg 1970:38–60). Overeducation for available jobs is found particularly among males who have graduated from college and females with high school degrees or some college, and appears to have increased between 1950 and 1960.

Proposition (2): *Formal education provides required job skills.* This proposition may be tested in two ways: (a) Are better educated employees more productive than less educated employees? (b) Are vocational skills learned in schools, or elsewhere?

(a) *Are better educated employees more productive?* The evidence most often cited for the productive effects of education is indirect, consisting of relationships between *aggregate* levels of education in a society and its overall economic productivity. These are of three types:

(i) The national growth approach involves calculating the proportion of growth in the U.S. Gross National Product attributable to conventional inputs of capital and labor; these leave a large residual, which is attributed to improvements in skill of the labor force based on increased education (Schultz 1961; Denison 1965). This approach suffers from difficulty in clearly distinguishing among technological change affecting productive arrangements, changes in the abilities of workers acquired by experience at work with new technologies, and changes in skills due to formal education and motivational factors associated with a competitive or achievement-oriented society. The assignment of a large proportion of the residual category to education is arbitrary. Denison (1965) makes this attribution on the basis of the increased income to persons with higher levels of education interpreted as rewards for their contributions to productivity. Although it is a common assumption in economic argument that wage returns reflect output value, wage returns cannot be used to prove the productive contribution of education without circular reasoning.

(ii) Correlations of education and level of economic development for nations show that the higher the level of economic development of a country, the higher the proportion of its population in elementary, secondary, and higher education (Harbison and Myers 1964). Such correlations beg the question of causality. There are considerable variations in school enrollments among countries at the same economic level, and many of these variations are explicable in terms of political demands for access to education (Ben-David 1963–64). Also, the overproduction of educated personnel in countries whose level of economic development cannot absorb them suggests the demand for education need not come directly from the economy, and may run counter to economic needs (Hoselitz 1965).

(iii) Time-lag correlations of education and economic development show that increases in the proportion of population in elementary school precede increases in economic development after a takeoff point at approximately 30–50% of the 7–14 years old age-group in school. Similar anticipations of economic development are suggested for increases in secondary and higher education enrollment, although the data do not clearly support this conclusion (Peaslee 1969). A pattern of advances in secondary school enrollments preceding advances in economic development is found only in a small number of cases (12 of 37 examined in Peaslee 1969). A pattern of growth of university enrollments and subsequent economic development is found in 21 of 37 cases, but the exceptions (including the United States, France, Sweden, Russia, and Japan) are of such importance as to throw serious doubt on any *necessary* contribution of higher education to economic development. The main contribution of education to economic productivity, then, appears to occur at the level of the transition to mass literacy, and not significantly beyond this level.

Direct evidence of the contribution of education to *individual* productivity is summarized by Berg (1970:85–104, 143–76). It indicates that the better educated employees are not generally more productive, and in some cases are less productive, among samples of factory workers, maintenance men, department store clerks, technicians, secretaries, bank tellers, engineers, industrial research scientists, military personnel, and federal civil service employers.

(b) *Are vocational skills learned in school, or elsewhere?* Specifically vocational education in the schools for manual positions is virtually independent of job rate, as graduates of vocational programs are not more likely to be employed than high school dropouts (Plunkett 1960; Duncan 1964). Most skilled manual workers acquire their skills on the job or casually (Clark and Sloan 1966:73). Retraining for important technological changes in industry has been carried out largely informally on-the-job; in only a very small proportion of jobs affected by technological change is formal retraining in educational institutions used (Collins 1969:147–158; Bright 1958).

The relevance of education for nonmanual occupational skills is more difficult to evaluate. Training in specific professions, such as medicine, engineering, scientific or scholarly research, teaching, and law can plausibly be considered vocationally relevant, and possibly essential. Evidences comparing particular degrees of educational success with particular kinds of occupational performance or success are not available, except for a few occupations. For engineers, high college grades and degree levels generally predict high levels of technical responsibility and high participation in professional activities, but not necessarily high salary or supervisory responsibility (Perrucci and Perrucci 1970). At the same time, a number of practicing engineers lack college degrees

(about 40% of engineers in the early 1950s; see Soderberg 1963:213), suggesting that even such highly technical skills may be acquired on the job. For academic research scientists, educational quality has little effect on subsequent productivity (Hagstrom and Hargens 1968). For other professions, evidence is not available on the degree to which actual skills are learned in school rather than in practice. In professions such as medicine and law, where education is a legal requirement for admission to practice, a comparison group of noneducated practitioners is not available, at least in the modern era.

Outside of the traditional learned professions, the plausibility of the vocational importance of education is more questionable. Comparisons of the efforts of different occupations to achieve "professionalization" suggest that setting educational requirements and bolstering them through licensing laws is a common tactic in raising an occupation's prestige and autonomy (Wilensky 1964). The result has been the proliferation of numerous pseudo-professions in modern society; nevertheless these fail to achieve strong professional organization through lack of a monopolizable (and hence teachable) skill base. Business administration schools represent such an effort. (See Pierson 1959:9, 55–95, 140; Gordon and Howell 1959:1–18, 40, 324–37). Descriptions of general, nonvocational education do not support the image of schools as places where skills are widely learned. Scattered studies suggest that the knowledge imparted in particular courses is retained only in small part through the next few years (Learned and Wood 1938:28), and indicate a dominant student culture concerned with nonacademic interests or with achieving grades with a minimum of learning (Coleman 1961; Becker et al. 1968).

The technical-function theory of education, then, does not give an adequate account of the evidence. Economic evidence indicates no clear contributions of education to economic development, beyond the provisions of mass literacy. Shifts in the proportions of more skilled and less skilled jobs do not account for the observed increase in education of the American labor force. Education is often irrelevant to on-the-job productivity and is sometimes counter-productive; specifically vocational training seems to be derived more from work experience than from formal school training. The quality of schools themselves, and the nature of dominant student cultures suggest that schooling is very inefficient as a means of training for work skills.

Functional and Conflict Perspectives

It may be suggested that the inadequacies of the technical-function theory of education derive from a more basic source: the functional approach to stratification. A fundamental assumption is that there is a generally fixed set of positions, whose various requirements the labor force must satisfy. The fixed demand for skills of various types, at any given time, is the basic determinant of who will be selected for what positions. Social change may then be explained by specifying how these functional demands change with the process of modernization. In keeping with the functional perspective in general, the needs of society are seen as determining the behavior and the rewards of the individuals within it.

However, this premise may be questioned as an adequate picture of the fundamental processes of social organization. It may be suggested that the "demands" of any occupational position are not fixed, but represent whatever behavior is settled upon in bargaining between the persons who fill the positions and those who attempt to control them. Individuals want jobs primarily for the rewards to themselves in material goods,

power, and prestige. The amount of productive skill they must demonstrate to hold their positions depends on how much clients, customers, or employers can successfully demand of them, and this in turn depends on the balance of power between workers and their employers.

Employers tend to have quite imprecise conceptions of the skill requirements of most jobs, and operate on a strategy of "satisfying" rather than optimizing—that is, setting average levels of performance as satisfactory, and making changes in procedures or personnel only when performance falls noticeably below minimum standards (Dill et al. 1962; March and Simon 1958:140–41). Efforts to predict work performance by objective tests have foundered due to difficulties in measuring performance (except on specific mechanical tasks) and the lack of control groups to validate the tests (Anastasi 1967). Organizations do not force their employees to work at maximum efficiency; there is considerable insulation of workers at all levels from demands for full use of their skills and efforts. Informal controls over output are found not only among production workers in manufacturing but also among sales and clerical personnel (Roy 1952; Blau 1955; Lombard 1955). The existence of informal organization at the managerial level, the widespread existence of bureaucratic pathologies such as evasion of responsibility, empire-building, and displacement of means by ends ("red tape"), and the fact that administrative work is only indirectly related to the output of the organization, suggest that managers, too, are insulated from strong technological pressures for use of technical skills. On all levels, wherever informal organization exists, it appears that standards of performance reflect the power of the groups involved.

In this light, it is possible to reinterpret the body of evidence that ascriptive factors continue to be important in occupational success even in advanced industrial society. The social mobility data summarized at the onset of this [chapter] show that social origins have a direct effect on occupational success, even after the completion of education. Both case studies and cross-sectional samples amply document widespread discrimination against Negroes. Case studies show that the operation of ethnic and class standards in employment based not merely on skin color but on name, accent, style of dress, manners, and conversational abilities (Noland and Bakke 1949; Turner 1952; Taeuber et al. 1966; Nosow 1956). Cross-sectional studies, based on both biographical and survey data, show that approximately 60 to 70% of the American business elite come from upper-class and upper-middle-class families, and fewer than 15% from working-class families (Taussig and Joslyn 1932:97; Warner and Abegglen 1955:37–68; Newcomer 1955: 53; Bendix 1956:198–253; Mills 1963:110– 39). These proportions are fairly constant from the early 1800s through the 1950s. The business elite is overwhelmingly Protestant, male, and completely white, although there are some indications of a mild trend toward declining social origins and an increase of Catholics and Jews. Ethnic and class background have been found crucial for career advancement in the professions as well (Ladinsky 1963; Hall 1946). Sexual stereotyping of jobs is extremely widespread (Collins 1969:234–38).

In the traditional functionalist approach, these forms of ascription are treated as residual categories: carry-overs from a less advanced period, or marks of the imperfections of the functional mechanism of placement. Yet available trend data suggest that the link between social class origins and occupational attainment has remained constant during the twentieth century in America (Blau and Duncan 1967:81–113); the proportion of women in higher occupational levels has changed little since the late nine-teenth century (Epstein 1970:7); and the few available comparisons between elite groups in traditional and modern societies suggest comparable levels of mobility (Marsh 1963). Declines in racial and ethnic discrimination that appear to have occurred at periods in twentieth-century America may be plausibly explained as results of political mobilization of particular minority groups rather than by an increased economic need to select by achievement criteria.

Goode (1967) has offered a modified functional model to account for these disparities: that work groups always organize to protect their inept members from being judged by outsiders' standards of productivity, and that this self-protection is functional to the organizations, preventing a Hobbesian competitiveness and distrust of all against all. This argument re-establishes a functional explanation, but only at the cost of undermining the technological view of functional requirements. Further, Goode's conclusions can be put in other terms: it is to the advantage of groups of employees to organize so that they will not be judged by strict performance standards; and it is at least minimally to the advantage of the employer to let them do so, for if he presses them harder he creates dissension and alienation. Just how hard an employer *can* press his employees is not given in Goode's functional model. That is, his model has the disadvantage common to functional analysis in its most general form, of covering too many alternative possibilities to provide testable explanations of specific outcomes. Functional analysis too easily operates as a justification for whatever particular pattern exists, asserting in effect that there is a proper reason for it to be so, but failing to state the conditions under which a particular pattern will hold rather than another. The technical version of job requirements has the advantage of specifying patterns, but it is this specific form of functional explanation that is jettisoned by a return to a more abstract functional analysis.

A second hypothesis may be suggested: the power of "ascribed" groups may be the *prime* basis of selection in all organizations, and technical skills are secondary considerations depending on the balance of power. Education may thus be regarded as a mark of membership in a particular group (possibly at times its defining characteristic), not a mark of technical skills or achievement. Educational requirements may thus reflect the interests of whichever groups have power to set them. Weber (1968:1000) interpreted educational requirements in bureaucracies, drawing especially on the history of public administration in Prussia, as the result of efforts by university graduates to monopolize positions, raise their corporate status, and thereby increase their own security and power vis-à-vis both higher authorities and clients. Gusfield (1958) has shown that educational requirements in the British Civil Service were set as the result of a power struggle between a victorious educated upper-middle-class and the traditional aristocracy.

To summarize the argument to this point: available evidence suggests that the technical-functional view of educational requirements for jobs leaves a large number of facts unexplained. Functional analysis on the more abstract level does not provide a testable explanation of which ascribed groups will be able to dominate which positions. To answer this question, one must leave the functional frame of reference and examine the conditions of relative power of each group.

A Conflict Theory of Stratification

The conditions under which educational requirements will be set and changed may be stated more generally, on the basis of a conflict theory of stratification derived from Weber (1968:926–39; see also Collins 1968), and from advances in modern organization theory fitting the spirit of this approach.

A. *Status Groups.* The basic units of society are associational groups sharing common cultures (or "subcultures"). The core of such groups is families and friends, but they may be extended to religious, educational, or ethnic communities. In general, they comprise all persons who share a sense of status equality based on participation in a common culture: styles of language, tastes in clothing and decor, manners and other ritual observances, conversational topics and styles, opinions and values, and preferences in sports, arts, and media. Participation in such cultural groups gives individuals their fundamental sense of identity, especially in contrast with members of other associational groups in whose everyday culture they cannot participate comfortably. Subjectively, status groups distinguish themselves from others in terms of categories of *moral evaluation* such as "honor," "taste," "breeding," "respectability," "propriety," "cultivation," "good fellows," "plain folks," etc. Thus the exclusion of persons who lack the ingroup culture is felt to be normatively legitimated.

There is no *a priori* determination of the number of status groups in a particular society, nor can the degree to which there is consensus on a rank order among them be stated in advance. These are not matters of definition, but empirical variations, the causes of which are subjects of other developments of the conflict theory of stratification. Status groups should be regarded as ideal types, without implication of *necessarily distinct* boundaries; the concepts remain useful even in the case where associational groupings and their status cultures are fluid and overlapping, as hypotheses about the conflicts among status groups may remain fruitful even under these circumstances.

Status groups may be derived from a number of sources. Weber outlines three: (a) differences in life style based on economic situation (i.e., class); (b) differences in life situation based on power position; (c) differences in life situation deriving directly from cultural conditions or institutions, such as geographical origin, ethnicity, religion, education, or intellectual or aesthetic cultures.

B. *Struggle for Advantage.* There is a continual struggle in society for various "goods"—wealth, power, or prestige. We need make no assumption that every individual is motivated to maximize his rewards; however, since power and prestige are inherently scarce commodities, and wealth is often contingent upon them, the ambition of even a small proportion of persons for more than equal shares of these goods sets up an implicit counter-struggle on the part of others to avoid subjection and disesteem. Individuals may struggle with each other, but since individual identity is derived primarily from membership in a status group, and because the cohesion of status groups is a key resource in the struggle against others, the primary focus of struggle is between status groups rather than within them.

The struggle for wealth, power, and prestige is carried out primarily through organizations. There have been struggles throughout history among organizations controlled by different status groups, for military conquest, business advantage, or cultural (e.g., religious) hegemony, and intricate sorts of interorganizational alliances are possible. In the more complex societies, struggle between status groups is carried on in large part *within* organizations, as the status groups controlling an organization coerce, hire, or culturally manipulate others to carry out their wishes (as in, respectively, a conscript army, a business, or a church). Or-

ganizational research shows that the success of organizational elites in controlling their subordinates is quite variable. Under particular conditions, lower or middle members have considerable *de facto* power to avoid compliance, and even to change the course of the organizations (see Etzioni 1961).

This opposing power from below is strengthened when subordinate members constitute a cohesive status group of their own; it is weakened when subordinates acquiesce in the values of the organization elite. Coincidence of ethnic and class boundaries produces the sharpest cultural distinctions. Thus, Catholics of immigrant origins have been the bulwarks of informal norms restricting work output in American firms run by WASPs, whereas Protestants of native rural backgrounds are the main "rate-busters" (O. Collins et al. 1946). Selection and manipulation of members in terms of status groups is thus a key weapon in intraorganizational struggles. In general, the organization elite selects its new members and key assistants from its own status group and makes an effort to secure lower-level employees who are at least indoctrinated to respect the cultural superiority of their status culture.[3]

Once groups of employees of different status groups are formed at various positions (middle, lower, laterally differentiated) in the organization, each of these groups may be expected to launch efforts to recruit more members of their own status group. This process is illustrated by conflicts among whites and blacks, Protestants and Catholics and Jews, Yankee, Irish and Italian, etc. found in American occupational life (Hughes 1949; Dalton 1951). These conflicts are based on ethnically or religiously founded status cultures; their intensity rises and falls with processes increasing or decreasing the cultural distinctiveness of these groups, and with the succession of advantages and disadvantages set by previous outcomes of these struggles which determine the organizational resources available for further struggle. Parallel processes of cultural conflict may be based on distinctive class as well as ethnic cultures.

C. *Education as Status Culture*. The main activity of schools is to teach particular status cultures, both in and outside the classroom. In this light, any failure of schools to impart technical knowledge (although it may also be successful in this) is not important; schools primarily teach vocabulary and inflection, styles of dress, aesthetic tastes, values and manners. The emphasis on sociability and athletics found in many schools is not extraneous but may be at the core of the status culture propagated by the schools. Where schools have a more academic or vocational emphasis, this emphasis may itself be the content of a particular status culture, providing sets of values, materials for conversation, and shared activities for an associational group making claims to a particular basis for status.

Insofar as a particular status group controls education, it may use it to foster control within work organizations. Educational requirements for employment can serve both to select new members for elite positions who share the elite culture and, at a lower level of education, to hire lower and middle employees who have acquired a general respect for these elite values and styles.

Tests of the Conflict Theory of Educational Stratification

The conflict theory in its general form is supported by evidence (1) that there are distinctions among status group cultures—based both on class and on ethnicity—in modern societies (Kahl 1957:127–56, 184–220); (2) that status groups tend to occupy different occupational positions within organizations (see data on ascription cited above);

and (3) that occupants of different organizational positions struggle over power (Dalton 1959; Crozier 1964). The more specific tests called for here, however, are of the adequacy of conflict theory to explain the link between education and occupational stratification. Such tests may focus either on the proposed mechanism of occupational placement, or on the conditions for strong or weak links between education and occupation.

Education as a Mechanism of Occupational Placement

The mechanism proposed is that employers use education to select persons who have been socialized into the dominant status culture: for entrants to their own managerial ranks, into elite culture; for lower-level employees, into an attitude of respect for the dominant culture and the elite which carries it. This requires evidence that: (a) schools provide either training for the elite culture, or respect for it; and (b) employers use education as a means of selection for cultural attributes.

(a) Historical and descriptive studies of schools support the generalization that they are places where particular status cultures are acquired, either from the teachers, from other students, or both. Schools are usually founded by powerful or autonomous status groups, either to provide an exclusive education for their own children, or to propagate respect for their cultural values. Until recently most schools were founded by religions, often in opposition to those founded by rival religions; throughout the 19th century, this rivalry was an important basis for the founding of large numbers of colleges in the U.S., and the Catholic and Lutheran school systems. The public school system in the U.S. was founded mainly under the impetus of WASP elites with the purpose of teaching respect for Protestant and middle-class standards of cultural and religious propriety, especially in the face of Catholic, working-class immigration from Europe (Cremin 1961; Curti 1935). The content of public school education has consisted especially of middle-class, WASP culture (Waller 1932:15–131; Becker 1961; Hess and Torney 1967).

At the elite level, private secondary schools for children of the WASP upper class were founded from the 1880s, when the mass indoctrination function of the growing public schools made them unsuitable as means of maintaining cohesion of the elite culture itself (Baltzell 1958:327–72). These elite schools produce a distinctive personality type, characterized by adherence to a distinctive set of upper-class values and manners (McArthur 1955). The cultural rule of schools has been more closely studied in Britain (Bernstein 1961; Weinberg 1967), and in France (Bourdieu and Passeron 1964), although Riesman and his colleagues (Riesman 1958; Jencks and Riesman 1968) have shown some of the cultural differences among prestige levels of colleges and universities in the United States.

(b) Evidence that education has been used as a means of cultural selection may be found in several sources. Hollingshead's (1949:360–88) study of Elmtown school children, school dropouts, and community attitudes toward them suggests that employers use education as a means of selecting employees with middle-class attributes. A 1945–1946 survey of 240 employers in New Haven and Charlotte, N.C. indicated that they regarded education as a screening device for employees with desirable (middle-class) character and demeanor; white-collar positions particularly emphasized educational selection because these employees were considered most visible to outsiders (Noland and Bakke 1949:20–63).

A survey of employers in nationally prominent corporations indicated that they regarded college degrees as important in hiring potential managers, not because they were thought to ensure technical skills, but rather to indicate "motivation" and "social experience" (Gordon and Howell 1959: 121). Business school training is similarly regarded, less as evidence of necessary training (as employers have been widely skeptical of the utility of this curriculum for most positions) than as an indication that the college graduate is committed to business attitudes. Thus, employers are more likely to refuse to hire liberal arts graduates if they come from a college which has a business school than if their college is without a business school (Gordon and Howell 1959:84–87; see also Pierson 1959:90–99). In the latter case, the students could be said not to have had a choice; but when both business and liberal arts courses are offered and the student chooses liberal arts, employers appear to take this as a rejection of business values.

Finally, a 1967 survey of 309 California organizations (Collins 1971) found that educational requirements for white-collar workers were highest in organizations which placed the strongest emphasis on normative control over their employees.[4] Normative control emphasis was indicated by (i) relative emphasis on the absence of police record for job applicants; (ii) relative emphasis on a record of job loyalty; (iii) Etzioni's (1961) classification of organizations into those with high normative control emphasis (financial, professional services, government, and other public services organizations) and those with remunerative control emphasis (manufacturing, construction, and trade). These three indicators are highly interrelated, thus mutually validating their conceptualization as indicators of normative control emphasis. The relationship between normative control emphasis and educational requirements holds for managerial requirements and white-collar requirements generally, both including and excluding professional and technical positions. Normative control emphasis does not affect blue-collar education requirements.

Variations in Linkage between Education and Occupation

The conflict model may also be tested by examining the cases in which it predicts education will be relatively important or unimportant in occupational attainment. Education should be most important where two conditions hold simultaneously: (1) the type of education most closely reflects membership in a particular status group, and (2) that group controls employment in particular organizational contexts. Thus, education will be most important where the fit is greatest between the culture of the status groups emerging from schools, and the status group doing the hiring; it will be least important where there is the greatest disparity between the culture of the school and of the employers.

This fit between school-group culture and employer culture may be conceptualized as a continuum. The importance of elite education is highest where it is involved in selection of new members of organizational elites, and should fade off where jobs are less elite (either lower level jobs in these organizations, or jobs in other organizations not controlled by the cultural elite). Similarly, schools which produce the most elite graduates will be most closely linked to elite occupations; schools whose products are less well socialized into elite culture are selected for jobs correspondingly less close to elite organizational levels.

In the United States, the schools which produce culturally elite groups, either by virtue of explicit training or by selection of students from elite backgrounds, or both, are the private prep schools at the secondary level; at the higher level, the elite colleges (the Ivy League, and to a lesser degree the major state universities); at the professional training level, those professional schools attached to the elite colleges and universities. At the secondary level, schools which produce respectably socialized, nonelite persons are the public high schools (especially those in middle-class residential areas); from the point of view of the culture of WASP employers, Catholic schools (and all-black schools) are less acceptable. At the level of higher education, Catholic and black colleges and professional schools are less elite, and commercial training schools are the least elite form of education.

In the United States, the organizations most clearly dominated by the WASP upper class are large, nationally organized business corporations, and the largest law firms (Domhoff 1967:38–62). Those organizations more likely to be dominated by members of minority ethnic cultures are the smaller and local businesses in manufacturing, construction, and retail trade; in legal practice, solo rather than firm employment. In government employment, local governments appear to be more heavily dominated by ethnic groups, whereas particular branches of the national government (notably the State Department and the Treasury) are dominated by WASP elites (Domhoff 1967:84–114, 132–37).

Evidence on the fit between education and employment is available for only some of these organizations. In a broad sample of organizational types (Collins 1971) educational requirements were higher in the bigger organizations, which also tended to be organized on a national scale, than in smaller and more localistic organizations.[5] The finding of Perrucci and Perrucci (1970) that upper-class social origins were important in career success precisely within the group of engineers who graduated from the most prestigious engineering schools with the highest grades may also bear on this question; since the big national corporations are most likely to hire this academically elite group, the importance of social origins within this group tends to corroborate the interpretation of education as part of a process of elite cultural selection in those organizations.

Among lawyers, the predicted differences are clear: graduates of the law schools attached to elite colleges and universities are more likely to be employed in firms, whereas graduates of Catholic or commercial law schools are more likely to be found in solo practice (Ladinsky 1967). The elite Wall Street law firms are most educationally selective in this regard, choosing not only from Ivy League law schools but from a group whose background includes attendance at elite prep schools and colleges (Smigel 1964: 39, 73–74, 117). There are also indications that graduates of ethnically-dominated professional schools are most likely to practice within the ethnic community; this is clearly the case among black professionals. In general, the evidence that graduates of black colleges (Sharp 1970:64–67) and of Catholic colleges (Jencks and Riesman 1968:357–66) have attained lower occupational positions in business than graduates of white Protestant schools (at least until recent years) also bolsters this interpretation.[6]

It is possible to interpret this evidence according to the technical-function theory of education, arguing that the elite schools provide the best technical training, and that the major national organizations require the greatest degree of technical talent. What is necessary is to test simultaneously for technical and status-conflict conditions. The most direct evidence on this point is the California employer study (Collins 1971), which examined the effects of normative control emphasis and of organizational prominence, while holding constant the organization's technological modernity, as measured by the

number of technological and organizational changes in the previous six years. Technological change was found to affect educational requirements at managerial and white-collar (but not blue-collar) levels, thus giving some support to the technical-function theory of education. The three variables—normative control emphasis, organizational prominence, and technological change—each independently affected educational requirements, in particular contexts. Technological change produced significantly higher educational requirements only in smaller, localistic organizations, and in organizational sectors not emphasizing normative control. Organizational prominence produced significantly higher educational requirements in organizations with low technological change, and in sectors de-emphasizing normative control. Normative control emphasis produced significantly higher educational requirements in organizations with low technological change, and in less prominent organizations. Thus, technical and normative status conditions all affect educational requirements; measures of association indicated that the latter conditions were stronger in this sample.

Other evidence bearing on this point concerns business executives only. A study of the top executives in nationally prominent businesses indicated that the most highly educated managers were not found in the most rapidly developing companies, but rather in the least economically vigorous ones, with highest education found in the traditionalistic financial and utility firms (Warner and Abegglen 1955:141–43, 148). The business elite has always been highly educated in relation to the American popoulace, but education seems to be a correlate of their social origins rather than the determinant of their success (Mills 1963:128; Taussig and Joslyn 1932:200; Newcomer 1955:76). Those members of the business elite who entered its ranks from lower social origins had less education than the businessmen of upper and upper-middle-class origins, and those businessmen who inherited their companies were much more likely to be college educated than those who achieved their positions by entrepreneurship (Bendix 1956:230; Newcomer 1955:80).

In general, the evidence indicates that educational requirements for employment reflect employers' concerns for acquiring respectable and well-socialized employees; their concern for the provision of technical skills through education enters to a lesser degree. The higher the normative control concerns of the employer, and the more elite the organization's status, the higher his educational requirements.

Historical Change

The rise in educational requirements for employment throughout the last century may be explained using the conflict theory, and incorporating elements of the technical-functional theory into it at appropriate points. The principal dynamic has centered on changes in the supply of educated persons caused by the expansion of the school system, which was in turn shaped by three conditions:

(1) Education has been associated with high economic and status position from the colonial period on through the twentieth century. The result was a popular demand for education as mobility opportunity. This demand has not been for vocational education at a terminal or commercial level, short of full university certification; the demand has rather focused on education giving entry into the elite status culture, and usually only those technically-oriented schools have prospered which have most closely associated themselves with the sequence of education leading to (or from) the classical

Bachelor's degree (Collins 1969:68–70, 86–87, 89, 96–101).

(2) Political decentralization, separation of church and state, and competition among religious denominations have made founding schools and colleges in America relatively easy, and provided initial motivations of competition among communities and religious groups that moved them to do so. As a result, education at all levels expanded faster in America than anywhere else in the world. At the time of the Revolution, there were nine colleges in the colonies; in all of Europe, with a population forty times that of America, there were approximately sixty colleges. By 1880 there were 811 American colleges and universities; by 1966, there were 2,337. The United States not only began with the highest ratio of institutions of higher education to population in the world, but increased this lead steadily, for the number of European universities was not much greater by the twentieth century than in the eighteenth (Ben-David and Zloczower 1962).

(3) Technical changes also entered into the expansion of American education. As the evidence summarized above indicates: (a) a mass literacy is crucial for beginnings of full-scale industrialization, although demand for literacy could not have been important in the expansion of education beyond elementary levels. More importantly, (b) there is a mild trend toward the reduction in the proportion of unskilled jobs and an increase in the promotion of highly skilled (professional and technical) jobs as industrialism proceeds, accounting for 15% of the shift in educational levels in the twentieth century (Folger and Nam 1964). (c) Technological change also brings about some upgrading in skill requirements of some continuing job positions, although the available evidence (Berg 1970:38–60) refers only to the decade 1950–1960. Nevertheless, as Wilensky (1964) points out, there is no "professionalization of everyone," as most jobs

do not require considerable technical knowledge on the order of that required of the engineer or the research scientist.

The existence of a relatively small group of experts in high-status positions, however, can have important effects on the structure of competition for mobility chances. In the United States, where democratic decentralization favors the use of schools (as well as government employment) as a kind of patronage for voter interests, the existence of even a small number of elite jobs fosters a demand for *large-scale* opportunities to acquire these positions. We thus have a "contest mobility" school system (Turner 1960); it produced a widely educated populace because of the many dropouts who never achieve the elite level of schooling at which expert skills and/or high cultural status are acquired. In the process, the status value of American education has become diluted. Standards of respectability are always relative to the existing range of cultural differences. Once higher levels of education become recognized as an objective mark of elite status, and a moderate level of education as a mark of respectable middle-level status, increases in the supply of educated persons at given levels result in yet higher levels, becoming recognized as superior, and previously superior levels become only average.

Thus, before the end of the nineteenth century, an elementary school or home education was no longer satisfactory for a middle-class gentleman; by the 1930s, a college degree was displacing the high school degree as the minimal standard of respectability; in the late 1960s, graduate school or specialized professional degrees were becoming necessary for initial entry to many middle-class positions, and high school graduation was becoming a standard for entry to manual laboring positions. Education has thus gradually become part of the status culture of classes far below the level of the original business and professional elites.

The increasing supply of educated persons has made education a rising requirement of jobs. Led by the biggest and most prestigious organizations, employers have raised their educational requirements to maintain both the relative prestige of their own managerial ranks and the relative respectability of middle ranks.[7] Education has become a legitimate standard in terms of which employers select employees, and employees compete with each other for promotion opportunities or for raised prestige in their continuing positions. With the attainment of a mass (now approaching universal) higher education system in modern America, the ideal or image of technical skill becomes the legitimating culture in terms of which the struggle for position goes on.

Higher educational requirements, and the higher level of educational credentials offered by individuals competing for position in organizations, have in turn increased the demand for education by the populace. The interaction between formal job requirements and informal status cultures has resulted in a spiral in which educational requirements and educational attainments become ever higher. As the struggle for mass educational opportunities enters new phases in the universities of today and perhaps in the graduate schools of the future, we may expect a further upgrading of educational requirements for employment. The mobilization of demands by minority groups for mobility opportunities through schooling can only contribute an extension of the prevailing pattern.

Conclusion

It has been argued that conflict theory provides an explanation of the principal dynamics of rising educational requirements for employment in America. Changes in the technical requirements of jobs have caused more limited changes in particular jobs. The conditions of the interaction of these two determinants may be more closely studied.

Precise measures of changes in the actual technical skill requirements of jobs are as yet available only in rudimentary form. Few systematic studies show how much of particular job skills may be learned in practice, and how much must be acquired through school background. Close studies of what is actually learned in school, and how long it is retained, are rare. Organizational studies of how employers rate performance and decide upon promotions give a picture of relatively loose controls over the technical quality of employee performance, but this no doubt varies in particular types of jobs.

The most central line of analysis for assessing the joint effects of status group conflict and technical requirements are those which compare the relative importance of education in different contexts. One such approach may take organization as the unit of analysis, comparing the educational requirements of organizations both to organizational technologies and to the status (including educational) background of organizational elites. Such analysis may also be applied to surveys of individual mobility, comparing the effects of education on mobility in different employment contexts, where the status group (and educational) background of employers varies in its fit with the educational culture of prospective employees. Such analysis of "old school tie" networks may also simultaneously test for the independent effect of the technical requirements of different sorts of jobs on the importance of education. Inter-nation comparisons provide variations here in the fit between types of education and particular kinds of jobs which may not be available within any particular country.

The full elaboration of such analysis would give a more precise answer to the historical question of assigning weight to various factors in the changing place of education in the stratification of modern societies. At the same time, to state the conditions under which status groups vary in organizational power, including the power to emphasize or limit the importance of technical skills, would be to state the basic elements of a comprehensive explanatory theory of the forms of stratification.

NOTES

1. The concern here is with these basic premises rather than with the theory elaborated by Davis and Moore to account for the universality of stratification. This theory involves a few further propositions: (C) in any particular form of society certain occupational positions are functionally most central to the operation of the social system; (D) the ability to fill these positions, and/or the motivation to acquire the necessary training, is unequally distributed in the population; (E) inequalities of rewards in wealth and prestige evolve to ensure that the supply of persons with the necessary ability or training meshes with the structure of demands for skilled performance. The problems of stating functional centrality in empirical terms have been subjects of much debate.

2. Proposition 3 is supported by Tables 1 and 2. The issue here is whether this can be explained by the previous propositions and premises.

3. It might be argued that the ethnic cultures may differ in their functionality: that middle-class Protestant culture provides the self-discipline and other attributes necessary for higher organizational positions in modern society. This version of functional theory is specific enough to be subject to empirical test: are middle-class WASPs in fact better businessmen or government administrators than Italians, Irishmen, or Jews of patrimonial or working class cultural backgrounds? Weber suggested that they were in the initial construction of the capitalist economy within the confines of traditional society; he also argued that once the new economic system was established, the original ethic was no longer necessary to run it (Weber

1930:180–83). Moreover, the functional explanation also requires some feedback mechanism whereby organizations with more efficient managers are selected for survival. The oligopolistic situation in large-scale American business since the late 19th century does not seem to provide such a mechanism; nor does government employment. Schumpeter (1951), the leading expositor of the importance of managerial talent in business, confined his emphasis to the formative period of business expansion, and regarded the large, oligopolistic corporation as an arena where advancement came to be based on skills in organizational politics (1951:122–24); these personalistic skills are arguably more characteristic of the patrimonial cultures than of WASP culture.

4. Sample consisted of approximately one-third of all organizations with 100 or more employees in the San Francisco, Oakland, and San Jose metropolitan areas. See Gordon and Thal-Larsen (1969) for a description of procedures and other findings.

5. Again, these relationships hold for managerial requirements and white-collar requirements generally, both including and excluding professional and technical positions, but not for blue-collar requirements. Noland and Bakke (1949:78) also report that larger organizations have higher educational requirements for administrative positions than smaller organizations.

6. Similar processes may be found in other societies, where the kinds of organizations linked to particular types of schools may differ. In England, the elite "public schools" are linked especially to the higher levels of the national civil service (Weinberg 1967:139–43). In France, the elite Ecole Polytechnique is linked to both government and industrial administrative positions (Crozier 1964:238–44). In Germany, universities have been linked principally with government administration, and business executives are drawn from elsewhere (Ben-David and Floczower 1962). Comparative analysis of the kinds of education of government officials, business executives, and other groups in contexts where the status group links of schools differ is a promising area for further tests of conflict and technical-functional explanations.

7. It appears that employers may have raised their wage costs in the process. Their behavior is nevertheless plausible, in view of these considerations: (a) the thrust of organizational research since Mayo and Barnard has indicated that questions of internal organizational power and control, of which cultural dominance is a main feature, take precedence over purely economic considerations; (b) the large American corporations, which have led in educational requirements, have held positions of oligopolistic advantage since the late 19th century, and thus could afford a large internal "welfare" cost of maintaining a well-socialized work force; (c) there are inter-organizational wage differentials in local labor markets, corresponding to relative organizational prestige, and a "wage-escalator" process by which the wages of the leading organizations are gradually emulated by others according to their rank (Reynolds 1951); a parallel structure of "educational status escalators" could plausibly be expected to operate.

REFERENCES

Anastasi, Anne. 1967. "Psychology, Psychologists, and Psychological Testing." *American Psychologist* 22:297–306.

Baltzell, E. Digby. 1958. *An American Business Aristocracy*. New York: Macmillan.

Becker, Howard S. 1961. "Schools and Systems of Stratification." Pp. 93–104 in *Education, Economy, and Society*, edited by A. H. Halsey, Jean Floud, and C. Arnold Anderson. New York: Free Press.

Becker, Howard S., Blanche Geer, and Everett C. Hughes. 1968. *Making the Grade: The Academic Side of College Life*. New York: Wiley.

Ben-David, Joseph. 1963–64. "Professions in the Class Systems of Present-Day Societies." *Current Sociology* 12:247–330.

Ben-David, Joseph and Awraham Zloczower. 1962. "Universities and Academic Systems in Modern Societies." *European Journal of Sociology* 31:45–85.

Bendix, Reinhard. 1956. *Work and Authority in Industry*. New York: Wiley.

Berg, Ivar. 1970. *Education and Jobs*. New York: Praeger.

Bernstein, Basil. 1961. "Social Class and Linguistic Development." Pp. 288–314 in *Education, Economy, and Society*, edited by A. H. Halsey, Jean Floud, and C. Arnold Anderson. New York: Free Press.

BLAU, PETER M. 1955. *The Dynamics of Bureaucracy.* Chicago: University of Chicago Press.

BLAU, PETER M. AND OTIS DUDLEY DUNCAN. 1967. *The American Occupational Structure.* New York: Wiley.

BOURDIEU, PIERRE AND JEAN-CLAUDE PASSERON. 1964. *Les Heritiers: Les Etudiants et la Culture.* Paris: Les Editions de Minuit.

BRIGHT, JAMES R. 1958. "Does Automation Raise Skill Requirements?" *Harvard Business Review* 36:85–97.

CLARK, BURTON R. 1962. *Educating the Expert Society.* San Francisco: Chandler.

CLARK, HAROLD F. AND HAROLD S. SLOAN. 1966. *Classrooms on Main Street.* New York: Teachers College Press.

COLEMAN, JAMES S. 1961. *The Adolescent Society.* New York: Free Press.

COLLINS, ORVIS, MELVILLE DALTON, AND DONALD ROY. 1946. "Restriction of Output and Social Cleavage in Industry." *Applied Anthropology* 5: 1–14.

COLLINS, RANDALL. 1968. "A Comparative Approach to Political Sociology." Pp. 42–67 in *State and Society,* edited by Reinhard Bendix et al. Boston: Little, Brown.

———. 1969. Education and Employment. Unpublished Ph.D. dissertation, University of California at Berkeley, Berkeley, CA.

———. 1971. "Educational Requirements for Employment: A Comparative Organizational Study." Unpublished manuscript.

CREMIN, LAWRENCE A. 1961. *The Transformation of the School.* New York: Knopf.

CROZIER, MICHEL. 1964. *The Bureaucratic Phenomenon.* Chicago: University of Chicago Press.

CURTI, MERLE. 1935. *The Social Ideas of American Educators.* New York: Scribners.

DALTON, MELVILLE. 1951. "Informal Factors in Career Achievement." *American Journal of Sociology* 56:407–415.

———. 1959. *Men Who Manage.* New York: Wiley.

DAVIS, KINGSLEY AND WILBERT MOORE. 1945. "Some Principles of Stratification." *American Sociological Review* 10:242–49.

DENISON, EDWARD F. 1965. "Education and Economic Productivity." Pp. 328–40 in *Education and Public Policy,* edited by Seymour Harris. Berkeley: McCutchen.

DILL, WILLIAM R., THOMAS L. HILTON, AND WALTER R. REITMAN. 1962. *The New Managers.* Englewood Cliffs, NJ: Prentice Hall.

DOMHOFF, G. WILLIAM. 1967. *Who Rules America?* Englewood Cliffs, NJ: Prentice Hall.

DUNCAN, BEVERLY. 1964. "Dropouts and the Un-employed." *Journal of Political Economy* 73: 121–34.

EPSTEIN, CYNTHIA FUCHS. 1970. *Woman's Place: Options and Limits in Professional Careers.* Berkeley: University of California Press.

ETZIONI, AMITAI. 1961. *A Comparative Analysis of Complex Organizations.* New York: Free Press.

FOLGER, JOHN K. AND CHARLES B. NAM. 1964. "Trends in education in relation to the occupational structure." *Sociology of Education* 38: 19–33.

GOODE, WILLIAM J. 1967. "The Protection of the Inept." *American Sociological Review* 32:5–19.

GORDON, MARGARET S. AND MARGARET THAL-LARSEN. 1969. *Employer Policies in a Changing Labor Market.* Berkeley: Institute of Industrial Relations, University of California.

GORDON, ROBERT A. AND JAMES E. HOWELL. 1959. *Higher Education for Business.* New York: Columbia University Press.

GUSFIELD, JOSEPH R. 1958. "Equalitarianism and Bureaucratic Recruitment." *Administrative Science Quarterly* 2:521–41.

HAGSTROM, WARREN O. AND LOWELL L. HARGENS. 1968. "Mobility Theory in the Sociology of Science." Paper delivered at Cornell Conference on Human Mobility, Ithaca, NY (October 31).

HALL, OSWALD. 1946. "The Informal Organization of the Medical Profession." *Canadian Journal of Economic and Political Science* 12:30–44.

HARBISON, FREDERICK AND CHARLES A. MYERS. 1964. *Education, Manpower, and Economic Growth.* New York: McGraw-Hill.

HESS, ROBERT D. AND JUDITH V. TORNEY. 1967. *The Development of Political Attitudes in Children.* Chicago: Aldine.

HOLLINGSHEAD, AUGUST B. 1949. *Elmtown's Youth.* New York: Wiley.

HOSELITZ, BERT F. 1965. "Investment in Education and Its Political Impact." Pp. 541–65 in *Education and Political Development,* edited by James S. Coleman. Princeton, NJ: Princeton University Press.

HUGHES, EVERETT C. 1949. "Queries Concerning Industry and Society Growing Out of the Study of Ethnic Relations in Industry." *American Sociological Review* 14:211–20.

JENCKS, CHRISTOPHER AND DAVID RIESMAN. 1968. *The Academic Revolution.* New York: Doubleday.

KAHL, JOSEPH A. 1957. *The American Class Structure.* New York: Rinehart.

KERR, CLARK, JOHN T. DUNLOP, FREDERICK H. HARBISON, AND CHARLES A. MYERS. 1960. *Industrialism and Industrial Man.* Cambridge: Harvard University Press.

LADINSKY, JACK. 1963. "Careers of Lawyers, Law Practice, and Legal Institutions." *American Sociological Review* 28:47–54.

LEARNED, W. S. AND B. D. WOOD. 1938. *The Student and His Knowledge.* New York: Carnegie Foundation for the Advancement of Teaching.

LOMBARD, GEORGE F. 1955. *Behavior in a Selling Group.* Cambridge: Harvard University Press.

MARCH, JAMES G. AND HERBERT A. SIMON. 1958. *Organizations.* New York: Wiley.

MARSH, ROBERT M. 1963. "Values, Demand, and Social Mobility." *American Sociological Review* 28:567–75.

MCARTHUR, C. 1955. "Personality Differences Between Middle and Upper Classes." *Journal of Abnormal and Social Psychology* 50:247–54.

MILLS, C. WRIGHT. 1963. *Power, Politics, and People.* New York: Oxford University Press.

NEWCOMER, MABEL. 1955. *The Big Business Executive.* New York: Columbia University Press.

NOLAND, E. WILLIAM AND E. WIGHT BAKKE. 1949. *Workers Wanted.* New York: Harper.

NOSOW, SIGMUND. 1956. "Labor Distribution and the Normative System." *Social Forces* 30:25–33.

PEASLEE, ALEXANDER L. 1969. "Education's Role in Development." *Economic Development and Cultural Change* 17:293–318.

PERRUCCI, CAROLYN CUMMINGS AND ROBERT PERRUCCI. 1970. "Social Origins, Educational Contexts, and Career Mobility." *American Sociological Review* 35:451–63.

PIERSON, FRANK C. 1959. *The Education of American Businessmen.* New York: McGraw-Hill.

PLUNKETT, M. 1960. "School and Early Work Experience of Youth." *Occupational Outlook Quarterly* 4:22–27.

REYNOLDS, LLOYD. 1951. *The Structure of Labor Markets.* New York: Harper.

RIESMAN, DAVID. 1958. *Constraint and Variety in American Education.* New York: Doubleday.

ROY, DONALD. 1952. "Quota Restriction and Goldbricking in a Machine Shop." *American Journal of Sociology* 57:427–42.

SCHULTZ, THEODORE W. 1961. "Investment in Human Capital." *American Economic Review* 51:1–16.

SCHUMPETER, JOSEPH. 1951. *Imperialism and Social Classes.* New York: Augustus M. Kelley.

SHARP, LAURE M. 1970. *Education and Employment: The Early Careers of College Graduates.* Baltimore: Johns Hopkins Press.

SMIGEL, ERWIN O. 1964. *The Wall Street Lawyer.* New York: Free Press.

SODERBERG, C. RICHARD. 1963. "The American Engineer." Pp. 203–30 in *The Professions in America,* edited by Kenneth S. Lynn. Boston: Beacon Press.

TAEUBER, ALMA F., KARL E. TAEUBER, AND GLEN G. CAIN. 1966. "Occupational Assimilation and the Competitive Process: A Reanalysis." *American Journal of Sociology* 72:278–85.

TAUSSIG, FRANK W. AND C. S. JOSLYN. 1932. *American Business Leaders.* New York: Macmillan.

TURNER, RALPH H. 1952. "Foci of Discrimination in the Employment of Nonwhites." *American Journal of Sociology* 58:247–56.

———. 1960. "Sponsored and Contest Mobility and the School System." *American Sociological Review* 25:855–67.

WALLER, WILLARD. 1932. *The Sociology of Teaching.* New York: Russell and Russell.

WARNER, W. LLOYD AND JAMES C. ABEGGLEN. 1955. *Occupational Mobility in American Business and Industry, 1928–1952.* Minneapolis: University of Minnesota Press.

WEBER, MAX.

———. 1930. *The Protestant Ethic and the Spirit of Capitalism.* New York: Scribner's.

———. 1968. *Economy and Society.* New York: Bedminster Press.

WEINBERG, IAN. 1967. *The English Public Schools: The Sociology of Elite Education.* New York: Atherton Press.

WILENSKY, HAROLD L. 1964. "The Professionalization of Everyone?" *American Journal of Sociology* 70:137–58.

Historical Accounts

11

BEYOND THE EDUCATIONAL FRONTIER
The Great American Dream Freeze

Samuel Bowles • Herbert Gintis

Those who take the meat from the table
Preach contentment. . . .
Those who eat their fill speak to the hungry
Of wonderful times to come. . . .
Those who lead the country into the abyss
Call ruling too difficult
For the ordinary.
—BERTOLT BRECHT, 1937

"Go West, young man!" advised Horace Greeley in 1851. A century later, he might have said: "Go to college!"

The Western frontier was the nineteenth-century land of opportunity. In open competition with nature, venturesome white settlers found their own levels, unfettered by birth or creed. The frontier was a way out—out of poverty, out of dismal factories, out of the crowded Eastern cities. The frontier was the Great Escape.

Few escaped. Railroad companies, mine owners, and, before long, an elite of successful farmers and ranchers soon captured both land and opportunity. The rest were left

with the adventure of making ends meet. But throughout the nineteenth century, the image of the frontier sustained the vision of economic opportunity and unfettered personal freedom in an emerging industrial system offering little of either.

With the closing of the Western frontier in the latter part of the nineteenth century and with the growing conflicts accompanying the spread of the now established "factory system," a new ideology of opportunity became the order of the day. The folklore of capitalism was revitalized: Education became the new frontier. Rapidly expanding educational opportunity in the twentieth century has met many of the functions served earlier by the Western frontier. Physical escape? Out of the question. But in school, an objective competition—as the story goes—provides an arena for discovering the limits of one's talents and, thence, the boundaries of one's life pursuit. Educational reformers have proposed an end run on economic strife by offering all children an equal opportunity to make it. Those who have failed to measure up have only themselves to blame.

For half a century or more, the educational system provided an admirable safety valve for the economic pressure cooker. Larger numbers of children completed high school and continued on to college every year. Most thought they were getting ahead, and many were. But by the late 1950s, the educational frontier was pressing its limits. Already a third of the age group was entering college; over the next decade, the fraction would rise to almost half. College graduates were driving cabs; others were collecting unemployment checks. Some were on welfare. The once relatively homogeneous appearance of the system of higher education was rapidly giving way to a hierarchy of colleges, dominated at the top by the elite Ivy League schools and descending through a fine gradation of private schools, state universities, and community colleges. Not surprisingly, a decade later, the expansion of education was slowed to a crawl. Between 1968 and 1973, the percentage of high-school graduates going on to college fell from 55 percent to 47 percent.[1] Public support for education began to wane. The fraction of all municipal school bond issues voted down in referenda doubled—from about a quarter in the mid-1960s to about a half in the early 1970s.[2] The percentage of national output devoted to educational expenditures, having more than doubled in the thirty years since 1940, fell slightly.[3]

Like the nineteenth-century prairie settler, the late twentieth-century student has come to realize the fancy of flight. The school system has been increasingly unable to support the myth of equal opportunity and full personal development. And the fading of the American Dream, hardly confined to education, has been a persistent theme of recent years.

The decade of the 1960s burst upon a complacent public in successive waves of political and cultural conflict. Their formative years untouched by depression, mobilization, and total world war, youth of the emerging generation were afforded more than a glimpse of the future of the American Dream. Large numbers were less than enthusiastic. Discontent often took the form of sporadic, but intense, political assaults against economic inequality in the United States. Minorities, women, welfare recipients, students, and working people have periodically brought the issue of inequality into the streets, forced it onto the front pages, and thrown it into the legislature and the courts. The dominant response of the privileged has been concern, tempered by a hardy optimism that social programs can be devised to alleviate social distress and restore a modicum of social harmony. Not exempt from this optimism has been modern academic economics and sociology. At the core of this conventional wisdom has rested the conviction that, within the "free enterprise" system of the United States, significant social progress can be achieved through a combination of enlightened persuasion and governmental initiative, particularly in the spheres of education and vocational training.

The social movements of the sixties and seventies did not limit their attack to inequality. The period witnessed a growing reaction against authoritarian and repressive social relationships. Wildcat strikes, worker insubordination, and especially, absenteeism became a serious problem for union bosses and for employers. Black people in open revolt against centuries of discrimination demanded control of their communities. Armed students seized administration buildings, general strikes swept the colleges, and police patrolled high-school study halls. What appeared to many as the cornerstone of social stability—the family itself—was rocked by a women's movement which challenged the sexual division of labor and the monopolization of personal and social power by males.

While the "law-and-order" forces gathered guns and adherents, the liberal community sought a more flexible answer. The "soft" human relations school of labor management enjoyed a boom. Civil rights legislation was passed. Some of the more oppressive laws defining women's place were repealed. But the key response to the movement against repressive social relations appeared in education. A free-school movement, reflecting the highest ideals of progressive students and parents, was welcomed by major foundations and supported by the U.S. Office of Education. The "open classroom" was quickly perceived by liberal educators as a means of accommodating and circumscribing the growing antiauthoritarianism of young people and keeping things from getting out of hand. Free schools proliferated.

The educational system, perhaps more than any other contemporary social institution, has become the laboratory in which competing solutions to the problems of personal liberation and social equality are tested and the arena in which social struggles are fought out. The school system is a monument to the capacity of the advanced corporate economy to accommodate and deflect thrusts away from its foundations. Yet at the same time, the educational system mirrors the growing contradictions of the larger society, most dramatically in the disappointing results of reform efforts.

By now, it is clear to many that the liberal school-reform balloon has burst. The social scientists and reformers who provided the intellectual impetus and rationale for compensatory education, for school integration, for the open classroom, for Project Headstart and Title I, are in retreat. In political as much as in intellectual circles, the current mood is one of retrenchment. In less than a decade, liberal preeminence in the field of educational theory and policy has been shattered. How did it happen?

The disappointing results of the War on Poverty and, in a larger sense, the persistence of poverty and discrimination in the United States have decisively discredited liberal social policy. The record of educational reform in the War on Poverty has been just short of catastrophic. A major Rand Corporation study, assessing the efficacy of educational programs, concluded that ". . . virtually without exception all of the large surveys of the large national compensatory educational programs have shown no beneficial results on the average."[4] The dissemination of the results of the Office of Education's Survey of Educational Opportunity—the Coleman Report—did nothing to bolster the fading optimism of the school reformers.[5] Coleman's massive 1966 study of 600,000 students in over 4,000 schools had been mandated by the Civil Rights Act of 1964; ostensibly, it was designed to provide statistical support for a policy of financial redistribution that would correct educational inequality. But while Coleman and his associates did identify positive effects of a few aspects of the school— such as teacher quality—the weight of the evidence seemed to point to the virtual irrelevance of educational resources or quality as a determinant of educational outcomes. Studies by economists in the latter 1960s revealed an unexpectedly tenuous relationship of schooling to economic success for blacks.[6] By the early 1970s, a broad spectrum of social-science opinion was ready to accept the view put forward by Jencks et al. in their highly publicized study, *Inequality:* that a more egalitarian school system would do little to create a more equal distribution of income or opportunity.[7]

The barrage of statistical studies in the late 1960s and early 1970s—the Coleman Report, Jencks' study, the evaluation of compensatory education, and others—cleared the ground for a conservative counterattack. Most notably, there has been a revival of the genetic interpretation of IQ. Thus Arthur Jensen—sensing the opportunity afforded by the liberal debacle—began his celebrated article on the heritability of IQ with: "Compensatory education has been tried and apparently it has failed."[8] In the ensuing debate, an interpretation of the role of IQ in the structure of inequality has been elaborated: The poor are poor because they are intellectually incompetent; their incompetence is particularly intractable because it is inherited from their poor, and also intellectually deficient, parents.[9] An explanation of the failure of egalitarian reform is thus found in the immutability of genetic structure. (This idea is not new: An earlier wave of genetic interpretations of economic inequality among ethnic groups followed the avowedly egalitarian, but largely unsuccessful, educational reforms of the Progressive Era.[10]) Others—Edward C. Banfield and Daniel P. Moynihan prominent among them—have found a ready audience for their view that the failure of liberal reform is to be located not in the genes, but in the attitudes, time perspectives, family patterns, and values of the poor.[11]

Free schools have fared better than egalitarian school reform. But not much—the boom peaked in the early 1970s. Today, much of the free-school rhetoric has been absorbed into the mainstream of educational thinking as a new wrinkle on how to get kids to work harder. Surviving free schools have not developed as their originators had hoped. The do-your-own-thing perspective found little favor with the majority of parents. Financial support has become harder to locate. Critics of the free-school movement increasingly raise the time-honored question: Are the majority of youth—or their elders—capable of making good use of freedom? Minus some of the more petty regulations and anachronistic dress codes, perhaps the schools are about all that can be expected—human nature being what it is, the complexity of modern life, and so forth.

These times, then, project a mood of inertial pessimism. Not a healthy conservatism founded on the affirmation of traditional values, but a rheumy loss of nerve, a product of the dashed hopes of the past decades. Even the new widespread search for individual solutions to social ills is not rooted in any celebration of individuality. Rather, to many people—viewing the failure of progressive social movements—the private pursuit of pleasure through consumption, drugs, and sexual experimentation is seen as the only show in town. Liberal social reform has been reduced to a program of Band-Aid remedies whose most eloquent vision is making do with the inevitable. In the camp of the optimists, there remain only two groups: One, those who mouth old truths and trot out tired formulas for social betterment in the vain hope that the past decade has been a quirk, a perverse and incomprehensible tangle in the history of progress which will—equally incomprehensibly—shake itself out. The other group, like ourselves, have been driven to explore the very foundation of our social order and have found there both a deeper understanding of our common situation and a conviction that our future is indeed a hopeful one.

We began our joint work together in 1968 when, actively involved in campus political movements, and facing the mass of contradictory evidence on educational reform, we became committed to comprehensive intellectual reconstruction of the role of education in economic life. Setting out to bring the total theoretical, empirical, and historical evidence of the social sciences to bear on the problem of rendering education a potent instrument of progressive social reform, we fully expected the results of this analysis to take novel and even radical forms. Moreover, we approached this task with a single overarching preconception: the vision of schools which promote economic equality and positive human development. Beyond this, we have questioned everything; we have found the social changes required to bring about what we would call a good educational system to be—while eminently feasible—quite far-reaching.

Some of the statistical results of this investigation, which will be reported in detail in later chapters, shed light on what are and are not reasons for the faltering of reform efforts. First, liberal strategies for achieving economic equality have been based on a fundamental misconception of the historical evolution of the educational system. Education over the years has never been a potent force for economic equality. Since World War I, there has been a dramatic increase in the general level of education in the United States, as well as considerable equalization of its distribution among individuals. Yet economic mobility—i.e., the degree to which economic success (income or occupational status) is independent of family background of individuals—has not changed measurably. And the total effect of family background on educational attainment (years of schooling) has remained substantially constant. Thus the evidence indicates that, despite the vast increase in college enrollments, the probability of a high-school graduate attending college is just as dependent on parental socioeconomic status as it was thirty years ago. Moreover, despite the important contribution of education to an individual's economic chances, the substantial equalization of educational attainments over the years has not led measurably to an equalization in income among individuals.

Second, the failure of reform efforts as well as the feeble contribution of education to economic equality cannot be attributed to inequalities among individuals in IQ or other measured cognitive capacities, whether of genetic or environmental origin. Thus while one's race and the socioeconomic status of one's family have substantial effect on the amount of schooling one receives, these racial and family background effects are practically unrelated to socioeconomic or racial differences in measured IQ. Similarly, while family background has an important effect on an individual's chances of economic success, this effect is not attributable to the genetic or environmental transmission of mea-

sured IQ. Thus the bitter debate of recent years over the "heritability of intelligence" would seem to be quite misplaced. Indeed, the salience of these issues in educational circles appears to be part of a widespread overestimation of the importance of mental performance in understanding education in the United States and its relationship to economic life. The intensive effort to investigate the effect of educational resources on the cognitive attainments of different races and social classes loses much of its rationale given the wide variety of statistical sources which indicate that the association of income and occupational status with an individual's educational attainment is not due to measured mental skills. More surprising, perhaps, for the bulk of the population, the dollar payoff to increased education—while strongly dependent on race and sex—is related to IQ only tenuously, if at all. Thus the standard educational practice of using IQ and test scores as a criterion for access to higher educational levels has little merit in terms of economic (not to mention educational) rationality and efficiency, except perhaps for the extremes of the IQ-distribution curve.

These results suggest that it is a mistake to think of the educational system in relation to the economy simply in "technical" terms of the mental skills it supplies students and for which employers pay in the labor market. To capture the economic import of education, we must relate its social structure to the forms of consciousness, interpersonal behavior, and personality it fosters and reinforces in students. This method gives rise to our third comment on the reform process. The free-school movement and related efforts to make education more conducive to full human development have assumed that the present school system is the product of irrationality, mindlessness, and social backwardness on the part of teachers, administrators, school boards, and parents. On the contrary, we believe the available evidence indicates that the pattern of social relationships fostered in schools is hardly irrational or accidental. Rather, the structure of the educational experience is admirably suited to nurturing attitudes and behavior consonant with participation in the labor force. Particularly dramatic is the statistically verifiable congruence between the personality traits conducive to proper work performance on the job and those which are rewarded with high grades in the classroom. Like the egalitarian reformers, the free-school movement seems to have run afoul of social logic rather than reaction, apathy, inertia, or the deficiencies of human nature.

As long as one does not question the structure of the economy itself, the current structure of schools seems eminently rational. Reform efforts must therefore go beyond the application of logical or moral argument to a public who probably understand these social realities far better than most advocates of the liberated classroom. Indeed, an impressive statistical study by Melvin Kohn indicates that parents are significantly affected by their job experiences—particularly those of dominance and subordinacy in work—and that these, in turn, are realistically reflected in the attitudes they exhibit toward the rearing and training of their children. Moreover, our historical investigations suggest that, for the past century and a half at least, employers have been similarly aware of the function of the schools in preparing youth psychologically for work. They have applied their considerable political influence accordingly.

How can we best understand the evidently critical relationship between education and the capitalist economy? Any adequate explanation must begin with the fact that schools produce workers. The traditional theory explains the increased value of an educated worker by treating the worker as a machine.[12] According to this view, workers have certain technical specifications (skills and motivational patterns) which in any given production situation determine their economic productivity. Productive traits are enhanced through schooling. We believe this worker-as-machine analogy is essentially incorrect. . . .

The motivating force in the capitalist economy is the employer's quest for profit. Profits are made through hiring workers and organizing production in such a way that the price paid for the worker's time—the wage—is less than the value of the goods produced by labor. The difference between the wage and the value of goods produced is profit, or surplus value. The production of surplus value requires as a precondition the existence of a body of wage workers whose sole source of livelihood is the sale of their capacity to work, their labor power. Opposing these wage workers is the employer, whose control of the tools, structures, and goods required in production constitutes both the immediate basis of his power over labor and his legal claim on the surplus value generated in production.

Capitalist production, in our view, is not simply a technical process; it is also a social process. Workers are neither machines nor commodities but, rather, active human beings who participate in production with the aim of satisfying their personal and social needs. The central problem of the employer is to erect a set of social relationships and organizational forms, both within the enterprise and, if possible, in society at large, that will channel these aims into the production and expropriation of surplus value.[13] Thus as a social process, capitalist production is inherently antagonistic and always potentially explosive. Though class conflicts take many forms, the most basic occurs in this struggle over the creation and expropriation of surplus value.

It is immediately evident that profits will be greater, the lower is the total wage bill paid by the employer and the greater is the productivity and intensity of labor. Education in the United States plays a dual role in the social process whereby surplus value, i.e., profit, is created and expropriated. On the one hand, by imparting technical and social skills and appropriate motivations, education increases the productive capacity of workers. On the other hand, education helps defuse and depoliticize the potentially explosive class relations of the production process, and thus serves to perpetuate the social, political, and economic conditions through which a portion of the product of labor is expropriated in the form of profits.

This simple model, reflecting the undemocratic and class-based character of economic life in the United States, bears a number of central implications which will be elaborated upon and empirically supported in the sequel.

First, we find that prevailing degrees of economic inequality and types of personal development are defined primarily by the market, property, and power relationships which define the capitalist system. Moreover, basic changes in the degree of inequality and in socially directed forms of personal development occur almost exclusively—if sometimes indirectly—through the normal process of capital accumulation and economic growth, and through shifts in the power among groups engaged in economic activity.

Second, the educational system does not add to or subtract from the overall degree of inequality and repressive personal development. Rather, it is best understood as an institution which serves to perpetuate the social relationships of economic life through which these patterns are set, by facilitating a smooth integration of youth into the labor force. This role takes a variety of forms. Schools legitimate inequality through the ostensibly meritocratic manner by which they reward and promote students, and allocate them to distinct positions in the occupational hierarchy. They create and reinforce patterns of social class, racial and sexual identification among students which allow them to relate "properly" to their eventual standing in the hierarchy of authority and status in the production process. Schools foster types of personal development compatible with the relationships of dominance and subordinacy in the economic sphere, and finally, schools create surpluses of skilled labor sufficiently extensive to render effective the prime weapon of the employer in disciplining labor—the power to hire and fire.

Third, the educational system operates in this manner not so much through the conscious intentions of teachers and administrators in their day-to-day activities, but through a close correspondence between the social relationships which govern personal interaction in the work place and the social relationships of the educational system. Specifically, the relationships of authority and control between administrators and teachers, teachers and students, students and students, and students and their work replicate the hierarchical division of labor which dominates the work place. Power is organized along vertical lines of authority from administration to faculty to student body; students have a degree of control over their curriculum comparable to that of the worker over the content of his job. The motivational system of the school, involving as it does grades and other external rewards and the threat of failure rather than the intrinsic social benefits of the process of education (learning) or its tangible outcome (knowledge), mirrors closely the role of wages and the specter of unemployment in the motivation of workers. The fragmented nature of jobs is reflected in the institutionalized and rarely constructive competition among students and in the specialization and compartmentalization of academic knowledge. Finally, the relationships of dominance and subordinacy in education differ by level. The rule orientation of the high school reflects the close supervision of low-level workers; the internalization of norms and freedom from continual supervision in elite colleges reflect the social relationships of upper-level white-collar work. Most state universities and community colleges, which fall in between, conform to the behavioral requisites of low-level technical, service, and supervisory personnel.

Fourth, though the school system has effectively served the interests of profit and political stability, it has hardly been a finely tuned instrument of manipulation in the hands of socially dominant groups. Schools and colleges do indeed help to justify inequality, but they also have become arenas in which a highly politicized egalitarian consciousness has developed among some parents, teachers, and students. The authoritarian classroom does produce docile workers, but it also produces misfits and rebels. The university trains the elite in the skills of domination, but it has also given birth to a powerful radical movement and critique of capitalist society. The contradictory nature of U.S. education stems in part from the fact that the imperatives of profit often pull the school system in opposite directions. The types of training required to develop productive workers are often ill suited to the perpetuation of those ideas and institutions which facilitate the profitable employment of labor. Furthermore, contradictory forces external to the school system continually impinge upon its operations. Students, working people, parents, and others have attempted to use education to attain a greater share of the social wealth, to develop genuinely critical capacities, to gain material security, in short to pursue objectives different—and often diametrically opposed—to those of capi-

tal. Education in the United States is as contradictory and complex as the larger society; no simplistic or mechanical theory can help us understand it.

Lastly, the organization of education—in particular the correspondence between school structure and job structure—has taken distinct and characteristic forms in different periods of U.S. history, and has evolved in response to political and economic struggles associated with the process of capital accumulation, the extension of the wage-labor system, and the transition from an entrepreneurial to a corporate economy.

We believe that current educational reform movements reflect these dynamics of the larger society. Thus the free-school movement and, more generally, youth culture are diffuse reactions to the reduced status and personal control of white-collar labor and its expression in repressive schooling. The extent to which the educational establishment will embrace free schooling depends to some extent on the political power of the parents and children pressing these objectives. But the long-run survival of the free school as anything but an isolated haven for the overprivileged will depend on the extent to which the interpersonal relationships it fosters can be brought into line with the realities of economic life. The increasing complexity of work, the growing difficulty of supervising labor and the rampant dissatisfaction of workers with their lack of power may foretell a sustained effort by employers to redesign jobs to allow limited worker participation in production decisions. Experiments with job enlargement and team work are manifestations of what may become a trend in the soft human relations school of personnel management. A co-opted free-school movement, shorn of its radical rhetoric, could play an important role in providing employers with young workers with a "built-in" supervisor. In this, it would follow the Progesssive Movement of an earlier era. This much, at least, is clear: the possibility of schooling which promotes truly self-initiated and self-conscious personal development will await a change in the work place more fundamental than any proposed by even the softest of the soft human relations experts. For only when work processes are self-initiated and controlled by workers themselves will free schooling be an integral part of the necessary process of growing up and getting a job. Nor, we suggest, are these necessary changes limited to the work place alone; they entail a radical transformation of the very class structure of U.S. society.

The impact of the current movement for equalization of schooling—through resource transfers, open enrollment, and similar programs—likewise hinges on the future of economic institutions. Education plays a major role in hiding or justifying the exploitative nature of the U.S. economy. Equal access to educational credentials, of course, could not arise by accident. But were egalitarian education reformers to win spectacular victories—the social relationships of economic life remaining untouched—we can confidently predict that employers would quickly resort to other means of labeling and segmenting working people so as to fortify the structure of power and privilege within the capitalist enterprise.

In short, our approach to U.S. education suggests that movements for educational reform have faltered through refusing to call into question the basic structure of property and power in economic life. We are optimistic indeed concerning the feasibility of achieving a society fostering economic equality and full personal development. But we understand that the prerequisite is a far-reaching economic transformation. An educational system can be egalitarian and liberating only when it prepares youth for fully democratic participation in social life and an equal claim to the fruits of economic activity. In the United States, democratic forms in the electoral sphere of political life are paralleled by highly dictatorial forms in the economic sphere. Thus we believe that the key to reform is the democratization of economic relationships: social ownership, democratic and participatory control of the production process by workers, equal sharing of socially necessary labor by all, and progressive equalization of incomes and destruction of hierarchical economic relationships. This is, of course, socialism, conceived of as an extension of democracy from the narrowly political to the economic realm.

In this conception, educational strategy is part of a revolutionary transformation of economic life. Under what conditions and by what means such a movement might be successful is discussed toward the end of our investigation. But the broad outlines of such an educational strategy are clear. We must press for an educational environment in which youth can develop the capacity and commitment collectively to control their lives and regulate their social interactions with a sense of equality, reciprocity, and communality. Not that such an environment will of itself alter the quality of social life. Rather, that it will nurture a new generation of workers—white and blue collar, male and female, black, white, brown, and red—unwilling to submit to the fragmented relationships of dominance and subordinacy prevailing in economic life.

· · ·

NOTES

1. U.S. Department of Labor, *Monthly Labor Review* (September 1974), p. 50.
2. Irene A. King, *Bond Sales for Public School Purposes* (1974), U.S. Department of Health, Education and Welfare, Publication No. (OE)–73–11406.
3. U.S. Department of Labor (1974), op. cit.
4. Harvey Averch, et al., *How Effective Is School-*

ing: A Critical Review and Synthesis of Research Findings (Santa Monica: The Rand Corporation, 1972), p. 125.

5. James S. Coleman et al., *Equality of Educational Opportunity* (Washington, DC: U.S. Government Printing Office, 1966). For a discussion of some of the shortcomings of the Coleman Report, see Samuel Bowles and Henry Levin, "The Determinants of Scholastic Achievement: An Appraisal of Some Recent Evidence," *Journal of Human Resources* (Winter 1968); and "More on Multicollinearity and the Effectiveness of Schools," *Journal of Human Resources* (Summer 1968).

6. Giora Hanoch, "An Economic Analysis of Earnings and Schooling," in *Journal of Human Resources,* no. 2 (Summer 1967); Randall Weiss, "The Effects of Education on the Earnings of Blacks and Whites," in *Review of Economics and Statistics,* no. 52 (May 1970); Bennett Harrison, *Education, Training, and the Urban Ghetto* (Baltimore: Johns Hopkins University Press, 1972).

7. Jencks, Smith, Ackland, Bane, Cohen, Gintis, Heyns, Michelson, *Inequality: A Reassessment of the Effects of Family and Schooling in America* (New York: Basic Books, 1972).

8. Arthur A. Jensen, "How Much Can We Boost IQ and Scholastic Achievement?" *Harvard Educational Review*, vol. 39, no. 1 (1969), p. 1.

9. Jensen (1969), op cit.; Richard Herrnstein, "IQ," *Atlantic Monthly*, vol. 228, no. 3 (September 1971); J. Eysenck, *The IQ Argument* (New York: Library Press, 1971); Arthur A. Jensen, *Educability and Group Differences* (New York: Harper and Row, 1975).

10. Clarence Karier, "Testing for Order and Control in the Corporate Liberal State," in *Education Theory*, vol. 22 (Spring 1972); Leon Kamin, *The Science and Politics of IQ* (Potomac, MD: Erlbaum Associates, 1974).

11. Edward Banfield, *The Unheavenly City* (Boston: Little, Brown and Company, 1968); Daniel Patrick Moynihan, *The Negro Family* (Cambridge, MA: MIT Press, 1967).

12. We have confined our attention to education in the United States. For an excellent treatment of education on a world-wide basis, see Martin Carnoy, *Education as Cultural Imperialism* (New York: McKay, 1974).

13. For a more extensive treatment, see Samuel Bowles and Herbert Gintis, "The Problem with Human Capital . . . A Marxian Critique," *American Economic Review* (May 1975).

12

THE RISING TIDE OF COEDUCATION IN THE HIGH SCHOOL

David Tyack • Elisabeth Hansot

Many of the pioneers in creating public high schools believed that the sexes should be educated separately, and in the early years often regarded public secondary education

David Tyack and Elisabeth Hansot, excerpt from "The Rising Tide of Coeducation in the High School" from *Learning Together: A History of Coeducation in American Public Schools.* Copyright © 1992 by Russell Sage Foundation. Reprinted with the permission of the publishers.

for girls as an experiment. Most early advocates of the high school could not foresee, and probably would not have approved of, what actually happened. In the last three decades of the nineteenth century four facts were becoming clear:

1. Public secondary education was overwhelmingly coeducational. In an 1882 survey, only 19 of 196 cities reported that they had separate-sex high schools. By the end of the century, only 12 cities out

of 628 reported that they had single-sex high schools.[1]

2. With few exceptions, girls and boys studied the same subjects. The curriculum was not significantly differentiated by gender.[2]

3. Girls at least equalled and often outperformed boys in their academic studies.[3]

4. Girls substantially outnumbered boys as both students and graduates of high schools, accounting for 57 percent of the students and 65 percent of the graduates in 1890. In 1889 the U.S. commissioner of education estimated that only about one-quarter of the students in the high schools of the ten biggest cities were boys.[4]

Trying to understand why high schools developed such gender patterns is like fitting together pieces of a complicated jigsaw puzzle.

An important part of the story is the institutional character of public high schools. The early history of the high school is still obscure, though conservatives relish nostalgic images of a golden age, with dignified temples of learning in which the teachers were scholars, the pupils were studiously preparing for college, the academic mission of the institution was simple and strong, and the public was well satisfied with its creation. There were a few privileged high schools that achieved this ideal, but, as a whole, public secondary education during the nineteenth century was diverse, controversial, and ambiguously connected with the larger society.

Urban educators developed bureaucratic visions of high schools as the capstone of a meritocratic and unified urban school system. They expected a competitive high-school entrance examination to pressure elementary-school administrators to standardize their curricula and to stimulate the ambitions and industry of talented students. They hoped that the high school would rival in quality the best private academies so that prosperous parents would enroll their children, but thought it should also be the people's college, a place where the children of janitors were welcome, too.

Despite hopeful rhetoric, most high schools were small and short of funds and hence had tiny faculties and limited curricula. Few young people attended them, and these were disproportionately from middle-class families. A high percentage of students, particularly boys, dropped out.

One reason for the shortage of students was the lack of a demonstrated connection between high-school studies and later life. Only a small proportion of public-high-school students were preparing for college. Although educators considered high-school attendance a reward for diligent work in the lower grades, boys often regarded secondary education as irrelevant to their futures, for they could obtain a variety of white-collar jobs without going to high school. The situation was different for girls. They had few opportunities to do nonmanual work. The late-nineteenth-century high school enrolled mostly native-born and middle-class students and thus seemed a safe haven for the proper urban girl, a place to spend one's adolescent years preparing to be a better wife and mother. In addition, the high school was a gateway for many young women into teaching careers, one of the few white-collar jobs open to women at the time.

Educators had good organizational reasons to adopt coeducation in high schools. In most cities, the elementary schools were coeducational, and mixing the sexes in the high schools maintained the symmetry and uniformity of the system. Girls performed better than boys in the lower grades, and it would have been a denial of meritocratic principles to forbid their admission to secondary schools. Besides, the number of students in high school were so paltry that creating separate-sex secondary schools would have been prohibitively expensive. Indeed, one might argue that in most places high schools could not have been justified economically if girls had not populated the classrooms.

The inclusion of girls in coeducational high schools, then, might be explained as the logical product of ideology (republican equality and preparation for the female sphere), economy (the financial necessity of coeducation in small schools), and organizational development (the high school as the upward extension of a coeducational bureaucracy). But this would be too neat. Because high schools were contested ground in politics, the path of their development was not straight and logical but winding and shaped by conflicting public opinions. In a series of case studies of the creation of secondary schools in diverse cities we trace this winding path, looking first at school districts that chose to educate girls in separate high schools and then at the movement toward coeducation.

. . .

A Diverse and Controversial Institution

. . .

Public high schools were controversial from their very beginning and throughout their development, in part because their constituencies and purposes were multiform. Even their advocates had different visions. Some used the traditional republican rhetoric: high schools would train virtuous citizens and principled leaders. Others regarded high schools as an upward extension of the public school system that would prepare students for white-collar employment. Still other high-school promoters wanted to attract the children of the wealthy and thereby gain support for public as opposed to private schooling.[5]

Many urban school superintendents saw high schools as meritocratic institutions. They developed competitive examinations for entrance into the high school that served as a template for the grammar-school curriculum. Grammar-school masters felt pressure to teach to the test since the examination results were often listed by school. In Chicago a newspaper called this entrance exam a form of academic "Olympic games." High-school promoters often argued that this competition for entrance motivated grammar pupils to excel, making the whole system more efficient. In most large cities educators added "normal departments" to high schools in order to train young women to teach the standardized curriculum in the approved manner, thereby further bureaucratizing the whole system.[6]

College officials had their own visions of an effective high school: one that would effectively prepare students to meet the requirements for admission to higher education. In the Midwest, state universities took the lead in accrediting high schools and shaping their curriculum to assure a steady flow of qualified students. Disenchanted with the hodgepodge of secondary-school curricula, Harvard's Charles William Eliot called the high school the "gap" between the elementary schools and the colleges and worked to upgrade precollegiate instruction.[7]

The opponents of the high school were even more diverse than the proponents. Issues of social class often arose. Working-class critics of the high school complained that it attracted chiefly the children of the prosperous and thus was an elitist institution. Studies of the social origins of high-school students do show high proportions of middle-class students—typically two-thirds or more—and relatively few from the working class. David Labaree, for example, has found that in Philadelphia students from middle-class backgrounds "outnumbered the working class at the high school by a ratio of two to one, [although] in the city as a whole workers outnumbered the middle-class by a margin of three-to-one." Sensitive to the criticism that high schools were elitist, educators broadcast stories of friendships between working-class students and children of the wealthy in the high schools. A principal in Newburyport, Massachusetts, wrote about two girls walking "with their arms closely entwined about each others' necks. . . . [one was] a daughter of one of our first merchants, the other has a father worse than none, who obtains a livelihood from one of the lowest and most questionable occupations, and is himself most degraded." In Boston the principal of the boys' high school declared that "some of our best scholars are sons of coopers, lamplighters, and day laborers."[8]

Critics of the high school asked why taxpayers should subsidize the teaching of subjects like Latin and French. Sometimes citizens challenged in the courts the legality of instructing pupils in subjects beyond the common-school curriculum, as in Michigan's Kalamazoo case of 1874. In revising the California Constitution in 1879, the Workingmen's Party in California tried "to exclude high schools from the school system of the State" and to discourage their growth. The Oakland high-school principal fought the Workingmen's notion that "free schools should instruct in the elements only, and that anything further should be left to private enterprise." The rapid development of the economy demanded that youth be trained in advanced subjects, he argued, and, in turn, these "changes in our relations to the material world have rendered our social and civil relations more complex. . . . Permit the coming generations to grow up in ignorance of all those principles which underlie good government . . . and [workingmen's protest] will be the muttering thunder which precedes the tempest."[9]

In some communities opposition came not from those on the bottom of the social structure but from those on top, the rich. They claimed that the high school gave unfair competition to private schools by providing free secondary education and argued that high schools spoiled workers. A conservative newspaper editor in Portland, Oregon, remarked in 1879 that the high school graduated "whole regiments of sickly sentimentalists: young gentlemen unused and unfit for work." School leaders countered by showing that graduates did go on to work, college, or useful lives as wives and mothers. The Oakland principal reported that at a meeting of the alumni of the high school in 1880 no graduate could be found who was "an example of the so-called pernicious effects of over-education."[10]

Countering the claim that the public high school invigorated and unified the common school, some critics objected that it diverted funds away from the elementary schools and brought an undesirable centralization. Especially in times of retrenchment—in the periodic panics of the nineteenth century—the high school struck many people as a costly luxury. In addition to the expense of the public high school, other critics objected to the grand plans of the professional educators. As Carl Kaestle has shown, much of the educational politics of the nineteenth century was a contest between localists and centralizers, between those who wished to retain local control and those who wished to create unified systems. As a symbol and instrument of centralization, the high school became a lightning rod for those who opposed the bureaucratization of the schools.[11]

Given such controversy, it is perhaps surprising that the high school took hold as firmly as it did in the nineteenth century. It is possible, however, that the very ambiguity of the high school's purpose and constituency may have shielded it. By claiming that the high school might be all things to all people, its advocates blunted attacks and co-opted the uncommitted.

Conflict over gender policies occurred in some communities, but in general these were less potent sources of controversy than the charge of class bias. The high school was originally designed for boys and indeed was regarded by some observers as a distinctly masculine institution, yet girls became model students who outperformed boys in a system that prided itself on being meritocratic. In a period when citizens strenuously maintained separate ideological and practical spheres for men and women, both sexes learned a similar curriculum. Many foreign observers of American high schools regarded coeducation and the predominance of female students as the most distinctive—and disturbing—features of American secondary education. Relatively few nineteenth-century Americans, however, worried about the implications of the number and performance of female high-school students for a society which decreed separate and unequal opportunities for the sexes in adult life.[12]

At the time of the origin of the high school, it was by no means clear, however, that coeducation would become the standard gender practice. Americans had more qualms about mixing teenage boys and girls than about educating younger children together. But by the early 1870s about nine out of ten public high schools were coeducational. In the modal high school at that time, teachers were about equally divided between men and women. Although some policymakers called for differentiation of high-school studies by gender, they failed to have much impact until the twentieth century.[13]

Although the term *coeducational public high school* came to designate a particular type of institution after the Civil War, each word in the phrase was ambiguous in the antebellum period. A separate school was

straightforward enough: it meant that only one sex attended classes in a school building. Prior to the 1820s, girls had been excluded from the sole form of public secondary education, the old Latin grammar schools. The first high schools open to girls were generally segregated by sex. Only a relatively few cities, however, chose to educate girls in separate buildings. A more common practice was to house both boys and girls in the same building but to separate them on different floors or in different "departments." Even when separate boys' and girls' departments were abandoned—in part because it was so expensive to teach small numbers of boys and girls in separate classes—the sexes were often segregated in study halls, required to use separate entrances, cloakrooms, and playgrounds, and allowed to mix only when reciting in academic classes. In some cases, certain courses of study were open to only one sex—for example, the normal (or teacher-training) program for girls and the classical course that prepared boys for admission to college. But as fears about the consequences of coeducating adolescent boys and girls faded, girls and boys generally studied the same subjects side by side in their regular classes in high schools, just as in primary and grammar schools. This came to be the generally understood meaning of *coeducation.*[14]

Like the word *coeducational*, the term *public* carried many meanings in education in the first half of the nineteenth century. Eventually it would designate a school that was free, supported by taxation, and controlled by clearly designated public authorities (usually a mix of state and local). Until the 1880s, however, the majority of secondary schools could not be described as public using these criteria. These "private" schools usually had self-perpetuating boards of trustees, charged tuition, recruited and selected students from a geographical area wider than the public school districts, and operated under charters that gave them authority as private corporations invested with the public interest. They far outnumbered public high schools. In Ohio, for example, there were ninety-three academies chartered before 1850, thirty-two seminaries, thirty institutes, and fourteen private high schools; only nine school districts had received legislative mandates to found public high schools. In some parts of the country, states gave private academies public funds. In New York the state subsidized the education of students preparing to become teachers, while in Illinois academies received funds from federal land grants. The charters of some academies specified that the trustees should be elected by the voters of the towns where they were located. As the public-high-school movement gained momentum, many towns simply incorporated academies into the public school system as high schools. Even in public high schools students often paid tuition, private benefactors provided endowments, and admission was highly selective, based on stiff entrance tests.[15]

Similarly, the name *high school* was ambiguous. The universe of secondary education, of which public high schools formed a part, included a variety of institutions, whose diversity is reflected in the multiplicity of names given to secondary schools: academy, classical school, English school, institute, grammar school, union school, college, select school, seminary, boarding school, graded school, and many permutations of these and other titles. The educational specialist of the U.S. Census complained as late as 1893 that the term "high school" designated a multitude of types of institutions and levels of instruction. Some high schools in the larger cities were elite academic institutions that competed with the best private academies, while in Tennessee a "high school" was defined by law as grades six, seven, and eight of the common school.[16]

. . .

Although high schools were a hodgepodge, some educational leaders sought to articulate a common definition of the high school and a vision of its potential. Henry Barnard was one of the earliest and most influential of these advocates. In his 1848 report as superintendent of the Rhode Island schools, he described a high school as "a public or common school for the older and more advanced scholars of the community . . . [with] a course of instruction adapted to their age, and intellectual and moral wants, and, to some extent, to their future pursuits in life." He continued: "It would be a mockery of the idea of such a school . . . if the course of instruction pursued is not higher and better than can be got in public schools of a lower grade; or if it does not meet the needs of the wealthiest and best educated families, or, if the course of instruction is liberal, and at the same time the worthy and talented child of a poor family is shut out from its privileges by a high rate of tuition." Barnard walked a fine line: the high school was to be an academically elite school fit for the first families, but it was not to be restricted by social class.[17]

To justify public support through taxation, "the advantages of such a school must accrue to the whole community," he wrote. The public high school would make the lower grades more efficient by removing advanced scholars who required extra time and attention from teachers and by rewarding the hard work of talented students who wished to continue their education. The high school was not for all: it was to be a meritocratic institution with strict entrance examinations and academic standards. Its influence would reach down into the lower schools by forcing the standardization of the curriculum and offering an opportunity for the ambitious. A well-ordered high school, said Barnard, would not only attract the wealthy away from private schools but would place "the privileges of a good school . . . within the reach of all classes of the community, and will actually be enjoyed by children of the same age from families of the most diverse circumstances as to wealth, education, and occupation."[18]

The school should teach boys subjects directly useful in later life in a wide array of occupations, such as "navigation, bookkeeping, surveying, botany, chemistry, and kindred studies, which are connected with success in the varied departments of domestic and inland trade, with foreign commerce, with gardening, agriculture, the manufacturing and domestic arts." But Barnard also wanted pupils to learn "astronomy, physiology, the history of our own state and nation, the principles of our state and national constitutions, political economy, and moral science." The result would be "such a course of study as . . . shall prepare every young man . . . for business or college."[19]

The high school, in Barnard's eyes, was not for boys alone. It would be open to girls as well but would prepare them for a much narrower sphere. Barnard argued that "the great influence of the female sex, as daughters, sisters, wives, mothers, companions, and teachers, in determining the manners, morals, and intelligence of the whole community, leaves no room to question the necessity of providing for the girls the best means of intellectual and moral culture." In their rationale for secondary education for girls, Barnard and other advocates of coeducational public high schools borrowed freely from Beecher and Willard.[20]

In the plans of Barnard and his fellow reformers, the urban high school occupied a pivotal position in relation both to other educational agencies and other school-related institutions. They believed that the high school should unify the lower schools and motivate students to work harder and continue their education. As a citywide institution, the high school would link together isolated districts, Barnard claimed, and lessen the "estrangements which now divide and subdivide the community." Because it trained some students in subjects required for college admission, the high school also connected city systems to higher education. By educating boys in skills useful in white-collar jobs, high schools were connected with the labor market. And secondary education offered girls from the urban middle class a place to spend their teenage years productively preparing for marriage and motherhood, thus reinforcing the family and the traditional female sphere in the home.[21]

Despite the blueprints of educators like Barnard, who sought to create institutional coherence in the high school and win broad support for public secondary education, in practice high schools remained contested terrain, ambiguous in purpose and diverse in character.

. . .

The High School through the Lens of Gender, 1870–1900

We began this chapter with four observations: that high schools were coeducational, that girls and boys studied mostly the same subjects, that girls equalled or outperformed boys academically, and that girls outnumbered boys as students and as graduates. We now return to these characteristics and ask how they connected with the nature of the high school as an institution during the period from 1870 to 1900 when the high school became rapidly institutionalized. We also

TABLE 12.1   Statistics on Urban Public High Schools, 1873

Number of schools	536
Average number of pupils per school	85
Average daily attendance per school	62
Percentage of all urban public school students enrolled in high schools	4
Average number of teachers per school	3
Percentage of female teachers	53

Source: U.S. Commissioner of Education, *Report for 1873*, pp. xliii–xliv.

look briefly at how the high school connected with the workplace and the life cycle of girls in the family to explore why there were fewer male than female students.

High schools of this era had small enrollments and high attrition. One should be cautious and skeptical in using almost all nineteenth-century educational statistics, and nowhere more so than in analyzing the very ambiguous institution called the high school. But by using federal, state, and local sources, one can create a rough statistical portrait of public secondary education. Consider, for example, the report on city high schools in 1873 cited in Table 12.1.

This table captures some of the essential institutional features of the modal public high school in 1873: it had a small enrollment; its teaching force was tiny and balanced between men and women; and it enrolled only a tiny fraction of the students attending public schools. Averages can of course mask variability. The census of 1870 makes it possible to group the average size of high schools by states, the more urban states having the larger schools: six states had an average high school enrollment of 35 to 50 pupils; fourteen states, an average of 51 to 100; six states, an average of 101 to 150; and three states, an average of 151 or more.[22]

Similar high-school characteristics were apparent in census statistics collected in 1890 and 1900. In 1890 the number of students in high schools represented only 3 per-cent of the number in elementary schools. The average number of students in public high schools was 80 in 1890, and 86 in 1900. The typical high school had 3.6 teachers in 1890, and 3.4 in 1900. Women constituted 58 percent of high-school teachers in 1890, and 50 percent in 1900. But again, it is useful to compare the sizes of high schools in different sizes of communities. In 1903 the statistics on high schools were disaggregated in a way that permits comparison of cities with populations greater than eight thousand, in which the average number of pupils was 355 and the number of teachers was 12, whereas in communities smaller than eight thousand, the average number of students was 52 and number of instructors was 2. Clearly such differences of scale greatly influenced what the high schools could offer their students and how they could group them for instruction.[23]

. . .

The size of high schools also helps to explain why both boys and girls studied the same, largely academic curriculum in coeducational classrooms (Table 12.2). In a school of sixty to ninety students and only two or three teachers, it was simply impossible to offer separate classes for the two sexes or to provide a sexually differentiated course of studies. Educators found it expedient to mix the sexes as a way of achieving better classification of students by subject as well as by age and proficiency, as in the grammar school.

. . .

High-school promoters justified the institution on meritocratic grounds, and this, too, helps explain why girls were welcome. The grammar schools were coeducational; to pass the high-school-entrance test was the ambition of both sexes. According to the common rationale for coeducation in the lower grades, girls and boys encouraged in

TABLE 12.2 Boys and Girls Enrolled in Certain High School Subjects, 1900

	Boys (%)	Girls (%)
Physics	19.5	18.7
Chemistry	8.2	7.4
Physiology	28.0	27.0
Physical geography	23.6	23.2
Algebra	57.0	55.8
Geometry	27.0	27.7
Latin	47.1	55.8
Greek	3.7	2.6
French	6.6	8.7
German	13.4	15.0
History	36.1	39.6
Rhetoric	37.5	39.2
English literature	40.7	42.9

Source: John Francis Latimer, *What's Happened to Our High Schools* (Washington, DC: Public Affairs Press, 1958), p. 149.

each other a more ardent and balanced form of academic achievement—an argument also applied to the high school.[24]

From the start, girls proved that they could meet the meritocratic standard for admission to high school and could perform at least as well as the boys in their courses. Already accustomed to the superior work of girls in the lower grades, superintendents also found that girls carried off more than their normal share of scholastic honors in high schools. In the Somerville, Massachusetts, high-school girls were usually the valedictorians, for example. In St. Louis, academic records for the period from 1870 to 1885 demonstrated that girls did slightly better than boys. In 1900 the superintendent of the Kansas City school system reported by sex on the rate of failures in different courses in the high schools. Although boys constituted only 36 percent of the students in the four high schools of the city, they accounted for 43 percent of the failures in mathematics, 50 percent in foreign languages, 49 percent in science, and 44 percent in history and related subjects. A study of failure rates by sex

in Indiana cities and rural schools concluded that "the boys are much less successful than the girls. The difference in the per cent of failures varies for the different subjects, but in practically all instances the per cent of failures and also the per cent of conditions is noticeably higher for the boys than for the girls. In many cases it is more than double. Even in mathematics the girls show a slight superiority."

As the phrase "even in mathematics" suggests, educators were surprised that girls did well not only in literary subjects—often gendered as feminine in a society that seemed to reserve high culture for women—but also in mathematics, a field typically gendered as male. Hence, when educational researchers began to collect evidence on the performance of girls in mathematics, they were surprised to find that females did well there, too. In 1903 Edward T. Thorndike and a superintendent of schools administered a test to twenty-eight boys and forty-nine girls in a high school in Albion, Indiana. The test itself showed a marked male bias: of twelve mentions of gender, eleven referred to men or boys, while the problem situations were typically masculine. Nonetheless, they reported, the girls did about 5 percent better than the boys. Suspicious of their results, they made the surmise—comforting to males—that probably the more able boys had already left school (an odd kind of school where the leavers were smarter than the ones who persisted).[25]

High school was one environment where effort paid off for young women, even though success in high-school studies did not generally translate into enhanced opportunities in later life. Competitive entrance examinations to normal classes and a competitive examination to qualify for teaching jobs strengthened the meritocratic underpinnings of the high school and justified the expense of creating high schools in the first place. Normal training classes firmly linked the high school to the improvement of the whole system in a meritocratic way and motivated girls to do well in high school in order to obtain a job after graduation.[26]

Of course not all girls aspired to teach. For most girls the high school years probably represented a moratorium between the parental and the conjugal family, a safe and productive way to spend youthful years, free from the dangers of the workplace and rich in cultural and human associations. In the Victorian era, middle-class parents in cities increasingly viewed the adolescence of girls as a time of special promise and jeopardy, and a whole literature emerged on what Joan Jacobs Brumberg has called "the iconography of girlhood." Jane Hunter has found that the diaries of schoolgirls were full of positive allusions to their classmates and school experiences.[27]

Despite educators' rhetoric about the high school as "the people's college" and their desire to prove that it served a cross-section of the population, high schools continued to attract mostly the sons and daughters of what was broadly called the "middle class"—professional people, shopkeepers, clerks, skilled laborers, and the like. The class composition of high schools no doubt varied according to the character of the community. In Erie, Pennsylvania, for example, the high-school principal claimed that over half his pupils came from homes where the parents had property assessments of less than $500, and in Adrian, Michigan, the principal found more children of farmers, railroad employees, and widows than of businessmen or professionals. But Selwyn Troen has found that in St. Louis in 1880, 80 percent of the sons of professional fathers and 64 percent of the sons of white-collar workers between the ages of thirteen and sixteen were in school, compared with only 32 percent of the sons of unskilled workers. In Philadelphia that same year, 46 percent of the students in Central High School came from what David Labaree calls the "proprietary middle class" (or "occupational groups that are self-employed") and only 3.5 percent from the unskilled working class.[28]

Because the high school was basically a middle-class institution and employed both female and male teachers, middle-class parents could be confident that a coeducational high school was a secure environment for girls who were no longer needed to help about the home in many urban households. Meeting boys in such a controlled setting and obtaining the cultural capital deemed appropriate to young women may have enhanced their daughters' standing in the marriage market. Indeed, contemporary observers of the high school claimed that more and more middle-class girls attended school because it was "the social thing to do." Sara Burstall, an English educator, wrote that high-school graduation could give girls "a certain social advantage." In 1894 the Atlanta schools reported that alumnae from its girls' high school were "adorning the highest ranks of society in the state."[29]

Boys faced a different kind of decision than girls did in choosing whether to attend a public high school in the years from 1870 to 1900. For boys going to school meant forgoing paid employment. They had a much wider array of white-collar and skilled jobs to choose from, even as teenagers, and less stigma was attached to young men's work than to most of the jobs young women could obtain. The high-school principal in Alameda, California, lamenting that only 30 percent of his students were boys, wrote that "this undesirable condition can be accounted for by the fact that boys of High School age have a strong desire to earn money and get a start in the world, while girls as a rule have not this impulse and are encouraged to continue their studies by pride, ambition, encouragement of parents, and in many cases by the desire to prepare themselves as teachers."[30]

Boys often found a quicker educational route to their goals than attending high school. Public-school leaders complained, for example, that private business schools that offered a short course of practical subjects were draining off boys from the more academic high school. Indeed, in 1890, 64,163 young men were attending such schools, almost three times the number of young women. Likewise, among boys who planned to go to college in 1900, almost 35,000 bypassed high schools by attending the "preparatory" departments of colleges and universities, outnumbering girls there three to two. One can explain the relative absence of boys from high schools in part as a function of their greater range of choices or the pressures to go to work or college at an earlier age.

At the turn of the century, however, the dearth of boys in high schools—increasingly referred to as "the boy problem"—came to be explained as the result of the "feminization" of public education. Some doctors and psychologists now worried that the high school was too masculine for the health of the girls, while others depicted the high school as too sissy for boys.

NOTES

1. U.S. Bureau of Education, *Coeducation of the Sexes in the Public Schools of the United States,* Circular of Information, no. 2-1883 (Washington, DC: GPO, 1883), pp. 12, 24; *U.S. Com. Ed. Report for 1900–1901,* pp. 1221.
2. *U.S. Com. Ed. Report for 1888–89,* 2:775; *Report for 1889–90,* 2:1388; John Francis Latimer, *What's Happened to Our High Schools?* (Washington, DC: Public Affairs Press, 1958), pp. 144–46.
3. James M. Greenwood, "Report on High School Statistics," *NEA Addresses and Proceedings, 1900,* p. 347, and citations on achievement given below.
4. U.S. Bureau of Education, *Biennial Survey of Education, 1918–20* (Washington, DC: GPO, 1923), p. 497; *U.S. Com. Ed. Report for 1889,* 2:775.
5. Some of these themes are skillfully developed by David F. Labaree, *The Making of an American High School: The Credentials Market and the Central High School of Philadelphia* (New Haven: Yale University Press, 1988); see also case studies below and local school reports for the rationale of the high school.
6. David B. Tyack, *The One Best System: A History of American Urban Education* (Cambridge: Harvard University Press, 1974), pp. 56–59. For an anguished complaint when the high school did not operate in this meritocratic manner, see *Lowell, Mass., Report for 1851,* pp. 56–58.
7. Charles W. Eliot, "The Gap Between the Elementary Schools and the Colleges," *NEA Addresses and Proceedings, 1890,* pp. 522–33. For arguments about the purposes of the early high school, see David Tyack, ed., *Turning Points in American Educational History* (Waltham, MA: Blaisdell Publishing, 1967), pp. 352–411; for the post–1880 period, a standard work is Edward A. Krug, *The Shaping of the American High School, 1880–1920* (New York: Harper and Row, 1964).
8. Principals quoted in Henry Barnard, "Public High School," *Rhode Island Report for 1848,* p. 258; Labaree, *American High School,* pp. 41, 45; Michael B. Katz, *The Irony of Early School Reform: Educational Innovation in Mid-Nineteenth Century Massachusetts* (Cambridge: Harvard University Press, 1968), pp. 271, 39; Joel A. Perlmann, *Ethnic Differences* (Cambridge, England: Cambridge University Press); Selwyn K. Troen, *The Public and the Schools: Shaping the St. Louis School System, 1838–1920* (Columbia: University of Missouri Press, 1975), p. 232; Krug, *Shaping the American High School,* pp. 12–13.
9. Principal quoted in *Oakland Report for 1881,* pp. 82–84; David Tyack, Thomas James, and Aaron Benavot, *Law and the Shaping of Public Education, 1785–1954* (Madison: University of Wisconsin Press, 1987), pp. 102–4; State of California, *Debates and Proceedings of the Constitutional Convention of the State of California, 1878–79,* 3 vols. (Sacramento: State Printer, 1880–81).
10. *Oakland Report for 1881,* p. 73; editor quoted in David B. Tyack, "Bureaucracy and the Common School: The Example of Portland, Oregon, 1851–1913," *American Quarterly* 19(1967): 489.
11. Mary Abigail Dodge, *Our Common School System* (Boston: Estes and Lauriat, 1880), pp. 21–

44; Carl Kaestle, *Pillars of the Republic: Common Schools and American Society, 1780–1860* (New York: Hill and Wang, 1983); Vinovskis, *Beverly High School.*

12. One report of the U.S. Office of Education that attempted to explain coeducation to foreign critics was U.S. Bureau of Education, *Coeducation of the Sexes.*

13. Our estimate that 90 percent of public high schools were coeducational is computed from *U.S. Com. Ed. Report for 1873,* table 5, pp. 586–617.

14. Emit Duncan Grizzell, *Origin and Development of the High School in New England Before 1865* (New York: Macmillan, 1923); Arnold Jack Keller, "An Historical Analysis of the Arguments for and against Coeducational Public High Schools in the United States," Ed.D. dissertation, Teachers College, Columbia University, 1971.

15. E. A. Miller, "High Schools in Ohio Prior to 1850," *School Review* 28 (1920): 454–69; Paul E. Belting, *The Development of the Free Public High School in Illinois to 1860* (Springfield, IL: Illinois State Historical Society Journal, 1919); Theodore Sizer, *The Age of the Academy* (New York: Teachers College, 1964).

16. *U.S. Com. Ed. Report for 1873,* pp. 586–643; James H. Blodgett, *Report on Education in the United States at the Eleventh Census, 1890* (Washington, DC: GPO, 1893), pp. 26–33; Theodore R. Sizer, *Secondary Schools at the Turn of the Century* (New Haven: Yale University Press, 1964), pp. 21–22, 39.

17. Barnard, "Public High School," p. 253.

18. Ibid., pp. 253, 254–59.

19. Ibid., pp. 254–55.

20. Ibid., pp. 254.

21. Barnard, "Public High School," p. 255; Labaree, *The Making of an American High School;* Jane Hunter, "Victorian Schoolgirls and Their Diaries: A Perspective on American Adolescence" (unpublished paper, Colby College, 1987).

22. *Census of 1870,* table 13, pp. 461–70.

23. Blodgett, *Report on Education in the United States,* p. 123; U.S. Bureau of Education, *Bien-* *nial Survey of Education, 1918–1920,* p. 497; *U.S. Com. Ed. Report for 1903,* 2:1818.

24. David Labaree found that while social class served as a filter for entrance to Central High School, once a student was enrolled, a rough form of meritocracy prevailed inside the institution. The best predictor of graduation was not class background but grades in courses; see Labaree, *The Making of an American High School,* chap. 3. See also the meritocratic assumptions underlying the report by the Committee of Ten on Secondary School Studies, *Report* (New York: American Book, 1894), p. 41.

25. Patricia Cline Cohen, *A Calculating People: The Spread of Numeracy in Early America* (Chicago: University of Chicago Press, 1982), pp. 139–49; W. A. Fox and Edward T. Thorndike, "The Relationships Between the Different Abilities Involved in the Study of Arithmetic and Sex Differences in Arithmetical Ability," in Edward T. Thorndike, ed., *Hereditary, Correlation, and Sex Differences in School Abilities* (New York: Macmillan, 1903), pp. 34, 38.

26. *Philadelphia Report for 1904,* pp. 23–30; John D. Philbrick, *City School Systems in the United States,* U.S. Bureau of Education, Circular of Information no. 1-1885 (Washington, DC: GPO, 1885), pp. 41–47; *Sketch of the Philadelphia Normal School for Girls* (Washington, DC: GPO, 1882); *San Francisco Report for 1898,* pp. 13–16.

27. Letter of Joan Jacobs Brumberg to authors, November 30, 1983; Hunter, "Victorian Schoolgirls."

28. Krug, *Shaping the American High School,* pp. 12–13; Troen, *The Public and the Schools,* p. 127; Labaree, *The Making of an American High School,* p. 42.

29. Joseph F. Kett, *Rites of Passage: Adolescence in America, 1790 to the Present* (New York: Basic Books, 1977), p. 138; Sara Burstall, *Impressions of American Education in 1908* (London: Longmans, Green, 1909), p. 57; *Atlanta Report for 1894,* p. 16.

30. *Alameda Report for 1900,* p. 27.

PART II
Stratification within and between Schools

When thinking about the structure of schooling in the United States, one must recognize that schools are not created equal. Schools may have different characteristics based on whether they are public or private, segregated or integrated, abundantly endowed or poorly financed. Even within the same school, curricular tracking provides a variety of different experiences and opportunities for students. Such differences between and within schools are consequential for student outcomes and attainment because they structure educational opportunity. The readings in Part II focus on some important areas of stratification between and within schools.

The readings in the first section look at how school sector structures educational experiences. In an ethnography of elite private boarding schools, Peter Cookson and Caroline Hodges Persell provide an extreme example of one side of the stratification between schools. They describe elite private schools that primarily cater to the most privileged members of society. Rather than relying on objective measures of student ability for admittance, private boarding schools are careful to maintain a student body with enhanced social status. In subsequent chapters of Cookson and Hodges' book (not included here), they demonstrate how the already fortunate students who attend private boarding schools are further advantaged by the schools' elite peer environment, generous resource endowment, and extensive linkages to prestigious colleges and universities.

In the next reading in this section, Anthony Bryk, Valerie Lee, and Peter Holland look at a second type of private educational institution: Catholic high schools. They demonstrate that in spite of "ordinary" instructional methods in the classroom, students in these schools possess a high level of interest and engagement in classroom activities. Teacher involvement, they argue, leads to high student engagement. In portions of their work not included here, Bryk and colleagues also discuss how traditional curricular offerings in Catholic high schools (as opposed to "shopping mall" selections of courses that public schools provide) serve as a strong integrating force among students. Less advantaged students tend to benefit from such an arrangement because they are "forced" to enroll in core academic courses, whereas in public school they often have many nonacademic alternatives.

The readings in the second section address the important issues of racial segregation and resource inequality between schools. These interrelated issues have long plagued the educational history of our nation. Although U.S. courts in the not-too-distant past endorsed the concept of "separate but equal" (the 1896 Supreme Court case of *Plessy v. Ferguson* was the basis of law until 1954), few historic examples exist in which subordinate minority groups were segregated without concurrent denial of equal access to resources and opportunity. "The problem of the twentieth century," W. E. B. Du Bois (1903) correctly foresaw, "is the problem of the color line." Since *Brown v. Board of Education* (1954), U.S. courts have outlawed intentional *de jure* racial segregation by public authorities. *De facto* racial segregation, however, still occurs in many U.S.

schools. One must remember this history when recognizing that issues of racial segregation are implicitly related to issues of educational resource inequality.

Perhaps because of the political implications inherent in research on educational resource inequality, there has been continued debate in the education literature about whether increasing financial resources to schools affects student outcomes. For example, conservative economist Eric Hanushek (1994, 1989) has been a harsh critic of plans to increase funding to schools, arguing that school resources are unrelated to student success. More sophisticated empirical research, however, has failed to support Hanushek's position. Recent work by economists Card and Krueger (1992), for example, demonstrates that for every 10 fewer students in a classroom, students can be expected to attain an additional half-year of education and 4 percent more income per year for each and every year of their labor market experience. Research in Tennessee based on the methodologically preferable use of randomized student assignment also provides clear and persuasive support for the conclusion that resources are related to student outcomes (Finn and Achilles 1990). In our own research, we too have found a clear association between increased educational resources and improved student outcomes (Arum and Beattie 1999, Arum 1998, Arum 1996).

The second section begins with a selection that is commonly referred to as "The Coleman Report." The report focused on the interrelated issues of racial segregation and resource inequality. James Coleman and his colleagues demonstrated that peer composition in schools and a student's family background have significant effects on student outcomes. Although the statistical analysis is rudimentary by contemporary standards, the results of the study were influential in the promotion of government plans to bus students to diminish racial segregation and provide equality of educational opportunity.

The second reading in this section is a portion of the results from a prominent study of inequality in the early 1970s. Christopher Jencks and others maintained that differences between schools did not account for variation in student educational attainment. Instead, the authors argued, family background was the crucial determinant of educational attainment. These results have important (if controversial) implications for policy: the best way to affect educational achievement is to invest in families, not in schools. Christopher Jencks has recently backed away from this policy recommendation, as is apparent in the selection by Jencks and Phillips in Part III.

In the next reading, Jonathan Kozol provides a journalistic description of the structure of funding in American schools. Kozol became a well-known writer on education with the publication of *Death at an Early Age* (1967), an account of his experiences as a first-year teacher in the Boston public schools. In the current selection, Kozol focuses on a low-income school district in Texas and discusses Supreme Court cases to demonstrate how current education funding schemes are inherently unequal. Economically disadvantaged families, by and large, must send their children to economically disadvantaged schools.

The fourth reading, by Gary Orfield, looks at the persistence of racial segregation in schools. This research is part of the Harvard Project on School Desegregation, in which Orfield has worked tracking patterns of racial segregation and desegregation in the United States. This reading illustrates that, in spite of *Brown v. Board of Education*, segregation by race has actually increased in many areas of the country. Strict court mandates for school desegregation in southern states have created the lowest levels of racial segregation in the country now in the South. Segregated schools result from a number of important structural factors in society, such as residential segregation, immigration patterns, and birth rates. Orfield calls for a recognition of segregation as something other than purely a racial issue, recognizing the economic and political causes and consequences that interplay to structure different educational opportunities for people of different backgrounds.

In the final reading in this section, Doris Entwisle, Karl Alexander, and Linda Steffel Olson look at stratification between elementary schools. Racial segregation and economic polarization exist for even the youngest students as they make their way through the public schools. The authors propose that because the early grades are so critical for cognitive development and later educational attainment, inequalities between elementary schools have profound effects on children's outcomes. In their previous work, Entwisle and Alexander (1992) demonstrated that low socioeconomic status has more detrimental effects on young student math achievement than does the racial composition of schools. Both black and white students from impoverished economic origins lose ground in math over the summer while school is not in session. However, the authors emphasize that the racial mix of a school can be important: even the poorest African American children do better in integrated schools.

The third section of readings in Part II focuses on stratification systems that operate within schools—specifically, tracking. Often, secondary school students are tracked, or sorted, into academic, general, or vocational tracks. Critics of this practice maintain that it is inherently inequitable, while proponents believe that it promotes more effective learning opportunities. In the first reading of this section, Maureen Hallinan provides an overview of tracking research. She argues that tracking has significant drawbacks, including inadvertently segregating students from one another by race and socioeconomic status. However, she believes that these problems are not inherent in tracking *per se*, but rather that they arise from the way tracking is implemented in schools. Therefore, instead of calling for a wholesale elimination of tracking, Hallinan calls for improvements in its implementation.

The next reading is a portion of Jeannie Oakes's influential ethnographic study *Keeping Track*. Oakes is an outspoken critic of tracking in schools. Here, she argues that tracking structures different opportunities for students in different tracks through distribution of knowledge and level of teacher expectations. Her results suggest that the types of skills learned by high-track students help them get ahead, while the skills taught to low-track students keep them at the bottom.

In the final reading in this section, prominent educational researcher Adam Gamoran asks the question, "Is Ability Grouping Equitable?" Gamoran draws on recent research to demonstrate that tracking rarely bolsters overall achievement in a school and often contributes to inequality between individuals. Thus, he believes, the use of ability grouping is inequitable and should be both reduced and reformed. Although researchers are nearly unanimous in their condemnation of general track programs that fail to prepare students for either college or the workforce, recent research suggests vocational programs—particularly when they are adequately funded—provide positive outcomes for students (Arum and Beattie 1999, Arum 1998, Arum and Shavit 1995).

REFERENCES

ARUM, RICHARD. 1998. "Invested Dollars or Diverted Dreams: The Effect of Resources on Vocational Students' Educational Outcomes." *Sociology of Education* 71:130–51.

ARUM, RICHARD AND IRENEE R. BEATTIE. 1999. "High School Experience and the Risk of Adult Incarceration." *Criminology* (forthcoming).

ARUM, RICHARD AND YOSSI SHAVIT. 1995. "Secondary Vocational Education and the Transition from School to Work." *Sociology of Education* 68:187–204.

CARD, DAVID AND ALAN B. KRUEGER. 1992. "Does School Quality Matter?" *Journal of Political Economy* 100:1–40.

ENTWISLE, DORIS R. AND KARL L. ALEXANDER. 1992. "Summer Setback: Race, Poverty, School Composition, and Mathematics Achievement in the First Two Years of School." *American Sociological Review* 57:72–84.

FINN, JEREMY AND CHARLES ACHILLES. 1990. "Answers and Questions about Class Size: A Statewide Experiment." *American Educational Research Journal* 27:557–77.

HANUSHEK, ERIC. 1989. "The Impact of Differential Expenditures on School Performance." *Educational Researcher* 18:45–65.

HANUSHEK, ERIC ET AL. 1994. *Making Schools Work: Improving Performance and Controlling Costs.* Washington, DC: Brookings Institute.

KOZOL, JONATHAN. 1967. *Death at an Early Age.* Boston, MA: Houghton Mifflin.

School Sector

13

THE CHOSEN ONES

Peter Cookson • Caroline Hodges Persell

For the vast majority of public high-school students, admission to school is a straightforward process. Students either attend the school in their community or, if they have special talents or needs, they may be admitted to a specialized public school where admission is based on openly stated criteria. Private schools, including boarding schools, are rarely democratic from the standpoint of admission. Like private corporations, country clubs, and cooperative real estate holdings, private schools have the right to choose whom they will or will not admit. And while

it is their stated policy not to discriminate on the basis of race or religion, the social traditions of the schools have meant that their student bodies have tended to be homogeneous in terms of family background, religion, and race.

Acceptance into an elite boarding school is in itself a form of ritual, the first step in the prep rite of passage. There was a time when a parent simply rang up the head or dropped by the school and a deal was struck, but by and large those days are gone. Today, applicants and their families must find their way through a maze of forms, letters of recommendation, transcripts, school visits, and interviews. Tenacity is essential to mastering the ritual of acceptance because for the majority of students entrance into the status seminary is not easy, nor is it meant to be. The schools have certain standards to uphold, and often those standards have less to do with ability or willingness than background and style. Tradition weighs heavily in the admissions process and parvenus are at somewhat of a disadvantage in the scramble for acceptance, as they may have yet to learn the subtlety of the prep code, or worse, may not know that such a code exists.

The schools must strike a balance between their ideal class and the class that can be formed from the applicant pool; generally the more elite the school the more carefully the class can be crafted. Tuition at the elite schools is very high and many heads feel obligated to "sell" their schools as good economic and social investments for families. A headmaster at a select 16 school calculated that it cost a family approximately $45 a day to send their child to his school. Where else, he maintained, could you get three meals a day, outstanding facilities, and the best possible education for such a small amount?

Part of the appeal of boarding schools for many parents and students is that they have a choice among a number of different types of schools. The power of choice may indeed be one of the hallmarks of upper-class and high-status life-styles. To hand tailor a child's education by selecting an appropriate school may be worth considerably more than $45 a day for many parents—it may be considered essential for the proper transmission of status.

. . .

Getting In: Raw Material and Prep Poise

When heads appoint teachers to various positions within a school, there is room for a certain margin of error. If a young English teacher turns out to be a magnificent educator, but a mediocre third-string soccer coach,

the foundations of the school are not rocked. But when a head appoints an admissions director, he or she is entrusting the future of the school to that individual, because the admissions director is the school's most important gatekeeper. Aside from those students that are admitted on the basis of what the British call "headmaster's choice," all incoming students must, ultimately, measure up to the standards set by the admissions office. Loyalty, discretion, and judgment are the essential qualities of an admissions officer, and a certain amount of sophistication, good looks, and humor do not hurt. The admissions director must have an acute awareness of the school's needs, as well as the expectations of parents.

Parents expect the elite schools to look elite. Most schools have spacious admissions offices where the emphasis is on understatement and traditional tastes. The antique clock and furniture, along with the original oil paintings and Persian rugs, create an aura of exclusiveness. Some schools wear their status openly by displaying the portraits or busts of their more illustrious alumni. In general, one would hesitate to raise one's voice in the admissions offices of the most elite schools.

Admissions officers and admissions committees are adept at creating student bodies that are tailored specifically for their schools. Certain basic qualities are required of each class admitted; they must be demographically distributed according to the school's admissions goals, ambitious, and reasonably athletic. Schools vary widely on the number of scholarship students they will accept and on the emphasis placed on prior academic ability. Every class must have musicians, artists, athletes, and thinkers if they are to be successful.

A school filled with "brains" stands the risk of driving away the less brainy but wealthier families. A school that is entirely "prepped out" may find its reputation among college admissions officers slipping. Too many "jocks" make teachers unhappy, too few jocks make students and alumni unhappy. Moreover, the picture is complicated by the search for diversity. Girls at coed schools must be as strong academically and socially as boys, otherwise they cannot hold their own.

It is generally believed that prep school students are highly qualified. At the more selective schools, students must take the Secondary School Aptitude Test (SSAT). Unlike colleges, however, the prep schools do not uniformly publish the range and average scores of entering students on these tests. Although entering freshmen in some select 16 schools, such as Groton and Exeter, have high median SSAT scores, other elite schools admit a number of students whose scores fall below the average.[1] Student grades and recommendations are also required for admission, although how the schools evaluate these measures is not known, underscoring the private nature of these institutions.

It is not by chance that most prep school students have shiny, well-combed hair, are trim, healthy, and at least reasonably attractive. The social psychiatrist Robert Coles contrasts the attention to appearance and self of privileged children with that of other children:

> With none of the other American children I have worked with have I heard such a continuous and strong emphasis put on the "self." In fact, other children rarely if ever think about themselves in the way children of well-to-do and rich parents do—with insistence, regularity, and, not least, out of a learned sense of obligation. These privileged ones are children who live in homes with many mirrors. They have mirrors in their rooms, large mirrors in adjoining bathrooms. When they were

three or four they were taught to use them; taught to wash their faces, brush their teeth, comb their hair. Personal appearance matters and becomes a central objective for such children. (Coles 1997:380)

Part of the screening process is to weed out those who will not fit in. Discovering what "fitting in" actually meant to admissions officers was difficult, however, because they were guarded in how much information they would reveal. After all, merit is only part of the criteria for admission; other intangibles, such as family wealth and social standing, also count for a great deal.

Thus the admissions process remains relatively secretive, although even the most casual observation of the students who go to the most elite schools leads one to believe that the presentation of the self plays an important role in how students are selected for admission. Part of the prep presentation of self is the public display of confidence and control—poise. The first step on the road to "being somebody" is to "act like somebody," even if you are not quite sure who that somebody is.

Schools vary in how they actually go about deciding who will be offered a place, who will be put on the waiting list, and who will "not be invited to attend"—reject is not a boarding school word. Most schools claim to need all the information on applicants by the end of January, although many will entertain applications after that date. Some schools have rolling admissions, evaluating applications more or less continually. Generally, a set of complete folders is read by a committee composed of faculty members from different departments, some coaching staff and, very probably, the admissions director and one or two assistants. Each member of a committee will read a great number of applications, ensuring that the biases of any single reader do not unduly influence the decision-making process. Naturally, these group readings entail a certain amount of horse trading and informal information sharing: children of alumni will have certain advantages, as will outstanding students and athletes.

An important element in the decision-making process is trying to estimate which families will send their children to a particular school if they are admitted. No school wants to admit a large number of students who then choose to go to other schools. Not only is a school's prestige on the line, but, practically speaking, there is a problem of determining the ratio of acceptances to enrollments. If too many students enroll, there is overcrowding; if too few enroll, the consequences are obvious. So the question of determining which parents are serious about sending their children to a prospective school is an important consideration. A waiting list, therefore, becomes a school's insurance policy against finding itself, come fall, under-enrolled.

Rejection from an applicant's school of choice can be traumatic to both students and their families. The families have invested themselves in the admissions process and rejection implies not only a lack of academic attainment, but a lack of social standing as well. Often rejection notices are couched in terms not of the student's failure, but of the school simply not having enough places. Some schools will counsel parents on alternative boarding schools that might be appropriate for their child. A student who fails to gain admission to a top boarding school may have to be content with a school with a somewhat less prestigious reputation. Competition among schools of similar prestige is intense, but it is minimal among schools of differing prestige.

Like the minuet of the seventeenth century, the admissions dance is highly stylized and a bit baroque. The complexity of the admissions process, of course, is not accidental. Boarding schools must retain a firm grip on who they admit, because, if the "wrong" students are admitted, then the historical mission of the schools to mold patrician and parvenu into an elite cadre will be jeopardized. The raw material must be suitable to the "treatment."

An examination, then, of who actually goes to boarding schools reveals a great deal about the schools and their perception of their place within the larger educational and social system. If people can be known by the company they keep, cannot schools be known by the students they admit?

Prep School Families

Income

F. Scott Fitzgerald is reputed to have once said to Ernest Hemingway, "The rich are different from you and I." To which Hemingway replied, "Yes, they have more money." If Fitzgerald had said, "Preps are different than you and I," Hemingway's response would have been the same: One only has to glance at the endowments of most of the major schools to see that their alumni are affluent. It is not uncommon for an elite school to net more than a million dollars a year in their annual fund drive. Happen by an elite school during a parents' weekend, and the collective value of the automobiles in the parking lot would be enough to build a reasonably well-equipped public school in a low-income neighborhood.

. . .

Forty-six percent of the boarding school families in our sample of twenty schools have annual incomes of more than $100,000 a year. An additional 20 percent of boarding school families have incomes between $75,000 and $100,000 per year. Only 3 percent have incomes of less than $15,000, 7 percent fall into the $15,000 to $25,000 a year range, and 24 percent fall between $25,001 and $75,000 a year. By contrast, in 1981, 9.7 percent of all American families earned more than $50,000 a year, and the median family income was slightly less than $24,000 a year. Forty-one percent of American families made less than $20,000 a year which, after taxes, equals about what it costs to send one child to boarding school for one year.

Students who board at school are only slightly more affluent than day students, but the families that send their daughters to girls schools are very well off indeed, even compared to other boarding school families; 58 percent have incomes in excess of $100,000 a year. Students at all-boys schools also come from affluent families; 53 percent have incomes in excess of $100,000 a year.

Foreign students are as affluent as the Americans, as are the Asian-American students in our sample. Among black students, these are also affluent families; 15 percent come from $100,000 or more a year homes. There were no major differences between freshmen and seniors in our sample, although freshmen appeared to come from slightly wealthier families (perhaps because they can afford four years of boarding school, whereas seniors, due to finances, may not have attended for all four years). A wealthy group of students come from Jewish homes, 41 percent having incomes of $100,000 a year or more. Presbyterians, Episcopalians, and Catholics are the next most wealthy groups, although Catholics are a weak fourth in affluence.

Parents who are prep school graduates have higher incomes than those who are not prep school graduates, and students who reported three or more relatives as boarding school alumni are proportionately more

wealthy; 54 percent of these families have incomes exceeding $100,000 a year.

Parental Education and Occupations

Income alone, however, is inadequate as a single descriptor of American boarding school families. This is a world where money matters, but other things matter as well. Boarding school families in our sample are well educated; 85 percent of the fathers have B.A.'s, as do 75 percent of the mothers. Nearly two-thirds of the fathers have attended graduate or professional school, compared to less than one-tenth of the fathers of high-school seniors nationally. One-third of boarding school mothers have attended graduate or professional schools, while nationally less than one in twenty mothers of high-school students have attended graduate school.

Given the high educational level of these families, it is not surprising that 50 percent of the fathers are professionals and 40 percent are managers. Specifically, 12 percent of our sample's fathers are doctors, 10 percent are attorneys, and 9 percent are bankers, with other professions following far behind. The academies attract some children of teachers, writers, and editors, but, proportionately, their number is small compared to the children of doctors, lawyers, and bankers. Progressive schools attract the children of doctors, girls schools attract bankers' and lawyers' daughters, with lawyers also preferring Episcopal schools for their children. College teachers seem to choose progressive schools, with academies running second.

Sixty-three percent of the mothers of boarding school students work, slightly less than the national average for mothers of high-school students, 71 percent of whom work. Of those who are not working, most are housewives. Boarding school mothers are less likely than the fathers, but more likely than either men or women in the national population, to occupy professional and managerial jobs. Slightly more than one-third of these mothers are professionals, and one in eight are managers or administrators. One out of thirteen are clerical workers. The rest are scattered across various other occupations.

Marital Status

Boarding school families in this sample are stable in terms of the percentage who remain married. Seventy-five percent of the parents in this sample are married. This is virtually the same figure reported by the recent National Association of Independent Schools (NAIS)[2] survey (Talbot 1983). Thirteen percent of the parents in our sample are divorced, 2 percent separated and 4 percent widowed. The remaining 6 percent of the students are living with step-parents or other relatives. Foreign families are also stable: 82 percent of the parents are married. Families that send their children to Episcopal, Catholic, or academy schools are the most stable, with the marriage rate above 80 percent. Western schools tend to attract a higher percentage of students whose parents are divorced, while less than one-half of progressive school parents are married.

Geographical Origins

In a survey of the catalogues of the 55 schools we visited, we found that it is not uncommon for a school with between 500 and 600 students to have representatives from thirty or more states and students from at least two dozen foreign countries. Even smaller schools, with between 200 and 300 students, will have students from twenty or more states and ten or more foreign countries. Some schools, however, count students as coming from foreign countries when, in fact, they are children of United States citizens serving overseas, often in the State Department or with multinational corporations. Based on our questionnaires at 20 schools, we found that foreign students, that is, non-U.S. citizens, make up between 3 percent and 11 percent of the schools' student bodies. On average, 7 percent of American boarding school students are non-citizens. Catholic schools have the most foreign students, while Episcopal schools have the fewest. Many foreign students come from high-income families in the Middle East, South America, and Asia.

While most boarding schools do have cosmopolitan student bodies, they also support local constituencies. A Massachusetts school will have a good number of students from that state and nearby states, and there are generally a large number of Californians in California schools. Despite the conscious attempts by several large schools to draw "national student bodies," the majority of students even at those schools live within a five-hour drive. Smaller schools draw even more heavily from their immediate state or region.

Global Travel

Boarding school families travel a great deal and they take their children with them. Sixty-nine percent of the students in the questionnaire sample of 20 schools have traveled outside of the United States, half of them have been to Europe, 15 percent to Asia, 13 percent to South America, 8 percent to Africa, and 4 percent to Australia. Progressive, entrepreneurial, academy, and western school families must be hopping on and off planes regularly, as less than 13 percent of these students have never been outside of the United States. Jewish families are the top travelers—only 12 percent have not been outside the United States. Among black students, 44 percent have never been outside of the United States.

It is by no means unusual that boarding school students, no matter what their grade level, are better traveled than their teachers, creating an interesting paradox. In the teaching of geography, for instance, one may wonder who is the expert and who is the learner? And many of those students are not just tourists. Quite often they visit foreign families and stay for extended periods. This sense of internationalism is an important part of boarding school culture, and undoubtedly some students feel that the world is their oyster.

Books and Computers

Boarding school families in the questionnaire sample own a great many books: 51 percent have 500 books or more in their home, and less than one percent have fewer than 25 books. Progressive school parents must be inveterate readers, as 70 percent have libraries of more than 500 books, as do 60 percent of Episcopalian families. Western school families tend to read less than other boarding school families, or, at least, collect fewer books, since only 40 percent of them have more than 500 books. Academy school families have only slightly larger than average libraries, as do entrepreneurial school families. Catholics own fewer books than the average boarding school family, and minorities do not appear to make heavy investments in books.

Despite the linear orientation of boarding school families, they are entering the computer age, with 21 percent owning computers. Western school families are most likely to own a computer, nearly one-third do, while Catholic school families have the fewest home computers. Thirty-six percent of Asian boarding school families have computers, as do 28 percent of Jewish families. Nationally only 8 percent of households have home computers, and even in Silicon Valley

only an estimated 25 percent of households have them (Rogers and Larsen 1984, 171).

Legacies

Elite schools vary in the number of alumni they admit or attract and in the last decades former public school families have been attracted to them. A 1983 National Association of Independent Schools study of boarding schools found that 57 percent of their students had come from public school and that 41 percent of their respondents' parents had never attended an independent school. For 53 percent of the students in the NAIS study at least one member of their extended family had attended boarding school. In our study, we found a similar percentage—54—of those attending boarding school have at least one relative who attended boarding school. These "legacy" students create a critical mass at many boarding schools, especially at the Episcopal, girls and academy schools whose student bodies are between 55 and 75 percent legacy students.

Legacy students differ from their non-legacy peers in terms of their backgrounds. They are more likely to be white and Episcopalian, their fathers are more educated and their mothers slightly more educated than non-legacy parents. No matter what legacy students' religious backgrounds, their parents are far more likely to hold prestigious occupational positions, and earn more than non-legacy families. Sixty percent of the students in our questionnaire sample who came from families earning more than $100,000 a year are legacies; only 2 percent have incomes of less than $15,000 a year.

For our study, we created a measure we called deep-prep. Deep-prep students are those who have had three or more relatives who attended boarding school. Over 26 percent of our questionnaire sample were deep-prep students, and they were predominantly Episcopalian, Presbyterian, and other Protestant denominations. Episcopalian schools have as many as 42 percent of their students come from deep-prep families. Girls schools also have many deep-prep families, and apparently the progressive tradition has become intergenerational, because the progressive schools attract a number of deep-preps. Academies have relatively few—16 percent—deep-preps. Girls are slightly more likely to come from deep-prep families than boys. Sixty-six percent of deep-prep fathers have graduate or professional degrees, and their wives are nearly all college graduates.

Because boarding schools have historically educated the sons and daughters of America's Protestant Establishment, we created a measure that identified those Episcopalian and Presbyterian students who have at least one relative who was a boarding school alumnus, are white, and who have an estimated family income of more than $100,000 a year. Eight percent of the sample fell into this category. These families tend to send their children to the entrepreneurial, girls, academy, and Episcopal schools. One-sixth of all girls schools' families are Protestant Establishment, as are 40 percent of the students at Episcopal schools—to no one's surprise.

. . .

Boarding School Student Bodies

. . .

Day Students

Overall, 24 percent of the respondents in our sample were day students. The lowest percent of day students at any school was 2 percent and the highest proportion was 62 percent. The entrepreneurial, girls, and Catholic schools are likely to be one-third day students, the academies, Episcopal, and progressive schools have less than 20 per-cent, and the western schools less than 10 percent. Select 16 schools have more boarding students (85 percent) than other schools (68 percent).

Day students, as a group, are quite similar to boarding students in terms of their family backgrounds. Much like freshman-senior comparisons, one is struck by the homogeneity between day and boarding students. If anything, day students are from more stable homes (81 percent of their parents are married), are better traveled, and have slightly larger libraries than boarding students. Day families have as high incomes as boarding families, and many day-school fathers are doctors. In general, day-school fathers have slightly higher occupational prestige scores than boarding-school fathers. Less than 2 percent of day students are black. The day-school population appears to be composed primarily of the children of local professionals. The number of day girls and day boys is nearly equal and there are more freshmen day students than senior day students.

The Issue of Diversity

"Diversity" is a prep school watchword. In the last twenty years, boarding schools have been proud of the increasing diversity of their student bodies. But how truly diverse is the boarding school world?

It is no surprise that the boarding school world is basically white. Ninety percent of boarding school students are Caucasian,[3] compared to 83 percent for the population at large. Episcopal, girls, and Catholic schools are more than 90 percent white.

Through private programs such as *A Better Chance*, black students from disadvantaged backgrounds are given opportunities to attend boarding schools, yet their representation in boarding schools is below their representation in society; 12 percent of the American population and 19 percent of the public high-school population was black in 1982. No private boarding school comes close to this number of black students. Some boarding schools have as few as one percent black students and, on average, 4 percent of boarding-school students are black. While a number of these students have low-income backgrounds, and receive scholarships, boarding schools also attract a great number of the black middle class; 29 percent of the black students in the sample had a relative who had attended boarding school, and 36 percent of the black fathers in the sample had obtained a graduate or professional degree. Thirty-two percent of the mothers had obtained a graduate or professional degree and 22 percent of the fathers owned their own business. Compared to the statistics for the black population in general, the divorce rate among black boarding school families is low, and their income is high. Eighty percent of black mothers work, and one-third of the black students are Baptists.

Surprisingly, there are more Asian students in this sample than blacks. Five percent is Asian. The academies, entrepreneurial, and western schools enroll a high number of Asian students. At least one-third of them are non-U.S. citizens, although 53 percent of these students indicated that one or more of their relatives attended boarding school. Seventy-four percent of the fathers have obtained a professional or graduate degree and 42 percent own their own business. Asian families have the lowest divorce rate of any group (93 percent have married parents) and have traveled a great deal, especially in North America and Asia. One-quarter of the Asian fathers earn $100,000 or more a year.

Religion

There was a time when elite schools simply did not accept non-Protestants, but today one-quarter of all boarding-school students are now Catholic, close to the 27 percent of Catholic-Americans. Naturally, the Catholic schools attract Catholics in large numbers, but academies, entrepreneurial, girls, and to a lesser extent, the western schools also attract them. Episcopal and progressive schools have the fewest Catholics.

The accusation of anti-Semitism has been laid at the doorstep of boarding schools since the late nineteenth century. But today 11 percent of the students in our sample of 2,475 are Jewish, compared to less than 3 percent in the general population. Entrepreneurial schools enroll a particularly high number of Jewish students (16 percent), followed by progressive schools, western schools, and the academies. In our sample there were no Jewish respondents at either the Episcopal schools or the Catholic schools. Jewish families have fewer legacies than any other group except blacks. They are the most highly educated group: 71 percent of Jewish fathers have professional or graduate degrees, and 45 percent of Jewish mothers have the same level of education. Sixty-five percent of Jewish fathers own their own business, and 22 percent of Jewish mothers own their own business. The divorce rate among Jewish families is relatively high in our sample, compared to other religious groups.

Sex

Another major admissions decision within the last two decades has been to admit girls to what were formerly all-boys schools. Overall, 39 percent of our sample were females. Progressive schools, western schools, and public schools come close to having equal numbers of girls and boys, partly, of course, because many of them have always been coeducational. The girls at boarding schools have similar family backgrounds to the boys'. Proportionately, there are a few more girls who come from Episcopalian homes. Girls who attend coed schools come from families with slightly lower incomes than do the boys at coed schools. Girls' mothers tend to work outside of the home a little more often than boys' mothers and, interestingly, they tend to come from families with a strong boarding-school tradition. Girls' mothers are slightly more educated than boys' mothers and slightly more likely to be divorced.

Stability and Continuity in the Prep School World

In sum, boarding school students are overwhelmingly from high-income professional and managerial families. Three-quarters of their parents are married, only 7 percent are non-citizens, 5 percent are Asians, and 4 percent are black. More than half (54 percent) of the students have one or more relatives who also attended boarding school. The students and their families travel widely; nearly three-quarters have traveled outside of the United States.

The students have a high degree of self-esteem and efficacy and value having strong friendships more than anything else as their life goal, although they seek even higher status occupations than the already high ones held by their parents.

The schools exhibit a rather remarkable capacity to maintain stability in the students they admit. Whether it is comparisons between day and boarding students, freshmen and seniors, or boys and girls, the relatively new arrivals closely resemble their traditional counterparts. Yet, there does appear to be some increase in the racial and religious diversity of current student bodies compared to traditional ones.

Boarding school students, by any reasonable standard, are elite—whether they come from the old monied patrician families or upwardly mobile parvenu families. Boarding schools not only choose their students, they can create their student bodies with precision. With the exception of coeducation, change has been slow in the boarding school world, and decisions are made carefully with a view to their long-term effect. Public schools and even many private day schools simply do not have this option. The select 16 boarding schools can be particularly selective in who they admit.

NOTES

1. The median score nationally on the SSAT is 309 and a score of 348 places a student in the 99th percentile. The median score for Groton and Exeter is 325.5 (*Independent Schools: A Handbook*, 1982).
2. The NAIS is a national organization that many private schools join. In the 1981 *Handbook of Private Schools'* population of 289 leading secondary boarding schools, 78 percent belong to NAIS.
3. The exact percentage of whites in the questionnaire sample of twenty schools is 90.3, of blacks, 4.3, and of Asians, 5.3. Due to rounding, the total percent equals 99 rather than 100.

REFERENCES

COLES, ROBERT. 1977. *Children of Privilege*. Boston: Little, Brown.

ROGERS, EVERETT M. AND JUDITH K. LARSEN. 1984. *Silicon Valley Fever: The Growth of High-Tech Culture*. New York: Basic Books.

TALBOT, MARJO. 1983. "The New Student Marketing Survey." Report, Committee on Boarding Schools, National Association of Independent Schools, Boston, Massachusetts.

14

CLASSROOM LIFE

Anthony Bryk ● *Valerie Lee* ● *Peter Holland*

. . .

General Features of Instruction

Use of Instructional Materials

In the classes we visited, teachers relied extensively on textbooks as the major instructional source, especially in mathematics, science, and foreign language courses. In English, social studies, and religion classes we were more likely to find some teacher-produced materials being used. Most instruction took place in conventional classrooms, although we noted a few classes in such makeshift settings as a corner of an auditorium or part of a basement cafeteria. The traditional seating pattern in the classrooms placed students in rows of desks or tables facing the teacher in the front. An occasional class had a seminar arrangement, with students and teacher seated in a small circle facing each other, but the sheer number of students made this seating plan infeasible for most classes.[1] Although the physical resources within classrooms were modest, teachers had access to the basic instructional materials required to perform their job: books, audiovisual equipment, maps, globes, posters, and charts.

Teachers chose various approaches to decorating their rooms. Bulletin boards often displayed posters, diagrams, and color pictures relevant to the current instructional unit. Items encouraging a strong school spirit were common, as were slogans expressing pride in the school: "We are the Royal Family!" (at St. Peter's, where the team nickname is the Royals). Posters exhorted attendance at school events: "May the Force Be with Us against Aquinas Prep on Friday! Get Your Ticket for THE GAME Today." Students' art projects, their collages for religion classes, and examples of their writing were also prominently exhibited in classrooms. These displays conveyed two clear images: we are a community, and your individual contributions are valued here.

Classroom Activities

During our second round of field research, we employed a structured observation protocol to document teachers' use of class time in fifty-seven classrooms within our seven field sites. Substantial proportions of classroom time were spent in discussion, teachers' introduction of new material in the form of lectures and demonstrations, review of previous homework, and in-class writing assignments (see Table 14.1). Virtually all of these activities were directed by the teacher and involved the whole class. Student-led discussion and cooperative work among students in small groups were uncommon. External interruptions such as public address announcements or classroom visitors were

TABLE 14.1   Amount of time spent on various classroom activities in Catholic high schools (based on observed classes in field-sample schools)

Activity	Time Spent (in minutes)	Time Spent (%)
Discussion	12.4	27.0
Instruction, new material	10.3	22.5
Homework review	6.7	14.6
Assigned work in class	5.9	12.9
Clerical	2.6	5.7
Quiz, drill	2.1	4.9
Review of quiz, drill	1.8	3.9
Oral reading	1.8	3.9
Review of previous work	1.6	3.5
Silent reading	0.5	1.1
PA announcements	0.1	0.2
Total	45.8	100.0

also rare. Similar time-use statistics have been reported elsewhere. A recent large-scale survey of Catholic high schools serving low-income youth showed a heavy emphasis on teacher-directed activities with the whole class. A large survey of public high school classrooms reported a similar allotment of time.[2]

Virtually every class we visited used some amount of time for the teacher to lecture the whole group. In most classes some individual coaching of students by the teacher occurred, typically during drill and practice activities based on in-class worksheets or homework. Although some classroom discussion time (particularly in English, religion, and social studies) involved give-and-take . . . , much of the discussion had a recitation quality; teachers asked questions to which students were expected to respond with the "correct" answer.

Regular testing and assigned homework are basic components of teaching. Teachers typically gave at least one quiz per week. The data in Table 14.1 actually underreport the amount of class time devoted to testing activities, because in order to maximize the information gained during our field research, we did not observe classrooms in which a full-period test was under way. All testing time referred to in Table 14.1 was devoted to short quizzes. Data from surveyed teachers indicated that full-period tests occur, on average, every two or three weeks.[3]

About two-thirds of the teachers in our field sites reported assigning homework at least three times a week, and over half the students reported spending more than five hours per week on homework. Data from *High School and Beyond* . . . indicate that such responses are typical of Catholic secondary school students. Most teachers (62 percent) indicated that they "always" or "usually" graded the homework they had assigned.

Student Engagement

Assessing the engagement of students in classroom instruction can be an elusive task, because it involves assessing cognitive processes that are not directly observable. We approached this problem in two ways. First, we looked for indicators of noninvolvement in classroom activities, such as students whose heads were on their desks or who were staring out the window; students who were without books, paper, or pencils; or students who talked to others during class instructions. Second, we noted signs of active student participation, such as contributing to class discussions, working out problems at the board, reading aloud from the text, or asking questions. At two predetermined points, 10 minutes into each class and 10 minutes before the end of each class, we recorded what each student was doing. In the fifty-seven classes we observed, almost 90 percent of the students were engaged at the initial checkpoint, and slightly

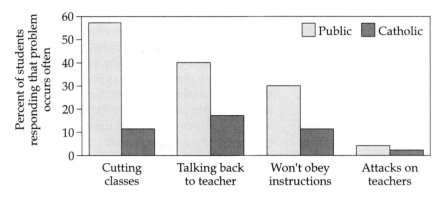

FIGURE 14.1   Student reports about classroom discipline problems: Percentage of students who indicate that these problems occur "often." Data from *High School and Beyond.*

under 80 percent were engaged at the later assessment.

These data suggest a high level of student engagement in classroom instruction.[4] Even more important, however, is that the relatively small proportion of students not engaged in class activities refrained from interfering with the engagement of others. Across all the classes we visited, we did not observe a single incident of disruptive student behavior. Teacher questionnaire data suggest that the absence of disruption is a general characteristic of classroom life within these schools. Fewer than 5 percent of the teachers reported *any* of the following problems: student fights in class, students under the influence of alcohol or drugs, physical or verbal abuse of students, students ridiculing other students, and excessive absences or tardiness. Failure to do homework and minor infractions were cited by fewer than 15 percent of the teachers as regular problems within their classes.

Data from *High School and Beyond* allow us to generalize these findings about the infrequency of disruptive behavior in Catholic high schools (see Figure 14.1). The incidence of students' cutting classes, refusing to obey instructions, talking back to teachers, and instigating physical attacks on teachers is very low, both in comparison with public schools and in absolute terms.

The absence of disruptive behavior is further complemented by student attitudes that are very positive about their schools and teachers. The vast majority of students express a strong interest in school (both on their part and on the part of their friends), believe that the academic quality of their school is either good or excellent, and agree almost unanimously that their school has a good reputation within the community (see Figure 14.2). Moreover, despite the rather ordinary character of instruction in many Catholic school classrooms, students describe their teachers as unusually patient, respectful, and happy with their work (see Figure 14.3).

. . . Teachers are firm and committed to high standards in classroom work, but they simultaneously display a strong personal interest in students, both in and outside of the classroom. Both their language and their behavior bespeak a strong sense of commitment to individual students and to a school life permeated with Christian personalism.

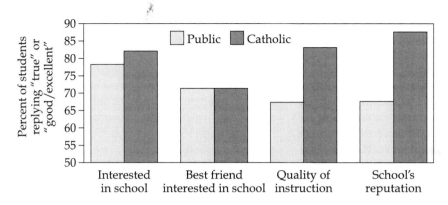

FIGURE 14.2 Student reports about their interest in school and school ratings (good or excellent). Data from *High School and Beyond.*

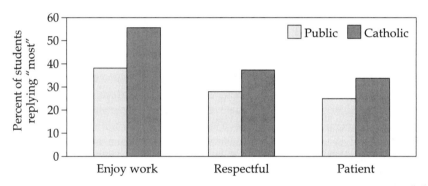

FIGURE 14.3 Student reports about their teachers. Data from *High School and Beyond.*

The Character of Work

Teachers' Work Load

Teachers in our field schools reported spending an average of 8.25 hours at their schools each day. Typically, a teacher arrives shortly after 7:30 A.M. and leaves at approximately 3:45 in the afternoon. He or she normally teaches five 45-minute periods per day, which might include a single section in one course and two sections each in two others. In addition to the almost 4 hours of class each

day, teachers might spend about 45 minutes on class preparation, approximately an hour on lunch and other personal business, and 30 minutes in passing between classes. The remainder of the typical teacher's time on campus is spent correcting papers and working with students individually.

After the instructional day, many teachers coach athletic teams or supervise other extracurricular activities. Half of the teachers in the schools we visited took responsibility for at least one after-school activity, which might consume another 6 hours per week of their time. For those with coaching responsibility, the time demands were somewhat greater, averaging nearly 11 hours per week during the athletic season. Half of the teachers also averaged over 8 hours per week on school-related responsibilities such as bingo, fund-raising, and parents' meetings. More generally, over 80 percent of our field-sampled teachers reported that they frequently worked with individual students beyond the school day, either before or after school. Similarly, over 80 percent were actively involved in attending extracurricular activities such as athletics, drama, or music presentations.

In addition to over 40 hours at school, teachers reported devoting an extra 8 to 10 hours per week at home on correcting papers, reading for class assignments, preparing for class and other school-related work. The combination of regular teaching, extracurricular activities, and home preparation time meant that many teachers in our field sites were spending well over 50 hours per week on their work. Similar data have been reported for Catholic secondary schools serving low-income youth; about a third of the teachers in that sample of 106 Catholic high schools indicated that they devoted more than 55 hours per week to school responsibilities.[5]

A brief look at a typical day for a Catholic secondary school teacher—in this case, Margie McDaniel, a second-year English teacher at St. Peter's—helps to pull these numbers together into a more coherent picture. Arriving at school at 7:45, McDaniel begins her teaching day with homeroom at 8:15. Between 8:30 and 9:20, she teaches an English I class for students of average ability. Her next instructional period, a remedial reading section for fifteen students, begins immediately thereafter. During her free period (10:10 to 11:00), she corrects papers or prepares materials for one of her later classes. The period

from 11:00 to 11:50 finds her teaching an honors section of English I. Lunch with faculty colleagues consumes only 20 minutes, with the remaining half hour of the lunch break usually spent meeting with students from one of the activities for which she takes responsibility. Her second section of English I begins at 12:40, followed immediately by a regular English II section.

The seasons dictate the remainder of her afternoon schedule. In the winter she coaches the girls' varsity basketball team from 2:45 to 4:15, which is normally followed by an hour or so of administrative chores associated with her position as girls' athletic director. The fall finds her coaching junior varsity volleyball; in the spring she assists with softball. On the few days without athletic practice, she might spend a few afternoon hours on her duties as English department chair. Rarely does she leave St. Peter's before 5 P.M., and on many occasions she is there well into the evening, either for athletic events or for parents' meetings. In addition, McDaniel often spends some portion of her weekend time at the school for various extracurricular activities.

Despite this large commitment of time, McDaniel was enthusiastic about her teaching and coaching at St. Peter's, and especially about the school's community spirit. Knowing the students both academically and personally and influencing their personal growth has been rewarding. Although the hectic schedule sometimes overwhelms her, she claims to have gained both organizational skills and the ability to use time productively.

Teachers frequently offered comments linking positive testimony about school life with remarks about how stressful it could be. In particular, they mentioned the daily demands of correcting papers, admonishing students, monitoring cafeterias and hallways, meeting with parents, and extended workdays. While expressing a real love for their work, they also worried about how long they could keep up the pace.

Even so, interviews and surveys from teachers in our field schools suggest a high level of job satisfaction among Catholic high school teachers, observations that are corroborated by survey data from NCEA (1986) and from *HS&B*.[6] Compared with their public school counterparts, Catholic high school teachers are more likely to be satisfied with their work, to feel personally efficacious, and to feel that good performance is recognized. They are also much less likely to report that their job requires excessive time for administrative tasks. Most of these teachers would advise young people to pursue teaching careers. The teachers' major discordant perception involves their salaries—Catholic school teachers are only half as likely as public school teachers to report that teaching allows them to earn a decent income. Because the average salaries in Catholic high schools are only about 70 percent of those in public schools, this response is not surprising.

Role Perspectives

Another distinctive feature of teaching in Catholic high schools is the view teachers have of their work. In general, teachers see their role in broad terms, involving considerably more than just specialized instruction in a subject area. These teachers are as concerned about the kind of person that each student becomes as about how much a student knows. Many teachers describe their work as a kind of ministry and their role as one of shaping young adults. We observed numerous instances of teacher behaviors consistent with these reports. Frequent personal accounts from both students and parents provided further corroboration.

We interviewed teachers about their views of their role within the school, their reason for teaching in a Catholic school, and their feelings about their work. To tell this story, we rely heavily on their comments. Virtually every teacher saw his or her work as extending beyond the five-class, seven-hour day. Although committed to teaching, class preparation, and the importance of the instructional programs, they also emphasized the personal values and the sense of community at their schools. A woman religious teacher at St. Cornelius' described her work: "I don't view it as a job. What I see here, and one of the reasons our religious community is here, is for the education of the poor . . . I think the importance of this work is not only in the academics but also because we teach personal values and are concerned about meeting students' other needs as part of what we do."

A faculty member at St. Edward's responded to our questions:

> I see what we do as teachers on three levels. We are role models, in that we are living examples of the beliefs that are taught in religion classes. We also have an obligation to teach values. I used to think that I was a Spanish and French teacher. Now I know that my values are at least as important as the content I teach. Finally, I remind myself that we play a four-year part in these students' lifetimes . . . What we have to transmit is a vision for the future to help them mold themselves into the kind of persons they want to become.

A faculty member at St. Frances' spoke about the importance of integrating life within learning in her classes: "As far as I'm concerned . . . besides the background on literature, grammar, and the like, we discuss life and the problems that students are likely to encounter. It is just as important that they learn about life while they are here as that they learn about academics."

Teachers in Catholic high schools see themselves as role models for their students. One teacher stated quite succinctly a view that was expressed by many others: "Even if teachers don't teach religion, we teach by our lives. Basically, this school is a good environment, and we teach by our example and who we are. We strive to make students more conscious of the world around them and how they fit into it."

Some teachers spoke about their work as "helping people, being involved, and feeling fulfilled as a result," an important part of which involves supporting students with troubled families. Principals and counselors frequently commented on the growing number of students whose families were experiencing divorce, unemployment, or other problems. One teacher described the surrogate-parent role that teachers and schools served for some students: "It's amazing when you hear them talk about their families. It's like they don't have any stability at home. Their life here at the school is about the only thing that is stable in their environment. I feel at times that we function almost like parents for some students."

In broad terms, many faculty view their multiple roles with the school—teacher, coach, counselor, and adult model—as a form of ministry.[7] The character of the social encounters that results from this view is pervasive and readily apparent. A field observer in another study of Catholic schools echoed our experience: "There's a feeling here that is hard to miss if you spend any time here . . . a tremendous rapport between students and faculty. The faculty is extremely concerned about the kids, not only academically. A number of people are involved in other areas nobody even knows about. I think at any one time probably the whole faculty is involved in something, for somebody."[8] This is personalism lived, day in and day out.

The character of instruction in Catholic high school appears quite traditional in format, setting, use of materials, and pedagogy. We observed some examples of excellent teaching, but, on average, the technical aspects of teaching in Catholic high schools can be described as "ordinary." Although we saw more emphasis on testing and homework than appears to be the case in public high schools, in most other respects the teaching techniques employed in Catholic secondary schools are quite similar to what have been reported for public schools.

The first surprise for us in our fieldwork findings was students' positive reactions to this rather ordinary teaching and their high levels of engagement with classroom activities. The prevailing professional rhetoric at the time we undertook these visits argued that a more appealing and diverse curriculum and more scintillating instruction were necessary in order to promote greater student engagement in learning. Neither of these two desiderata was especially prevalent in Catholic high schools, yet engagement was occurring. Trying to make sense of this observation eventually led us to a new dimension of inquiry, focusing on the quality of human relations within the school, and to the evolution of a set of ideas about communal school organization.

Similarly, the roles teachers assumed in Catholic high schools were broader and the perspectives they offered on their work different from what we had expected. The typical teacher's work load was heavy, including multiple class preparations and extensive extracurricular involvement. Low salaries were a major source of dissatisfaction, especially given the commitments involved. Nonetheless, these teachers spoke very positively about their work and the considerable psychic rewards it afforded them.[9] To them, teaching values and shaping the lives of young people by their actions and their example was as important as the subject matter presented in classes. This broad concern and extended teacher role was not lost on students, who saw their instructors as interested in them, as patient and understanding, yet also as firm and committed to high standards. Such teacher personalism, which seemed to pervade the myriad social encounters within the schools, was infectious, pulling students strongly toward engagement in school life.

Initially we saw little connection between our observations of teacher commitment and student engagement. Although both were quite common in all the schools we visited, we did not at first understand or link them. As our work proceeded, however, we came to appreciate the influence of tradition in these schools. We also slowly began to see these events as subsidiarity at work—fomenting social ties, building social solidarity—where both the academic structure and the communal organization of the school were key contributors.

NOTES

1. The rectangular row and column seating arrangement appears to be a universal characteristic of secondary education. Other researchers, such as Goodlad (1984) and Sizer (1984), have found similar arrangements in the field sites they visited.
2. For Catholic high schools, see NCEA (1986), pp. 141–2. For public high schools, see Goodlad (1984), p. 107.
3. The teachers in NCEA (1986) report that about 10 percent of their class time is devoted to tests and quizzes. These results are reasonably consistent with our data if we factor in a full-period test every three weeks, in addition to the 2.1 minutes of quiz time we observed.
4. These engagement rates appear to be higher than those reported in field studies of public high school classrooms. See, for example, the descriptive accounts in Sizer (1984). See also Powell, Farrar, and Cohen (1985).

5. NCEA (1986), p. 140.
6. Ibid., p. 142. The *ATS* survey of teachers in *HS&B* schools . . . supports these findings, in particular the finding of job satisfaction that is considerably higher in Catholic than in public schools. See also Lee, Dedrick, and Smith (1991).
7. In a recent national survey of Catholic high school teachers, "a view of teaching as ministry" was the third most important reason cited for teaching in Catholic high schools. The first two reasons given were "a desire to teach in this kind of educational environment" and "a love of teaching." See Benson and Guerra (1985), p. 17.
8. NCEA (1986), p. 143.
9. The importance of intrinsic or psychic rewards to teachers has been well documented in the seminal work of Lortie (1975). As in our research, Lortie found that the main rewards in teaching derived from the positive feelings associated with success in working with individual students. External rewards such as income were less influential.

REFERENCES

BENSON, P. L. AND M. J. GUERRA. 1985. *Sharing the Faith: The Beliefs and Values of Catholic High School Teachers*. Washington, DC: National Catholic Educational Association.

GOODLAD, F. 1984. *A Place Called School: Prospects for the Future*. New York: McGraw-Hill.

LEE, V. E., R. F. DEDRICK, AND J. B. SMITH. 1991. "The Effect of the Social Organization of Schools on Teacher Satisfaction." *Sociology of Education*, 64:190–208.

LORTIE, D. C. 1975. *Schoolteacher*. Chicago: University of Chicago Press.

NATIONAL CATHOLIC EDUCATIONAL ASSOCIATION (NCEA). 1986. *Catholic High Schools: Their Impact on Low-Income Students*. Washington, DC: National Catholic Educational Association.

POWELL, A. G., E. FARRAR, AND D. K. COHEN. 1985. *The Shopping Mall High School: Winners and Losers in the Educational Marketplace*. Boston: Houghton-Mifflin.

SIZER, T. R. 1984. *Horace's Compromise: The Dilemma of the American High School*. Boston: Houghton-Mifflin.

Racial Segregation and Resource Inequality

15

THE COLEMAN REPORT

James Coleman • Ernest Campbell • Carol Hobson • James McPartland • Alexander Mood • Frederick Weinfeld • Robert York

1.1 Segregation in the Public Schools

The great majority of American children attend schools that are largely segregated—that is, where almost all of their fellow students are of the same racial background as they are. Among minority groups, Negroes are by far the most segregated. Taking all groups, however, white children are most segregated. Almost 80 percent of all white pupils in 1st grade and 12th grade attend schools that are from 90 to 100 percent white. And 97 percent at grade 1, and 99 percent at grade 12, attend schools that are 50 percent or more white.

For Negro pupils, segregation is more nearly complete in the South (as it is for whites also), but it is extensive also in all the other regions where the Negro population is concentrated: the urban North, Midwest, and West.

More than 65 percent of all negro pupils in the first grade attend schools that are between 90 and 100 percent Negro. And 87 percent at grade 1, and 66 percent at grade 12, attend schools that are 50 percent or more

Excerpt from "Summary Report" from *Equality of Educational Opportunity*, Washington, D.C.: U.S. Government Printing Office, 1966.

Negro. In the South most students attend schools that are 100 percent white or Negro.

The same pattern of segregation holds, though not quite so strongly, for the teachers of Negro and white students. For the Nation as a whole, the average Negro elementary pupil attends a school in which 65 percent of the teachers are Negro; the average white elementary pupil attends a school in which 97 percent of the teachers are white. White teachers are more predominant at the secondary level, where the corresponding figures are 59 and 97 percent. The racial matching of teachers is most pronounced in the South, where by tradition it has been complete. On a nationwide basis, in cases where the races of pupils and teachers are not matched, the trend is all in one direction: white teachers teach Negro children but Negro teachers seldom teach white children; just as, in the schools, integration consists primarily of a minority of Negro pupils in predominantly white schools but almost never of a few whites in largely Negro schools.

In its desegregation decision of 1954, the Supreme Court held that separate schools for Negro and white children are inherently unequal. This survey finds that, when measured by that yardstick, American public education remains largely unequal in most regions of the country, including all those where Negroes form any significant proportion of the population. Obviously, however, that is not the only yardstick. The next section of the summary describes other characteristics by means of which equality of educational opportunity may be appraised.

1.2   The Schools and Their Characteristics

The school environment of a child consists of many elements, ranging from the desk he sits at to the child who sits next to him, and including the teacher who stands at the front of his class. A statistical survey can give only fragmentary evidence of this environment.

Great collections of numbers such as are found in these pages—totals and averages and percentages—blur and obscure rather than sharpen and illuminate the range of variation they represent. If one reads, for example, that the average annual income per person in the State of Maryland is $3,000, there is a tendency to picture an average person living in moderate circumstances in a middle-class neighborhood holding an ordinary job. But that number represents at the upper end millionaires, and at the lower end the unemployed, the pensioners, the charwomen. Thus the $3,000 average income should somehow bring to mind the tycoon and the tramp, the showcase and the shack, as well as the average man in the average house.

So, too, in reading these statistics on education, one must picture the child whose school has every conceivable facility that is believed to enhance the educational process, whose teachers may be particularly gifted and well educated, and whose home and total neighborhood are themselves powerful contributors to his education and growth. And one must picture the child in a dismal tenement area who may come hungry to an ancient, dirty building that is badly ventilated, poorly lighted, overcrowded, understaffed, and without sufficient textbooks.

Statistics, too, must deal with one thing at a time, and cumulative effects tend to be lost in them. Having a teacher without a college degree indicates an element of disadvantage, but in the concrete situation, a child may be taught by a teacher who is not only without a degree but who has grown up and received his schooling in the local community, who has never been out of the State, who has a 10th-grade vocabulary, and who shares the local community's attitudes.

One must also be aware of the relative importance of a certain kind of thing to a certain kind of person. Just as a loaf of bread means more to a starving man than to a sated one, so one very fine textbook or, better, one very able teacher, may mean far more to a deprived child than to one who already has several of both.

Finally, it should be borne in mind that in cases where Negroes in the South receive unequal treatment, the significance in terms of actual numbers of individuals involved is very great, since 54 percent of the Negro population of school-going age, or approximately 3,200,000 children, live in that region.

All of the findings reported in this section of the summary are based on responses to questionnaires filled out by public school teachers, principals, district school superintendents, and pupils. The data were gathered in September and October of 1965 from 4,000 public schools. All teachers, principals, and district superintendents in these schools participated, as did all pupils in the 3d, 6th, 9th, and 12th grades. First-grade pupils in half the schools participated. More than 645,000 pupils in all were involved in the survey.

. . .

TABLE 15.1 Percent (except Where Average Specified) of Pupils in Secondary Schools Having the School Characteristics Named at Left, Fall 1965

Characteristic	Whole Nation						Nonmetropolitan						Metropolitan									
							North and West		South		Southwest		Northeast		Midwest		South		Southwest		West	
	MA	PR	IA	OA	Neg.	Maj.	Neg.	Maj.	Neg.	Maj.	Neg.	Maj.	Neg.	Maj.	Neg.	Maj.	Neg.	Maj.	Neg.	Maj.	Neg.	Maj.
Age of main building:																						
Less than 20 years	48	40	49	41	60	53	64	35	79	52	76	44	18	64	33	43	74	84	76	43	53	79
20 to 40 years	40	31	35	32	26	29	15	26	13	33	22	46	41	20	38	37	18	14	16	56	46	19
At least 40 years	11	28	15	26	12	18	21	38	3	15	3	10	40	15	29	20	3	0	6	1	2	3
Average pupils per room	32	33	29	32	34	31	27	30	35	28	22	20	35	28	54	33	30	34	28	42	31	30
Auditorium	57	68	49	66	49	46	32	27	21	36	56	68	77	72	51	44	49	40	67	57	72	45
Cafeteria	72	80	74	81	72	65	55	41	65	78	78	97	88	73	55	54	77	97	75	63	77	79
Gymnasium	78	88	70	83	64	74	51	52	38	63	71	71	90	90	75	76	52	80	70	77	99	95
Shop with power tools	96	88	96	98	89	96	97	96	85	90	88	91	67	97	99	100	89	90	92	97	100	100
Biology laboratory	95	84	96	96	93	94	99	87	85	88	93	96	83	94	100	99	95	100	100	97	100	100
Chemistry laboratory	96	94	99	99	94	98	98	97	85	91	92	95	99	99	100	100	94	100	100	97	100	100
Physics laboratory	90	83	90	97	80	94	80	90	63	83	74	93	92	99	94	96	83	100	96	97	76	100
Language laboratory	57	45	58	75	49	56	32	24	17	32	38	19	47	79	68	57	48	72	69	85	95	80
Infirmary	65	77	77	69	70	75	47	56	53	45	23	47	96	99	70	83	83	83	74	63	71	87
Full-time librarian	84	93	85	98	87	83	53	58	69	76	67	61	97	99	99	94	96	99	71	97	100	99
Free textbooks	74	79	78	88	70	62	42	53	51	43	94	92	98	91	67	39	58	34	98	57	99	86
Sufficient number of textbooks	92	89	90	96	85	95	99	99	79	91	97	100	94	99	98	100	69	97	94	82	96	96
Texts under 4 years old	58	68	65	55	61	62	77	56	64	54	73	66	55	59	51	67	56	65	99	59	59	67
Average library books per pupil	8.1	6.2	6.4	5.7	4.6	5.8	4.5	6.3	4.0	6.1	8.1	14.8	3.8	5.3	3.5	4.8	4.5	5.7	5.6	3.7	6.5	6.3
Free lunch program	66	80	63	75	74	62	58	54	89	88	61	82	66	52	74	63	79	79	89	52	47	54

Note: The group identifications are abbreviated as follows: MA—Mexican American; PR—Puerto Rican; IA—Indian American; OA—Oriental American; Neg.—Negro; and Maj.—Majority or white.

Facilities

Table 15.1 lists certain school characteristics and the percentages of pupils of the various races who are enrolled in schools which have those characteristics. Where specified by "average" the figures represent actual numbers rather than percentages. Reading from left to right, percentages or averages are given on a nationwide basis for the six groups; then comparisons between Negro and white access to the various facilities are made on the basis of regional and metropolitan-nonmetropolitan breakdowns.

[F]or the Nation as a whole white children attend elementary schools with a smaller average number of pupils per room (29) than do any of the minorities (which range from 30 to 33). . . .

Table 15.1 shows that secondary school whites have a smaller average number of pupils per room than minorities, except Indians. Looking at the regional breakdown, however, one finds much more striking differences than the national average would suggest: In the metropolitan Midwest, for example, the average Negro has 54 pupils per room—probably reflecting considerable frequency of double sessions—compared with 33 per room for whites. Nationally, at the high school level the average white has 1 teacher for every 22 students and the average Negro has 1 for every 26 students.

It is thus apparent that the table must be studied carefully, with special attention paid to the regional breakdowns, which often provide more meaningful information than do the nationwide averages. Such careful study will reveal that there is not a wholly consistent pattern—that is, minorities are not at a disadvantage in every item listed—but that there are nevertheless some definite and systematic directions of differences. Nationally, Negro pupils have fewer of some of the facilities that seem most related to academic achievement: They have less access to

physics, chemistry, and language laboratories; there are fewer books per pupil in their libraries; their textbooks are less often in sufficient supply. To the extent that physical facilities are important to learning, such items appear to be more relevant than some others, such as cafeterias, in which minority groups are at an advantage.

Usually greater than the majority-minority differences, however, are the regional differences. Table 15.1, for example, shows that 95 percent of Negro and 80 percent of white high school students in the metropolitan Far West attend schools with language laboratories, compared with 48 and 72 percent, respectively, in the metropolitan South, in spite of the fact that a higher percentage of Southern schools are less than 20 years old.

Finally, it must always be remembered that these statistics reveal only majority-minority average differences and regional average differences; they do not show the extreme differences that would be found by comparing one school with another.

Programs

Table 15.2 summarizes some of the survey findings about the school curriculum, administration, and extracurricular activities. The table is organized in the same way as Table 15.1 and should be studied in the same way, again with particular attention to regional differences.

The pattern that emerges from study of this table is similar to that from Table 15.1. Just as minority groups tend to have less access to physical facilities that seem to be related to academic achievement, so too they have less access to curricular and extracurricular programs that would seem to have such a relationship.

Secondary school Negro students are less likely to attend schools that are regionally accredited; this is particularly pro-

TABLE 15.2 Percent of Pupils in Secondary Schools Having the Characteristic Named at Left, Fall 1965

Characteristic	Whole Nation						Nonmetropolitan								Metropolitan							
							North and West		South		Southwest		Northeast		Midwest		South		Southwest		West	
	MA	PR	IA	OA	Neg.	Maj.	Neg.	Maj.	Neg.	Maj.	Neg.	Maj.	Neg.	Maj.	Neg.	Maj.	Neg.	Maj.	Neg.	Maj.	Neg.	Maj.
Regionally accredited schools	77	78	71	86	68	76	69	65	40	59	30	62	74	74	75	86	72	81	92	86	100	100
Music teacher, full-time	84	94	88	96	85	88	87	87	65	61	85	77	95	97	96	96	87	100	91	82	99	97
College preparatory curriculum	95	90	96	98	88	96	98	95	74	92	81	83	93	99	99	100	87	100	89	82	100	100
Vocational curriculum	56	50	55	68	56	55	49	64	51	62	52	34	42	35	60	60	58	21	89	80	65	65
Remedial reading teacher	57	76	55	81	53	52	35	32	24	20	4	9	81	66	62	57	46	65	63	62	100	97
Accelerated curriculum	67	60	66	80	61	66	42	46	46	58	25	25	60	82	64	78	72	81	87	55	74	73
Low IQ classes	54	56	50	85	54	49	44	47	23	20	46	12	75	62	86	59	37	34	64	14	98	98
Speech impairment classes	28	58	28	51	21	31	18	33	10	6	1	11	43	44	48	42	0	10	14	3	45	57
Use of intelligence test	91	57	84	86	80	89	87	93	83	90	97	100	59	87	86	86	78	100	94	75	89	92
Assignment practice other than area or open	4	20	9	3	19	4	5	0	32	14	2	0	14	5	0	0	36	9	4	0	0	0
Use of tracking	79	88	79	85	75	74	41	48	55	57	21	24	94	92	74	90	80	80	92	82	99	98
Teachers having tenure	65	86	71	85	61	72	47	73	33	41	2	3	100	98	97	83	50	79	24	15	96	88
Principal's salary $9,000 and above	73	89	73	91	66	72	54	64	31	37	59	63	99	99	76	91	61	46	86	18	100	100
School newspaper	89	95	86	97	80	89	71	72	50	81	67	71	95	93	99	97	87	100	66	94	100	100
Boys' interscholastic athletes	94	90	98	99	95	98	99	99	97	100	96	93	80	95	100	97	93	100	95	100	100	100
Girls' interscholastic athletes	58	33	59	37	57	54	32	32	80	69	89	81	51	60	50	43	45	80	89	97	38	35
Band	92	88	92	98	91	95	97	97	80	76	84	81	92	97	100	100	93	100	99	100	100	100
Drama club	95	93	89	92	92	93	75	91	87	75	91	88	92	88	93	99	94	94	100	97	100	100
Debate team	51	32	46	50	39	52	43	48	27	36	80	67	27	46	49	69	42	58	68	63	37	48

Note: The group identifications are abbreviated as follows: MA—Mexican American; PR—Puerto Rican; IA—Indian American; OA—Oriental American; Neg.—Negro; and Maj.—Majority or white.

nounced in the South. Negro and Puerto Rican pupils have less access to college preparatory curriculums and to accelerated curriculums; Puerto Ricans have less access to vocational curriculums as well. Less intelligence testing is done in the schools attended by Negroes and Puerto Ricans. Finally, white students in general have more access to a more fully developed program of extracurricular activities, in particular those which might be related to academic matters (debate teams, for example, and student newspapers).

Again, regional differences are striking. For example, 100 percent of Negro high school students and 97 percent of whites in the metropolitan Far West attend schools having a remedial reading teacher (this does not mean, of course, that every student uses the services of that teacher, but simply that he has access to them (compared with 46 percent and 65 percent, respectively, in the metropolitan South—and 4 percent and 9 percent in the nonmetropolitan Southwest.

· · ·

Student Body Characteristics

Table 15.3 present[s] data about certain characteristics of the student bodies attending various schools. Th[is] table must be read the same as those immediately preceding. Looking at the sixth item on Table 15.3, one should read: the average white high school student attends a school in which 82 percent of his classmates report that there are encyclopedias in their homes. This does not mean that 82 percent of all white pupils have encyclopedias at home, although obviously that would be approximately true. In short, [this table] attempt[s] to describe the characteristics of the student bodies with which the "average" white or minority student goes to school.

Clear differences are found on these items. The average Negro has fewer classmates whose mothers graduated from high school; his classmates more frequently are members of large rather than small families; they are less often enrolled in a college preparatory curriculum; they have taken a smaller number of courses in English, mathematics, foreign language, and science.

On most items, the other minority groups fall between Negroes and whites, but closer to whites, in the extent to which each characteristic is typical of their classmates.

Again, there are substantial variations in the magnitude of the differences, with the difference usually being greater in the Southern States.

1.3   Achievement in the Public Schools

The schools bear many responsibilities. Among the most important is the teaching of certain intellectual skills such as reading, writing, calculating, and problem solving. One way of assessing the educational opportunity offered by the school is to measure how well they perform this task. Standard achievement tests are available to measure these skills, and several such tests were administered in this survey to pupils at grades 1, 3, 6, 9, and 12.

These tests do not measure intelligence, nor attitudes, nor qualities of character. Furthermore, they are not, nor are they intended to be, "culture free." Quite the reverse: they are culture bound. What they measure are the skills which are among the most important in our society for getting a good job and moving up to a better one, and for full participation in an increasingly technical world. Consequently, a pupil's test results at the end of public school provide a good measure of

TABLE 15.3 For the Average Minority and White Pupil, the Percent of Fellow Pupils with the Specified Characteristics, Fall 1965

Level of School and Pupil Characteristic	Whole Nation						Nonmetropolitan								Metropolitan							
							North and West		South		Southwest		Northeast		Midwest		South		Southwest		West	
	MA	PR	IA	OA	Neg.	Maj.	Neg.	Maj.	Neg.	Maj.	Neg.	Maj.	Neg.	Maj.	Neg.	Maj.	Neg.	Maj.	Neg.	Maj.	Neg.	Maj.
Elementary schools:																						
Mostly white classmates last year	59	52	66	63	19	89	59	91	17	91	19	72	33	87	26	91	7	91	27	91	20	86
All white teachers last year	75	68	77	74	53	88	71	89	53	87	57	84	60	89	52	88	49	89	51	89	52	85
Encyclopedia in home	62	57	64	70	54	75	62	72	36	65	48	64	71	84	60	80	51	80	57	72	64	83
Secondary schools:																						
Mostly white classmates last year	72	56	72	57	10	91	77	96	12	94	23	88	41	90	40	89	4	95	14	96	35	81
All white teachers last year	73	57	75	57	25	89	79	93	11	93	23	90	44	84	45	88	3	92	16	95	46	79
Encyclopedia in home	77	76	75	82	69	82	76	78	52	75	66	75	82	87	80	86	67	88	73	83	78	83
Mother high school graduate or more	49	47	50	53	40	58	51	58	23	45	44	48	51	63	49	63	37	58	41	49	53	65
Taking college preparatory course	36	38	35	41	32	41	29	35	22	33	28	32	39	53	43	46	34	44	29	31	34	46
Taking some vocational course	27	30	28	32	27	23	22	24	23	20	25	20	30	20	28	25	27	16	37	38	35	30
2½ years or more of science	36	38	38	38	39	42	41	41	41	38	47	39	43	55	32	38	43	43	42	31	26	34
1½ years or more of language	37	41	35	43	35	40	29	30	25	26	19	23	49	60	36	44	38	44	34	23	37	50
3½ years or more of English	77	73	80	76	69	83	68	78	66	89	75	84	79	91	73	79	67	89	71	87	62	72
2½ years or more of math	47	45	44	47	44	49	40	39	43	46	50	52	47	63	41	50	46	55	58	45	37	47

Note: The group identifications are abbreviated as follows: MA—Mexican American; PR—Puerto Rican; IA—Indian American; OA—Oriental American; Neg.—Negro; and Maj.—Majority or white.

TABLE 15.4 Nationwide Median Test Scores for 1st- and 12th-Grade Pupils, Fall 1965

Test	Racial or Ethnic Group					
	Puerto Ricans	*Indian Americans*	*Mexican- Americans*	*Oriental Americans*	*Negro*	*Majority*
1st grade:						
Nonverbal	45.8	53.0	50.1	50.6	43.4	54.1
Verbal	44.9	47.8	46.5	51.6	45.4	53.2
12th grade:						
Nonverbal	43.3	47.1	45.0	51.6	40.0	52.0
Verbal	43.1	43.7	43.8	40.0	40.0	52.1
Reading	42.6	44.3	44.2	48.8	42.2	51.9
Mathematics	43.7	45.9	45.5	51.3	41.8	51.8
General information	41.7	44.7	43.3	49.0	40.6	52.2
Average of the 5 tests	43.1	45.1	44.4	50.1	41.1	52.0

the range of opportunities open to him as he finishes school—a wide range of choice of jobs or colleges if these skills are very high; a very narrow range that includes only the most menial jobs if these skills are very low.

Table 15.4 gives an overall illustration of the test results for the various groups by tabulating nationwide median scores (the score which divides the group in half) for 1st-grade and 12th-grade pupils on the tests used in those grades. For example, half of the white 12th-grade pupils had scores above 52 on the nonverbal test and half had scores below 52. (Scores on each test at each grade level were standardized so that the average over the national sample equaled 50 and the standard deviation equaled 10. This means that for all pupils in the Nation, about 16 percent would score below 40 and about 16 percent above 60.)

With some exceptions—notably Oriental Americans—the average minority pupil scores distinctly lower on these tests at every level than the average white pupil. The minority pupils' scores are as much as one standard deviation below the majority pupils' scores in the 1st grade. At the 12th grade, results of tests in the same verbal and nonverbal skills show that, in every case, the minority scores are farther below the ma-

jority than are the 1st-graders. For some groups, the relative decline is negligible; for others, it is large.

Furthermore, a constant difference in standard deviations over the various grades represents an increasing difference in grade level gap. For example, Negroes in the metropolitan Northeast are about 1.1 standard deviations below whites in the same region at grades 6, 9, and 12. But at grade 6 this represents 1.6 years behind; at grade 9, 2.4 years; and at grade 12, 3.3 years. Thus, by this measure, the deficiency in achievement is progressively greater for the minority pupils at progressively higher grade levels.

For most minority groups, then, and most particularly the Negro, schools provide little opportunity for them to overcome this initial deficiency; in fact they fall farther behind the white majority in the development of several skills which are critical to making a living and participating fully in modern society. Whatever may be the combination of nonschool factors—poverty, community attitudes, low educational level of parents—which put minority children at a disadvantage in verbal and nonverbal skills when they enter the first grade, the fact is the schools have not overcome it.

Some points should be borne in mind in reading the table. First, the differences shown should not obscure the fact that some minority children perform better than many white children. A difference of one standard deviation in median scores means that about 84 percent of the children in the lower group are below the median of the majority students—but 50 percent of the white children are themselves below that median as well.

A second point of qualification concerns regional differences. By grade 12, both white and Negro students in the South score below their counterparts—white and Negro—in the North. In addition, Southern Negroes score farther below Southern whites than Northern Negroes score below Northern whites. The consequences of this pattern can be illustrated by the fact that the 12th-grade Negro in the nonmetroplitan South is 0.8 standard deviation below—or, in terms of years, 1.9 years behind—the Negro in the metropolitan Northeast, though at grade 1 there is no such regional difference.

Finally, the test scores at grade 12 obviously do not take account of those pupils who have left school before reaching the senior year. In the metropolitan North and West, 20 percent of the Negroes of ages 16 and 17 are not enrolled in school—a higher dropout percentage than in either the metropolitan or nonmetropolitan South. If it is the case that some or many of the Northern dropouts performed poorly when they were in school, the Negro achievement in the North may be artificially elevated because some of those who achieved more poorly have left school.

1.4 Relation of Achievement to School Characteristics

If 100 students within a school take a certain test, there is likely to be great variation in their scores. One student may score 97 percent, another 13; several may score 78 percent. This represents variability in achievement within the particular school.

It is possible, however, to compute the average of the scores made by the students within that school and to compare it with the average score, or achievement, of pupils within another school, or many other schools. These comparisons then represent variations between schools.

When one sees that the average score on a verbal achievement test in school X is 55 and in school Y is 72, the natural question to ask is: What accounts for the difference?

There are many factors that may be associated with the difference. This analysis concentrates on one cluster of those factors. It attempts to describe what relationship the school's characteristics themselves (libraries, for example, and teachers and laboratories, and so on) seem to have to the achievement of majority and minority groups (separately for each group on a nationwide basis, and also for Negro and white pupils in the North and South).

The first finding is that the schools are remarkably similar in the way they relate to the achievement of their pupils when the socioeconomic background of the students is taken into account. It is known that socioeconomic factors bear a strong relation to academic achievement. When these factors are statistically controlled, however, it appears that differences between schools account for only a small fraction of differences in pupil achievement.

The schools do differ, however, in their relation to the various racial and ethnic groups. The average white student's achievement seems to be less affected by the strength or weakness of his school's facilities, curriculums, and teachers than is the average minority pupil's. To put it another way, the achievement of minority pupils depends more on the schools they attend than does the achievement of majority pupils. Thus, 20 percent of the achievement of Negroes in the South is associated with the particular schools they go to, whereas only 10 percent of the achievement of whites in the South is. Except for Oriental Americans, this general result is found for all minorities.

The inference might then be made that improving the school of a minority pupil may increase his achievement more than would improving the school of a white child increase his. Similarly, the average minority pupil's achievement may suffer more in a school of low quality than might the average white pupil's. In short, whites, and to a lesser extent Oriental Americans, are less affected one way or the other by the quality of their schools than are minority pupils. This indicates that it is for the most disadvantaged children that improvements in school quality will make the most difference in achievement.

All of these results suggest the next question: What are the school characteristics that are most related to achievement? In other words, what factors in the school seem to be most important in affecting achievement?

It appears that variations in the facilities and curriculums of the schools account for relatively little variation in pupil achievement insofar as this is measured by standard tests. Again, it is for majority whites that the variations make the least difference; for minorities, they make somewhat more difference. Among the facilities that show some relationship to achievement are several for which minority pupils' schools are less well equipped relative to whites. For example, the existence of science laboratories showed a small but consistent relationship to achievement, and Table 15.1 shows that minorities, especially Negroes, are in schools with fewer of these laboratories.

The quality of teachers shows a stronger relationship to pupil achievement. Further-

more, it is progressively greater at higher grades, indicating a cumulative impact of the qualities of teachers in a school on the pupil's achievement. Again, teacher quality seems more important to minority achievement than to that of the majority.

It should be noted that many characteristics of teachers were not measured in this survey; therefore, the results are not at all conclusive regarding the specific characteristics of teachers that are most important. Among those measured in the survey, however, those that bear the highest relationship to pupil achievement are first, the teacher's score on the verbal skills test, and then his educational background—both his own level of education and that of his parents. On both of these measures, the level of teachers of minority students, especially Negroes, is lower.

Finally, it appears that a pupil's achievement is strongly related to the educational backgrounds and aspirations of the other students in the school. Only crude measures of these variables were used (principally the proportion of pupils with encyclopedias in the home and the proportion planning to go to college). Analysis indicates, however, that children from a given family background, when put in schools of different social composition, will achieve at quite different levels. This effect is again less for white pupils than for any minority group other than Orientals. Thus, if a white pupil from a home that is strongly and effectively supportive of education is put in a school where most pupils do not come from such homes, his achievement will be little different than if he were in a school composed of others like himself. But if a minority pupil from a home without much educational strength is put with schoolmates with strong educational backgrounds, his achievement is likely to increase.

This general result, taken together with the earlier examinations of school differences, has important implications for equalcity of educational opportunity. For the earlier tables show that the principal way in which the school environments of Negroes and whites differ is in the composition of their student bodies, and it turns out that the composition of the student bodies has a strong relationship to the achievement of Negro and other minority pupils.

   This analysis has concentrated on the educational opportunities offered by the schools in terms of their student body composition, facilities, curriculums, and teachers. This emphasis, while entirely appropriate as a response to the legislation calling for the survey, nevertheless neglects important factors in the variability between individual pupils within the same school; this variability is roughly four times as large as the variability between schools. For example, a pupil attitude factor, which appears to have a stronger relationship to achievement than do all the "school" factors together, is the extent to which an individual feels that he has some control over his own destiny. . . . The responses of pupils to questions in the survey show that minority pupils, except for Orientals, have far less conviction than whites that they can affect their own environments and futures. When they do, however, their achievement is higher than that of whites who lack that conviction.

   Furthermore, while this characteristic shows little relationship to most school factors, it is related, for Negroes, to the proportion of whites in the schools. Those Negroes in schools with a higher proportion of whites have a greater sense of control. This finding suggests that the direction such an attitude takes may be associated with the pupil's school experience as well as his experience in the larger community.

1.5   Other Surveys and Studies

. . .

School Enrollment and Dropouts

Another extensive study explored enrollment rates of children of various ages, races, and socioeconomic categories using 1960 census data. The study included also an investigation of school dropouts using the October 1965 Current Population Survey of the Bureau of the Census. This survey uses a carefully selected sample of 35,000 households. It was a large enough sample to justify reliable nationwide estimates for the Negro minority but not for other minorities. In this section the word "white" includes the Mexican American and Puerto Rican minorities.

   According to the estimates of the Current Population Survey, approximately 6,960,000 persons of ages 16 and 17 were living in the United States in October 1965. Of this number 300,000 (5 percent) were enrolled in college, and therefore, were not considered by the Census Bureau study. Of the remaining, approximately 10 percent, or 681,000 youth of 16 and 17, had left school prior to completion of high school.

   The bottom line of Table 15.5 shows that about 17 percent of Negro adolescents (ages 16 and 17) have dropped out of school whereas the corresponding number for white adolescents is 9 percent. . . .

   Table 15.6 is directed to the question of whether the dropout rate is different for different socioeconomic levels. The data suggest that it is, for whereas the nonenrollment rate was 3 percent for those 16- and 17-year-olds from white-collar families, it was more than four times as large (13 percent) in the case of those from other than white-collar families (where the head of household was in a blue-collar or farm occupation, unemployed, or not in the labor force at all).

TABLE 15.5 Enrollment Status of Persons 16 and 17 Years Old Not in College by Sex and Race, for the United States: October 1965. (Numbers in thousands. Figures are rounded to the nearest thousand without being adjusted to group totals, which are independently rounded.)

Enrollment status	Total	Both Sexes		Male		Female	
		White	*Negro*	*White*	*Negro*	*White*	*Negro*
Total not in college, 16–17 years	6,661	5,886	775	3,001	372	2,885	403
Enrolled:							
Private school	588	562	26	281	11	281	15
Public school	5,198	4,588	610	2,363	299	2,225	311
Not enrolled:							
High school graduate	194	183	11	66	2	117	9
Non-high-school graduate	681	553	128	201	60	262	68
Nonenrollment rate[1]	10	9	17	10	16	9	17

[1] Percent "not enrolled, non-high-school graduates" are of "total not in college, 16–17 years."

TABLE 15.6 Enrollment Status of Persons 16 and 17 Years Old by Sex, Race, and Occupation of Household Head, for the United States: October 1965. (Numbers in thousands. Percent not shown where base is less than 40,000.)

Enrollment Status and Occupation of Household Head	Total	Both Sexes		Male		Female	
		White	*Negro*	*White*	*Negro*	*White*	*Negro*
White Collar							
Total not in college, 16–17 years	2,065	2,017	48	1,081	31	936	17
Enrolled:							
Private school	275	257	18	135	11	122	7
Public school	1,680	1,654	26	893	18	762	8
Not enrolled:							
High school graduate	44	42	2	14	2	28	0
Non-high-school graduate	65	63	2	39	0	24	2
Nonenrollment rate[1]	3	3	4	4	—	3	—
Not White Collar							
Total not in college, 16–17 years	4,596	3,869	727	1,920	341	1,949	384
Private school	313	305	8	146	0	159	8
Public school	3,517	2,933	584	1,470	281	1,463	303
Not enrolled:							
High school graduate	150	141	9	52	0	89	9
Non-high-school graduate	616	490	126	252	660	238	64
Nonenrollment rate[1]	13	13	17	13	18	12	17

[1] Percent "not enrolled, non-high-school graduates" are of "total not in college, 16–17 years."

Furthermore, this difference in nonenrollment by parental occupation existed for both male and female, Negro and white adolescents.

The racial differences in the dropout rate are thus sharply reduced when socioeconomic factors are taken into account. Then the difference of 8 percentage points between all Negro and white adolescent dropouts becomes 1 percent for those in white-collar families, and 4 percent for those in other than white-collar families.

. . .

Relations of Integration to Achievement

An education in integrated schools can be expected to have major effects on attitudes toward members of other racial groups. At its best, it can develop attitudes appropriate to the integrated society these students will live in; at its worst, it can create hostile camps of Negroes and whites in the same school. Thus, there is more to "school integration" than merely putting Negroes and whites in the same building, and there may be more important consequences of integration than its effect on achievement.

Yet the analysis of school factors described earlier suggests that in the long run, integration should be expected to have a positive effect on Negro achievement as well. An analysis was carried out to seek such effects on achievement which might appear in the short run. This analysis of the test performance of Negro children in integrated schools indicates positive effects of integration, though rather small ones. Results for grades 6, 9, and 12 are given in Table 15.7 for Negro pupils classified by the proportion of their classmates the previous year who were white. Comparing the averages in each row, in every case but one the highest average score is recorded for the Negro pupils where more than half of their classmates were white. But in reading the rows from left to right, the increase is small and often those Negro pupils in classes with only a few white pupils score lower than those in totally segregated classes.

Table 15.8 was constructed to observe whether there is any tendency for Negro pupils who have spent more years in integrated schools to exhibit higher average achievement. Those pupils who first entered integrated schools in the early grades record consistently higher scores than the other groups, although the differences are again small.

No account is taken in these tabulations of the fact that the various groups of pupils may have come from different backgrounds.

TABLE 15.7   Average Test Scores of Negro Pupils, Fall 1965

| Grade | Region | Reading Comprehension—Proportion of White Classmates Last Year | | | | Math Achievement—Proportion of White Classmates Last Year | | | |
		None	Less Than Half	Half	More Than Half	None	Less Than Half	Half	More Than Half
12	Metropolitan Northeast	46.0	43.7	44.5	47.5	41.5	40.6	41.1	44.5
12	Metropolitan Midwest	46.4	43.2	44.0	46.7	43.8	42.6	42.9	44.8
9	Metropolitan Northeast	44.2	44.8	44.8	47.1	43.1	43.5	43.7	47.2
9	Metropolitan Midwest	45.3	45.2	45.3	46.4	44.4	44.3	44.1	46.6
6	Metropolitan Northeast	46.0	45.4	45.8	46.6	44.0	43.4	43.6	45.6
6	Metropolitan Midwest	46.0	44.7	44.9	45.1	43.8	42.8	42.9	44.1

TABLE 15.8   Average Test Scores of Negro Pupils, Fall 1965

Grade	Region	Grade of First Time with Majority Pupils	Proportion of Majority Classmates Last Year				Total
			None	*Less Than Half*	*Half*	*More Than Half*	
9	Metropolitan Northeast	1, 2, or 3	45.9	46.7	46.9	48.1	46.8
		4, 5, or 6	45.2	43.3	44.4	44.4	44.8
		7, 8, or 9	43.5	42.9	44.6	45.0	44.0
		Never	43.2	—	—	—	43.2
9	Metropolitan Midwest	1, 2, or 3	45.4	46.6	46.4	48.6	46.7
		4, 5, or 6	44.4	44.1	45.3	46.7	44.5
		7, 8, or 9	44.4	43.4	43.3	45.2	43.7
		Never	46.5	—	—	—	46.5
12	Metropolitan Northeast	1, 2, or 3	40.8	43.6	45.2	48.6	46.2
		4, 5, or 6	46.7	45.1	44.9	46.7	45.6
		7, 8, or 9	42.2	43.5	43.8	49.7	48.2
		10, 11, or 12	42.2	41.1	43.2	46.0	44.1
		Never	40.9	—	—	—	40.9
12	Metropolitan Midwest	1, 2, or 3	47.4	44.3	45.6	48.3	46.7
		4, 5, or 6	46.1	43.0	43.5	46.4	45.4
		7, 8, or 9	46.6	40.8	42.3	45.6	45.3
		10, 11, or 12	44.8	39.5	43.5	44.0	44.3
		Never	47.2	—	—	—	47.2

When such account is taken by simple cross-tabulations on indicators of socioeconomic status, the performance remains highest in those schools which have been integrated for the longest time. Thus, although the differences are small, and although the degree of integration within the schools is not known, there is evident, even in the short run, an effect of school integration on the reading and mathematics achievement of Negro pupils.

. . .

16

INEQUALITY IN EDUCATIONAL ATTAINMENT

Christopher Jencks • Marshall Smith • Henry Acland
• Mary Jo Bane • David Cohen • Herbert Gintis
• Barbara Heyns • Stephan Michelson

[S]chools have rather modest effects on the degree of cognitive and noncognitive inequality among adults. Most people find this argument difficult to accept. Highly educated people differ from uneducated people in many important ways, and most people assume that schools must cause many of these differences. In response we have argued that people who stay in school and attend college would differ from people who now drop out even if they all had exactly the same amount of school. We have argued, in other words, that schools serve primarily as selection and certification agencies, whose job is to measure and label people, and only secondarily as socialization agencies, whose job is to change people. This implies that schools serve primarily to legitimize inequality, not to create it. With this in mind, we turn to the question of who gets educational credentials, and why.

Schools do not have to be certification agencies. Nor does certification have to depend on time spent in school. Certification could be done strictly by examinations. Such a system exists to some extent in many European countries, where schools prepare students for national examinations, and the results of these examinations determine certification. A student can often take the examinations without having attended school. Conversely, merely attending school is no guarantee that he will pass the examinations.

In America, however, there is no national certification system. Free enterprise fills the gap, with thousands of schools and colleges issuing their own separate diplomas and degrees. The primary criterion for certifying a student is usually the amount of time he has spent in school, not the skills he has learned. This arrangement guarantees the schools a captive audience. It also guarantees that young people will be kept out of the labor market. Imagine, for example, what would happen to high school enrollment if states allowed anyone, regardless of age, to take a high school equivalency examination. Most capable students would probably leave high school by the time they were 16. The only way to keep many of these students in school is to make continued school attendance the quickest route to certification.

A second reason schools have become certification agencies is that this serves the interest of a society that wants people sorted and graded but does not know precisely what standards it wants to use. If high school diplomas or other certificates of competence were given solely for passing examinations, there would have to be political agreement on what the examination should cover. This would be hard to get. Delegating the problem to the schools is a way of sweeping it under the rug. A third advantage of relying on schools to certify students is that employers are at least as interested in whether their workers behave properly and do what they are told as in the workers' cognitive skills. This means that employers need a certification system that includes some direct observation of an individual "at work." Schools can provide this. Examination boards cannot.

This chapter investigates the effects of turning certification over to the schools. It asks what kinds of people schools certify and what kinds of people they fail to certify. This is obviously a complex question. Schools and colleges issue an enormous variety of diplomas and degrees. In order to get an overall picture of the relationship between educational certification and other kinds of inequality, we will have to simplify the question by assuming that the value of any given credential depends solely on how long it takes to acquire. We will assume, in other words, that the value of an individual's credentials is proportional to the highest grade of school he has completed. We will call this "educational attainment."

This approach has at least two limitations. First, it treats each extra year of school or college as if it were exactly as valuable as the next. This is clearly an oversimplification. An extra year of college increases a man's earning power more than an extra year of high school. Completing the last year of either high school or college also brings more economic benefits than completing any of the three preceding years. Nonetheless, the differences are relatively modest. Assuming that one year of school or college is just like the next reduces our ability to explain adult economic success by only 3 to 5 percent, and it greatly simplifies our analysis.

A second major limitation of our approach is that we make no qualitative distinctions between types of certification or

types of institutions. A Master's degree in Engineering is harder to get than a Master's degree in Education, and it is more valuable economically. Similarly, a B.A. in English from an Ivy League college is harder to get than a B.A. in English from a state college, and the economic benefits are greater. Once again, however, the effects of these distinctions among types of B.A.s and higher degrees is rather modest.

The remainder of this chapter examines the factors that determine how long people stay in school. The next 4 sessions deal with the effects of economic background, race, family background, and academic aptitude on who gets academic credentials. We then turn to the effects of schools on their students' eventual attainment. We conclude by examining the policy implications of our findings.

· · ·

The Effects of Economic Background

· · ·

There are several possible reasons why children with economically successful parents get more credentials than children with unsuccessful parents. First, they are more likely to have a home environment in which they acquire the intellectual skills they need to do well in school. Second, they are more likely to have genes that facilitate success in school. Third, they seldom have to work or borrow money to attend college. Fourth, they may feel that they ought to stay in school, even if they have no special aptitude for academic work and dislike school life. Fifth, they may attend better schools, which induce them to go to college rather than to drop out.

· · ·

Overall, the data lead us to three general conclusions. First, economic origins have a substantial influence on the amount of schooling people get. Second, the difference between rich and poor children is partly a matter of academic aptitude and partly a matter of money. Third, cultural attitudes, values, and taste for schooling play an even larger role than aptitude and money. Even if a middle-class child does not enjoy school, he evidently assumes that he will have to stay in school for a long time. Children with working-class parents or lower-class parents evidently assume that if they dislike school they can and should drop out. As we shall see, students who plan to drop out usually assume they will have to take low-status jobs. But such jobs evidently seem more acceptable to working-class students than to most upper-middle class children. This suggests that if we want to equalize the educational attainment of children from different economic backgrounds, we will probably have to change not only their test scores and financial resources, but also their attitudes and values.

The Effects of Race

Since 1990, the educational attainment of blacks has risen faster than that of whites. Blacks born at the turn of the century averaged 3 years less schooling than whites. Blacks born during World War II averaged 1 year less than whites.[1]

. . .

Surveys have repeatedly found that blacks said they wanted more schooling than whites with comparable test scores and economic backgrounds. This is often presumed to mean that blacks have unrealistic expectations. This does not appear to be the case. Blacks not only want but get more schooling than whites with similar test scores.

These findings suggest two conclusions. First, the overall difference between black and white educational attainment is much smaller than the difference between black and white test scores, occupational status, income, or almost anything else we can think of. Young blacks have nearly caught up with whites in terms of educational credentials. This has not enabled them to catch up in terms of other things, or at least not yet. Second, differences between black and white attainment can today be explained by differences in their test scores. The effects of test scores are, moreover, partially offset by the high level of black educational aspirations. Discrimination seems to have trivial effects.

. . .

Academic Aptitude and Academic Credentials

There has always been a conflict in American education between the idea that academic credentials should measure competence and the idea that they should reward effort. The result has been a series of battles between those who want to maintain standards by failing students who do poor work and those who want to encourage academic effort by conferring diplomas and degrees on people who have tried to do academic work, regardless of whether they did it well or poorly.

Many schools and colleges have ended up awarding credentials primarily for effort rather than performance. Thus, high schools have largely abandoned the idea that students should have to know anything in particular in order to earn a diploma. The student who has spent 12 years in attendance is generally felt to have "earned" some kind of diploma, and it seems "unfair" to send him away empty handed. Colleges also flunk out fewer and fewer students. The same is true of graduate schools. In many institutions admission has become a virtual guarantee of graduation, at least for students who are willing to go through the required motions.

Yet the very fact that admission guarantees graduation has made colleges and professional schools more careful about whom they admit. Instead of letting in large numbers and failing the less competent, many institutions now have elaborate procedures for excluding in advance those whom they think unworthy of a degree. This spares the faculty the unpleasant task of flunking students whom they may know personally. Instead, they can simply send polite letters of rejection to the less promising applicants, saying there was not enough room for everyone, however well qualified. Arrangements of this kind have increased the apparent importance of aptitude test scores, which are often explicitly used in choosing among candidates for admissions. Grades, while still used along with test scores in making admissions decisions, are rarely used to deny a student the diploma or degree of the institution in which he is enrolled. This means that mastery of subject matter probably plays less of a role than it used to play in determining who gets certified.

. . .

We can sum up our conclusions about the effects of academic aptitude on educational attainment in the following generalizations:

1. Academic aptitude has slightly more influence than economic background on a student's chances of acquiring educational credentials.
2. About a quarter of the correlation between test scores and attainment can be explained by the fact that students with high test scores tend to come from economically successful families.
3. Another quarter of the correlation can probably be explained by other subtler family background characteristics.

4. The factors influencing educational attainment are overwhelmingly social, not biological.

One final observation about the relationship between test scores and educational credentials is in order. Attending school increases most cognitive skills. This means that even if those who got a lot of schooling had the same aptitudes as everyone else when they started school, they would often have more information and more skills than other people by the time they had finished. The correlation between attainment and test scores in adulthood is therefore considerably higher than the correlation between attainment and scores in childhood. The skills measured on standardized tests, such as adult intelligence tests or the Armed Forces Qualification Test, correlate 0.60 to 0.70 with educational attainment. This means that an employer who is looking for workers with high test scores can do moderately well if he recruits on the basis of educational attainment. Still, he could do considerably better if he simply gave a test himself.

The Effects of School Quality on Educational Attainment

[Q]ualitative differences between schools had relatively little impact on students' test scores, especially at the high school level. This section shows that differences between schools also have relatively little effect on students' eventual educational attainment. We will look first at high schools, then at elementary schools, and finally at the cumulative impact of elementary and secondary schools together.

High Schools

Both Project Talent and EEOS provide some information on the educational attainment of students who attend different high schools.

Just as with cognitive skills, there is much more inequality in the educational attainment of different students in the same high school than between the average student in one high school and the average student in another high school. If, for example, we rank ninth graders in the same high school according to how much education they eventually get, the top 20 percent typically get nearly 7 years more education than the bottom 20 percent. If we rank high schools in this same way, we estimate that ninth graders from the top fifth of all high schools get only 2 or 3 years more schooling than ninth graders from the bottom fifth.

Another point that emerges from both Project Talent and EEOS is that differences between high schools can be largely explained by the characteristics of their entering students. In Project Talent, for example, differences in comprehensive high schools' effects on their students explain no more than 2 percent of the variation in the students' eventual educational attainment. If we compare students from typical socioeconomic backgrounds who have typical ninth grade aspirations and test scores, about 50 percent of those in the most effective fifth of all high schools go to college, compared to 30 percent of those in the least effective fifth of all schools. ("Effectiveness" here is defined solely in terms of keeping students in school and getting them to attend college.) Putting it slightly differently, attending a high school in the top fifth boosts the average student's eventual attainment about half a year above the expected level, while attending a high school in the bottom fifth lowers his probable attainment about half a year.

Elementary Schools

No one has ever collected comparative data on the eventual educational attainment of children who attend different elementary schools. When we began our work on educational attainment, however, we assumed that if an elementary school did an unusually good job in raising verbal, reading, and math scores, its alumni would have an unusually good chance of earning good grades in junior high school, being placed in a college preparatory program, doing well on college entrance examinations, and eventually earning impressive educational credentials. Unfortunately, the scanty available data offer little support for this assumption.

In order to test our assumptions, we matched 127 northern urban high schools in EEOS with the elementary schools from which they normally received students. Then we ranked these elementary school feeder systems according to their effectiveness in boosting sixth grade verbal, reading, and math scores. High schools drawing their students from the most effective fifth of all elementary feeder systems were sending 44.0 percent of their students to college, whereas high schools drawing their students from the least effective fifth of all elementary systems were sending 38 percent of their students to college. This implies an eventual difference in mean educational attainment of about a tenth of a year.

We do not have data on college entrance rates for the alumni of different elementary schools in the same high school. There could be appreciable differences. We can be almost certain, however, that attending an elementary school that ranks in the top rather than the bottom fifth in terms of its effect on test scores will not increase the average student's eventual educational attainment more than 0.8 years, and our best guess is that the effect is far smaller.

We have no evidence on the extent to which differences between elementary schools influence students' eventual appetite for more schooling. Nor do we know whether elementary schools that raise aspirations are the same as those that boost test scores. Our guess, however, is that elementary schools have very few permanent effects of this kind.

Cumulative Effects of Schools

Conventional wisdom tells us that effective elementary schools are usually found in the same district as effective secondary schools. This is because effective schools are presumed to be those which have ample budgets and middle-class students. But the conventional wisdom is wrong. The next sections will show that there is no correlation between what a high school spends and its impact on students' attainment, nor is there any consistent correlation between a high school's social composition and its impact on attainment. Furthermore, elementary schools that boost achievement are not especially likely to be found in the same districts as secondary schools that boost educational attainment. This means that an individual whose test scores rise as a result of attending a good elementary school is as likely to attend a high school that discourages college attendance as a high school that encourages it.

For these reasons, living in the "right" school district seems to make relatively little difference to an individual's educational attainment. Our best guess is that the cumulative impact of school quality alters the average student's educational attainment less than half a year. Attending the right school may, of course, make an enormous difference to particular students. But the school that is right for one student seems very often to be wrong for another. The average effect of any given school is therefore small.

The Effects of High School Resources

High schools with ample resources have slightly fewer dropouts and send slightly more students to college than high schools with scanty resources. But this is because high schools with ample resources enroll students with slightly more successful parents, higher test scores, and higher initial aspirations than the average high school. If students are alike in these respects, they end up with the same amount of schooling, regardless of how much their high school spends.

Our 91 Project Talent high schools reported their expenditures per pupil, the expenditures per pupil in the entire school system, the average salary of their teachers, and the number of teachers per student. If we compare ninth graders with similar aspirations, test scores, and economic backgrounds, we find that those who got the most education attended high schools which spent less money than average, had worse-paid teachers, and had larger classes.

The reader should not, of course, jump to the conclusion that raising per pupil expenditures increases the dropout rate or lowers the proportion of students who attend college. A more plausible theory is that our 91 Project Talent schools are simply atypical. This view is supported by the fact that teacher salaries and class size are not associated with college entrance rates in the EEOS sample, once ninth graders' characteristics are taken into account.

None of the specific things high schools buy with their money seems to affect dropout rates or college entrance rates. Both Project Talent and EEOS sent long questionnaires to principals. EEOS also collected information from teachers. These questionnaires yield hundreds of different measures of school policies and resources. A few of these measures show nonrandom (i.e. statistically significant) relationships to the students' estimated educational attainment, even after controlling the students' characteristics when they entered a high school. But the length of the school day is the only policy or resource that has a statistically significant relation to attainment in both Project Talent and the EEOS national sample. Even in this case, there is no consistency between EEOS results for the North and the South, for urban and rural areas, or for blacks and whites.

Two additional examples should suffice to illustrate the general pattern. First, let us consider the impact of high school guidance counselors on educational attainment. In Project Talent, students in schools with one or more guidance counselor got about a fifth of a year less schooling than similar students in schools without counselors. In the EEOS national sample, students from schools with counselors were less likely to go to college than students with similar ninth grade aspirations and socio-economic backgrounds who were in schools without counselors. These findings do not mean that counselors keep students out of college. They may mean that schools acquire more counselors when they have a dropout problem, or when they are not sending as many students to college as the school board thinks they should. In our EEOS regional and ethnic samples (urban North, rural North, white rural South, black rural South) the relationship between counselors and college entrance rates is entirely random.[2]

Another school characteristic that might reasonably be expected to influence the percentage of students going to college is the percentage of ninth graders whom a school assigns to the college preparatory curriculum. In both Project Talent and EEOS, however, the percentage of ninth graders who said they were in a college curriculum had no relationship whatever to the percentage who attended college, once the characteristics of entering students were taken into account. EEOS did find a consistent relationship between the percentage of twelfth graders who said they were in the college curriculum and the percentage who attended college. We suspect, however, that

this derived from the fact that students who planned to attend college were likely to say they were in a college preparatory curriculum no matter what they were studying.

Examples of this kind could be enumerated more or less indefinitely. We can sum up the overall pattern by saying that while some schools are unusually effective both in preventing dropouts and in encouraging college attendance, none of the policies or resources about which surveys habitually obtain information has a consistent relationship to this kind of effectiveness. A high school's impact on individual students seems to depend on relatively subtle "climatic" conditions, not on the size of the budget or the presence of the resources professional educators claim are important.

. . .

The Effects of Segregation

We turn next to the effects of economic and racial segregation on students' chances of earning educational credentials. Once again, the evidence comes mostly from high schools and is generally discouraging.

Economic Segregation

Research on the relationship between a high school's socio-economic composition and its students' college plans became a minor sociological industry during the 1960s. Most investigators found that students in predominantly middle-class high schools had higher aspirations than students in predominantly working-class high schools. These differences persisted even after various statistical adjustments had been made to take account of initial differences between the students entering middle-class and working-class schools. In recent years, however, sociologists have gathered better data and have become more sophisticated in their use of statistics. The best recent studies have concluded that the socio-economic composition of a high school has virtually no effect on students' aspirations.[3]

Our own research has followed this same course. We began by looking at aspirations. We first investigated whether students in different EEOS high schools said they wanted to attend college and whether they had taken steps to implement their hopes (like writing for a college catalogue). We found that students in middle-class high schools were much more likely to plan to attend college than students with similar test scores and socio-economic backgrounds in working-class high schools. EEOS was not a longitudinal study, however, so we could not rule out the possibility that students who attended middle-class high schools had higher aspirations before they entered these schools.

We therefore turned to [the study of] 91 white comprehensive Project Talent high schools. . . . Instead of looking at high school seniors' plans, we looked at whether students actually entered college the year after high school. When we compared the 18 schools with the most middle-class students to the 18 schools with the fewest, we found that the former sent 38 percent of their tenth graders to college, while the latter sent 15 percent.[4] We then compared the educational attainment of students with the same ninth grade test scores, aspirations, and economic background. To our surprise, students in the middle-class schools were *less* likely to finish high school and enter college than similar students in the working-class schools.

How are we to explain this? We assumed that students made new friends in high school. We therefore expected students who attended high schools where most of the other students planned to attend college to acquire friends who planned to attend college also. Both common sense and quantitative social science suggest that friends

have some influence on one another's college plans.[5] We therefore expected that attending a school where other students went to college would encourage an ambivalent student to attend. Yet this did not happen.

The most plausible explanation of our findings is that middle-class high schools have two contradictory effects on students. On the one hand, they increase a student's chances of making college-oriented friends. This raises the probability that the student will go to college. On the other hand, middle-class high schools have higher academic standards than working-class high schools. This means that if a student at any given ability level enters a middle-class school, he is likely to rank lower in his class than if he enters a working-class school. He is likely to find this discouraging. The college of his choice may also hold it against him.

If this explanation were correct, we would expect a student's chances of attending college to be greatest if he attended a high school where the other students had high aspirations but low test scores. We would expect his chances to be lowest in a high school where the other students had high test scores but low aspirations. We would not expect his chances of attending college to be affected much either way if he entered a high school where the other students had both high test scores and high aspirations, or where they had both low test scores and low aspirations. Since most schools fall into one of the two latter categories, we would not expect social composition to have much impact in most cases.

The data from our 91 Project Talent high schools are consistent with this theory. When we examined the effect of classmates' aspirations and test scores on individual students, we found that classmates with high aspirations seemed to raise the average student's eventual attainment, while classmates with high test scores seemed to lower it. In an analysis of this complexity, a sample of only 91 schools might yield such results entirely by chance. The Educational Testing Service has, however, conducted a much larger study of 35,330 students in 518 schools, which also tried to disentangle the effects of academic and socio-economic context on aspirations. The results were consistent with ours. College students' chances of attending graduate school also seem to be lowered if they attend academically selective colleges.[6]

All in all, the evidence indicates that a white student with a given test score and family background is no more likely to end up with impressive educational credentials if he attends a middle-class high school than if he attends a working-class high school. Neither is he any more likely to end up with high test scores.

Racial Segregation

When we turn from economic to racial segregation, our conclusions have to be more tentative. Very little of the research on aspirations discussed earlier in this chapter covered high schools with appreciable numbers of black students. Project Talent did not collect information on students' race until 1965, and it has never managed to locate most of the blacks who were presumably in the 1960 sample. EEOS provides information on blacks and whites in both segregated and desegregated high schools, but it provides no data on whether their aspirations changed between ninth and twelfth grade.

Despite these limitations, we have reanalyzed EEOS data on aspirations, and our findings require brief comment. The reader will recall that when we compared twelfth graders who had similar test scores and socio-economic backgrounds, those in predominantly middle-class schools had substantially higher aspirations than those in working-class schools. Since middle-class schools tend to be predominantly white, and

since black schools tend to be predominantly working class, we expected to find a relationship between a school's racial composition and twelfth graders' aspirations. Surprisingly, the relationship turned out to be nil. When we compared individuals with similar family backgrounds and test scores, those in predominantly black schools had the same aspirations as those in predominantly white schools.

This finding probably reflects the "big fish in a small pond" phenomenon described earlier. Blacks at any given economic level have lower test scores than whites. This means that a student at any given ability level will rank higher in his class if he attends a predominantly black school than if he attends a predominantly white school. In addition, blacks have higher aspirations than whites of similar ability and economic origins. This means that students are more likely to have friends who want to attend college if they attend predominantly black schools than if they attend academically and economically similar white schools. Thus while aspirations are lower in working-class than in middle-class schools, they are higher in black working-class than in white working-class schools.

Having found that the racial composition of a high school did not seem to affect students' aspirations, we still suspected that students in predominantly white high schools might find it easier to realize their aspirations than students in predominantly black high schools. EEOS data did not support this suspicion. Once the aspirations, socio-economic status, and test scores of the ninth graders had been taken into account, the racial composition of a high school had no relationship to the percentage of students whom the principal said dropped out before graduating, or to the percentage he said entered college. The principals of these schools were also specifically asked how many blacks attended college. Principals in predominantly black schools reported slightly more blacks attending college than principals in predominantly white schools.[7]

These 1965 findings are hard to reconcile with survey data on blacks who attended desegregated schools prior to 1960. Among blacks brought up in the North, those who attended racially mixed elementary and secondary schools came from the same economic and educational backgrounds as those who attended all-black schools. But those who attended racially mixed schools ended up with half a year more schooling than those who attended all-black schools. Perhaps desegregation at the elementary level increases attainment, whereas desegregation at the secondary level does not. Or perhaps attending a desegregated high school was more of an asset to a black prior to 1960 than in 1965. Neither explanation seems fully convincing.

The foregoing comparisons all deal with northern schools that were desegregated because blacks and whites lived in the same area. Such "natural experiments" may or may not be relevant to the current controversy over busing. We know only one study of such a situation. The study deals with black students who were voluntarily bused from Boston to predominantly white suburban high schools outside Boston. These students were somewhat more likely to attend college than their older siblings. This is, however, a highly publicized program, and the mere fact of being in it may increase a student's chances of getting into college.

Taking all the evidence together, we can find no convincing evidence that racial desegregation affects students' eventual educational attainment one way or the other. This holds for both blacks and whites. Admittedly, the evidence is not good enough to be regarded as final. There is still a real need for studies of districts where high schools

have been desegregated by court order or by deliberate administrative changes in attendance patterns. In addition, we do not know whether desegregating elementary schools affects either students' aspirations or their ability to cope with the demands made by high schools and colleges. Still, the most reasonable assumption at present is that desegregation makes little or no difference to students' college prospects.

Conclusions about Desegregation

[W]e have seen that high school segregation probably has no effect on students' chances of earning educational credentials. These findings may convince some readers that segregation is not so bad after all, and that reformers should devote themselves to other causes.

We must therefore emphasize once again that the outcomes of schooling discussed [here] are not all-embracing. Test scores and credentials may be the two products of schooling most likely to influence economic success, but even this is not certain. We must also emphasize that the most important effects of school desegregation may be on adults, not on students. School desegregation can be seen as part of an effort to make blacks and whites rethink their historic relationship to one another. If blacks and whites attend the same schools, then perhaps they will feel more of a stake in each other's well-being than they have in the past. If that does not happen—if blacks and whites emerge from desegregated schools as alien from one another as before—the struggle will have been in vain. This will be so even if the racial disparity in test scores and educational credentials is slightly reduced in the process—which is far from certain. The question, then, is how desegregation affects the attitudes of children and of adults. It is easy to construct theories showing either that desegregation will make things better or that it will make them worse. Past experience can also be cited to support either view. Our own prejudice is that in most contexts desegregation will probably increase tension in the short run and reduce it in the long run. But we have no real evidence for this. All we have is a conviction that the debate over desegregation ought to focus on this issue, not on test scores and college entrance rates.

The Effects of Curriculum Placement

We have already noted that there is far more variation in educational attainment between different students in the same school than between the average student in one school and the average student in another school. Almost every high school has some dropouts, some students who take a diploma but do not attend college, and some students who enter college. Nationally, the ratio of these groups to one another is now about 20–40–40. Relatively few high schools deviate dramatically from these norms. Most fall between 40–40–20 and 10–30–60. This makes the reasons for unequal attainment within any given school considerably more important than the reasons for disparities between schools.

In general, we expect students to remain in school and enter college if they are good at doing the things schools value and reward. We expect them to drop out of school if they are bad at doing these things. Of course, we also expect exceptions. Some students will drop out even though they have done very well in school, both socially and intellectually. Others stay in school and attend college despite poor grades, conflict with the school authorities, or both. In general, however, we view persistence in school and college as a measure of how agreeable a student finds life in these institutions, and we believe most students find school life

agreeable if they are good at the tasks schools set. We also think that different American schools set quite similar tasks.

Ideally, we would like to be able to evaluate the impact of all sorts of rewards and punishments on students' persistence in school. In practice, we do not have enough data to do this. We know, for example, that students are less likely to finish high school or enter college if they receive low grades. But we do not know whether low grades actually *cause* attrition. We do not know of any controlled experiments in which schools or teachers have given out grades randomly and then tried to assess the results. We suspect that if poor students are given higher grades than they deserve, their subsequent performance improves. Classical pedagogic theory predicts the opposite, and habitual cynicism predicts no significant change of any sort.

Neither do we know much about the effects of tracking. We suspect that if students of comparable ability and personality are assigned to different tracks in elementary school, those in the fast track are more likely to end up in the college curriculum in high school, more likely to earn a diploma, and more likely to enter college. We would need controlled experiments to test this theory. Simply comparing the fate of students with similar test scores in different tracks tells us relatively little, since there are probably noncognitive differences between students who get assigned to different tracks.

The same problem arises when we try to assess the impact of high school curriculum assignment on college entrance rates. Project Talent shows, for example, that about 60 percent of the ninth graders who were in college preparatory curriculums in 1960 entered college in 1964, compared to 18 percent of those in other curriculums. But students in the college curriculum came from more affluent families and had higher grades, test scores, and educational aspirations in the ninth grade than those in noncollege curriculums. If we compare students who were at national norms in all these respects, about 44 percent of those who said they were in the college curriculum in ninth grade entered college, compared to 32 percent of those who said they were in other curriculums.

Viewing the issue in a different way, we can divide students into those who would go to college regardless of what curriculum they ended up in, those who would not go regardless of curriculum, and those whose fate depends on which curriculum they enter. The latter group apparently constitutes something like 12 percent of the total high school population, though the exact figure could be anywhere from 5 to 20 percent. This way of formulating our results makes it clear that curriculum assignment is not the main explanation for differences in educational attainment among students in the same high school. Nonetheless, the effect is not trivial. It is similar for both high and low aptitude students.

In light of these findings, one might reasonably expect schools with large college curriculums to send more students to college than schools with similar students and smaller college curriculums. This does not seem to be the case.

Thus it is hard to argue that curriculum assignment influences educational attainment by preparing students for college academically. If that were the case, trying to teach algebra and history to more students ought to increase the proportion who went to college. Nor can we argue that curriculum assignment affects the distribution of school resources. If that were the case, providing the entire school with more resources should make more students attend college.[8] Our findings require a "zero-sum" theory, in which assigning an individual to the college curriculum gives him an advantage relative to his classmates, but assigning more students to the college curriculum does not increase the overall level of well-being. The most plausible theory is that assigning a student to the college curriculum is like giving him a high grade; it tells the student that he is going to go farther than his classmates, but it does not tell him how far. Schools cannot convince all their students that they will "get ahead," because teachers cannot believe this and neither can the students. Students can, however, believe that they are going to get ahead if they can see that someone else is going to get left behind. This means that if a few students are assigned to a college curriculum they see themselves as an elite and react accordingly. If more students are assigned to the college curriculum, the significance of the distinction diminishes. If everyone is assigned to the college curriculum, the distinction loses its meaning entirely, as an "A" loses its meaning when everyone gets one.

Conclusions about Educational Attainment

This chapter has investigated the reasons why some people end up with more impressive educational credentials than others. We have shown that the most important determinant of educational attainment is family background. The impact of family background is accounted for partly by measurable economic differences between families and partly by more elusive noneconomic differences. Except for family background, the most important determinant of educational attainment is probably cognitive skill. The precise effect of cognitive skill is hard to determine, however, since we do not know to what extent test scores are a proxy for unmeasured, noncognitive differences between home environments. Race now seems to affect educational attainment almost entirely by affecting test scores and aspirations.

Qualitative differences between high schools seem to explain about 2 percent of the variation in students' educational attainment. Unfortunately, we cannot say what qualities of a high school boost its college entrance rates and what qualities lower it. School resources do not appear to influence students' educational attainments at all. Attending high school with bright, highly motivated classmates seems to have both positive and negative effects on a student's chances of attending college. The curriculum to which a student is assigned is the one measurable factor that influences attainment, and it explains differences within rather than between schools.

What are the policy implications of all this? The answer is not that "nothing matters." It is true that making high schools more alike would have a negligible effect on the distribution of credentials. But if colleges altered their criteria for admitting students and awarding degrees, some groups would gain and some would lose. This is why there is now so much political pressure to alter admissions procedures in various ways.

Suppose, for example, that America adopted a certification system based entirely on standardized tests of the kind now used in college admissions. Such a system would benefit white working-class children and reduce the advantage now enjoyed by white middle-class children by about a third. But while such a system would benefit poor whites, it would not benefit blacks. Blacks now seem to get slightly more education than whites with comparable test scores. They would lose this advantage if test scores were the sole basis for awarding diplomas and degrees.

A system in which credentials were distributed entirely on the basis of grades, and in which standardized tests played no part, would improve the position of working-class students and reduce the advantage of the middle classes even more than a system based entirely on test scores. This may be one reason why admission to public colleges has traditionally depended largely on high school grades, while private colleges have usually weighted grades and test scores about equally.

A system in which all students end up with as much education as they think they can stand would have less predictable effects. Suppose all education were free and no institution had admission or graduation requirements. If we judge by the amount of schooling people now say they would like, the relative advantage of middle-class over working-class students would not decline at all. A system which gave everyone as much education as he wanted would, however, slightly reduce the correlation between educational attainment and cognitive skill. If aspirations remained unchanged, then, and credentials remained equally valuable, such a system would create an elite no less hereditary, but slightly less clever than the present elite. If aspirations *did* change, the consequences might be more appealing.

Without some evidence about the way in which society would operate if credentials were distributed on a different basis, we cannot really choose among these alternatives. If cognitive skills are important for on-the-job success, for example, a credentialing system which ignores cognitive skills will not work. If competence depends mainly on noncognitive traits, a drastic change in the present system may be more feasible. . . .

NOTES

1. This improvement is partly attributable to the fact that educational inequality in general has diminished. But even in relative terms, blacks are better off than they used to be. . . .
2. Details of this analysis are reported in Jencks, "The Effects of High Schools on Their Students."
3. See Sewell and Armer, "Neighborhood Con-

text," and Hauser, "Stratification Process." See also, the controversy generated by Sewell and Armer's work in the October 1966 issue of the *American Sociological Review.*

4. College entrance rates were estimated from principals' reports. The socio-economic classification was based on data supplied by ninth grade students.

5. For empirical evidence to support this assumption, see Campbell and Alexander, "Structural Effects"; Erickson, "Normative Influence"; and Duncan et al., "Peer Influences."

6. See Davis, "The Campus As a Frog Pond." Davis is responsible for the introduction of the "frog pond" metaphor into this line of research. It is interesting to speculate about why sociologists talk about frog ponds, when the metaphor in common usage involves big *fish* in little ponds, and vice versa. We are inclined to favor the fish metaphor, since the variance in the size of both fish and fish ponds is greater than that for frogs. This should produce more

reliable estimates. As far as we know, however, no empirical studies of this have been done. The results might be different if we compared fish only to other fish of their own species, rather than to fish in general. It is possible that the coefficient of variation for the size of, say, small-mouth bass is less than that for frogs. Additional research seems needed here, since regional interactions may be important.

7. This may, of course, only mean that principals in predominantly black schools overstate the percentage of blacks attending college, while principals in predominantly white schools understate it.

8. Thus Heyns, in "Curriculum Assignment," shows that students in the college curriculum see counselors more than other students. Yet we have already cited evidence that schools with more counselors do not send more students to college. We must therefore reject the theory that extra counseling time raises college chances in the college curriculum.

17

THE DREAM DEFERRED, AGAIN, IN SAN ANTONIO

Jonathan Kozol

When low-income districts go to court to challenge the existing system of school funding, writes John Coons, the natural fear of the conservative is "that the levelers are at work here sapping the foundations of free enterprise."

In reality, he says, there is "no graver threat to the capitalist system than the pres-

Jonathan Kozol, excerpt from "The Dream Deferred, Again, in San Antonio" from *Savage Inequalities: Children in America's Schools.* Copyright © 1991 by Jonathan Kozol. Reprinted with the permission of Crown Publishers, Inc.

ent cyclical replacement of the 'fittest' of one generation by their artificially advantaged offspring. Worse, when that advantage is proffered to the children of the successful *by the state*, we can be sure that free enterprise has sold its birthright. . . . To defend the present public school finance system on a platform of economic or political freedom is no less absurd than to describe it as egalitarian. In the name of all the values of free enterprise, the existing system [is] a scandal."

There is something incongruous, he goes on, about "a differential of any magnitude" between the education of two children, "the sole justification for which is an imaginary school district line" between those children. The reliance of our public schools on property taxes and the localization of the uses of those taxes have combined to make the public school into an education for the educated rich and a keeper for the uneducated poor. There exists no more powerful force for rigidity of social class and the frustration of natural potential. . . ."

The freedom claimed by a rich man, he says, "to give his child a preferential education, and thereby achieve the transmission of advantage by inheritance, denies the children of others the freedom inherent in the notion of free enterprise." Democracy "can stand certain kinds and amounts" of inherited advantage. "What democracy cannot tolerate is an aristocracy padded and protected by the state itself from competition from below. . . ." In a free enterprise society, he writes, "differential provision by the public schools marks the intrusion [of] heresy, for it means that certain participants in the economic race are hobbled at the gate—and hobbled by the public handicapper."

According to our textbook rhetoric, Americans abhor the notion of a social order in which economic privilege and political power are determined by hereditary class. Officially, we have a more enlightened goal in sight: namely, a society in which a family's wealth has no relation to the probability of future educational attainment and the wealth and station it affords. By this standard, education offered to poor children should be at least as good as that which is provided to the children of the upper-middle class.

If Americans had to discriminate directly against other people's children, I believe most citizens would find this morally abhorrent. Denial, in an active sense, of other people's children is, however, rarely necessary in this nation. Inequality is mediated for us by a taxing system that most

people do not fully understand and seldom scrutinize. How this system really works, and how it came into existence, may enable us to better understand the difficulties that will be confronted in attempting to revise it.

The basic formula in place today for education finance is described as a "foundation program." First introduced during the early 1920s, the formula attempts to reconcile the right of local districts to support and govern their own schools with the obligation of the state to lessen the extremes of educational provision between districts. The former concern derives from the respect for liberty—which is defined, in this case, as the freedom of the district to provide for its own youth—and from the belief that more efficiency is possible when the control of local schools is held by those who have the greatest stake in their success. The latter concern derives from the respect for equal opportunity for all schoolchildren, regardless of their parents' poverty or wealth.

The foundation program, in its pure form, operates somewhat like this: (1) A local tax upon the value of the homes and businesses within a given district raises the initial funds required for the operations of the public schools. (2) In the wealthiest districts, this is frequently enough to operate an adequate school system. Less affluent districts levy a tax at the same rate as the richest district—which assures that the tax burden on all citizens is equally apportioned—but, because the property is worth less in a poor community, the revenues derived will be inadequate to operate a system on the level of the richest district. (3) The state will then provide sufficient funds to lift the poorer districts to a level ("the foundation") roughly equal to that of the richest district.

If this formula were strictly followed, something close to revenue equality would be achieved. It would still not satisfy the greater needs of certain districts, which for instance may have greater numbers of retarded, handicapped, or Spanish-speaking children. It would succeed in treating districts, but not children, equally. But even this degree of equal funding has not often been achieved.

The sticking point has been the third and final point listed above: what is described as the "foundation." Instead of setting the foundation at the level of the richest district, the states more frequently adopt what has been called "a low foundation." The low foundation is a level of subsistence that will raise a district to a point at which its schools are able to provide a "minimum" or "basic" education, but not an education on the level found in the rich districts. The notion of a "minimum" (rather than a "full") foundation represents a very special definition of the idea of equality. It guarantees that every child has "an equal minimum" but not that every child has the same. Stated in a slightly different way, it guarantees that every child has a building called "a school" but not that what is found within one school will bear much similarity, if any, to that which is found within another.

The decision as to what may represent a reasonable "minimum" (the term "sufficient" often is employed) is, of course, determined by the state officials. Because of the dynamics of state politics, this determination is in large part shaped by what the richer districts judge to be "sufficient" for the poorer; and this, in turn, leads to the all-important question: "sufficient" for what purpose? If the necessary outcome of the education of a child of low income is believed to be the capability to enter into equal competition with the children of the rich, then the foundation level has to be extremely high. If the necessary outcome is, however, only the capacity to hold some sort of job—perhaps a job as an employee of the

person who was born in a rich district—then the foundation could be very "minimal" indeed. The latter, in effect, has been the resolution of this question.

This is not the only factor that has fostered inequality, however. In order to win backing from the wealthy districts for an equalizing plan of any kind, no matter how inadequate, legislatures offer the rich districts an incentive. The incentive is to grant some portion of state aid to *all* school districts, regardless of their poverty or wealth. While less state aid is naturally expected to be given to the wealthy than the poor, the notion of giving something to all districts is believed to be a "sweetener" that will assure a broad enough electoral appeal to raise the necessary funds though statewide taxes. As we have seen in several states, however, these "sweeteners" have been so sweet that they have sometimes ended up by deepening the preexisting inequalities.

All this leads us to the point, acknowledged often by school-finance specialists but largely unknown to the public, that the various "formulas" conceived—and reconceived each time there is a legal challenge—to achieve some equity in public education have been almost total failures. In speaking of the equalizing formula in Massachusetts, for example, the historian Joel Weinberg makes this candid observation: "The state could actually have done as well as if it had made no attempt to relate its support system to local ability [i.e., local wealth] and distributed its 'largesse' in a completely random fashion"—as, for example, "by the State Treasurer throwing checks from an airplane and allowing the vagaries of the elements to distribute them among the different communities." But even this description of a "random" distribution may be generous. If the wind had been distributing state money in New Jersey, for example, it might have left most disparities unchanged, but it would not likely have increased disparities consistently for 20 years, which *is* what the state formula has done without exception.

The contest between liberty and equity in education has, in the past 30 years, translated into the competing claims of local control, on the one hand, and state (or federal) intervention on the other. Liberty, school conservatives have argued, is diminished when the local powers of school districts have been sacrificed to centralized control. The opposition to desegregation in the South, for instance, was portrayed as local (states') rights as a sacred principle infringed upon by federal court decisions. The opposition to the drive for equal funding in a given state is now portrayed as local (district) rights in opposition to the powers of the state. While local control may be defended and supported on a number of important grounds, it is unmistakable that it has been historically advanced to counter equity demands; this is no less the case today.

As we have seen, the recent drive for "schools of excellence" (or "schools of choice") within a given district carries this historic conflict one step further. The evolution of a dual or tripartite system in a single district, as we have observed in New York City and Chicago, has counterposed the "freedom" of some parents to create some enclaves of selective excellence for their own children against the claims of equity made on behalf of all the children who have been excluded from these favored schools. At every level of debate, whether it is states' rights versus federal intervention, local district versus state control, or local school versus the district school board, the argument is made that more efficiency accrues from local governance and that equity concerns enforced by centralized authority inevitably lead to waste and often to corruption. Thus, "efficiency" joins "liberty" as a rhetorical rebuttal to the claims of equal opportunity and equal funding. "Local control" is the sacred principle in all these arguments.

Ironically, however, as we saw in the New Jersey situation, "local control" is readily ignored when state officials are dissatisfied with local leadership. A standard reaction of state governors, when faced with what they judge to be ineptitude at local levels, is to call for less—and not more—local governance by asking for a state takeover of the failing district. The liberty of local districts, thus, is willingly infringed on grounds of inefficiency. It is only when equal funding is the issue that the sanctity of district borders becomes absolute.

But this is not the only way in which the states subvert local control. They do it also by prescription of state guidelines that establish uniform curricula for all school districts, by certifying teachers on a statewide basis, and—in certain states like Texas, for example—by adopting textbooks on a statewide basis. . . .

. . .

We may ask again, therefore, what "local governance" in fact implies in public education. The local board does not control the manufacture of the textbooks that its students use. It does not govern teacher preparation or certification. It does not govern political allegiance. It does not govern the exams that measure math and reading. It does not govern the exams that will determine or prohibit university admissions. It does not even really govern architecture. With few exceptions, elementary schools constructed prior to ten years ago are uniform boxes parted by a corridor with six rooms to the left, six to the right, and maybe 12 or 24 more classrooms in the same configuration on the floor or floors above.

What the local school board *does* determine is how clean those floors will be; how well the principal and teachers will be paid; whether the classrooms will be adequately heated; whether a class of 18 children will have 18 textbooks or whether, as in some cities we have seen, a class of 30 children will be asked to share the use of 15 books; whether the library is stocked with up-to-date encyclopedias, computers, novels, poetry, and dictionaries or whether it's used instead for makeshift classrooms, as in New York City; whether the auditorium is well equipped for real theatrical productions or whether, as in Irvington, it must be used instead to house 11 classes; whether the gymnasium is suitable for indoor games or whether it is used for reading classes; whether the playground is equipped with jungle gyms and has green lawns for soccer games and baseball or whether it is a bleak expanse of asphalt studded with cracked glass.

If the school board has sufficient money, it can exercise some real control over these matters. If it has very little money, it has almost no control; or rather it has only negative control. Its freedom is to choose which of the children's needs should be denied. This negative authority is all that local governance in fact implies in places such as Camden and Detroit. It may be masked by the apparent power to advance one kind of "teaching style," one "approach," or one "philosophy" over another. But, where the long-standing problems are more basic (adequate space, sufficient teachers for all classrooms, heating fuel, repair of missing windowpanes and leaking roofs and toilet doors), none of the pretended power over tone and style has much meaning. Style, in the long run, is determined by the caliber and character of teachers, and this is an area in which the poorest schools have no real choice at all.

Stephen Lefelt, the judge who tried the legal challenge in New Jersey, concluded from the months of testimony he had heard, that "local control," as it is presently interpreted to justify financial inequality, denies poor districts *all* control over the things that matter most in education. So, in this respect, the age-old conflict between liberty and equity is largely nonexistent in this setting. The wealthy districts have the first and seldom think about the second, while the very poor have neither.

In surveying the continuing tensions that exist between the claims of local liberty and those of equity in public education, historians have noted three distinguishable trends within this century. From the turn of the century until the 1950s, equity concerns were muted and the courts did not intrude much upon local governance. From 1954 (the year in which *Brown v. Board of Education* was decided) up to the early 1970s, equity concerns were more pronounced, although the emphasis was less on economic than on racial factors. From the early 1970s to the present, local control and the efficiency agenda have once again prevailed. The decisive date that scholars generally pinpoint as the start of the most recent era is March 21 of 1973: the day on which the high court overruled the judgment of a district court in Texas that had found the local funding scheme unconstitutional—and in this way halted in its tracks the drive to equalize the public education system through the federal courts.

We have referred to the Texas case above. It is time now to examine it in detail.

A class-action suit had been filed in 1968 by a resident of San Antonio named Demetrio Rodriguez and by other parents on behalf of their own children, who were students in the city's Edgewood district, which was very poor and 96 percent nonwhite. Although Edgewood residents paid one of the highest tax rates in the area, the district could raise only $37 for each pupil. Even with the "minimum" provided by the state, Edgewood ended up with only $231 for each child. Alamo Heights, meanwhile, the richest section of the city but incorporated as a separate schooling district, was able to raise $412 for each student from a lower tax rate and, because it also got state aid (and federal aid), was able to spend $543 on each pupil. Alamo Heights, then as now, was a predominantly white district.*

The difference between spending levels in these districts was, moreover, not the widest differential to be found in Texas. A sample of 110 Texas districts at the time showed that the ten wealthiest districts spent an average of three times as much per pupil as the four poorest districts, even with the funds provided under the state's "equalizing" formula.

Late in 1971, a three-judge federal district court in San Antonio held that Texas was in violation of the equal protection clause of the U.S. Constitution. "Any mild equalizing effects" from state aid, said the court, "do not benefit the poorest districts."

It is this decision which was then appealed to the Supreme Court. The majority opinion of the high court, which reversed the lower court's decision, noted that, in order to bring to bear "strict scrutiny" upon the case, it must first establish that there had been "absolute deprivation" of a "fundamental interest" of the Edgewood children. Justice Lewis Powell wrote that education is not "a fundamental interest" inasmuch as education "is not among the rights afforded explicit protection under our Federal Constitution." Nor, he wrote, did he believe that "absolute deprivation" was at stake. "The argument here," he said, "is not that the children in districts having relatively low assessable property values are receiving a poorer quality education; rather, it is that they are receiving a poorer quality education than that available to children in districts having more assessable wealth." In cases where wealth is involved, he said, "the

*Per pupil expenditures presented here, as elsewhere in this [chapter], are not adjusted for inflation.

Equal Protection Clause does not require absolute equality. . . ."

Attorneys for Rodriguez and the other plaintiffs, Powell wrote, argue "that education is itself a fundamental personal right because it is essential to the exercise of First Amendment freedoms and to intelligent use of the right to vote. [They argue also] that the right to speak is meaningless unless the speaker is capable of articulating his thoughts intelligently and persuasively. . . . [A] similar line of reasoning is pursued with respect to the right to vote.

"Yet we have never presumed to possess either the ability or the authority to guarantee . . . the most *effective* speech or the most *informed* electoral choice." Even if it were conceded, he wrote, that "some identifiable quantum of education" is a prerequisite to exercise of speech and voting rights, "we have no indication . . . that the [Texas funding] system fails to provide each child with an opportunity to acquire the basic minimal skills necessary" to enjoy a "full participation in the political process."

This passage raised, of course, some elemental questions. The crucial question centered on the two words "minimal" and "necessary." In the words of O. Z. White of Trinity University in San Antonio: "We would always want to know by what criteria these terms had been defined. For example, any poor Hispanic child who could spell three-letter words, add and subtract, and memorize the names and dates of several presidents would have been viewed as having been endowed with 'minimal' skills in much of Texas 50 years ago. How do we update those standards? This cannot be done without the introduction of subjective notions as to what is needed in the present age. Again, when Powell speaks of what is 'necessary' to enjoy what he calls 'full participation' in the nation's politics, we would want to know exactly what he has in mind by 'full' participation. A lot of wealthy folks in Texas think the schools are doing a sufficiently good job if the kids of poor folks learn enough to cast a vote—just not enough to cast it in their own self-interest. They might think it fine if kids could write and speak—just not enough to speak in ways that make a dent in public policy. In economic terms, a lot of folks in Alamo Heights would think that Edgewood kids were educated fine if they had all the necessary skills to do their kitchen work and tend their lawns. How does Justice Powell settle on the level of effectiveness he has in mind by 'full participation'? The definition of this term is at the essence of democracy. If pegged too low, it guarantees perpetuation of disparities of power while still presenting an illusion of fair play. Justice Powell is a human being and his decision here is bound to be subjective. When he tells us that the Edgewood kids are getting all that's 'full' or 'necessary,' he is looking at the world from Alamo Heights. This, I guess, is only natural. If he had a home here, that is where he'd likely live.

"To a real degree, what is considered 'adequate' or 'necessary' or 'sufficient' for the poor in Texas is determined by the rich or relatively rich; it is decided in accord with their opinion of what children of the poor are fitted to become, and what their social role should be. This role has always been equated with their usefulness to us; and this consideration seems to be at stake in almost all reflections on the matter of the 'minimal' foundation offered to schoolchildren, which, in a sense, is only a metaphor for 'minimal' existence. When Justice Powell speaks of 'minimal' skills, such as the capacity to speak, but argues that we have no obligation to assure that it will be the 'most effective' speech, he is saying something that may seem quite reasonable and even commonplace, but it is something that would make

more sense to wealthy folks in Alamo than to the folks in Edgewood."

Powell, however, placed great emphasis on his distinction between "basic minimal" skills, permitting some participation, and no skills at all, which might deny a person all participation; and he seemed to acquiesce in the idea that some inequity would always be inevitable. "No scheme of taxation . . . ," he wrote, "has yet been devised which is free of all discriminatory impact."

In any case, said Justice Powell in a passage that anticipates much of the debate now taking place, "experts are divided" on the question of the role of money in determining the quality of education. Indeed, he said, "one of the hottest sources of controversy concerns the extent to which there is a demonstrable correlation between educational expenditures and the quality of education."

In an additional comment that would stir considerable reaction among Texas residents, Powell said the district court had been in error in deciding that the Texas funding system had created what is called "a suspect class"—that is to say, an identifiable class of unjustly treated people. There had been no proof, he said, that a poor district such as Edgewood was necessarily inhabited mainly or entirely by poor people and, for this reason, it could not be said that poverty was the real cause of deprivation, even if there *was* real deprivation. There is, said Powell "no basis . . . for assuming that the poorest people . . . are concentrated in the poorest districts." Nor, he added, is there "more than a random chance that racial minorities are concentrated" in such districts.

Justice Thurgood Marshall, in his long dissent, challenged the notion that an interest, to be seen as "fundamental," had to be "explicitly or implicitly guaranteed" within the Constitution. Thus, he said, although the right to procreate, the right to vote, the right to criminal appeal are not guaranteed, "these interests have nonetheless been afforded special judicial consideration . . . because they are, to some extent, interrelated with constitutional guarantees." Education, Marshall said, was also such a "related interest" because it "directly affects the ability of a child to exercise his First Amendment interests both as a source and as a receiver of information and ideas. . . . [Of] particular importance is the relationship between education and the political process."

Marshall also addressed the argument of Justice Powell that there was no demonstrated "correlation between poor people and poor districts." In support of this conclusion, Marshall wrote, the majority "offers absolutely no data—which it cannot on this record. . . ." Even, however, if it were true, he added, that *all* individuals within poor districts are not poor, the injury to those who *are* poor would not be diminished. Nor, he went on, can we ignore the extent to which state policies contribute to wealth differences. Government zoning regulations, for example, "have undoubtedly encouraged and rigidified national trends" that raise the property values in some districts while debasing them in others.

Marshall also challenged the distinction, made by Justice Powell, between "absolute" and "relative" degrees of deprivation, as well as Powell's judgment that the Texas funding scheme, because it had increased the funds available to local districts, now provided children of low income with the "minimum" required. "The Equal Protection Clause is not addressed to . . . minimal sufficiency," said Marshall, but to equity; and he cited the words of *Brown* to the effect that education, "where the State has undertaken to provide it, is a right which must be made available to all on equal terms."

On Justice Powell's observation that some experts questioned the connection between spending and the quality of education, Marshall answered almost with derision: "Even an unadorned restatement of this contention is sufficient to reveal its absurdity." It is, he said, "an inescapable fact that if one district has more funds available per pupil than another district," it "will have greater choice" in what it offers to its children. If, he added, "financing variations are so insignificant" to quality, "it is difficult to understand why a number of our country's wealthiest school districts," which, he noted, had no obligation to support the Texas funding scheme, had "nevertheless zealously pursued its cause before this Court"—a reference to the *amicus* briefs that Bloomfield Hills, Grosse Pointe and Beverly Hills had introduced in their support of the defendants.

On the matter of local control, Marshall said this: "I need not now decide how I might ultimately strike the balance were we confronted with a situation where the State's sincere concern for local control inevitably produced educational inequality. For, on this record, it is apparent that the State's purported concern with local control is offered primarily as an excuse rather than as a justification for interdistrict inequality. . . . [If] Texas had a system truly dedicated to local fiscal control one would expect the quality of the educational opportunity provided in each district to vary with the decision of the voters in that district as to the level of sacrifice they wish to make for public education. In fact, the Texas scheme produces precisely the opposite result." Local districts, he observed, *cannot* "choose to have the best education in the State" because the education offered by a district is determined by its wealth—"a factor over which local voters [have] no control."

If, for the sake of local control, he concluded, "this court is to sustain interdistrict discrimination in the educational opportunity afforded Texas schoolchildren, it should require that the State present something more than the mere sham now before us. . . ."

Nonetheless, the court's majority turned down the suit and in a single word—"reversed"—Justice Powell ended any expectations that the children of the Edgewood schools would now be given the same opportunities as children in the richer districts. In tandem with the *Milliken* decision two years later, which exempted white suburban districts from participating in desegregation programs with the cities, the five-to-four decision in *Rodriguez* ushered in the ending of an era of progressive change and set the tone for the subsequent two decades which have left us with the present-day reality of separate and unequal public schools.

Unlike the U.S. Constitution, almost all state constitutions are specific in their references to public education. Since the decision in the Texas case, therefore, the parents of poor children have been centering their legal efforts on the various state courts, and there have been several local victories of sorts. In the absence of a sense of national imperative, however, and lacking the unusual authority of the Supreme Court, or the Congress, or the president, local victories have tended to deliver little satisfaction to poor districts. Even favorable decisions have led frequently to lengthy exercises of obstruction in the legislative process, eventuating often in a rearrangement of the old state "formula" that merely reconstructs the old inequities.

There is another way, however, in which legal victories have been devalued by the states, and this is seen most vividly in California. Even before the Texas case had been reversed, parents from Southern California had brought suit in the state courts, alleging that the funding system was unconstitutional because of the wide differential between funding for the children of the rich and poor. At the time of the trial, for example, Baldwin Park, a low-income city near Los Angeles, was spending $595 for each student while Beverly Hills was able to spend $1,244, even though the latter district had a tax rate less than half that of the former. Similar inequities were noted elsewhere in the state.

The court's decision found the California scheme a violation of both state *and* federal constitutions. For this reason, it was not affected by the later finding in the Texas case. In 1974 a second court decision ordered the state legislature to come up with a different system of school funding. A new system was at last enacted in the spring of 1977. As soon as Californians understood the implications of the plan—namely, that funding for most of their public schools would henceforth be approximately equal—a conservative revolt surged through the state. The outcome of this surge, the first of many tax revolts across the nation in the next ten years, was a referendum that applied a "cap" on taxing and effectively restricted funding for *all* districts. Proposition 13, as the tax cap would be known, may be interpreted in several ways. One interpretation was described succinctly by a California legislator: "This is the revenge of wealth against the poor. 'If the schools must actually be equal,' they are saying, 'then we'll undercut them all.'"

It is more complex than that, but there is an element of truth in this assessment and there is historic precedent as well. Two decades earlier, as U.S. Commissioner of Education Francis Keppel had observed, voters responded to desegregation orders in the South by much the same approach. "Throughout much of the rural South," he wrote, "desegregation was accompanied by lowering the tax base for [the] public schools [while] granting local and state tax exemptions for [a parallel system of private white] academies. . . ."

Today, in all but 5 percent of California districts, funding levels are within $300 of each other. Although, in this respect, the plaintiffs won the equity they sought, it is to some extent a victory of losers. Though the state ranks eighth in per capita income in the nation, the share of its income that now goes to public education is a meager 3.8 percent—placing California forty-sixth among the 50 states. Its average class size is the largest in the nation.

These developments in California, which may soon be replicated in some other states as local courts begin to call for equitable funding of the schools, tell us much about the value we assign to "excellence." If excellence must be distributed in equitable ways, it seems, Americans may be disposed to vote for mediocrity.

Meanwhile, for the children of the rich and very rich in California, there is still an open door to privileged advancement. In the affluent school districts, tax-exempt foundations have been formed to channel extra money into local schools. Afternoon "Super Schools" have been created also in these districts to provide the local children with tutorials and private lessons. And 5 percent of California's public schools remain outside the "spread" ($300) that exists between the other districts in official funding. The consequence is easily discerned by visitors. Beverly Hills still operates a high school that, in academic excellence, can rival those of Princeton and Winnetka. Baldwin Park still operates a poorly funded and inferior system. In Northern California, Oakland remains a mainly nonwhite, poor and troubled system while the schools that serve the Piedmont district, separately incorporated though it is surrounded on four sides by Oakland, remains richly funded, white, and excellent. The range of district funding in the state is still extremely large: The poorest districts spend less than $3,000 while the wealthiest spend more than $7,000.

For those of the affluent who so desire, there are also private schools; and because the tax cap leaves them with more money,

wealthy parents have these extra funds available to pay for private school tuition—a parallel, in certain ways, to the developments that Keppel outlined in the South after the *Brown* decision.

The lesson of California is that equity in education represents a formidable threat to other values held by many affluent Americans. It will be resisted just as bitterly as school desegregation. Nor is it clear that even an affirmative decision of the high court, if another case should someday reach that level, would be any more effective than the California ruling in addressing something so profoundly rooted in American ideas about the right and moral worth of individual advancement at whatever cost to others who may be less favored by the accident of birth.

Despite the evidence, suburbanites sometimes persist in asking what appears at first a reasonable question: "So long as every child has a guarantee of education, what harm can it really be to let us spend a little more? Isn't this a very basic kind of freedom? And is it fair to tell us that we *cannot* spend some extra money if we have it?"

This sentiment is so deeply held that even advocates for equity tend to capitulate at this point. Often they will reassure the suburbs: "We don't want to take away the good things that you have. We just want to lift the poorer schools a little higher." Political accommodation, rather than conviction, dictates this approach because, of course, it begs the question: Since every district is competing for the same restricted pool of gifted teachers, the "minimum" assured to every district is immediately devalued by the district that can add $10,000 more to teacher salaries. Then, too, once the richest districts go above the minimum, school suppliers, textbook publishers, computer manufacturers adjust their price horizons—just as teachers raise their salary horizons—and the poorest districts are left where they were before the minimum existed.

Attorneys in school-equalization suits have done their best to understate the notion of "redistribution" of resources. They try instead, wherever possible, to speak in terms that seem to offer something good for everyone involved. But this is a public relations approach that blurs the real dynamics of a transfer of resources. No matter what devices are contrived to bring about equality, it is clear that they require money-transfer, and the largest source of money is the portion of the population that possesses the *most* money. When wealthy districts indicate they see the hand of Robin Hood in this, they are clear-sighted and correct. This is surely why resistance to these suits, and even to court orders, has been so intense and so ingeniously prolonged. For, while, on a lofty level, wealthy districts may be fighting in defense of a superb abstraction—"liberty," "local control," or such—on a mundane level they are fighting for the right to guarantee their children the inheritance of an ascendant role in our society.

There is a deep-seated reverence for fair play in the United States, and in many areas of life we see the consequences in a genuine distaste for loaded dice; but this is not the case in education, health care, or inheritance of wealth. In these elemental areas we want the game to be unfair and we have made it so; and it will likely so remain.

Let us return, then, for a final time in San Antonio—not to the city of 1968, when the *Rodriguez* case was filed, but to the city of today. It is 23 years now since Demetrio Rodriguez went to court. Things have not changed very much in the poor neighborhoods of Texas. After 23 years of court disputes and numerous state formula revisions, per-pupil spending ranges from $2,000 in

the poorest districts to some $19,000 in the richest. The minimum foundation that the state allows the children in the poorest districts—that is to say, the funds that guarantee the minimal basic education—is $1,477. Texas, moreover, is one of the ten states that gives no financial aid for school construction to the local districts.

In San Antonio, where Demetrio Rodriguez brought his suit against the state in 1968, the children of the poor still go to separate and unequal schools.

"The poor live by the water ditches here," said O. Z. White as we were driving through the crowded streets on a hot day in 1989. "The water is stagnant in the ditches now but, when the rains come, it will rise quite fast—it flows south into the San Antonio River. . . .

"The rich live on the high ground to the north. The higher ground in San Antonio is Monte Vista. But the very rich—the families with old money—live in the section known as Alamo Heights."

Alamo Heights, he told me, is a part of San Antonio. "It's enclosed by San Antonio but operated as a separate system. Dallas has a similar white enclave known as Highland Park, enclosed on four sides by the Dallas schools but operated as a separate district. We call these places 'parasite districts' since they give no tax support to the low-income sections.

"Alamo Heights is like a different world. The air is fresher. The grass is greener. The homes are larger. And the schools are richer."

Seven minutes from Alamo Heights, at the corner of Hamilton and Guadalupe, is Cassiano—a low-income housing project. Across the street from Cassiano, tiny buildings resembling shacks, some of them painted pastel shades, house many of the children who attend the Cooper Middle School, where 96 percent of children qualify by poverty for subsidized hot lunches and where 99.3 percent are of Hispanic origin. At Cooper, $2,800 is devoted to each child's education and 72 percent of children read below grade level. Class size ranges from 28 to 30. Average teacher salary is $27,000.

In Alamo Heights, where teachers average $31,000, virtually all students graduate and 88 percent of graduates go on to college. Classes are small and $4,600 is expended yearly on each child.

Fully 10 percent of children at the Cooper Middle School drop out in seventh and eighth grades. Of the survivors, 51 percent drop out of high school.

In 1988, Alamo Heights spent an average of $46 per pupil for its "gifted" program. The San Antonio Independent District, which includes the Cooper Middle School, spent only $2 for each child for its "gifted" program. In the Edgewood District, only $1 was spent per child for the "gifted" program.

Although the property tax in Alamo Heights yielded $3,600 for each pupil, compared to $924 per pupil in the San Antonio district and only $128 in Edgewood, Alamo Heights also received a share of state and federal funds—almost $8,000 yearly for a class of 20 children. Most of this extra money, quite remarkably, came to Alamo Heights under the "equalizing" formula.

Some hope of change was briefly awakened in the fall of 1989 when front-page headlines in the *New York Times* and other leading papers heralded the news that the school funding system in the state of Texas had been found unconstitutional under state law. In a nine-to-zero decision, the state supreme court, citing what it termed "glaring disparities" in spending between wealthy and poor districts, said that the funding system was in violation of the passage in the Texas constitution that required Texas to maintain an education system for "the general diffusion of knowledge" in the state. The court's decision summarized some of the

most extreme inequities: District spending ranged from $2,112 to $19,333. The richest district drew on property wealth of $14 million for each student while the poorest district drew on property worth only $20,000 for each student. The 100 wealthiest districts taxed their local property, on the average, at 47 cents for each $100 of assessed worth but spent over $7,000 for each student. The 100 poorest districts had an average tax rate more than 50 percent higher but spent less than $3,000 for each student. Speaking of the "evident intention" of "the framers of our [Texas] Constitution to provide equal educational advantages for all," the court said, "Let there be no misunderstanding. A remedy is long overdue." There was no reference this time to the U.S. Constitution.

Stories related to the finding dominated the front page and the inside pages of the *San Antonio Express-News.* "Students cheered and superintendents hugged lawyers in an emotional display of joy," the paper said. In the library of John F. Kennedy High School in the Edgewood district, Demetrio Rodriguez put his hand on his chest to fight back tears as students, teachers and community leaders cheered his vindication and their victory. As the crowd rose to applaud the 64-year-old man, Rodriguez spoke in halting words: "I cried this morning because this is something that has been in my heart. . . . My children will not benefit from it. . . . Twenty-one years is a long time to wait." Rodriguez, a sheet-metal worker at a nearby U.S. Air Force base, had lived in San Antonio for 30 years. "My children got caught in this web. It wasn't fair . . . but there is nothing I can do about it now." The problem, he said to a reporter, should have been corrected 20 years before.

In an editorial that day, the paper said that what the court had found "should have been obvious to anyone" from the beginning.

The Edgewood superintendent, who had been the leader in the latest round of litigation, spoke of the attacks that he had weathered in the course of years. He had been a high school principal in 1974 when the original *Rodriguez* finding had been overruled by the U.S. Supreme Court. "It was like somebody had died. . . ." he said. In the years since, he had gone repeatedly to the state capital in Austin, where he was met by promises from legislators that they would "take care of it," he said. "More and more task forces studied education," he recalled, while another generation of poor children entered and passed through the Edgewood schools. At length, in 1984, Edgewood joined with seven other poor school districts and brought suit against the state and 48 rich districts. The suit was seen by some as a class war, he said. He was accused of wanting to take away the "swimming pools," the "tennis courts" and "carpeted football fields" from wealthy districts. "They'd say I was being Robin Hood . . . ," he said. The district, he assured reporters, was not looking to be given swimming pools. All the district wanted was "to get us up to the average. . . ." Children in Edgewood, he said, had suffered most from being forced to lower their horizons. "Some of the students don't . . . know how to dream. . . . They have accepted [this]," he said, as if it were "the way [that] things should be."

The governor of Texas, who had opposed the suit and often stated he was confident the court would find against the claims of the poor districts, told the press of his relief that the Supreme Court hadn't mandated an immediate solution: "I am extremely pleased," he said, "that this is back in the hands of the legislature. . . ."

The chairman of the Texas Railroad Commission, who was running for governor as a Republican, voiced his concern that people might use this court decision to impose an income tax on Texas.

The U.S. Secretary of Education, Lauro Cavazos, came to Texas and provided fuel for those who sought to slow down implementation of the court's decision. "First," he said, "money is clearly not the answer. . . ." Furthermore, he said, "there is a wide body of research" to support that view and, he added, in apparent disregard of the conclusions of the court, "the evidence here in Texas corroborates those findings." He then went on to castigate Hispanic parents for not caring about education.

Meanwhile, the press observed that what it termed "the demagoguery" of "anti-tax vigilantes" posed another threat. "Legions of tax protestors" had been mobilized, a local columnist said. It was believed that they would do their best to slow down or obstruct the needed legislative action. Others focused on the likelihood that wealthy people would begin to look outside the public schools. There were already several famous private schools in Texas. Might there soon be several more?

Predictions were heard that, after legislative red tape and political delays, a revised state formula would be developed. The court would look it over, voice some doubts, but finally accept it as a reasonable effort. A few years later, O. Z. White surmised, "we'll discover that they didn't do the formula 'exactly' right. Edgewood probably will be okay. It's been in the news so it will have to be a showpiece of improvement. What of the children in those other districts where the poor Hispanic families have no leaders, where there isn't a Rodriguez? Those are the ones where children will continue to be cheated and ignored.

"There's lots of celebration now because of the decision. Wait a year. Watch and see the clever things that people will contrive. You can bet that lots of folks are thinking hard about this 'Robin Hood' idea. Up in Alamo Heights I would expect that folks have plenty on their minds tonight. I don't blame them. If I lived in Alamo Heights, I guess I'd be doing some hard thinking too. . . .

. . .

It is now the spring of 1991. A year and a half has passed since these events took place. The Texas legislature has at last, and with much rhetoric about what many legislators call "a Robin Hood approach," enacted a new equalizing formula but left a number of loop-holes that perpetuate the fiscal edge enjoyed by very wealthy districts. Plaintiffs' attorneys are guarded in their expectations. If the experience of other states holds true in Texas, there will be a series of delays and challenges and, doubtless, further litigation. The implementation of the newest plan, in any case, will not be immediate. Twenty-three years after Demetrio Rodriguez went to court, the children of the poorest people in the state of Texas still are waiting for an equal chance at education.

. . .

18

THE GROWTH OF SEGREGATION
African Americans, Latinos, and Unequal Education

Gary Orfield

Segregation grew in the early 1990s. For the first time since the Supreme Court overturned segregation laws in 1954, southern public schools returned to greater segregation. Southern segregation grew significantly from 1988 to 1991 and segregation of African American students across the United States also increased. Latino students remained in an unbroken pattern of increasing segregation dating to the time national data was first collected in the late 1960s.[1] These trends surfaced even before the Supreme Court opened the door to large-scale resegregation. Those decisions were likely to accelerate the trend.

National data show that most segregated African American and Latino schools are dominated by poor children but that 96 percent of white schools have middle-class majorities. The extremely strong relationship between racial segregation and concentrated poverty in the nation's schools is a key reason for the educational differences between segregated and integrated schools. One of the most consistent findings in research on education has been the powerful relationship between concentrated poverty and virtually every measure of school-level academic results. Schools with large numbers of impoverished students tend to have much lower test scores, higher dropout rates, fewer students in demanding classes, less well-prepared teachers, and a low percentage of students who will eventually finish college. Low-income families and communities can provide much less for children and their schools have much weaker links with colleges and good jobs.

Gary Orfield, excerpt from "Leading Decisions on Desegregation" and excerpt from "The Growth of Segregation: African Americans, Latinos, and Unequal Education" from *Dismantling Desegregation: The Quiet Reversal of Brown v. Board of Education.* Copyright © 1996 by Gary Orfield. Reprinted with the permission of the author and The New Press.

Segregated schools are far more likely to face intense social and personal problems related to poverty.

Such problems include: low levels of competition and expectation, less qualified teachers who leave as soon as they get seniority, deteriorated schools in dangerous neighborhoods, more limited curricula, peer pressure against academic achievement and supportive of crime and substance abuse, high levels of teen pregnancy, few connections with colleges and employers who can assist students, little serious academic counseling or preparation for college, and powerless parents who themselves failed in school and do not know how to evaluate or change schools.

Poor children face a variety of family problems that make their way into the classroom every day and deeply affect the school environment. Poor families are more likely to move frequently for lack of rent money, disrupting school continuity. Children of jobless parents are more likely to encounter violence, alcoholism, abuse, divorce, and desertion related to joblessness and poverty. Poor children are much more likely to come to school sick, sometimes with severe long-term problems that limit their ability to see or hear in school. Students in concentrated poverty communities and schools often grow up without experience preparing them to function effectively in the middle-class settings of college or well-paying jobs.

In contemporary debates, desegregation plans are often ridiculed as reflecting a belief that there is "something magic about sitting next to whites." In fact, however, a student moving from a segregated African American or Latino school to a white school is usually moving from a school of concentrated poverty with many social and educational shortcomings to a school with fewer burdens and better resources to prepare students for college or jobs. Attendance at an integrated rather than a segregated city high school greatly increases the probability that an African American or Latino student will finish college, even if both students start college with the same test scores.[2] Black disenchantment is most likely when the desegregation plan is not able to provide access to strong middle-class schools for black children, a particular problem in plans in older central cities with few remaining middle-class families—cities that have been cut off from suburbia by *Milliken I*.

Resegregation in the Late 1980s

The proportion of black students in schools with more than half minority students rose from 1986 to 1991, to the level that had existed before the Supreme Court's first busing decision in 1971.[3] The share of black students in intensely segregated (90–100 percent minority) schools, which had actually declined during the 1980s, also rose. The consistent trend toward greater segregation of Latino students continued unabated on both measures. During the 1991 school year, they were far more likely than blacks to be in predominantly minority schools and slightly more likely to be in intensely segregated schools.

Since there has been little effort to desegregate Latino students, they will be far less affected than blacks by many of the changes analyzed here. However, any discussion of the future of segregation in U.S. schools must keep in mind the trends affecting what will be the nation's largest minority community.[4] The Latino share of U.S. enrollment has more than doubled since 1968. Current legal trends are dismantling the tools that could be used to provide desegregated education in middle-class schools to Latinos.

Another segregation measure, the exposure index, provides a second way of describing the changes. The average share of whites in the school attended by a black or

Latino student fell. This reversed a trend toward greater integration for African Americans and continued the trend toward increasing segregation for Latinos.

. . .

Race and Poverty

One of the fundamental problems in thinking through possible remedies for metropolitan educational inequality is the complex interaction of issues related to race and poverty. To a considerable extent, concentrated school poverty is a problem affecting minority students only. In our studies of metropolitan areas, for instance, white high schools with concentrated poverty were rare.

In other words, the existing patterns of income distribution and residential segregation make it almost impossible to disentangle the problems of race and poverty in American schools. Though there are millions of poor whites, they have more residential options. They are much more likely to be only temporarily poor (as a result of divorce, health problem, or job loss) and to be able to continue living in a nonpoor area.[5] White schools are overwhelmingly middle-class schools. Even in central cities with large nonwhite school majorities, whites tend to be in schools with less poverty than are Latinos and African Americans.

. . .

Race and poverty are confounded politically as well as statistically. The Fourteenth Amendment and the civil rights laws prohibit unequal treatment of racial minorities in public institutions, but they provide little, if any, protection against unequal treatment of the poor. In the housing market it is illegal to exclude families on the basis of race but perfectly legal to use lot size, zoning, and other local legal powers to exclude all housing affordable by any but the top five or 10 percent of families in terms of income. Many of the inequalities in schools, however, derive from the concentrated poverty that is the result both of historic and contemporary job discrimination and housing segregation.

Unfortunately, the framing of the issue in racial terms often leads both blacks and whites to conclude that desegregation plans assume that black institutions are inferior and that black gains are supposed to come from sitting next to whites in school. But the actual benefits come primarily from access to the resources and connections of institutions that have always received preferential treatment, and from the expectations, competition, and values of successful middle-class educational institutions that routinely prepare students for college. Segregated schools are unequal not because of anything inherent in race but because they reflect the long-term corrosive impact on neighborhoods and families from a long history of racial discrimination in many aspects of life. If those inequalities and the stereotypes associated with them did not exist, desegregation would have little consequence. The fact that they do exist means that desegregation has far more significance than those who think of it merely as "race-mixing" could understand.

Regional Differences

Trends in segregation and concentrated poverty differ from region to region across the country. The much clearer legal requirements imposed on the South and the fact that the racial composition of school districts made desegregation more feasible within single districts there meant that much more progress was achieved in the South and that black students there became more integrated than blacks in other regions. This was true even though the South had by far the largest share of African American students in its total enrollment.

The fact that enforcement was concentrated in the South and desegregation was never achieved in some of our largest and most influential cities may help explain the belief that desegregation cannot work. Leaders in intensely segregated and visible cities like New York, Washington, and Los Angeles often assume that things are worse in the South and that desegregation was an unfortunate failure. Both African American and Latino students, however, continue to face the most intense segregation in the Northeast. Millions of African American children in the southern and border states attend schools that are still well-integrated decades after the first court orders. Understanding regional differences is essential when examining current realities and future choices in desegregation policy.

. . .

Blacks have more contact with whites in schools in the South than in any other region. More than half of all blacks in the United States live in the South. The exposure index shows that blacks in the southern and border states are in schools, on average, where almost two-fifths of the students are white. The Northeast and Midwest, which have much larger white majorities, provide much less integration for blacks. Latinos experience the least contact with whites in the Northeast, the South (which includes Texas), and the West.[6]

. . .

Although regional variations in segregation are large, variations among states are even greater. The regional variations reflect, particularly in the case of African Americans, the effects of differences in law and enforcement activity, while variations among the states relate more closely to the impact of particular court decisions, the state's reliance on small or countywide school districts, and patterns of demographic change and immigration.

For more than a decade, the same four states, Illinois, Michigan, New York, and New Jersey, have been at the top of the list of intensely segregated states for African Americans. Segregation is most intense in the largest, older industrial metropolises where the central city and its school districts were hemmed in by independent suburbs a century or more ago and where housing segregation is intense. There were large increases in intense segregation in Michigan, New Jersey, Tennessee, Alabama, Maryland, and Connecticut. The resegregation in the South is beginning to challenge the high segregation levels of parts of the urban North.[7]

The level of segregation for Latino students was high across the country but most severe in the Northeast, in the Chicago area, and in the two states in which a substantial majority of all Latino children go to school—California and Texas. New York State has had the highest segregation for Latino students for a generation. New York led the nation in segregation levels since 1980, leading in all three methods of measuring segregation in 1991. Rounding out the list of the five most segregated states for Latinos are Texas, California, New Jersey, and Illinois. This means that the most important settlement centers for both Mexican Americans and Puerto Ricans have become severely segregated.

Compared to earlier rankings from 1970, almost all states with significant Latino enrollment have become more segregated. The changes in California have been dramatic. In 1970, the typical California Latino student was in a school with 54.4 percent white students; a decade later the white percentage was down to 35.9 percent, and by 1991 it was 27.0 percent. Blacks in Alabama and Mississippi are significantly less segregated, according to this measure, than Latinos in California.

One reason for the increase in segregation of Latino students is the tremendous increase in the number and proportion of these students in most of the areas in which the group has been concentrated since the 1960s. In all of the states with high Latino enrollments except New York and New Mexico, increases have been explosive, greatly outpacing overall enrollment gains. Latinos experience severe problems in school, particularly in terms of a high school dropout rate that is very much higher than that of blacks. Latinos are more isolated in high-poverty schools than blacks. In the most isolated areas, many students needing to acquire English for college and jobs are attending schools with few native speakers of English.

School District Fragmentation

There is a relationship between district size and severity of segregation. States with smaller districts tend to break up urban housing markets into more segregated school districts. For Hispanics, the relationship between district structure and intensity of segregation is clearer because there are few desegregation plans to offset its effects. Six of the states with fragmented districts had higher levels of intense segregation than any of the states with larger districts.

· · ·

African American and Latino students who live in towns, rural areas, and in the suburbs of small metropolitan areas are the most likely to be experiencing integrated education. By far the most serious segregation is in the large central cities, followed by the smaller central city communities where *Milliken I* made lasting desegregation impossible.

In the big central cities, fifteen of every sixteen African American and Latino students are in schools where most of the students are nonwhite. In the smaller central cities, 63 percent of African Americans and 70 percent of Latinos attend such schools. About 30 percent of African American and Latino students (almost five times the big city level) attend majority white schools in those smaller metropolitan area cities.[8]

· · ·

Why These Trends?

The huge changes in the racial composition of American public schools and the segregation of African American and Latino students over the past half century have often been misunderstood. The great increase in the proportion of nonwhite students has not been a consequence of "white flight" from public to private schools, but rather of basic changes in birth rates and immigration patterns. In fact, there has been no significant redistribution between public and private schools. During the period from 1970 to 1984, there was a small increase in the share of students in private schools, but between 1984 and 1991 public enrollment grew 7 percent while private enrollment dropped 9 percent.[9] U.S. Department of Education projections indicate that between 1994 and 2004 public school enrollment would climb 12 percent while private enrollment would rise 11 percent.[10] Even as many Americans believe there is flight from public schools, many believe that desegregation is something that was tried a generation ago but did not last. Both beliefs reflect the political rhetoric of the 1980s, not what actually happened in the society.

According to the Census Bureau, the number of black students in public schools in the United States increased 3 percent from 1972 to 1992, the first two decades of widespread busing plans. In contrast, Latino enrollments soared 89 percent and white enrollments fell 14 percent. These trends led to many claims that whites were abandoning public education because of resistance to integration. The decline was not, however, the result of whites leaving public schools.

The white drop was not balanced by growth in white private school enrollment. The Census Bureau reports that there were 18 percent fewer white students in private elementary schools and 23 percent fewer whites in private high schools than two decades ago.[11] The proportion of whites in public schools was actually increasing. The underlying cause, of course, was a dramatic drop in the white birth rate. Contrary to many claims by politicians, these overall changes had nothing to do with desegregation. Public schools were actually holding a growing share of a declining group of school-age white children.

In 1992, 89 percent of whites, 95 percent of blacks, and 92 percent of Latinos attended public schools at the elementary level. Even among upper-income whites, only one-sixth of the children were in private schools. At the high school level, 92 percent of American children were in public schools, including 92 percent of whites, 95 percent of Latinos, and 97 percent of blacks. Private high schools were more popular among affluent whites, but served only one-eighth of their children.[12]

White and middle-class enrollments have been shrinking in all of the largest central city school districts for decades. In fact, the total number of white students in the United States fell sharply from 1968 to 1986 as a result of plummeting white birth rates.[13] In 1986, the nation's twenty-five largest urban school districts served only 3 percent of whites.[14] In metropolitan Atlanta, for example, 98 percent of the area's white high school students attended suburban schools by 1986.[15]

There is no evidence that these trends will reverse or that changes in school desegregation plans will reverse these patterns. Middle-class suburbanization is continuing. Census Bureau studies of migration patterns between 1985 and 1990 show that each year "central cities lost 1.6 to 3.0 million residents while their suburbs . . . gained 1.9 to 3.2 million persons."[16] The overwhelming majority of those who left central cities for the suburbs were white and/or middle class. Central cities were left with increasing concentrations of minority and low-income families. The growth of minority middle-class population is now largely suburban as well, though the suburbs are also segregated, especially for blacks. It would be ironic if *Milliken I,* a decision that was intended to protect the suburbs from unwanted racial change, ended up undermining the ability to cope successfully with vast demographic changes sweeping across the entire nation.

The loss of white and middle-class families and students in central cities occurred in cities that always had neighborhood schools and even in cities that abandoned desegregation orders. Atlanta, for example, decided against a busing plan in 1973 but experienced one of the most drastic losses in white students; similarly, the rapid decline in Los Angeles in the number of white students did not end or reverse itself after elimination of all mandatory desegregation in 1981.[17] The largest cities that never had a mandatory busing plan but experienced large white declines include New York, Chicago, and Houston. Los Angeles bused children for only eighteen months at the middle school level before it returned to neighborhood schools in search of a stability that has not materialized. American cities were changing rapidly long before busing and continue to change where busing stops. Certain kinds of mandatory city-only plans may accelerate the change; others may slow it.

The Feasibility of Desegregation Strategies

While some desegregation plans have proven ineffective in either producing lasting desegregation or creating opportunity for all students to attend quality schools, there is evidence that school desegregation on a metropolitan level is a feasible strategy with major benefits. A metropolitan plan is one in which desegregation takes place both in the central city and in the suburbs. Most of these plans are found in states with county-wide school districts where single districts include the central city and much of suburbia. Also, in a handful of other districts, the courts have ordered students transferred across city-suburban boundaries. Experience with such plans shows that the strategy that the Supreme Court blocked in the *Milliken II* case may have been the key to realizing the goals of *Brown*. The first metropolitan desegregation plans were implemented almost twenty-five years ago, and there is now a rich body of experience that permits comparison of their results with city-only desegregation and with neighborhood schools.

Metropolitanwide desegregation is advantageous because it produces by far the highest levels of integration and the most stable enrollment patterns. The achievement of integration is more likely through metropolitan plans than through city-only plans to provide African American and Latino children access to high-achieving middle-class schools, since it provides far more access to suburban schools where most middle-class white students live. Metropolitan plans also

establish a framework for interracial area-wide concern for and involvement in the same institutions of public schooling.

Separate and Unequal Schools

Contemporary metropolitan educational inequalities are dramatically demonstrated in comparisons of achievement test scores, dropout rates, course offerings, and teacher preparedness. Metropolitan areas are characterized by two-tiered educational systems: one tier serving the mostly white and suburban children of affluent and middle-class families, and the other for the mostly minority and urban students from low-income families and communities.

Inequalities in the Midwest's largest metropolitan region—Chicago—exemplify the big city pattern. (The Chicago and Detroit public schools, because of residential segregation, had the majority of all-black public school students living in the huge Midwestern region from Ohio to Minnesota in 1988.) In 1988, 1,081,000 children were enrolled in public schools in the Chicago metropolitan area, of whom 30 percent of them were black, 13 percent Latino, and slightly more than 50 percent were white. Most attended schools that were intensely segregated. A total of 223,000 black children (69 percent) attended schools that were 90 to 100 percent minority; only 3,350 white students were enrolled in these schools, resulting in a black/white ratio of 70:1. Similarly, 63 percent of the white students—390,000—along with only 5,500 black students, were enrolled in schools that were 90 to 100 percent white—a ratio of 71:1.[18] In other words, more than 60 percent of the children in public schools in the Chicago metropolitan area attended schools where seventy of every seventy-one students had the same skin color. All but one of the 90 to 100 percent white schools were in the suburban communities surrounding Chicago, and 94 percent of the students in 90 to 100 percent minority schools were within the city of Chicago. In the city schools an average of 73 percent of the students were poor (receiving free or reduced-price lunch), compared with 12 percent in suburban schools.[19]

Achievement Inequalities

The intense segregation of minority and low-income students in urban schools is a critical factor in analyzing educational opportunity because it is systematically connected to patterns of low achievement. In virtually every large metropolitan area studied that lacks city-suburban desegregation, low-income minority students and middle-class white students attend schools that are not only separate, but profoundly unequal.

In metropolitan Chicago, the average suburban school had 35 to 40 percent of its students in the top quartile on nationally normed math tests; students in Chicago city schools, in contrast, ranged from a high of 22 percent in the top quartile in the third grade to fewer than 8 percent by the tenth grade. These patterns were very closely tied to race and concentrated poverty. A breakdown of tenth-grade test scores by race and location shows that only 6 percent of the black tenth-graders in Chicago public schools performed in the top quartile nationally, compared with 36 percent of white tenth-graders in the Chicago suburbs. Latino students performed somewhat better than African American students, but still well below national averages and far behind whites.[20] Test scores varied dramatically by income as well. In nonmagnet Chicago area elementary schools with 90 to 100 percent low-income students, only an average of 23 percent of their students scored above the national median in math, compared to 74 percent of suburban students.[21] This means that inner-city children experienced a far lower level of competition and far less stimulation than their equally talented and motivated suburban counterparts. The same relationships among race, community wealth, and achievement hold in other large urban communities, suggesting that these relationships are systemic and structural. In Ohio, for example, in the state's seventeen large urban districts—characterized by low average incomes, large minority populations, and high proportions of families receiving AFDC benefits—an average of only 43 percent of their students scored at the test's version of the national median on achievement tests in math, reading, and language in grades four, six, eight, and ten. In the thirty-seven most affluent suburbs, in contrast, an average 78 percent of their students scored at the same level. Even suburbs with only average wealth significantly outperformed urban districts, averaging 55 percent of their students scoring above the national median.[22]

. . .

Nationally, central city districts have annual dropout rates of 5.7 percent, close to double the 3.2 percent rate of suburban districts,[23] but the differences are generally greater in larger metropolitan areas. In metropolitan Philadelphia, for example, the dropout rate in the city was four times that in the four suburban counties surrounding the city.[24] One study, typical of most dropout studies, of New Jersey urban school districts, concluded that "there are really two school systems in New Jersey—one consisting of most suburban and rural districts, which have relatively low dropout rates and few major academic problems; the other consisting of a much smaller number of big, needy urban districts, many of which have [four-year] dropout rates of from 40 to 60 percent."[25]

Moreover, the differences in dropout rates between urban and suburban districts are not only in the number of dropouts, but in who drops out, and when. In the Milwaukee public schools (MPS), students who drop out tend to do so earlier than their suburban counterparts.[26] In Los Angeles County, 55 percent of African Americans and Latino dropouts left school by the tenth grade; only 41 percent of white dropouts left schools as early.[27]

Unequal Curriculum

Some may argue that correlations between race, class, and educational success alone are not evidence of unequal opportunity. Data on curricular offerings and teacher credentials, however, provide evidence that the stark differences in achievement are linked to equally stark differences in opportunity.

Low-income and minority students are concentrated in schools within metropolitan areas that tend to offer different and inferior courses and levels of competition, creating a situation where the most disadvantaged students receive the least effective preparation for college. A fundamental reason is that schools do not provide a fixed high school curriculum taught at a common depth and pace. The actual working curriculum of a high school is the result of the ability of teachers, the quality of counseling, and enrollment patterns of students. Schools with high concentrations of well-prepared students offer rewarding teaching experiences and often attract highly qualified teachers in precollegiate subjects. Schools with poorly prepared students in less desirable areas to work may have trouble staffing some courses. Even if teachers offering demanding courses can be found, they may not have enough students to keep a teacher fully occupied. In such circumstances, the classes normally either disappear or are watered down so that they are no longer equivalent to similar courses elsewhere. Even if advanced classes are offered, one key compo-

nent—challenging engagement and interaction with other excellent students—may be lacking. The practical barriers to excellent precollegiate instruction in high-poverty schools are recognized to be so severe that the accomplishments of one teacher, Jaime Escalante, who taught Advanced Placement (AP) calculus in one Latino school in California, were celebrated across the United States. He became a hero, though the same course is routinely offered in a great many suburban schools.

As a result of staffing difficulties and high school students' course selections (themselves often the result, in predominantly low-income schools, of inadequate advice from school counselors), low-income urban schools do not offer the same range and level of courses as their more affluent suburban counterparts. The differences in curricula are relatively small in elementary schools, but grow dramatically by the time students reach middle and high school. Middle schools in suburban low-poverty communities, for example, are more than twice as likely as urban predominantly low-income and minority middle schools to offer their students the opportunity to take algebra (25 percent v. 11 percent) and foreign language instruction (30 percent v. 13 percent).[28]

By high school, the differences are more pronounced. Nationally, roughly 34 percent of classes in high schools with fewer than 10 percent minority children are classified as homogeneously grouped, high-ability classes; in high schools with more than 90 percent minority students, only 11 percent of classes are classified the same way. Similarly, wealthy high schools offer three times as many high-ability classes as low-ability classes; high-poverty schools offer roughly equal proportions of each.[29]

Not only do white and wealthy schools offer proportionately more high-ability classes—two to three times as many AP courses per student as low-income, predominantly minority schools—but a larger share of their students take such classes.[30]

Segregated minority high-poverty schools have to spend much larger shares of their resources on remedial courses, special education, dealing with out-of-school problems and crises, managing violence, teaching students in other languages, and other special functions. UCLA Professor Jeannie Oakes also found that 59 percent of all disproportionately minority math and science classes were general level courses, while 85 percent of disproportionately white courses were either academic or advanced-level courses.[31]

The striking differences in course offerings and tracking are compounded by differences in the teaching pools available in urban and suburban schools. Suburban schools, particularly those in communities that are predominantly wealthy and white, report fewer vacancies and fewer difficulties filling science and mathematics positions. For example, 37 percent of principals in high-poverty schools, more than 50 percent in 90+ percent minority schools, and 40 percent in inner-city schools reported difficulties finding qualified biology teachers, compared to only 10 percent in wealthy schools, 15 percent in 90+ percent white schools, and 15 percent in suburban schools.[32]

Young teachers working in high poverty inner-city schools find the job less rewarding and are more likely to consider leaving teaching. Among many other problems, they report that they are vastly less likely to have the materials they need for their teaching. Among teachers in schools with no poor children, 25 percent of teachers reported that they got everything they needed; another 59 percent said that they got most of the necessary materials and resources. Among those schools with 30 percent or more poor children, only 11 percent of the teachers said

that they got everything they needed; another 30 percent said that they received most of the necessary supplies. In other words, 16 percent of the teachers in affluent schools reported significant voids compared to 59 percent of those in the higher poverty schools.[33]

As a result, schools serving poor and minority children often end up hiring less qualified teachers than do advantaged schools. In metropolitan Chicago, suburban teachers were much more likely to have advanced degrees and degrees from more selective institutions than their urban counterparts. Moreover, even within the city, the most qualified teachers were found in schools with the smallest minority and low-income populations, which means that "minority and low-income students tend to be in schools and school districts with less well-prepared teachers and counselors [and] larger class sizes."[34] Research conducted by Jeannie Oakes for the Rand Corporation found a similar pattern for secondary teachers on a national level.[35]

While school success is dependent on many complex factors, it is certainly true that students learn more with better opportunities for learning, whether at school, in the community, or at home. If the schools lack certified teachers, offer few academically challenging courses, and track disadvantaged students disproportionately into low-level courses; if the community is economically depressed, with few libraries, museums, and other out-of-school educational resources; and if a large number of adults with high school diplomas are unable to find adequate employment, disadvantaged students face more barriers and receive less reinforcement to succeed in school.

Segregation is powerfully related to educational inequalities. The most important dimensions of these inequalities—such as the level of competition, qualifications of teachers, and the level of instruction—

Leading Decisions on Desegregation 1896–1995

Plessy v. Ferguson, 163 U.S. 537 (1896). This case involved a challenge from Homer Plessy, a black man, to a Louisiana state law requiring that blacks and whites use separate train car facilities. The Supreme Court concluded that racial segregation did not constitute discrimination under the Fourteenth Amendment, so long as the separate facilities were equal. The doctrine of "separate but equal" meant that the federal government sanctioned segregation. Subsequently, laws requiring racial segregation in education and other social and political domains were enacted throughout the South.

Brown v. Board of Education of Topeka, 347 U.S. 483 (1954) ("Brown I"). In this decision, the Supreme Court unanimously concluded that state-imposed segregated schools were "inherently unequal" and must be abolished. This decision, regarded by many as the landmark Supreme Court decision of this century, struck down the "separate but equal" doctrine.

Brown II, 349 U.S. 294 (1955). Coming a year after *Brown I,* this was the Supreme Court's first attempt to define how and when school desegregation would be achieved. In Brown II, the Court hedged on Brown I's powerful anti-segregation stand, setting no standard or deadline for desegregation to occur. Desegregation, the Court said, should occur with "all deliberate speed" in plans developed in federal district courts. Consequently, desegregation was delayed in many Southern districts.

. . .

Milliken v. Bradley, 418 U.S. 717 (1974). In this decision, the Supreme Court blocked efforts for interdistrict, city-suburban desegregation remedies as a means to integrate racially isolated city schools. The Court prohibited such remedies unless plaintiffs could demonstrate that the suburbs or the state took actions that contributed to segregation in the city. Because proving suburban and state liability is often difficult, *Milliken* effectively shut off the option of drawing from heavily white suburbs in order to integrate city districts with very large minority populations.

. . .

Missouri v. Jenkins, 115 S. Ct. 2038 (1995). The Supreme Court ruled that *Milliken* . . . equalization remedies should be limited in time and extent and that school districts need not show any actual correction of the education harms of segregation. The Court defined rapid restoration of local control as the primary goal in desegregation cases.

---

cannot be readily changed within a context of segregation by race, poverty, and educational background.

Some of the reasons why these issues may become desegregation issues are apparent in the metropolitan Hartford, Connecticut lawsuit against the state government for desegregation and educational equalization. In a typical class of twenty-three students in the Hartford public schools, an average of twenty-one students are either African American or Latino; three were born to mothers on drugs, five to teen mothers; three were born underweight. In addition, eight live in poverty; fifteen live with a single parent; nine have parents with less than a high school education; eight live in households with an excessive housing cost burden, ten are in households where a member is involved in criminal activity; and nine live with parents who are not working and have given up looking for work.

The suburbs have few such problems. If we expect these segregated city schools to provide educational opportunities equal to those of suburban communities, we will have to find support for a long-term policy of treating these schools much better than suburban schools, in terms of resources and assignments of teachers and administrators. Schools that must cope with homelessness, severe health and nutrition problems in communities menaced by gangs, violence, and joblessness face massive obstacles. The only alternative will be to try to open up the suburban schools and their opportunities to city students.

As segregation grows in the country, demographic trends and divisions among school districts point to increasing separation by race and poverty. This isolation is deeply and systematically linked to educational inequality, both in educational experiences and results. It is not likely to be self-correcting since the most troubled are also those with the fewest resources, organizational skills, and political power. Teacher recruitment and assignment practices are likely to increase rather than diminish this gap. To try to provide equal opportunities within segregated schools and districts, school officials would have to set up mechanisms to provide the most resources to the most disadvantaged, who happen to be the most powerless. Given the operation of local and state school politics there is no probability that such money, resources, special programs would stay in place. The depth and severity of the inequalities and their self-perpetuating character help explain why desegregation cases continue to seek ways to reconstruct the basic structures of educational segregation.

NOTES

1. Much of the data included in this chapter was first released by the Harvard Project on School Desegregation in a report issued by the National School Boards Association. See Gary Orfield with Sara Schley and Sean Reardon, *The Growth of Segregation in American Schools* (Alexandria, VA: National School Boards Association, 1993).
2. Eric M. Cambum, "College Completion among Students from High Schools Located in Large Metropolitan Areas," *American Journal of Education,* 98 no. 4 (August 1990) pp. 551–69.
3. U.S. Department of Education Office for Civil Rights Data in Gary Orfield, *Public School Desegregation in the United States,* 1968–1980, Tables 1 and 10, and 1991 Center for Education, Statistics, Common Core of Data Public Education Agency Universe.
4. 1994 Census Bureau projections indicated that Latinos will be the largest minority by 2020, with nearly 16 percent of the population. See "Americans in 2020: Less White, More Southern," *New York Times,* 22 April 1994. The Census Bureau has projected that the U.S. population will be 22 percent Latino and 14 percent African American by 2050 if trends in the early 1990s continue. The Latino share of the U.S. school enrollment should surpass the African American share in the early twenty-first century. See U.S. Bureau of the Census, P25-1104, Tables A, 2, 3, cited in *Population Bulletin,* 49, no. 2 (September 1994), p. 9.
5. Greg J. Duncan, *Years of Poverty, Years of Plenty* (Ann Arbor, MI: Institute for Social Research, 1984).
6. Gary Orfield, *The Growth of Segregation in American Schools: Changing Patterns of Separation and Poverty Since 1968* (Alexandria, VA: National School Boards Association, 1993), Table 4.
7. Orfield, *Growth of Segregation,* Table 7.
8. Ibid., Table 8.
9. *The Condition of Education 1993,* p. 100.
10. *The Condition of Education 1994,* p. 110.
11. U.S. Census Bureau, *School Enrollment, 1992,* Table A1, Table C.
12. Ibid.
13. Gary Orfield, Franklin Monfort, and Melissa Aaron, *Status of School Desegregation, 1968–1986. Segregation, Integration, and Public Policy: National, State, and Metropolitan Trends in Public Schools* (Alexandria, VA: National School Boards Association, 1989), 1.
14. Gary Orfield and Franklin Monfort, *Racial Change and Desegregation in Large School Districts: Trends Through the 1986–1987 School Year* (Alexandria, VA: National School Boards Association, 1988).
15. Orfield and Ashkinaze, 1991, p. 113.
16. U.S. Bureau of the Census, 1991b, p. 5.
17. Orfield and Ashkinaze, 1991, p. 111; Orfield and Monfort, 1988, p. 11.

18. Orfield and Monfort, "Racial Change," U.S. Civil Rights Commission, *New Evidence on School Desegregation*, 1987.

19. Peter Scheirer, "Poverty Not Bureaucracy," working paper, Metropolitan Opportunity Project, University of Chicago, 1991; the following chapter segment draws heavily on Orfield and Sean Reardon, "Race, Poverty, and Inequality."

20. Ibid.

21. Peter Scheirer, "Metropolitan Chicago Public Schools: Concerto for Grades, Schools, and Students in F Major," Metropolitan Opportunity Project, University of Chicago, 1989.

22. Computations from Ohio Department of Education data by Sean Reardon.

23. P. Kaufman and M. M. McMillen, *Dropout Rates in the United States* (Washington, DC: National Center for Education Statistics, 1990), p. 5.

24. Because dropout rates are calculated a number of different ways, rates may not always be comparable across districts or metropolitan areas. In this [chapter], we cite two basic kinds of dropout rates—*annual* (or *event*) rates and *cohort* rates. Annual rates give the percentage of students entering a particular grade (usually ninth or tenth) who have dropped out by the time their cohort graduates four or three years later. There is a great deal of variation even among the way these rates are calculated in different studies and in different cities. Therefore, in this [chapter] we present dropout rates from only one study at a time, and then only to compare districts within a particular metropolitan area. Our intention is not to provide definitive reports of actual dropout rates, but only to show that they differ sharply by race, SES and location.

25. Philip Burch, *The Dropout Problems in New Jersey's Big Urban Schools: Educational Inequality and Government Inaction* (New Brunswick, NJ: Rutgers Bureau of Government Research, 1992), p. ix.

26. Study Commission on the Quality of Education in the Metropolitan Milwaukee Public Schools, 1985; John F. Witte and Daniel J. Walsh, *Metropolitan Milwaukee District Performance Assessment Report,* staff report to the Study Commission on the Quality of Education in the Metropolitan Milwaukee Public Schools, August 1, 1985.

27. Los Angeles County Office of Education, *The Demographic and Education Conditions of Public Schools in Los Angeles County 1987–1988: A Statistical Report*, 1989.

28. Henry Jay Becker, *Opportunities for Learning Curriculum and Instruction in the Middle Grades*, Report No. 37 (Baltimore: Center for Research on Elementary and Middle Schools, Johns Hopkins University, 1990); Doug MacIver and Joyce Epstein, *How Unequal Are Opportunities for Learning in Disadvantaged and Advantaged Middle Grade Schools?*, Report No. 7 (Baltimore: Johns Hopkins University Center for Research on Effective Schooling for Disadvantaged Students, 1990).

29. See Jeannie Oakes, *Multiplying Inequalities: The Effects of Race, Social Class, and Tracking on Opportunities to Learn Mathematics and Science* (Santa Monica: RAND, 1990), Figure 2.3.

30. Ibid., Figures 3.4 and 3.5.

31. Ibid.

32. Ibid., Figure 4.3.

33. NAEP data reported in Educational Testing Service, *The State of Inequality* (Princeton: ETS, 1988).

34. Gary Orfield, Howard Mitzel et al., *The Chicago Study of Access and Choice in Higher Education*, University of Chicago, Committee on Public Policy Studies, 1984, p. 117.

35. Oakes, *Multiplying Inequalities*, 66.

19

THE NATURE OF SCHOOLING

Doris R. Entwisle • *Karl L. Alexander* • *Linda Olson*

The nation remains skeptical that schools can reduce social inequality among children. Historically, this skepticism springs from two main sources, one, the early evaluations of Headstart that reported little benefit for children attending preschools, and the other, a consensus inherited from the Coleman Report (1996), that said differences in school quality had little bearing on students' achievement. These two lines of research strongly deflected public policy analysts and laypersons away from seeing schools as institutions that could reduce social inequality. In order to set aside old shibboleths and move ahead toward a fresh and more realistic view of children's early schooling, each of these lines of research will be briefly summarized and reinterpreted in turn.

Headstart

According to early evaluations, Headstart programs raised disadvantaged children's IQ's by only a few points and for only a relatively short period of time (Cicarelli 1969; McDill et al. 1969; Bronfenbrenner 1974). These conclusions, which were widely disseminated, were mistakenly pessimistic, and taking them at face value even led some

commentators to conclude that children's IQ's responded mainly to genetic rather than to environmental factors (Jensen 1969). These conclusions were modified a decade or so later when the early Headstart reports were re-evaluated by pooling data from all the major Headstart experiments, concentrating on those in which students were *randomly* assigned to experimental (preschool) and control (no preschool) groups (Lazar and Darlington 1982). The re-evaluations verified that preschooled children's IQ gains amounted to about 8 points in first grade and gradually faded after 2 or 3 years. But these re-evaluations found benefits that had not been uncovered earlier: compared to the control children, the Headstart children had better math achievement up through grade 5 and had more pride in their accomplishments throughout elementary school. Parents of Headstart children were also affected. Compared to mothers of control children, the mothers of the preschooled children were more satisfied with their children's school performance, even allowing for the level of that performance; also mothers of preschooled children had higher occupational aspirations for their children than other mothers did, and higher aspirations for their children than their children had for themselves. Most impressive, when the Headstart students reached seventh grade, only 14.6% of them were in Special Education compared to 34.9% of the control children, and only 19.9% had been retained compared to 34.9% of the control group. By twelfth grade, 18.9% more of the preschooled than the control group had avoided Special Education.

These findings in favor of Headstart are impressive because they come from hard experimental data analyzed by careful investigators who had no part either in designing or running the original Headstart programs. In addition, the re-evaluation included *every* experiment before 1969 in the United States that involved more than 100 children. It is hard to overrate the importance of helping youngsters avoid being held back or placed in Special Education because avoiding these placements makes a tremendous difference in their long-term life chances—more of them will continue in school, and not drop out before high school graduation, for example.

. . .

Some additional long-term effects also have emerged subsequent to the time of the 1982 evaluation. Headstart youngsters were more likely to graduate from high school, and after they left high school, 66% of the graduates who had no retentions were employed compared to 41% of those who had been retained (Consortium 1983: p. 443ff). The Headstart youngsters also adapted better to "mainstream society": they were more likely to be in some type of educational program, including high school or the military; they were more likely to be either employed or temporarily laid off; they were more likely to be living with a working spouse/companion. By contrast, the non-Headstart group was more likely not to be employed or looking for work, and more likely to be in prison or a non-student on public assistance. Many of these positive findings come from the Perry Preschool Project (Berrueta-Clement et al. 1984), one of the experiments with the longest time frame and a particularly intensive intervention.

. . .

Secondary Schools

Another large-scale and famous study, the Coleman Report (1966), can also be interpreted to support the idea that schools reduce social inequality, although originally it was taken to prove the opposite. Coleman et al. concluded that *differences* among youngsters' families and not differences among their high schools affected students' achievement. Narrowly interpreted, this conclusion is correct: secondary school quality does account for less of the *difference* among high school students' achievement than do personal and family background factors (see also Hauser 1971; Jencks et al. 1972; Mosteller and Moynihan 1972; Alexander and Eckland 1975). Still, to say that secondary schools have little differential influence on students' learning is not to say that attending high school has no influence: if children who attended one high school gained 100 points on some standardized test while those who attended another high school gained 98 points, the 2-point difference is rightly judged negligible, but the 98-point gain that they all make is not negligible. If schools act to negate social inequalities, they *would* produce this lack of variability in achievement across secondary schools because they would boost the performance of the less advantaged children to equal that of the more advantaged.

Unfortunately, the negative interpretation of the Coleman data discouraged similar research at the elementary level, so that, without directly examining new data, Jencks wrote (1972, p. 89): "Differences between elementary schools may be somewhat more important [than those between high schools] . . . but the average effect of attending the best rather than the worst fifth of all elementary schools is almost certainly no more than 10 [IQ] points and probably no more than 5."[1] At the same time though, Jencks (p. 89) was careful to note the early work of Hayes and

Grether (1969), which shows that children's differential growth in summer is the major source of the differences in achievement between children of different socioeconomic levels. (See also Mosteller and Moynihan 1972, p. 48.) In this sense, Jencks anticipated Heyns' (1978) Atlanta study that demonstrated substantial effects of schooling independent of home background for sixth and seventh graders. She brought to light seasonal differences in learning that make the school's contribution much clearer.

Seasonal Learning

Heyns' research provided a major breakthrough. By comparing children's cognitive growth when schools are open (in winter) to children's growth when schools are closed (in summer), she separated effects of home background from effects of school. In winter both school and home can affect children's growth but in summer only home influence can affect their growth.

Heyns determined that attending school reduces the achievement gap separating economically advantaged from disadvantaged children, a gap which increases as they progress up through the grades, i.e., she demonstrated that the distance between the achievement of well-off and poor students narrows during the school year. She showed . . . that the *school-year* gain for white children from the most favored backgrounds is 1.00 grade-equivalent unit, and is very close to the 0.96 unit gain seen for those in the next lower income category (a difference of only .04 units). Over the summer, however, the better-off white children in her study gained .11 units more than students in the next lower economic category (.29 versus .18). For African Americans, the seasonal contrasts were even more striking; gains in the school year for children in the highest income categories differed by only .03 units

(.62 and .59), but differed by .34 units in summer (−.12 plus .22). Thus, achievement differences between children from advantaged and disadvantaged home backgrounds emerged mainly in the summer months when schools were closed. When schools were open, poor children gained just about as much as better-off children did. Rather than making no difference, it seems Atlanta schools actually made up for shortfalls in resources in low socioeconomic status children's homes.

Heyns was not the first to identify seasonal differences in learning (see Hayes and Grether 1969; Murnane 1975), but she developed a conceptual framework, including multivariate models with "summer parameters," and carried out a large scale study on summer learning that produced two solid findings: (1) the gains children made in the school year exceeded those they made in the summer, and (2) children's summer gains were inversely related to their socioeconomic status; that is, poorer children gained about the same amount as other children in winter but gained less in summer. In summers, almost all the African American children in Atlanta *lost* ground, in fact.

A subsequent study of summer learning (Klibanoff and Haggart 1981), based on three years' data for more than 100,000 students in over 300 elementary schools, bore out Heyns' conclusions. Economically disadvantaged students grew at a slower rate over the summer than did their more advantaged counterparts, and as in the Atlanta sample, the least advantaged children consistently lost ground over the summer in reading and math (see Heyns 1986).

Why have these findings about "summer learning" not energized educators and policy makers? Mainly because in most educational research, children's school progress is assessed only once a year. Any variation in rates of learning during the year is thereby obscured. If students are tested every June, then the annual increment in their achievement is computed as this June's score minus last June's score. The relationship between social background and learning is then necessarily assumed to be constant throughout the year, and all the causes of that learning are necessarily taken to operate in the same way over that period. Only when score gains are computed by season, separately for winter and summer, is the strong inverse relation between socioeconomic status and children's lack of summer achievement apparent.

To understand how schooling counteracts social inequality, it is essential to separate "home" from "school" learning. The effect of schooling *by itself* is hard to isolate, because children learn around the clock, and on week-ends as well as on week days. Indeed, they spend more time outside school than inside, and much of that time is spent at home. Accordingly, much of what children learn could be learned at home, not at school. Better-off families travel, go to museums and libraries, and spend time with youngsters in ways that could enhance their cognitive growth, while families who are not so well-off have fewer resources to help children develop. It would not be surprising then, if children from relatively advantaged backgrounds improved their academic skills substantially over the summer, when school is closed, while children from poor backgrounds did not. (See Entwisle and Alexander 1992, 1994; and Alexander and Entwisle 1996.)

Seasonal patterns in learning square well with the long-time impression that schooling helps disadvantaged more than it helps advantaged children (St. John 1975; Coleman 1966). In fact, in periods when school is open, disadvantaged children in Baltimore learn as much as their more advantaged counterparts do (Alexander and Entwisle 1996). Only when school is closed does Baltimore children's achievement vary

by socioeconomic status level. The seasonal variation in learning seen in Heyns' and other data (Entwisle and Alexander 1992, 1994; Murnane 1975) highlights the idea that schools *mitigate* social inequality because differences in children's learning across socioeconomic status groups are virtually absent in winter. . . . Heyns (1978) shows that African American children with less than $4,000 income have a "school gain" (.42) plus a "summer gain" (−.28) that produces a net gain of .14 points. Parallel gains for African Americans in the highest income group came to .84 points. The highest and lowest income groups are thus separated by .70 points, but the "winter" part of that differential is .20 while the "summer" part is .50. Therefore, most of the difference in gains between the two groups (71% of it) comes from the considerable progress that better-off children made in summer when school was closed. All but the very poorest African American children in Atlanta gained roughly the same amounts of word knowledge when school was in session (.51, .59, .62). In summer, however, all of the poorer groups lost ground; only the most affluent group gained. The major differences in children's overall achievement are thus traceable to family background, as the Coleman Report concluded, but when schools are in session they are highly successful at reducing effects of social inequality. Seasonal learning data thus provide a strong counterpoint to the Coleman Report and other large national studies that have been interpreted so as to negate the role of schools in reducing inequality.

The Beginning School Study that we carried out in Baltimore builds directly on Heyns' research. It sees children's cognitive development as temporal in two key respects. The first is consistent with Heyns— schooling occurs in some seasons of the year, not in others, and the pace of children's cognitive growth reflects the school calendar. The second emphasizes that cognitive growth is temporal in quite another sense: it is much more rapid early in life than later. Jencks (1985) estimates the rate of cognitive growth in first grade is ten times the rate in high school. Consistent with this, Beginning School Study data show that children's cognitive growth is much more rapid over the first two elementary years than the later years. The reading comprehension gain that children made in year one (64 points) is well over twice the gain in year five (26 points), for example (see Entwisle and Alexander 1996). Because students' capacity to profit from schooling is greatest in the early primary grades, their rapid rate of growth in the early years means that effects of social inequality are probably greatest in the early years of schooling.

Dimensions of Inequality

This [chapter] covers just a few dimensions of social inequality: children's socioeconomic status, age, and gender, plus school and family organization. The first three of these are characteristics of *individual* children and are closely related to the "risk factors" often discussed in connection with schooling (Pallas, Natriello, and McDill 1989). As we will later point out, organizational factors in school and family also impose "risks" that can help or hinder children's schooling. Before considering these, a few words are needed about the individual risks, however, especially socioeconomic status.

Children from families of low socioeconomic status suffer from multiple risks including two major ones that overlap: family economic status or income, and the level of their parents' education. Low family income and reduced education go together, because, other things equal, persons who finish high school or better can anticipate a much higher standard of living throughout their lives than those who do not. In 1992, for example, for U.S. families in the lowest income quintile, 22% of household heads had less than a 9th grade education and only 5% had earned a bachelor's degree. By contrast, among families in the highest income quintile, 54% of heads had at least a bachelor's degree and only 1% had not reached the 9th grade. Similarly, high school completion rates for household heads in the highest income quintile stood at 96%, while among those in the lowest income quintile, only 57% had earned a high school diploma (U.S. Bureau of the Census 1993).

Children who come from economically disadvantaged families are at greater risk of failing a grade, getting low test scores and marks, or having behavior problems in school. (See Zill 1996.) The odds are 8% greater that a child from a higher income family will be in the upper half of the class than a child from a lower income family will be, for example. Children in low-income families are also more likely to fail a grade, and those whose families were in the lowest income quintile in 1992 had a dropout rate of close to 25% versus a rate of only 2% for children from families in the highest income quintile (Smith et al. 1994). (See also U.S. Department of Education 1994.) Bianchi (1984) used national school enrollment data to show that among sons of high school dropout parents living in poverty, retention rates reached 50%, compared with rates of 18% to 19% for sons in an "average household" (a husband–wife family with income above the poverty level, in which the wife had a high school education and either did not work outside the family or worked part-time). Similarly the NELS-88 survey shows that, in the lowest quartile of family socioeconomic status, over 31% of children had repeated a grade versus 8% in the highest quartile (National Center for Education Statistics 1990).

Parental education level is an alternative measure of family socioeconomic status that also predicts children's school performance. The proficiency tests administered in 1990 by the National Assessment of Educational Progress reveal a consistent relationship between achievement and parental education. Among 9 year olds, scores in reading ranged from 193 for students whose parents did not have a high school diploma, to 218 for those whose parents had more than a high school education. Math scores ranged from 210 for 9 year olds whose parents lacked a high school education, to 238 for those whose parents were college graduates (U.S. Bureau of the Census 1994). The relationship between students' achievement and how far their parents have gone in school is thus strong and consistent. (See also U.S. Department of Education 1994; U.S. Department of Education 1991.) As a consequence, research studies often merge family income and parent education level, as happens when father's occupation is used to measure family socioeconomic standing.

Baltimore data clearly illustrate the specific risks posed by low family economic status for young children's school achievement in reading and math. Grade equivalent scores[2] in reading and math in all 122 elementary schools in Baltimore in the spring of 1987, classified by quartiles according to the percentage of children in the school eligible for subsidized meals, show that in schools where less than 50% of the children were on subsidy, scores are above grade level in every year. . . . At the end of grade 2, for example, these children were already reading above the third grade level (3.19), and by the second semester of grade 5, they were reading above the seventh grade level (7.15). At the other extreme, however, in schools where almost everyone (89% or more) was on subsidy, children at the end of grade 2 were reading almost half a grade (2.53) below the third grade level. By the end

of elementary school, the difference in reading proficiency was well over one full grade equivalent between children in schools where students were at the two extremes of meal subsidy rates.

The risk factor approach is unattractive for many reasons, however, one being that this approach focuses on characteristics of *individual* children. Many influences on children's schooling are organizational or institutional, a prime example being the school's socioeconomic mix. The "risk" associated with children's low economic status could be mitigated or reinforced depending upon the fit between the socioeconomic characteristics of the school and those of the child who attends. On the one hand, placing poor children in schools where the majority of other children are well-off can promote higher achievement in those who are poor (Coleman et al. 1966). On the other hand, placing first grade African American youngsters in integrated schools (where they are often poorer than their white classmates) may make it harder for them to learn to read than it is for their counterparts in segregated schools (Entwisle and Alexander 1994).

The risk factor approach is limited for another reason, too. A risk factor is essentially the kernel of a probability statement where "risk" means an elevated probability of some event. It is easy to slide into causal imagery—that is, to say "low economic status causes children to drop out." To invoke causality requires more than an elevated likelihood, however; it requires pinpointing why and how low family income hinders children's schooling. Does family economic deprivation shunt children away from attending "good" schools, does the lack of infrastructure in poor children's neighborhoods undercut their learning outside of school, do poor families lack books and other learning materials in the home, or what? Rating individuals according to risks is a useful starting point in terms of suggesting hypotheses to test, but this approach cannot shed much light on social processes or social contexts. Also, so far the risk factor approach focuses mainly on *negative* relationships. The "risk" of doing better in school than would be predicted is hardly ever considered even though many children from economically disadvantaged and/or single-parent families do well in school (Pallas et al. 1987). The "risk" label has a negative ring to it, which is not necessary but which, nevertheless, leads to a neglect of "upside" risk.

Life Course Perspective

Issues related to social inequality and schooling can best be joined by taking a life course perspective. Risk factors, as just noted, somehow direct attention to shortfalls or failure, while a life course perspective directs attention to *all* outcomes, the positive *and* the negative. Many economically disadvantaged youngsters manage to finish high school, complete college, and go on to successful careers. A key question is how these children manage to do well despite economic disadvantage. Also a life course approach requires thinking in terms of how early schooling affects students over their entire life span. The schooling process in adolescence and early adulthood can be understood only in light of students' earlier school histories. In middle school, for example, children who take a foreign language and algebra and so are in line for the college preparatory program in high school, are those same students who have done well in elementary school (Dauber et al. 1996; Dauber 1993). Thus, to understand high school tracking requires an assessment of where students stood before they started high school. As yet, however, a dearth of longitudinal research with elementary school children examines effects of economic disad-

vantage, minority status, family type, and other social inequities in relation to school outcomes over the long term. In fact, to our knowledge, no national study of test scores in elementary schools continues into secondary schools even though various local studies suggest the correlation between early test scores and educational attainment is greater than .50, perhaps almost .60 in some instances (see Jencks, p. 323 . . .).

A life course approach also highlights the importance of school transitions. School transitions are times when children's social roles and obligations change, so they provide a window through which we can get a clearer view of how social forces affect schooling. They are strategically advantageous because they are points of maximum continuity/discontinuity in people's lives. In a bicycle race, it is hard to make distinctions among people when all are pedaling ahead on the straightaway and so bunched close together. Encountering a hill, however, spreads cyclists out, and it is easier to see who is ahead or behind as they pump uphill. Likewise, it is hard to tell who is ahead or behind when children stay in the same school, but school transitions are like "hills" when people are challenged and the differences among them tend to widen. Expanding the range along which people can be measured (spreading them out) is a technical advantage, because when people are more spread out we can estimate their positions relative to one another more accurately and so have a better chance to identify what propelled them ahead or behind. For example, if children are only one or two points apart on an achievement test, say 300 versus 302 on the California Achievement Test in reading when they began first grade, we cannot tell who is doing better or worse because the random error in the test is bigger than one or two points. If John gets 302 and Harry gets 300, we are hard pressed to say John's true score is actually greater than Harry's because if the test were repeated, Harry could easily outscore John. If scores are separated by many points, however, we have more confidence in our decision as to which person is first, which is second, and so on.

Children's long-term success can be made more certain or placed in jeopardy by how they negotiate school transitions. By studying the details of their performance over such problematic periods, researchers usually can learn more than they learn from studying a life period that is static. The beginning school transition is a very difficult transition for children. Because of the way schools are organized, it is also the time when social inequality may exact its heaviest toll on their long-term life chances. As noted earlier, the rate of retention is higher in first grade than in any subsequent grade (Shepard and Smith 1989; Reynolds 1992; Alexander, Entwisle, and Dauber 1994). With other things equal, poor children are more likely than better-off children to be held back, so socioeconomic inequality at this stage can exact a price that may never be repaid (Pallas 1984).

The "excess" retention rate in first grade for children from poor families illustrates how social inequity present at the time children begin school can provoke serious consequences for later schooling. Or, to take another example, single parents have lower expectations than married parents do for children's school performance at the beginning of first grade . . . and lower parent expectations act to depress their children's reading marks. Given the importance of early reading skills for all other kinds of academic performance, a small difference in parents' expectations for their children's reading performance at the start of first grade, when added on to the debit linked to the low income of single parents, can make the difference between children who pass or fail first grade (Sundius 1996).

It is puzzling why so little research examines children's success in negotiating the transition into full-time schooling because children's starting points are strong determinants of their trajectory patterns. Those who have an early lead have a marked tendency to stay ahead (Ensminger and Slusarcick 1992; Harnqvist 1977; Husén and Tuijnman 1991; Kraus 1973; Alexander, Entwisle, and Dauber 1994; Kerckhoff 1993; Luste and McAdoo 1996). As discussed earlier, the advantage of Headstart youngsters in the early grades that put them slightly ahead of their non-preschooled counterparts persisted far into adulthood. The Consortium (1983) and other related analyses (Luster and McAdoo 1996) provide a compelling example of how even a slight edge early in the game can mediate remarkable long-term advantages.

Children's personal characteristics are easier to study than the social contexts of schools, and so are more often investigated, but the two are intertwined. If two children of the same ability attend different schools, for example, such that one school has a student body of higher socioeconomic status than the other, the student attending the "low" school could well receive less instruction than the student in the "high" school. Yet because his/her reference group could contain many more students of lower ability than him/herself, the student's academic self-image in the "low" school could exceed that of the student in the "high" school. The social milieu as well as the student's individual characteristics need to be considered in understanding schooling.

Teachers' personal characteristics are part of the school milieu that students experience. All else equal, higher status teachers in the Beginning School Study rated disadvantaged or minority children lower than they rated advantaged or majority children (Alexander et al. 1987). Compared to children with the same test scores but of higher socioeconomic status, high status teachers held lower expectations for the future performance of students from low social backgrounds and saw them as less active participants in class.

Teachers' feelings about their work environment can form still another part of the school's social milieu. Beginning School Study first graders who did exceptionally well in first grade had teachers who rated the social climate of their school higher than did other teachers (Pallas et al. 1987). Specifically, if teachers found teaching in their school "pleasant" (versus "unpleasant") and found trying to do their job right as "very rewarding" (versus "frustrating"), their students did better than did students of less satisfied teachers. Perhaps the enthusiasm of teachers who think well of their school spreads to their students, or perhaps these schools provide settings that make teacher-student interactions more productive. Whatever the case, these examples show how subtleties of the school context can help or hinder young students.

Social Inequality and Early Schooling in Perspective

This chapter started by looking back at two large research studies, one on Headstart and the other the Coleman Report, which both initially seemed to provide strong evidence that schools do *not* mitigate social inequality. The consensus about these earlier studies has now changed: attending high quality preschool programs certainly reduces effects of social inequality on students' later school success, and secondary schools serve to equalize the achievement of students of varying economic backgrounds in winter when they are open (Heyns 1978). In fact, . . . schooling at any level probably offsets ef-

fects of social inequity because home resources are critical for students' development mainly when schools are closed.

NOTES

1. His emphasis on the "smallness" of 10 IQ points can be questioned. The standard deviation of most IQ tests is 15 points—two thirds of a standard deviation on each side of the mean includes 49% of the population. Or, from another point of view, the 10 point difference between an average score (100) and the score (110) is often cited as appropriate for a cutoff for college admissions.
2. Grade equivalents classify test scores by grade level. For example, a child who can complete tests in reading at the beginning third grade level is rated at 3.0 Grade Equivalent Units (G.E.'s). One who can complete tests equivalent to those of children in the middle of grade 3 would be rated at 3.5 G.E.

REFERENCES

ALEXANDER, KARL L. AND BRUCE K. ECKLAND. 1975. "School Experiences and Status Attainment." Pp. 171–210 in *Adolescence in the Life Cycle,* edited by S. E. Dragastin and Glen H. Elder. New York: Wiley.

—— AND DORIS R. ENTWISLE. 1996. "Educational Tracking in the Early Years: First Grade Placements and Middle School Constraints." Pp. 83–113 in *Generating Social Stratification: Toward a New Research Agenda,* edited by Alan C. Kerckhoff. New York: Westview Press.

——, DORIS R. ENTWISLE, AND SUSAN L. DAUBER. 1994. *On the Success of Failure: A Reassessment of the Effects of Retention in the Primary Grades.* Cambridge, MA: Cambridge University Press.

——, DORIS R. ENTWISLE, AND MAXINE S. THOMPSON. 1987. "School Performance, Status Relations and the Structure of Sentiment: Bringing the Teacher Back In." *American Sociological Review* 52:665–82.

BIANCHI, SUSAN M. 1984. "Children's Progress Through School: A Research Note." *Sociology of Education* 57:184–92.

BRONFENBRENNER, URIE. 1974. "Is Early Intervention Effective?" *Teachers College* 76:279–303.

CICARELLI, VICTOR ET AL. 1969. *The Impact of Head Start: An Evaluation of Head Start on Children's*

Cognitive and Affective Development. Report presented to the Office of Economic Opportunity, Pursuant to Contract B89-4536. Report No. PB 184 328. U.S. Institute for Applied Technology: Westinghouse Learning Corporation for Federal Scientific and Technical Information.

COLEMAN, JAMES S., ERNEST Q. CAMPBELL, CHARLES J. HOBSON, JAMES McPARTLAND, ALEXANDER MOOD, F. D. WEINFELD, AND R. L. YORK. 1966. *Equality of Educational Opportunity.* Washington, DC: U.S. Government Printing Office.

CONSORTIUM OF LONGITUDINAL STUDIES. 1983. *As the Twig Is Bent: Lasting Effect of Preschool Programs.* Hillsdale, NJ: Erlbaum.

ENSMINGER, MARGARET E. AND ANITA L. SLUSARCICK. 1992. "Paths to High School Graduation or Dropout: A Longitudinal Study of a First-Grade Cohort." *Sociology of Education* 65: 95–113.

ENTWISLE, DORIS R. AND KARL L. ALEXANDER. 1992. "Summer Setback: Race, Poverty, School Composition, and Mathematics Achievement in the First Two Years of School." *American Sociological Review* 57: 72–84.

—— AND KARL L. ALEXANDER. 1994. "Winter Setback: School Racial Composition and Learning to Read. *American Sociological Review* 59: 446–60.

—— AND KARL L. ALEXANDER. 1996. "Further Comments on Seasonal Learning." Pp. 125–36 in *Family–School Links: How Do They Affect Educational Outcomes?* edited by Alan Booth and Judith F. Dunn. Mahwah, NJ: Erlbaum.

HARNQVIST, K. 1977. "Enduring Effects of Schooling: A Neglected Area in Educational Research." *Educational Researcher* 6: 5–11.

HAUSER, ROBERT M. 1971. *Socioeconomic Background and Educational Performance.* American Sociological Association. Washington, DC: Rose Monograph Series.

HAYES, DONALD P. AND JUDITH GRETHER. 1969. "The School Year and Vacations: When Do Students Learn?" Paper presented at the Eastern Sociological Association meeting. New York, April. Subsequently Published in *Cornell Journal of Social Relations* 17 (1983): 56–71.

HEYNS, BARBARA. 1978. *Summer Learning and the Effects of Schooling.* New York: Academic Press.

HUSÉN, TORSTEN AND ALBERT TIUJNMAN. 1991. "The Contribution of Formal Schooling to the Increase in Intellectual Capital." *Educational Researcher* 20: 17–25.

JENCKS, CHRISTOPHER, MARSHALL SMITH, HENRY ACLAND, MARY JO BANE, DAVID COHEN, HERBERT GINTIS, BARBARA HEYNS, AND STEPHAN MICHELSON. 1972. *Inequality: A Reassessment of the Effects of Family and Schooling in America.* New York: Basic.

——. 1985. "How Much Do High School Students Learn?" *Sociology of Education* 58: 128–53.

JENSEN, ARTHUR R. 1969. "How Much Can We Boost I.Q. and Scholastic Achievement?" *Harvard Educational Review* 39: 1–123.

KERCKHOFF, ALAN C. 1993. *Diverging Pathways: Social Structure and Career Deflections.* New York: Cambridge University Press.

KLIBANOFF, LEONARD S. AND SUE A. HAGGART. 1981. *Report # 8: Summer Growth and the Effectiveness of Summer School.* Technical Report to the Office of Program Evaluation. U.S. Department of Education, Mountain View, CA: RMC Research Corporation.

KRAUS, PHILIP E. 1973. *Yesterday's Children.* New York: Wiley.

LAZAR, IRVING AND RICHARD DARLINGTON. 1982. "Lasting Effects of Early Education: A Report from the Consortium for Longitudinal Studies." *Monographs of the Society for Research in Child Development* 47: 2–3.

LUSTER, TOM AND HARRIETTE McADOO. 1996. "Family and Child Influences on Educational Attainment: A Secondary Analysis of the High/Scope Perry Prechool Data." *Developmental Psychology* 32: 26–39.

McDILL, EDWARD L., MARY S. McDILL, AND J. TIMOTHY SPREHE. 1969. *Strategies for Success in Compensatory Education: An Appraisal of Evaluation Research.* Baltimore: Johns Hopkins University Press.

MOSTELLER, FREDERICK AND DANIEL P. MOYNIHAN. 1972. *On Equality of Educational Opportunity.* New York: Vintage.

MUESER, PETER. 1979. "The Effects of Non-Cognitive Traits." Pp. 122–58 in *Who Gets Ahead? The Determinants of Economic Success in America,* edited by Christopher Jencks. New York: Basic.

MURNANE, RICHARD J. 1975. *The Impact of School Resources on the Learning of Inner City Children.* Cambridge, MA: Ballinger.

NATIONAL CENTER FOR EDUCATION STATISTICS. 1990. *A Profile of the American Eighth Grader: NELS 88 Student Descriptive Summary.* U.S. Department of Education, Office of Educational Research and Improvement. Washington, DC: U.S. Government Printing Office.

PALLAS, AARON M. 1984. "The Determinants of High School Dropouts." Unpublished doctoral dissertation. Baltimore: Johns Hopkins University.

——, DORIS R. ENTWISLE, KARL L. ALEXANDER, AND DORIS CADIGAN. 1987. "Children Who Do Exceptionally Well in First Grade." *Sociology of Education* 60:257–71.

——, GARY NATRIELLO, AND EDWARD L. MCDILL. 1989. "The Changing Nature of the Disadvantaged Population: Current Dimensions and Future Trends." *Educational Researcher* 18:16–22.

REYNOLDS, ARTHUR J. 1992. "Grade Retention and School Adjustment: An Explanatory Analysis." *Educational Evaluation and Policy Analysis* 14:101–21.

——. 1994. "Effects of a Preschool plus Follow-On Intervention for Children at Risk." *Developmental Psychology* 30:787–804.

SHEPARD, LORRIE A. AND MARY LEE SMITH. 1989. *Flunking Grades: Research and Policies on Retention.* London: Falmer.

SMITH, THOMAS M., GAYLE T. ROGERS, NABEEL ALSALAM, MARIANNE PERIE, REBECCA P. MAHONEY, AND VALERIE MARTIN. 1994. *The Condition of Education.* NCES 94-194. Washington, DC: U.S. Department of Education.

SØRENSEN, AAGE B. AND MAUREEN HALLINAN. 1984. "Effects of Race on Assignment to Ability Groups." Pp. 85–103 in *The Social Context of Instruction: Group Organization and Group Processes,* edited by Penelope L. Peterson, Louise Cherry Wilkinson, and Maureen T. Hallinan. New York: Academic.

ST. JOHN, NANCY. 1975. *School Desegregation: Outcomes for Children.* New York: Wiley.

SUNDIUS, M. JANE. 1996. "Making The Mark: Family Resources and Their Effect on Children's First Grade Report Cards." Unpublished doctoral dissertation. Baltimore, MD: Johns Hopkins University.

U.S. BUREAU OF THE CENSUS. 1973. "Characteristics of the Population. Part 22, Maryland." In *Census of the Population: 1970, Vol. 1.* Washington, DC: U.S. Government Printing Office.

——. 1983. *Census of Population: 1980 Vol. 1. Characteristics of the Population.* Washington, DC: U.S. Government Printing Office.

——. 1992. *Statistical Abstract of the U.S.* Washington, DC: Bureau of the Census.

——. 1993. *Money Income of Households, Families, and Persons in the United States: 1992.* Current Population Reports. P-60, No. 184. Washington, DC: U.S. Government Printing Office.

——. 1994. *Statistical Abstract of the U.S.* Washington, DC: Bureau of the Census.

——. 1995a. *Child Support for Custodial Mothers and Fathers: 1991.* August, 1995. Current Population Reports, Series P-20, No. 187. Washington, DC: U.S. Government Printing Office.

——. 1995b. *Statistical Abstract of the U.S.* Washington, DC: Bureau of the Census.

U.S. DEPARTMENT OF EDUCATION. 1991. *Trends in Academic Progress.* National Center for Education Statistics. Washington, DC: U.S. Department of Education.

——. 1994. *The Condition of Education.* National Center for Education Statistics 94-104. Washington, DC: U.S. Department of Education.

ZILL, NICHOLAS. 1996. "Family Change and Student Achievement: What We Have Learned, What It Means for Schools." Pp. 139–74 in *Family-School Links: How Do They Affect Educational Outcomes?* edited by Alan Booth and Judy Dunn. Mahwah, NJ: Erlbaum.

Tracking

20

TRACKING
From Theory to Practice

Maureen T. Hallinan

The term *tracking* refers to the practice of assigning students to instructional groups on the basis of ability. Originally, secondary school students were assigned to academic, general, or vocational tracks, with the courses within those tracks designed to prepare students for postsecondary education or careers. More recently, these track categories have been replaced by course levels, with students typically being assigned to advanced, honors, regular, or basic courses. These course levels continue to be referred to as tracks, with the regular and higher-level courses loosely equivalent to the academic track and the basic and lower courses loosely equivalent to the general and vocational tracks. Most secondary and junior high or middle schools track students for English and mathematics, and many schools track for social studies, science, language, and other courses.

Tracking is an organizational practice whose aim is to facilitate instruction and to increase learning. The theory of tracking argues that tracking permits teachers to tailor instruction to the ability level of their students. A good fit between a student's ability and the level of instruction is believed to maximize the effectiveness and efficiency of the instructional process. Thus, tracking is meant to promote cognitive development; it is not designed to influence or modify students' social or emotional growth.

The practice of tracking is currently a topic of intense debate. The concern focuses on two issues pertaining to the effectiveness and equity of tracking. The first is whether tracking is more effective in promoting students' learning than are other methods of grouping. The second is whether all students benefit from tracking to the same degree.

The tracking debate is fed by conjectures and assumptions about the way tracking operates and how it affects students. Among these beliefs are that track placement is determined primarily by academic criteria, that tracks are strictly homogeneous with respect to ability, that track assignments tend to be permanent, that tracking has a negative effect on the self-esteem of low-ability students, that low-ability students are difficult to teach because they are not highly motivated to learn, and that tracking limits the college options of low-track students.

Maureen T. Hallinan, excerpt from "Tracking: From Theory to Practice" from *Sociology of Education* 67 (April 1994). Copyright © 1994 by the American Sociological Association. Reprinted with the permission of the author and the American Sociological Association.

Research on Tracking

A number of fairly rigorous empirical studies, including both surveys and case studies, have provided information about how students are assigned to tracks and about the effects of track levels on students' learning. The findings of these studies are consistent with some of the commonly held beliefs about tracking, but contradict others. Empirical research supports the following conclusions about tracking.

Assignment to Tracks

1. In practice, the assignment of students to tracks is based not only on academic considerations, which would lead to strictly homogeneous groupings, but on nonacademic factors. Academic factors that influence track placement are grades, scores on standardized tests, teachers' and counselors' recommendations, prior track placement, and course prerequisites. Nonacademic considerations include course conflicts, cocurricular and extracurricular schedules, work demands, and teacher and curricular resources. A reliance on nonacademic factors increases the heterogeneity of ability groups and leads to overlapping ability distributions in adjacent tracks.

2. Schools vary in this constellation of factors on which they rely to assign students to tracks and in the weight they attach to each factor. As a result, track assignments are dependent, in part, on the schools that students attend.

3. Track assignments tend to be less permanent than is commonly believed. It is not uncommon for a student to change tracks during a school year and from one school year to the next. The flexibility of track assignments varies by school, by subject, and by grade level.

4. A greater proportion of minority and low-income students are assigned to the lower tracks. When academic achievement is controlled, the race–ethnicity and income effect on track assignment decreases, but does not disappear.

5. Higher social status is associated with placement in a higher track. The importance of track level for social status differs across schools.

Effects of Tracking

1. The quantity and quality of instruction increases with the level of the track. The curriculum and related instructional materials are more interesting and engaging in higher tracks. The amount of time spent on instruction, as opposed to administrative and disciplinary tasks, is greater in higher tracks. The relationship between track level and instructional characteristics differs among schools.

2. Students in high-ability tracks learn more and at a faster pace than do those in lower-ability tracks.

3. Tracking provide no advantage over heterogeneous grouping with respect to the achievement of students in the middle-ability range.

These conclusions indicate that tracking, as currently practiced, tends to be both inequitable and, at least for some students, ineffective. Tracking provides fewer learning opportunities for low-ability students than for those with higher ability. Since low ability is related to race, ethnicity, and socioeconomic status, tracking discriminates against students in these demographic categories. The disadvantages of tracking for low-ability students perpetuate the effects of background characteristics on achievement. Tracking also disadvantages lower-ability students by conveying on them lower social status. Differences among schools in the effectiveness and equity of tracking place additional constraints on access to learning opportunities for some students, usually those of lower ability.

In general, empirical research seems to provide the rationale for eliminating tracking as an organizational and pedagogical practice. However, the decision to detrack a school may be premature and unwarranted. To evaluate the effectiveness and equity of tracking in an effort to determine how it can be improved, rather than eliminated, it is necessary to examine its intended and unintended consequences.

Tracking as an Organizational Practice

Tracking is a way of organizing a student body. The intended purpose of tracking is to increase the effectiveness and efficiency of instruction. If tracking operated according to theory, students at all ability levels and from all backgrounds would learn more in tracked classes than in untracked ones. However, tracking produces unintended consequences that impede the attainment of its goal. Some of these consequences are inherent in the nature of tracking, whereas others are due to the failure of tracking practice to reflect tracking theory. These consequences make tracking less effective and less equitable than intended.

The task of an educational administrator who is faced with a decision about tracking is twofold: to determine whether the practice of tracking can be made more consistent with the theory and to ascertain whether negative features that are inherent in tracking can be outweighed by other school policies and practices. If the answer to these questions is affirmative, then it is reasonable to retain tracking, so teachers and students can benefit from the positive effects of the practice.

Modifying Negative Consequences

Segregation. One unintended negative consequence of tracking is the way it segregates students by race or ethnicity and socioeconomic status. Since academic achievement is related to students' background, minority and low-income students are disproportionately assigned to lower tracks. Even if the quality of instruction were the same across tracks, this segregating effect would concern educators and parents.

Although the segregation produced by tracking may be unavoidable, its negative effects can be countered by integrating students in their untracked classes and in other school activities. Ensuring that students spend a large part of their school day in integrated settings should lessen the negative effects of assignment to a small number of segregated classes. Furthermore, school authorities can create a school atmosphere that is intolerant of racism and that strongly supports positive social relations among different ethnic and racial groups.

Low social status. A second negative feature of tracking is its effects on students' social status. Tracking typically leads to a social hierarchy based on track level and academic performance. Students who are assigned to the lower tracks are apt to receive less respect from their peers and to be assigned lower status in the academic hierarchy. Lower status can have negative consequences for learning by decreasing a student's motivation and effort. In addition, rewards typically are given to higher-track students, which could further discourage or alienate lower-track students.

To counter the negative social dynamics created by tracking, school authorities need to create structures and methods to support the social and emotional experiences of lower-track students. Restructuring the reward system to broaden the bases for social recognition and respect is one way to enhance the status of low-track students.

Heterogeneous tracks. A third negative consequence of tracking results from the failure of authorities to create strictly homogeneous tracks. In practice, track levels are rarely as homogeneous as they could be. In most cases, the distribution of achievement in one track overlaps, to a surprising degree, with the distribution in adjacent tracks. Typically, students at the high end of the distribution in one track have higher achievement than do those at the low end of the distribution in the next higher track. The degree of heterogeneity among students in a track affects teachers' ability to direct instruction to the students' ability levels. Thus, the failure of students to benefit from tracking may be due partly to the failure of schools to create homogeneous tracks.

Moreover, students develop cognitively at different rates. Even when a track structure is homogeneous at the beginning of a school year, students' different rates of growth introduce heterogeneity into the tracks during the school year. When students' track placements are permanent, either across a school year or for longer periods, allowance is not made for the heterogeneity that arises from these differential rates of growth. Heterogeneity becomes greater with time, creating a wider departure from the conditions under which tracking is expected to be effective.

What is needed is a flexible tracking policy that allows for reassignments to preserve the homogeneity of tracks. Empirical data show that track assignments in many secondary schools are flexible, both across and within school years. However, changes in tracks are often made to accommodate a student's participation in other school activities, rather than for academic reasons. These changes usually create greater heterogeneity in tracks.

Frequent reassignments of students to tracks to increase the homogeneity of tracks are desirable. Periodic evaluations of the distribution of achievement in tracks and a policy of reassigning students to different tracks, when appropriate, should ensure a good fit between students' abilities and the level of instruction.

Slower achievement of students in low tracks. The most serious, unintended negative effect of tracking is the slower growth in achievement of students in low tracks. This effect is caused, in part, by instructional inadequacies in the lower tracks. Instruction in many low tracks can be characterized by uninteresting lessons and instructional materials, by teachers' low expectations and standards for their students' performance, by low standards for teachers' performance, and by a significant number of interruptions in instruction owing to disciplinary problems.

Educational authorities have the ability to modify each of these characteristics of instruction in lower tracks. Teachers can provide more interesting instructional materials without going beyond the students' level of comprehension. They also can alter their assumptions about the learning potential of low-ability students. Recent research on the multiple facets of intelligence, as well as new developments in learning theory that have identified different learning styles, should be helpful in this regard. Teachers can raise their expectations and requirements for students' performance. Principals can devise reward systems that are aimed at improving teachers' instruction, and teachers can provide rewards that motivate students to study. The school can consistently and publicly acknowledge the accomplishments of students in all academic tracks. Principals and counselors can devise methods of dealing with disciplinary problems without infringing on the teachers' instructional time.

Negative social psychological consequences. In addition, negative social psychological processes occur in lower tracks that further jeopardize learning for lower-ability students. These processes link a student's assignment to a lower track to his or her self-esteem and social status. Students are likely to view their assignments to low tracks as evidence that teachers have a low regard for their academic abilities and as an indication that they cannot be successful in school and should not aspire to go to college. This inference leads to a loss of self-confidence and decreases their motivation to achieve academically. Discouragement usually results in students' detachment from learning and often leads to disruptive behavior or withdrawal. This negative cycle tends to be self-perpetuating.

Change or intervention can occur at any point in the negative social psychological processes that interfere with learning. The principal and faculty of a school can make a determined effort to communicate a positive message about the meaning of different track levels. Teachers can increase the academic demands they place on lower-track students and challenge these students to achieve. They can offer students frequent opportunities to succeed and provide tangible and public rewards for success and improvement. The school can adhere to a policy of flexible track assignments, motivating students to work harder to advance to higher tracks if they so choose. In short, educators can forestall or reverse the negative social psychological dynamics that often accompany placements in low tracks by fostering a more positive attitude about track placement and students' potential. When accompanied by improved instruction in the lower tracks, this attitude adjustment should generate social psychological processes that encourage, rather than obstruct, learning in the lower tracks.

A common reaction to these unintended negative consequences of tracking is to call for the abandonment of tracking as an educational practice. A more tempered response would be to improve the way tracking is practiced, so it better fits the ideal, and to counter students' negative cognitive, social psychological, or behavioral responses to being tracked. The negative effect of tracking on integration in schools can be reduced by a committed effort to eliminate racism in a school and by avoiding segregation in nontracked classes and other school activities.

Objective versus Subjective Criteria

The effectiveness and equity of tracking are also influenced by the way students are assigned to track levels. Schools differ in the criteria they use to determine students' placements in tracks. Within a school, differences also occur in the criteria for assigning students to different track levels.

Assignments to tracks that are based strictly on objective, academic criteria, such as standardized test scores, academic grades, and prerequisites for courses, produce the most academically homogeneous groups. When more arbitrary criteria are applied, such as counselors' and teachers' recommendations, parents' and students' preferences, and schedule conflicts with other academic courses or with cocurricular and extracurricular activities, tracks tend to be more heterogeneous.

Secondary schools seem to use more objective criteria in assigning students to higher tracks and more arbitrary criteria in assigning students to lower tracks. This tendency creates greater homogeneity in the upper tracks, implying that students who are assigned to the upper tracks enjoy a more optimal instructional environment than do those assigned to the lower tracks.

Although subjective criteria may yield a more accurate assessment of students' potential than many objective measures, they usually do not because limitations on counselors' time leads to cursory evaluations, resulting in inappropriate assignments.

Schools differ in the criteria on which they base their decisions on track placements. Some schools rely heavily on objective measures, others use indicators of a student's improvement. Whether a school makes track placements on the basis of absolute, relative, or self-mastery standards has a direct impact on the track level to which a student is assigned. Differences in criteria among schools represent one way that tracking can transmit unequal learning opportunities to students.

School-district administrators, principals, and counselors establish their schools' criteria for placing students in tracks. Their challenge is to determine the most effective and equitable set of criteria to ensure the success of tracking. Most criteria that are defined at the district level are based on objective measures of ability or achievement, usually grades and standardized test scores. These are suitable measures generally, assuming that they correlate with students' ability, because they tend to create a fair degree of within-track homogeneity. Nevertheless, modifications of and exceptions to these criteria may be required to reduce heterogeneity further.

Although the use of objective measures of achievement as criteria for track placements increases the homogeneity of tracks, it creates other problems. Standardizing criteria for achievement results in the assignment of disproportionately fewer students to the upper tracks than to the lower tracks in some schools. Research has found that schools in which a small number of students qualify for admission to advanced tracks tend to lower their standards for admission to those tracks to increase the number of students in the advanced courses to a desired level. Thus, criteria for track placements may have to be defined at the school, rather than the district, level to take the characteristics of a school's population into account. Under these circumstances, careful counseling is called for when students change from one school to another.

A more serious consequence of standardizing criteria for admission to tracks and of basing admission primarily on objective measures of achievement is related to the equity of tracking. Administrators avoid setting objective criteria because doing so results in the assignment of fewer minority students to the higher tracks and disproportionately more minority students to the lower tracks. Since most administrators deplore this segregative aspect of tracking, they tend to prefer less objective measures of ability. To resolve this dilemma, it is necessary to compromise between the two desired goals of effectiveness and equity. In addition, however, schools need to make systematic, concerted efforts to improve the performance of low-ability students, so these students can meet the criteria for admission to higher tracks.

Conclusion

Tracking clearly has many shortcomings. Some of them, such as its segregative aspect and its effects on students' social status, are difficult to eliminate. However, schools have a number of opportunities to reduce these negative effects of tracking by ensuring that nontracked classes and other school activities are integrated and by expanding the bases of social status to include nonacademic talents.

Other shortcomings of tracking result not from the organizational technique itself, but from the way tracking is practiced in schools. Efforts to reform the practice should be directed toward improving the quantity and quality of instruction at all track levels, particularly the lower ones, to eliminate the instructional disadvantages of tracking that some students experience. Schools also need to guard against lessening the motivation of lower-track students by providing support mechanisms and reward systems for all students, including those in the lower tracks.

Finally, to ensure that tracking works as intended, great care is needed in making initial track assignments and in permitting students to change tracks when their original placements are no longer appropriate. Improving the fit of track assignments is a complex task. It requires school authorities to choose criteria that are valid measures of students' abilities and that reduce the likelihood of inappropriate placements. In the design of a student's schedule, track placement must take priority over other scheduling considerations. However, deviation from a rigid admissions policy is appropriate if it attains another objective, such as the integration of tracks, without having a major negative effect on the homogeneity of tracks.

In general, many of the criticisms leveled against tracking can be avoided by improving, rather than eliminating, tracking. The compelling advantage of retaining tracking, at least in certain subjects, is that it facilitates instruction and learning. The many teachers who favor tracking have concluded, from pedagogical experience, that teaching heterogeneously grouped students without additional resources, such as teacher aides and supplementary material, is a formidable task. Moreover, the outcome of detracking in less-than-ideal circumstances may be as unsatisfactory as that of tracking that is not practiced according to principle. If educators are willing to put serious efforts into creating a tracking system that attempts to maximize effectiveness and equity, the results should benefit students at all levels of ability.

21

THE DISTRIBUTION OF KNOWLEDGE

Jeannie Oakes

There has been a considerable amount of interest in tracking and some scholarly effort spent analyzing it. As a result, we know quite a bit about the outcomes of tracking—

Jeannie Oakes, excerpt from "The Distribution of Knowledge" from *Keeping Track: How Schools Structure Inequality.* Copyright © 1985 by Yale University. Reprinted with the permission of Yale University Press.

what happens to students as a result of being in one or another track, how their academic learning is affected, and what behaviors and attitudes they are likely to exhibit. Other studies have considered the factors that are important in determining who gets placed in which track level. Much of this inquiry has revolved around the question of fairness and has tried to assess the extent to which student placements are based on social class or on "merit." This question has not yet been resolved to everyone's satisfaction, because underlying the issue is a whole hotbed of other concerns: the definition of "merit," the objectivity of standardized tests, and probably the most volatile of all, the relationship between race and scholastic aptitude.

We looked at tracking from a slightly different, but not unrelated, perspective. Consistent with the focus of A Study of Schooling, we were interested in learning the content and process of classrooms under tracking systems. We wanted to know what actually goes on in classes at different track levels and how they are similar or different from one another. We wanted to know specific information about what students were being taught, how teachers carried out their instruction, what classroom relationships were like, and how involved students seemed to be in classroom learning. We also wanted to know about what kinds of student attitudes were characteristic of class rooms: attitudes students had toward themselves, their classrooms, and their schools. Essentially, we wanted to know details about what different kinds of classes were like for students and how students felt about being in them.

. . .

Who Goes Where

[T]here is a pattern of relationships between students' socioeconomic positions—and important in this is their ethnicity—and their chances of being placed in a particular track level. While there is certainly no automatic placement of poor and minority students in low tracks or of affluent white students in upper tracks, the odds of being assigned into particular tracks are not equal. In virtually every study that has considered this question, poor and minority students have been found in disproportionately large percentages in the bottom groups.

In our study of twenty-five schools, we found this same pattern operating We were able to examine it directly in two ways— related to student race and ethnicity—and indirectly—related to other socioeconomic characteristics. For one thing, we were able to look closely at the schools with racially mixed populations to determine who got placed in which track levels at those schools. And second, we were able to look at vocational education programs at all the schools and assess the differences in programs taught to white and nonwhite students. While these two considerations are related directly to race and ethnicity and tracking, they relate indirectly to other socioeconomic status factors as well, for not surprisingly, the minority students in our schools tended to be poorer than the whites. Moreover, the relationships we uncovered were the strongest at schools where the minority students were at the lowest income levels.

Academic Tracking and Race

Our twenty-five schools were very diverse in a number of ways, as we have seen. But one of the most noticeable ways in which they differed was in the racial and ethnic characteristics of the students who attended them. Seven senior highs and six junior highs were attended almost exclusively by white students. These were the schools in the Vista, Crestview, Woodlake, Atwater, Bradford, Euclid, and Dennison communities. The Rosemont schools were Mexican-American, and the Manchester schools black. The other eight schools were racially or ethnically mixed: Fairfield Junior and Senior highs were about half Mexican-American and half white, the Laurel and Palisades schools about half black and half white. Laurel's schools were part of a mixed, although hardly integrated rural community. The blacks at the two Palisades schools were bused in to this affluent white community. The Newport schools, located in a highly diverse metropolitan suburb, were unique among our group. The student population at these schools represented a rich variety of ethnic and racial groups. Slightly less than half of the students at each of the schools were white; the others were Mexican-American, black, or Asian, and a scattering of students were from a number of other distinct ethnic groups. Together, the thirteen white schools enrolled 10,783 students; the four nonwhite schools, 8,248 students; and the eight mixed schools, 4,287 white and 4,546 nonwhite students.

The relationship between student ethnicity and tracking could be seen at six of our mixed schools: Fairfield, Laurel, and Palisades. At these schools we recorded the race or ethnic background of every student in the classes we studied. By looking at how students from various groups were tracked into the English and math classes at these six schools, we could check to see if the schools followed the pattern that has been found so consistently in other research.

The white student populations at these six mixed schools ranged from a low of 46 percent to a high of 53 percent with an average for the six of 50 percent. Within these schools, an average of 62 percent of the students in high-track English classes were white, a considerably larger proportion than in the student population as a whole. Only 29 percent of the students in low-track English classes at these six schools were white, a substantially smaller percentage than in the total student population.[1]

Eight high-track and ten low-track English classes were included in the sample at these six multiracial schools. Of these eighteen classes, fourteen followed the predominant pattern of racial composition, with disproportionately large percentages of white students in high-track classes and of nonwhite students in low-track classes. Of the four classes that did not conform to this racial pattern, three were high-track classes with between 32 and 46 percent white students; the other, a low-track class, had 67 percent white students.

These four classes, however, shared some common characteristics. All four were located in the Palisades community, which, as we have seen, was a middle- to upper-middle-class suburb of a large city. The minority students were middle- and upper-middle-class blacks voluntarily bused to the school. At the other four multiracial schools, the minority populations were considerably less affluent. Additionally, three of these four nonconforming classes were elective subjects—speech, journalism, and creative writing. Only one was a standard language arts class, and that class had the largest white population of any of the three high-track classes (46 percent).

Math classes, too, evidenced this disproportionate allocation of racial groups in track levels. An average of 60 percent of the students in high-track math classes at the six schools were white, compared to only 37 percent of the students in the low-track math classes. As with the English classes, these percentages differed markedly from the percentage of white students in the total population at these multiracial schools.

Six high-track and twelve low-track math classes were studied at these schools. Of these eighteen math classes, only five did not follow the predominant pattern in racial composition—larger percentages of white students in high-track classes and smaller percentages of whites in low-track classes than in the schools as a whole. Of these five nonconforming classes, two were high-track classes—one with 44 percent white students and one with 29 percent—and three were low-track classes with a percentage of whites ranging from 55 to 65 percent. Like the exceptional English classes, three of these five math classes were located in the Palisades community, which had the more affluent black students.

From the information about these six schools, then, it is clear that in our multiracial schools minority students were found in disproportionately small percentages in high-track classes and in disproportionately large percentages in low-track classes. And, as we have seen, this pattern was most consistently found in schools where minority students were also poor. These findings are consistent with virtually every study that has considered the distribution of poor and minority students among track levels in schools. In academic tracking, then, poor and minority students are most likely to be placed at the lowest levels of the schools' sorting system.

. . .

Who Learns What

QUESTION: What is the most important thing you have learned or done so far in this class?

We were interested in finding out what students regarded as the most important learnings in their classroom experience. We gave them a considerable amount of empty space on their questionnaires to tell us what they thought. Students in high-track classes tended to write answers like these:

RESPONSES: I've learned to analyze stories that I have read. I can come with an open mind and see each character's point of view. Why she or he responded the way they did, if their response was stupidity or an heroic movement. I like this class because he [the teacher] doesn't put thoughts into your head; he lets you each have a say about the way it happened.

High-track English—senior high

Basic concepts and theories have been most prevalent. We have learned things that are practiced without taking away some in-depth studies of the subject.

High-track Science—senior high

Learning political and cultural trends in relation to international and domestic events.

High-track Social Studies—senior high

I have learned a lot about molecules and now am able to reason and figure out more things.

High-track Science—senior high

It teaches you how to do research in a college library.

High-track English—senior high

Learned to analyze famous writings by famous people, and we have learned to understand people's different viewpoints on general ideas.

High-track English—junior high

Things in nature are not always what they appear to be or what seems to be happening is not what really is happening.

High-track Science—senior high

Greek philosophy, Renaissance philosophy, humanities. How to write essays and do term papers. The French Revolution. HISTORY!

High-track Social Studies—junior high

We learned how to do experiments.

High-track Science—junior high

I've really learned the whole idea and meaning behind economics and how to apply economics to my life.

The bases of our economic system and the way the business world is.

*High-track Vocational Education—
senior high*

About businesses—corporations, monopolies, oligopolies, etc., and how to start, how they work, how much control they have on the economy—prices, demand, supply, advertising.

We've talked about stocks—bonds and the stock market and about the business in the U.S.A.

High-track Vocational Education—junior high

We have learned about business deals. We have also learned about contracts.

High-track Vocational Education—senior high

Learned many new mathematical principles and concepts that can be used in a future job.

High-track Math—senior high

Learning to change my thought processes in dealing with higher mathematics and computers.

High-track Math—senior high

How to write successful compositions, how to use certain words and their classifications. What to expect in my later years of schooling.

High-track English—junior high

The most important thing that we have done is to write a formal research paper.

High-track English—senior high

There is no one important thing I have learned. Since each new concept is built on the old ones, everything I learn is important.

High-track Math—senior high

To me, there is not a most important thing I learned in this class. Everything or mostly everything I learn in here is *IMPORTANT.*

High-track English—junior high

I have learned to do what scientists do.

High-track Science—junior high

Students in low-track classes told us the following kinds of things:

How to blow up light bulbs.

Low-track Vocational Education—junior high

Really I have learned nothing. Only my roman numerals. I knew them, but not very good. I could do better in another class.

Low-track Math—junior high

I've learned how to get a better job and how to act when at an interview filling out forms.

Low-track English—junior high

How to ride motorcycles and shoot trap.

Low-track Science—senior high

How to cook and keep a clean house. How to sew.

Low-track Vocational Education—junior high

The most important thing I have learned in this class I think is how to write checks and to figure the salary of a worker. Another thing is the tax rate.

Low-track Math—senior high

To be honest, nothing.

Low-track Science—senior high

Nothing outstanding.

Low-track Science—senior high

Nothing I'd use in my later life; it will take a better man than I to comprehend our world.

Low-track Science—senior high

I don't remember.

Low-track Social Studies—junior high

The only thing I've learned is how to flirt with the chicks in class. This class is a big waste of time and effort.

Low-track Science—senior high

I learned that English is boring.

Low-track English—senior high

I have learned just a small amount in this class. I feel that if I was in another class, that I would have a challenge to look forward to each and every time I entered the class. I feel that if I had another teacher I would work better.

Low-track Math—junior high

I can distinguish one type rock from another.

Low-track Science—senior high

To spell words you don't know, to fill out things where you get a job.

Low-track English—junior high

Learned about how to get a job.

Low-track English—junior high

Job training.

Low-track English—junior high

How to do income tax.

Low-track Math—senior high

A few lessons which have not very much to do with history. (I enjoyed it).

Low-track Social Studies—junior high

Most Americans believe that the school curriculum is fairly standard. From what we remember of our own experiences and what we saw represented in the media, we have an impression of sameness. Tenth-grade English at one school seems, with only slight variations here and there, to be tenth-grade English everywhere. This seems to be so much so that we would expect a tenth-grader who moves in the middle of the year from Pittsburgh or Pensacola to Petaluma to slip quite easily into a familiar course of study—a little Shakespeare, some famous short stories, a few Greek myths, lists of vocabulary words from the College Entrance Exams, and guidelines for well-developed paragraphs and short expository themes. The same beliefs hold for most academic subjects. For example, isn't eighth-grade math everywhere a review of basic operations, an introduction to algebraic and geometric concepts, with some practice in graphing and scientific notation and a brief glimpse at function and inequalities? How much could eleventh-grade American history differ from class to class or from place to place? Or ninth-grade introductory biology?

Don't misunderstand, however. We, as a society, have no expectation that all tenth-, or eighth-, or eleventh-graders will finish these classes having *learned* all the same things. We know well that some students are more or less interested than others and that some find it more or less difficult than others do. But most of us do assume that the material itself—facts and concepts to be learned, pieces of knowledge and works of scientific literacy or cultural merit to be appreciated—is at least paraded by everyone as they proceed through school. We assume that everyone is at least *exposed*. In our study of twenty-five schools we found these assumptions and beliefs to be unsubstantiated by our observations of what actually went on in classrooms.

One of the particulars we were most interested in finding out about was whether students who were placed in different track levels in subjects had the same opportunities to learn the *content* of those subjects. Were students in different track levels being exposed to the same or similar material? If so, were the differences among tracks merely ones of mode of presentation or pace of instruction? If actual content differences did exist, were they socially or educationally important ones—that is, was what some students were exposed to more highly valued by society than what other students were presented? We also wanted to know whether students in different track levels were experiencing about the same amount of learning time. Were some groups of students getting more instruction than others? Were effective instructional techniques being used more in one track than in another? Did teachers seem to perform better with some groups of students than with others?

We studied each of these questions carefully because we knew that the implications of what we found could be far-reaching. We believe that these issues go to the very heart of the matter of educational equity. For beyond the issue of what schools students have access to is the issue of what knowledge and learning experiences students have access to within those schools. If there are school-based or system-related differences in what students are exposed to, are these differences fair? Do they interfere with our commitment to educational equality?

We have long acknowledged and perhaps even overemphasized the ways in which differences among students influence their learning in school. Cultural and socioeconomic patterns have been carefully studied with an eye toward how those patterns characteristic of poor children, and especially poor and minority children, interfere with their opportunities to achieve in school. We have also given attention to the influence of family characteristics, such as support and encouragement, on school success. Measured aptitude for learning or intelligence has received a huge share of research time and money in the search for explanations of differences in student learning outcomes. All these attributes are alike in that they are seen to reside in the student. They are clearly important in the school-learning process, but they are not factors over which schools have much control. As conceived, there is little school people can do to alter them.

We have not, however, paid so much attention to the role of school opportunities in determining what and how much students learn. For, ultimately, students can learn *in*

school only those things that the school exposes them to. And this learning is restricted by the time allotted for it and the mode of instruction employed. Perhaps this is so obvious that it is clearly understood. I suspect, rather, that it is so obvious that it is usually overlooked as important. But the implications of these simple facts of schooling are tremendous. If schools, perhaps in response to differences students bring with them from home, provide them with different kinds of opportunities to learn, then the schools play an active role in producing differences in what and how much students actually learn. The different educational opportunities schools provide to students become the boundaries within which what different students learn *must* be confined. Further, if these opportunities differ in ways that may be important in influencing children's future opportunities both in and out of school, then the differences in learning that schools help produce have profound social and economic as well as educational consequences for students.

We found in our twenty-five schools that students in some classes had markedly different access to knowledge and learning experiences from students in other classes. In nearly every school, some groups of students experienced what we typically think of as tenth-grade English, eighth-grade math, eleventh-grade history, and ninth-grade science. We found also, again in nearly every school, that other groups of students encountered something quite different. And we found that these differences were directly related to the track level of the classes students were in.

In our study we used several sources of information about the 299 English and math classes to shed light on this question of differences in what was likely to be taught and learned in classes in different track levels. Teachers had compiled packages of materials for us about their classes, including lists of the instructional topics they cover during the year, the skills they teach their students, the textbooks they use, and the ways they evaluate their students' learning. Many teachers also gave us copies of sample lesson plans, worksheets, and tests. The teachers were interviewed, and as part of the interview they were asked to indicate the five most important things they wanted their students to learn during the year with them.

In analyzing all these data we looked for similarities and differences in the content of what students were expected to learn in classes at various track levels. We looked both at the substance of what they were exposed to and at the intellectual processes they were expected to use.

We analyzed these similarities and differences systematically[2] and from a particular point of view. We did not assume that all knowledge presented in schools is equally valuable in terms of societal worth, as exchange for future educational, social, and economic opportunities. On the contrary, we began with the recognition that some kinds of knowledge are far more valuable in this way than are others.

We were not thinking, of course, about the value of knowledge in a pure—that is, culture-free—sense. The issue of what is worth knowing in this abstract sense is a question philosophers will continue to grapple with. Nor were we thinking about the value of knowledge in a purely educational sense. Again, it is not clear what kinds of learnings may be better than others in the development of a person who is a learner. This is likely to vary dramatically in groups, even those composed of very similar individuals.

These two issues ignore the social and economic ties attached to learning when it becomes housed in schools. Schools, as social institutions, do far more than impart knowledge and skills to students. They do more than pass on the traditions and values, the folkways and mores of the culture, to the young. Schooling is both more and less than education in the purest sense. It includes as an important function the preparation of youth for future adult roles and for their maintenance of the social structure and organizational patterns of society. And because our social structure is a hierarchical one, with different and fairly specific criteria for entry at various levels, schooling becomes what Joel Spring has called a "sorting machine."[3] By this he meant that the form and substance of the educative process that occurs in schools also select and certify individuals for adult roles at *particular* levels of the social hierarchy. This sorting process results in part from students' access to socially meaningful knowledge and educational experiences.

We analyzed the differences in the content of classes from this perspective. We wanted to explore whether students in different track levels were systematically given access to knowledge that would point them toward different levels in the social and economic hierarchy.

We found considerable differences in the kinds of knowledge students in various tracks had access to. We found also that these differences were not merely equally valued alternative curricula. Rather than being neutral in this sense, they were differences that could have important implications for the futures of the students involved.

For example, students in high-track English classes were exposed to content that we might call "high-status" knowledge in that it would eventually be required knowledge for those going on to colleges and universities. These students studied standard works of literature, both classic and modern. Some classes traced the historical development of literature, some studied the characteristics of literary genres (the novel, the short story, poetry, the essay), and others analyzed literary elements in these works (symbolism, irony, metaphoric language).

Students in these classes were expected to do a great deal of expository writing, both thematic essays and reports of library research. In some classes, too, students were taught to write in particular styles or to learn the conventions of writing in the various literary forms. These students were expected to learn the vocabulary they would encounter on the College Board Entrance (SAT) exams and practice the type of reading comprehension exercises they would find there as well. Some, although not many, of these classes studied language itself, including historical analyses and semantics.

Low-track English classes rarely, if ever, encountered these kinds of knowledge or were expected to learn these kinds of skills. Not only did they not read works of great literature, but we found no evidence of good literature being read *to* them or even shown to them in the form of films. What literature they did encounter was so-called young-adult fiction—short novels with themes designed to appeal to teenagers (love, growing pains, gang activity) and written at a low level of difficulty. These novels constituted part of the focus of low-track classes on basic literary skills. Prominent in these classes was the teaching of reading skills, generally by means of workbooks, kits, and reading texts in addition to young-adult fiction. The writing of simple, short narrative paragraphs and the acquisition of standard English usage and functional literacy skills (filling out forms, applying for jobs) were also frequently mentioned as course content in low-track classes.

It is probably not surprising, given the differences in *what* they were learning, that the differences in the intellectual processes expected of students in classes at different levels were substantial. Teachers of the high-track classes reported far more often than others that they had students do activities that demanded critical thinking, problem solving, drawing conclusions, mak-

ing generalizations, or evaluating or synthesizing knowledge. The learning in low-track classes, in nearly all cases, required only simple memory tasks or comprehension. Sometimes low-track students were expected to apply their learnings to new situations, but this kind of thinking was required far less frequently than were memorization and simple understanding.

The teachers of classes intended for "average" students gave us information indicating that the learnings encountered in their classes were somewhere in between the high- and low-track extremes. But it is worth noting that the kinds of knowledge and intellectual skills emphasized in these average English classes were far more like those in the high track than in the low. It is more appropriate to consider these classes as watered-down versions of high-track classes than as a mixture of the other two levels. Low-track classes seemed to be distinctly different.

Math classes followed a similar pattern of differences with one major exception. The knowledge presented in high-track classes in math, as in English, was what we could call "high status"; it was highly valued in the culture and necessary for access to higher education. Topics frequently listed included mathematical *ideas*—concepts about numeration systems, mathematical models, probability, and statistics—as well as computational procedures which became increasingly sophisticated at the higher grades.

In contrast, low-track classes focused grade after grade on basic computational skills and arithmetic facts—multiplication tables and the like. Sometimes included in these classes were simple measurement skills and the conversion of the English system into the metric. Many low-track classes learned practical or consumer math skills as well, especially at the high school level—the calculation of simple and compound interest, depreciation, wages, and so on. Few mathematical ideas as such seemed to be topics of instruction in these classes. In essence, while the content was certainly useful, almost none of it was of the high-status type.

As in the English classes, the average math classes were considerably more like the high-track classes in their content than like the low. And, too, the content of average math classes can be considered a diluted version of that of the high classes. This was especially true at the junior highs and through about grade ten at the senior highs. From that point on in our schools, math was usually no longer a required subject, and only what would be considered high-track classes were offered to those students wishing to go on in math.

Math classes did differ from English classes in the intellectual processes demanded of students in classes at the various track levels. While the topics of math classes differed considerably—and the differences in the conceptual difficulty of these topics is dramatic—students at all levels of math classes were expected to perform about the same kinds of intellectual processes. That is, at all levels, a great deal of memorizing was expected, as was a basic comprehension of facts, concepts, and procedures. Students at all levels were also expected to apply their learnings to new situations—whether it was the application of division facts to the calculation of automobile miles per gallon of gasoline in low-track classes or the application of deductive logic learned in geometry to the proof of theorems and corollaries in calculus.

It is clear that both the knowledge presented and the intellectual processes cultivated in English classes and the access to mathematical content in math classes were quite different at different track levels. Moreover, these differences seem to be more than simply a result of accommodating individ-

ual needs—a major reason given for such curricular variation. The types of differences found indicate that, whatever the motives for them, social and educational consequences for students are likely to flow from them. The knowledge in which different groups of students had access differed strikingly in both educationally and socially important ways.

Much of the curricular content of low-track classes was such that it would be likely to lock students into that track level—not so much as a result of the topics that were included for instruction but because of the topics that were omitted. Many of the topics taught almost exclusively to students in low-track classes may be desirable learnings for all students—consumer math skills, for example. But these topics were taught to the exclusion of others—introduction to algebraic equations, for example—that constitute prerequisite knowledge and skills for access to classes in different, and higher, track levels. So, by the omission of certain content from low-track classes, students in effect were denied the opportunity to learn material essential for mobility among track levels. This content differentiation was found as early as grade six. Contrary to the suspicions of many, this line of thinking, however, does not imply that all students need the same things in school. Moreover, it is not in conflict with the view that schools should accommodate differences among individuals in learning speed and style, nor does it deny that some students need remediation in fundamental prerequisite skills. But it suggests, given the importance of some curricular topics for students' future educational opportunities, that individualization and remediation should take place within the context of a core of educationally and socially important learnings—thus at least providing equal access to these topics.

. . .

NOTES

1. The analysis of the distribution of white and nonwhite students into high- and low-track classes in six multiracial schools yielded a chi-square significant at the .001 level with 1 df. See J. Oakes, *A Question of Access: Tracking and Curriculum Differentiation in a National Sample of English and Mathematics Classes,* A Study of Schooling Technical Report no. 24 (Los Angeles: University of California, 1981), available from the ERIC clearinghouse on teacher education, for a complete presentation of this analysis.

2. The findings presented here are the results of discriminant analyses conducted separately for each construct in each subject area at each of the two levels of schooling. For a detailed presentation of these analyses and precise definitions of the variables and summary statistics, see the report cited above.

3. J. H. Spring, *The Sorting Machine* (New York: David McKay, 1976).

22

IS ABILITY GROUPING EQUITABLE?

Adam Gamoran

Ability grouping is one of the most common responses to the problem of providing for student differences, but is it an *equitable* response? Few questions about education have evoked more controversy.

Grouping has different effects in different circumstances. As currently practiced, it typically leads to *inequitable* outcomes. To place the debate in its proper perspective, we must remember that decisions about grouping are preliminary and that what matters most comes next: decisions about what to do with students *after* they've been assigned to classes. Given poor instruction, neither heterogeneous nor homogeneous grouping can be effective; with excellent instruction, either may succeed.

Drawing on the best research we have on grouping, I want to describe conditions that make one system or the other more likely to result in high achievement that is equitably distributed. Then I'll look at the challenges educators face depending on which approach to grouping they take. But, first, let's clarify two terms.

Tracking versus Grouping

"Curriculum tracking" and "ability grouping" are sometimes used interchangeably. I use "tracking" to mean broad, programmatic divisions that separate students for all academic subjects. For example, high school tracks divide students into academic, general, and vocational programs. Elementary schools "track" students when they divide them into separate classes for the entire day.

I use "ability grouping" to refer to divisions among students for particular subjects, such as special class assignments for math or within-class groups for reading. "Ability," strictly speaking, however, is not usually the

Adam Gamoran, "Is Ability Grouping Equitable?" from *Educational Leadership and Administration* 50 (1992). Reprinted with the permission of the author.

criterion for grouping. Rather, students are typically divided according to measured or perceived performance in school. Because school performance is related to social inequality outside the school, such divisions contribute to the separation of students from different racial, ethnic, and social background (Oakes et al. 1992).

Achievement Effects of Grouping and Tracking

To consider the effects of ability grouping, we need to keep two questions in mind. First, how does grouping affect the overall *level* of achievement in the school? This is a question about "productivity." Would the school produce higher achievement if ability grouping were eliminated?

Second, how does grouping affect the *distribution* of achievement in the school? This is a question about "inequality." Would achievement be more equally distributed in the absence of ability grouping? In the past, advocates of grouping have tended to focus on the first question, and critics have emphasized the second. To engage in a balanced discussion, we must examine both.

Grouping and productivity. Little evidence supports the claim that tracking or grouping by ability produces higher overall achievement than heterogeneous grouping. At the elementary level, most grouping systems fail to raise achievement. Some forms of subject-specific grouping—particularly within-class grouping for math and cross-grade grouping for reading—tend to have positive effects on overall achievement (Slavin 1987). The issue has received less attention at the secondary level, probably because almost all American secondary schools have some degree of tracking (Oakes 1985).

In a well-designed British study, Fogelman (1983) and Kerckhoff (1986) followed

more than 9,000 students in grouped and ungrouped secondary schools for a five-year period, finding little difference in average scores on standardized tests of math and reading achievement.[1] The absence of overall differences between types of schools, however, masked important differences that occurred *within* the grouped schools.

Grouping and inequality. In the British study, there were no average differences between grouped and ungrouped schools because within the grouped schools, high-group students performed better than similar students in ungrouped schools, but low-group students did worse. Students in remedial classes performed especially poorly compared to ungrouped students with similar family backgrounds and initial achievement. With low-group losses offsetting high-group gains, the effects on productivity were about zero, but the impact on inequality was substantial.

In the United States, high school tracking results in similar increases in inequality. In a national survey that followed more than 20,000 student from grades 10–12, academic track students gained significantly more on test of math, science, reading, vocabulary, writing, and civics, compared to similar students in general and vocational tracks (Gamoran 1987). In fact, achievement gaps between students in different tracks widened more than the overall disparity between students who dropped out of school after 10th grade and those who stayed in school. This means that which program a student pursued in high school mattered more for achievement than whether or not he or she was in school! Unfortunately, studies like this one do not show whether increasing inequality occurred in the context of rising or falling achievement for the school as a whole, because tracked and untracked schools were not compared.

Elementary school studies also show increasing inequality over time (Weinstein

1976, Hallinan and Sorensen 1983, Gamoran 1986). Even when overall achievement rises, inequality may grow because high-group students often gain more than students in low-ability groups (Oakes et al. 1992).

Slavin's "best evidence syntheses." Perhaps the most comprehensive and careful reviews of research on ability grouping are Robert Slavin's reports of grouping and achievement in elementary (1987) and secondary (1990) schools. Other than the elementary school exceptions noted above, Slavin argued that ability grouping has no effects on either productivity or inequality: grouped and ungrouped schools produce about the same level of achievement, and neither high, nor low, nor average groups obtain any special benefit or suffer a particular loss due to grouping. Slavin reached these conclusions after examining a diverse array of studies conducted over a 60-year period. Some of the studies showed positive effects, others yielded negative results, for productivity and inequality, as a result of ability grouping. Because the results averaged out to about zero, Slavin concluded that ability grouping has no effects and that the effects that appeared in many studies resulted from random or systematic errors of measurement (Slavin 1990).

I think another interpretation is more likely: the diversity of results does not mean the true effects are zero but, rather, that ability grouping has different effects depending on where and how it is implemented. The studies Slavin reviewed provided almost no information on what occurred inside the classrooms after students were assigned. In some studies, teachers may have provided exactly the same instruction to the grouped and ungrouped classes, and there would be little reason to expect achievement benefits *or* detriments to ability grouping. In other studies, teaching quality may have favored one group or the other, leading to outcomes that differed by group. Slavin's ultimate con-

clusion echoes a finding that is more than half a century old: ability grouping has no effects on achievement unless teachers use it to provide different instruction to different groups.

I conclude that grouping and tracking rarely add to overall achievement in a school, but they often contribute to inequality. This finding is most consistent for high school tracking, but it is not uncommon in other forms and at other levels. Typically, it means that high-track students are gaining and low-track students are falling farther behind. But the effects of ability grouping are not the same in every context, and we need to discover how they come about in order to improve productivity and reduce inequality.

Sources of Achievement Inequality

Why does tracking often benefit high achievers but not their counterparts in other groups? Most research on grouping and achievement has failed to consider how students were treated after they were assigned to their classes. Fortunately, a number of case studies and a few surveys provide information on what goes on in different groups and tracks. These reports suggest that the quality of instruction and the climate for learning favors high-level groups and honors classes over low groups and remedial classes.

Unequal instruction. At the elementary level, several researchers have documented fast-paced reading instruction in high-level groups and slow-moving progress in low groups. This occurs for both within-class and between-class groupings (Barr and Dreeben 1983, Gamoran 1986, Rowan and Miracle 1983). From these studies, one cannot tell whether slower instruction in low groups meets the needs of these students or unnecessarily holds them back. When middle- and low-group students of similar prior achievement are compared, middle-group students gain more, suggesting that slow-paced instruction contributes to the low-group deficit. This interpretation is bolstered by a recent survey of elementary school mathematics classes, in which middle- and low-group students were significantly more likely than high-group students to say their class was too easy (Coley et al. 1992). Other researchers indicate that low reading groups offer a less conducive learning environment, with more interruptions than middle and high groups (Allington 1980, Eder 1981).

Differences in context and climate have also been described at the secondary level. First, college-track students take more academic courses than students in other tracks, contributing to their achievement advantage (Gamoran 1987). Second, observers report that high-track teachers are more enthusiastic and spend more time preparing (Rosenbaum 1976, Oakes 1991). Teachers may compete for the opportunity to teach honors and accelerated classes, and those with more experience or better reputations tend to win the privilege (Finley 1984, Oakes 1991). Although problem solving and critical thinking are not especially common, they are more likely to occur in high tracks than low tracks (Oakes 1985, Gamoran and Nystrand 1990). In contrast, low-track instruction tends to be fragmented, emphasizing worksheets and recitation (Page 1992). Teachers in low-track classes spend more time on behavior management and less time on instruction (Oakes 1985).

Unequal behavior and attitudes among students. These differences cannot be ascribed solely to teachers, however, because *students' responses* to instruction also differ across tracks and ability groups. Low-track students are off-task more often, spend less time on homework, and turn in fewer assignments (Oakes 1985, Gamoran and Nystrand 1990). Current data do not indicate whether low-track students respond less

well because instruction is less engaging or whether instruction is less engaging because students are not responsive. Both processes are probably at work. Case study writers have long contended that tracking polarizes the student body into "pro-school" and "anti-school" groups (for example, Lacey 1970, Abraham 1989). The latest survey research supports this claim: Berends (1991) found that college- and noncollege-track students differ more over time in the extent of disciplinary problems, in engagement with schoolwork, and in expectations for future schooling.

What Can Be Done?

Although the research is not definitive, it does suggest two actions: reduce the use of tracking and grouping and improve the way ability grouping is used where it is retained.

Reduce the use of tracking and grouping. Generally, the more rigid the tracking system, the more research studies have found no benefits to overall school achievement and serious detriments to equity. Students who report being assigned to different tracks in high school become more unequal in their achievement over time, and the increase in inequality is greatest in schools where students rarely change tracks (Gamoran 1992). In elementary schools, between-class grouping for the entire school day is least likely to show any benefits (Slavin 1987). As Slavin (1987) explains, rigid tracking systems are likely to fail because when a single division by ability is made for all subjects, classes remain heterogeneous on most skills, so there is no improvement in the fit between students' needs and the provision of instruction. In addition, rigid tracking systems may be more likely to induce polarized attitudes toward schooling (Gamoran 1992). In moving to reduce the use of grouping, then, the first step should be to eliminate the most rigid forms of tracking, such as broad, inflexible program assignment in high schools and between-class tracking for the whole day in elementary schools.

Efforts to reduce tracking must grapple with the fact that in at least some cases, high-track students perform better than similar students in heterogeneous classes. The elimination of grouping must be accompanied by staff development opportunities for teachers to learn strategies for enhancing the learning of all students in classes that are more diverse than those to which they are accustomed. At the same time, those who strive to maintain ability grouping out of concern for high-track students must come to grips with the growth in inequality that occurs in many cases.

Improve the use of ability grouping. To the extent that grouping is not completely eliminated, it must be implemented more effectively than is typical. First, it is essential to avoid locking in teachers and students to their track assignments. Permanent assignments result in a vicious cycle in which the expectations of teachers and students enter a downward spiral (Page 1992). Schools must make at least two sorts of investments to bring greater flexibility to their grouping systems: (1) they must reassess students' capabilities and take new information into account when making assignment decisions, and (2) they must enable students to make up curricular material they may have missed —for example, in tutorials during the school year or the summer—so that those who are ready to advance are not held back by lack of curriculum coverage. The latter requires investment not just by schools, but by students as well, who must undertake extra work to catch up. Implementing more flexible grouping systems also means rotating teachers so that all students have opportunities to learn from the most effective teachers and to prevent the loss of morale that some-

times occurs for teachers who are assigned to low tracks year after year.

Second, those who use ability grouping must improve instruction in low groups. This could, at the same time, reduce the inequality that often results from grouping and raise the overall level of achievement in the school. This recommendation is extremely difficult to follow—indeed, were it not so difficult, ability grouping would be a lot less controversial! It is difficult because (1) by virtue of their assignment, teachers and students in low tracks have low expectations for academic work; and (2) low-track students often resist challenging academic work. One observer found that low-track students preferred worksheets to discussion, because the seatwork kept private what students did and did not know (Metz 1978).

Is it even possible? Can high-quality instruction ever take place in low-status groups? We have many more examples of unsuccessful low-track classes than successful ones, but there are some circumstances under which low-group students receive effective instruction. At the elementary level, grouping systems that divide students on the basis of skills closely related to the curriculum and those that adjust curriculum and instruction to address students' needs are more likely to be effective. This conclusion is based on studies of within-class grouping for math and cross-grade, subject-specific grouping for reading (Slavin 1987), but the conclusion is probably generally valid.

At the secondary level, a few case studies suggest that low-track classes may serve their remedial purpose—that is, they allow students to catch up, or at least prevent them from falling further behind—under the following conditions:

• Teachers hold high expectations, manifested by their emphasis on academic work.

- Teachers exert extra effort, compared to their efforts in other classes.
- Teachers and students have opportunities for extensive oral interaction.
- There is no procedure in place that assigns weak or less experienced teachers to the lower track (Page and Valli 1990, Gamoran 1991).

These case studies rely on private schools mostly with middle-class students, and we have as yet no evidence that they generalize well to other situations.

One 9th grade English teacher I observed, whose low-group students kept pace with their peers in other classes, told her students: "I know it's not easy, you guys—I know it's not easy—but we're not going to read *Weekly Reader* in this class. All right? You deserve to have this information, so stick with it." With such a persistent teacher, and equally persistent students, low-track classes may be effective, but the phenomenon is too rare for one to have confidence that it will become the general case anytime soon. All the more reason to curtail tracking and grouping where possible.

NOTES

1. The British study is remarkable in its comprehensiveness: it began with nearly every child born in England, Scotland, and Wales during the first week of March 1958 and followed them from birth to age 23. The ability-grouping analyses covered the period from age 11 to 16. The study is also especially valuable because it includes a large number of comparable schools that used and did not use tracking, or "streaming" as it is called in Britain. In the United States, it is impossible to find a representative sample of secondary schools in which students are not grouped in math and English.
2. These differential gains occurred for students who were statistically equated in prior achievement and background characteristics. In general, students in the different tracks are far

from equal in these areas, so the gross differences between tracks were much larger.
3. Slavin has stated: "For ability grouping to be effective at the elementary level, it must create true homogeneity on the specific skill being taught, and instruction must be closely tailored to students' levels of performance" (1987, p. 323). For the secondary level, he remarked: "The lesson to be drawn from research on ability grouping may be that unless teaching methods are systematically changed, school organization has little impact on student achievement" (1990, p. 491). Compare these to what Ethel L. Cornell concluded in 1936: "The results of ability grouping seem to depend less upon the fact of grouping itself than upon . . . the differentiations in [curricular] content, method, and speed, and the technique of the teacher" (p. 304).

REFERENCES

ABRAHAM, J. 1989. "Testing Hargreaves' and Lacey's Differentiation-Polarization Theory in a Settled Comprehensive." *British Journal of Sociology* 40:46–81.

ALLINGTON, R. L. 1980. "Teacher Interruption Behaviors During Primary-Grade Oral Reading." *Journal of Educational Psychology* 72:371–74.

BARR, R. AND R. DREEBEN. 1983. *How Schools Work.* Chicago: University of Chicago Press.

BERENDS, M. 1991. *High School Tracking and Students' School Orientations.* Madison, WI: National Center on Effective Secondary Schools.

COLEY, R. J., R. EKSTROM, J. GANT, A. M. VILLEGAS, R. MITCHELL, AND S. M. WATTS. 1992. *On the Right Track.* Princeton, NJ: Educational Testing Service.

CORNELL, E. L. 1936. "Effects of Ability Grouping Determinable from Published Studies." In *The Grouping of Pupils.* Yearbook of the National Society for the Study of Education, vol. 35, part I, edited by G. M. Whipple. Bloomington, IL: Public School Publishing.

EDER, D. 1981. "Ability Grouping as a Self-Fulfilling Prophecy: A Microanalysis of Teacher-Student Interaction." *Sociology of Education* 54: 151–61.

FINLEY, M. K. 1984. "Teachers and Tracking in a Comprehensive High School." *Sociology of Education* 57:233–43.

FOGELMAN, K. 1983. "Ability Grouping in the Secondary School." In *Growing Up in Great*

Britain: Papers from the National Child Development Study, edited by K. Fogelman. London: Macmillan.

GAMORAN, A. 1986. "Instructional and Institutional Effects of Ability Grouping." *Sociology of Education* 59:185–98.

GAMORAN, A. 1987. "The Stratification of High School Learning Opportunities." *Sociology of Education* 60:135–55.

GAMORAN, A. 1991. *Alternative Uses of Ability Grouping: Can We Bring High-Quality Instruction to Low-Ability Classes?* Madison, WI: Center on Organization and Restructuring of Schools.

GAMORAN, A. 1992. *The Variable Effects of High School Tracking.* Madison, WI: Center on Organization and Restructuring of Schools.

GAMORAN, A. AND M. NYSTRAND. 1990. "Tracking, Instruction, and Achievement." Paper presented at the World Congress of Sociology, Madrid.

HALLINAN, M. T. AND A. B. SORENSEN. 1983. "The Formation and Stability of Instructional Groups." *American Sociological Review* 48: 838–51.

KERCKHOFF, A. C. 1986. "Effects of Ability Grouping in British Secondary Schools." *American Sociological Review* 51:842–58.

LACEY, C. 1970. *Hightown Grammar.* Manchester: Manchester University Press.

METZ, M. H. 1978. *Classrooms and Corridors: The Crisis of Authority in Desegregated Secondary Schools.* Berkeley: University of California Press.

OAKES, J. 1985. *Keeping Track: How Schools Structure Inequality.* New Haven, CT: Yale University Press.

OAKES, J. (1991). *Multiplying Inequalities: The Effects of Race, Social Class, and Tracking on Opportunities to Learn Mathematics and Science.* Santa Monica, CA: RAND.

OAKES, J., A. GAMORAN, AND R. N. PAGE. 1992. "Curriculum Differentiation: Opportunities, Outcomes, and Meanings." In *Handbook of Research on Curriculum,* edited by P. W. Jackson. Washington, DC: American Educational Research Association.

PAGE, R. N. 1992. *Lower Track Classrooms: A Curricular and Cultural Perspective.* New York: Teachers College Press.

PAGE, R. N. AND L. VALLI, eds. 1990. *Curriculum Differentiation: Interpretive Studies in U.S. Secondary Schools.* Albany, NY: SUNY Press.

ROSENBAUM, J. E. 1976. *Making Inequality: The Hidden Curriculum of High School Tracking.* New York: Wiley.

ROWAN, B. AND A. W. MIRACLE, JR. 1983. "Systems of Ability Grouping and the Stratification of Achievement in Elementary Schools." *Sociology of Education* 56:133–44.

SLAVIN, R. E. 1987. "Ability Grouping nd Achievement in Elementary Schools: A Best-Evidence Synthesis." *Review of Educational Research* 57: 293–336.

SLAVIN, R. E. 1990. "Achievement Effects of Ability Grouping in Secondary Schools: A Best-Evidence Synthesis." *Review of Educational Research* 60:471–99.

WEINSTEIN, R. S. 1976. "Reading Group Membership in First Grade: Teacher Behavior and Student Experiences Over Time." *Journal of Educational Psychology* 68:103–16.

Author's note: This paper was written at the Center on Organization and Restructuring of Schools, Wisconsin Center for Education Research. University of Wisconsin-Madison, which is supported by a grant from the Office of Educational Research and Improvement (Grant No. OERI-R117-Q00005). Any opinions, findings, or conclusions expressed here are those of the author and do not necessarily reflect the views of these agencies or the U.S. Department of Education.

Class, Race, and Gender

Part III examines in greater depth how access to educational opportunities are stratified along the dimensions of class, race, and gender. Selections in this part build on the readings about stratification within and between schools. Specifically, the readings here suggest that class, race, and gender are often the social categories used to structure access to educational opportunities. Obviously, numerous other characteristics such as disability, sexual orientation, age, language ability, and immigrant status can magnify existing inequalities within and between schools for individual students. Rather than provide superficial coverage of inequality along all these relevant dimensions, we focus instead on the key divisions of class, race, and gender. Such an approach allows a more in-depth treatment of the mechanisms underlying educational inequality.

The first section identifies the effects of class background on educational attainment and school experiences. Hans-Peter Blossfeld and Yossi Shavit summarize the results of a seminal, cross-national study that modeled the effect of class background on educational transitions in 13 countries for a series of cohorts over the past century. This work continues the tradition of status attainment research. The cross-national study demonstrates that although class background matters less for different educational transitions today than it did in the past, its determining influence on educational attainment continues to persist. Only in countries that have enacted progressive social democratic policies (Sweden and the Netherlands) have the effects of class background on educational attainment been reduced.

The second reading on class, an excerpt from a study by Paul Willis, examines how young men from working-class backgrounds end up in working-class jobs. This study emerged from the British cultural studies tradition that sought to demonstrate how working-class culture, meanings, and understandings were continuously recreated through localized social interaction and communication. Using this cultural studies framework, Willis's ethnography of an English comprehensive high school demonstrates how the social reproduction of workers occurs in school settings. The working-class "lads" create a culture of resistance to school knowledge and authority—complete with their own language, rules of behavior, and attitudes toward outsiders. Ironically, the counter-school culture adopted by the "lads" effectively ensures that their resistance to class inequality will ultimately reproduce their own subordinate class position. The excerpt provides descriptive details of youth language and behavior that illustrate the self-destructive and self-defeating resistance characterizing the "lads" culture.

The third reading on class, Jay MacLeod's "Teenagers in Clarendon Heights," is an ethnographic study of working-class teenagers in an American high school setting. The study, informed by the methodological and theoretical approach taken by Willis, demonstrates how similar class issues are at work in U.S. cities. MacLeod focuses on the language and culture of two groups of teenagers: the "Hallway Hangers" and the "Brothers." His analysis illustrates how the orientations, experiences, and attitudes that working-class students bring to the classroom can affect their educational experiences. MacLeod conducted this research as an undergraduate honor's thesis while he was a senior at Harvard University.

In the final reading on class, Annette Lareau takes a step beyond Willis and MacLeod to demonstrate how social class affects broader aspects of the relationship between schools and community. Not only does class affect adolescent culture, it also significantly affects larger relations between schools and families. The position and culture of middle-class parents provides them with more information about schooling and better social networks in school communities than their working-class counterparts. It is the structure of schools that privileges middle-class membership, Lareau argues, rather than any intrinsic value attributable to middle-class culture.

The second section provides four readings on the importance of race in school settings. Rather than discussing the divergent experiences of different racial and ethnic groups, all three readings compare the experiences of African Americans and whites in U.S. schools. This focused approach allows for in-depth exploration of mechanisms underlying racial issues and the inclusion of a variety of perspectives that illustrate recent debates in the academic literature on race and schooling. A broader coverage of a range of racial minority groups, although more inclusive, would also be shallower and more superficial. When reading this section, keep in mind that the structure of schooling has different effects on individuals from different racial and ethnic backgrounds (see, e.g., Bean and Tienda 1987, Kao and Tienda 1998). For example, contemporary debates about education, immigration, and language suggest that Latino students face different sets of issues than do African Americans. Indeed, recent data show that African Americans are almost as likely to graduate from high school as whites,

whereas Latinos are almost three times more likely to drop out of high school than students from either of the other two racial groups.

The first reading in this section is Signithia Fordham and John U. Ogbu's "Black Students' School Success: Coping with the 'Burden of "Acting White."'' Ogbu is an anthropologist whose ideas have received wide attention from sociologists (see, e.g., Farkas 1996). Ogbu rearticulated earlier sociological insights on immigrant achievement, and maintained that immigrant minorities do better in school than nonimmigrant minority children due to collective orientations and a heightened sense of community. Here, Fordham and Ogbu argue that the fear among African American high school students of being accused of "acting white" causes a social and psychological orientation that diminishes black students' academic effort and thus leads to underachievement. The authors use data from an ethnographic study of a Washington, D.C., high school to draw these conclusions. Recent research has challenged Fordham and Ogbu's findings. In a quantitative analysis of the school attitudes of various racial and ethnic groups, Ainsworth-Darnell and Downey (1998) demonstrate African Americans maintain more pro-school values and greater regard for high-achieving peers than do whites. African Americans are hindered in their academic success, they believe, by a lack of material conditions and *not* by a burden of "acting white." Additionally, Cook and Ludwig (1997) demonstrate that racial group differences in peer attitudes do not account for the black–white gap in educational attainment. Racial differences, they conclude, are largely accounted for by inequities between the family backgrounds of whites and blacks.

In the second reading in this section, Amy Stuart Wells and Robert Crain look at all African American urban schools in St. Louis, Missouri. Their analysis demonstrates the importance of attending to structural factors—which is largely ignored by Fordham and Ogbu—when explaining race differences in school achievement. They show how racially segregated schools shape and limit the opportunities available to students who attend them. Further, students who attend these schools often remain because their parents lack the information and sense of empowerment necessary to help them transfer to higher-status suburban schools. The lack of power experienced by these families strongly determines schooling decisions, Wells and Crain maintain, because it is embedded in many aspects of their social and economic lives.

In the final reading on race, Christopher Jencks and Meredith Phillips examine why African American students tend to score lower on achievement tests than whites and recommend policies to close the gap between the groups. Jencks and Phillips contend that both differences in school resources and student experiences in families explain some of the black–white test gap. However, they indicate that existing explanations of the test gap are rife with uncertainty and that more research must be conducted in order to isolate the cause. The authors provide a prescription for narrowing the test score gap that requires altering the way schools, communities, families, and individuals operate. It is important to note that Jencks in this reading has shifted from his earlier contention that increasing school resources is an ineffectual policy—here he clearly indicates that increased resources can foster student success (see Jencks et al., Part II).

Gender in schools is the focus of the final section in Part III. In the first reading, Roslyn Arlin Mickelson addresses the question: In view of the limited rewards that women are likely to receive for education, why do they do as well and attain as much education as they do? Mickelson reviews four possible hypotheses that might offer insight on the anomaly of women's achievement and concludes that each explanation suffers from shortcomings. She notes that the theories discussed are especially weak in explaining the educational attainment of women from various race and class backgrounds. This reading calls attention to the criticism that sociological theories, often developed to explain the behaviors of white men, are at times inadequate when applied to the experiences of women and people of color.

In spite of women's anomalous achievement and attainment, research nonetheless shows that girls often experience institutionalized bias in schools. Lee, Marks, and Byrd (1994), for example, have examined instances of sexism in single-sex and coeducational private school classrooms. In their analysis, the authors find sexism present in both single-sex and coed environments. The forms of sexism vary somewhat by the gender composition of schools and by the subject area of the classroom. Although all-girls secondary schools pay the most attention to gender equity, they often exhibit a harmful form of sexism that involves watering down the curriculum and providing less rigorous instruction to the students. Chemistry classrooms exhibit the most explicit sexism in the form of discrimination and gender domination. The authors contend that school policies for gender equity in enrollment, teacher hiring, and personal relations exhibit the greatest amount of gender equity. In all the classrooms studied, sexism is both subtle and pervasive, and thus likely to elude national standards and policies created to reduce it.

The second reading on gender, Barrie Thorne's "Boys and Girls Together . . . But Mostly Apart," looks at the everyday social worlds of kids in elementary schools. Through an ethnography of students at two working-class elementary schools in northern California, Thorne illustrates that patterns of gender segregation among children are amplified by school settings. These patterns, however, are not merely the result of adult intervention and are not simply created by schools. They result from a complex interaction of the characteristics of family, neighborhood, school, and classroom settings that contributes to the geography of gender separation in school.

In the final reading of this section, Michael Apple addresses another important aspect of gender in schools. Apple takes a historical look at the teaching profession and describes how teaching became a "women's profession" as well as how the prevalence of women changed the vocation. At the end of the 1800s, teaching was predominantly performed by men. However, decreasing wages coupled with increased certification requirements led many men to abandon teaching for more lucrative alternatives. Women filled the gaps after their successful fight to gain entrance to education and employment outside the home. Greater involvement of women in teaching resulted in a de-skilling of the profession. The feminization of teaching also led to a de-powering of the profession such that outside administrators—who were usually men—dictated classroom policies. Because this reading deals with employment, an arena in which sex segregation is more readily apparent, the effects of gender discrimination are clearly ascertained. Teaching has been one of the few professional oppor-

tunities available to educated women. In 1970, 41 percent of college-educated, employed women worked as teachers; by 1990, 19 percent of college-educated women were teachers, compared to 6 percent of college-educated men (Hanushek and Rivkin 1996).

REFERENCES

AINSWORTH-DARNELL, JAMES W. AND DOUGLAS B. DOWNEY. 1998. "Assessing the Oppositional Culture Explanation for Racial/Ethnic Differences in School Performance." *American Sociological Review* 63:536–53.

BEAN, FRANK AND MARTA TIENDA. 1987. *The Hispanic Population of the United States.* New York: Russell Sage.

COOK, PHILLIP AND JENS LUDWIG. 1997. "Weighing the Burden of Acting White: Are There Race Differences in Attitudes Toward Education?" *Journal of Policy Analysis and Management* 16:411–29.

FARKAS, GEORGE. 1996. *Human Capital or Cultural Capital? Ethnicity and Poverty Groups in an Urban School District.* New York: Aldine de Gruyter.

HANUSHEK, ERIC AND STEVEN RIVKIN. 1996. "Understanding the Twentieth-Century Growth in U.S. School Spending." *Journal of Human Resources* 32:35–68.

KAO, GRACE AND MARTA TIENDA. 1998. "Educational Aspirations of Minority Youth." *American Journal of Education* 106:349–85.

LEE, VALERIE, HELEN MARKS, AND TINA BYRD. 1994. "Sexism in Single-Sex and Coeducational Independent Secondary School Classrooms." *Sociology of Education* 67:92–120.

Class

23

PERSISTING BARRIERS
Changes in Educational Opportunities in Thirteen Countries

Hans-Peter Blossfeld • Yossi Shavit

Introduction

During the twentieth century, industrial societies have experienced a remarkable process of social and economic change. In the occupational system, there has been a long-term shift in employment from the primary to the secondary sector, and from the secondary to the tertiary sector (Erikson and Goldthorpe 1985; Haller 1989). In most industrialized countries this shift has been accompanied by a change in class composition and an upgrading of the occupational structure; the major decreases in agricultural and manual employment have been in the less skilled rather than the more skilled jobs, and the greatest increases in non-agricultural and non-manual employment have occurred not in relatively low-level clerical, sales, and personal service grades but in professional, administrative, and managerial occupations

Hans-Peter Blossfeld and Yossi Shavit, excerpt from "Persisting Barriers: Changes in Educational Opportunities in Thirteen Countries" from *Persistent Inequality*. Copyright © 1993 by Westview Press. Reprinted with the permission of Westview Press, a member of Perseus Books Group LLC.

(Goldthorpe 1986). For all industrial countries, the twentieth century has also been a period of increased bureaucratization and rationalization, as ever greater proportions of the work force have been employed in larger and more formalized organizations and firms (Blau and Duncan 1967). This tendency has been intensified in many countries—particularly in the 1960s and 1970s—by a rapid expansion of the welfare state and an increase in public employment (Flora 1981, 1988; Esping-Andersen 1990).

Industrialization, bureaucratization, and the expansion of the (welfare) state did not occur in isolation from changes in the educational system. Changes in the class structure and the upgrading of the occupational distribution have increased the demand for better education (Bell 1974; Featherman and Hauser 1978; Blossfeld 1985, 1989, 1990). The progressive rationalization and bureaucratization of working life have enhanced the value of educational and skill qualifications for job opportunities (Blau and Duncan 1967; Arrow 1973; Spence 1973; Mincer 1974; Thurow 1976). This is particularly true for public sector employment, which tends to be based on formal educational qualifications (Müller and Mayer 1976; Müller 1990). Thus, throughout the twentieth century, we observe the increasing importance in industrial societies of the role of education, together with a long-term growth in the enrollment of men and women in the educational system. From one birth cohort to another, the expansion of the educational system has enabled ever larger proportions of children from all social strata to complete primary and secondary education, and to attend tertiary education. Indeed, in almost all industrial countries primary, and even some types of lower secondary education, are now virtually universal (Meyer et al. 1977). The distribution of educational credentials has shifted upward and the average level of educational attainment has risen.

Given this long-term process of educational expansion, reinforced in many countries by educational reforms, one might expect a drop in the impact of social background on educational opportunity. Boudon (1974), for example, argued that if school attendance rates increase over time, then inequalities in educational opportunity will steadily decline, because the lower socioeconomic classes can increase their attendance rates by more percentage points than the upper classes whose rates are already high and constrained by ceiling effects.

Surprisingly, however, empirical studies showed that inequality of educational opportunity between social strata has been quite stable over time. For the United States, Featherman and Hauser (1976, 1978) reported that the effects of social background on years of schooling during the first half of the twentieth century have remained more or less unchanged. For England and Wales, Halsey, Heath, and Ridge (1980) showed that in the inter-war period the working class increased their chances of securing a place at a selective secondary school from 20% to 26%, while the service class increased theirs from 70% to 77%. The relative growth was greater for the working class, but the absolute differ-

ence between the classes increased. This led Halsey and his associates to conclude that the effect of educational expansion in equality of opportunity is dependent on the starting points of the various classes, and on the saturation levels of the educational institutions themselves. "If the working-class starting point is very low . . . there can be a high rate of growth but low absolute gains. A higher starting point, on the other hand, may yield a lower rate of growth but, providing it is still well short of the saturation level, the absolute gains can be large, and class differences can decline." (Halsey, Heath, and Ridge 1980: 217). Thus, Halsey and his associates were convinced that in the early stages of educational growth, expansion would lead to greater inequality and that only in the later stages would it reduce social inequality in the attainment of a given level of schooling.

The comments of Boudon, and the analyses of Featherman and Hauser together with those of Halsey and his associates, reflect a certain ambiguity as regards the concept of inequality of educational opportunity and its measurement (see also Sorensen 1983, 1986; Sorensen and Blossfeld 1989). Should we measure change in inequality of educational opportunity by the change in effect of social origin variables on the mean number of school years completed? Or in terms of change in class-specific proportion completing a given level of schooling? Or again, in terms of change in the ratio between such proportions? Mare (1980) clarified this matter by showing that previously employed measures of changes in equality of educational opportunity fail to make a clear distinction between two different processes: the expansion of the educational system and the processes of selection and allocation of students. He proposes a model of change in inequality of educational opportunity whose parameters are not affected by the degree of educational expansion or contraction. The model views the educational attainment process as a sequence of transitions (for example, from first to second grade, from second to third grade, etc.). At each level of the sequence a student can either make the transition or discontinue. The odds of making the transition are determined by various exogenous variables such as students' parental education, family size, etc. . . .

. . .

An important implication of Mare's work is the reformulation of the original research question. Rather than simply ask "How have educational attainment processes changed historically?" we now distinguish between changes in the process which are due to the changing distribution of schooling and changes in the association between educational transition and social strata.

Following Mare's study, there have been several analyses of changes in educational opportunities in European countries. . . .

. . .

In sum, the various studies report different patterns of change or stability in the parameters of educational attainment and educational transition models for the different countries. Why these differences? Clearly, they may reflect interesting social differences in the structures of educational systems and in the processes of educational stratification. However, most of these studies focus on single countries (see, for example, Matějů 1984, and Peschar 1990) and do not attempt to explore the role of societal factors in producing differences in the educational attainment process. Furthermore, there are major methodological differences between the studies that hinder a systematic comparison of results. For example, there are differences between studies in the definition and measurement of key variables, and in the time-span covered by the data. In addition, some studies focus on men while others analyze data for both sexes.

This [chapter summarizes and synthesizes] the results of thirteen very similar studies of educational attainment in thirteen different countries. The countries offer a range of variation in important variables such as industrial development and culture, political systems and history, and types of educational structures. The countries included in this comparison are the United States, the (former) Federal Republic of Germany, the Netherlands, Sweden, England and Wales, Italy, Switzerland, Taiwan, Japan, Poland, Hungary, Czechoslovakia, and Israel. . . . Each study was conducted by researchers who have an intimate understanding of the country in question. Most of these studies employed relatively recent nationally representative data, covering cohorts educated over a broad historical period (with the exception of Switzerland). . . . In particular, we studied change in the educational opportunities for cohorts who attended school before and after major educational reforms or changes in attendance rates. We also employed very similar statistical models although we preferred to avoid complete standardization of method, because the institutional structure of the educational system varies from country to country. For example, in some countries, there is formal and rigid streaming or tracking (e.g., Germany, Poland), while in others there is less rigid curricular differentiation (e.g., the United States). Furthermore, the important independent variables in the educational attainment process vary across societies. For example, in some societies, ethnicity or race are important independent variables in the educational process while other societies are ethnically homogenous. A completely standardized analysis would have lost these unique features of the different societies. We did, however, attempt to maintain sufficient standardization to enable a systematic comparison of the results. . . .

. . .

Theoretical Perspectives and Hypotheses

The basic question which is addressed by the comparative analysis can be stated as follows: *To what extent has the relationship between parental socioeconomic characteristics and educational opportunities changed over time and why?* In the following we will concentrate on theoretical perspectives which have guided the comparative study of this question.

Cultural and Economic Theories of Educational Stratification

Socioeconomic differences in educational attainment are broad and pervasive in all industrialized societies: children from working-class or farming families attain less education on average than children from higher socioeconomic origins (Gambetta 1987). Among the possible hypotheses explaining the pervasive class and ethnic inequalities of educational attainment, the two most prominent highlight different aspects of the issue: *cultural capital theory* and the *economic constraint thesis.*

The cultural capital theory, first advanced by Bourdieu and Passeron (Bourdieu and Passeron 1964, 1977; Bourdieu 1966), contends that children from families with a low level of parental education are likely to lack those abilities normally transmitted by the family and valued and rewarded by schools. In particular, cultural resources such as dominant societal values, attitudes, language skills, and styles of interaction are acquired in school more quickly by children already familiar with them. Consequently,

selection in school favors children from those families that already possess dominant cultural advantages.

By contrast to the cultural capital thesis, Boudon's (1974) economic constraint thesis contends that in most countries, education must be financed by family resources which include direct costs (e.g., tuition fees, learning materials, and transportation) and forgone earnings. Thus, it is reasonable to expect that education is particularly dependent on the economic resources of the family of origin. Although it is true that in many countries lower-class families now send their children to school for longer periods, it does not contradict the basic statement that poor families ". . . need at the same time to make heavier sacrifices and to have relatively stronger ambitions" than families which are better off (Gambetta 1987:80). Thus, cultural and economic inequalities between classes and status groups combine to produce educational inequalities among their children.

Theories of Change in Educational Stratification

Parsons (1970) and Treiman (1970), two main exponents of *modernization theory,* have suggested that the educational system expands in response to the functional requirements of an industrial society and that education plays an increasingly important role in the process of status attainment (Lenski 1966; Treiman 1970). It has been argued that as the level of educational requirements in industrial societies rises, educational qualifications become more important for occupational placement. It has also been assumed that with increasing modernization and the expansion of the educational system, educational selection tends to become more meritocratic. Hence, inequality of educational opportunity, as measured by its dependence on socioeconomic and sociocultural characteristics, should decrease across all educational levels over time.[1] As we shall see, this hypothesis is turned on its head in the final section of this chapter.

By contrast, *cultural reproduction theorists* (see, for example, Collins 1971) claim that educational certificates actually serve to exclude members of subordinate and low status groups from desirable positions in the occupational structure. Education-based selection and allocation in the labor market are used to maintain the hegemony and privilege of dominant social groups (Bowles and Gintis 1976, Bourdieu 1973; Collins 1971). Educational credentials therefore mirror the class structure and help legitimize inequality of job opportunity.

Reproduction theorists recognize, however, that there is an inherent conflict between the socialization role of education and its selective function. On the one hand, schooling is an effective institution by which children of subordinate group origins are socialized into the dominant value system of the society. Therefore, representatives of the dominant groups may pressure the political system to expand the educational institutions and to absorb children of ethnic minorities or working class origins. This is consistent with the demands of the subordinate groups themselves for more education. Consequently, the attainment of primary and even some types of secondary schooling may become increasingly independent of social background. On the other hand, if the dominant groups want to maintain their privileges in the status system, they must retain their advantage in the attainment of higher educational qualifications. Thus, students of subordinate group origins are diverted from higher education by various means. These range from the expansion of non-academic educational alternatives (see, for example, Karabel 1972; Shavit 1984), to raising the admission standards in universities. Thus, the

effect of social background on the attainment of higher educational qualification is not reduced despite the democratization of graded schooling.

In summary, although both the modernization and reproduction approaches agree that educational expansion—whether the result of functional imperatives of economic modernization or an outcome of competition between status groups—leads to greater equality of educational opportunities at the lower levels of the educational system over time, they disagree as to the predicted trends in inequality of education at the higher levels of the educational hierarchy: modernization theorists predict a decreasing trend of inequality of education over time; and reproduction theorists expect an unchanged or even an increasing importance of social origin.

Raftery and Hout (1990) suggested a more radical version of reproduction theory. They argue that inequality in *educational opportunity is "maximally maintained."* This means that in modern societies, the effects of social origin at all levels of education do not change, except when the enrollment of advantaged groups is already so high at a given level that further expansion is only feasible by increasing the opportunity of disadvantaged groups to make the transition. Accordingly, where grade-saturation occurs, educational expansion is the consequence of the demands for education made by advantaged groups, which increase their proportion in the course of the upgrading of the occupational structure. As long as these advantaged groups are not fully integrated at a given level of education, they strongly support efforts to expand educational participation by eliminating tuition fees, lowering admissions standards, increasing capacity, etc. Expansion in participation at these given levels of education, however, does not lead to more educational equality between social groups because the increases for the advantaged groups will be greater as these groups favor higher education more. Therefore, expansion of education does not lead to a better chance for disadvantaged groups to make the transition and will not change the association between social origins and given educational transitions. This was the case in England and Wales during the 1950s and 1960s (Halsey, Heath, and Ridge 1980), and in Ireland (Raftery and Hout 1990). Only where for a given level of education, the participation is saturated for the advantaged groups (this means if the advantaged groups already have transition rates close to 100%), and there is further expansion, will the association between social origin and grade progression decline. In particular, it is suggested that, if primary and lower secondary education is nearly universal for the privileged groups, then any further expansion of secondary education may lead to declining effect of social origin on these transitions.

Reproduction theory views education as an instrument by which dominant social elite exclude other classes from attaining desirable occupations. When the elite are replaced by previously subordinate classes, one would expect the educational system to open up for these (previously) less privileged strata. Thus, one can expect that the association between the socioeconomic origins of students and their educational transition rates should have declined in the decades following the socialist transformations in Eastern and Central Europe after World War II. As noted, this hypothesis is consistent in part with the results of earlier studies of formerly socialist societies where the effects of socioeconomic origins declined on the earlier educational transitions. However, these studies also reported no change in the effects on later transitions. The *socialist transformation hypothesis* also suggests that once the new elite establish their privilege and gain control of the school system, they take steps to secure the educational advantages of their own children. Thus, we can expect an increase in the impact of social origins in the later years of socialist regimes. This hypothesis is discussed in some detail in the studies on Hungary and Czechoslovakia by Szelényi and Aschaffenburg, and by Matějů respectively.

As noted earlier, previous studies on educational transition have found that the effect of social origin is strong at the beginning of the educational career and then declines for later transitions. One hypothesis to explain this pattern is that younger pupils are more dependent on the preferences of their parents and the economic conditions of their families of origin than older ones. *With increasing age, students will increasingly be able to decide on their own what they want and will rely less on parental resources,* particularly in countries where higher education is not connected with high costs for the family of origin (Müller 1990:9). An alternative explanation for this finding is that *children from lower social classes meet very severe selection barriers at the earlier educational transitions.* Thus, only the brightest working-class children make it to higher levels of the school system. By contrast, middle-class and upper-class children progress into secondary schools and universities with greater ease. Consequently, among candidates for later transitions, socioeconomic origin is less and less correlated with scholastic aptitude and with other student characteristics—such as motivation—that determine educational success. Therefore, the indirect effect of origins that is mediated by aptitude and motivation, is reduced or eliminated, and its effect is small (Mare 1981).

Thus we have two possible explanations for the decline in the effects of origins on successive transitions: an explanation that hinges on arguments about life course differences in dependence on family, and one which relates it to the selection process. These two explanations suggest competing hypotheses regarding cohort differences in the parameters of the educational transitions process. The *life-course hypothesis* states that if primary and lower secondary education become universal and lead to a decrease in the effect of social origin at these earlier levels, then the effects of social origin on higher grade progression will stay small across cohorts because older pupils are less dependent on the preferences and the economic conditions of their families than younger ones. This means that expansion of primary and secondary education does not only abolish or drastically reduce earlier severe selection barriers for disadvantaged groups, but will also lead to more equality of origin-specific educational opportunity across cohorts.

By contrast, the *differential selection hypothesis* states that if the proportion of successive birth cohorts in the risk set to make a transition increases, so will the observed association between social origin and the transition probability. This is simply an implication of the argument concerning unmeasured variables (such as ability, ambition, and motivation) within different social groups: as growing proportions of all social groups reach higher levels of schooling across cohorts, the social groups become more equal with respect to unmeasured variables which leads to a greater effect of observed socioeconomic factors across cohorts.

To summarize, we have suggested the following six hypotheses regarding change in the effects of social origins on educational transitions:

- Modernization hypothesis: the effects of social origins on all transitions decline;
- Reproduction hypothesis: the effects of social origins decline on earlier transitions but not on later transitions;
- Hypothesis of maximally maintained inequality: the effects will only decline at those transitions for which the attendance rates of the privileged classes are saturated;
- Socialist transformation hypothesis: socialist transformations brought about an initial reduction in the effects. This will then be followed by increased effects;
- Life-course hypothesis: the effects decline across transitions but are stable across cohorts;
- Differential selection hypothesis: the effects decline across cohorts but the effects on later transitions increase across cohorts.

The Comparative Project: Countries and Methods

The Countries

Thirteen industrialized countries are included in the study. They may be classified according to their basic cultural and economic system into three major groups: (1) Western capitalist countries: the United States of America, the (former) Federal Republic of Germany, England and Wales (see also, Health and Clifford 1990), Italy, Switzerland, the Netherlands, and Sweden; (2) non-Western capitalist countries: Japan and Taiwan; and (3) Western formerly socialist countries: Poland, Hungary, and Czechoslovakia. In addition, and in order to enrich the selection of societies examined here, we have also included a study on Arabs living in Israel: in the mid-twentieth century, the Arab population in Israel shifted from being a society of mass illiteracy to one with nearly universal primary education. Of recent cohorts, large proportions have also completed secondary education. Moreover, this population also shifted from a peasant to a proletariat society. As such, it is a striking example of a society which has undergone radical structural changes.

These societies do not constitute a representative sample of all industrialized societies, but do represent considerable variations in the following: the level and timing of industrialization (compare for example, England and Wales with Taiwan and Sweden): the political system (democracies, socialist states, and non-democratic states); the structure of the distributive systems (market-based vs. bureaucratically determined, ethnic vs. class stratification); the organizational form of the school systems (nationally centralized in most societies, decentralized in the United States, and regional in Germany and Switzerland) including the degree of "tracking" (mostly rigid with the exception of the United States and Sweden), and educational attendance rates; and formal public commitment to equality of opportunity. Thus, the array of countries enables an evaluation of the hypotheses listed earlier in a variety of societies.

. . .

Results of the International Comparison

. . .

Patterns of Educational Expansion

We begin by focusing on inter-cohort changes in highest educational attainment. . . . [E]ducational expansion is strong and universal in all countries, whether socialist or capitalist, Western or non-Western. The average level of educational attainment has risen across cohorts. . . . In all thirteen societies, primary and even some types of lower secondary education have become nearly universal during the period under study. . . . This means that in all these societies, deci-

sions about the educational continuation of children are no longer taken at a very early age. As we shall see, this has important implications for equality of educational opportunity. In all the societies, the major branching point between continuation and discontinuation of schooling occurs at the transition from primary to secondary education.

The expansion of the educational systems [is] evaluated relative to the changing sizes of cohorts. Thus, expansion of a given level of schooling is defined as an increase in the proportions of successive cohorts who attended that level. In all societies, expansion has been strong at the lower secondary level, less pronounced at the upper secondary level, and modest at the tertiary level. In some countries tertiary education increased only slightly, or failed to increase at all, relative to the changing sizes of the cohorts to which it catered (Netherlands, Taiwan, Hungary, and Poland). Educational systems appear to open up more fully at the bottom than at higher educational levels. Higher levels of education do not expand fast enough to absorb the growing proportions of graduates from lower levels of the school system, and educational bottlenecks can become quite severe, especially in the transition from secondary to tertiary education.

It would seem that there is a universal pattern of educational expansion policies. Educational systems open up step-by-step from the bottom up. In the process, successive birth cohorts improve their chances to move up a small step within the educational hierarchy. However, higher levels of education still remain fairly exclusive. This pattern of expansion leans towards the arguments of reproduction theory rather than towards modernization theory. A persistent rationing of higher credentials restricts the pool of candidates to positions of privilege at the top of the occupational hierarchy, and thus legitimizes inequality of job opportunities.

In several countries (Germany, Switzerland, Sweden, Poland, and for Israeli Jews see Shavit [1990]), this basic pattern of educational expansion has been accompanied by an impressive expansion of tracking and vocational education as an alternative to academic secondary or higher secondary education. In some cases, vocational training opens employment opportunities in a wide range of occupations. It is attractive for children from lower socioeconomic backgrounds because it provides rapid access to a skill. Thus, the availability of vocational education enables the educational system to absorb disadvantaged groups at the secondary level without disturbing the basic social interests of advantaged groups at higher levels in the school system (Shavit 1989).

. . . Ten of the thirteen studies analyze data for both sexes. All ten studies report a substantial reduction in the differences between the mean educational attainment of men and women. In some societies (United States, Germany, Hungary, Poland, and Sweden), women's mean attainment in recent cohorts even surpassed those of men. This indicates that women in particular have profited from educational expansion in industrial countries.

Socioeconomic Inequalities in Educational Attainment

Given the long-term process of educational expansion in all of the industrialized countries, one might expect a drop in inequality of educational opportunity between socioeconomic strata. As noted earlier, each of the studies in the project estimated the traditional linear regressions of educational attainment (measured as number of school years) on measures of social background for successive cohorts. Changes in equality of educational opportunity are operationalized as cohort differences in the effects of social origins on educational attainment. . . . In

one country in particular (the Netherlands), there is a decline in the effect of both father's education and father's occupation across cohorts. In six of the societies examined there has not been any significant change in the effects of either indicator of social origins on educational attainment (Germany, England and Wales, Switzerland, Hungary, Poland, and the case of the Israeli Arabs). The remaining five studies report mixed results: a decrease in the effect of one variable, and stability or increase in the effect of the other (United States, Italy, Taiwan, Japan, and Czechoslovakia). Interestingly, the study for Czechoslovakia reports a decline in the effect of father's education on educational attainment for cohorts educated immediately after the introduction of the socialist reforms. However, this was followed by an increase in the effects for more recent birth cohorts.

Thus, although there is a uniform trend of educational expansion in the participant societies, there is no uniform outcome with respect to educational inequality. Most notably, in most cases, expansion has not entailed greater equality of educational opportunity among socioeconomic strata. With the exceptions of Sweden and the Netherlands, the studies do not reveal a consistent decline in the associations between social origins and educational attainment. Stability is somewhat more common with respect to the effect of father's occupation than with respect to the effect of father's education.

Educational Transitions: Stability with the Same Two Exceptions

As noted earlier, cohort differences in linear regression effects of socioeconomic origins on educational attainment confound two distinct components: cohort differences in the proportions continuing to successive levels of education, and changes in the associations between educational transition rates and social origin (Mare 1980). The former component is a reflection of educational expansion, whereas the latter is a reflection of the social and institutional arrangements which govern the educational selection of different social strata. . . .

. . . With the exception of Switzerland, the effects of social origins are strongest at the beginning of the educational career and then decline for subsequent educational transitions. In some countries (for example, the Netherlands, Sweden, and Germany) the effects of social origin on the transitions to tertiary education are so small as to be insignificant. Thus, it would seem that social selection is most pronounced at very early stages of the educational career.

Earlier, we mentioned two hypotheses explaining this declining effect of social origin across transitions: the differential selection hypothesis, and the life-course hypothesis. The later postulates that the effects of family diminish with age, as children become less dependent on their families. The data employed by the thirteen studies do not allow for a direct test of the two hypotheses because we have not been able to control for unmeasured variables such as ability or motivation. However, the implication of the differential selectivity hypothesis is that as growing proportions of *all* social groups reach higher levels of schooling across cohorts, there is greater heterogeneity on unmeasured variables at higher level of schooling. This should result in increasing effects of *observed* socioeconomic variables across cohorts, but this has not been the case in our study. Although we observe a long-term and strong educational expansion in all countries . . . , there is no universal increase in the effect of social background on grade progression. In most countries, there is no change in the logit effects of social origin on educational transitions,[2] and some report declining effects.

This pattern suggests that variation in unmeasured heterogeneity is not a single cause for the decline in the logit effects across transitions. . . . Mare shows that controlling for unmeasured heterogeneity in family characteristics eliminates the decline in the effects of father's education across the early educational transitions. However, even when heterogeneity is controlled, the effect of father's education *declines sharply* for the completion of university or college. This also suggests that the decline in the effects across the first transitions is best explained by a life-course hypothesis. Presumably, older students are less dependent on family resources—cultural and material—in their educational decision-making.

Focusing on change in the association between social origins and educational transitions, we find virtual stability across cohorts. The two exceptions are Sweden and the Netherlands, where the associations have declined for transitions within secondary education. These two exceptions are highly significant for our study. First, in neither case have the privileged classes been saturated with secondary education before the associations declined. Thus, both cases counter the Maximally Maintained Inequality (MMI) hypothesis (Raftery and Hout 1990). The MMI hypothesis is also inconsistent with the results for the United States . . . , in which the middle class *has been saturated,* or nearly saturated, with secondary education but in which the association has actually *increased* at that level. Second, the Swedish model of the welfare state has been very effective in reducing class differences in everyday life chances and life styles (see, for example, Erikson 1983; Erikson and Goldthorpe 1987). Jonsson therefore suggests that the equalization of living conditions in Sweden is probably the major explanation for the declining association between social origins and educational opportunity. As social classes become more equal in their living conditions, the factors which differentiate their educational opportunity (for example, differences in cultural, capital, and material resources) also diminish. Moreover, the Netherlands is undergoing a similar historic process of opening-up and equalization in the long-run. In sum, these two deviant cases suggest that long-term commitments to socioeconomic equality may lead to an equalization of educational opportunities between classes and socioeconomic strata.

On the other hand, the common experience of the three formerly socialist states in the study tell a quite different story. In all three cases studied, there has been an expansion of educational opportunity at the primary and secondary level similar to that found in other countries. And yet, despite the nominal commitment of their regimes to equality and equality of educational opportunity, the data reveal stability in the relationship between social origins and educational attainment. The Socialist Transformation Hypothesis suggested that the transformation was followed by an initial equalization of educational opportunity, especially at the bottom levels of the school system, followed by greater inequality in subsequent decades. In view of the data, the hypothesis now appears too optimistic. Only in Czechoslovakia was there some indication that inequalization of educational opportunity at the lower level declined somewhat, and there too, it was followed by a return to its initial level.

In sum, despite the marked expansion of all the educational systems under study, in most countries there has been *little change in socioeconomic inequality of educational opportunity*. Even in extreme cases of industrial transformation (such as Taiwan, Japan, and Italy), and radical changes of the occupational structure (Israeli Arabs), the parameters of the educational stratification process remain stable (see also Smith and Cheung 1986). This is a clear refutation of the modernization hypothesis. Only in Sweden and the Netherlands has there been a consistent equalization of educational opportunity by socioeconomic strata.

The Effects of Educational Reforms

Several of the educational systems studied . . . have undergone major structural reforms during the decades covered by the data. Most notable of course, were the transformations of educational systems during the socialist transformations in Eastern and Central Europe. But major reforms were also made in England and Wales in 1944, in Sweden during the early 1960s, in Japan after World War II, in Israel during the 1960s and 1970s, and during the 1968 Mammoth Reform in the Netherlands. Less dramatic transformations of the educational system were introduced in other countries. The details of the reforms for each country are described in the respective chapters of this volume. The finding which is common to all our studies is, however, that the reforms did not lead to a reduction in the association between social origins and any of the educational transitions. Even in Sweden and the Netherlands, which report a decline in the association, this is not attributable to the educational reforms. In Poland, educational policy was designed to form "a new Communist man" with the technical skills for productive labor, but the major effect seems in fact to have been the displacement of men by women in the conventional elite academic tracks (see Heyns and Bialecki in Blossfeld and Shavit 1993).

Summary and Conclusion

The synthesis of the empirical studies . . . suggest seven major conclusions. First, whereas earlier studies of changes in the process of educational stratification in some of the countries yielded divergent results, the results of the present study are more homogeneous. Two major patterns are identified: an equalization among socioeconomic strata in educational opportunity for Sweden and the Netherlands, and virtual stability in other countries.

Second, in all thirteen countries, there was a marked educational expansion during the periods examined. This is equally true for industrializing and for advanced industrialized societies, for capitalist and for socialist states, and for Western and non-Western countries. Furthermore, in most cases, expansion was not uniform across all educational levels. Instead, educational systems expanded much more rapidly at the primary and secondary levels than at the post-secondary level. Consequently, as larger proportions of successive cohorts enter and complete secondary education, they encounter severe bottlenecks in the transitions to tertiary education. In some cases, access to tertiary education actually declined across cohorts, as the pool of candidates increased dramatically.

In some countries (e.g. Germany, Switzerland, Sweden, Poland, and Israel [Shavit 1989]), the expansion of secondary education has been accompanied by a growing differentiation into academic and vocational tracks or programs. The expansion of vocational, non-college education enabled these systems to incorporate growing proportions of children from lower strata who would complete secondary education but would not be considered for further academic education. This led to an opening up of secondary education without disturbing the basically exclusive character of higher education.

Third, the analyses of linear regressions of educational attainment reveal a mixed pattern. In two countries (Sweden and the Netherlands) there is a clear overall decline in the effect of social background for the first two transitions across cohorts, whereas, in six countries the effects of socioeconomic origin on education attainment have remained virtually stable. In the remaining five countries there have been both a decline and stability or even increases in the effects. Thus, expansion of education does not consistently reduce the association between social origins of students and their educational attainment.

Fourth, the effect of social origin on grade progression is strong at the beginning of the educational career and declines for later educational transitions (except for Switzerland). Thus, socioeconomic selection occurs at early stages of the educational career. This is partly due to the fact that school systems select students on the basis of characteristics which are correlated with their socioeconomic origins (Mare 1980, 1981 . . .). However, there is also some indication that the effects of socioeconomic origins decline across educational transitions because older students are less dependent on the family of origin in making (and financing) educational decisions.

Fifth, while the effects of students' origins decline across transitions, there is little change in these effects across cohorts. There are only two exceptions to this pattern: Sweden and the Netherlands, in which the effects of father's occupation and education on the low and intermediate transitions declined. Both the Dutch (De Graaf and Ganzeboom) and Swedish (Jonsson) authors attribute the declining effects to a general policy of equalization of socioeconomic conditions in their countries. In Sweden, there has been an equalization of life chances for the different social strata, and in the Netherlands there has been a long-term opening up in many aspects of the stratification system (van Kersberger and Becker 1988; Esping-Andersen 1990). In both countries the decline occurred before saturation of attendance of the privileged groups has taken place. This means that part of the hypothesis of maximally maintained inequality is incorrect: inequalities of educational opportunities can decline before saturation is reached. Furthermore, . . . for the United States, saturation does not necessarily reduce class inequality in the odds of making transitions.[3] Also interestingly, the radical social policies of the socialist states did not reduce the effect of social origin. This is consistent with the assertion that under socialism, the bureaucratic elites were as effective in protecting the interests of their children as elites in other types of society. The stability in the association between social origins and educational transitions in eleven of the thirteen societies indicates that educational selection persistently favors children of privileged social origins. This is consistent with the argument that dominant social classes manage to resist changes in the school system might diminish their relative advantage in the educational process (Erikson and Goldthorpe 1992).

Sixth, for ten of the thirteen societies, data were available on both men and women. In all ten cases, the data reveal a marked reduction in gender differences in means of educational attainment. In some cases, most notably, in Poland, the United States, Germany, and Sweden, the educational gender gap has actually been reversed, with girls being more likely to benefit from the expansion of educational systems than lower class boys. In addition, the association between gender and educational transitions has declined in each of the studies in which it was estimated. Two important causes for this decline are suggested: girls are less often fed into dead-end vocational tracks (Heyns and Bialecki), and families' discrimination against girls has declined, especially among the middle classes (Jonsson).

Finally, the impact of educational reforms on changes in educational stratification seems to be negligible. Nowhere have they reduced inequalities of educational opportunity between socioeconomic strata. Even in Sweden and the Netherlands, which report declines in the association, the decline is not attributable to the educational reforms, but occurred before the educational reforms.

The thirteen societies represent very different social and educational structures. We noted that some were socialist, others capitalist, and some in between the two. Some have highly centralized educational systems whilst in others the systems are locally controlled (e.g. the United States, Switzerland, Germany). The countries also display marked cultural variations. And yet, in all but two cases, there are two marked similarities between them all. They all experienced dramatic educational expansions during the twentieth century, and they all exhibit stability of socioeconomic inequalities of educational opportunities. Thus, whereas the proportions of all social classes attending all educational levels have increased, the relative advantage associated with privileged origins persists in all but two of the thirteen societies.

Many people will still be somewhat surprised that rapid educational expansion did *not* reduce inequalities of educational opportunities. The reason may be that "educational opportunity" is still a rather vague and unspecified concept. Educational opportunity—as we understand it—means the *chance* to attain a specific educational level, rather than its actual *attainment*. It is a relative, not an absolute, concept. As a consequence of educational expansion societies can produce a higher average level of educational attainment from one birth cohort to the next, without changing the educational opportunities of children from different social strata. Thus, educational expansion may even account for the stable patterns of educational stratification. It is a well-known fact that the larger the pie, the less the conflict as to the relative size of the slices. For example, class conflict is more pronounced during periods of decline than during periods of economic growth. Similarly, there are two mechanisms through which the education of disadvantaged classes may be enhanced: through educational expansion whereby the educational attainment of all classes is increased, and/or through a change of the rules that govern educational selection and reduce or eliminate the disadvantage of lower social strata. As long as the educational attainment of lower social strata is rapidly increasing, political attention can neglect any parallel increases among the privileged classes. Thus, educational expansion can alleviate political pressure to reduce inequalities. This is the essence of Halsey, Heath, and Ridge's assertion which is discussed extensively at the beginning of this chapter. It is also similar to the position of Raftery and Hout who too view educational expansion and the equalization of educational opportunity to a certain extent as competing alternatives. Thus, the modernization theorists' hypothesis that educational expansion results in greater equality of educational opportunity must be turned on its head: expansion actually facilitates to a large extent the persistence of inequalities in educational opportunity.

NOTES

1. It should be noted that increased meritocratic selection does not necessarily reduce socioeconomic inequalities in educational attainment. If scholastic ability is highly correlated with socioeconomic origins, educational selection on ability may produce a correlation between origins and educational attainment. Most studies of change in the effect of socioeconomic origins on educational attainment do not explicitly consider the role of ability in the process. Hence, they are not able to distinguish between those components of change in these effects that are mediated by ability and those mediated by other factors.
2. There are only two exceptions: the United States and Switzerland. For the United States, the authors attribute the increasing effect of parental education on high school graduation across cohorts to the various factors of urban disorganization. For Switzerland, for men the increase of social background on the transition to university is probably connected with the

specific meaning of these transitions in the Swiss educational system.
3. If the upper class actually reached an attendance rate of 100%, any increase in lower class attendance would lead to a declining logit effect. However, if the upper class reaches near saturation (around 95%), it is no longer a mathematical necessity that lower class increased attendance need reduce the effects.

REFERENCES

ARROW, K. 1973. "Higher Education as a Filter." *Journal of Public Economics* 2:83–102.

BELL, D. 1974. *The Coming of the Post-Industrial Society.* London: Heinemann.

BLAU, P. M. AND O. D. DUNCAN. 1967. *The American Occupational Structure.* New York: Wiley.

BLOSSFELD, H.-P. 1983. "Höherqualifizierung und Verdrängung–Konsequenzen der Bildungsexpansion in den Siebziger Jahren." *Beschäftigungssystem im gesellschaftlichen Wandel,* edited by M. Haller and W. Müller. Frankfurt am Main and New York: Campus.

———. 1985. *Bildungsexpansion und Berufschancen.* Frankfurt am Main and New York: Campus.

———. 1989. *Kohortendifferenzierung und Karriereprozeß–Eine Längsschnittstudie über die Veränderung der Bildungs- und Berufschancen im Lebenslauf.* Frankfurt am Main and New York: Campus.

———. 1990. "Changes in Educational Careers in the Federal Republic of Germany." *Sociology of Education* 63:165–77.

BOUDON, R. 1974. *Education, Opportunity and Social Inequality.* New York: Wiley.

BOURDIEU, P. 1966. "L'Ecole conservatrice." *Revue Française de Sociologie* 7:325–47.

———. 1973. "Cultural Reproduction and Social Reproduction." In *Knowledge, Education, and Cultural Change,* edited by R. Brown. London: Tavistock.

BOURDIEU, P. AND J.-C. PASSERON. 1964. *Les Heritiers.* Paris: Editions de Minuit.

———. 1977. *Reproduction in Education, Society and Culture.* Beverly Hills, CA: Sage.

BOWLES, S. AND H. GINTIS. 1976. *Schooling in Capitalist America.* New York: Basic Books.

COLLINS, R. 1971. "Functional and Conflict Theories of Educational Stratification." *American Sociological Review* 36:1002–19.

ERIKSON, R. 1983. "Changes in Social Mobility in Industrial Nations: The Case of Sweden." *Research on Social Stratification and Mobility* 2:165–95.

ERIKSON, R. AND J. H. GOLDTHORPE. 1985. "Are American Rates of Social Mobility Exceptionally High? New Evidence on an Old Issue." *European Sociological Review* 1:1–22.

———. 1987. "Commonality and Variation in Social Fluidity in Industrial Nations I: A Model for Evaluating the 'FJH-Hypothesis.'" *European Sociological Review* 3:54–77.

———. 1992. *The Constant Flux: A Study of Class Mobility in Industrial Societies.* Oxford: Clarendon Press.

ESPING-ANDERSEN, G. 1990. *The Three Worlds of Welfare Capitalism.* Cambridge (U.K.): Polity Press.

FEATHERMAN, D. L. AND R. M. HAUSER. 1976. "Equality of Schooling: Trends and Prospects." *Sociology of Education* 49:99–120.

———. 1978. *Opportunity and Change.* New York: Academic Press.

FLORA, P. 1981. "Solution or Source of Crises? The Welfare State in Historical Perspective." In *The Emergence of the Welfare State in Britain and Germany,* edited by W. J. Mommsen. London: Croom Helm.

———. 1988. *Westeuropa im Wandel.* Frankfurt am Main and New York: Campus.

GAMBETTA, D. 1987. *Were They Pushed or Did They Jump?* Cambridge (U.K.): Cambridge University Press.

GOLDTHORPE, J. H. 1986. "Employment, Class and Mobility: A Critique of Liberal and Marxist Theories of Long-term Change." Conference on Social Change and Development, Berkeley, CA.

HALLER, M. 1989. *Klassenstrukturen und Mobilität in fortgeschrittenen Gesellschaften.* Frankfurt am Main and New York: Campus.

HALSEY, A. H., A. HEATH, AND J. M. RIDGE. 1980. *Origins and Destinations.* Oxford: Clarendon Press.

HEATH, A. F. AND P. CLIFFORD. 1990. "Class Inequalities in the Twentieth Century." *Journal of the Royal Statistical Society,* Series A, 153:1–16.

KARABEL, J. 1972. "Community Colleges and Social Stratification." *Harvard Education Review* 42:521–62.

LENSKI, G. 1966. *Power and Privilege.* New York: McGraw-Hill.

———. 1978. "Marxist Experiments in Destratification: An Appraisal." *Social Forces* 57:364–83.

MARE, R. D. 1980. "Social Background and School Continuation Decisions." *Journal of the American Statistical Association* 75:295–305.

———. 1981. "Change and Stability in Educa-

tional Stratification." *American Sociological Review* 46:72–87.

MATĚJŮ, P. 1984. "Democratization of Education and the Development of Educational Mobility in Czechoslovakia and Hungary." ISA Research Committee on Social Stratification, Budapest.

MEYER, J. W., F. O. RAMIREZ, R. RUBINSON, AND J. BOLI-BENNETT. 1977. "The World Educational Revolution, 1950–1970." *Sociology of Education* 50:242–58.

MINCER, J. 1974. *Schooling, Experience, and Earnings.* Cambridge: National Bureau of Economic Research.

MÜLLER, W. 1990. "Does Education Matter? Evidence from Cross-national Comparisons." Manuscript, University of Mannheim.

MÜLLER, W. AND K.-U. MAYER. 1976. "Chancengleichheit durch Bildung? Untersuchungen über den Zusammenhang von Ausbildungsabschlüssen und Berufsstatus." *Deutscher Bildungsrat, Studien und Gutachten der Bildungskommission,* Vol. 42. Stuttgart: Klett.

PARSONS, T. 1970. "Equality and Inequality in Modern Society, or Social Stratification Revisited." In *Social Stratification,* edited by E. O. Lauman. Indianapolis: Bobbs-Merrill.

PESCHAR, J. L., ed. 1990. *Social Reproduction in Eastern and Western Europe.* Nijmegen: Institute for Applied Social Sciences (ITS).

RAFTERY, A. E. AND M. HOUT. 1990. "Maximally Maintained Inequality: Expansion, Reform, and Opportunity in Irish Education, 1921–1975." ISA Research Committee on Social Stratification, Madrid.

SHAVIT, Y. 1984. "Tracking and Ethnicity in Israeli Secondary Education." *American Sociological Review* 49:210–20.

———. 1989. "Tracking and the Educational Spiral: Arab and Jewish Educational Expansion." *Comparative Education Review* 33:216–31.

———. 1990. "Segregation, Tracking and Educational Attainment of Minorities: Arabs and Oriental Jews in Israel." *American Sociological Review* 55:115–26.

SMITH, H. L. AND P. P. L. CHEUNG. 1986. "Trend in the Effects of Family Background on Educational Attainment in the Philippines." *American Journal of Sociology* 91:1387–1408.

SORENSEN, A. B. 1983. "The Structure of Allocation to Open and Closed Positions in the Social Structure." *Zeitschrift für Soziologie* 12:203–24.

———. 1986. "Theory and Methodology in Social Stratification." In *The Sociology of Structure and Action,* edited by U. Himmelstrand. New York: Sage.

SORENSEN, A. B. AND H.-P. BLOSSFELD. 1989. "Socioeconomic Opportunities in Germany in the Postwar Period." *Research in Social Stratification and Mobility* 8:85–106.

SPENCE, A. M. 1973. "Job Market Signaling." *Quarterly Journal of Economics* 87:355–74.

THUROW, L. C. 1976. *Generating Inequality.* London: Macmillan.

TREIMAN, D. J. 1970. "Industrialization and Social Stratification." In *Social Stratification: Research and Theory for the 1970s,* edited by E. O. Lauman. Indianapolis: Bobbs-Merrill.

VAN KERSBERGER, K. AND U. BECKER. 1988. "The Netherlands: A Passive Social Democratic Welfare State in a Christian Democratic Ruled Society." *Journal of Social Policy* 17:477–99.

24

ELEMENTS OF A CULTURE

Paul Willis

Opposition to Authority and Rejection of the Conformist

The most basic, obvious and explicit dimension of counter-school culture is entrenched general and personalized opposition to "authority." This feeling is easily verbalized by "the lads" (the self-elected title of those in the counter-school culture).

[in a group discussion on teachers]

JOEY: (. . .) they're able to punish us. They're bigger than us, they stand for a bigger establishment than we do, like, we're just

little and they stand for bigger things, and you try to get your own back. It's, uh, resenting authority I suppose.

EDDIE: The teachers think they're high and mighty 'cos they're teachers, but they're nobody really, they're just ordinary people ain't they?

BILL: Teachers think they're everybody. They are more, they're higher than us, but they think they're a lot higher and they're not.

SPANKSY: Wish we could call them first names and that . . . think they're God.

PETE: That would be a lot better.

PW: I mean you say they're higher. Do you accept at all that they know better about things?

—

JOEY: Yes, but that doesn't rank them above us, just because they are slightly more intelligent.

Paul Willis, excerpts from *Learning to Labor: How Working Class Kids Get Working Class Jobs,* 1981. Republished with permission of Columbia University Press, 562 West 113th Street, New York, NY 10025. Reproduced by permission of the publishers via Copyright Clearance Center, Inc.

BILL: They ought to treat us how they'd like us to treat them.

. . .

PW: You think of most staff as kind of enemies (. . .)?
— Yeah.
— Yeah.
— Most of them.
JOEY: It adds a bit of spice to yer life, if you're trying to get him for something he's done to you.

This opposition involves an apparent inversion of the usual values held up by authority. Diligence, deference, respect—these become things which can be read in quite another way.

[*in a group discussion*]

PW: Evans [the Careers Master] said you were all being very rude (. . .) you didn't have the politeness to listen to the speaker [during a careers session]. He said why didn't you realize that you were just making the world very rude for when you grow up and God help you when you have kids 'cos they're going to be worse. What did you think of that?
JOEY: They wouldn't. They'll be outspoken. They wouldn't be submissive fucking twits. They'll be outspoken, upstanding sort of people.
SPANKSY: If any of my kids are like this, here, I'll be pleased.

This opposition is expressed mainly as a style. It is lived out in countless small ways which are special to the school institution, instantly recognized by the teachers, and an almost ritualistic part of the daily fabric of life for the kids. Teachers are adept conspiracy theorists. They have to be. It partly explains their devotion to finding out "the truth" from suspected culprits. They live

surrounded by conspiracy in its most obvious—though often verbally unexpressed—forms. It can easily become a paranoic conviction of enormous propositions.

. . .

Of course individual situations differ, and different kinds of teaching style are more or less able to control or suppress this expressive opposition. But the school conformists—or the "ear 'oles" for the lads—have a visibly different orientation. It is not so much that they support teachers, rather they support *the idea* of teachers. Having invested something of their own identities in the formal aims of education and support of the school institution—in a certain sense having foregone their own right to have a "laff"—they demand that teachers should at least respect the same authority. There are none like the faithful for reminding the shepherd of his duty.

[*in a group discussion with conformists at Hammertown Boys*]

GARY: Well, I don't think they'm strict enough now (. . .) I mean like Mr Gracey, and some of the other teachers, I mean with Groucho, even the first years play him up (. . .) they [the lads] should be punished like, so they grow up not to be cheeky (. . .) Some of the others, you can get on with them all right. I mean from the very beginning with Mr Peters everybody was quiet and if you ain't done the work, you had to come back and do it. I mean some of the other teachers, say from the first years, they give you homework, say you didn't do it, they never asked for it, they didn't bother.

It is essentially what appears to be their enthusiasm for, and complicity with, immediate authority which makes the school conformists—"ear 'oles" or "lobes"—the second great target for "the lads." The term "ear 'ole" itself connotes the passivity and absurdity of the school conformists for "the lads." It seems that they are always listening, never *doing:* never animated with their own internal life, but formless in rigid reception. The ear is one of the least expressive organs of the human body: it responds to the expressivity of others. It is pasty and easy to render obscene. That is how "the lads" liked to picture those who conformed to the official idea of schooling.

Crucially, "the lads" not only reject but feel *superior* to the "ear 'oles." The obvious medium for the enactment of this superiority is that which the "ear 'oles" apparently yield—fun, independence and excitement: having a "laff."

[*in a group discussion*]

PW: (. . .) why not be like the ear 'oles, why not try and get CSEs?

[1]: They don't get any fun, do they?

DEREK: Cos they'm prats like, one kid he's got on his report now, he's got five As and one B.

[2]: —Who's that?

DEREK: Birchall.

SPANKSY: I mean, what will they remember of their school life? What will they have to look back on? Sitting in a classroom, sweating their bollocks off, you know, while we've been . . . I mean look at the things we can look back on, fighting on the Pakis, fighting on the JAs [i.e. Jamaicans]. Some of the things we've done on teachers, it'll be a laff when we look back on it.

(. . .)

PERCE: Like you know, he don't get much fun, well say Spanksy plays about all day, he gets fun. Bannister's there sweating, sweating his bollocks off all day while

Spanksy's doing fuck all, and he's enjoying it.

. . .

Opposition to staff and exclusive distinction from the "ear 'oles" is continuously expressed amongst "the lads" in the whole ambience of their behavior, but it is also made concrete in what we may think of as certain stylistic/symbolic discourses centering on the three great consumer goods supplied by capitalism and seized upon in different ways by the working class for its own purposes: clothes, cigarettes and alcohol. As the most visible, personalized and instantly understood element of resistance to staff and ascendancy over 'ear 'oles' clothes have great importance to "the lads." The first signs of a lad "coming out" is a fairly rapid change in his clothes and hairstyle. The particular form of this alternative dress is determined by outside influences, especially fashions current in the wider symbolic system of youth culture. At the moment the "lads' look" includes longish well-groomed hair, platform-type shoes, wide collared shirt turned over waisted coat or denim jerkin, plus the still obligatory flared trousers. Whatever the particular form of dress, it is most certainly *not* school uniform, rarely includes a tie (the second best for many heads if uniform cannot be enforced), and exploits colors calculated to give the maximum distinction from institutional drabness and conformity. There is a clear stereotypical notion of what constitutes institutional clothes—Spike, for instance, trying to describe the shape of a collar: "You know, like a teacher's!"

We might note the importance the wider system of commercial youth culture has here in supplying a lexicography of style, with already connoted meanings, which can be adapted by "the lads" to express their own more located meanings Though much of this style, and the music associated with it, might be accurately described as arising from purely commercial drives and representing no authentic aspirations of its adherents, it should be recognized that the way in which it is taken up and used by the young can have an authenticity and directness of personal expression missing from its original commercial generation.

It is no accident that much of the conflict between staff and students at the moment should take place over dress. To the outsider it might seem fatuous. Concerned staff and involved kids, however, know that it is one of their elected grounds for the struggle over authority. It is one of the current forms of a fight between cultures. It can be resolved, finally, into a question about the legitimacy of school as an institution.

Closely related with the dress style of "the lads" is, of course, the whole question of their personal attractiveness. Wearing smart and modern clothes gives them the chance, at the same time as "putting their finger up" at the school and differentiating themselves from the "ear 'oles," to also make themselves more attractive to the opposite sex. It is a matter of objective fact that "the lads" do go out with girls much more than do any other groups of the same age and that a good majority of them are sexually experienced. Sexual attractiveness, its association with maturity, and the prohibition on sexual activity in school is what valorizes dress and clothes as something more than an artificial code within which to express an institutional/cultural identity. This double articulation is characteristic of the counter-school culture.

If manner of dress is currently the main apparent cause of argument between staff and kids, smoking follows closely. Again we find another distinguishing characteristic of "the lads" against the "ear 'oles." The majority of them smoke and, perhaps more importantly, are *seen* to smoke. The essence of

schoolboy smoking is school gate smoking. A great deal of time is typically spent by "the lads" planning their next smoke and "hopping off" lessons "for a quick drag." And if "the lads" delight in smoking and flaunting their impertinence, senior staff at least cannot ignore it. There are usually strict and frequently publicized rules about smoking. If, for this reason, "the lads" are spurred, almost as a matter of honor, to continue public smoking, senior staff are incensed by what they take to be the challenge to their authority. This is especially true when allied to that other great challenge: the lie.

[*in a group discussion on recent brushes with staff*]

SPIKE: And we went in, I says "We warn't smoking," he says (. . .) and he went really mad. I thought he was going to punch me or summat.

SPANKSY: "Call me a liar," "I'm not a liar," "Get back then," and we admitted it in the end; we was smoking (. . .) He was having a fit, he says "Callin' me a liar." We said we warn't smoking, tried to stick to it, but Simmondsy was having a fit.

SPIKE: He'd actually seen us light up.

. . .

Again, in a very typical conjunction of school-based and outside meanings cigarette smoking for "the lads" is valorized as an act of insurrection before the school by its association with adult values and practices. The adult world, specifically the adult male working class world, is turned to as a source of material for resistance and exclusion.

As well as inducing a "nice" effect, drinking is undertaken openly because it is the most decisive signal to staff and "ear 'oles" that the individual is separate from the school and has a presence in an alternative, superior and more mature mode of social being. Accounts of staff sighting kids in pubs are excitedly recounted with much more relish than mere smoking incidents, and inaction after being "clocked boozing" is even more delicious proof of a traitor/sympathizer/weakling in the school camp than is the blind eye to a lighted "fag." Their perception of this particular matrix of meanings puts some younger and more progressive members of staff in a severe dilemma. Some of them come up with bizarre solutions which remain incomprehensible to "the lads": this incident involves a concerned and progressive young teacher.

[*in a group discussion about staff*]

DEREK: And Alf says, er, "Alright sir" [on meeting a member of staff in a public house] and he dayn't answer, you know, and he says, "Alright, sir?," and he turned around and looked at him like that, see, and er . . . and he dayn't answer and he says, in the next day, and he says, "I want you Alf," goes to him and he says, "What was you in there last night for?" He says, "I was at a football meeting," he says, "Well don't you think that was like kicking somebody in the teeth?" "No," he says. "What would you feel like if I kicked you in the teeth?" he says "What do you mean?" he says. "Saying hello like that down there," he says, "what would you expect me to say?" He says, "Well don't speak to me again unless I speak to you first." He says, "Right sir, I won't say hello again," he says, "even if I see you in the drive."

Certainly "the lads" self-consciously understand the symbolic importance of drinking as an act of affiliation with adults and opposition to the school. It is most important to them that the last lunchtime of their last term should be spent in a pub, and that the maximum possible alcohol be consumed. This is the moment when they finally break

free from school, the moment to be remembered in future years.

. . .

In the pub there is indeed a very special atmosphere amongst the Hammertown "lads." Spike is expansively explaining that although he had behaved like a "right vicious cunt" sometimes, he really likes his mates and will miss them. Eddie is determined to have eight pints and hold the "record"—and is later "apprehended drunk," in the words of the head, at the school and ingloriously driven home by him. Fuzz is explaining how he had nearly driven Sampson (a teacher) "off his rocker" that morning and had been sent to see the head, "but he wasn't off or anything, he was joking." Most important, they are accepted by the publican and other adult customers in the pub, who are buying them drinks and asking them about their future work. At closing time they leave, exchanging the adult promises which they have not yet learned to disbelieve, calling to particular people that they will do their plumbing, bricklaying or whatever.

That they have not quite broken loose, and that staff want to underline this, is shown when "the lads" return to the school late, smelling of alcohol and in some cases quite drunk. In a reminder that the power of the school is backed ultimately by the law and state coercion, the head has called in the police. A policeman is waiting outside the school with the head. This frightens "the lads" and a bizarre scenario develops as they try to dodge the policeman.

. . .

Eventually "the lads" are rounded up and delivered in an excited state to the head's study, where they are told off roughly by the policeman: "He picked me up and bounced me against the wall"—Spike (I did not see this incident myself). The head subsequently writes to all of their parents threatening to withhold their final testimonials until an apology is received: In the case of Spike he wrote:

> . . . your son had obviously been drinking, and his subsequent behavior was generally uncooperative, insolent, and almost belligerent. He seemed bent on justifying his behavior and went as far as describing the school as being like Colditz . . . as is my practice, I wish to give the parents of the boys an opportunity to come and see me before I finally decide what action to take.

Even sympathetic young staff find the incident "surprising," and wondered why "the lads" had not waited until the evening, and then "really done it properly." The point is, of course, that the drinking has to be done at lunchtime, and in defiance of the school. It is not done simply to mark a neutral transition—a mere ritual. It is a decisive rejection and closing off. They have, in some way, finally beaten the school in a way which is beyond the "ear 'oles" and nearly unanswerable by staff. It is the transcendence of what they take to be the mature life, the *real* life, over the oppressive adolescence of the school—represented by the behavior both of the "ear 'oles" *and* of the teachers.

Some of the parents of "the lads" share their sons' view of the situation. Certainly none of them take up the head's offer to go and see him.

[*in a group discussion*]

WILL: Our mum's kept all the letters, you know, about like the letters Simmondsy's sent [about the drinking]. I says, "What you keeping them for?" She says, "Well, it'll be nice to look back on to, won't it," you know, "show your kids like you know, what a terror you was." I'm keeping 'em, I am.

[*individual interview at work*]

PW: Did your old man understand about having a drink the last day of term?
SPANKSY: Oh ah (. . .) he laughed, he said, "Fancy them sending a letter," you know. Joey's father come and had a little laugh about it you know.

No matter what the threats, and the fear of the law, the whole episode is "worth it" to "the lads." It is the most frequently recounted, embellished and exaggerated school episode in the future working situation. It soon becomes part of a personalized folklore. As school uniform and smoking cease to be the most obvious causes of conflict in schools as more liberal regimes develop, we may expect drinking to become the next major area where the battle lines are drawn.

The Informal Group

. . .

In many respects the opposition we have been looking at can be understood as a classic example of the opposition between the formal and the informal. The school is the zone of the formal. It has a clear structure: the school building, school rules, pedagogic practice, a staff hierarchy with powers ultimately sanctioned—as we have seen in small way—by the state, the pomp and majesty of the law, and the repressive arm of state apparatus, the police. The "ear 'oles" invest in this formal structure, and in exchange for some loss in autonomy expect the official guardians to keep the holy rules—often above and beyond their actual call to duty. What is freely sacrificed by the faithful must be taken from the unfaithful.

Counter-school culture is the zone of the informal. It is where the incursive demands of the formal are denied—even if the price is the expression of opposition in style, micro-interactions and non-public discourses. In working class culture generally opposition is frequently marked by a withdrawal into the informal and expressed in its characteristic modes just beyond the reach of "the rule."

Even though there are no public rules, physical structures, recognized hierarchies or institutionalized sanctions in the counter-school culture, it cannot run on air. It must have its own material base, its own infrastructure. This is, of course, the social group. The informal group is the basic unit of this culture, the fundamental and elemental source of its resistance. It locates and makes possible all other elements of the culture, and its presence decisively distinguishes "the lads" from the "ear 'oles."

. . .

The essence of being "one of the lads" lies within the group. It is impossible to form a distinctive culture by yourself. You cannot generate fun, atmosphere and a social identity by yourself. Joining the counter-school culture means joining a group, and enjoying it means being with the group:

[*in a group discussion on being "one of the lads"*]

JOEY: (. . .), when you'm dossing on your own, it's no good, but when you'm dossing with your mates, then you're all together, you're having a laff and it's a doss.
BILL: If you don't do what the others do, you feel out.
FRED: You feel out, yeah, yeah. They sort of, you feel, like, thinking the others are . . .
WILL: In the second years . . .
SPANKSY: I can imagine . . . you know, when I have a day off school, when you come back the next day, and something happened like in the day you've been off, you feel, "Why did I have that day off," you know, "I could have been enjoying myself." You know what I mean? You

come back and they're saying, "Oorh, you should have been here yesterday," you know.
WILL: (. . .) like in the first and second years, you can say er'm . . . you're a bit of an ear 'ole right. Then you want to try what it's like to be er'm . . . say, one of the boys like, you want to have a taste of that, not an ear 'ole, and so you like the taste of that.

Though informal, such groups nevertheless have rules of a kind which can be described—though they are characteristically framed in contrast to what "rules" are normally taken to mean.

PW: (. . .) Are there any rules between you lot?
PETE: We just break the other rules.
FUZZ: We ain't got no rules between us though, have we?

(. . .)

PETE: Changed 'em round.
WILL: We ain't got rules but we do things between us, but we do things that y'know, like er . . . say, I wouldn't knock off anybody's missus or Joey's missus, and they wouldn't do it to me, y'know what I mean? Things like that or, er . . . yer give 'im a fag, you expect one back, like, or summat like that.
FRED: T'ain't rules, it's just an understanding really.
WILL: That's it, yes.
PW: (. . .) What would these understandings be?
WILL: Er . . . I think, not to . . . meself, I think there ain't many of us that play up the first or second years, it really is that, but y'know, say if Fred had cum to me

and sez, "er . . . I just got two bob off that second year over there," I'd think, "What a cunt," you know.

(. . .)

FRED: We're as thick as thieves, that's what they say, stick together.

There is a universal taboo amongst informal groups on the yielding of incriminating information about others to those with formal power. Informing contravenes the essence of the informal group's nature: the maintenance of oppositional meanings against the penetration of "the rule." The Hammertown lads call it "grassing." Staff call it telling the truth. "Truth" is the formal complement of "grassing." It is only by getting someone to "grass"—forcing them to break the solemnest taboo—that the primacy of the formal organization can be maintained. No wonder then, that a whole school can be shaken with paroxysms over a major incident and the purge which follows it. It is an atavistic struggle about authority and the legitimacy of authority. The school has to win, and someone, finally, has to "grass": this is one of the ways in which the school itself is reproduced and the faith of the "ear'oles" restored. But whoever has done the "grassing" becomes special, weak and marked.

. . .

The group also supplies those contacts which allow the individual to build up alternative maps of social reality, it gives the bits and pieces of information for the individual to work out himself what makes things tick. It is basically only through the group that other groups are met, and through them successions of other groups. School groups coalesce and further link up with neighborhood groups, forming a network for the passing on of distinctive kinds of knowledge and perspectives that progressively place school at a tangent to the overall experience of being a working class teenager in an industrial city. It is the infrastructure of the informal group which makes at all possible a distinctive kind of *class* contact, or class culture, as distinct from the dominant one.

. . .

Dossing, Blagging and Wagging

Opposition to the school is principally manifested in the struggle to win symbolic and physical space from the institution and its rules and to defeat its main perceived purpose: to make you "work." Both the winning and the prize—a form of self-direction—profoundly develop informal cultural meanings and practices. The dynamic aspects of the staff/pupil relationship will be examined later on. By the time a counter-school culture is fully developed its members have become adept at managing the formal system, and limiting its demands to the absolute minimum. Exploiting the complexity of modern regimes of mixed ability groupings; blocked timetabling and multiple RSLA options, in many cases this minimum is simply the act of registration.

[*in a group discussion on the school curriculum*]

JOEY: (. . .) of a Monday afternoon, we'd have nothing right? Nothing hardly relating to school work, Tuesday afternoon we have swimming and they stick you in a classroom for the rest of the afternoon, Wednesday afternoon you have games and there's only Thursday and Friday afternoon that you work, if you call that work. The last lesson Friday afternoon we used to go and doss, half of us wagged out o' lessons and the other half go into the classroom, sit down and just go to sleep (. . .)

SPANKSY: (. . .) Skive this lesson, go up on the bank, have a smoke, and the next lesson go to a teacher who, you know, 'll call the register (. . .)

BILL: It's easy to go home as well, like him [Eddie] . . . last Wednesday afternoon, he got his mark and went home (. . .)

EDDIE: I ain't supposed to be in school this afternoon, I'm supposed to be at college [on a link course where students spend one day a week at college for vocational instruction]

PW: What's the last time you've done some writing?

WILL: When we done some writing?

FUZZ: Oh are, last time was in careers, 'cos I writ "yes" on a piece of paper, that broke me heart.

PW: Why did it break your heart?

FUZZ: I mean to write, 'cos I was going to try and go through the term without writing anything. 'Cos since we've cum back, I ain't dun nothing [it was half way through term].

Truancy is only a very imprecise—even meaningless—measure of rejection of school. This is not only because of the practice of stopping in school for registration before "wagging off" (developed to a fine art amongst "the lads"), but also because it only measures one aspect of what we might more accurately describe as informal student mobility. Some of "the lads" develop the ability of moving about the school at their own will to a remarkable degree. They construct virtually their own day from what is offered by the school. Truancy is only one relatively unimportant and crude variant of this principle of self-direction which ranges across vast chunks of the syllabus and covers many diverse activities: being free out of class, being

in class and doing no work, being in the wrong class, roaming the corridors looking for excitement, being asleep in private. The core skill which articulates these possibilities is being able to get out of any given class: the preservation of personal mobility.

[in a group discussion]

PW: But doesn't anybody worry about your not being in their class?

FUZZ: I get a note off the cooks saying I'm helping them (. . .)

JOHN: You just go up to him [a teacher] and say, "Can I go and do a job." He'll say, "Certainly, by all means," 'cos they want to get rid of you like.

FUZZ: Specially when I ask 'em.

PETE: You know the holes in the corridor, I didn't want to go to games, he told me to fetch his keys, so I dropped them down the hole in the corridor, and had to go and get a torch and find them.

For the successful, there can be an embarrassment of riches. It can become difficult to choose between self-organized routes through the day.

WILL: (. . .) what we been doing, playing cards in this room 'cos we can lock the door.

PW: Which room's this now?

WILL: Resources center, where we're making the frames [a new stage for the deputy head], s'posed to be.

PW: Oh! You're still making the frames!

WILL: We should have had it finished, we just lie there on top of the frame, playing cards, or trying to get to sleep (. . .) Well, it gets a bit boring, I'd rather go and sit in the classroom, you know.

PW: What sort of lessons would you think of going into?

WILL: Uh, science, I think, 'cos you can have a laff in there sometimes.

This self-direction and thwarting of formal organizational aims is also an assault on official notions of time. The most arduous task of the deputy head is the construction of the timetables. In large schools, with several options open to the fifth year, everything has to be fitted in with the greatest of care. The first weeks of term are spent in continuous revision, as junior members of staff complain, and particular combinations are shown to be unworkable. Time, like money, is valuable and not to be squandered. Everything has to be ordered into a kind of massive critical path of the school's purpose. Subjects become measured blocks of time in careful relation to each other. Quite as much as the school buildings the institution over time *is* the syllabus. The complex charts on the deputy's wall shows how it works. In theory it is possible to check where every individual is at every moment of the day. But for "the lads" this never seems to work. If one wishes to contact them, it is much more important to know and understand their own rhythms and patterns of movement. These rhythms reject the obvious purposes of the timetable and their implicit notions of time. The common complaint about "the lads" from staff and the "ear'oles" is that they "waste valuable time." Time for "the lads" is not something you carefully husband and thoughtfully spend on the achievement of desired objectives in the future. For "the lads" time is something they want to claim for themselves now as an aspect of their immediate identity and self-direction. Time is used for the preservation of a state—being with "the lads"—not for the achievement of a goal—qualifications.

Of course there is a sense of urgency sometimes, and individuals can see the end of term approaching and the need to get a job. But as far as their culture is concerned time is importantly simply the state of being free from institutional time. Its own time all passes as essentially the same thing, in the same units. It is not planned, and is not counted in loss, or expected exchange.

"Having a Laff"

"Even communists laff" (Joey)

The space won from the school and its rules by the informal group is used for the shaping and development of particular cultural skills principally devoted to "having a laff." The "laff" is a multi-faceted implement of extraordinary importance in the counter-school culture. As we saw before, the ability to produce it is one of the defining characteristics of being one of "the lads"—"We can make them laff, they can't make us laff." But it is also used in many other contexts: to defeat boredom and fear, to overcome hardship and problems—as a way out of almost anything. In many respects the "laff" is the privileged instrument of the informal, as the command is of the formal. Certainly "the lads" understand the special importance of the "laff":

[in an individual discussion]

JOEY: I think fuckin' laffing is the most important thing in fuckin' everything. Nothing ever stops me laffing (. . .) I remember once, there was me, John, and this other kid, right, and these two kids cum up and bashed me for some fuckin' reason or another. John and this other kid were away, off (. . .) I tried to give 'em one, but I kept fuckin' coppin' it . . . so I ran off, and as I ran off, I scooped a handful of fuckin' snow up, and put it right over me face, and I was laffing me bollocks off. They kept saying, "You can't fuckin' laff." I should have been scared but I was fuckin' laffing (. . .)

PW: What is it about having a laugh, (. . .) why is it so important?

JOEY: (...) I don't know why I want to laff, I dunno why it's so fuckin' important. It just is (...) I think it's just a good gift, that's all, because you can get out of any situation. If you can laff, if you can make yourself laff, I mean really convincingly, it can get you out of millions of things (...) You'd go fuckin' berserk if you didn't have a laff occasionally.

The school is generally a fertile ground for the "laff." The school importantly develops and shapes the particular ambience of "the lads'" distinctive humor.... We can note the ways in which specific themes of authority are explored, played with and used in their humor. Many of their pranks and jokes would not mean the same thing or even be funny anywhere else. When a teacher comes into a classroom he is told, "It's alright, sir, the deputy's taking us, you can go. He said you could have the period off." "The lads" stop second and third years around the school and say, "Mr Argyle wants to see you, you'm in trouble I think." Mr. Argyle's room is soon choked with worried kids. A new teacher is stopped and told, "I'm new in the school, the head says could you show me around please." The new teacher starts to do just that before the turned away laughs give the game away. As a rumor circulates that the head is checking everyone's handwriting to discover who has defaced plaster in the new block, Fuzz boasts, "The fucker can't check mine, I ain't done none." In a humorous exploration of the crucial point where authority connects with the informal code through the sacred taboo on informing, there is a stream of telltale stories half goading the teacher into playing his formal role more effectively: "Please sir, please sir, Joey's talking/pinching some compasses/picked his nose/killing Percival/having a wank/let your car tyres down."

. . .

Of course "the lads" do not always look to external stimulants or victims for the "laff." Interaction and conversation in the group frequently take the form of "pisstaking." They are very physical and rough with each other, with kicks, punches, karate blows, arm-twisting, kicking, pushing and tripping going on for long periods and directed against particular individuals often almost to the point of tears. The ribbing or "pisstaking" is similarly rough and often directed at the same individuals for the same things. Often this is someone's imagined stupidity. This is ironic in view of "the lads" general rejection of school work, and shows a ghost of conventional values which they would be quick to deny. Though "the lads" usually resist conventional ways of showing their abilities, certainly the ablest like to be thought of as "quick." Certain cultural values, like fast talking and humor, do anyway register in some academic subjects. Joey, for instance, walks a very careful tightrope in English between "laffing" with "the lads" and doing the occasional "brilliant" essay. In certain respects obvious stupidity is penalized more heavily amongst "the lads" than by staff, who "expected nothing better." Very often the topic for the "pisstake" is sexual, though it can be anything—the more personal, sharper and apposite the better. The soul of wit for them is disparaging relevance: the persistent searching out of weakness. It takes some skill and cultural know-how to mount such attacks, and more to resist them:

[*a group of "lads" during break-time*]

EDDIE: X gets his missus to hold his prick, while he has a piss. [Laughter]
WILL: Ask him who wipes his arse. [Laughter]

SPIKE: The dirty bastard . . . I bet he changes her fucking rags for her.
SPANKSY: With his teeth! [More laughter]

[*X arrives*]

SPANKSY: Did you have a piss dinnertime?
BILL: Or a shit?
SPANKSY: You disgusting little boy . . . I couldn't do that.
BILL: Hold on a minute, I want you to hold my cock while I have a piss. [Laughter]
X: Why am I . . .
WILL (INTERRUPTING): He don't even know.
BILL: Does your missus hold your cock for you when you go for a piss?
X: Who does? [Laughter and interruptions]
— You do
X: Who?
— You
X: When?
SPIKE: You did, you told Joey, Joey told me.

Plans are continually made to play jokes on individuals who are not there: "Let's send him to Coventry when he comes," "Let's laugh at everything he says," "Let's pretend we can't understand and say, 'How do you mean' all the time." Particular individuals can get a reputation and attract constant ribbing for being "dirty," or "as thick as two short planks," or even for always wearing the "same tatty jacket." The language used in the group, especially in the context of derision and the "pisstake," is much rougher than that used by the "ear 'oles," full of spat-out swearwords, vigorous use of local dialect and special argot. Talking, at least on their own patch and in their own way, comes very naturally to "the lads":

[*in a group discussion on skiving*]

JOEY: (. . .) You'm always looking out on somebody [when skiving] and you've al-

ways got something to talk about . . . something.
PW: So what stops you being bored?
JOEY: Talking, we could talk forever, when we get together, it's talk, talk, talk.

Sexism

Two other groups against whom "the lads" exclusivity is defined, and through which their own sense of superiority is enacted, are girls and ethnic minority groups.

Their most nuanced and complex attitudes are reserved for the opposite sex. There is a traditional conflict in their view of women: they are both sexual objects and domestic comforters. In essence this means that whilst women must be sexually attractive, they cannot be sexually experienced.

Certainly desire is clear on the part of "the lads." Lascivious tales of conquest or jokes turning on the passivity of women or on the particular sexual nature of men are regular topics of conversation. Always it is their *own* experience, and not that of the girl or of their shared relationship, which is the focus of the stories. The girls are afforded no particular identity save that of their sexual attraction.

. . .

Although they are its object, frank and explicit sexuality is actually denied to women. There is a complex of emotion here. On the one hand, insofar as she is a sex object, a commodity, she is actually diminished by sex; she is literally worthless; she has been romantically and materially partly consumed. To show relish for this diminution is seen as self-destructive. On the other hand, in a half recognition of the human sexuality they have suppressed, there is a fear that once a girl is sexually experienced and has known joy from sex at all, the floodgates of her desire will be opened and she will be completely promiscuous.

Y: After you've been with one like, after you've done it like, well they're scrubbers afterwards, they'll go with anyone. I think it's that once they've had it, they want it all the time, no matter who it's with.

Certainly reputations for "easiness"—deserved or not—spread very quickly. "The lads" are after the "easy lay" at dances, though they think twice about being seen to "go out" with them.

The "girlfriend" is a very different category from an "easy lay." She represents the human value that is squandered by promiscuity. She is the loyal domestic partner. She cannot be held to be sexually experienced—or at least not with others. Circulated stories about the sexual adventures of "the missus" are a first-rate challenge to masculinity and pride. They have to be answered in the masculine mode:

[*in an individual discussion*]

X: He keeps saying things, he went out with me missus before like, and he keeps saying things what I don't like, and y'know like, it gets around . . . he won't learn his fucking lesson, he does summat, he sez summat, right, I bash him for it, he won't hit me back, he runs off like a little wanker, then he sez something else (. . .) he ain't been to school since Friday (. . .) when I fuckin' cop him I'm gonna kill 'im, if I get 'im on the floor he's fucking dead.

Courtship is a serious affair. The common prolepsis of calling girlfriends "the missus" is no accident amongst "the lads." A whole new range of meanings and connotations come into play during serious courting. Their referent is the home: dependability and domesticity—the opposite of the sexy bird

on the scene. If the initial attraction is based on sex, the final settlement is based on a strange denial of sex—a denial principally, of course, of the girl's sexuality for others, but also of sexuality as the dominant feature of their own relationship. Possible promiscuity is held firmly in check by domestic glue:

[*in an individual interview*]

SPIKE: (. . .) I've got the right bird, I've been goin' with her for eighteen months now. Her's as good as gold. She wouldn't look at another chap. She's fucking done well, she's clean. She loves doing fucking housework. Trousers I brought yesterday, I took 'em up last night, and her turned 'em up for me (. . .) She's as good as gold and I wanna get married as soon as I can.

The model for the girlfriend is, of course, the mother and she is fundamentally a model of limitation. Though there is a great deal of affection for "mum," she is definitely accorded an inferior role: "She's a bit thick, like, never knows what I'm on about," "She don't understand this sort of stuff, just me dad." And within the home there is a clear sense that men have a right to be waited on by the mother:

[*in an individual interview*]

SPANKSY: (. . .) it shouldn't be done, you shouldn't need to help yer mother in the house. You should put your shoes away tidy and hang your coat up, admittedly, but, you know, you shouldn't vacuum and polish and do the beds for her and (. . .) her housekeeping and that.

The resolution amongst working class girls of the contradiction between being sexually desirable but not sexually experienced leads to behavior which strengthens "the lads'" sense of superiority. This resolution takes the form of romanticism readily fed by teenage magazines. It turns upon the "crush," and sublimation of sexual feeling into talk, rumors and message-sending within the protective circle of the informal female group. This is not to say that they never have sex—clearly a good proportion must do—but that the dominant social form of their relationship with boys is to be sexy, but in a girlish, latter day courtly love mold which falls short of actual sexual proposition. The clear sexual stimulus which in the first place attracts the boy can thus be reconverted into the respectable values of the home and monogamous submission. If ever the paranoic thought strikes the boy that, having got the "come on" himself, why shouldn't others, he can be calmed with the thought, "she's not like that, she's soft inside." In this way, still, romanticism brokes the sexual within a patriarchal society. It allows sexual display without sexual promise, being sexy but not sexual.

What "the lads" see of the romantic behavior they have partly conditioned in the girls, however, is a simple sheepishness, weakness and a silly indirectness in social relationships: "saft wenches giggling all the time." Since the girls have abandoned the assertive and the sexual, they leave that ground open to the boys. It is they who take on the drama and initiative, the machismo, of a sexual drive. They have no reservations about making their intentions clear, or of enjoying a form of their sexuality. However, they take it as an aspect of their inherent superiority that they can be frank and direct and unmystified about their desires. The contortions and strange rituals of the girls are seen as part of their girlishness, of their inherent weakness and confusion. Their romanticism is tolerated with a knowing masculinity, which privately feels it knows much more about the world. This sense of masculine pride spreads over into the expressive confidence of the rest of "the lads" culture. It adds a zest to their language, physical and boisterous relations with each other, humiliation of "ear 'oles," and even to a particular display style of violence.

The combination of these various factors gives a special tone to interaction between the sexes. "The lads" usually take the initiative in conversation and are the ones who make suggestive comments. The girls respond with giggles and talk amongst themselves. Where girls do make comments they are of the serious, caring or human kind. It is left to "the lads" to make the jokes, the hard comments, the abrasive summations and to create a spectacle to be appreciated by the girls. The girls are clearly dominated, but they collude in their own domination:

[*a mixed group talking "by the sheds" at dinner time*]

JOAN: We'm all gonna start crying this afternoon, it's the last.

BILL: You've only got two weeks left ain't yer, we'm gonna laugh when we leave (. . .)

JOAN: I like your jumper.

BILL: You can come inside if yer like!

WILL: Ain't it terrible when you see these old women with bandages round their ankles.

MARY: I ain't got 'em, and I ain't fat.

WILL: I dayn't say you had, I said it was terrible.

BILL: I'm gonna nick Mary's fags and smoke 'em all. [Giggles]

(. . .)

EDDIE: It's time you lot were back in school, go on. [Giggles and whispering about someone who "fancies" Eddie]. These wenches don't half talk about you behind your back, me ears are burning. [Loud burp from one of "the lads"]

MAGGIE: Oh, you pig, shut up.

BILL: [Handling cigarettes around] He'are.

MAGGIE: No thanks, I'll have a big one.

BILL: She likes big ones! He's got a big one, ask him, he'll let you have a look.

THE REST: [Singing] He's got a big one, he's got a big one . . . [Bill takes his coat off]

EDDIE: Have it off.

BILL: [To Mary] Have you ever had it off?

WILL: I've had it off twice today already [Laughter] Do you like having it off? [To Maggie]

MAGGIE: You cheeky sod.

WILL: I mean your coat.

. . .

Racism

Three distinct groups—Caucasians, Asians and West Indians—are clearly visible in most school settings. Though individual contacts are made, especially in the youth wing, the ethnic groups are clearly separated by the fourth year. Divisions are, if anything, more obvious in informal settings. For a period the head of upper school allows fifth years to use form rooms for "friendship groups" during break time. This is yet another, this time defensive and accommodating, variant of the continuous if subtle struggle to contain opposition. Its results, however, demonstrate for us what are the clear informal patterns of racial culture beneath and sometimes obscured by the official structures of the school.

HEAD OF UPPER SCHOOL: We have got the Martins (Bill), Croft (Joey), Rustin, Roberts (Will), Peterson (Eddie), Jeffs (Fuzz) and Barnes (Spike) in the European room. Bucknor, Grant, Samuels, Spence in the West Indian room and Singh, Rajit and co in the Asiatic room. So much for integration! There are three distinct rooms. You go into the white room and you will probably sit down and have a cup of tea made. You go into the Indian room and

they are all playing cards and they are jabbering to each other, and then you go into the West Indian room and they are all dancing to records. In the West Indian room they are sort of stamping around, twisting.

From the point of view of "the lads" the separation is certainly experienced as rejection of others. There is frequent verbal, if not actual, violence shown to "the fuckin' wogs," or the "bastard pakis." The mere fact of different color can be enough to justify an attack or intimidation. A clear demarcation between groups and a derogatory view of other racial types is simply assumed as the basis for this and other action: it is a daily form of knowledge in use.

SPANKSY: We had a go at the Jamaicans, 'cos you know, we outnumbered them. We dayn't want to fight them when they was all together. We outnumbered them.

SPIKE: They was all there though.

SPANKSY: They was all there, but half of them walked off dayn't they, there was only a couple left. About four of us got this one.

JOEY: Not one of us was marked . . . that was really super.

Racial identity for "the lads" supplants individual identity so that stories to friends concern not "this kid," but "this wog." At Hammertown Boys there is an increasing and worrying tension between the ethnic groups, particularly the Caucasians and the Asians, which sometimes flares up into violence. The deputy head then gets everyone into the hall and lectures them, but this only suppresses the immediate expression of dislike:

[In a group discussion on recent disturbances at the school]

JOEY: He [the deputy in the hall after an incident] even started talking about the Israeli war at one stage, "This is how war starts. . . . Pack it in."

PW: (. . .) was he convincing you a bit?

JOEY: He was just talking, we were just listening thinking, "Right you black bastard, next time you start, we'll have you"— which we will.

This curiously self-righteous readiness to express and act on dislike is reinforced by what "the lads" take to be a basically collusive attitude of staff—no matter what the public statements. This is perhaps even an unconscious effect and certainly where racism exists amongst staff it is much less virulent than that in the counter-school culture. There is, however, by and large much less sympathy and rapport between (a massively white) staff and ethnic minorities than between staff and whites. In an almost automatic cultural reflex minorities are seen as strange and less civilized—not "tea," but "jabbering to each other" and "stamping around." Certainly it is quite explicit that many senior staff associate the mass immigration of the 1960s with the break up of the "order and quietness" of the 1950s and of what is seen more and more retrospectively as their peaceful, successful schools. Both "lads" and staff do share, therefore, a sense in their different ways of resentment for the disconcerting intruder. For racism amongst "the lads" it provides a double support for hostile attitudes. The informal was, for once, backed up by at least the ghost of the formal.

The racism in the counter-school culture is structured by reified though somewhat differentiated stereotypes. Asians come off worst and are often the target for petty intimidation, small pestering attacks, and the physical and symbolic jabbing at weak or unprotected points in which "the lads" specialize. Asians are seen both as alien, "smelly" and probably "unclean," and as sharing some of the most disliked "ear 'ole" characteristics. They are doubly disliked for the contradictory way in which they seem simultaneously to be both further off, and closer to received English cultural models. They are interlopers who do not know their station and try to take that which is not rightfully theirs but which is anyway disliked and discredited on other grounds.

. . .

25

TEENAGERS IN CLARENDON HEIGHTS: THE HALLWAY HANGERS AND THE BROTHERS

Jay MacLeod

On any given day, except during the coldest winter months, the evening hours in Clarendon Heights are filled with activity. At one end of the housing development, elderly women sit on wooden benches and chat. In the center of the project, children play street hockey, kickball, stickball, or football, depending on the season. At the other end, teenage boys congregate in the stairwell and on the landing of one of the entries—doorway #13.

The Hallway Hangers: "You Gotta Be Bad"

This doorway and the area immediately outside it are the focus of activity for the Hallway Hangers, one of the two main peer groups of high-school-age boys living in Clarendon Heights. Composed of a core of eight youths, but including up to ten additional people who are loosely attached to the group, the Hallway Hangers are tough, streetwise, individuals who form a distinctive subculture. Except for Boo-Boo, who is black, and Chris, who is of mixed racial parentage, the Hallway Hangers are white boys

of Italian or Irish descent. The eight members considered here range in age from sixteen to nineteen. Five have dropped out of school, two graduated last year, and one continues to attend high school. They all smoke cigarettes, drink regularly, and use drugs. All but two have been arrested. . . .

. . .

These boys come together in the late afternoon or early evening after dinner and "hang" in doorway #13 until late at night. They come to "see what's up," to "find out what's goin' down," to "shoot the shit," and, generally, to just pass the time. Smelling of urine, lined with graffiti, and littered with trash and broken glass, this hallway is the setting for much playful banter, some not so playful "capping" (exchange of insults), and an occasional fight. The odors of cigarette smoke, beer, and marijuana are nearly always present. During the weekend, there may be a case or two of beer, a nearly constant circulation of joints, and some cocaine, mescaline, or "angel dust" (PCP). Late at night, one occasionally stumbles upon a lone figure shooting up heroin.

In an inversion of the dominant culture's vocabulary and value scheme, the subculture of the Hallway Hangers is a world in which to be "bad" is literally to be good. A common characteristic of lower-class teenage peer cultures, this emphasis on being bad is inextricably bound up with the premium put on masculinity, physical toughness, and street wisdom in lower-class culture. Slick, in articulating the prominence of this value for the Hallway Hangers, states in definite terms what being bad often involves.

(in an individual talk)

SLICK: You hafta make a name for yourself, to be bad, tough, whatever. You hafta be, y'know, be with the "in" crowd. Know what I mean? You hafta—it's just all part of growing up around here—you hafta do certain things. Some of the things you hafta do is, y'know, once in awhile you hafta, if you haven't gotten into a fight, if you have a fight up the high school, you're considered bad. Y'know what I mean? If you beat someone up up there, especially if he's black, around this way . . . if you're to be bad, you hafta be arrested. You hafta at least know what bein' in a cell is like.

(in a group discussion)

JM: So how is it that to be what's good down here, to be respected . . .
SLICK: You gotta be bad.
FRANKIE: Yeah, if you're a straight A student, you get razzed.
SLICK: Then you're a fucking weirdo, and you shouldn't be living here in the first place.
SHORTY: No, you got people down here who don't drink and don't smoke.
SLICK: Who? Name one.
SHORTY: Crane. Bruce Crane.
FRANKIE: Yeah, but like he's sayin', whadda we think of Bruce Crane?
SHORTY: Fucking shithead (*all laugh*).

Thus, good grades in school can lead to ostracism, whereas time spent in prison earns respect. To be bad is the main criterion for status in this subculture; its primacy cannot be overemphasized, and its importance is implied continually by the boys.

. . .

For the Hallway Hangers, being bad entails the consumption of alcohol and the use of drugs on a regular basis. The boys are intoxicated for a good portion of almost every weekend and drink heavily during the week. During the summer, the level of drinking reaches staggering proportions, often involving the consumption of two or more "beer balls" (the equivalent of two and half cases of beer pressurized into a plastic ball about two feet in diameter) a day for a group of eight or ten boys. Although none of the Hallway Hangers is drunk constantly, Frankie, Shorty, Slick, and Chris all consider themselves alcoholics.

FRANKIE: See, the way we are right now, technically we are alcoholics. Y'know, I can go days without drinking alcohol. It ain't like I need it, but right now I want it, y'know; it helps me get through. Y'know, get through problems, whatever; it helps me get through. Take away all the fucking problems down here, and there would be no problems with alcohol.

Shorty is honest about the debilitating effects of his dependence on alcohol.

(in a group discussion)

SHORTY: I think when you're an alcoholic like me, man, you ain't gonna be able to hold no fucking job. You say things you fucking forget.
FRANKIE: Yeah, yeah. I hear ya.
SHORTY: I mean, I don't remember trying to stab my own brother in the back; my other brother caught me. That's when I knew I was dead-up an alcoholic. Then I stabbed myself and three other people.
JM: How'd you get to be an alcoholic in the first place?
SHORTY: Being with these motherfuckers (*all laugh*). These got me going. Frankie always used to drink before me. I only used to drink about a beer a night, and I used

to get buzzed every night. It's like this now: six pack—Monday through Friday. Friday, it's a case, and when summer comes, it's . . .

ALL: Beer balls!

Most of these boys began drinking beer regularly at the age of thirteen or fourteen; their preferences now include whiskey and Peppermint Schnapps.

The Hallway Hangers also began smoking marijuana when they were twelve or thirteen years old, a tendency that has led many to use an assortment of heavier drugs as well. Most of them describe stages in their adolescence during which they used PCP, mescaline, valium, or THC (the chief intoxicant in marijuana). . . .

. . .

Having moderated what they now see as their youthful enthusiasm for different drugs, the Hallway Hangers generally limit themselves to marijuana and cocaine. All the Hallway Hangers smoke a great deal of marijuana; Chris, Jinks, and Stoney acknowledge their dependence on the drug. Marijuana joints circulate in doorway #13 almost as often as cans of beer, and all admit they get high before and during school.

. . .

Obviously, underage drinking and drug use are illegal, and the Hallway Hangers have made their share of trips to the police station and the courthouse. Stoney has three convictions, twice for possession of narcotics and once for passing stolen property. Boo-Boo has been arrested for "hot boxes" (stolen cars). Chris has assault with a deadly weapon in addition to some less serious convictions on his record. Shorty has been to court for larceny, assault with a deadly weapon, and other less substantial crimes. One of the older teenagers on the fringes of the Hallway Hangers was convicted of rape and sen-

tenced to eighteen months in the maximum security state prison after his sophomore year in high school.

These, of course, represent only the crimes at which the Hallway Hangers have been caught. Their criminal activity is actually much more widespread. Those trusted by the Hallway Hangers are occasionally approached with offers for good deals on bicycles, stereo equipment, or musical instruments, all of which have been stolen. Chris makes serious money dealing drugs. Other Hallway Hangers make small amounts of cash selling drugs to friends and acquaintances.

JINKS: We all know how to make a fast buck on the street. Buy the pot, roll up joints, sell 'em for two bucks a joint. Pay thirty for a bag; get twenty-five bones out of a bag—there's fifty bucks for thirty bucks.

Jimmy Sullivan, an experienced and perceptive teacher of the adjustment class in which Frankie, Shorty, and Steve are, or were at one time, enrolled, gives a good description of the Hallway Hangers' criminal careers.

JS: One thing about these kids: Crime pays, and they know it. . . . It's so easy to go over to the hallowed halls across the street there [a large university] and pick up a bike. I know three or four stores in the city that will pay thirty to forty dollars for a good bike, no questions asked. They'll turn it over for a hundred fifty or two hundred bucks. What do these kids need money for? What do they care about? Beer, sneakers, joints. They're not going to work when they can make easy money through virtually riskless criminal enterprises. Only suckers are gonna work for that. As long as their expectations stay low and they only need a hundred bucks a week—as Steve said, "All I want is my beer money"—they're all set. Up to when they're seventeen years old there's no risk. But when they turn about eighteen, the peer group doesn't accept that anymore. If they could go on stealing bikes for the rest of their lives, I think they would. But when you're seventeen or eighteen and someone says, "Hey man, where'd you get the cash?" it's unacceptable to say, "Oh, stealing bikes, man." You've got to be into cars, dealing drugs, or holding people up. That's when the risk and fear start coming into it. For many of them, the easiest route is to get a job. Of course, some of them don't, and they end up in jail.

Although this dynamic certainly plays a role in the Hallway Hangers' rationale, the legal system's distinction between a juvenile and an adult is more important in their determination of whether or not crime pays.

(in a group interview)

JM: Most of you are seventeen or over now?

SLICK: Only Chris is sixteen.

JM: Doesn't that make a big difference in terms of what you're doing to get money?

SHORTY: Hey, I'm doin' good. I don't deal no more, Jay. I got a good job coming at the weapons lab; most likely I'm gonna get my brother one there.

FRANKIE: Yeah, you slow down. Seventeen—you're an adult.

SLICK: Yeah, at seventeen you start slowing down.

SHORTY: You gotta start thinking.

(in a separate interview)

FRANKIE: Now that I think about it, I should've did more crime when I was a juvenile cuz when you're a juvenile you get arrested a good eight or nine times before they put you away. So I could've did a lot more crime, but I don't really mind. It was all right. But yeah, that's what most people do is once they go to

seventeen, they smarten up and say that's big-time prison. And I've had many good examples of what not to do. I know jail ain't no place for nobody, even though some of my brothers make a living out of it.

Like many urban slums, the teenage underworld of Clarendon Heights is characterized by predatory theft, and some of the Hallway Hangers specialize in "cuffing" drugs, stolen merchandise, and money off those who themselves are involved in illegal activity. Shorty and Frankie have sold hundreds of fake joints, robbed other drug pushers, and forced younger or less tough boys to give them a share of their illegal income. The consensus among the Hallway Hangers is that this type of thievery is morally more defensible than conventional theft. More importantly, there is less risk of detection, for the authorities are unlikely to become involved.

. . .

For those raised with a strong sense of law and order, these attitudes are difficult to fathom. The Hallway Hangers, for their part, however, cannot understand the contempt and disdain the upper classes display for their lifestyle and launch a counterattack of their own.

(in a group interview)

SLICK: All right, you get people making fucking over fifty thousand dollars, and they fucking ask us why do we hang there? What the fuck, man?

CHRIS: What else are we gonna do?

JINKS: They can go fuck themselves.

CHRIS: They want us to deal the drugs so they can buy them.

SLICK: See, they don't know what the deal is. See, they're just doing what we're doing, except they're doing it in a more respectable way. They're ripping off each other up there. That's all they're doing. They're all ripping each other off up there. But they're doing it in a fucking legal way.

FRANKIE: Yeah, check this out.

SHORTY: We ain't doin' it behind anybody's back.

FRANKIE: All them fucking businessmen, man. All them stockbrokers and shit in New York. All them motherfuckers are out to rip people off. There's more fucking scamming going on up there. They're like legally ripping everyone off.

SLICK: We're just doing it illegally.

This is an insightful, if incomplete, critique of the social order, but not one about which the Hallway Hangers get particularly upset. Rather, they accept it as a simple fact of life with an acquiescent attitude that is typical of their outlook.

An important characteristic of the subculture of the Hallway Hangers is group solidarity. Membership in the Hallway Hangers involves a serious commitment to the group: a willingness to put out for others and to look out for the rest of the group's well-being as well as one's own. This loyalty is the glue that holds the group together, and honoring it is essential. The requirements and limits of this commitment to the group are seldom expressed, but are such that Slick would not leave Shorty "hanging with the cops," even though to stay with Shorty resulted in his own arrest.

SHORTY: See, that's how Slick was that day we were ripping off the sneakers [from a nearby factory]. He figured that if he left me that would be rude, y'know? If he just let me get busted by myself and he knew I had a lot of shit on my head, that's what I call a brother. He could've. I could've pushed him right through that fence, and he coulda been *gone*. But no,

he waited for me, and we both got arrested. I was stuck. My belly couldn't get through the fucking hole in the fence.

This cohesion between members of the Hallway Hangers is a striking characteristic of their subculture and one to which they constantly draw attention. Not only are they proud of their adoption of communitarian values, but they also see their "brotherhood" as inconsistent with conventional middle- and upper-class attitudes.

(in a group discussion)

SLICK: What it is, it's a brotherhood down here. We're all fucking brothers. There's a lot of backstabbing going on down here, down in the streets. But we're always there for each other. No shit. There's not a guy in here that wouldn't put out for one of the rest of us. If he needs something and I got it, I'll give it to him. Period. That's the way it works. It's a brotherhood. We're not like them up there—the rich little boys from the suburbs or wherever. There's a line there. On this side of the line we don't fuck with each other; we're tight.

FRANKIE: We'd chump them off [rob] on the other side, though.

SLICK: Fucking right. If he's got four hundred bucks in his pocket, there's more where that came from. Fuck him. But they also chump each other off; only they do it legally. How do you think they got rich—by fucking people over. We don't do that to each other. We're too fucking tight. We're a group. We don't think like them; we think for all of us.

.   .   .

These comments bear ample testimony to the solidarity that characterizes the subculture of the Hallway Hangers. This solidarity is not an ideal to which they only pay lip service; shared money, shared drugs, and shared risks in criminal activity are all facts of life in doorway #13.

At the same time that these boys affirm the lifestyle and values of people in their neighborhood, they assert with peculiar constancy their deeply felt desire to move with their families out of Clarendon Heights. Many of them want to make enough money to get their families out of the projects forever.

(all in separate discussions, unsolicited by me)

SLICK: Most of the kids down here, most of 'em wanna make money so they can help their families and help themselves to get out of this place. . . . My main concern is to get my family out of the projects.

CHRIS: I just wanna get my mother out of the projects, that's all.

SHORTY: All's I'm doing, I'm gonna get enough money, save enough money to get my mother the fuck out of here.

These statements are evidence of the stigma the Hallway Hangers, as public housing tenants, feel as a matter of course. Their pride in their lifestyle is pierced by the dominant culture's negative judgments. One implication of the culture's achievement ideology is that those of low socioeconomic stature are personally deficient. This negative evaluation and the inability of the Hallway Hangers to shield themselves completely from it combine to produce the deep ambivalence the boys feel toward themselves and their community.

. . .

Growing up in Clarendon Heights is indeed tough, and the frustrations of project life find release through the racist attitudes held by the boys. Racism among members of the Hallway Hangers runs very deep. Frankie and Shorty are violent in their prejudice against black people, while Slick, Steve,

and Stoney are racist in a less strident manner. Only Jinks has a measure of empathy and respect for blacks.

According to the Hallway Hangers, their antipathy toward blacks stems from an incident in the early 1970s. At that time, a full-scale riot erupted in Clarendon Heights between the project's mostly white residents and black youths from the predominantly black Emerson Towers housing project a half mile away. The conflict lasted several days and involved the National Guard and riot police. Frankie describes how this event crystallized his own racist attitudes.

JM: So why is it, why is there like this tension between the whites and the blacks?

FRANKIE: Well, when I grew up here, when I was fucking second, third grade, there was racial riots right in front of my window every night. My brothers, I have seven brothers, were all out there, y'know, stabbin' niggers, beating niggers up. I was brought up thinking fucking niggers suck. Went over to Hoover School, no fuckin' black people there at all. Y'know, third grade, we had one black kid. His name was Sonny. Y'know, everyone fucked him up. So it was this through the racial riots. I was brought up to hate niggers.

Although the riots contributed to the racism of the Hallway Hangers, surprisingly enough, they also account for the acceptance of Boo-Boo and Chris into the group.

(in an interview with Jinks and Chris)

JM: Now Chris, you're an interesting case cuz, except when Boo-Boo's around, you're the only black guy out there. How'd that come about?

CHRIS: It goes back to the days of the riots.

JINKS: Back in the days of the riots, when the whites used to fight the blacks at the Heights . . .

CHRIS: Nobody fucked with my family.

JINKS: Chris's family was always like neutral. They'd help out anybody. And besides, as he's grown older, I've related to him more because my brother married a black lady. And I got nieces and nephews that are like him: mulatto. I've just related to him more. I see things from his point of view more. Cuz I know how he feels when people start capping on him: "Hey Breed."

. . .

Other factors have contributed to Chris's and Boo-Boo's affiliation with the Hallway Hangers. Boo-Boo's family was one of the first black households to be moved by the city's Housing Authority into the Heights. When he was growing up, he naturally made friends with white youngsters. His younger brother Derek went to a private grammar school; most other black youths who now live in Clarendon Heights had yet to move in. Boo-Boo's expressed reason for being a Hallway Hanger is simple: "I grew up with them, since I was real small."

The situation was much the same for Chris; in addition, his acceptance into the Hallway Hangers has been facilitated because he is half white.

(in a group interview)

FRANKIE: It ain't like he's living with his black daddy; he's living with his white mommy.

SHORTY: His white brothers.

(in a separate discussion)

JINKS: My brothers always liked his family though . . .

CHRIS: Cuz my brothers were white, y'know.

JINKS: His brothers were mulatto, but they looked like a white person. . . . It just looked like he had a nice tan all year

round. And he was one of my brother's best friends. Y'know, it's just families hanging around.

Although both Chris and Boo-Boo are full members of the Hallway Hangers, their position often seems tenuous because of their race. Both take a lot of ribbing for their skin color. Chris routinely is referred to as nigs, nigger, breed, half-breed, or oreo; Boo-Boo gets less direct abuse but is the butt of racist jokes and occasional taunts. Both tend to deal with it in the same way: They "play it off," make a joke of it, or ignore it.

(in an individual discussion)

JM: So you naturally hung with Frankie and them. Are there any problems with you being black?

BOO-BOO: No. They say things but they're just fooling around. I take it as a joke. They're just fooling around. It doesn't bother me at all. If they hit me or something, that's a different story.

Chris occasionally will play along with the other Hallway Hangers by agreeing with their racist statements and denigrating other blacks.

. . .

Chris will go so far as to shout racial epithets at fellow blacks and to show enthusiasm for fighting with the Hallway Hangers against other black youths.

Much of this attitude, however, is expedient posturing that enables Chris to maintain his sometimes tenuous status in the group. His real feelings are quite different.

CHRIS: I've lived here for fourteen years. I've always hung with these guys. I dunno, maybe it's cuz I never knew many black people back then. These guys are all right though. They fuck with me some, but not like with some kids. I mean, after fourteen fucking years you get used to them calling you nigger every ten minutes. It doesn't do no good to get upset. I just let it slide. Fuck it. I've gotten used to it. I'm glad you're not prejudiced though. The only time they get real bad is when they've been drinking; then I gotta watch myself. I know how these guys think. That's something too—understanding how they think. I've been here fourteen fucking years, and I know how these motherfuckers think. Like, I can tell when they're gonna fuck with me. When they're trashed, they'll be looking at me a certain way and shit. Then another one will do it. I get the fuck out of there because I know they're gonna fuck with me. Yeah, when they're drunk, they'll get like that. Fucking assholes. But when they haven't been pounding the beers, they're the most dynamite people around. Really.

The rest of the Hallway Hangers are quick to deny any animosity toward Chris.

(in a group interview)

JM: Chris, it can't be easy coming from down here and being half black and half white.
SHORTY: The blacks bother him cuz he hangs with whites—us.
JM: Yeah, and you fuck with him cuz he's black.
FRANKIE: No, see, cuz we just razz him because he's black.
SHORTY: We done that all his life and he knows it.
CHRIS: It don't bother me.

Nevertheless, outright hostility toward Chris does come to the surface at times, especially when people are under the influence of alcohol or drugs. It seems that whenever Chris threatens the status of others in the group

with his street hockey ability, his knack for making a fast buck selling drugs, or his success with girls, racial antagonism comes to the fore. One particular incident is illustrative of this dynamic. Frankie and I were talking in the doorway when we noticed two white girls giving Chris a few lines of cocaine on the landing above us. As they came down the stairs on their way out, Frankie demanded in a very abrasive tone, "What are you getting that fuckin' *nigger* high for? You don't fucking do that." As the door slammed behind them, Frankie muttered, "They want to suck his black cock, that's why. Fuckin' cunts."

Although the Hallway Hangers attribute their racist attitudes to the riots that occurred in Clarendon Heights during their childhoods, such an explanation cannot account for the racial antagonism that gave rise to the riots in the first place. Racism in Clarendon Heights is a complex phenomenon that does not lend itself to easy interpretation or explanation. Nevertheless, in the attitudes and comments of the Hallway Hangers, it is possible to discern evidence in support of the proposition that racism in lower-class communities stems from competition for scarce economic resources. Shorty, for example, bitterly attributes his brother's unemployment to affirmative action policies: "He got laid off because they hired all Puerto Rican, blacks, and Portegis (Portuguese). It's cuz of the fuckin' spics and niggers." In a separate discussion of the harshness of unemployment, Smitty, an older youth on the fringes of the Hallway Hangers, put forth a similar view.

SMITTY: All the fuckin' niggers are getting the jobs. Two of them motherfuckers got hired yesterday [at a construction site]; I didn't get shit. They probably don't even know how to hold a fuckin' shovel either.
FRANKIE: Fuckin' right. That's why we're hanging here now with empty pockets.

The perceived economic threat blacks pose to the Hallway Hangers contributes to their racism. The racial prejudice of the Hallway Hangers, a subject of academic interest in its own right, also has important ramifications for social reproduction. . . . we see how it not only harms blacks but is ultimately self-estructive as well.

Although the Hallway Hangers can be hostile to Boo-Boo and Chris, their real racial venom is directed against the Brothers, the black peer group at Clarendon Heights. Interestingly, when considering each member of the Brothers individually, the Hallway Hangers admit respect and esteem for a number of them. Considered as a group, however, there is little feeling aside from bitter racial enmity. As with Chris, the enmity is at its sharpest when the Brothers are perceived as threatening in some way. The following interview segment, quoted at length, captures the essence of the Hallway Hangers' attitude toward the Brothers.

. . .

SHORTY: I've lived here all my fucking life, and no new nigger is gonna move in and fucking start [a fight] with me.

FRANKIE: And I'll tell ya, I'll stick any of them; I'll beat any of them. Fuck them fucking niggers.

SHORTY: Jay, listen to this. They move in here, right?

JM: But how do they move in here, huh?

SHORTY: They just move in here, y'know?

JM: But wait. Into the projects? It's not like you pick which one you wanna move into.

SHORTY: Bullshit!

JM: I think they said, "There's too many white people in here and people been complaining." So they started moving black people in here.

FRANKIE: (*still yelling*) Yeah, that's what happened last time. They moved too many

fucking niggers in, and then in '71 and '72 we had the fucking riots.

SHORTY: The last time they did that was ten years ago. Watch!

JM: All's I'm sayin' is that it's not their fault that they moved in. It's the Housing Authority that sends 'em in.

SHORTY: Will you fucking listen, Jay?

JM: Yeah, but I mean, if you were black, would you wanna live here? I fucking wouldn't.

FRANKIE: (*very angrily*) They come in here with a fucking *attitude,* man. They ain't gettin' no [inaudible] attitude. Fucking niggers are getting *hurt* this summer. I'm telling you, man.

. . .

The resentment the Hallway Hangers feel toward blacks and the destructive consequences that flow from this hatred could not be more plainly exposed. By pointing to the economic and social factors that feed this racism, I do not mean to absolve the Hallway Hangers of responsibility for their racist attitudes and beliefs, much less for the violence to which these give rise. Racism is a sickness that rots American society, but those who see it simply as a matter of individual pathology overlook the social conditions that contribute to its outbreak and spread. We can blame the Hallway Hangers, but we also must blame the economic and social conditions of lower-class life under competitive capitalism.

The Brothers: Conspicuous by Their Conventionality

In contrast to the Hallway Hangers, the Brothers accommodate themselves to accepted standards of behavior and strive to fulfill socially approved roles. It is the white peer group from Clarendon Heights that is at odds with mainstream American culture. Nonconformity fascinates the sociologist, and if in this [chapter] undue attention is given to the distinctive cultural novelty of the Hallway Hangers, it should be borne in mind that the Brothers also pose an interesting and in many ways exceptional case. However, because my primary interest is the role that aspirations play in social reproduction, and because the Hallway Hangers undergo the process of social reproduction in a unique fashion, my emphasis in both the presentation of ethnographic material and in its analysis inevitably falls on the Hallway Hangers.

The most obvious difference between the two peer groups is in racial composition: The Brothers have only one white member. When one considers that this peer group emerges from the same social setting as do the Hallway Hangers, other striking differences become apparent. Composed of a nucleus of seven teenagers and expanding to twelve at times, this peer group is not a distinctive subculture with its own set of values defined in opposition to the dominant culture. The Brothers attend high school on a regular basis. None of them smokes cigarettes, drinks regularly, or uses drugs. None has been arrested.

· · ·

The Brothers, in contrast to the Hallway Hangers, are not a distinctive subculture with its own set of shared values. The Brothers accept the dominant culture's definitions of success and judge themselves by these criteria. A night in the city jail would permanently tarnish a Brother's reputation rather than build it up. In the eyes of the Brothers, John Grace, the bartender who was involved in the shootout in Clarendon Heights, only would be worthy of disdain, and perhaps pity, rather than the respect Frankie accords him. While the Hallway Hangers have little concern for the judgments of the dominant culture, the Brothers become uncomfortable and embarrassed when recounting disciplinary problems they have had at home or in

school. Such a "confession" for a member of the Hallway Hangers, on the other hand, might be accompanied by laughter and a sense of triumph.

Just as the Brothers accept the values of the dominant culture, their behavior generally conforms to societal expectations. Whereas the Hallway Hangers are conspicuous in their consumption of cigarettes and beer, the Brothers reject both. Although many of the Brothers drink beer in moderation every once in a while at a party or on a similar occasion, their consumption of alcohol is very limited. Likewise, although most of the Brothers have tried marijuana, they rarely smoke it, and they never use other drugs.

The Brothers are uncomfortable with simply "hanging"; they cannot tolerate such inactivity. They often can be found playing basketball in the park or the gym. If a pick-up game of basketball cannot be mustered in the immediate neighborhood, they often will walk a half mile to the Salvation Army gym or another housing project. Energetic and spirited, the Brothers dislike the idleness of the Hallway Hangers.

DEREK: I would never hang with them. I'm not interested in drinking, getting high, or making trouble. That's about all they do. . . . I don't like to just sit around.

Although the Brothers do not adopt these practices that symbolize rejection of authority or basic societal values, their peer group does have its own distinctive attributes. The Brothers carry themselves in ways familiar to most urban black Americans, although somewhat scaled down. Their style of dress, mode of speech, and form of greeting clearly set them apart from other residents of Clarendon Heights. However, the caps, neck chains, and open shirts so prevalent among teenagers in the predominantly black sections of the city are lacking among the Brothers, whose residency in a white neighborhood has important implications for much more than their dress.

Athletics is one activity into which the Brothers channel their energies. Many excel in organized youth, church, and school basketball leagues as well as in regular pick-up games. Mike, Super, and Mokey also play on the school football team. Only Juan and Derek are not good athletes, and even they maintain an interest in sports, often rounding out the teams for a pick-up game of basketball.

Girls also claim much of the Brothers' time. A frequent topic of conversation, their interest in girls seems much more widespread than is the case for the Hallway Hangers. While the Hangers tend to go out with girls on a casual basis (typically for a weekend), the Brothers often have steady girlfriends, with whom they are constantly speaking on the phone, to whose house they are forever headed, and about whom they always are boasting. Whereas the Hallway Hangers focus on their beer and drugs, the Brothers have their basketball and girlfriends.

Since Juan bought an old worn-out Vega for two hundred dollars and fixed it up complete with paint job and functioning engine, cruising the streets also has become a favorite pastime for the Brothers. It gives them access to the "Port" and the "Coast," the black sections of the city. Considering the tense racial atmosphere of the Clarendon Heights community, it is no wonder that the Brothers do not spend as much time in the vicinity of the Heights as the Hallway Hangers do and instead prefer the black neighborhoods.

In addition to being the objects of many of the Hallway Hangers' racist slurs and insults, the Brothers suffer from even more substantive racial abuse. Super tells how the windows of his family's car have been broken year after year and how one morning last spring he awoke to find "KKK" drawn in spray paint in the side of the car. Juan

recounts with anger accompanied by matter-of-fact acceptance how his mother was taunted by some members of the Hallway Hangers, which led his father into a confrontation with them. His father was lucky to escape unharmed from the ensuing argument. Juan has a measure of understanding for the Hallway Hangers: "When they call me a nigger, I usually don't let it bother me none. They drunk or high, y'know. They don't know what they're doing." In his freshman year of high school, however, Juan was beaten up by Shorty for no apparent reason; he still bears the scar on his lip from the fight, and the memory of it burns in his mind, fueling the resentment he feels toward the Hallway Hangers.

Although the Brothers are not submissive in the face of racial animosity from the Hallway Hangers, they are outnumbered and outmatched, and they usually find it expedient to walk away before a confrontation explodes into a street fight. They are accustomed to the violent racial prejudice of the Hallway Hangers. In fact, Craig, instead of being upset that a simple basketball game threatened to erupt into a racial brawl, merely commented, "That was good of Shorty to come over and tell us we better leave before his friends start all sorts of trouble." Although the Brothers are hesitant to answer openly the insults of the Hallway Hangers, they do vent their contempt for the Hallway Hangers in private discussions.

(all in separate interviews)

JUAN: I don't like their attitude, their gig, what they do. . . . They'll be there, hanging in front of the Heights, fighting and arguing and stuff like that. . . . It wasn't until I moved here that I heard the word "nigger." I had heard about people in the projects; I knew they'd be a pain in the ass sometimes. . . . I swear, if I ever see one of them touching my mother or doing something to my car, I don't care, I'll kill them. Cuz I don't like none of them. I'm afraid I'm gonna hurt one of them real bad. Every time I hear them call me nigger, I just don't say anything, but I can't take the pressure of people getting on my case every time, y'know?

CRAIG: I don't know why they just hang out there being crazy and getting drunk and bothering people. Maybe cuz they need attention or something. They got nuttin' better to do so they might as well cause trouble so people will think they're bad and stuff. They're just lazy. They wanna take the easy way out—that is, hang around outside all day.

JAMES: They're not gonna get anywhere except for standing at the same corner going (*imitating someone who is very benumbed*), "Hey man, got some pot, man? Hey Frank, let's get high."

DEREK: We just have different attitudes. We like to stay away from the projects as much as possible, or they'll give us trouble. That's about all they do: make trouble.

SUPER: They smoke reefer; they drink. They ain't friendly like people, y'know what I'm sayin'? They go around the street laughing at people, ragging them out, y'know what I mean? They just disrespect people.

MIKE: They're just a bunch of fuck-ups.

Such perceptions are often voiced by the Brothers. The situation between the two peer groups, however, is not one of constant strife. Rather, there is a constant underlying tension that surfaces occasionally—often during basketball games or when the Hallway Hangers have been drinking excessively—but that threatens to erupt into considerable violence.

Aside from racial factors, the character of the two peer groups differs markedly in other ways. The Brothers have no pecking order based on fighting ability. Although Craig is generally respected most, there is no hierarchy in the group, hidden or otherwise; the Brothers do not playfully abuse each other, physically or verbally. Loose and shifting cliques develop among the members and sometimes encompass outsiders. Friendships wax and wane according to the season and the extracurricular activities and responsibilities of the boys. During the winter, for example, Craig is so tied up with the basketball team that he effectively drops out of the group, and his best friend, Super, becomes closer to Derek and Mokey. During the school day, the Brothers often see little of each other and, once out, invariably break up into smaller friendship groups, coming all together only once in awhile. In short, the Brothers are no more than a peer group, whereas the Hallway Hangers are a much more cohesive unit with its own subculture.

The Hallway Hangers, who reject the values of the dominant culture and subscribe to their own distinctive cultural norms, have a sense of solidarity that is noticeably absent form the Brothers' peer group. Internal cohesion and the adoption of communitarian values, in which the Hallway Hangers take pride, are missing among the Brothers. Although all the Brothers would support each other in a fight, the ties that bind them are not as strong and are not as strongly affirmed as those that bind the Hallway Hangers.

The Brothers do not compare themselves to members of the upper classes, nor do they feel as keenly the stigma or shame associated with life in public housing. . . .

Daily life for the Brothers is far less circumscribed than it is for the Hallway Hangers. Active, enthusiastic, and still in school, the Brothers are not preoccupied with mere survival on the street. Their world extends into the classroom and onto the basketball court, and it extends into the home a great deal more than does the world of the Hallway Hangers. . . .

26

SOCIAL CLASS DIFFERENCES IN FAMILY–SCHOOL RELATIONSHIPS: THE IMPORTANCE OF CULTURAL CAPITAL

Annette Lareau

The influence of family background on children's educational experiences has a curious place within the field of sociology of education. On the one hand, the issue has dominated the field. Wielding increasingly sophisticated methodological tools, social scientists have worked to document, elaborate, and replicate the influence of family background on educational life chances (Jencks et al. 1972; Marjoribanks 1979). On the other hand, until recently, research on this issue focused primarily on educational *outcomes;* very little attention was given to the *processes* through which these educational patterns are created and reproduced.

Over the past fifteen years, important strides have been made in our understanding of social processes inside the school. Ethnographic research has shown that classroom learning is reflexive and interactive and that language in the classroom draws unevenly from the sociolinguistic experiences of children at home (Bernstein 1975, 1982; Cook-Gumperez 1973; Heath 1982, 1983; Labov 1972; Diaz, Moll, and Mehan 1986; Mehan and Griffin 1980). Studies of the curriculum, the hidden curriculum, the social organization of the classroom, and the authority relationships between teachers and students

have also suggested ways in which school processes contribute to social reproduction (Aggleton and Whitty 1985; Anyon 1981; Apple 1979; Erickson and Mohatt 1982; Gearing and Epstein 1982; Gaskell 1985; Taylor 1984; Valli 1985; Wilcox 1977, 1982).

Surprisingly, relatively little of this research has focused on parental involvement in schooling. Yet, quantitative studies suggest that parental behavior can be a crucial determinant of educational performance (Epstein 1984; Marjoribanks 1979). In addition, increasing parental participation in education has become a priority for educators, who believe it promotes educational achievement (Berger 1983; Seeley 1984; National Education Association 1985; Robinson 1985; Trelease 1982; Leichter 1979).

Those studies that have examined parental involvement in education generally take one of three major conceptual approaches to understanding variations in levels of parental participation. Some researchers subscribe to the culture-of-poverty thesis, which states that lower-class culture has distinct values and forms of social organization. Although their interpretations vary, most of these researchers suggest that lower-class and working-class families do not value education as highly as middle-class families (Deutsch 1967). Other analysts trace unequal levels of parental involvement in schooling back to the educational institutions themselves. Some accuse schools of institutional discrimination, claiming that they make middle-class families feel more welcome than working-class and lower-class families (Lightfoot 1978; Ogbu 1974). In an Australian study of home-school relationships, for example, Connell et al. (1982) argue that working-class parents are "frozen out" of schools. Others maintain that institutional differentiation, particularly the role of teacher leadership, is a critical determinant of parental involvement in schooling (Epstein and Becker 1982; Becker and Epstein 1982).

A third perspective for understanding varying levels of parental involvement in schooling draws on the work of Bourdieu and the concept of cultural capital. Bourdieu (1977a, 1977b; Bourdieu and Passeron 1977) argues that schools draw unevenly on the social and cultural resources of members of the society. For example, schools utilize particular linguistic structures, authority patterns, and types of curricula; children from higher social locations enter schools already familiar with these social arrangements. Bourdieu maintains that the cultural experiences in the home facilitate children's adjustment to school and academic achievement, thereby transforming cultural resources into what he calls cultural capital (Bourdieu 1977a, 1977b).

This perspective points to the structure of schooling and to family life and the dispositions of individuals (what Bourdieu calls habitus [1977b, 1981]) to understand different levels of parental participation in schooling. The standards of schools are not neutral; their requests for parental involvement may be laden with the social and cultural experiences of intellectual and economic elites. Bourdieu does not examine the question of parental participation in schooling, but his analysis points to the importance of class and class cultures in facilitating or impeding children's (or parents') negotiation of the process of schooling. . . .

In this [chapter] I argue that class-related cultural factors shape parents' compliance with teachers' requests for parental partici-

pation in schooling. I pose two major questions. First, what do schools ask of parents in the educational experience of young children? Are there important variations in teachers' expectations of parental involvement in elementary schooling? Second, how do parents respond to schools' requests? In particular, how does social class influence the process through which parents participate in their children's schooling? The analysis and conclusions are based on an intensive study of home-school relationships of children in the first and second grades of a white working-class school and an upper-middle-class school.

. . .

Research Methodology

The research presented here involved participant-observation of two first-grade classrooms located in two different communities. Also, in-depth interviews of parents, teachers, and principals were conducted while the children were in first and second grade. Following other studies of social class differences in family life (Rubin 1976; Kohn 1977), I chose a white working-class community and a professional middle-class community. I sought a working-class community in which a majority of the parents were high school graduates or dropouts, employed in skilled or semiskilled occupations, paid an hourly wage, and periodically unemployed. For the professional middle-class school, I sought a community in which a majority of the parents were college graduates and professionals who had strong career opportunities and who were less vulnerable to changes in the economy. The two communities described here met these criteria.

Colton School (fictitious name) is located in a working-class community. Most of the parents of Colton students are employed in semiskilled or unskilled occupations (see Table 26.1). School personnel report that most of the parents have a high school education; many are high school dropouts. The school has about 450 students in kindergarten, first grade, and second grade. Slightly over one half of the children are white, one third are Hispanic, and the remainder are black or Asian, especially recent Vietnamese immigrants. About one half of the children qualify for free lunches under federal guidelines.

Prescott School (fictitious name) is in an upper-middle-class suburban community about 30 minutes from Colton. Most of the parents of Prescott students are professionals (Table 26.1). Both parents in the family are likely to be college graduates, and many of the children's fathers have advanced degrees. The school enrolls about 300 students from kindergarten to fifth grade. Virtually all the students are white, and the school does not offer a lunch program, although the Parents' Club sponsors a Hot Dog Day once a month.

For a six-month period, January to June 1982, I visited one first-grade classroom at each school. My visits averaged once or twice a week per school and lasted around two hours. During this time, I observed the classroom and acted as a volunteer in the class,

passing out paper and helping the children with math and spelling problems.

At the end of the school year, I selected six children in each class for further study. The children were selected on the basis of reading-group membership; a boy and a girl were selected from the high, medium, and low reading groups. To prevent the confounding effects of race, I chose only white children. I interviewed one single mother in each school; the remaining households had two parents. In both of the schools, three of the mothers worked full time or part time, and three were at home full time. All of the Colton mothers, however, had worked in recent years, when their children were younger. The Prescott mothers had worked prior to the birth of their children but had not been in the labor force since that time.

When the children finished first grade, I interviewed their mothers individually. When they finished second grade, I interviewed their mothers for a second time, and in separate sessions, I interviewed most of their fathers. I also interviewed the first- and second-grade teachers, the school principals, and a resource specialist at one of the schools. All the interviews were semistructured and lasted about two hours. The interviews were tape recorded, and all participants were promised confidentiality.

TABLE 26.1   The Percentage of Parents in Each Occupational Category, by School

Occupation	Colton	Prescott
Professionals, executives, managers	1	60
Semiprofessionals, sales, clerical workers, and technicians	11	30
Skilled and semiskilled workers	51	9
Unskilled workers (and welfare recipients)	23	1
Unknown	20	—

Note: The figures for Prescott school are based on the principal's estimation of the school population.
Source: California Department of Education 1983.

Teachers' Requests for Parental Involvement

The research examined the formal requests from the teachers and school administrators asking parents to participate in schooling, particularly surrounding the issue of achievement. It also studied the quality of interaction between teachers and parents on the school site. Although there were some variations among the teachers in their utilization of parents in the classrooms, all promoted parental involvement and all be-

lieved there was a strong relationship between parental involvement (particularly
reading to children) and academic performance. At both schools, the definition of
the ideal family–school relationship was the
same: a partnership in which family life and
school life are integrated.

In the course of the school year, teachers
in both schools actively promoted parental
involvement in schooling in several ways.
For example, newsletters were used to notify
families of school events and to invite them to
attend. Teachers also reminded children verbally about school events to which parents
had been invited and encouraged the children to bring their parents to classroom and
schoolwide events.

In their interactions with parents, educators urged parents to read to their children. The principal at Prescott school, for example, told the parents at Back to School
Night that they should consider reading the
child's homework. In every class at Colton
school, there was a Read at Home Program,
in which the teacher kept track of the number
of hours a child read to an adult at home or
was read to by a sibling or adult. A chart
posted in the classroom marked hours of
reading in 15-minute intervals. A child could
choose a free book after eight hours of reading at home. This emphasis on reading also
surfaced in the routine interactions between
parents and teachers and between teachers
and children. In the classroom, the teachers
suggested that children check out library
books, read to their parents, or have their parents read to them at home. At parent–teacher
conferences, teachers suggested that parents
read to their child at home. In one 20-minute
parent–teacher conference, for example, the
teacher mentioned five times the importance
of reading to the child at home.

Other requests of parents were made as
well. Teachers encouraged parents to communicate any concerns they had about their
child. In their meetings with parents, teach-

ers also expressed a desire for parents to review and reinforce the material learned in
class (e.g., to help their children learn their
spelling words). Generally, teachers at both
schools believed that the relationship between parental involvement and academic
performance was important, and they used a
variety of approaches to encourage parents
to participate in education.

Teachers and administrators spoke of
being "partners" with parents, and they
stressed the need to maintain good communication, but it was clear that they desired
parents to defer to their professional expertise. For example, a first-grade teacher at
Prescott did not believe in assigning homework to the children and did not appreciate parents communicating their displeasure
with the policy by complaining repeatedly to
the principal. Nor did principals welcome
parents' opinions that a teacher was a bad
teacher and should be fired. Teachers wanted
parents to support them, or as they put it, to
"back them up."

Although generally persuaded that parental involvement was positive for educational growth, some teachers, particularly in
the upper-middle-class school, were ambivalent about some types of parental involvement in schooling. The Prescott teachers were
very concerned that some parents placed too
much pressure on their children. Parental involvement could become counterproductive
when it increased the child's anxiety level and
produced negative learning experiences. As
one Prescott teacher put it,

> It depends on the parent. Sometimes it
> can be helpful, sometimes it creates too
> much pressure. Sometimes they learn
> things wrong. It is better for them to
> leave the basics alone . . . and take them
> to museums, do science, and other en-
> richment activities.

As Becker and Epstein (1982) have found,
there was some variation among the teachers

in the degree to which they took leadership roles in promoting parental involvement in schooling, particularly in the area of classroom volunteers. Although all the teachers in the study requested parents to volunteer and had parents in the classroom, there were other teachers in the school who used parents more extensively. Teachers also varied in how they judged parents. While the extreme cases were clear, the teachers sometimes disagreed about how supportive parents were or about how much pressure they were putting on their children. For example, the first-grade teacher at Prescott thought one boy's father placed too much pressure on him, but the second-grade teacher judged the family to be supportive and helpful. Thus, there were variations in teachers' styles as well as in the way they implemented the model of home–school partnerships.

This study does not, however, support the thesis that the different levels of parental involvement can be traced to institutional differentiation or institutional discrimination, i.e., to teachers' pursuit of different kinds of relationships with working-class and middle-class families (Connell et al. 1982; Epstein and Becker 1982). All of the first- and second-grade teachers in the study made similar requests to parents. In both schools, teachers made clear and repeated efforts to promote parental involvement in the educational process.

Educational Consequences of Family–School Relationships

Parents who agreed with the administrators' and teachers' definition of partnership appeared to offer an educational advantage to their children; parents who turned over the responsibility of education to the professional could negatively affect their child's schooling.

Teachers' methods of presenting, teaching, and assessing subject matter were based on a structure that presumed parents would help children at home. At Colton, for example, spelling words were given out on Monday and students were repeatedly encouraged to practice the words at home with their parents before the test on Friday. Teachers noticed which children had practiced at home and which children had not and believed it influenced their performance.

This help at home was particularly important for low achievers. At Prescott, teachers encouraged parents of low achievers to work with them at home. In one case, a girl missed her spelling lessons because she had to meet with the reading resource teacher. Rather than fall behind in spelling, she and her mother did her spelling at home through most of the year. Colton teachers also tried to involve parents in the education of low achievers. One Colton teacher arranged a special conference at a student's home and requested that the parents urge the student to practice reading at home. The teacher complained that the girl didn't "get that much help at home." The teacher believed that if the parents had taken an active role in schooling, the child would have been promoted rather than retained.

In other instances, the initiative to help children at home came from parents. For example, at Prescott, one mother noticed while volunteering in the classroom that her son was somewhat behind in his spelling. At her request, she and her son worked on his spelling every day after school for about a month, until he had advanced to the lesson that most of the class was on. Prior to the mother's actions, the boy was in the bottom third of the class in spelling. He was not, however, failing spelling, and it was unlikely that the teacher would have requested the parent to take an active role. After the mother and son worked at home, he was in the top third of the class in his spelling work. The teacher was very impressed by these efforts and believed that the mother's active involvement in schooling had a positive effect on her son's performance:

> She is very supportive, very committed. If she didn't work in the class [volunteering] her boys wouldn't do too well. They are not brilliant at all. But they are going to do well. She is just going to see that they are going to get a good foundation. A child like that would flounder if you let him.

Not all parental involvement in schooling was so positive, however. There is a dark side to the partnership, which is not usually addressed in the literature aimed at increasing parental participation in education (Epstein and Becker 1982; Seeley 1984). Particularly in the upper-middle-class school, teachers complained of the pressure parents placed on teachers and children for academic performance. One mother reported that her son had been stealing small objects early in first grade, a pattern the pediatrician and the mother attributed to the boy's "frustration level" in schooling. A girl in the lowest reading group began developing stomach aches during the reading period in first grade. Teachers at Prescott mentioned numerous cases in which parental involvement was unhelpful. In these cases, parents had usually challenged the professional expertise of the teachers.

Generally, however, the teachers believed that the relationship between parental participation and school performance was positive. These results provide indications that teachers take *parental performance* in schooling very seriously. Teachers recall which parents participate and which parents fail to participate in schooling. They believe that their requests of parents are reasonable and that all parents, regardless of social

position, can help their children in first and second grade.

Parents' Involvement in Schooling

Although teachers at both schools expressed a desire for parental participation in schooling, the amount of contact varied significantly between the sites. The response of parents to teachers' requests was much higher at the upper-middle-class school than at the working-class school.

Attendance at School Events

As Table 26.2 shows, the level of attendance at formal school events was significantly higher at Prescott than at Colton. Virtually all Prescott parents attended the parent–teacher conferences in the fall and spring, but only 60 percent of Colton parents attended. Attendance at Open House was almost three times higher at Prescott than at Colton.

The difference between the two schools was apparent not only in the quantity of interaction but in the quality of interaction. Although teachers at both schools asked parents to communicate any concerns they had about their children, Colton parents rarely initiated contact with teachers. When Colton parents did contact the school, they frequently raised nonacademic issues, such as lunchboxes, bus schedules, and playground activities. One of the biggest complaints, for

TABLE 26.2 Percentage of Parents Participating in School Activities, by School, First Grade Only, 1981–1982

Activity	Colton (n = 34)	Prescott (n = 28)
Parent–teacher conferences	60	100
Open house	35	96
Volunteering in classroom	3	43

example, was that children had only 15 minutes to eat lunch and that slower eaters were often unable to finish.

At Colton, the interactions between parents and teachers were stiff and awkward. The parents often showed signs of discomfort: nervous shifting, blushing, stuttering, sweating, and generally looking ill at ease. During the Open House, parents wandered around the room looking at the children's pictures. Many of the parents did not speak with the teacher during their visit. When they did, the interaction tended to be short, rather formal, and serious. The teacher asked the parents if they had seen all of their children's work, and she checked to see that all of the children had shown their desk and folder of papers to their parents. The classrooms at Colton often contained only about 10 adults at a time, and the rooms were noticeably quiet.

At Prescott, the interactions between parents and teachers were more frequent, more centered around academic matters, and much less formal. Parents often wrote notes to the teacher, telephoned the teacher at school, or dropped by during the day to discuss a problem. These interactions often centered around the child's academic progress; many Prescott parents monitored their children's education and requested additional resources for them if there were problems. Parents, for example, asked that children be signed up to see the reading resource teacher, be tested by the school psychologist, or be enrolled in the gifted program. Parents also asked for homework for their children or for materials that they could complete at home with their children.

The ease with which Prescott parents contacted the school was also apparent at formal school events. At the Open House, almost all of the parents talked to the teacher or to the teacher's aide; these conversations were often long and were punctuated by jokes and questions. Also, many of the parents were friends with other parents in the class, so there was quite a bit of interaction between families. In inviting me to the Open House, the teacher described the event as a "cocktail party without cocktails." The room did indeed have the noisy, crowded, and animated atmosphere of a cocktail party.

In sum, Colton parents were reluctant to contact the school, tended to intervene over nonacademic matters, and were uncomfortable in their interactions in the school. In contrast, although Prescott parents varied in the level of supervision and scrutiny they gave their child's schooling, they frequently contacted teachers to discuss their child's academic progress.

. . .

In addition, Prescott parents played a more active role in reinforcing and monitoring the school work of their children. Colton parents were asked by teachers to help review and reinforce the material at school, particularly spelling words. Though a few parents worked with their children, Colton teachers were disappointed in the response. Colton parents were also unfamiliar with the school's curriculum and with the specific educational problems of their children. Parents of children with learning disabilities, for example, knew only that their children's grades "weren't up to par" or that their children "didn't do too well" in school. Moreover these parents were unaware of the teacher's specific efforts to improve their child's performance.

Prescott parents, on the other hand, carefully followed their children's curriculum. They often showed children the practical applications of the knowledge they gained at school, made up games that strengthened and elaborated children's recently acquired knowledge, and reviewed the material presented in class with their children. Parents of low achievers and children with learning problems were particularly vigorous in these efforts and made daily efforts to work with children at home. Parents knew their child's specific problems and knew what the teacher was doing to strengthen their child's performance. Parents' efforts on behalf of their children were closely coordinated with the school program.

There were some variations in parents' response to teachers' requests in the two school communities. Notably, two of the Colton parents (who appeared to be upwardly mobile) actively read to their children at home, closely reviewed their children's school work, and emphasized the importance of educational success. The teachers were very impressed by the behavior of these parents and by the relatively high academic performance of their children. At Prescott, parents differed in how critically they assessed the school and in their propensity to intervene in their children's schooling. For example, some parents said that they "felt sorry for teachers" and believed that other parents in the community were too demanding. The child's number of siblings, birth order, and temperament also shaped parental intervention in schooling. There was some variation in the role of fathers, although in both schools, mothers had the primary responsibility for schooling.

There were important differences, then, in the way in which Colton and Prescott parents responded to teachers' requests for participation. These patterns suggest that the relationship between families and schools was *independent* in the working-class school, and *interdependent* in the middle-class school.

Factors Structuring Parents' Participation

Interviews and observations of parents suggested that a variety of factors influenced parents' participation in schooling. Parents'

educational capabilities, their view of the appropriate division of labor between teachers and parents, the information they had about their children's schooling, and the time, money, and other material resources available in the home all mediated parents' involvement in schooling.

Educational Capabilities

Parents at Colton and Prescott had different levels of educational attainment. Most Colton parents were high school graduates or high school dropouts. Most were married and had their first child shortly after high school. They generally had difficulties in school as children; several of the fathers, for example, had been held back in elementary school. In interviews, they expressed doubts about their educational capabilities and indicated that they depended on the teacher to educate their children. As one mother stated,

> I know that when she gets into the higher grades, I know I won't be able to help her, math especially, unless I take a refresher course myself. . . . So I feel that it is the teacher's job to help her as much as possible to understand it, because I know that I won't be able to.

Another mother, commenting on her overall lack of educational skills, remarked that reading preschool books to her young son had improved her reading skills:

> I graduated from high school and could fill out [job] applications, but when I was nineteen and married my husband, I didn't know how to look up a word in the dictionary. When I started reading to Johnny, I found that *my* reading improved.

Observations of Colton parents at the school site and in interviews confirmed that parents' educational skills were often wanting. Prescott parents' educational skills, on the other hand, were strong. Most were college graduates and many had advanced degrees.

Parents in the two communities also divided up the responsibility between home and school in different ways. Colton parents regarded teachers as "educated people." They turned over the responsibility for education to the teacher, whom they viewed as a professional. As one mother put it,

> My job is here at home. My job is to raise him, to teach him manners, get him dressed and get him to school, to make sure that he is happy. Now her [the teacher's] part, the school's part, is to teach him to learn. Hopefully, someday he'll be able to use all of that. That is what I think is their part, to teach him to read, the writing, any kind of schooling.

Education is seen as a discrete process that takes place on the school grounds, under the direction of a teacher. This mother's role is to get her son to school; once there, his teacher will "teach him to learn."

This mother was aware that her son's teacher wanted him to practice reading at home, but neither she nor her husband read to their son regularly. The mother's view of reading was analogous to her view of work. She sent her children to school to learn for six hours a day and expected that they could leave their schooling (i.e., their work) behind them at the school site, unless they had been given homework. She believed that her seven-year-old boy's afternoons and evenings were time for him to play. In this context, her son's reading at home was similar to riding his bike or to playing with his truck. The mother did not believe that her child's academic progress depended upon his activities at home. Instead, she saw a separation of spheres.

Other parents had a different conception of their role in schooling. They believed education was a shared responsibility: They were *partners* with teachers in promoting their children's academic progress. As one mother stated,

> I see the school as being a very strong instructional force, more so than we are here at home. I guess that I am comfortable with that, from what I have seen. It is a three-to-one ratio or something, where out of a possible four, he is getting three quarters of what he needs from the school, and then a quarter of it from here. Maybe it would be better if our influence was stronger, but I am afraid that in this day and age it is not possible to do any more than that even if you wanted to.

Prescott parents wanted to be involved in their child's educational process in an important way. In dividing up the responsibility for education, they described the relationship between parents and teachers as a relationship between equals, and they believed that they possessed similar or superior educational skills and prestige. One Prescott father discussed his relationship with teachers in this way:

> I don't think of teachers as more educated than me or in a higher position than me. I don't have any sense of hierarchy. I am not higher than them, and they are not higher than me. We are equals. We are reciprocals. So if I have a problem I will talk to them. I have a sense of decorum. I wouldn't go busting into a classroom and say something. . . . They are not working for me, but they also aren't doing something I couldn't do. It is more a question of a division of labor.

Prescott parents had not only better educational skills and higher occupational status than Colton parents but also more disposable income and more flexible work schedules.

These material resources entered into the family–school relationships. Some Colton mothers, for example, had to make a series of complicated arrangements for transportation and child care to attend a school event held in the middle of the afternoon. Prescott parents, on the other hand, had two cars and sufficient resources to hire babysitters and housecleaners. In addition, Prescott parents generally had much greater flexibility in their work schedules than Colton parents. Material resources also influenced the educational purchases parents made. Colton parents reported that most of the books they bought for their children came from the flea market. Prescott parents had the financial flexibility to purchase new books if they desired, and many of the parents of low achievers hired tutors for their children during the summer months.

Information about Schooling

Colton parents had only limited information about most aspects of their children's experience at school; what they did know, they learned primarily from their children. For example, the Colton mothers knew the names of the child's teacher and the teacher's aide, the location of the classroom on the school grounds, and the name of the janitor, and they were familiar with the Read at Home Program. They did not know details of the school or of classroom interaction. The amount of information Colton parents had did not seem to vary by how much contact they had with the school.

In the middle-class community, parents had extensive information about classroom and school life. For example, in addition to knowing the names of their child's current classroom teacher and teacher's aide, the mothers knew the names and academic reputations of most of the other teachers in the school. The mothers also knew the academic rankings of children in the class (e.g., the best

boy and girl in math, the best boy and girl in reading). Most of the mothers knew the composition of their child's reading group, the math and spelling packet the child was working on, and the specific academic problems to which the child was being exposed (e.g., adding single-digit numbers). Other details of classroom experience were also widely known, including the names of children receiving the services of the reading resource specialist, occupational therapist, and special education teacher. Although a few fathers had very specific information about the school, most depended on their wives to collect and store this information. The fathers were, however, generally apprised of the reputations of teachers and the dissatisfactions that some parents had with particular teachers.

Much of the observed difference between the schools in parents' information about schooling may be traced to differences in family life, particularly in social networks and childrearing patterns. Prescott families saw relatively little of their relatives; instead, many parents socialized with other parents in the school community. Colton parents generally had very close ties with relatives in the area, seeing siblings or parents three times per week or more. Colton parents had virtually no social contact with other parents in the school, even when the families lived on the same street. The social networks of the middle-class parents provided them with additional sources of information about their child's school experience; the networks of working-class parents did not (see Bott 1971; Litwack and Szeleny 1971).

The childrearing patterns of the two groups also differed, particularly in the leisure time activities they encouraged. At Colton, children's after-school activities were informal: bike riding, snake hunting, watching television, playing with neighbor children, and helping parents with younger siblings. Prescott children were enrolled in formal socialization activities, including swimming lessons, soccer, art and crafts lessons, karate lessons, and gymnastics. All the children in the classroom were enrolled in at least one after-school activity, and many were busy every afternoon with a lesson or structured experience. The parents took their children to and from these activities. Many stayed to watch the lesson, thus providing another opportunity to meet and interact with other Prescott parents. Discussions about schools, teachers' reputations, and academic progress were frequent. For many parents, these interactions were a major source of information about their children's schooling, and parents believed that the discussions had an important effect on the way in which they approached their children's schooling.

Discussion

Teachers in both schools interpreted parental involvement as a reflection of the value parents placed on their children's educational success (see Deutsch 1967; Strodbeck 1958). As the principal at Prescott commented,

> This particular community is one with a very strong interest in its schools. It is a wonderful situation in which to work. Education is very important to the parents and they back that up with an interest in volunteering. This view that education is important helps kids as well. If parents value schooling and think it is important, then kids take it seriously.

The teachers and the principal at Colton placed a similar interpretation on the lack of parental participation at the school. Speaking of the parents, the principal remarked,

> They don't value education because they don't have much of one them-

selves. [Since] they don't value education as much as they could, they don't put those values and expectations on their kids.

Interviews and observations of parents told a different story, however. Parents in both communities valued educational success, all wanted their children to do well in school, and all saw themselves as supporting and helping their children achieve success at school. Middle- and working-class parents' aspirations differed only in the level of achievement they hoped their children would attain. Several Colton parents were high school dropouts and bitterly regretted their failure to get a diploma. As one mother said, "I desperately want her to graduate. If she can do that, that will satisfy me." All of the Prescott parents hoped that their children would get a college diploma, and many spoke of the importance of an advanced degree.

Although the educational values of the two groups of parents did not differ, the ways in which they promoted educational success did. In the working-class community, parents turned over the responsibility for education to the teacher. Just as they depended on doctors to heal their children, they depended on teachers to educate them. In the middle-class community, however, parents saw education as a shared enterprise and scrutinized, monitored, and supplemented the school experience of their children. Prescott parents read to their children, initiated contact with teachers, and attended school events more often than Colton parents.

Generally, the evidence demonstrates that the level of parental involvement is linked to the class position of the parents and to the social and cultural resources that social class yields in American society. By definition, the educational status and material resources of parents increase with social class.

These resources were observed to influence parental participation in schooling in the Prescott and Colton communities. The working-class parents had poor educational skills, relatively lower occupational prestige than teachers, and limited time and disposable income to supplement and intervene in their children's schooling. The middle-class parents, on the other hand, had educational skills and occupational prestige that matched or surpassed that of teachers; they also had the necessary economic resources to manage the child care, transportation, and time required to meet with teachers, to hire tutors, and to become intensely involved in their children's schooling.

These differences in social, cultural, and economic resources between the two sets of parents help explain differences in their responses to a variety of teacher requests to participate in schooling. For example, when asked to read to their children and to help them at home with school work, Colton parents were reluctant to comply because they felt that their educational skills were inadequate for these tasks. Prescott parents, with their superior educational skills, felt more comfortable helping their children in these areas. Parents at Colton and Prescott also differed in their perceptions of the appropriate relationship between parents and teachers. Prescott parents conceived of schooling as a partnership in which parents have the right and the responsibility to raise issues of their choosing and even to criticize teachers. Colton parents' inferior educational level and occupational prestige reinforced their trust in and dependence on the professional expertise of educators. The relatively high occupational position of Prescott parents contributed to their view of teachers as equals.[1] Prescott parents occasionally had more confidence in their right to monitor and to criticize teachers. Their occupational prestige levels may have helped both build this confi-

dence and demystify the status of the teacher as a professional.

Finally, more straightforward economic differences between the middle- and working-class parents are evident in their different responses to requests to attend school events. Attendance at parent–teacher conferences, particularly those held in the afternoon, requires transportation, child care arrangements, and flexibility at the workplace—all more likely to be available to Prescott parents than to Colton parents.

The literature on family life indicates that social class is associated with differences in social networks, leisure time, and childrearing activities (Bott 1971; Kohn 1977; Rubin 1976). The observations in this study confirm these associations and, in addition, indicate that social class differences in family life (or class cultures) have implications for family–school relationships. Middle-class culture provides parents with some information about schooling and promotes social ties among parents in the school community. This furthers the interdependence between home and school. Working-class culture, on the other hand, emphasizes kinship and promotes independence between the spheres of family life and schooling.

Because both schools promote a family–school relationship that solicits parental involvement in schooling and that promotes an interdependence between family and school, the class position and the class culture of middle-class families yield a social profit not available to working-class families. In particular, middle-class culture provides parents with more information about schooling and also builds social networks among parents in the school community. Parents use this information to build a family–school relationship congruent with the schools' definition of appropriate behavior. For example, they may request additional educational resources for their children, monitor the behavior of the teacher, share costs of a tutor with other interested parents, and consult with other parents and teachers about their children's educational experience.

It is important to stress that if the schools were to promote a different type of family–school relationship, the class culture of middle-class parents might not yield a social profit. The data do not reveal that the social relations of middle-class culture are intrinsically better than the social relations of working-class culture. Nor can it be said that the family–school relationships in the middle class are objectively better for children than those in the working class. Instead, the social profitability of middle-class arrangements is tied to the schools' definition of the proper family–school relationship.

. . .

Family–School Relationships and Cultural Capital

The results suggest that social class position and class culture become a form of cultural capital in the school setting (Bourdieu 1977a; Bourdieu and Passeron 1977). Although working-class and middle-class parents share a desire for their children's educational success in first and second grade, social location leads them to construct different pathways for realizing that success. Working-class parents' method—dependence on the teacher to educate their child—may have been the dominant method of promoting school success in earlier periods within the middle class. Today, however, teachers actively solicit parents' participation in education. Middle-class parents, in supervising, monitoring, and overseeing the educational experience of their children, behave in ways that mirror the requests of schools. This appears to provide middle-class children with educational advantages over working-class children.

The behavior of parents in this regard is not fully determined by their social location. There are variations within as well as between social classes. Still, parents approach the family–school relationship with different sets of social resources. Schools ask for very specific types of behavior from all parents, regardless of their social class. Not all cultural resources are equally valuable, however, for complying with schools' requests. The resources tied directly to social class (e.g., education, prestige, income) and certain patterns of family life (e.g., kinship ties, socialization patterns, leisure activities) seem to play a large role in facilitating the participation of parents in schools. Other aspects of class and class cultures, including religion and taste in music, art, food, and furniture (Bourdieu 1984) appear to play a smaller role in structuring the behavior of parents, children, and teachers in the family–school relationship. (These aspects of class cultures might, of course, influence other dimensions of schooling.)

These findings underline the importance of studying the significance of cultural capital within a social context. In recent years, Bourdieu has been criticized for being overly deterministic in his analysis of the role of cultural capital in shaping outcomes (Giroux 1983; Connell et al. 1982). Connell et al., for example, argue that cultural capital

> practically obliterates the person who is actually the main constructor of the home/school relationship. The student is treated mainly as a bearer of cultural capital, a bundle of abilities, knowledges and attitudes furnished by parents. (p. 188)

Moreover, Bourdieu has focused almost exclusively on the social profits stemming from high culture. Although he is quite clear about the arbitrary character of culture, his emphasis on the value of high culture could be misinterpreted. His research on the cultural capital of elites may be construed as suggesting that the culture of elites is intrinsically more valuable than that of the working class. In this regard, the concept of cultural capital is potentially vulnerable to the same criticisms that have been directed at the notion of the culture of poverty (Valentine 1968).

. . .

Implications for Further Research

Educators and policymakers may seek to increase parental involvement in schooling by boosting the educational capabilities and information resources of parents. For sociologists interested in family, schools, and social stratification, a somewhat different task is in order. Families and schools, and family–school relationships, are critical links in the process of social reproduction. For most children (but not all), social class is a major predictor of educational and occupational achievement. Schools, particularly elementary and secondary schools, play a crucial role in this process of social reproduction; they sort students into social categories that award credentials and opportunities for mobility (Collins 1979, 1981c). We know relatively little about the stages of this social process.

The concept of cultural capital may help by turning our attention to the structure of opportunity and to the way in which individuals proceed through that structure (see also Collins 1981a, 1981b; Knorr-Cetina and Cicourel 1981). Moreover, the concept does not overlook the importance of the role of the individual in constructing a biography within a social structure. Class provides social and cultural resources, but these resources must be invested or activated to become a form of cultural capital. Analyzing the role of cultural capital in structuring family–school relationships, particularly parental participation in education, provides a rich setting for analyzing the linkages between micro and macro levels of analysis.

NOTE

1. Some Prescott parents, however, did report that they felt intimidated by a teacher on some occasions.

REFERENCES

AGGLETON, PETER J. AND GEOFF WHITTY. 1985. "Rebels without a Cause? Socialization and Subcultural Style among the Children of the New Middle Classes." *Sociology of Education* 58: 60–72.

ANYON, JEAN. 1981. "Social Class and School Knowledge." *Curriculum Inquiry* 11:1–42.

APPLE, MICHAEL W. 1979. *Ideology and Curriculum.* London: Routledge and Kegan Paul.

BECKER, HENRY JAY AND JOYCE L. EPSTEIN. 1982. "Parent Involvement: A Survey of Teacher Practices." *Elementary School Journal* 83:85–102.

BERGER, EUGENIA H. 1983. *Beyond the Classroom: Parents as Partners in Education.* St. Louis: Mosby.

BERNSTEIN, BASIL. 1975. *Class, Codes and Control.* Vol. 3. London: Routledge and Kegan Paul.

———. 1982. "Codes, Modalities and the Process of Cultural Reproduction: A Model." Pp. 304–55 in *Cultural and Economic Reproduction in Education*, edited by Michael W. Apple. London: Routledge and Kegan Paul.

BOTT, ELIZABETH. 1971. *Family and Social Networks.* New York: Free Press.

BOURDIEU, PIERRE. 1977a. "Cultural Reproduction and Social Reproduction." Pp. 487–511 in *Power and Ideology in Education*, edited by J. Karabel and A. H. Halsey. New York: Oxford University Press.

———. 1977b. *Outline of a Theory of Practice.* Cambridge, England: Cambridge University Press.

———. 1981. "Men and Machines." Pp. 304–17 in *Advances in Social Theory: Toward an Integration of Micro- and Macro-Sociologies*, edited by K. Knorr-Cetina and A. V. Cicourel. Boston: Routledge and Kegan Paul.

———. 1984. *Distinction: A Social Critique of the Judgment of Taste.* Translated by Richard Nice. Cambridge, MA: Harvard University Press.

BOURDIEU, PIERRE AND JEAN-CLAUDE PASSERON. 1977. *Reproduction in Education, Society and Culture.* Translated by Richard Nice. Beverly Hills: Sage.

CALIFORNIA DEPARTMENT OF EDUCATION. 1983. *California Assessment Program 1981–1982.* Sacramento: California Department of Education.

COLLINS, RANDALL. 1979. *The Credential Society.* New York: Academic Press.

———. 1981a. "Micro-Translation as a Theory-Building Strategy." Pp. 81–108 in *Advances in Social Theory: Toward an Integration of Micro- and Macro-Sociologies,* edited by K. Knorr-Cetina and A. V. Cicourel. Boston: Routledge and Kegan Paul.

———. 1981b. "On the Micro-Foundations of Macro-Sociology." *American Journal of Sociology* 86:984–1014.

———. 1981c. *Sociology Since Midcentury: Essays in Theory Cumulation.* New York: Academic Press.

CONNELL, R. W., D. J. ASHENDON, S. KESSLER, AND G. W. DOWSETT. 1982. *Making the Difference: Schools, Families and Social Division.* Sydney: George Allen and Unwin.

COOK-GUMPEREZ, JENNY. 1973. *Social Control and Socialization: A Study of Class Difference in the Language of Maternal Control.* Boston: Routledge and Kegan Paul.

COOKSON, PETER W., JR. AND CAROLINE H. PERSELL. 1985. *Preparing for Power: America's Elite Boarding Schools.* New York: Basic Books.

DEUTSCH, MARTIN. 1967. "The Disadvantaged Child and the Learning Process." Pp. 39–58 in *The Disadvantaged Child,* edited by M. Deutsch. New York: Basic Books.

DIAZ, STEPHAN, LUIS C. MOLL, AND HUGH MEHAN. 1986. "Sociocultural Resources in Instruction: A Context-Specific Approach." Pp. 187–230 in *Beyond Language: Social and Cultural Factors in Schooling Language Minority Students,* edited by the Bilingual Education Office. Los Angeles: California State University, Evaluation, Dissemination, and Assessment Center.

EPSTEIN, JOYCE. 1984. "Effects of Teacher Practices and Parent Involvement on Student Achievement." Paper presented at the annual meetings of the American Educational Research Association, New Orleans.

EPSTEIN, JOYCE AND HENRY JAY BECKER. 1982. "Teachers' Reported Practices of Parent Involvement: Problems and Possibilities." *Elementary School Journal* 83:103–13.

ERICKSON, FREDERICK AND GERALD MOHATT. 1982. "Cultural Organization of Participation Structures in Two Classrooms of Indian Students." Pp. 132–75 in *Doing the Ethnography of Schooling,* edited by G. Spindler. New York: Holt, Rinehart and Winston.

GASKELL, JANE. 1985. "Course Enrollment in the High School: The Perspective of Working-Class Females." *Sociology of Education* 58:48–59.

GEARING, FREDERICK AND PAUL EPSTEIN. 1982. "Learning to Wait: An Ethnographic Probe into the Operation of an Item of Hidden Curriculum." Pp. 240–67 in *Doing the Ethnography of Schooling,* edited by G. Spindler. New York: Holt, Rinehart and Winston.

GIROUX, HENRY A. 1983. *Theory and Resistance in Education.* South Hadley, MA: Bergin and Harvey.

HEATH, SHIRLEY B. 1982. "Questioning at Home and at School: A Comparative Study." Pp. 102–31 in *Doing the Ethnography of Schooling,* edited by G. Spindler. New York: Holt, Rinehart and Winston.

———. 1983. *Ways with Words.* London: Cambridge University Press.

JENCKS, CHRISTOPHER ET AL. 1972. *Inequality.* New York: Basic Books.

KNORR-CETINA, KARIN AND AARON V. CICOUREL. 1981. *Advances in Social Theory: Toward an Integration of Micro- and Macro-Sociologies.* Boston: Routledge and Kegan Paul.

KOHN, MELVIN L. 1977. *Class and Conformity.* Chicago: University of Chicago Press.

LABOV, WILLIAM. 1972. *Sociolinguistic Patterns.* Philadelphia: University of Pennsylvania Press.

LEICHTER, HOPE JENSEN. 1979. "Families and Communities as Educators: Some Concepts of Relationships." Pp. 3–94 in *Families and Communities as Educators,* edited by H. J. Leichter. New York: Teachers College Press.

LIGHTFOOT, SARA LAWRENCE. 1978. *Worlds Apart.* New York: Basic Books.

LITWACK, EUGENE AND I. SZELENY. 1971. "Kinship and Other Primary Groups." Pp. 149–63 in *Sociology of the Family,* edited by M. Anderson. Middlesex, England: Penguin.

MARJORIBANKS, KEVIN. 1979. *Families and Their Learning Environments: An Empirical Analysis.* London: Routledge and Kegan Paul.

MEHAN, HUGH AND PEG GRIFFIN. 1980. "Socialization: The View from Classroom Interactions." *Social Inquiry* 50:357–98.

NATIONAL EDUCATION ASSOCIATION. 1985. "Teacher–Parent Partnership Program, 1984–1985 Status Report." Unpublished paper. Washington, DC: National Education Association.

OGBU, JOHN. 1974. *The Next Generation.* New York: Academic Press.

ROBINSON, SHARON. 1985. "Teacher–Parent Co-operation." Paper presented at the annual meetings of the American Educational Research Association, Chicago.

RUBIN, LILLIAN B. 1976. *Worlds of Pain.* New York: Basic Books.

SEELEY, DAVID. 1984. "Home-School Partnership." *Phi Delta Kappan* 65:383–93.

STRODBECK, F. L. 1958. "Family Interaction, Values, and Achievement." Pp. 131–91 in *Talent and Society,* edited by D. D. McClelland. New York: Van Nostrand.

TAYLOR, SANDRA. 1984. "Reproduction and Contradiction in Schooling: The Case of Commercial Studies." *British Journal of Sociology of Education* 5:3–18.

TRELEASE, JAMES. 1982. *The Read-Aloud Handbook.* New York: Penguin.

VALENTINE, CHARLES A. 1968. *Culture and Poverty.* Chicago: University of Chicago Press.

VALLI, LINDA. 1985. "Office Education Students and the Meaning of Work." *Issues in Education* 3:31–44.

WILCOX, KATHLEEN A. 1977. "Schooling and Socialization for Work Roles." Ph.D. dissertation, Harvard University.

———. 1982. "Differential Socialization in the Classroom: Implications for Equal Opportunity." Pp. 269–309 in *Doing the Ethnography of Schooling,* edited by G. Spindler. New York: Holt, Rinehart and Winston.

Race

27

BLACK STUDENTS' SCHOOL SUCCESS
Coping with the "Burden of 'Acting White'"

Signithia Fordham • John U. Ogbu

. . .

Our main point in this [chapter] is that *one major reason* black students do poorly in school is that they experience inordinate ambivalence and affective dissonance in regard to academic effort and success. This problem arose partly because white Ameri-

Signithia Fordham and John U. Ogbu, excerpts from "Black Students' School Success: Coping with the 'Burden of "Acting White"'" from *The Urban Review* 18, no. 3 (1986). Copyright © 1986 by Agathon Press, Inc. Reprinted with the permission of the Plenum Publishing Corporation.

cans traditionally refused to acknowledge that black Americans are capable of intellectual achievement, and partly because black Americans subsequently began to doubt their own intellectual ability, began to define academic success as white people's prerogative, and began to discourage their peers, perhaps unconsciously, from emulating white people in academic striving, i.e., from "acting white." Because of the ambivalence, affective dissonance, and social pressures, many black students who are academically able do not put forth the necessary effort and perseverance in their schoolwork and, consequently, do poorly in school. Even black students who do not fail generally perform well below their potential for the same reasons. We will illustrate this phenomenon with data from a recent ethnographic study of both successful and unsuccessful students in a predominantly black high school in Washington, D.C.

. . .

"Acting White" at Capital High

The setting of the study, Capital High School and its surrounding community, has been described in detail elsewhere (Fordham 1982b, 1984, 1985). Suffice it here to say that Capital High is a predominantly black high school (some 99% black—1,868 out of 1,886 students at the start of the research effort in 1982). It is located in a historically black section of Washington, D.C., in a relatively low-income area.

The influence of fictive kinship [that is, the specific worldview of those persons who are appropriately labeled "black"] is extensive among the students at Capital High. It shows up not only in conflicts between blacks and whites and between black students and black teachers, who are often perceived to be "functionaries" of the dominant society, but also in the students' constant need to reassure one another of black loyalty and identity. They appear to achieve this group loyalty by defining certain attitudes and behaviors as "white" and therefore unacceptable, and then employing numerous devices to discourage one another from engaging in those behaviors and attitudes, i.e., from "acting white."

Among the attitudes and behaviors that black students at Capital High identify as "acting white" and therefore unacceptable are: (1) speaking standard English; (2) listening to white music and white radio stations; (3) going to the opera or ballet; (4) spending a lot of time in the library studying; (5) working hard to get good grades in school; (6) getting good grades in school (those who get good grades are labeled "brainiacs"); (7) going to the Smithsonian; (8) going to a Rolling Stones concert at the Capital Center; (9) doing volunteer work; (10) going camping, hiking, or mountain climbing; (11) having cocktails or a cocktail party; (12) going to a symphony orchestra concert; (13) having a party with no music; (14) listening to classical music; (15) being on time; (16) reading and writing poetry; and (17) putting on "airs," and so forth. This list is not exhaustive, but indicates kinds of attitudes and behaviors likely to be negatively sanctioned and therefore avoided by a large number of students.

As operationally defined in this reading, the idea of "coping with the burden of 'acting white'" suggests the various strategies that black students at Capital High use to resolve, successfully or unsuccessfully, the tension between students desiring to do well academically and meet the expectations of school authorities on the one hand and the demands of peers for conformity to group-sanctioned attitudes and behaviors that validate black identity and cultural frame on the other. Black students at Capital High who choose to pursue academic success are perceived by their peers as "being kind of white" (Weis 1985, p. 101) and therefore not truly black. This gives rise to the tension between those who want to succeed (i.e., who in the eyes of their peers want to "act white") and others insisting on highlighting group-sanctioned attitudes and behaviors. Under the circumstance, students who want to do well in school must find some strategy to resolve the tension. This tension, along with the extra responsibility it places on students who choose to pursue academic success in spite of it, and its effects on the performance of those who resolve the tension successfully and those who do not, constitute "the burden of 'acting white.'" The few high-achieving students, as we will show, have learned how to cope successfully with the burden of acting white; the many underachieving students have not succeeded in a manner that enhances academic success. It is this tension and its effects on black students' academic efforts and outcomes that are explored in the case study of Capital High students.

Ethnographic data in the study were collected over a period of more than one year. During the study some 33 students in the eleventh grade were studied intensively, and our examples are drawn from this sample.

Underachieving Students

Underachieving black students in the sample appear to have the ability to do well in school, at least better than their present records show. But they have apparently decided, consciously or unconsciously, to avoid "acting white." That is, they choose to avoid adopting attitudes and putting in enough time and effort in their schoolwork because their peers (and they themselves) would interpret their behaviors as "white." Their main strategy for coping with the burden of acting white tends, therefore, to be *avoidance*.

. . . Like most students in the sample, Sidney took the Preliminary Scholastic Aptitude Test (PSAT) and did fairly well, scoring at the 67th percentile on the math section of the test and at the 54th percentile on the verbal section. His scores on the Comprehensive Test of Basic Skills (CTBS) in the ninth grade indicate that he was performing well above grade level: His composite score in reading was 12.2; he scored at the college level on the language component (13.6); on the math component he scored just above eleventh grade (11.3), making his total battery on these three components 11.8. He scored above college level in the reference skills, science, and social studies sections. On the whole, his performance on standardized tests is far higher than that of many high-achieving males in our sample.

In spite of this relatively good performance on standardized tests, his grade point average is only C. Sidney is surprised and disgusted with his inability to earn grades comparable to those he earned in elementary and junior high school. While he takes most of the courses available to eleventh graders from the Advanced Placement sequence, he is not making the A's and B's at Capital High that he consistently made during his earlier schooling.

Sidney is an outstanding football player who appears to be encapsulated in the very forces which he maintains are largely responsible for the lack of upward mobility in the local black community. He is very much aware of the need to earn good grades in school in order to take advantage of the few opportunities he thinks are available to black Americans. However, he appears unable to control his life and act in opposition to the forces he identifies as detrimental to his academic progress.

His friends are primarily football players and other athletes. He is able to mix and mingle easily with them despite the fact that, unlike most of them, he takes advanced courses; he claims that this is because of his status as an athlete. His friends are aware of his decision to take these advanced courses, and they jokingly refer to him as "Mr. Advanced Placement."

Sidney readily admits that he could do a lot better in school, but says that he, like many of his friends, does not value what he is asked to learn in school. He also reluctantly admits that the fear of being called a "brainiac" prevents him from putting more time and effort into his schoolwork. According to him, the term "brainiac" is used in a disparaging manner at Capital High for students who do well in their courses:

ANTHROPOLOGIST: Have you heard the word "brainiac" used here?

SIDNEY: Yes. [When referring to students who take the Advanced Placement courses here.] That's a term for the smartest person in class. Brainiac—jerk—you know, those terms. If you're smart, you're a jerk, you're a brainiac.

ANTHRO: Are all those words synonyms?

SIDNEY: Yes.

ANTHRO: So it's not a positive [term]?

SIDNEY: No, it's a negative [term], as far as brilliant academic students are concerned.

ANTHRO: Why is that?

SIDNEY: That's just the way the school population is.

Although Sidney takes the Advanced Placement Courses, he is not making much effort to get good grades; instead, he spends his time and effort developing a persona that will nullify any claims that he is a brainiac, as can be seen in the following interview excerpt:

ANTHROPOLOGIST: Has anyone ever called you a [brainiac]?

SIDNEY: Brainiac? No.

ANTHRO: Why not?

SIDNEY: Well, I haven't given them a reason to. And, too, well, I don't excel in all my classes like I *should* be—that's another reason. . . . I couldn't blame it on the environment. I have come to blame it on myself—for partaking *in* the environment. But I *can* tell you that—going back to what we *were* talking about—another reason why they don't call me a "brainiac," because I'm an athlete.

ANTHRO: So . . . if a kid is smart, for example, one of the ways to limit the negative reaction to him or her, and his or her brilliance, is. . . .

SIDNEY: Yeah, do something extracurricular in the school . . . [like] being an athlete,

cheerleader squad, in the band—like that. . . . Yeah, *something that's important* [emphasis added], that has something to do with—that represents your school.

Sidney admits that the fear of being known as a brainiac has negatively affected his academic effort a great deal. The fear of being discovered as an "imposter" among his friends leads him to choose carefully those persons with whom he will interact within the classroom; all of the males with whom he interacts who also take Advanced Placement courses are, like him, primarily concerned with "mak[ing] it over the hump."

He also attributes his lack of greater effort in school to his lack of will power and time on task. And he thinks that his low performance is due to his greater emphasis on athletic achievement and his emerging manhood, and less emphasis on the core curriculum. He does not study. He spends very little time completing his homework assignments, usually fifteen minutes before breakfast. On the whole, Sidney is not proud of his academic record. But he does not feel that he can change the direction of his school career because he does not want to be known as a brainiac.

. . .

High-Achieving Students

Students at Capital High who are relatively successful academically also face the problem of coping with the "burden of 'acting white.'" But they have usually adopted strategies that enable them to succeed. These students decide more or less consciously (a) to pursue academic success and (b) to use specific strategies to cope with the burden of acting white.

. . .

Katrina's performance on the math component of the PSAT was at the 95th percentile. Only one other student . . . scored higher and another student had a comparable score. Katrina's score on the verbal component was not as high, being at the 75th percentile. But her overall score far surpassed those of most other students. Her performance on the CTBS was equally impressive, with an overall grade equivalent of 13.6, or college level, in every section—math, reading, and language, and in every subsection, as well as in the ancillary sections, namely, reference skills, social studies, and science. She also performed well on the Life Skills examination which measures students' ability to process information in nine different areas. Katrina scored 100% in each of the nine areas.

In the classroom her performance has been equally outstanding. She had A in all subjects except handwriting in the elementary school. Her final grades in the ninth grade (i.e., junior high school) were all A's; and in the tenth grade, her first year at Capital High, her final grades were all A's.

Katrina has heard of the term "brainiac" not only at Capital High, but as far back as at the elementary and junior high school levels. And she is very much aware of the nuances associated with the term. She explains:

> When they [other students] call someone a "brainiac," they mean he's always in the books. But he probably isn't always in the books. Straight A, maybe—you know, or A's and B's. A Goody-Two-Shoes with the teacher, maybe—you know, the teacher always calling on them, and they're always the leaders in the class or something.

She acknowledges that she is often referred to as a brainiac, but that she always denies it because she does not want her peers to see her that way. To treat her as a brainiac "blows her cover" and exposes her to the very forces she has sought so hard to avoid:

alienation, ridicule, physical harm, and the inability to live up to the name.

How does Katrina avoid being called a brainiac and treated with hostility while at the same time managing to keep up her outstanding academic performance? Katrina admits that she has had to "put brakes" on her academic performance in order to minimize the stress she experiences. She says that she is much better at handling subject matter than at handling her peers. To solve the peer problem, she tries not to be conspicuous. As she puts it:

> Junior high, I didn't have much problem. I mean, I didn't have—there were always a lot of people in the classroom who did the work, so I wasn't like, the only one who did this assignment. So—I mean, I might do better at it, but I wasn't the only one. And so a lot of times, I'd let other kids answer—I mean, not *let* them, but. . . . All right, I *let* them answer questions [laughter], and I'd hold back. So I never really got into any arguments, you know, about school and my grades or anything.

She is extremely fearful of peer reactions if she were identified as acting white. Since she wants to continue doing well in school, she chooses to "go underground," that is, not to bring attention to herself. Her reluctance to participate in Capital High's "It's Academic" Club, a TV competition program, illustrates her desire to maintain a low profile. "It's Academic" is perhaps the most "intellectual" extracurricular activity at the school. To participate in the three-person team, a student must take a test prepared by the faculty sponsoring it. The three top scores are eligible to represent the school in the TV competition. Katrina reluctantly took the test at the suggestion of her physics teacher, the club sponsor. However, she had a prior agreement that she would not be selected to participate on the team *even if she had the top score.* She was one of the three top scorers, but because of the prior agreement was made only an alternate member of the team.

. . .

To summarize, . . . high-achieving students wrestle with the conflict inherent in the unique relationship of black people with the dominant institution: the struggle to achieve success while retaining group support and approval. In school, the immediate issue is how to obtain good grades and meet the expectations of school authorities without being rejected by peers for acting white. . . . [S]uccessful students at Capital High generally adopt specific strategies to solve this problem.

. . .

Summary and Implications

We have suggested . . . that black students' academic efforts are hampered by both external factors and within-group factors. We have tried to show that black students who are academically successful in the face of these factors have usually adopted specific strategies to avoid them. Although we recognize and have described elsewhere in detail the external, including school, factors which adversely affect black adolescents' school performance (Fordham 1982a, 1985; Ogbu 1974, 1978), our focus . . . is on the within-group factors, especially on how black students respond to other black students who are trying to "make it" academically.

. . .

Fictive kinship is, then, not only a symbol of social identity for black Americans, it is also a medium of boundary maintenance vis-a-vis white Americans. The school experi-

ence of black children is implicated because, under the circumstance, schooling is perceived by blacks, especially by black adolescents, as learning to act white, as acting white, or as trying to cross cultural boundaries. And, importantly, school learning is viewed as a subtractive process. In our view, then, the academic learning and performance problems of black children arise not only from a limited opportunity structure and black people's responses to it, but also from the way black people attempt to cope with the "burden of 'acting white.'" The sources of their school difficulties—perceptions of and responses to the limited opportunity structure and the burden of acting white—are particularly important during the adolescent period in the children's school careers.

We chose to focus our analysis on the burden of acting white and its effects on the academic effort and performance of black children because it seems to us to be a very important but as yet widely unrecognized dilemma of black students, particularly black adolescents. In other words, while we fully recognize the role of external forces—societal and school forces—in creating academic problems for the students, *we also argue that how black students respond to other black students who are trying to make it is also important in determining the outcome of their education.*

In the case study of Capital High School in Washington, D.C., we showed that coping with the burden of acting white affects the academic performance of both underachieving and high-achieving students. Black students who are encapsulated in the fictive kinship system or oppositional process experience greater difficulty in crossing cultural boundaries; i.e., in accepting standard academic attitudes and practices of the school and in investing sufficient time and effort in pursuing their educational goals. Some of the high-achieving students do not identify with the fictive kinship system; others more or less deliberately adopt sex-specific strategies to camouflage their academic pursuits and achievements.

The strategies of the academically successful students include engaging in activities which mute perceptions of their being preoccupied with academic excellence leading eventually to individual success outside the group, i.e., eventual upward mobility. Among them are athletic activities (which are regarded as "black activities") and other "team"-oriented activities, for male students. Other high-achieving students camouflage their academic effort by clowning. Still others do well in school by acquiring the protection of "bullies" and "hoodlums" in return for assisting the latter in their schoolwork and homework. In general, academically successful black students at Capital High (and probably elsewhere) are careful not to brag about their achievements or otherwise bring too much attention to themselves. We conclude, however, from this study of high-achieving students at Capital High, that they would do much better if they did not have to divert time and effort into strategies designed to camouflage their academic pursuit.

There are several implications of our analysis, and the implications are at different levels. As this analysis clearly demonstrates, the first and critically important change must occur in the existing opportunity structure, through an elimination of the job ceiling and related barriers. Changes in the opportunity structure are a prerequisite to changes in the behaviors and expectations of black adolescents for two salient reasons: (1) to change the students' perceptions of what is available to them as adult workers in the labor force and (2) to minimize the exacerbation of the extant achievement problem of black adolescents who are expected to master the technical skills taught and condoned in the school context but who are, nonetheless, unable to find employment in areas where they demonstrate exemplary expertise. Barring changes in the opportunity structure, the perceptions,

behaviors, and academic effort of black adolescents are unlikely to change to the extent necessary to have a significant effect on the existing boundary-maintaining mechanisms in the community. Therefore, until the perceptions of the nature and configuration of the opportunity structure change (see J. Williams 1985), the response of black students in the school context is likely to continue to be one which suggests that school achievement is a kind of risk which necessitates strategies enabling them to cope with the "burden of acting white." Second, educational barriers, both the gross and subtle mechanisms by which schools differentiate the academic careers of black and white children, should be eliminated.

Third, and particularly important in terms of our analysis, *the unique academic learning and performance problems created by the burden of acting white should be recognized and made a target of educational policies and remediation effort.* Both the schools and the black community have important roles to play in this regard. School personnel should try to understand the influence of the fictive kinship system in the students' perceptions of learning and the standard academic attitudes and practices or behaviors expected. The schools should then develop programs, including appropriate counseling, to help the students learn to divorce academic pursuit from the idea of acting white. The schools should also reinforce black identity in a manner compatible with academic pursuit, as in the case of Sargent (1985).

The black community has an important part to play in changing the situation. The community should develop programs to teach black children that academic pursuit is not synonymous with one-way acculturation into a white cultural frame of reference or acting white. To do this effectively, however, the black community must reexamine its own perceptions and interpretations of school learning. Apparently, black children's general perception that academic pursuit is "acting white" is learned in the black community. The ideology of the community in regard to the cultural meaning of schooling is, therefore, implicated and needs to be reexamined. Another thing the black community can do is to provide visible and concrete evidence for black youths that the community appreciates and encourages academic effort and success. Cultural or public recognition of those who are academically successful should be made a frequent event, as is generally done in the case of those who succeed in the fields of sports and entertainment.

· · ·

REFERENCES

FORDHAM, S. 1982a. "Black Student School Success as Related to Fictive Kinship: An Ethnographic Study in the Washington, DC, Public School System." Research proposal submitted to the National Institute of Education.

————. 1982b. "Cultural Inversion and Black Children's School Performance." Paper presented at the 81st Annual Meeting, American Anthropological Association, Washington, DC, December 3–7.

————. 1984. "Ethnography in a Black High School: Learning Not to Be a Native." Paper presented at the 83rd Annual Meeting, American Anthropological Association, Denver, November 14–18.

————. 1985. "Black Students School Success as Related to Fictive Kinship." Final Report. Washington, DC: The National Institute of Education.

OGBU, J. U. 1974. *The Next Generation: An Ethnography of Education in an Urban Neighborhood.* New York: Academic Press.

————. 1978. *Minority Education and Caste: The American System in Cross-Cultural Perspective.* New York: Academic Press.

SARGENT E. 1985. "Freeing Myself: Discoveries That Unshackle the Mind." *The Washington Post* (February 10).

[WEIS, L. 1985.] *Between Two Worlds: Black Students in an Urban Community College.* Boston: Routledge and Kegan Paul.

28

CONSUMERS OF URBAN EDUCATION

Amy Stuart Wells • Robert Crain

Our valedictorian, a very nice young man, chose to go to St. Louis University. And when the woman from there came here, I said, "How is he doing?" and she said, "Well, he went into remedial this summer and I kept him in remedial and January" because, she said, there are a lot of skills people from the all-black city schools have to learn. There are social skills, too, you know, and it's sad because [she was] saying how could we have better prepared him. . . . But it is just very, very discouraging because they have a very hard time making it. It's just a handful, you know.

—English Teacher from an All-Black
High School in St. Louis

Amy Stuart Wells and Robert Crain, excerpt from "Consumers of Urban Education" from *Stepping Over the Color Line: African-American Students in White Suburban Schools.* Copyright © 1997 by Yale University. Reprinted with the permission of Yale University Press.

The more we learned about the St. Louis public schools and the racial politics that drives the system, the more curious we became about the students who attend the all-black schools in North St. Louis. Who are these "consumers" of urban education, and why do they stay in racially segregated urban schools as their friends and neighbors leave for suburban and magnet schools? Too often policy makers and researchers oversimplify the process by which students and parents make school choices, as though it were similar to shopping for a car or a household appliance (Chubb and Moe 1990). But the African-American students and parents of St. Louis, who, because of a voluntary metropolitan-wide desegregation plan, have more than 100 schools in 17 school districts to choose from, explain that the process is not that simple. When the choice is between a nearby and familiar all-black school in a low-income neighborhood and a faraway, mostly white suburban school, the decision is never easy nor is it necessarily based on "objective" standards of school quality. Race, social class, segregation, and alienation all play a significant and interconnected role in where students "choose" to go to school.

This chapter is about the experiences of the "city students" who have chosen not to choose a suburban school.[1] The first author, accompanied by an African-American woman researcher from St. Louis, got to know the families of twelve tenth-grade city students, interviewing them and their parents about why they attend all-black urban high schools as opposed to suburban or magnet schools. In addition, we have drawn on other studies of African-American city and transfer students in St. Louis to better understand who chooses to step over the color line, who does not, and what the consequences are for each. In listening to the stories of students and their parents, we have come to a clearer understanding of the inherent possibilities and shortcomings of this inter-district transfer plan and how school choice and school

desegregation policies might be improved to provide greater opportunities for all urban students.

. . .

The three neighborhoods and their high schools differ dramatically in many respects. For instance, the percentage of residents in the Northwest high neighborhood who own their homes is 55 percent, one of the highest home ownership rates among all the neighborhoods on the city's north side. By comparison, near Sumner, about 30 percent of families own their homes, as opposed to about 2 percent of families who live near Vashon. Poverty rates for the three neighborhoods also show that Vashon High School draws from the lowest-income households in the city, with more than 50 percent of all families living below the poverty line. Near Sumner, Census data show that 40 percent of all families live below the poverty line. For families in the northernmost part of the city, near Northwest High School, the poverty rate is less than 20 percent.

We wanted to talk with city, transfer, and return students in each of these neighborhoods to better understand how African-American students and their parents living in very different inner-city neighborhoods make sense of the inter-district desegregation plan and thus their school choices.

City Parents: The Beat Down

To know these city students and their families is to gain a deeper understanding of how alienation and powerlessness, which grow out of the poverty and isolation experienced by many inner-city black families, shape their view of the larger social structure and where they fit into it (Bourdieu and Passeron 1979). This view shapes their achievement ideology, their racial attitudes, and their hopes for the future. In short, we found many of these students and their parents to be living under what West (1993a) calls nihilism: "the lived experience of coping with a life of horrifying meaninglessness, hopelessness, and (most important) lovelessness" (p. 14). Many of these parents and students were "beat down" by the burden of racism and severe poverty in a society that understands the weight of neither.

Perhaps the most striking finding from our interviews with the city students and their parents is that the key factor influencing the decision of an African-American student from the north side of St. Louis to transfer to a county school or to remain in an all-black neighborhood school appears to be the degree of parental involvement in the decision. In general, parents who were most involved in their children's educational decisions—indeed, those who *made* the decisions for their children—were those who insisted that their children attend county schools. Only one of the city parents felt strongly about her son remaining in a city school. The others were willing to let their children decide.

Our interviews reveal that students, for the most part, have to be pushed onto a bus heading for the county by a parent who is convinced that the benefits of going to a county school will, in the long run, outweigh the inconvenience, discomfort, and prejudice that the transfer entails. While there are a few exceptions, overall parental involvement in the students' education and the degree to which parents direct and control their children's educational decisions varied greatly between city and transfer students, and, to a lesser degree, between city and return students, with the city parents almost always leaving the school-choice decision to their children.

The city parents' lack of involvement echoes what teachers and principals in the all-black schools told us. Most of these educators insisted that the desegregation plan had resulted less in a "brain drain"

of the highest achieving students from the city schools than in a drain of students with the most active and involved parents. One teacher referred to the phenomenon as the "motivation drain." Of course the correlation between student achievement and parental involvement has traditionally been quite high (see Epstein 1990), so involved parents and high-achieving students often go hand in hand. But what these urban educators notice first is that many of the efficacious parents who provided a spark of momentum in their neighborhood schools and a more critical voice in the city school system have transferred their children to the suburbs in search of a better opportunity (see Witte, Baily, and Thorn 1993).

A teacher in one of the city's all-black high schools said that she was "doing good" if she has five parents show up to open house to talk about their children's progress. "And we are here from 12:30 to 7:00 all day and have five people show up. If you ever get ten you have the record; people will say you are kidding. That's sad if you think about how many youngsters you have, and you get such a small percentage of parents involved."

In all but one case, "powerless" best describes the parents we interviewed whose children remain in the all-black city schools. They were generally shy and withdrawn, typifying, much more so than either the parents of transfer or return students, what Comer (1980) describes as alienated inner-city parents with deep distrust of educators and an inability to act on their child's behalf in the world of the school. Eight of the eleven city parents we spent time with said the decision that their son or daughter remain in a city school was made by the student alone.[2] Half of these parents said that they did not discuss this decision with their child.

The powerlessness and alienation that city parents experience in their own lives seems to preclude them from helping their children to make educational decisions. We know, for instance, from the demographic information we collected from the families we studied that city parents in any of the three neighborhoods are less educated and hold lower-status jobs than the transfer parents in all three neighborhoods. Furthermore, unlike the transfer or return parents, none of the city parents works in the county or goes to the county on a regular basis. In fact, many of these city parents have never been to the predominantly white areas of St. Louis County, where the suburban schools that their children could choose to attend are located. The different educational backgrounds and lack of exposure to the suburbs seem to affect their perceptions of the transfer program.

Minnie Liddell, in an interview about the impact of the court case that bears her son's name, said that many African-American parents who keep their children in the all-black schools in the city are overwhelmed by just trying to survive in the impoverished north side of St. Louis: "You know, day-to-day living is their number one priority. . . . They don't have any hope for themselves so they don't have a lot of hope that Johnny or Mary is going to be a scientist anyway. So you know, he just goes to school where the law says he has to go to school. [So] you got that group too, where just living is a chore with them 'cause things are so hard for them."

What becomes more apparent as one gets to know these city parents is that all of them want what is best for their children; they all want their children to make it and be more successful than they have been. Like most parents, they care deeply about their children. But the degree to which they feel they can help their child attain the best—the best education, the best job after graduation, and so on—depends on their own self-concept and experiences in integrated settings.

The teenagers who are left to choose a school on their own are likely to choose city over county, familiar over unfamiliar—the path of least resistance. Meanwhile, the way

that familiar versus unfamiliar is defined has much to do with geography and race—the result of living in a highly segregated society in which African Americans have been systematically denied opportunities to live in whiter and wealthier neighborhoods. The frustration of generations of African Americans who have been told by a predominantly white society that they are inferior reverberate in the voices of city students as they tell us they are afraid of not being accepted in a suburban school or of not being able to compete with the white students in these schools. In a survey of African-American tenth-graders from the city of St. Louis attending nonintegrated, integrated, magnet, and suburban schools, Lissitz (1994) found that students in the nonintegrated or all-black city schools are much less likely to agree with the following statements than are students who transfer to a suburban school:

1. Going to school with members of another race will help prepare me for life.
2. A student of another race could be my friend.
3. All racial groups are equally worthwhile.

These racial attitudes, coupled with the alienation of city students and their parents from the county and its suburban school districts, play a significant role in the school processes of these families and their decision not to cross the color line.

. . .

The city parents' sometimes contradictory responses to questions of likes and dislikes about the city schools and the lack of involvement in their children's choice of schools suggest a high level of alienation or powerlessness, which Seeman (1959) has described as the "expectancy or probability held by an individual that his own behavior cannot determine the occurrence of the outcomes, or reinforcements, he seeks" (1959,

p. 784). Like West's (1993a) more recent conception of nihilism in the isolated inner-city neighborhoods, notions of alienation and powerlessness help to explain why city parents, with the exception of Leo's mother, do not view themselves as important actors in shaping the educational outcomes of their children.

Expressions of these parents' beliefs in their own powerlessness are sprinkled throughout their responses to questions concerning the city's schools and their children's education: "I don't know a heck of a lot about it," "I don't know what to say; I can't think about it," "I don't know; I can't speak to that." These are juxtaposed with several positive comments that these parents have heard about the county schools from parents who send their children there: "Better curriculum and more attention," "Children learn more and better in the county than in the city," and "They don't want their kids to be around a lot of fighting." Only two city parents—Chandra's mother and Leo's mother—even suggested that such positive appraisals of the county schools are false or exaggerated. When asked how the city schools compare to the county schools, seven of the eleven city parents stated that they did not know enough about the county schools to draw a comparison.

Another example of the level of alienation experienced by these parents is their eager adoption of a can-achieve-anywhere philosophy—the notion that the particular school does not matter and that academic success is entirely up to the student. Seven of the city parents we interviewed expressed some form of this philosophy, which helps to explain their lack of involvement in the school-choice process and their lack of information about the transfer program: "If the child wants to learn he can do it anywhere," "It's up to the child, not the school," and "I left it up to her to succeed. . . . [She] can achieve in city schools as well as county."

While this ideology is supposed to motivate children to try harder in school, it also allows parents to absolve themselves of the weighty responsibility of helping their son or daughter choose the "best" school. The process of gathering information, evaluating one school against another, and making an active decision about the educational options available is one that these parents have not engaged in since the transfer plan created greater school choices for them and their children. Ignoring the transfer program and leaving school choice decisions to their children is one way of dealing with the feeling of powerlessness. Except for Leo's mother, who is determined that her son will not be subjected to the racism and unfair treatment that she is certain exists in the suburban schools, these parents are too beat down to take an active stance. Meanwhile, their children are choosing to remain in the schools in which they feel most comfortable and familiar.

Another sign of the city parents' powerlessness and seeming helplessness is found in their responses to questions concerning their expectations for their children. For instance, when asked what they would like for their son or daughter to be doing in five years, four parents stated that they either "didn't know" or would leave that entirely up to the student to decide—"I can't pick for her." Three additional parents gave such general answers as "Working—on her own," "See him stand on his own two feet," and "To be an upstanding young man—get ahead."

The remaining parents were slightly more specific, with all four speaking of college. Leo's mother stated that she "knew" what her son would be doing in five years: "He will be graduating from college with an engineering degree." Chandra's mother said that she hopes her daughter will be "coming out of college." Casey's mother said her son will need to go into the service to "get that college" because she cannot afford to send him. And Erin's father wanted his daughter to be finished with college and "on her own" in five years.

Yet when asked whether their child's city high school was preparing their son or daughter for that future, only two of the parents—Venicia's mother and Erin's father—answered with an affirmative yes. Troy's mother said, "Yeah, they have nice teachers." Six parents said, "I think so," "I don't know," "It's hard to tell," or "I can't answer that." Leo's mother and Kally's stepmother said that the city high school was not preparing their son or daughter for the future. Leo's mother said that she and her husband were paying to send their son to a special blueprint class because it was not offered at his school. According to her, Northwest High School is not preparing Leo for his career as an engineer, "his parents are."

Related to the powerlessness expressed by the city parents were their racial attitudes, reflected in their opinions of city-versus-county schools. Many of these parents told us they thought mostly white schools are better than all-black schools and that white students are generally smarter than black students. School desegregation is a good thing, according to these parents, but it will work only for the very "smart" black students. For the rest of the African-American students the city schools are perceived to be good enough.

Salina's grandmother said she worried about what will happen to Salina, who has been classified as a high school junior for three years in a row and is receiving no guidance from the school about her future. Meanwhile, one of her daughters sends her son, Salina's cousin, to a county school because "he's real smart." The grandmother says he likes the county school and has excelled there academically and athletically. When asked whether she thought it was better for African-American students from the city to attend county schools, she nodded. "I just think it's not as loud in the county schools—it's more

like Catholic schools. There's more time for learning." But for Salina, who loves babies and likes to take care of them at her church each Sunday, the grandmother never considered a county school—"Never thought about it," she said, "because of her not being real smart."

Manny's father expressed a similar sentiment toward the county schools and his son's ability to succeed there. He said he would not have dared send Manny to a county school because his grades in the city schools were not strong enough. He also said that Summer High School would be a lot better if it were "mixed" or integrated. He said that is why he sent two of his children to private schools when they were younger: "The teachers were Caucasian and the board was mixed." He adds that "most Caucasian people I have been around are very serious about family," and he wishes more blacks were that way.

This deprecation of their own children or grandchildren and of blacks in general is also accounted for in research on poor people and members of oppressed racial groups; it is a perspective that grows out of years of being treated as the other or as less than wealthier people or members of higher-status racial or religious groups (see, for instance, Bourdieu and Passeron 1979, and West 1993b). In other words, this deprecation is part of the self-fulfilling prophecy of racial prejudice, which indicates that blacks have been told overtly and covertly for so many years that they are inferior to whites that some have come to believe it and even accommodate society's expectations by playing the part (Snyder 1988).

When asked about the benefits of an all-black school, seven of the city parents said that they either did not know or did not think there would be any benefits. "It's just a school," said Venicia's mother. "All black, that's about the size of it," said Manny's father. Mildly positive reactions came from Casey's mother, who said that being in an all-black school could keep her son out of trouble, and Paulette's mother, who said that the benefit of an all-black school is that her daughter is "adjusted to her color, her race." Yet when asked about the benefits of an integrated school, Paulette's mother said her daughter "would learn to adjust herself to black and white." A cost-benefit analysis of an all-black versus an integrated school and the ramifications of each choice had clearly not been conducted by any of the city parents except Leo's mother.

As the one parent who stands out from the rest when it comes to the impact of racial attitudes on school choices, Leo's mother maintains a firm separatist attitude that reflects her resistance to African-American assimilation into a white world. The benefit of an all-black school, she states emphatically, is that "my baby will know who he is." She adds that black people are "crazy to ship" their children out to the county. "Black folk used to get educated in a dark shack. Why do they have to sit next to white folk to get an education? . . . Many of the people who moved out there [to the county] did so because they did not want to live next to blacks." Why, Leo's mother wants to know, would black parents send their children out to schools full of white students whose parents fled the city and the African Americans who live there. "If there were true integration," she adds, "for every black student who goes out there [to a suburban school], they should have a white student come in here."

Because she taught at Northwest High School, Leo's mother was fully aware of the school's shortcomings. Yet, instead of blaming the black students for the decline of the city schools, she faults the racial politics of the St. Louis Board of Education for allowing the county schools and the city's magnet schools to cream off the best students or those with the most involved parents, leaving the all-black schools on the city's north side with few resources and many of the

hardest to educate students. "All of the problems I have with this school are the result of Board of Ed policy." She noted, for instance, that many of the long fluorescent light bulbs in her classroom were burned out for as long as five years before she got them changed. The Board of Education has hired only twelve electricians to service the more than 100 school buildings in the district. "The all-black schools are deliberately allowed to fall down while the magnet schools look gorgeous," she said. Leo's mother has a clear vision of the causes of decline in the black community: racial discrimination and the politics that endorse it.

City Students: Comfort and Hopelessness

The city students, while perhaps not as shy as their parents, were more defensive than either the transfer or return students when talking to a white interviewer about their neighborhood high school and the transfer program. This is probably to be expected in a discussion of black versus predominantly white schools between a white researcher and black students who chose to remain in all-black schools, but some of these students appeared very uneasy and uncertain. Others seemed swallowed up in hopelessness. They, like many of their parents, argued that it didn't really matter where they went to school. Yet what is most striking about the city students and their discussions of why they choose to stay in their neighborhood schools is the degree to which they are attracted to that which is familiar and comfortable.

. . .

[T]he city students who stated what they dislike about their high schools were focused on factors that make their daily school experience less pleasant, especially the actions of their fellow students. Three students—Venicia, Kally, and Paulette, all of whom attended Northwest High School and live in the same middle-class neighborhood—cited the fighting and the juvenile behavior of students as the aspect they disliked the most about their school. "They act like they was eleven years old," said Paulette of her classmates. Several city students mentioned that the students at their schools do not respect the teachers.

Still, students . . . defend their decisions not to transfer with the can-achieve-anywhere philosophy voiced by many of the city parents. "There are a lot of honors students at Northwest; if you want to learn—you got the ability, you will," [Venicia] said. Yet when asked why some black students from the city choose to transfer to county schools, Venicia explained, "Maybe it's more advanced to them than the public [city] schools. Maybe they think there are more computers or they can learn a little more . . . , maybe they don't think the public school teachers will teach them enough. . . . I wouldn't want to teach them either."

. . .

Meanwhile, most of the city students we interviewed said that black students who want to go to county schools are doing the right thing by transferring. "I have no disagreement with kids who go to the county," said Salina. "They should have the freedom to go wherever they want to." Other responses to the question of whether transfer students are doing the right thing contained hints of defensiveness and insecurity on the part of city students. "If they think they can handle it, they should go," said Venicia. According to Chandra, "They're just trying to show off. They are not better."

The extent to which racial attitudes and a fear of competing with whites affect the city students' perceptions of comfortable and uncomfortable territory is obvious in Salina's fear of not being able to understand what is

not taught in a county school. This suggests that she feels less knowledgeable than the mostly white students in county schools. As Bourdieu and Passeron (1979) might posit, Salina fears she does not have the "cultural capital" needed to succeed in an upper-middle-class, predominantly white school.

When asked the more general questions of "What are the benefits of going to an all-black school?" and "What are the benefits of going to an integrated school?" city students revealed their racial attitudes. Seven responded by either criticizing all-black schools or blacks in general:

VENICIA: There isn't any benefit—any benefit at all; it's just an all-black school.
KALLY: It's good because when they [black students] get around other people—white persons—they pick on white kids. When they get around white persons, they get worse. . . . I'm a good person, the rest are like animals.
CHANDRA: The teachers teach real well—just students, they don't want to learn—they be carrying on and partying too much.
GWENN: None. When us black people get together, we don't know how to act. We try to appear more than ourselves when with our own kind.

Only two of the city students had anything remotely positive to say about all-black schools. Leo said that at all-black schools there are fewer problems with racial tension. Manny noted that in all-black schools students have a good chance of getting into a nice college because they have better opportunities for receiving financial aid. The remaining three city students made rather benign comments about the "benefits" of an all-black school, such as, "It's close to home" and "All-black or all-white, it shouldn't matter."

Furthermore, two of the city students' responses to the question concerning the benefits of going to a racially mixed school indicate a sense of racial inferiority and insecurity. Salina, for instance, said the benefit of going to an integrated school is that "whites are more mature. Black students play in the halls, skip class." Angie stated that she would like to go to a "mixed" school but added, "I don't know how they would react to me."

Meanwhile, four of the city students referred to the importance of integration and improved race relations as a benefit of attending an integrated school:

VENICIA: Maybe you could learn more about each other's culture. How they grew up, the things they know—how we grew up, the things we know.
LEO: You learn to relate with other races better.
CASEY: Being able to interact with different races and know kids from suburbs.
GWENN: Be better dealing with many different types of people—that's about it.

These responses to questions pertaining to race and school choice suggest that many of these students who remain in all-black schools buy into the notion that white schools in general are superior to all-black ones. But they have chosen for themselves the schools that are more safe, comfortable, and perhaps less challenging. This finding causes us to wonder whether the level of alienation from the larger, whiter world that was exhibited by their parents has been passed down to the next generation.

Choosing Not to Choose

The evidence cited here paints a portrait of twelve black students who end up in all-black inner-city schools for several reasons that have nothing to do with the quality of education offered. Many are the children of tired, beat down parents who have not actively investigated the educational options.

They often come from homes where day-to-day survival taps so much energy that little is left for gathering information on schools of choice. They attend city schools because the schools are close to their homes and host many familiar faces.

In other words, most of these city students attend their neighborhood schools because their parents never said they could not. Their parents, for the most part, do not feel capable of making major educational decisions for their children. And the result is the choice not to choose. When parents left the choice to the students, the students followed the path of least resistance. This is not the story of self-maximizing families who have evaluated their options and their long-term goals and decided that a city school would serve their needs better than a county school. Empowerment did not result from a voluntary transfer plan, because the lack of power that these families experience is embedded in several aspects of their social and economic lives. Offering these students the choice of higher-status schools will not free them from the fear and insecurity they face in a world that places them at the bottom of the social structure.

NOTES

1. Throughout the . . . chapter we refer to the African-American students who remain in the all-black city schools as "city students." The African-American students who have transferred out of the city to one of the suburban school districts and remained enrolled in those schools are referred to as "transfer students." The African-American students who have attended a suburban school at some point but who are no longer participating in the transfer program are referred to as "return students."
2. Nearly all of the African-American parents and students we interviewed refer to the St. Louis public schools as simply "public" schools—as opposed to city schools—and the schools in the suburbs as "county" schools, as though the urban schools were public and the suburban schools were not.

REFERENCES

BOURDIEU, P. 1984. *Distinction.* Cambridge, MA: Harvard University Press.

BOURDIEU, P. AND J. PASSERON. 1979. *The Inheritors: French Students and Their Relation to Culture.* Translated by R. Nice. Chicago: University of Chicago.

CHUBB, J. E. AND T. M. MOE. 1990. *Politics, Markets, and America's Schools.* Washington DC: Brookings Institution.

COMER, J. P. 1980. *School Power: Implications of an Intervention Project.* New York: Free Press.

EPSTEIN, J. L. 1990. "School and Family Connections: Theory, Research, and Implications for Integrating Sociologies of Education and Family." Pp. 99–126 in *Families in Community Settings: Interdisciplinary Perspectives,* edited by D. G. Unger and M. B. Sussman. New York: Haworth.

LISSITZ, R. W. December 1994. *Assessment of Student Performance and Attitude Year IV—1994: St. Louis Metropolitan Area Court Ordered Desegregation Effort.* Report submitted to the Voluntary Interdistrict Coordinating Council. St. Louis: Voluntary Interdistrict Coordinating Council.

SEEMAN, M. 1959. "On the Meaning of Alienation." *American Sociological Review* 24:783–91.

———. 1972. "Alienation and Knowledge-Seeking: A Note on Attitude and Action." *Social Problems* 20:3–17.

SNYDER, M. 1988. "Self-Fulfilling Stereotypes." In *Racism and Sexism: An Integrated Study,* edited by P. S. Rothenberg. New York: St. Martin's Press.

WEST, C. 1993a. *Race Matters.* Boston: Beacon.

———. 1993b. "The New Cultural Politics of Difference." In *Race Identity and Representation in Education,* edited by C. McCarthy and W. Crichlow. New York: Routledge.

WITTE, J. F., A. B. BAILY, AND C. A. THORN. 1993. *Third-Year Report: Milwaukee Parental Choice Program.* Madison: Department of Political Science and The Robert La Follette Institute of Public Affairs, University of Wisconsin.

29

AMERICA'S NEXT ACHIEVEMENT TEST
Closing the Black–White Test Score Gap

Christopher Jencks • Meredith Phillips

African Americans currently score lower than European Americans on vocabulary, reading, and math tests, as well as on tests that claim to measure scholastic aptitude and intelligence. This gap appears before children enter kindergarten, and it persists into adulthood. It has narrowed since 1970, but the median American black still scores below 75 percent of American whites on most standardized tests. On some tests the typical American black scores below more than 85 percent of whites.

The black–white test score gap does not appear to be an inevitable fact of nature. It is true that the gap shrinks only a little when black and white children attend the same schools. It is also true that the gap shrinks only a little when black and white families have the same amount of schooling, the same income, and the same wealth. But despite endless speculation, no one has found genetic evidence indicating that blacks have less innate intellectual ability than whites. Thus while it is clear that eliminating the test score gap would require enormous effort by both blacks and whites and would probably take more than one generation, we believe it can be done. This conviction—supported at greater length in the new collection of studies we have edited, *The Black–White Test Score Gap*, . . . published by the Brookings Institution—rests mainly on three facts:

• *IQ and achievement scores are sensitive to environmental change.* Scores on nonverbal IQ tests have risen dramatically throughout the world since the 1930s. The average white scored higher on the Stanford–Binet test in 1978 than 82 percent of whites who took the test in 1932.

• *Black–white differences in academic achievement have also narrowed throughout the twentieth century.* The best trend data come from the National Assessment of Educational Progress (NAEP), which has been testing seventeen-year-olds since 1971 and has repeated many of the same items year after year. From 1971 to 1996, the black–white reading gap shrank by almost half and the math gap by a third. . . . According to a study by two sociologists, Min-Hsiung Huang and Robert Hauser, the black–white vocabulary gap also shrank by half among adults born between 1909 and 1969.

• *When black or mixed-race children are raised in white rather than black homes, their preadolescent test scores rise dramatically.* Black adoptees' scores seem to fall in adolescence, but this is what we would expect if, as seems likely, their social and cultural environment comes to resemble that of other black adolescents and becomes less like that of the average white adolescent.

Why Test Scores Matter

In a country as racially polarized as the United States, no single change taken in isolation could possibly eliminate the entire legacy of slavery and Jim Crow or usher in an era of full racial equality. But if racial equality is America's goal, reducing the black–white test score gap would probably do more to promote this goal than any other strategy that could command broad political support. Reducing the test score gap is probably both necessary and sufficient for substantially reducing racial inequality in educational attainment and earnings. Changes in education and earnings would in turn help reduce racial differences in crime, health, and family structure, although we do not know how large these effects would be.

This judgment contradicts the conclusion of *Inequality*, a study published in 1972 by one of us (Christopher Jencks), which argued that reducing cognitive inequality would not do much to reduce economic inequality. The reason for the contradiction is simple: the world has changed. In 1972, the best evidence about what happened to black workers with high test scores came from a study by Phillips Cutright, who had analyzed the 1964 earnings of men in their thirties who had taken the Armed Forces Qualification Test (AFQT) between 1949 and 1953. Overall, employed black men earned 57.5 percent of what whites earned. Among men with AFQT scores above the national average, black men earned 64.5 percent of what whites earned. In such a world, eliminating racial differences in test performance did not seem likely to reduce the earnings gap very much.

Today's world is different. The best recent data on test scores and earnings come from the National Longitudinal Survey of Youth (NLSY), which gave the Armed Services Vocational Aptitude Battery to a national sample of young people in 1980. Among employed men who were 31 to 36 years old in 1993, blacks earned 67.5 percent of what whites earned—a modest but significant improvement over the situation in 1964. The big change occurred among blacks with test scores near or above the white average. Among men who scored between the thirtieth and forty-ninth percentiles nationally, black earnings rose from 62 to 84 percent of the white average. Among men who scored above the fiftieth percentile, black earnings rose from 65 to 96 percent of the white average. [See "More-Equal Scores Now Bring More-Equal Earnings." Figure 29.1] In this new world, raising black workers' test scores looks far more important than it did in the 1960s.

Some skeptics have argued that scores on tests of this kind are really just proxies for family background. Family background does affect test performance. If we compare random pairs of children, their IQ scores differ by an average of 17 points. Among pairs of children who have been adopted into the same family, the difference averages about 15 points. Even if we compare pairs of biological siblings reared in the same family, their IQ scores still differ by an average of 12 or 13 points. The claim that test scores are only a proxy for family background is therefore false. Furthermore, test score differences between siblings raised in the same family have sizable effects on their educational attain-

ment and earnings. Thus while it is true that eliminating the black–white test score gap would not eliminate the black–white earnings gap, the effect would surely be substantial.

Reducing the black–white test score gap would reduce racial disparities in educational attainment as well as earnings. The nationwide "High School and Beyond" survey tested twelfth graders in 1982 and followed them up in 1992, when they were in their late twenties. At the time of the follow-up only 13.3 percent of the blacks had earned a bachelor's degree, compared to 30 percent of the non-Hispanic whites. Many observers blame this disparity on black parents' inability to pay college bills, black students' lack of motivation, or the hostility that black students encounter on predominantly white college campuses. All these factors probably play some role. Nonetheless, when we compare blacks and whites with the same twelfth-grade test scores, blacks are *more* likely than whites to complete college. Once we equalize test scores, High School and Beyond blacks' 16.7-point disadvantage in college graduation rates turns into a 5.9-point advantage.

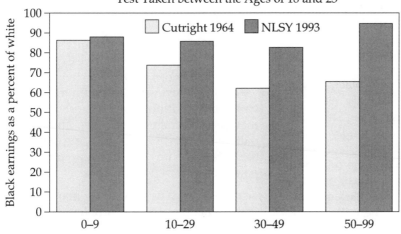

Ratio of Black to White Annual Earnings in 1964 and 1993 for Employed Men in Their Early Thirties, by Percentile Score on a Military Test Taken between the Ages of 18 and 23

FIGURE 29.1 More-Equal Scores Now Bring More-Equal Earnings
Sources: Cutright and authors' quotations from the National Longitudinal Survey of Youth (NLSY). Cutright's version of the AFQT included vocabulary, arithmetic, and societal relations. Our NLSY appropriation of Cutright's AFQT included world knowledge, numerical operations, and mechanical reasoning. See our introduction to *The Black–White Test Score Gap* for details on the samples and standard errors.

Eliminating racial differences in test performance would also allow colleges, professional schools, and employers to phase out the racial preferences that have caused so much political trouble over the past generation. If selective colleges based their admission decisions solely on applicants' predicted college grades, their undergraduate enrollment would currently be 96 or 97 percent white and Asian. To avoid this, almost all selective colleges and professional schools admit African Americans and Hispanics whom they would not admit if they were white. If selective colleges could achieve racial diversity without making race an explicit factor in their admission decisions, blacks would do better in college and whites would nurse fewer political grudges.

Advocates of racial equality might be more willing to accept our argument that narrowing the test score gap is crucial to achieving their goals if they believed that narrowing the gap was really feasible. But pessimism on this front has become almost universal. In the 1960s, racial egalitarians routinely blamed the test score gap on the combined effects of black poverty, racial segregation, and inadequate funding for black schools. That analysis implied obvious solutions: raise black children's family income, desegregate their schools, and equalize spending on schools that remain racially segregated. All these steps still look useful, but none has made as much difference as optimists expected in the early 1960s.

- The number of affluent black parents has grown substantially since the 1960s, but their children's test scores still lag far behind those of white children from equally affluent families. Income inequality between blacks and whites appears to play some role in the test score gap, but it is quite small.
- Most southern schools desegregated in the early 1970s, and southern black nine-

year-olds' reading scores seem to have risen as a result. Even today, black third graders in predominantly white schools read better than initially similar blacks who have attended predominantly black schools. But large racial differences in reading skills persist even in desegregated schools, and a school's racial mix has little effect on reading scores after sixth grade or on math scores at any age.

- Despite glaring economic inequalities between a few rich suburbs and nearby central cities, the average black child and the average white child now live in school districts that spend almost exactly the same amount per pupil. Black and white schools also have the same average number of teachers per pupil, the same pay scales, and teachers with almost the same amount of formal education and teaching experience. The most important resource difference between black and white schools seems to be that both black and white teachers in black schools have lower test scores than their counterparts in white schools.

For all these reasons, the number of people who think they know how to eliminate racial differences in test performance has shrunk steadily since the mid-1960s. While many people still think the traditional liberal remedies would help, few now believe they would suffice.

Demoralization among liberals has given new legitimacy to conservative explanations for the test score gap. From an empirical viewpoint, however, the traditional conservative explanations are no more appealing than their liberal counterparts. These explanations fall into three overlapping categories: the culture of poverty, the scarcity of two-parent black families, and genes.

- In the 1960s and 1970s many conservatives blamed blacks' problems on a culture of poverty that rejected school achievement, the work ethic, and the two-parent family in favor of instant gratification and episodic violence. In the 1980s conservatives (as well as some liberals) characterized the "black underclass" in similar terms. But this description fits only a tiny fraction of the black population. It certainly cannot explain why children from affluent black families have much lower test scores than their white counterparts.

• Conservatives invoke the decline of the family to explain social problems almost as frequently as liberals invoke poverty. But once we control for a mother's family background, test scores, and years of schooling, whether she is married has even less effect on her children's test scores than whether she is poor.

• Scientists have not yet identified many of the genes that affect test performance, so we have no genetic evidence regarding innate cognitive differences between blacks and whites. But we have accumulated a fair amount of indirect evidence since 1970. Most of it suggests that whether children live in a "black" or "white" environment has far more impact on their test performance than the number of Africans or Europeans in their family tree. . . .

Culture and Schooling

Taken as a whole, then, what we have characterized as the "traditional" explanations for the black–white test score gap do not take us very far. This has led some people to dismiss the gap as unimportant, arguing that the tests are culturally biased and do not measure skills that matter in the real world. Few scholars who spend time looking at quantitative data like that in [Figure 29.1] accept either of these arguments, so they have had to look for new explanations of the gap. These new explanations can mostly be grouped under two overlapping headings: schooling and culture.

Social scientists' thinking about "school effects" has changed substantially since the late 1960s. The 1966 Coleman Report and subsequent studies convinced most economists and quantitative sociologists (including Jencks) that school resources had little impact on achievement. Since 1990, however, new statistical methods, new data, and a handful of genuine experiments have suggested that additional resources may in fact have sizable effects on student achievement. The notion that resources matter cannot in itself explain the black–white achievement gap, because most school resources are now fairly equally distributed between blacks and whites. But certain crucial resources, like teachers with high test scores, are still quite unequally distributed. And other resources, like small classes and teachers with high expectations, may help blacks more than whites.

Equally important is the fact that predominantly black schools enroll far more children with severe academic and behavioral problems than white schools do. Such children consume many times more resources than the average child. To begin with, they are often assigned to very small classes (for the "educably mentally retarded," for example). In addition, schools where many children have serious academic, emotional, or disciplinary problems need more reading specialists, more psychologists, and more security guards. That leaves less money for regular teachers. Finally, children with serious problems consume a disproportionate share of their teachers' time when they are in regular classes, leaving less time for other students. The net result is that while predominantly black schools spend about as much per pupil as predominantly white schools, ordinary black children without special problems are likely to be in larger classes, get less attention, and have less academically skilled teachers than similar white children.

Nonetheless, disparities between black and white schools cannot explain why black children enter preschool with smaller vocabularies than white children. This fact must reflect differences between black and white children's experiences before they enter school. While racial disparities in income, parental education, family size, and the like explain some of the test score gap among preschool children, they do not explain most of it. That fact has forced many scholars to take cultural explanations more seriously.

In the late 1960s and early 1970s, many liberals and radicals dismissed cultural explanations of the test score gap as an effort to put down blacks for not thinking and acting like upper-middle-class whites. Since then, cultural explanations have enjoyed a slow but steady revival. In 1978, the Nigerian anthropologist John Ogbu suggested that caste-like minorities throughout the world tended to do poorly in school, even when they were visually indistinguishable from the majority. Later, Ogbu made this argument more specific, suggesting that because of their caste-like status, blacks developed an "oppositional" culture that equated academic success with "acting white." By linking black culture directly to oppression, Ogbu made it much easier for liberals to talk about cultural differences. Jeff Howard and Ray Hammond added another important strand to this argument when they suggested that academic competence develops partly through competition, and that "rumors of inferiority" make blacks reluctant to compete in the academic arena. More recently, Claude Steele has argued that people of all races avoid situations in which they expect others to have negative stereotypes about them, even when they know that the stereotype does not apply. According to Steele, many

black students "disidentify" with school because constructing a personal identity based on academic competence entails a commitment to dealing with such stereotypes on a daily basis. In a series of elegant experiments with Stanford students, Steele has also shown that merely asking test-takers to report their race or telling them that a test measures intellectual ability lowers black students' scores.

Cutright's 1964 finding that blacks with high test scores earned little more than those with low test scores may also help explain why blacks did so badly on these tests. In an economy where high-scoring blacks had very limited job opportunities, few blacks had any reason to suppose that they would win anyone's respect by acquiring a larger vocabulary, better mathematical skills, or more information about science, history, and literature. As we have seen . . . , the world has changed since 1964. But it always takes several generations for any group to adjust to a new reality, especially when the adjustment has significant costs (spending more time studying). The message that nerds will do well as adults is always hard to sell to children, but it is doubly hard to sell when it has only recently become true.

Can We Explain More of the Gap?

The available evidence shows that traditional explanations for the black–white test score gap do not work very well. If genes play any role, it is probably quite small. Poverty probably plays some role, but it too is modest. School desegregation probably reduced the black–white gap in the South during the 1970s, and desegregating northern elementary schools might raise blacks' reading scores today, but the gain would not be huge. Reducing class size in the early grades would probably raise scores more for blacks than whites, and reducing class size in later grades might help preserve these black gains, although this latter conclusion is based on conjecture rather than firm evidence. Screening teachers for verbal and mathematical competence (or raising the competence of those already employed) is also likely to raise black children's scores.

The United States should be conducting large-scale experiments aimed at reducing uncertainty about the effects of schools' racial mix, class size, teachers' test scores, ability grouping, and many other policies. We do such experiments to determine the effects of different medical treatments, different job training programs, and many other social interventions. But the U.S. Department of Education, which should in principle be funding experiments from which every state and school district would benefit, has shown almost no interest in this approach to advancing knowledge. The most important piece of educational research in the past generation, the Tennessee class size experiment, showed that small classes in the early grades made a big difference, especially for blacks—yet it was funded by the Tennessee legislature, not the U.S. Department of Education. Experimental assessments of other educational policies that have a major impact on school spending—salary levels, teacher selection systems, education for the physically and mentally disabled, and bilingual education, for example—have been almost nonexistent.

If we did more experiments, we might eventually develop better theories. At present, theorizing about the causes of the black–white gap is largely a waste of time, because there is no way to resolve theoretical disagreements without data that both sides accept as valid. Most theories about human behavior start out as hunches, anecdotes, or ideological predispositions. Such theories improve only when they have to confront evidence that the theorist cannot control. In education, that seldom happens.

Our best guess is that successful new theories about the causes of the black–white gap will differ from traditional theories in at least three ways:

• Instead of looking mainly for resource differences between predominantly black and predominantly white schools, successful theories will concentrate on differences in the way black and white schools spend the resources available to them—differences that probably derive in large part from the disproportionate number of black children with severe academic or psychological problems, but that probably prevent ordinary black children in the same schools from getting as much attention and support as their counterparts in white schools.

• Instead of concentrating on whether teachers treat black and white children differently, successful theories will probably pay more attention to the way black and white children respond to the same classroom experiences, such as having a teacher of a different race or having a teacher with low expectations for students who read below grade level.

• Instead of emphasizing families' economic and educational resources, successful theories will probably pay more attention to the way family members and friends interact with one another and with the outside world. A good explanation of why white four-year-olds have bigger vocabularies than black four-year-olds is likely to focus on how much parents talk to their children, how they deal with their children's questions, and how they react when their children either learn or fail to learn something, not on how much money the parents have in the bank.

· · ·

Gender

30

WHY DOES JANE READ AND WRITE SO WELL?
The Anomaly of Women's Achievement

Roslyn Arlin Mickelson

The evidence is in and the conclusion is clear: Women can and do achieve academically as well as do men. The myth of female under-achievement has been exposed by many studies that have indicated that women's motivation and behavior to achieve not only equal but often surpass that of men (Klein 1985; Maccoby and Jacklin 1974; National Center for Educational Statistics 1986; Stockard 1985; Stockard and Wood 1984; U.S. Bureau of the Census 1987). Today, as in the past, more girls than boys graduate from high school and more women than men receive baccalaureate degrees, and nationwide, women now outnumber men in master's degree programs. More men than women are enrolled only in professional and Ph.D. programs, but even here, the gaps between women and men are closing (National Center for Educational Statistics 1986; Stockard et al. 1980). Fields of specialization continue to be gender linked—mathematics, engineering, and the physical and biologi-

cal sciences are dominated by males, and the social sciences and humanities are dominated by females—but evidence from a study of undergraduates indicates that differences are disappearing here, too (Hafner and Shaha 1984).

If the picture of women's achievement and attainment is so positive, why do educators and researchers pay so much attention to the subject? One obvious answer lies in the different areas of achievement. Because high-paying careers (those with the best pay, benefits, working conditions, and career ladders) usually require strong backgrounds in mathematics and science, the fact that women continue to lag behind men in these areas is important. A second answer involves the links among schooling, work, and income. Even though women have all but closed the overall gap in educational attainment between the sexes, the occupational world fails to reward women equitably for their accomplishments. Research suggests strongly that the inequalities faced by women in the occupational world cannot be linked, except in the most tenuous ways, to differences in educational achievement and attainment (Stockard 1985:320).

The issue of structural inequality in the work world raises another question that is the focus of this [chapter]. In view of the limited rewards that women are likely to receive from education, why do they do as well and attain as much education as they do? In this society, in which educational credentials purportedly are linked to jobs, promotions, wages, and status, women's educational accomplishments appear anomalous because women continue to receive far fewer rewards for their educational credentials than do men with comparable credentials. One might expect that if women knew of the diminished opportunities that lay ahead, they would put less effort into school because these efforts are likely to yield smaller returns to them than to males who make similar efforts. Yet, this is not the case. This [chapter] explores why gender stratification in the opportunity structure appears to be of little relevance to young women's academic achievement and attainment. It examines the anomaly of females' achievement in light of four hypotheses and presents empirical evidence to assess each hypothesis.

Basis of the Anomaly

The academic achievement of female students is a curious reversal of a dynamic found among minority and working-class students. A study conducted by the author in 1983 indicated that both working-class and minority youths underachieve, in part, because of the poor returns they are likely to receive from education (Mickelson 1984, 1990). This research was inspired largely by the work of Ogbu (1979), which examined the American opportunity structure and its possible influence on the scholastic achievement of minority students. Ogbu argued that members of a social group that faces a job ceiling know that they do so, and this knowledge channels and shapes their children's academic behavior. The term "job ceil-

ing" refers to overt and informal practices that limit members of castelike minority groups (such as blacks and Chicanos) from unrestricted competition for the jobs for which they are qualified. Members of these groups are excluded from or not allowed to obtain their proportionate share of desirable jobs and hence are overwhelmingly confined to the least desirable jobs in the occupational structure. Ogbu contended that because the job ceiling faced by black adults prevents them from receiving rewards that are commensurate with their educational credentials, education is not the same bridge to adult status for blacks as it is for whites. Black children see that efforts in school often do not have the same outcomes for them as do similar efforts for members of socially dominant groups, such as middle-class white men. Thus, they tend to put less effort and commitment into their schoolwork and hence perform less well, on average, than do middle-class white youths. As Ogbu (1979:193) stated:

> I think their perception of the job ceiling is still a major factor that colors [minority] attitudes and school performance. . . . Given the premise that what motivates Americans to maximize their achievement efforts in school is their belief that the better education one has, the more money and more status [one will acquire] . . . . is it logical to expect Blacks and Whites to exert the same energy and perform alike in school when the job ceiling consistently underutilizes the black talent and ability and underrewards Blacks for their education?

The author's study tested Ogbu's thesis on minority underachievement but expanded the research to include class and gender—two additional social forces that are strongly related to differential occupational returns on education—by examining students' attitudes toward education in relation to their high school grades. In 1983, 1,193 seniors in nine comprehensive public high schools in the Los Angeles area completed a questionnaire that ascertained their attitudes toward education, family background, and educational and occupational aspirations, as well as various measures of school outcomes. The results showed that all students hold two sets of attitudes toward education, but only one set predicts their achievement in school. The first set of attitudes is composed of beliefs about education and opportunity, as found in the dominant ideology of U.S. society. These attitudes, which the author calls *abstract* attitudes toward education, embody the Protestant Ethic's promise that schooling is a vehicle for upward mobility and success (for example, "Education is the key to success in the future"). These beliefs are widely shared and vary little at this level of abstraction. Abstract attitudes, therefore, cannot predict achievement behavior. The second set of beliefs about education consists of *concrete* attitudes, which reflect the diverse material realities that people experience with regard to returns on education from the opportunity structure ("Based on their experiences, my parents say people like us are not always paid or promoted according to our education"). Agreement or disagreement with statements of concrete attitudes closely follow class and racial divisions in society. The overall findings indicate that concrete attitudes, not abstract ones, predict achievement in high school (see Mickelson 1990 for a complete presentation of the research).

This research demonstrates that the effort that students put into their schoolwork and their academic achievement is influenced by students' accurate assessments of the class- and race-linked occupational returns their education is likely to bring them as they make the transition to adulthood. It suggests that middle-class white youths correctly interpret their parents' experiences in the labor market as evidence that they, too,

can expect returns commensurate with their educational attainment; therefore, it is not surprising that they generally earn high grades and are likely to attend college. Following this same logic, working-class and black youths put less effort into their schoolwork because they judge that for people like themselves, the payoffs for schooling are limited; hence, they receive lower grades and go to college less often than do middle-class whites (Mickelson 1984, 1990).

Consequently, individuals who are reasonably aware of the realities of the opportunity structure that lie ahead should put more effort or less effort into schoolwork, depending on the occupational returns they are likely to receive. It is in this context that the achievement and attainment of females appear anomalous. If occupational opportunities help shape students' educational goals and achievements, as Ogbu and this author believe, women should not achieve as well or attain as much education as do men in comparable racial and class subgroups.

Yet women do not achieve as one might predict on the basis of gender inequalities in the opportunity structure. In other words, the relatively poor occupational return on educational investments does not appear to depress either their school performance or their willingness to earn advanced degrees. The anomaly considered in this article, then, is not "Why can't Jane read and write?" because she certainly does, but "Why does Jane read and write so well?"

Extent of the Anomaly

To capture the anomalous quality of women's educational achievement in light of the gender-linked job ceiling women face, the following discussion reviews the research on women's educational and occupational outcomes, with special attention to racial and class variations in each. It is important to note that most sociological studies, including those that compare the educational attainment of blacks and whites, tended, until recently, either to ignore women or to treat them as persons whose social status was a function of their father's or husband's positions (Acker 1973, 1980; Bernard 1981; Oakley 1974). Turner's (1964) was a classic study in this tradition; it measured women's goals and ambitions by the occupation they expected their husbands to attain. During the past two decades, however, many social scientists have turned their attention to women's unique experiences in achievement, education, and the labor market. It is these studies that are reviewed in this section.

Academic Achievement

Differences in the academic achievement of males and females involve issues of both performance and motivation. Differences in performance are mediated by age and by type of cognitive activity (Kaufman and Richardson 1982). For example, girls generally do better in school until puberty (Klein 1985). The new learning climate of the junior high school, which is more competitive and more individualistic than is the elementary school, works against girls' strengths, such as working cooperatively in groups (Eccles and Hoffman 1985; Steinkamp and Maehr 1984). Although the grade-point averages of boys and girls are comparable in high school, girls tend to outperform boys in verbal tasks, while boys do better in visual-spatial and quantitative activities. Boys and girls differ, however, in the kind of elective courses they choose in high school (there are few gender differences in the enrollment in mandatory high school courses). These gender differences appear particularly in vocational education, where the sex segregation of the work world is mirrored in the students' enrollment. Thus, boys are still more likely than are girls to enroll in higher level mathematics and science courses

(National Center for Educational Statistics 1984). Many researchers have attributed the gender differences in quantitative achievement to the different courses in which boys and girls enroll (Berryman 1983; Pallas and Alexander 1983).[1] Although the domains of academic achievement continue to differ by gender, once-popular stereotypes of girls as under- or nonachievers are now considered more mythical than factual (Stockard and Wood 1984).

Gender differences in the motivation to achieve are complex. Earlier research attributed differences in attainment and alleged achievement to girls' lower motivation to achieve. More recent studies, however, have confirmed Maccoby and Jacklin's (1974) conclusions that levels of motivation to achieve among women, including intellectual achievement, continue to equal or surpass those of men (Klein 1985; Lueptow 1980, 1984; Stockard 1985; Stockard and Wood 1984).[2]

Educational Attainment

Until recently, men and women differed in how much schooling they acquired. Alexander and Eckland (1974) showed that female status depressed educational attainment. Nevertheless, today, more women than men graduate from high school (National Center for Educational Statistics 1986; Stockard et al. 1980; U.S. Bureau of the Census 1987). Differences in the subjects in which women and men major at the undergraduate level contribute to differences at the graduate and professional levels (Berryman 1983). On the graduate level, gender differences in attainment appear both in the types of degrees that are sought (women are less likely to be found in science departments and professional schools) and in the completion of advanced degree programs (Astin 1969; Berryman 1983; Klein 1985). Structural factors, such as curricular placement and counseling practices in elementary and high schools, are likely contributors to these patterns in higher education. For example, Hallinan and Sorensen (1987) reported that among equally able girls and boys in elementary school, boys are more likely than girls to be placed in high-ability mathematics groups. However, in a personal communication (1987), Jeannie Oakes, a social scientist with the RAND Corporation, noted that she found no systematic evidence of gender differences in track placement among secondary students; girls are just as likely as boys to be found in academic tracks, although they are less likely to choose additional mathematics and science courses when they have fulfilled the minimum requirements for entrance into college.

Racial and Class Differences

Historically, white working-class women generally did not seek education beyond high school because they thought that the home and family were their careers and that their husbands' "family wage" would provide them with a decent life (Rubin 1976). Bernard (1981) noted that among working-class women, the lack of a job was evidence of their husbands' abilities as providers. Today, when working-class women work outside the home, they do so in the secondary labor market, in which advanced educational credentials are not necessary (Howe 1977; Rubin 1976). Nevertheless, they often have more education than their husbands because when they work, they work in clerical or service occupations that require writing and spelling skills. Although white middle-class women often went to college in the past, most of those who sought a higher education did not necessarily plan careers because work outside the home was not intrinsically desired or financially necessary. However, they might attempt to start careers after the children left home (Bernard 1981). Only since the 1970s,

with the decline of the "family wage," have middle- and working-class white women faced the economic and social realities that make employment and the concomitant educational credentials seem necessary.

The case of black women is strikingly different from that of white women. Black women from all classes have always worked outside their homes (Davis 1981). Because the labor market was highly segregated by gender and class, the vast majority of black women were excluded from all but the most menial domestic and service jobs. Nevertheless, black women were more likely than were black men to obtain an education, especially a higher education. This gender pattern of educational achievement represents a reversal of the pattern found historically among whites.

Consequently, the small cadre of educated middle-class blacks was composed primarily of women. Middle-class black women did not view their education as a credential for a desirable marriage or as "social finishing," as did many of their white counterparts. Instead, they believed that education was a bona fide credential for entry into the middle-class occupational structure. Although the vast majority of these women were confined to careers in teaching and, to a lesser degree, nursing or social work, they worked in their chosen occupations for which they were trained, albeit their careers were constrained severely by a race- and sex-segregated occupational structure. Today, black women, unlike white women, do not face the relatively new experience of having to work to survive; they have always had to do so (Davis 1981; Simms and Malveaux 1987; Wallace 1980).

Today, class differences in black women's educational attainment remain. Teenage motherhood, epidemic among poor blacks, has a devastating effect on educational outcomes (Children's Defense Fund 1985, 1988;

Rumberger 1983).[3] Black women from working- and lower-class backgrounds continue to attain less schooling than any ethnic group except Hispanics and Native Americans (Children's Defense Fund 1988; U.S. Bureau of the Census 1987).

Differences in Returns on Education

Members of the working-class, women, and minorities continue to receive lower returns on their education than do middle-class white men. In 1982, the U.S. Commission on Civil Rights reported that at every level of training, blacks, Hispanics, and women receive lower pay and have higher levels of under- and unemployment than do white middle-class men. Moreover, in many instances, the disparities are greater among female and minority workers with the most education (Treiman and Hartman 1981).

Treiman and Hartman (1981: 16) reported that "minority males employed full time earned 75.3 percent of the salary of similarly employed majority males; majority females earned 58.6 percent and minority females 55.8 percent." These disparities were present even after the authors controlled for differences in seniority, education, age, specific vocational training, local pay rates, average number of hours worked, number of weeks worked per year, and other characteristics.

A primary reason for the persistence of unequal returns is that men and women continue to work in sex-segregated labor markets that have different career ladders (Sewell, Hauser, and Wolf 1980). Rosenfeld (1980) examined career trajectories (the job histories of socioeconomic status and income over an individual's work life) by sex and race. She found that white men have a general advantage over all other groups in many as-

pects of their careers, including wages and status, and that women and nonwhite men have similar career profiles. Kanter (1977) described the problems faced by women in the corporate world: White men gain more status than does any other group and nonwhite women gain the least, and the differences between white men and other groups increase over time. The exception to this trend is the small number of black women with extremely high levels of education (Carrigan 1981; Jones 1987; Rosenfeld 1980; Wilkerson 1987). Among black women managers with MBAs, the evidence is mixed. Although their career mobility rates were nearly identical to those of men, personal and institutional factors affected their promotions differently than they did for men (Nkomo and Cox 1987). For example, mentors were more available to men than to women and men were more likely to be promoted if they had line positions, while women were more likely to be promoted if they worked in large, rather than small, firms.

Why do women continue to achieve and value education in the face of limited potential returns on their efforts? A review of the literature reveals at least four hypotheses as possible explanations for this anomaly. The following sections discuss these hypotheses and assess each in the light of some relevant research.

Differential Reference Groups

The first hypothesis is drawn from reference-group theory, which Nilson (1982: 1) summarized as follows:

> "[M]entally healthy" individuals realistically assess their statuses in comparison to others who are perceived to be fairly similar on at least one important, visible dimension of actual or expected

rewards or resources. It is only within a range of meaningful comparison that satisfaction or dissatisfaction is felt.

From reference-group theory, one can deduce that women are aware of their diminished status in relation to men but when they evaluate what a fair and just return on education might be, they look to other women, not to men, as a point of reference. Women's evaluations of whether returns on schooling are equitable are based on their awareness that there are two occupational structures, one for them and one for men (Treiman and Terrell 1975).[4] In this context, women are likely to believe that their education is rewarded. Empirical research indicates that women's incremental return on education is similar to men's, but the intercept of the regression equation is lower for women than for men. That is, year for year and credential for credential, both men and women receive more returns on more education but they start in different places in the opportunity structure. In addition, the internal career ladders in the female occupational structure are much more limited than are those in the male sector (England et al. 1988; Sewell, Hauser, and Wolf 1980).

Reference-group theory may explain why women do not consider their mothers', aunts', and older sisters' poor returns on education to be unfair. The returns are fair in terms of a sex-segregated occupational structure, particularly if a woman sees that her role model's education enabled her to move from an unskilled, tedious, dangerous laboring position to a higher-status, clean, pink-collar job. This is exactly what educational credentials have done for many women in the past 20 years: With education, a woman can move from cafeteria worker to secretary, from secretary to teacher, and from clerk to registered nurse.

. . .

The Pollyanna Hypothesis

According to this explanation, the typical young woman who graduates from high school is likely to be optimistic about her future. Although she may be aware of the sexism that her mother and aunts experienced in the workplace, she interprets it as the problem of the "older generation," which the women's movement has already addressed. Such a view is likely to be a product of this historical moment and of the limited world of high school seniors. Young women today have been exposed to 15 years of rhetoric from the women's movement. They have heard of affirmative action and Title IX. They see that society is changing; women can run for the vice-presidency of the United States. The major social institutions that they experience beyond the nuclear family are the mass media and the high school, where women appear to be moving toward gender equity. The rhetoric and the reality of their world outside the family converge into a picture in which women seemingly can achieve their potentials, largely unencumbered by sexism.

Adolescent girls have not yet faced situations that conflict with the rhetoric of equal opportunity for women. They are not yet in the job market, and they have yet to enter close relationships with men in which they may face the choice of subordinating their goals and ambitions to save the family unit. It will be two or three years before these young women achieve adult status and face these possibilities. In the Pollyannaish world of adolescent girls, their education will be treated just like a man's and their careers will not be compromised by family responsibilities because their husbands will be equal partners in a dual-career marriage. For these Pollyannas, sexism is a thing of the past; they need not worry about it because the battle for equality has been won.

. . .

The Pollyanna hypothesis suggests that today young women believe they have "come a long way"—that barriers to successful careers in both the marketplace and the home have fallen by the wayside. This belief may explain the anomaly of women's achievement: Women do well in school because they have no doubt that they will be able to take their rightful places in industry and the professions next to their comparably educated brothers. To explode the myth that the battle has been won, more comparable worth cases must make headlines and more Elizabeth Hishons, Christine Crafts, and Theda Skocpols may have to sue their employers for sexism.[5] Perhaps young women must encounter the gender-segregated occupational structure, the gap in the salaries of men and women, and the problems that most women face in "happily integrating" the career–husband–children "triad" before their attitudes toward education, career, and family reflect, to a greater degree, the realities of modern society.

Social Powerlessness

Theories of the social powerlessness of women are the basis of the third explanation for the apparent failure of sexism in the opportunity structure to affect women's motivations to achieve in school. This explanation posits that marriage is a consciously sought alternative to a career. Aware of the structural inequalities in the occupational world, women know that they cannot expect equitable returns on their education, no matter how well they have done in school, and realize that they must seek a husband if they wish to be socially and financially secure. In addition, they are aware of the economic plight of those who attempt to be independent of a male partner (breadwinner) or of those who are left to support young children alone. Thus, young women

strive for future status and success by choosing a "promising" husband rather than by focusing on a career. Education still has a role; it is essential for acquiring an appropriate husband.

Educational achievement in high school allows a woman to attend college, where she can meet men who are likely to have suitable futures as breadwinners. Accordingly, the primary evaluation of social returns on her educational achievement and attainment will not be made in the labor market, but in marriage. This hypothesis applies to the middle-class woman who must marry a college-educated man simply to maintain the social status and lifestyle of her childhood and to the working-class woman who aspires to upward mobility.

. . .

For both middle- and working-class women, black and white, education and marriage have different meanings for potential social status. Arguably, white adolescent girls are aware of the less-than-favorable occupational options that await them and know that for most women (at least for white women), the safest and most reliable route to high status as an adult may be through a good marriage. Although the situation is more ambiguous for young black women, marriage remains important to the economic survival of black families. Wilson (1988) made this point as well in his discussion of the structural origins of the underclass.[6] As Featherman (1978: 53) commented:

> [V]icarious achievement (through a spouse) remains a major mechanism for intergenerational continuity or change in status for women, supplementing or complementing the opportunities for achievement through independent pursuits outside marriage and the home economy.

Sex-Role Socialization

The fourth hypothesis with regard to the anomaly of women's achievement comes from the literature on sex-role socialization. According to the asymmetry model described by Kaufman and Richardson (1982), boys' achievement is motivated by the desire for mastery and other intrinsic rewards, while girls' achievement is directed toward winning social approval and other extrinsic rewards. Little girls want to please and be "good" so they will earn love and approval. Women's motivation for achievement, it is suggested, evolves from early childhood needs for love and the approval of others, more than for mastery and self-reliance, which underlies the motivation of men. Clearly, this distinction is rigidly simplistic. Marciano (1981) suggested a subtler explanation: The "center of gravity" of women's motivation to achieve is an orientation to others, while the "center of gravity" of men's motivation is a desire for mastery and self-gratification. Girls perform well in school because good performance is compatible with affiliative motives and consistent with the "good girl" role into which they are socialized (Kaufman and Richardson 1982; Maccoby and Jacklin 1974; Weitzman 1979, 1984).

The sex-role socialization hypothesis actually has two aspects. First, girls do well in school because they are socialized to be good. Being a "good girl" in school means dutifully following orders and instructions from teachers, being decorous and compliant, and accepting rules with little protest. This is the kind of behavior that is more compatible with female than with male sex roles. Weitzman (1984:172) explained how girls' early sex-role socialization produces a particular kind of motivation to achieve that is not found in boys:

The dependence and affection-seeking responses seen as normal for both boys and girls in early childhood become defined as feminine in older children. . . . [G]irls are not separated from their parents as sources of support and nurturance, and they are therefore not forced to develop internal controls and an independent sense of self. Instead, the self they value is the one that emanates from the appraisals of others. Consequently, girls develop a greater need for the approval of others . . . than do boys.

The second part of this argument revolves around the male sex role and achievement. Although the female sex role demands that girls be good and do well in school, the male sex role, particularly among working-class white boys, requires a degree of resistance to authority figures like teachers and a certain devaluation of schoolwork because it is "feminine" (Stockard et al. 1980; Willis 1977). The lived culture of working-class men glorifies manual labor, which involves physical strength, a willingness to get dirty, and an attitude of rebellion against and independence from superiors, as distinguished from the attitudes of submission and appeasement associated with women (Bologh 1986). Thus, the high achievement of female students may be due to two separate sex-role processes: Girls do well because they are socialized to be good and they do better than some boys because the sex-role socialization of boys requires a degree of academic underachievement. As Stockard et al. (1980) noted, good students display behavior that is generally sex typed as feminine. Therefore, it is understandable if boys do not conform to the role of good student because being a good student would mean acting feminine. Boys do not refuse to learn, but they may not reflect learning in the ways that are required for high grades. Until this century, even elite white men tempered their achievement in college to receive a "gentleman's C."[7]

. . .

Discussion

The anomaly with which this article began remains essentially unresolved. Why do women do so well in school when they can expect only relatively limited returns on their educational achievements? The rationale underlying the educational attainment of most men—gaining credentials that will bring higher pay, better jobs, and promotions—is, in many ways, inadequate for women. The academic achievement and attainment of women defy this logic because women continue to match (and often surpass) men without the same occupational returns from schooling that men receive.

The four hypotheses explored in the previous section offered a variety of perspectives on the question of why women achieve in school. The first three hypotheses examined how young women view the connection between education and the occupational structure, while the fourth ignored structure altogether. Although these hypotheses offer some insight into the question of women's achievement, all four hypotheses suffer from certain problems:

• Reference-group theory assumes that women are aware of the greater returns from education that men receive but do not care. This idea requires a major leap of faith.

• If one accepts the reference-group premise that young women are aware of a sex-segregated occupational structure, one must deny the Pollyanna and the social powerlessness hypotheses. The Pollyanna theory presumes that the basis of the reference-group hypothesis—a sex-segregated occupational structure—is a thing of the past. The social powerlessness hypothesis denies the direct relevance of occupational returns on education for women's decisions and proposes that good marriages, not careers, are the fundamental motivation behind women's educational attainment. If this is true, then a sex-segregated occupational structure is less relevant than is women's primarily dependent status in society.

• Furthermore, the Pollyanna theory and the social powerlessness theory are mutually exclusive. One denies that young women perceive sexism as a factor in the status-attainment process, but the other identifies sexism as such a prominent component of the status-attainment process that marriage appears to be the most reasonable alternative for women who seek social and financial security.

• The sex-role socialization hypothesis focuses completely on the individual and her early socialization experiences. It fails to link her behavior in school to such broad social-structural phenomena as those discussed in the other hypotheses. Any account of social behavior that fails to incorporate structure is limited in its explanatory power.

A final shortcoming of all the hypotheses discussed in this article is the uneven ability of the theories to explain the achievement and attainment behavior of women from diverse racial and class backgrounds. It is likely, for example, that the Pollyanna phenomenon is more characteristic of middle-class women, while reference group is a more likely explanation of working-class experiences. Social powerlessness theory is also relevant mainly to middle-class white women; it is especially inadequate for poor and working-class black women.

. . .

NOTES

1. Whether gender differences in quantitative achievement are due to sociobiological or environmental factors, such as socialization and exposure to different curricula, remains controversial. However, recent work by Professor Harold Stevenson and his colleagues in the Department of Psychology, University of Michigan, Ann Arbor (personal communication, 1987) strongly supports the idea that gender differences in the performance of American students in mathematics are due to socialization and experiences in school. These researchers compared the mathematics achievement of American schoolchildren with that of children from Japan, Taiwan, and China. They found that there are no significant gender differences in mathematics achievement among Asian students.
2. Although gender differences exist in vocational tracks, they are rooted in differences in the lived cultures of adolescent boys and girls, as well as in certain structural aspects of schooling, such as counseling practices. Valli's (1986) research on clerical education and Lee and Bryk's (1986) study of girls' achievement and attitudes in single-sex secondary schools suggest the importance of lived cultures for the achievement of females.
3. The "epidemic" is not confined to the black community; the rate of increase in teenage pregnancies is higher among white girls than among black girls (Children's Defense Fund 1985, 1988).
4. Waite (1981) confirmed that 75 percent of women work in occupations whose incumbents are more than 50 percent female and that 32 percent are in occupations whose incumbents are more than 90 percent female.
5. Elizabeth Hishon is the lawyer who won permission from the U.S. Supreme Court to sue her former employer, Atlanta's prestigious law firm King and Spalding, for sex discrimination because it failed to grant her or any other woman partnership in the 100-partner firm. Christine Craft is the television anchor who was fired because her employers thought she was not sufficiently attractive to report the news. Theda Skocpol is the sociologist who received tenure from Harvard University after winning a sex-discrimination suit against the university, which originally failed to grant her tenure.
6. Wilson (1988) has been criticized by those who interpret his discussion of the unavailability of marriageable men for underclass women as an argument that poor women are but a husband away from economic insolvency. Although he denies that this was his intent, the relative lack of a detailed discussion of the effects of the sex-segregated occupational structure lends support to his critics.
7. An interesting twist on this was reported by Fordham and Ogbu (1986), who described how able black students consciously hide their ability and temper their achievement lest they be labeled as "acting white." The similarities and differences between labeling achievement as either feminine or white behavior, an implication of pariahlike status in both cases, need further exploration.

REFERENCES

ACKER, J. 1973. "Women and Social Stratification: A Case of Intellectual Sexism." *American Journal of Sociology* 78:936–45.

———. 1980. "Women and Stratification: A Review of Recent Literature." *Contemporary Sociology* 9:25–39.

ALEXANDER, K. L. AND B. K. ECKLAND. 1974. "Sex Differences in the Educational Attainment Process." *American Sociological Review* 39:668–82.

ASTIN, H. 1969. *The Female Doctorate in America.* New York: Russell Sage Foundation.

BERNARD, J. 1981. *The Female World.* New York: Free Press.

BERRYMAN, S. E. 1983. *Who Will Do Science?* New York: Rockefeller Foundation.

BOLOGH, R. W. 1986. "Dialectical Feminism: Beyond Marx, Weber, and Masculine Theorizing." Paper presented at the Annual Meetings of the American Sociological Association, New York.

CARRIGAN, S. P. 1981. "Income Variation: A Comparison of Determinants for Men and Women." Unpublished doctoral dissertation, University of California at Los Angeles.

CHILDREN'S DEFENSE FUND. 1985. *Black Children, White Children.* Washington, DC: Children's Defense Fund.

———. 1988. *Children's Defense Budget FY 1989.* Washington, DC: Children's Defense Fund.

DAVIS, A. 1981. *Women, Race, and Class.* New York: Random House.

ECCLES, J. S. AND L. W. HOFFMAN. 1985. "Sex Roles, Socialization, and Occupational Behavior." Pp. 367–420 in *Research in Child Development and Social Policy,* vol. 1, edited by H. W. Stevenson and A. E. Siegel. Chicago: University of Chicago Press.

ENGLAND, P., G. FARKAS, B. KILBOURNE, AND T. DOU. 1988. "Explaining Occupational Sex Segregation and Wages: Findings from a Model with Fixed Effects." *American Sociological Review* 53:528–43.

FEATHERMAN, D. O. 1978. "Schooling and Occupational Careers: Constancy and Change in Worldly Success." Madison: Center for Demography and Ecology, University of Wisconsin.

FINLEY, M. 1983. "Transition from School to Work: The Education and Careers of Working Class Women." Unpublished manuscript, University of California at Los Angeles.

FORDHAM, S. AND J. U. OGBU. 1986. "Black Students' School Success: Coping with the Burden of 'Acting White.'" *Urban Review* 18:176–206.

HAFNER, A. L. AND S. SHAHA. 1984. "Gender Differences in the Prediction of Freshman Grades." Paper presented at the Annual Meeting of the American Educational Research Association, New Orleans (April).

HALLINAN, M. T. AND A. B. SORENSEN. 1987. "Ability Grouping and Sex Differences in Mathematics Achievement." *Sociology and Education* 60(2):63–73.

HOWE, L. K. 1977. *Pink Collar Workers*. New York: Avon Books.

JONES, B. A. P. 1987. "Black Women and Labor Force Participation: An Analysis of Sluggish Growth Rates." Pp. 11–32 in *Slipping Through the Cracks: The Status of Black Women*, edited by M. C. Simms and J. Malveaux. New Brunswick, NJ: Transaction Books.

KANTER, R. M. 1977. *Men and Women of the Corporation*. New York: Basic Books.

KAUFMAN, D. R. AND B. RICHARDSON. 1982. *Achievement and Women: Challenging the Assumptions*. New York: Free Press.

KLEIN, S., ed. 1985. *Handbook for Achieving Sex Equity through Education*. Baltimore, MD: Johns Hopkins University Press.

LEE, V. AND A. BRYK. 1986. "Effects of Single Sex Secondary Schools on Student Achievement and Attitudes," *Journal of Educational Psychology* 70(5):381–95.

LUEPTOW, L. B. 1980. "Social Change and Sex Role Change in Adolescent Orientation toward Life, Work, and Achievement: 1967–1975." *Social Psychology Quarterly* 43:48–59.

———. 1984. *Adolescent Sex Roles and Social Change*. New York: Columbia University Press.

MACCOBY, E. AND C. JACKLIN. 1974. *The Psychology of Sex Differences*. Palo Alto, CA: Stanford University Press.

MARCIANO, T. D. 1981. "Socialization and Women at Work." *National Forum* 71:24–25.

MICKELSON, R. A. 1984. "Race, Class, and Gender Differences in Adolescent Academic Achievement Attitudes and Behaviors." Unpublished doctoral dissertation, University of California at Los Angeles.

———. 1990. The Attitude-Achievement Paradox among Black Adolescents." *Sociology of Education* 63:44–61.

NATIONAL CENTER FOR EDUCATIONAL STATISTICS. 1984. "Science and Mathematics Education in American High Schools: Results from the High School and Beyond Study." *Bulletin of the U.S. Department of Education*. Washington, DC: U.S. Government Printing Office.

———. 1986. *Earned Degrees Conferred, Department of Education*. Washington, DC: U.S. Government Printing Office.

NILSON, L. B. 1982. "The Perceptual Distortions of Social Distance: Why the Underdog Principle Seldom Works." Paper presented at the meetings of the American Sociological Association, San Francisco.

NKOMO, S. M. AND T. COX. 1987. "Gender Differences in the Upward Mobility of Black Managers." Paper presented at the meetings of the National Academy of Management, New Orleans.

OAKLEY, A. 1974. *The Sociology of Housework*. New York: Pantheon Books.

OGBU, J. U. 1979. *Minority Education and Caste*. New York: Academic Press.

PALLAS, A. M. AND K. ALEXANDER. 1983. "Sex Differences in Quantitative SAT Performance: New Evidence on Differential Course Work Hypothesis." *American Educational Research Journal* 20:165–82.

ROSENFELD, R. 1980. "Race and Sex Differences in Career Dynamics." *American Sociological Review* 45:583–609.

RUBIN, L. 1976. *Worlds of Pain*. New York: Basic Books.

RUMBERGER, R. 1983. "Dropping Out of High School: The Influence of Race, Sex, and Family Background." *American Educational Research Journal* 20:199–220.

SEWELL, W., R. HAUSER, AND W. WOLF. 1980. "Sex, Schooling, and Occupational Status." *American Journal of Sociology* 86:551–83.

SIMMS, M. C. AND MALVEAUX. 1987. *Slipping Through the Cracks: The Status of Black Women*. New Brunswick, NJ: Transaction Books.

STEINKAMP, M. W. AND M. L. MAEHR. 1984. "Gender Differences in Motivational Orientation toward Achievement in School Science: A Quantitative Synthesis." *American Educational Research Journal* 21:39–59.

STOCKARD, J. 1985. "Education and Gender Equality: A Critical View." Pp. 299–326 in *Research in Sociology of Education and Socialization,* vol. 5. Greenwich, CT: JAI Press.

STOCKARD, J., P. A. SCHMUCK, K. KEMPNER, P. WILLIAMS, S. K. EDSON, AND M. A. SMITH. 1980. *Sex Equity in Education.* New York: Academic Press.

STOCKARD, J. AND J. W. WOOD. 1984. "The Myth of Female Underachievement: A Reexamination of Sex Differences in Academic Underachievement." *American Educational Research Journal* 21: 825–38.

TREIMAN, D. W. AND H. HARTMAN. 1981. *Women, Wages, and Work: Equal Pay for Equal Value.* Washington, DC: National Academy Press.

TREIMAN, D. W. AND K. TERRELL. 1975. "Sex and the Process of Status Attainment: A Comparison of Working Men and Women." *American Sociological Review* 40(20):174–200.

TURNER, R. 1964. *The Social Context of Ambition.* San Francisco: Chandler Publishing Co.

U.S. BUREAU OF THE CENSUS. 1987. Educational Attainment in the United States: March 1982–1985. *Current Population Reports,* Series P-20, No. 415. Washington, DC: U.S. Department of Commerce.

VALLI, L. 1986. *Becoming Clerical Workers.* Boston: Routledge Kegan Paul.

WAITE, L. J. 1981. *U.S. Women at Work.* Santa Monica, CA: The RAND Corp.

WALLACE, P. A. 1980. *Black Women in the Labor Force.* Cambridge, MA: MIT Press.

WEITZMAN, L. J. 1979. *Sex-Role Socialization.* Palo Alto, CA: Mayfield Publishing Co.

———. 1984. "Sex-Role Socialization: A Focus on Women." Pp. 157–237 in *Women. A Feminist Perspective,* edited by J. Freeman. Palo Alto, CA: Mayfield Publishing Co.

WILKERSON, M. B. 1987. "A Report on the Educational Status of Black Women During the UN Decade of Women: 1976–85." Pp. 83–96 in *Slipping Through the Cracks: The Status of Black Women,* edited by M. C. Simms and J. Malveaux. New Brunswick, NJ: Transaction Books.

WILLIS, P. 1977. *Learning to Labor.* New York: Columbia University Press.

WILSON, W. J. 1988. *The Truly Disadvantaged.* Chicago: University of Chicago Press.

31

BOYS AND GIRLS TOGETHER . . . BUT MOSTLY APART

Barrie Thorne

The landscape of contemporary childhood includes three major sites—families, neighborhoods, and schools. Each of these worlds contains different people, patterns of time and space, and arrangements of gender. Families and neighborhoods tend to be small, with a relatively even ratio of adults and children. In contrast, schools are crowded and bureaucratic settings in which a few adults organize and continually evaluate the activities of a large number of children.[1] Within schools, the sheer press of numbers in a relatively small space gives a public, witnessed quality to everyday life and makes keeping down noise and maintaining order a constant adult preoccupation. In their quest for order, teachers and aides continually sort students into smaller, more manageable groups (classes, reading groups, hallway lines, shifts in the lunchroom), and they structure the day around routines like lining up and taking turns. In this chapter I trace the basic organizational features of schools as they bear upon, and get worked out through, the daily gender relations of kids. As individuals, we always display or "do" gender, but this dichotomous difference (no one escapes being declared female or male) may be more or less relevant, and relevant in different ways, from one social context to another.

· · ·

The Choreography of Gender Separation and Integration

A series of snapshots taken in varied school settings would reveal extensive spatial separation between girls and boys. This phenomenon, which has been widely observed by researchers in schools, is often called "sex segregation among children," a term evoking images of legally enforced separation, like purdah in some Islamic societies. But school authorities separate boys and girls only occasionally. Furthermore, girls and boys sometimes interact with one another in relaxed and extended ways, not only in schools but also in families, neighborhoods, churches, and other settings. Gender separation—the word "segregation" suggests too total a pattern—is a variable and complicated process, an intricate choreography aptly summarized by Erving Goffman's phrase "with-then-apart."[2]

Boys and girls separate (or are separated) periodically, with their own spaces, rituals, and groups, but they also come together to become, in crucial ways, part of the same world. In the following verbal snapshots of classrooms, hallways, cafeterias, and school playgrounds, it is crucial to note that although the occasions of gender separation may seem more dramatic, the mixed-gender encounters are also theoretically and practi-

cally important. Note also that groups may be formed by teachers, aides, or by kids themselves, and that criteria of group formation may or may not be explicitly mentioned or even in conscious awareness.

The "With-Then-Apart" of Classrooms

In organizing classroom seating, teachers use a variety of plans, some downplaying and others emphasizing the significance of gender. When Mrs. Smith, the kindergarten teacher at Ashton School, assigned seats, she deliberately placed girls and boys at each table, and they interacted a great deal in the formal and informal life of the classroom. Mrs. Johnson, the second-grade teacher at the same school, also assigned seats, but she organized her classroom into pairs of desks aligned in rows. With the layout came a language—"William's row" . . . "Monica's row" . . . "Amy's row"—for the five desks lined up behind William, Monica, Amy, and the other three students seated at the front. The overall pattern mixed girls and boys, and they participated together in much of the classroom whispering and byplay.

I asked Mrs. Johnson, who was nearing retirement after many years of teaching, what she had in mind when she assigned classroom seats. She responded with weary familiarity: "Everybody is sitting somewhere for a reason—hearing, sight, height. No two in the same reading group sit together, so I make sure they do their own work in their workbook. Or they sit in a particular place because they don't get along, or get along too well, with someone else." Differences of hearing, sight, height, and reading performance cut across the dichotomous division between boys and girls; sorting the students according to these criteria led to largely gender-integrated seating. However, the last of Mrs. Johnson's criteria, the degree to which two children get along, embeds a gender skew. Since friends are usually of the same gender, splitting up close friends tends to mix girls and boys.

Instead of assigning seats, Miss Bailey, the teacher of the combined fourth-fifth grade in Oceanside School, let the students choose their own desks in a U-shaped arrangement open at the front of the room. Over the course of the school year there were three occasions of general choosing. Each time, the students' choices resulted in an almost total cleavage: boys on the left and girls on the right, with the exception of one girl, Jessie, who frequently crossed gender boundaries and who twice chose a desk with the boys and once with the girls. . . . The teacher and students routinely spoke of "a boys' side" and "a girls' side" in the classroom.[3]

Miss Bailey made clear that she saw the arrangement as an indulgence, and when the class was unusually noisy, she threatened to change the seating and "not have a boys' side and a girls' side." "You have chosen that," she said on one occasion, "you're sitting this way because you chose to do it at the first of the year. I may have to sit you in another way." The class groaned as she spoke, expressing ritualized preference for gender-separated seating. Miss Bailey didn't carry out her threat, and when she reseated individual students in the name of classroom order, she did so within each side. Miss Bailey framed the overall gender separation as a matter of student choice and as a privilege she had granted them, but she also built on and ratified the gender divide by pitting the girls against the boys in classroom spelling and math contests. . . .

Physical separation of girls and boys in regular classroom seating affects formal and informal give-and-take among students. One day Miss Bailey wrote sentences on the board and said she would go around the room and give each student a chance to find an error in spelling, grammar, or pronunciation. "We'll start with Beth," she said, gesturing to the right front of the U-shaped layout of the desks. Recognizing that to go around the room meant she would call on all the girls first, Miss Bailey added, "that leaves the hard part for the boys." Picking up the theme of gender opposition, several boys called out, "We're smart!" The divided seating pattern also channeled informal byplay, such as whispering, casual visiting, and collusive exchanges, among boys and among girls, whereas in classrooms with mixed-gender seating, those kinds of interaction more often took place between girls and boys.

When Miss Bailey divided the class into smaller work groups, gender receded informal organizational importance. On these occasions, the teacher relied on sorting principles like skill at reading or spelling, whether or not someone had finished an earlier task, counting off ("one-two-one-two"), or letting students choose from alternative activities such as practicing for a play or collectively making a map out of papier-mâché. Sometimes Miss Bailey asked the fourth- and fifth-graders to meet separately and work on math or spelling. These varied organizational principles drew girls and boys out of separate halves of the classroom and into groups of varied gender composition standing at the blackboard or sitting on the floor in front or at round tables at the side of the room. When they found places in these smaller groups, girls often scrambled to sit next to girls, and boys to sit next to boys. But if the interaction had a central focus such as taking turns reading aloud or working together to build a contour map, boys and girls participated together in the verbal give-and-take.

Although I did not do systematic counting, I noticed that during formal classroom instruction, for example, when Miss Bailey invited discussion during social studies lessons, boys, taken as a whole, talked more than girls. This pattern fits with an extensive body of research finding that in classroom interaction from the elementary through college levels, male students tend to talk more than female students.[4]

. . .

Life on the Line

When Mrs. Smith announced to her kindergarten class, "This is what you call a line . . . one at a time," she introduced a social form basic to the handling of congestion and delay in schools. In Ashton School, where classrooms opened onto an indoor hallway, kids rarely moved from the classroom unless they were in carefully regulated lines. The separate lines meandering through the hallways reminded me of caterpillars, or of planes on a runway slowly moving along in readiness to take off. In the layout of the Oceanside School each of the classrooms opened to the outside, an arrangement facilitated by the warm California climate. Although this lessened the problem of noise and thereby relaxed the amount of adult control, the Oceanside teachers still organized students into loose lines when they headed to and from the library and the playground and when they went to the lunchroom.

Gender threaded through the routines of lining up, waiting and moving in a queue, and dispersing in a new place. In Oceanside School it was customary for girls and boys to line up separately, a pattern whose roots in the history of elementary schooling are still evident on old school buildings with separate entrances engraved with the words "Girls" and "Boys."[5] Several adults who have told me their memories of elementary school recall boys and girls lining up separately to go to different bathrooms. One woman remembered waiting in the girls' line several feet away from a row of boys and feeling an urgent need to urinate; she held her legs tightly together and hoped no one—especially the boys—would notice. This experience of bodily shame gave an emotional charge to gender-divided lines.

Like the schools of these adult memories, Oceanside had separate girls' and boys' bathrooms shared by many classrooms. But unlike the remembered schools, Oceanside had no collective expeditions to the bathrooms. Instead individual students asked permission to leave the classrooms and go to either the boys' or girls' bathroom, both of which, like the classrooms, opened to the outside. In Ashton School, as in many contemporary school buildings, each classroom had its own bathroom, used one-at-a-time by both girls and boys. This architectural shift has eliminated separate and centralized boys' and girls' facilities and hence the need to walk down the hall to take turns going to the toilet.

In Oceanside School the custom of separate girls' and boys' lines was taken for granted and rarely commented on. One of the fourth graders told me that they learned to form separate boys' and girls' lines in kindergarten and had done it ever since. A first-grade teacher said that on the first day of school she came out to find the boys and the girls already standing in two different lines. When I asked why girls and boys formed separate lines, the teachers said it was the children's doing. With the ironic detachment that adults often adopt toward children's customs, Miss Bailey told me that she thought the gender-separated lines were "funny." A student teacher who joined the classroom for part of the year rhetorically asked the kids why they had a girls' line and a boys' line. "How come? Will a federal marshal come and get you if you don't?" There was no reply.

Miss Bailey didn't deliberately establish separate lines for boys and girls; she just told the students to line up. It took both attention and effort for the kids to continually create and recreate gender-separated queues. In organizing expeditions out of the classroom, Miss Bailey usually called on students by stages, designating individuals or smaller groups ("everyone at that side table"; "those practicing spelling over in the corner") to move into line as a reward for being quiet. Once they got to the classroom door—unless it was lunchtime, when boys and girls mixed in two lines designated "hot lunch" and "cold lunch"—the students routinely separated by gender. The first boy to reach the door always stood to the left; the first girl stood to the right, and the rest moved into the appropriate queue.

The kids maintained separate boys' and girls' lines through gestures and speech. One day when the class was in the library, Miss Bailey announced, "Line up to go to assembly." Judy and Rosie hurried near the door, marking the start of one line on the right; Freddy and Tony moved to the left of the door. Other girls lined up behind Rosie, who became a sort of traffic director, gesturing a boy who was moving in behind her that he should shift to the other line. Once when the recess bell had rung and they began to line up for the return to class, a boy came over and stood at the end of a row of girls. This evoked widespread teasing—"John's in the girls' line"; "Look at that girl over there"—that quickly sent him to the row of boys. Off-bounds to those of the other gender, the separate lines sometimes became places of sanctuary, as during the close of one recess when Dennis grabbed a ball from Tracy, and she chased after him. He squeezed into line between two boys, chanting "Boys' line, boy's line," an incantation that indeed kept her away and secured his possession of the ball.

. . .

The Gender Geography of Lunchroom Tables

Seating in school lunchrooms falls between the more fixed spaces of classroom desks and the arrangements kids improvise each time they sit on the floor of the classroom or the auditorium; an Oceanside teacher once referred to "their strange conglomeration way of sitting," describing the clusters, primarily of either girls or boys, arrayed on the floor. Eating together is a prime emblem of solidarity, and each day at lunchtime there is a fresh scramble as kids deliberately choose where, and with whom, to eat. The scrambling takes place within limits set by adults and defined by age-grading. In both schools, each classroom, in effect an age-grade, had two designated cafeteria tables, placed end to end from the wall.

Table seating takes shape through a predictable process: the first arrivals (who have cold lunches, a reason some children say they prefer to bring lunch from home) stake out territory by sitting and spreading out their possessions, usually at the far ends of each table. The tables fill through invitations, squeezing in, or individuals or groups going to an empty space. The groups who maneuver to eat together are usually friends and mostly of the same gender. The result is a pattern of separated clusters; many of the tables have a mix of girls and boys, but they are divided into smaller same-gender groupings. On the other hand, late-arriving individuals, who have less choice of where to sit, move into leftover spaces and tend to integrate the seating.

The collective table talk often includes both boys and girls, as do some daily rituals, like one that accompanied the opening of plastic bags of cutlery in both schools. As kids pulled out their plastic forks, they looked for and announced the small numbers stamped on the bottom: I'm twenty-four, how old are you?" "I must have flunked; I'm in the fourth grade and I'm forty-five." "Ninety-three." "You're stupid; you were really held back in school."

Even when boys and girls are seated at the same table, their same-gender clustering may be accompanied by a sense of being on separate turfs. This became apparent when there were temporary changes in the physical ecology at Oceanside School. The combined fourth–fifth-grade class usually had two tables, but one day when the kids arrived for lunch, one of the tables was temporarily designated for another class. The kids began to crowd around the remaining table. Sherry, who had a cold lunch and arrived first, chose her usual seat by the wall; girls usually filled up that end. Scott and Jeremy sat down across from her, while three girls with hot lunches chose seats at the other end of the table. Scott looked around and asked, "Where are all the boys? Where are all the boys?" Four boys arrived and sat across from Scott and Jeremy and next to Sherry, who began to crouch in her corner. In a small anxious voice she asked them, "What are you doing on the girls' side?" "There isn't room," one of the newly arrived boys explained.

Occasionally those who are already seated look around, take the lay of the developing table, and change places, sometimes with a gender-marking pronouncement. In the Ashton School lunchroom when the two second-grade tables were filling, a high-status boy walked by the inside table, which had a scattering of both boys and girls. He said loudly, "Oooo, too many girls," and headed for a seat at the other, nearly empty table. The boys at the inside table picked up their trays and moved to join him. After they left, no other boy sat at that table, which the pronouncement had made effectively taboo. So in the end, girls and boys ate at separate tables that day, although this was not usually the case.

. . .

Playground Divisions of Space and Activity

In classrooms, hallways, and lunchrooms boys and girls do the same core activities: working on math or spelling, moving from one area to another, or eating a meal. Same-gender groups might add their own, sometimes collusive agendas, such as a group of girls passing around a tube of lip gloss during a grammar lesson or a group of boys discussing sports or setting up arm wrestling during lunch. But there is no pronounced division of activity by gender.[6] In contrast, on the playground, an area where adults exert minimal control and kids are relatively free to choose their own activities and companions, there is extensive separation by gender. Activities, spaces, and equipment are heavily gender-typed; playgrounds, in short, have a more fixed geography of gender.

My inventories of activities and groups on the playground showed similar patterns in both schools. Boys controlled the large fixed spaces designated for team sports: baseball diamonds, grassy fields used for football or soccer, and basketball courts. In Oceanside School there was also a skateboard area where boys played, with an occasional girl joining in. The fixed spaces where girls predominated—bars and jungle gyms and painted cement areas for playing foursquare, jump rope, and hopscotch—were closer to the building and much smaller, taking up perhaps a tenth of the territory that boys controlled.[7] In addition, more movable activities—episodes of chasing, groups of younger children playing various kinds of "pretend," and groups milling around and talking—often, although by no means always, divided by gender. Girls and boys most often played together in games of kickball, foursquare, dodgeball, handball, and chasing or tag.

Kids and playground aides pretty much take these gender-divided patterns for granted; indeed, there is a long history in the United States of girls and boys engaging in different types of play, although the favored activities have changed with time. The Ashton School aides openly regarded the space close to the building as girls' territory and the playing fields "out there" as boys' territory. They sometimes shooed away children of the other gender from what they saw as inappropriate turf, especially boys who ventured near the girls' area and seemed to have teasing in mind.

. . .

Other Research on Gender Separation among Children

My observations of extensive separation in the activities and social relations of boys and girls echo a recurring finding in the research literature. In fact, in nearly every study of school situations where kids from age three through junior high are given the opportunity to choose companions of the same age, girls have shown a strong preference to be with girls, and boys with boys. (Because as much as 90 percent of research on children's peer groups has been done in schools, the finding of gender separation among children dominates the literature.[8] Studies of children's social relations in neighborhoods and a study in a children's museum have found much more mixing of girls and boys than is typical in schools.)

To grasp the magnitude of the gender divide, a number of researchers have counted the relative proportions of mixed and same-gender groups in various school settings. For example, Zella Luria and Eleanor Herzog did inventories of the playground groups of fourth- and fifth-graders in two elementary schools in Massachusetts. They found that in a private, upper-middle-class school, 63 percent of the groups were same-gender, compared with 80 percent same-gender groups in a middle-class public school of about the same size and racial composition. In another study on the East Coast, Marlaine Lockheed and Abigail Harris found that in twenty-nine fourth- and fifth-grade classrooms where students constituted their own work groups, 86 percent were same-gender.[9]

In short, there is ample evidence of extensive separation between girls and boys within contemporary coeducational schools. Numerical counts, moreover, may underestimate the degree of separation. Luria and Herzog note that their method of counting all playground clusters regardless of activity may overrate the extent and "quality" of cross-gender activity. For example, in the public school in their study, half of the 20 percent of play groups mixed by gender were integrated by one girl and hence were token situations.[10] The method of simply counting all-boy, all-girl, and boy-girl groups also neglects meanings. For example, by these researchers' counting methods, girls-chase-the-boys, a favorite game on both the Ashton and Oceanside playgrounds, would be chalked up as a mixed-gender group or interaction. However, . . . the organization of this activity dramatizes gender boundaries and maintains a sense of separation between the girls and the boys as distinctive groups.

Information not only about the quantity of gender separation, but also about the quality and meaning (e.g., the degree of felt intimacy or social distance) of kids' social relations can be found in their perceptions of friendship. Researchers who have asked kids of different ages to name their best friends have found that in at least 75 percent of the cases, boys name only boys and girls name only girls.[11] Sociometric studies that go beyond "best" friendships to ask about and map broader self-reported patterns of affiliation and avoidance have also documented a deep division by gender. For example, in a study of four fourth-, fifth-, and sixth-grade classrooms, Maureen Hallinan found that all the cliques that the students identified were either of girls or of boys; not one crossed the line of gender.[12] Although she observed, and the students reported, some cross-gender friendships, they were not integrated into the larger, more public and visible groupings or cliques.

In short, although girls and boys *are* together and often interact in classrooms, lunchrooms, and on the playground, these contacts less often deepen into friendship or stable alliances, while same-gender interactions are more likely to solidify into more lasting or acknowledged bonds. Much of the daily contact between girls and boys, as Janet Schofield comments, resembles that of "familiar strangers" who are in repeated physical proximity and recognize one another but have little real knowledge of what one another are like.[13] Some of the students in the middle school where Schofield observed felt that the gulf between boys and girls was so deep that it was fruitless to try to form cross-gender friendships, which they saw as different from romantic liaisons.

Whether painted with narrative or by numbers, the prevalence of gender separation, especially on school playgrounds and in patterns of children's friendship, is quite striking. But separation between boys and girls is far from total, and the "with" occasions should be sketched into view. In the next chapter I move in and around an obvious question: When given a choice, why do girls and boys so often separate from one another? The answers, I suggest, should be far more complex and contextual than the approaches currently offered by developmental psychologists.

NOTES

1. Philip W. Jackson (*Life in Classrooms*) highlights the centrality of *crowds, praise,* and *power* in the organization of schools.
2. Erving Goffman, "The Arrangement between the Sexes," p. 316.
3. Cynthia A. Cone and Berta E. Perez ("Peer Groups and the Organization of Classroom Space") observed a similar pattern. . . .
4. See reviews of research in Barrie Thorne et al., eds., *Language, Gender, and Society;* Jere E. Brophy and Thomas L. Good, *Teacher–Student Relations;* and in the American Association of University Women Educational Foundation

and the Wellesley College Center for Research on Women, *How Schools Shortchange Girls.*
5. See Tyack and Hansot, *Learning Together.*
6. Goffman observes that this "parallel organization," in which similar activities are organized in a segregated manner, provides a "ready base for elaborating differential treatment," such as having a row of girls file in before a row of boys ("The Arrangement between the Sexes," p. 306).
7. My observations resemble those of Janet Lever, who recorded differences in the playground activities of fifth-graders in Connecticut. She found that boys most often engaged in team sports, whereas girls focused on turn-taking play. (See Lever, "Sex Differences in the Games Children Play" and "Sex Differences in the Complexity of Children's Play and Games.")
8. This estimate comes from Willard W. Hartup, "Peer Relations."
9. Zella Luria and Eleanor W. Herzog, "Gender Segregation across and within Settings"; Marlaine S. Lockheed and Abigail M. Harris, "Cross-Sex Collaborative Learning in Elementary Classrooms."
10. Luria and Herzog, "Gender Segregation across and within Settings."
11. For example, when Maureen Hallinan and Nancy B. Tuma ("Classroom Effects on Change in Children's Friendships") asked fourth-, fifth-, and sixth-graders to name their "best friend," 77 percent named someone of the same gender.
12. Maureen Hallinan, "Structural Effects of Children's Friendships and Cliques."
13. Schofield, *Black and White in School.* Schofield found that race, as well as gender, was a barrier to the development of friendship; in the racially balanced middle school where she observed, close friendships between students of different genders *or* races were quite rare.

REFERENCES

American Association of University Women Educational Foundation and the Wellesley College Center for Research on Women. 1992. *How Schools Shortchange Girls.* Washington, DC: AAUW Educational Foundation.

Brophy, Jere E. and Thomas L. Good. 1974. *Teacher–Student Relations.* New York: Holt.

Cone, Cynthia A. and Berta E. Perez. 1986. "Peer Groups and the Organization of Classroom Space." *Human Organization* 45:80–88.

Goffman, Erving. 1977. "The Arrangement between the Sexes." *Theory and Society* 4: 301–336.

Hallinan, Maureen and Nancy B. Tuma. 1978. "Classroom Effects on Change in Children's Friendships." *Sociology of Education* 51:270–82.

Hartup, Willard W. 1983. "Peer Relations." Pp. 103–96 in *Handbook of Child Psychology, vol. 4: Socialization, Personality and Social Development,* 4th ed., edited by Paul H. Mussen and E. Mavis Heatherington. New York: Wiley.

Jackson, Philip W. 1968. *Life in Classrooms.* New York: Holt, Rinehart and Winston.

Lever, Janet. 1976. "Sex Differences in the Games Children Play." *Social Problems* 23:478–87.

Lockheed, Marlaine S. and Abigail M. Harris.-

1984. "Cross-Sex Collaborative Learning in Elementary Classrooms." *American Educational Research Journal* 21:275–94.

Luria, Zella and Eleanor W. Herzog. "Gender Segregation across and within Settings." Paper presented at annual meeting of the Society for Research on Child Development, Toronto, Canada, 1985.

Schofield, Janet W. 1982. *Black and White in School.* New York: Praeger.

Thorne, Barrie, Cheris Kramarae, and Nancy Henley, eds. 1983. *Language, Gender, and Society.* New York: Newbury House.

Tyack, David and Elizabeth Hansot. 1990. *Learning Together: A History of Coeducation in American Schools.* New Haven: Yale University Press.

32

TEACHING AND "WOMEN'S WORK"

Michael Apple

[W]omen's work is very often the target of both rationalization and attempts to gain control over it. Such attempts and the resistances to them become quite significant economically and politically, to say nothing of educationally, in schools. In this chapter, I would like to inquire into how it came about that women were in the position to be so targeted. Not only here in the United States, but in other countries as well, the control of teaching and curricula had a strong relationship to sexual and class divisions. I shall

focus historically here on the United States and England, though the arguments I shall present are not necessarily limited to these countries.

. . .

In general, there seems to be a relatively strong relationship between the entry of large numbers of women into an occupation and the slow transformation of the job. Pay is often lowered and the job is regarded as low-skilled so that control is "needed" from the outside. Added to this is the fact that "those occupations which became defined as female expanded at a time when the skills needed to do them were [seen as being] commonly held or easily learned and when there was a particularly high demand for labour, or an especially large pool of women seeking work."[1]

. . .

In my presentation of data to show the progression of teaching from being largely men's work to women's work, in many ways we shall want to pay close attention to how teaching may have changed and to the economic and gender conditions surrounding this. In essence, we may not be describing quite the same occupation after elementary school teaching became women's work. For jobs *are* transformed, often in significant ways, over time. A good example here is again clerical work. Like teaching, this changed from being a masculine occupation in the nineteenth century to being a largely female one in the twentieth. And the labor process of clerical work was radically altered during this period. It was deskilled, came under tighter conditions of control, lost many of its paths of upward mobility to managerial positions, and lost wages at the end of the nineteenth century in the United States and England as it became "feminized."[2] Given this, it is imperative that we ask whether what has been unfortunately called the feminization of teaching actually concerns the same job. I will claim, in fact, that in some rather substantive economic and ideological aspects it is not the same job. This transformation is linked in complex ways to alterations in patriarchal and economic relations that were restructuring the larger society.

Gender and Teaching over Time

Where does teaching fit in here? Some facts may be helpful. What has been called the "feminization" of teaching is clearly seen in data from England. Before the rapid growth of mass elementary education, in 1870, men actually outnumbered women slightly in the

TABLE 32.1   Teachers in Public Elementary Schools in England and Wales, 1870–1930

Year	Total Number	Number of Women Teachers per 100 Men Teachers
1870	13,729	99
1880	41,428	156
1890	73,533	207
1900	113,986	287
1910	161,804	306
1920	151,879	315
1930	157,061	366

Source: Reconstructed from Barry Bergen, "Only a Schoolmaster: Gender, Class, and the Effort to Professionalize Elementary Teaching in England, 1870–1910," *History of Education Quarterly* 22 (Spring 1982), p. 4.

teaching profession. For every 100 men there were only 99 women employed as teachers. This, however, is the last time men have a numerical superiority. Just ten years later, in 1880, for every 100 males there are now 156 women. This ratio rose to 207 to 100 in 1890 and to 287 in 1900. By 1910, women outnumbered men by over three to one. By 1930, the figure had grown to closer to four to one.[3]

Yet these figures would be deceptive if they were not linked to changes in the actual numbers of teachers being employed. Teaching became a symbol of upward mobility for many women, and as elementary schooling increased so did the numbers of women employed in it—points I shall go into in more detail later on. Thus, in 1870, there were only 14,000 teachers in England, of which more were men than women. By the year 1930, 157,061 teachers worked in state-supported schools in England and Wales, and close to 120,000 of these were women.[4] The definition of teaching as a female enclave is given further substantiation by the fact that these numbers signify something quite graphic. While the 40,000 men employed as teachers

TABLE 32.2   Teachers in Public Elementary Schools in the United States, 1870–1930

Year	Number of Men	Number of Women	Total Number of Teachers	Percentage of Women
1870	—	—	—	59 (estimate)
1880	—	—	—	60 (estimate)
1890	121,877	232,925	354,802	65.6
1900	116,416	286,274	402,690	71.1
1910	91,591	389,952	481,543	81.0
1920	63,024	513,222	576,246	89.1
1930	67,239	573,718	640,957	89.5

Source: Adapted from Willard S. Elsbree, *The American Teacher* (New York: American Book Co., 1939), p. 554, and Emery M. Foster, "Statistical Summary of Education, 1929–30," *Biennial Survey of Education 1928–1930,* Vol. 2 (Washington: U.S. Government Printing Office, 1932), p. 8.

around 1930 constitute less than 3 percent of the occupied male workers, the 120,000 women teachers account for nearly 20 percent of all women working for pay outside the home.[5]

If we compare percentages of male to female teachers in the United States with those of England for approximately the same time period, similar patterns emerge. While there was clear regional variation, in typical areas in, say, 1840, only 39 percent of teachers were women. By 1850, the figure had risen to 46 percent.[6] The increase later on is somewhat more rapid than the English experience. The year 1870 finds women holding approximately 60 percent of the public elementary school teaching positions. This figure moves up to 71 percent by 1900. It reaches a peak of fully 89 percent in 1920 and then stabilizes within a few percentage points over the following years.

Given the historical connection between elementary school teaching and the ideologies surrounding domesticity and the definition of "women's proper place," in which teaching was defined as an extension of the productive and reproductive labor women engaged in at home,[7] we should not be surprised by the fact that such changes occurred in the gendered composition of the teaching force. While there are clear connections between patriarchal ideologies and the shift of teaching into being seen as "women's work," the issue is not totally explained in this way, however. Local political economies played a large part here. The shift to non-agricultural employment in male patterns of work is part of the story as well. Just as important was the relationship between the growth of compulsory schooling and women's labor. As we shall see, the costs associated with compulsory schooling to local school districts were often quite high. One way to control such rising costs was in changing accepted hiring practices.[8] One simply hired cheaper teachers—women. Let us examine both of these dynamics in somewhat more detail. In the process, we shall see how class and gender interacted within the limits set by the economic needs of our social formation.

Some simple and well-known economic facts need to be called to mind at the outset. In the U.K., although women teachers outnumbered their male colleagues, the salaries they were paid were significantly lower. In fact, from 1855 to 1935, there was a remarkably consistent pattern. Women were paid approximately two-thirds of what their male counterparts received.[9] Indeed, Bergen claims that one of the major contributing factors behind the schools' increased hiring of women was that they would be paid less.[10]

In the United States, the salary differential was often even more striking. With the rapid growth of schooling stimulated by large rates of immigration as well as by struggles by a number of groups to win free compulsory education, school committees increased their rate of hiring women, but at salaries that were originally half to a third as much as those given to men.[11] But how did it come about that there were positions to be filled in the first place? What happened to the people who had been there?

Elementary school teaching became a woman's occupation in part because men *left* it. For many men, the "opportunity cost" was too great to stay in teaching. Many male teachers taught part-time (e.g., between harvests) or as a stepping stone to more lucrative or prestigious jobs. Yet with the growth of the middle class in the United States, with the formalization of schools and curricula in the latter half of the nineteenth century, and with the enlarged credentialling and certification requirements for teaching that emerged at this time, men began to, and were often able to, look elsewhere.

. . .

Thus, patriarchal familial forms in concert with changes in the social division of labor of capitalism combine here to create some of the conditions out of which a market for a particular kind of teacher emerges. (In England, we should add, a considerable number of men sought employment both there and abroad in the civil service. Many of the men who attended "training colleges," in fact, did so as a point of entry into the civil service, not into teaching.[12] The "Empire," then, had a rather interesting effect on the political economy of gendered labor.)

Faced with these "market conditions," school boards turned increasingly to women. Partly this was a result of women's successful struggle. More and more women were winning the battles over access to both education and employment outside the home. Yet partly it is the result of capitalism as well. Women were continuing to be recruited to the factories and mills (often, by the way, originally because they would sometimes be accompanied by children who could also work for incredibly low wages in the mills).[13] Given the exploitation that existed in the factories and given the drudgery of paid and unpaid domestic labor, teaching must have seemed a considerably more pleasant occupation to many single women. Finally, contradictory tendencies occurred at an ideological level. While women struggled to open up the labor market and alter patriarchal relations in the home and the paid workplace, some of the arguments used for opening up teaching to women were at the expense of reproducing ideological elements that had been part of the root causes of patriarchal control in the first place. The relationship between teaching and domesticity was highlighted. "Advocates of women as teachers, such as Catherine Beecher, Mary Lyon, Zilpah Grant, Horace Mann and Henry Barnard, argued that not only were women the ideal teachers of young children (because of their patience and nurturant qualities) but that teaching was ideal preparation for motherhood."[14] These same people were not loath to argue something else. Women were "willing to" teach at lower wages than those needed by men.[15] When this is coupled with the existing social interests, economic structures, and patriarchal relations that supported the dominance of an ideology of domesticity in the larger society, we can begin to get a glimpse at the conditions that led to such a situation.

Many men did stay in education, however. But as Tyack, Strober, and others have demonstrated, those men who stayed tended to be found in higher-status and higher-paying jobs. In fact, as school systems became more highly bureaucratized, and with the expansion of management positions that accompanied this in the United States, many more men were found in positions of authority than before. Some men stayed in education; but they left the classroom. This lends support to Lanford's claim that from 1870 to 1970, the greater the formalization of the educational system, the greater the proportion of women teachers.[16] It also tends to support my earlier argument that once a set of positions becomes "women's work," it is subject to greater pressure for rationalization. Administrative control of teaching, curricula, and so on increases. The job *itself* becomes different.

Thus, it is not that women had not been found in the teaching ranks before; of course they had. What is more significant is the increasing numbers of women at particular levels "in unified, bureaucratic, and public schools" with their graded curricula, larger and more formally organized districts, growing administrative hierarchies,[17] and, just as crucially, restructuring of the tasks of teachers themselves.

Such sex segregation was not an unusual occurrence in the urban graded school, for instance. At its very outset, proponents of these school plans had a specific labor force and labor process in mind. "Hiring, promotion and salary schedules were routinized." Rather than leaving it up to teachers, the curriculum was quite standardized along grade level lines, with both teachers and students divided into these grades. New managerial positions were created—the superintendent and non-teaching principal, for instance—thereby moving responsibility for managerial concerns out of the classroom. Again, women's supposed nurturing capabilities and "natural" empathic qualities and their relatively low salaries made them ideally suited for teaching in such schools. Even where there were concerns about women teachers' ability to discipline older students, this too could be solved. It was the principal and/or superintendent who handled such issues.[18]

This sexual division of labor within the school had other impacts. It enhanced the ability of urban school boards to maintain bureaucratic control of their employees and over curriculum and teaching practices.

. . .

Given these ideological conditions and these unequal relations of control, why would women ever enter such labor? Was it the stereotypical response that teaching was a temporary way-station on the road to marriage for women who loved children? While this may have been partly accurate, it is certainly overstated since in many instances this was not even remotely the case.

In her collection of teachers' writings from the nineteenth and twentieth centuries, Nancy Hoffman makes the point that most women did not enter teaching with a love of children or with marital plans as the main things in mind. Rather, uppermost in their minds was one major concern. They entered teaching in large part because they needed work. The teachers' comments often document the following facts:

> Women had only a few choices of occupation; and compared with most—laundering, sewing, cleaning, or working in a factory—teaching offered numerous attractions. It was genteel, paid reasonably well, and required little special skill or equipment. In the second half of the century and beyond, it also allowed a woman to travel, to live independently or in the company of other women, and to attain economic security and a modest social status. The issue of marriage, so charged with significance among male educators, emerges in stories of schoolmarms pressured reluctantly into marriage by a family fearful of having an 'old maid' on their

hands, rather than in teachers' accounts of their own eagerness or anxiety over marriage. There are also explicit statements, in these accounts, of teachers *choosing* work and independence over a married life that appeared, to them, to signify domestic servitude or social uselessness. Finally, the accounts of some women tell us that they chose teaching not because they wanted to teach children conventional right from wrong, but in order to foster social, political, or spiritual change: they wanted to persuade the young, move them to collective action for temperance, for racial equality, for conversion to Christianity. What these writings tell us, then, is that from the woman teacher's perspective, the continuity between mothering and teaching was far less significant than a paycheck and the challenge and satisfaction of work.[19]

We should be careful about overstating this case, however. Not a few women could and did train to be teachers and then worked for a relatively short period. As Angela John puts it, "Because the dominant ideology argued that woman's place was in the home, it conveniently enabled elementary teaching to be viewed in theory (if not in practice) as a profession for which women could train and work for a limited time."[20] Obviously, constructing the image of teaching as a transient occupation "permitted the perpetuation of low wages," since such waged labor was merely a way of "tiding women over until they were married."[21] Many women teachers in England, the United States, and elsewhere, however, never married and, hence, the situation is considerably more complicated than conventional stereotypes would have it.[22]

Yet while many teachers in the United States and undoubtedly in the U.K. approached their jobs with a sense that did not necessarily mirror the stereotypes of nurturance and preparation for marriage, this did not stop such stereotypes from creating problems. The increase in women teachers did not occur without challenge. Conservative critics expressed concern over the negative effects women teachers might have on their male pupils. Such concerns increased as the proportion of students going on to secondary schools rose. "While recognizing the beneficial effects on primary-level pupils, the continuation of the female teacher–male student relation into higher grades was viewed as potentially harmful."[23] (The longer tradition of single-sex schools in England partially mediated these pressures.) That this is not simply a historical dynamic is evident by the fact that even today the proportion of male teachers in high school is considerably higher than in the elementary school.

Class Dynamics and Teaching

The general picture I have painted so far has treated the constitution of teaching as primarily a part of the sexual division of labor over time. While this is crucially important, we need to remember that gender was not the only dynamic at work here. Class played a major part, especially in England, but most certainly in the United States as well.[24] Class dynamics operated at the level of who became teachers and what their experiences were.

It was not until the end of the nineteenth century and the outset of the twentieth that middle-class girls began to be recruited into teaching in England. In fact, only after 1914 do we see any large influx of middle-class girls entering state-supported elementary school teaching.[25]

Class distinctions were very visible. While the concept of femininity *idealized* for middle-class women centered around an image of the "perfect wife and mother," the middle-class view of working-class women often entailed a different sense of femininity. The waged labor of working-class women "tarnished" them (though there is evidence of between-class feminist solidarity).[26] Such waged labor was a departure from bourgeois ideals of domesticity and economic dependence. With the emergence of changes in such bourgeois ideals toward the end of the nineteenth century, middle-class women themselves began to "widen their sphere of action and participate in some of the various economic and social changes that accompanied industrialization" and both the restructuring of capitalism and the division of labor. Struggles over legal and political rights, over employment and education, came to be of considerable import. Yet because of a tension between the ideals of domesticity and femininity on the one hand and the struggle to enlarge the middle-class woman's economic sphere on the other, particular jobs were seen as appropriate for women. Teaching (and often particular kinds of stenographic and secretarial work) was one of the predominant ones.[27] In fact, of the white women who worked outside the home in the United States in the mid- to late nineteenth century, fully 20 percent were employed at one time or another as teachers.[28]

This entrance of women, and especially of middle-class women, into paid teaching created important pressures for improvements in the education of women in both the United States and England.[29] Equalization of curricular offerings, the right to enter into traditional male enclaves within universities, and so on, were in no small part related to this phenomenon. Yet we need to remember an important social fact here. Even though women were making gains in education and employment, most, say, middle-class women still found themselves *excluded* from the professions and other areas of employment.[30] Thus, a dynamic operated that cut both

ways. In being limited to and carving out this area of employment, women "held on to it as one of the few arenas in which they could exert any power, even at the expense of further reinforcing stereotypes about women's sphere."[31]

Having said this, we again should not assume that teachers were recruited primarily from middle-class homes in the United States or England. Often quite the opposite was the case. A number of studies demonstrate that working-class backgrounds were not unusual. In fact, one American study completed in 1911 presents data on the average woman teacher's economic background. She came from a family in which the father's income was approximately $800 a year, a figure that places the family among skilled workers or farmers rather than the middle class.[32]

These class differences had an impact not only on an ideological level, but in terms of education and employment within education as well. Girls of different class backgrounds often attended different schools, even when they might both wish to be teachers.[33] Furthermore, by the end of the nineteenth century in England, class differences created clear distinctions in patterns of where one might teach. While middle-class women teachers were largely found working in private secondary and single-sex schools "which catered especially to middle class girls" or as governesses, women teachers from working-class backgrounds were found elsewhere. They dominated positions within state-supported elementary schools—schools that were largely working-class and mixed-sex.[34] In many ways these were simply different jobs.

These class distinctions can hide something of considerably significance, however. Both groups still had low status.[35] To be a woman was still to be involved in a social formation that was defined in large part by the structure of patriarchal relations. But again patriarchal forms were often colonized and mediated by class relations.

For example, *what* was taught to these aspiring teachers had interesting relationships to the social and sexual divisions of labor. Many aspiring working-class "pupil teachers" in England were recruited to teach in working-class schools. Much of what they were expected to teach centered around domestic skills such as sewing and needlework in addition to reading, spelling, and arithmetic. For those working-class pupil teachers who might ultimately sit for an examination to enter one of the teacher training colleges, gender divisions were most pronounced. In Purvis's comparison of these entrance tests, the different expectations of what men and women were to know and, hence, teach are more than a little visible. Both men and women were examined in dictation, penmanship, grammar, composition, school management, history, geography, French, German, Latin, and Welsh. Yet only men were tested in algebra, geometry, Euclid, and Greek. Only women took domestic economy and needlework.

The focus on needlework is a key here in another way, for not only does it signify clear gender dynamics at work but it also points again to class barriers. Unlike the "ornamental sewing" that was more common in middle-class households, these working-class girls were examined on "useful sewing." Questions included how to make the knee part of "knickerbocker drawers" and the sewing together of women's petticoats of a gored variety. (This was one of the most efficient uses of material, since less material is needed if the fabric is cut and sewn correctly.)[36] The dominance of utility, efficiency, and cost saving is once more part of the vision of what working-class girls would need.[37] As Purvis notes, "it would appear then that female elementary teachers were expected to

teach those skills which were linked to that form of feminity deemed appropriate for the working classes."[38]

But teaching, especially elementary school teaching, was not all that well paid, to say the least, earning somewhat more than a factory operative but still only the equivalent of a stenographer's wages in the United States or England.[39] What would its appeal have been for a working-class girl? In England, with its very visible set of class relations and articulate class culture, we find answers similar to but—given these more visible class relations—still different from the United States. First, the very *method* by which girls were first trained in the 1870s to become teachers was a system of apprenticeship—a system that was "indigenous to working class culture." This was especially important since it was evident at the time that female pupil teachers were usually the daughters of laborers, artisans, or small tradesmen. Second, and here very much like the American experience, compared to occupations such as domestic service, working in factories, dressmaking, and so on—among the only jobs realistically open to working-class women—teaching had a number of benefits. It did increase status, especially among working-class girls who showed a degree of academic ability. Working conditions, though still nothing to write home about, were clearly better in many ways. They were relatively clean and, though often extremely difficult given the overcrowded conditions in schools, had that same potential for job satisfaction that was evident in my earlier quotation from Hoffman and that was frequently missing in other employment. And, just as significantly, since teaching was considered to be on the mental side of the mental/manual division of labor, it gave an opportunity—though granted a limited one—for a certain amount of social mobility.[40] (This question of social mobility and "respectability" may have been particularly important to those women and families newly within a "lower-middle-class" location, as well, given the increasing proportion of such people in teaching in England by the beginning of the second decade of this century.)

There was a price to pay for this "mobility" and the promise of improved working conditions that accompanied it. Women elementary school teachers became less connected to their class origins, and at the same time class differences in ideals of femininity still kept them from being totally acceptable to these classes above them. This contradictory situation is not an abstraction. The fact that it was lived out is made clear in these teachers' frequent references to their social isolation.[41] Such isolation was of course heightened considerably by other lived conditions of teachers. The formal and contractual conditions under which teachers were hired were not the most attractive. As many of you already know, women teachers in the United States, for example, could be fired for getting married, or if married, getting pregnant. There were prohibitions about being seen with men, about clothes, about makeup, about politics, about money, about nearly all of one's public (and private) life.

It would be wrong to trace all of this back to economic motives and class dynamics. For decades married women were prohibited from teaching on both sides of the Atlantic. While single women were often young, and hence were paid less, the notion of morality and purity as powerful symbols of a womanly teaching act undoubtedly played a large part. The above-mentioned array of controls of women's physicality, dress, living arrangements, and morals shows the importance of these concerns. Ideologies of patriarchy, with the teacher being shrouded in a domestic and maternal cloak—possibly combined with a more deep-seated male suspicion of female sexuality—are reproduced here.[42] It is the very combination of patriar-chal relations and economic pressures that continue to work their way through teaching to this day.

These controls are strikingly evident in a relatively standard teacher's contract from the United States for the year 1923. I reproduce it in its entirety since it condenses within itself so many of the ideological conditions under which women teachers worked:

TEACHERS CONTRACT 1923

This is an agreement between
Miss _____, teacher, and the Board
of Education of the _____ School,
whereby Miss _____ agrees to teach
for a period of eight months, beginning
Sept. 1, 1923. The Board of Education
agrees to pay Miss _____ the sum
of ($75) per month.
Miss _____ agrees:

1. Not to get married. This contract becomes null and void immediately if the teacher marries.

2. Not to keep company with men.

3. To be home between the hours of 8:00 P.M. and 6:00 A.M. unless in attendance at a school function.

4. Not to loiter downtown in ice cream stores.

5. Not to leave town at any time without the permission of the chairman of the Board of Trustees.

6. Not to smoke cigarettes. This contract becomes null and void immediately if the teacher is found smoking.

7. Not to drink beer, wine, or whiskey. This contract becomes null and void immediately if the teacher is found drinking beer, wine, or whiskey.

8. Not to ride in a carriage or automobile with any man except her brother or father.

9. Not to dress in bright colors.

10. Not to dye her hair.
11. To wear at least two petticoats.
12. Not to wear dresses more than two inches above the ankles.
13. To keep the schoolroom clean.
    a. to sweep the classroom floor at least once daily.
    b. to scrub the classroom floor at least once weekly with hot water and soap.
    c. to clean the blackboard at least once daily.
    d. to start the fire at 7:00 so the room will be warm at 8:00 A.M. when the children arrive.
14. Not to use face powder, mascara, or paint the lips.

In many ways, the contract speaks for itself. It is important to note, though, that this sort of thing did not end in 1923. Many of these conditions continued for decades, to be ultimately transformed into . . . more technical and bureaucratic forms of control. . . .

Let me give one further concrete example. The larger political economy, in combination with patriarchal ideological forms, shows its power once again whenever the question of married women who engage in waged work appears historically. By the turn of the century hundreds of thousands of married women had begun to work outside the home. Yet during the Depression, it was very common for married women to be fired or to be denied jobs if they had working husbands. The state played a large role here. In England, governmental policies and reports gave considerable attention to women's domestic role.[43] In the United States, in 1930–31 the National Association of Education reported that of the 1,500 school systems in the country 77 percent refused to hire married women teachers. Another 63 percent dismissed any woman teacher who got married during the time of her employment. This did not only occur at the elementary and second-ary levels. Some universities asked their married women faculty to resign. Lest we see this as something that only affected women teachers, the Federal government itself required in 1932 that if a married couple worked for the government, one must be let go. This law was applied almost invariably to women only.[44]

The very fact that these figures seem so shocking to us now is eloquent testimony of the sacrifices made and the struggles that women engaged in for decades to alter these oppressive relations. These struggles have been over one's control of one's labor and over the control of one's very life. Given the past conditions I have just pointed to, these historically significant struggles have actually brought no small measure of success. . . .

. . .

NOTES

1. Linda Murgatroyd, "Gender and Occupational Stratification," *Sociological Review* 30 (November 1982), p. 588.
2. Veronica Beechey, "The Sexual Division of Labour and the Labour Processes: A Critical Assessment of Braverman." P. 67 in *The Degradation of Work?* edited by Stephen Wood. London: Hutchinson, 1982.
3. Barry H. Bergen, "Only a Schoolmaster: Gender, Class, and the Effort to Professionalize Elementary Teaching in England, 1870–1910," *History of Education Quarterly* 22 (Spring 1982), p. 12.
4. Ibid.
5. Ibid., p. 5.
6. Myra Strober, "Segregation by Gender in Public School Teaching: Toward a General Theory of Occupational Segregation in the Labor Market." Unpublished manuscript, Stanford University, 1982, p. 16.
7. See, for example, Sheila Rothman, *Women's Proper Place* (New York: Basic Books, 1978), and Michele Barrett, *Women's Oppression Today* (London: New Left Books, 1980).
8. John Richardson and Brenda Wooden Hatcher, "The Feminization of Public School Teaching, 1870–1920," *Work and Occupations* 10 (February 1983), p. 84.
9. Bergen, "Only a Schoolmaster," p. 13.

10. Ibid., p. 14.
11. Nancy Hoffman, *Women's "True" Profession: Voices from the History of Teaching* (Old Westbury: The Feminist Press, 1981), p. xix.
12. See the discussion in Frances Widdowson, *Going Up into the Next Class: Women and Elementary Teacher Training, 1840–1914* (London: Hutchinson, 1983).
13. David Gordon, Richard Edwards, and Michael Reich, *Segmented Work, Divided Workers: The Historical Transformation of Labor in the United States* (New York: Cambridge University Press, 1982), p. 68.
14. Strober, "Segregation by Gender in Public School Teaching," p. 19.
15. Strober, "Segregation by Gender in Public School Teaching." This "willingness" often had *religious* roots.
16. Lanford, quoted in Strober, "Segregation by Gender in Public School Teaching," p. 21.
17. Richardson and Hatcher, "The Feminization of Public School Teaching," 82.
18. Myra Strober and David Tyack, "Why Do Women Teach and Men Manage?: A Report on Research on Schools," *Signs* 5 (Spring 1980), p. 499.
19. Hoffman, *Women's "True" Profession*, pp. xvii–xviii.
20. Angela V. John, "Foreword" to Widdowson, *Getting Up into the Next Class*, p. 9.
21. Ibid.
22. See, for example, Marta Danylewycz and Alison Prentice, "Teachers, Gender, and Bureaucratizing School Systems in Nineteenth Century Montreal and Toronto." *History of Education Quarterly* 24 (Spring 1984).
23. Richardson and Hatcher, "The Feminization of Public School Teaching," 87–88.
24. On the importance of thinking about the United States in class terms, see David Hogan, "Education and Class Formation: The Peculiarities of the Americans," in Michael W. Apple, ed., *Cultural and Economic Reproduction in Education: Essays on Class, Ideology and the State* (Boston and London: Routledge and Kegan Paul, 1982), pp. 32–78, and Erik Olin Wright, *Class, Crisis and the State* (London: New Left Books, 1978).
25. June Purvis, "Women and Teaching in the Nineteenth Century," in Dale et al., eds., *Education and the State*, Vol. 2, p. 372. See also Widdowson, *Going Up into the Next Class*.
26. See the interesting historical analysis of the place of socialist women here in Mari Jo Buhle, *Women and American Socialism, 1870–1920* (Urbana: University of Illinois Press, 1981).
27. Purvis, "Women and Teaching in the Nineteenth Century," pp. 361–63.
28. Carl Degler, *At Odds: Women and the Family in America from the Revolution to the Present* (New York: Oxford University Press, 1980), p. 381.
29. Purvis, "Women and Teaching in the Nineteenth Century," p. 372.
30. Strober and Tyack, "Why Do Women Teach and Men Manage?" p. 496.
31. Sandra Acker, "Women and Teaching: A Semi-Detached Sociology of a Semi-Detached Profession," in Stephen Walker and Len Barton eds., *Gender, Class and Education* (Barcombe, Sussex: Falmer Press, 1983), p. 134.
32. Degler, *At Odds*, p. 380. Paul Mattingly, too, argues that by the 1890s even many normal schools had become almost exclusively female and had directed their attention to a "lower-class" student body.
33. Interestingly enough, some believed that upper-middle-class young women were at an academic disadvantage compared to working-class young women in teacher training institutions in England. See Widdowson, *Going Up into the Next Class*.
34. Purvis, "Women and Teaching in the Nineteenth Century," p. 364.
35. Ibid.
36. Ibid., p. 366.
37. I wish to thank Rima D. Apple for this point.
38. Purvis, "Women and Teaching in the Nineteenth Century," p. 366.
39. Rotham, *Women's Proper Place*, p. 58.
40. Purvis, "Women and Teaching in the Nineteenth Century," p. 367.
41. Ibid.
42. See Barrett, *Women's Oppression Today*, pp. 187–226.
43. See Ann Marie Wolpe, "The Official Ideology of Education for Girls." Pp. 138–59 in *Educability, Schools and Ideology*, edited by Michael Flude and John Ahier. (London: Halsted Press, 1974).
44. Degler, *At Odds*, pp. 413–14.

PART IV

Student Behavior and Adolescent Subcultures

Schools are not only places at which societal inequalities are perpetuated or diminished; they are also settings in which children and adolescents spend an increasing amount of their lives. Over the last century, high school students have increasingly formed their peer relationships in school, generating what researchers term "adolescent subcultures." Additionally, at school students exhibit rebellious behavior toward one another, their teachers, and authority in general. Earlier selections in this reader attest to the importance of peer climates in determining student outcomes (e.g., Coleman and Hoffer, Part I; Cookson and Persell, Part II; Coleman et al., Part II). The readings in Part IV focus on the character of peer climates by investigating adolescent subcultures and student behavior. The readings span the past four decades and thus also provide a portrait of changing adolescent behavior in schools.

The first reading is a classic 1960 study of adolescent subcultures by James Coleman, which foreshadowed his later contention, in "The Coleman Report" (Part II), that peer reklationships are highly influential in structuring student outcomes. Coleman argues that an adolescent subculture has emerged in post–WWII society. He believes that the increased importance of peer relationships came about because of changes in family dynamics and labor market trends, which resulted in a prolonged period of adolescence, mostly spent in schools. Further, the growing capabilities of mass media to target a youth audience provided a common source of cultural information for adolescents. Although this study is 40 years old, the broad

patterns of peer orientations and gender experiences in schools today have remained strikingly similar to the schools Coleman once investigated.

In the second reading, Mary Metz studies classroom rebellion in the late 1970s. Metz moves away from a conception of individual student status frustration and toward an understanding of classroom dynamics informed by a symbolic interactionist perspective. Metz demonstrates how meanings and understandings about classroom life are generated from interactions between students and teachers. Rather than blaming the students for acting up without cause or reason, Metz views the rebellion as a logical product of teachers' inappropriate attempts to discipline students. Other researchers, such as Pedro Noguera (1992), have argued more broadly that student misbehavior is the logical outgrowth of the current structure of educational inequality.

In the final selection, John Devine presents a contemporary depiction of adolescent student behavior. Whereas the earlier readings suggest that student rebellion is nothing new, Devine demonstrates how modern social context alters the character of rebellion by providing adolescents with access to weapons. Neighborhood schools located in areas with concentrated poverty, crime, and drug dealing face student rebellion more violent in character than it was in the past. Over the twentieth century, raising the school-leaving age and expanding educational opportunity have changed the populations that schools serve, with children from more impoverished families gaining access to higher levels of education. Because the population of students has grown more inclusive, schools are encountering new sets of responsibilities and challenges in discipline and violence prevention (Toby 1995).

REFERENCES

NOGUERA, PEDRO. 1992. "Preventing and Producing Violence: A Critical Analysis of Responses to School Violence." *Harvard Educational Review*, pp. 189–212.

TOBY, JACKSON. 1995. "The Schools." Pp. 141–70 in *Crime*, edited by James Q. Wilson and Joan Petersilia. San Francisco, CA: Institute for Contemporary Studies.

33

THE ADOLESCENT CULTURE

James Coleman

The simple fact that adolescents are looking to each other rather than to the adult community for their social rewards has a number of significant implications for educational theory and practice. To be sure, parents and parental desires are of great importance to children in a long-range sense, but it is their peers whose approval, admiration, and respect they attempt to win in their everyday activities, in school and out. As a result, the old "levers" by which children are motivated—approval or disapproval of parents and teachers—are less efficient.

As long as meaningful social rewards could be directly supplied by adults, there was little need to be explicit about them in educational theory, for they were naturally provided by the very process of interaction between parent and child, or student and

teacher. To be sure, these rewards were often distributed in ways that reinforced the stratification system and took away the lower-class child's meager chance for equality; as some authors have shown very well, the middle-class backgrounds of teachers often made them unable to hold out reasonable rewards for reasonable achievement to lower-class children.[1] The situation, however, was fundamentally simpler than it is today, because teachers and parents had direct control over the levers they could apply to motivate children. Now the levers are other children themselves, acting as a small society, and adults must come to know either how to shape the directions this society takes, or else how to break down the adolescent society, thus re-establishing control by the old levers.

I suspect that this latter solution would be exceedingly difficult, for it flies in the face of large-scale social changes, and would seem to require a reorganization of work and community, which is hardly in the offing. The major thesis of this [chapter] is that it is possible to take the other tack, to learn how to control the adolescent community *as a community*, and to use it to further the ends of education.

The first step is to examine a number of adolescent communities themselves, in order to discover just what the value systems are. On what grounds do adolescents give approval to one another or withhold it? How does a boy or girl become a member of the "inner core" or "leading crowd"? What makes a boy or girl popular, admired, and imitated by his fellows? There are differences from community to community and from school to school, some of which will be examined in detail later; there are also similarities, which make it worthwhile investigating first the values of the general adolescent culture and the possible effects of these values on children. The similarities among different schools suggest there are some general elements in the role to which adolescents are relegated by the adult society. The differences indicate that it is not hopeless for adults to attempt to modify the adolescent cultures.

The General Interests and Activities of Teen-Agers

Because adolescents live so much in a world of their own, adults remain uninformed about the way teen-agers spend their time, the things that are important to them, and the things that friends have in common. Several questions were asked in the study that give a picture of these patterns of activities and interests. Every boy and girl was asked: (I.108) "What is your favorite way of spending your leisure time?"

The boys' responses (see Table 33.1) indicate that boys like to spend a great deal of their time in fairly active outdoor pursuits, such as sports, boating, and just going around with the fellows. They also spend

time on hobbies—the most frequent of which is working on their car—and on such passive pursuits as movies, television, records, and the like. Being with girls does not, as adults sometimes think, constitute a large part of their leisure activities—although it comes to occupy more time as they go from the freshman year to the senior year.

Girls' leisure-time activities show a sharp contrast in some categories. Girls' favorite leisure activities less often include the active outdoor pursuits of boys. More frequent are activities like "just being with their friends," watching television and movies, attending games, reading, and listening to records. Their more active pursuits include one that never exists for boys—dancing among themselves. Perhaps this is an activity that substitutes for the sports at which boys spend their time; in part, it is certainly preparation for dancing with boys. In any case, it suggests the oft-heard quip that boys are interested in sports and girls are interested in boys.

The general pattern of these leisure pursuits, showing considerably more activity among the boys, is indicative of a situation that seems to be quite general in the adolescent community: boys have far more to *do* than girls. Whether it is athletics, or cars, or hunting, or model-building, our society seems to provide a much fuller set of activities to engage the interests of boys. Thus, when girls are together, they are more often just "with the group" than are boys. A frequent afternoon activity is simply "going up town" to window shop and walk around.[2]

There is a point of particular interest in these responses, in relation to the school. Only one of the categories, organized sports, has any direct relation to school. Some of the hobbies and other activities may, of course, have their genesis in school, but except for such hobbies and organized sports, school-related activities are missing. No one

TABLE 33.1   Leisure Activities of Boys and Girls in the Nine
Public High Schools

	Boys	Girls
1. Organized outdoor sports—including football, basketball, tennis, etc.	22.0%	6.9%
2. Unorganized outdoor activities—including hunting, fishing, swimming, boating, horseback riding	14.7	11.3
3. "Being with the group," riding around, going up town, etc.	17.2	32.5
4. Attending movies and spectator events—athletic games, etc.	8.5	10.4
5. Dating or being out with opposite sex	13.6	11.6
6. Going dancing (girls only)		12.0
7. Hobby—working on cars, bicycles, radio, musical instruments, etc.	22.5	20.1
8. Indoor group activities—bowling, playing cards, roller skating, etc.	8.0	8.1
9. Watching television	19.4	23.6
10. Listening to records or radio	11.2	31.7
11. Reading	13.7	35.5
12. Other, e.g., talking on telephone	7.1	9.3
13. No answer	8.1	3.7
Number of cases	(4,020)	(4,134)

responds that doing homework is his favorite way of spending his leisure time. This is at least in part because homework is assigned work, and cannot be leisure. Yet athletics, which involves work during practice, manages to run over into leisure time, breaking the barrier that separates work from leisure. Perhaps it is not too much to expect that other in-school activities directly tied to learning could—if the right way were found—similarly spill over into leisure and be a favored way of spending free time.

. . .

The Leading Crowds in the Schools

Let us examine what it takes to "rate" in these schools, both among one's own sex, and with the other sex. What does it take to be in the "leading crowd" in school? This question, of course, presumes that there *is* a leading

crowd in school. To be sure, when students were asked such a question, some, particularly in the smallest school, did object to the idea that there was a leading crowd. Yet this kind of objection is in large part answered by one of the boys in another small school, Maple Grove, in a group interview. A friend of his denied that there was any leading crowd at all in the school, and he responded: "You don't see it because you're in it."

Another boy in the same school had this to say in an interview:

(What are some of the groups in school?)
You mean like cliques? Well, there's about two cliques. There's one that's these girls and boys—let's see, there's ———, ———, and ———. I'm in it, but as far as I'm concerned, I'm not crazy about being in it. I tell you, it wasn't any of my doing, because I'm always for the underdog myself. But

I'd rather be with a bunch like that, you know, than have them against me. So I just go along with them.

(What's the other clique?)

Well, I don't know too much about it, it's just another clique.

(Kind of an underdog clique?)

Sort of.

(Who are some of the kids in it?)

Oh—I couldn't tell you. I know, but I just can't think of their names.

(How do you get in the top clique?)

Well, I'll tell you, like when I came over here, I had played football over at ————. I was pretty well known by all the kids before I came over. And when I came there was ———— always picking on kids. He hit this little kid one day, and I told him that if I ever saw him do anything to another little kid that I'd bust him. So one day down in the locker he slammed this kid against the locker, so I went over and hit him a couple times, knocked him down. And a lot of the kids liked me for doing that, and I got on the good side of two or three teachers.

(What are the differences between these two cliques?)

Well, I'll tell you, I don't like this top clique, myself. Just to be honest with you, they're all scared of me, because I won't take anything off of them, and they know it. I've had a run-in with this one girl, she really thinks she's big stuff. And I don't like her at all, we don't get along, and she knows it and I know it, and they don't say nothing. But a lot of them in the big clique, they're my friends. I get along with them real good, and then I try to be real nice to the underdogs, the kids that haven't got—not quite as lucky— they haven't got as much money, they have a hard time, maybe they don't look as sharp as some of the others.

(What are the main interests of the top clique?)

Just to run everything, to be the big deal.

(Are most of the boys in athletics?)

Yeah—you couldn't really say that in this town, though. The really good athletes, a couple of them may be in the clique—the clique's a funny thing, it's just who they want to be in it. They don't want to have anybody in there they think might give them trouble. They want to rule the roost.

(Do most of them have fathers that have good jobs, are well-to-do?)

Most of them. They come from families that have money.

. . .

This account of the leading crowd in one school gives a vivid picture of how such crowds function; not that the leading crowd in every school functions in just the same way. Most interviews in other schools suggested a somewhat less closed circle than in this school, yet one that is not greatly different.

In every school, most students saw a leading crowd, and were willing to say what it took to get in it. This should not be surprising, for every adult community has its leading crowd, although adults are less often in such close and compelling communities. Adults, however, are often blind to the fact that the teen-agers in a high school *do* constitute a community, which *does* have a leading crowd. Consequently, adult concern tends to be with questions of better ways to teach "the child," viewed as an isolated entity—whether it is the "gifted child" or the "backward child."

The major categories of response to the question, "What does it take to get into the leading crowd in this school?" are shown in Figure 33.1. Consider first the girls' responses. Most striking is the great impor-

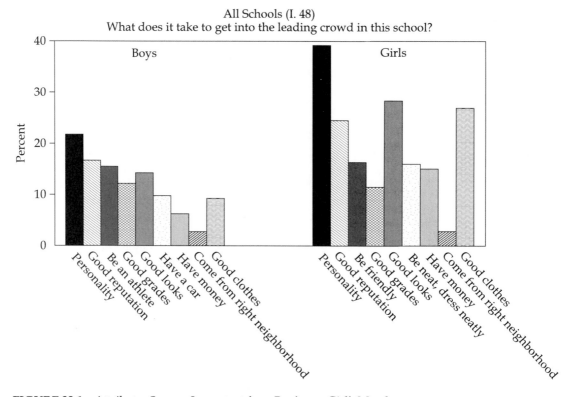

FIGURE 33.1 Attributes Seen as Important for a Boy's or a Girl's Membership in the Leading Crowd.

tance of "having a good personality." Not only is this mentioned most often in the total responses, but it is mentioned most often in seven of the nine schools.

The importance of having a good personality, or, what is a little different, "being friendly" or "being nice to the other kids," in these adolescent cultures is something that adults often fail to realize. Adults often forget how "person-oriented" children are; they have not yet moved into the world of cold impersonality in which many adults live. This is probably due to their limited range of contacts. In the world of grade school, a boy or girl *can* respond to his classmates as persons, with a sincerity that becomes impossible as one's range of contacts grows. One of the major transitions for some

children comes, in fact, as they enter high school and find that they move from classroom to classroom and have different classmates in each class.

After "a good personality" come a wide range of attributes and activities. The diversity of responses is indicated by the collection of remarks listed below—some respondents were hostile to the leading crowd, and, in their hostility, often thought it immoral; others were friendly to it, and, in their friendliness, attributed positive virtues to it.

(What does it take to get into the leading crowd in this school?)
Wear just the right things, nice hair, good grooming, and have a wholesome personality.

Money, clothes, flashy appearance, date older boys, fairly good grades.

Be a sex fiend—dress real sharp—have own car and money—smoke and drink—go steady with a popular boy.

Have pleasant personality, good manners, dress nicely, be clean, don't swear, be loads of fun.

A nice personality, dress nice without overdoing it.

Hang out at ———'s. Don't be too smart. Flirt with boys. Be co-operative on dates.

Among these various attributes, the graph shows "good looks," phrased in some fashion, to be second to "personality" in frequency. Having nice clothes, or being well dressed, is the third most frequent item mentioned. What it means to be well dressed differs sharply in a well-to-do suburb and in a working-class school, of course. Nevertheless, whether it is the number of cashmere sweaters a girl owns or simply having clean and attractive dresses, the matter of "having good clothes" is important. The importance of clothes appears to derive partially from the fact that clothes symbolize family status. However, it also appears to stem from the same source that gives importance to "good looks"; these items are crucial in making a girl attractive to boys. Thus, in this respect, the values of the girls' culture are molded by the presence of boys—and by the fact that success with boys is of overriding importance.

Another attribute required if one is to be in the leading crowd is indicated by the class of responses labeled "having a good reputation," which was fourth in number of times mentioned. In all these schools, this item was often mentioned, although in each school, some saw the leading crowd as composed of girls with bad reputations and immoral habits.

A girl's "reputation" is crucial among adolescents. A girl is caught in a dilemma, posed by the importance of good looks, on the one hand, and a good reputation, on the other. A girl must be successful with the boys, says the culture, but in doing so she must maintain her reputation. In some schools, the limits defining a good reputation are stricter than in others, but in all the schools, the limits are there to define what is "good" and what is "bad." The definitions are partly based on behavior with boys, but they also include drinking, smoking, and other less tangible matters—something about the way a girl handles herself, quite apart from what she actually does.

It is not such an easy matter for a girl to acquire and keep a good reputation, particularly if her mother is permissive in letting her date whom she likes as a freshman or sophomore. Junior and senior boys often date freshman and sophomore girls, sometimes with good intentions and sometimes not. One senior boy in Green Junction, in commenting upon the "wildness" of the leading girls in his class, explained it by saying that when his class was in the eighth grade, it was forced to go to school in the high-school building because of a classroom shortage. A number of the girls in the class, he explained, had begun dating boys in the upper classes of high school. This, to him, was where the problem began.

Another criterion for membership in the leading crowd was expressed by a girl who said simply: "Money, fancy clothes, good house, new cars, etc.—the best." These qualities are all of a piece: they express the fact that being born into the right family is a great help to a girl in getting into the leading crowd. It is expressed differently in different schools and by different girls—sometimes as "parents having money," sometimes as "coming from the right neighborhood," sometimes as "expensive clothes." These qualities differ sharply from some of those discussed above, for they are not something a girl can *change*.[3] Her position in the system is ascribed according to her parents' social position, and there is nothing she can do about it. If criteria such as these dominate, then we would expect the system to have a very different effect on the people in it than if other criteria, which a girl or boy could hope to meet, were the basis of social comparison. Similarly, in the larger society a caste system has quite different effects on individuals than does a system with a great deal of mobility between social classes.

It is evident that these family-background criteria play some part in these schools, but—at least, according to these girls—not the major part. (It is true, however, that the girls who are *not* in the leading crowd more often see such criteria, which are glossed over or simply not seen by girls who are in the crowd.) Furthermore, these criteria vary sharply in their importance in different schools. . . .

Another criterion for being in the leading crowd is scholastic success. According to these girls, good grades, or "being smart" or "intelligent," have something to do with membership in the leading crowd. Not much, to be sure: it is mentioned less than 12 percent of the time, and far less often than the attributes of personality, good looks, clothes, and the like. Nevertheless, doing well in school apparently counts for something. It is surprising that it does not count for more, because in some situations, the "stars," heroes, and objects of adulation are those who best achieve the goals of the institution. For example, in the movie industry, the leading crowd is composed of those who have achieved the top roles—they are, by consensus, the "stars." Or in a graduate school, the "leading crowd" of students ordinarily consists of the bright students who excel in their work. Not

so for these high school girls. The leading crowd seems to be defined primarily in terms of *social* success: their personality, clothes, desirability as dates, and—in communities where social success is tied closely to family background—their money and family.

Perhaps, however, achievement in other areas within the school is important in getting into the leading crowd. That is, participation in school activities of one sort or another may be the entree for a girl into the leading group.

A look at the frequency of responses in Figure 33.1 indicates that this is not true. Activities in school, such as cheerleading, and "being active in school affairs" were mentioned, but rather infrequently. The over-all frequency was 6.5 percent, and in none of the schools were these things mentioned as much as 10 percent of the time. It may very well be, of course, that activities help a girl's access to the leading crowd through an indirect path, bringing her to the center of attention, from whence access to the leading crowd is possible.

What about boys? What were their responses to this question about criteria for the leading crowd? Figure 33.1 shows the boys' responses, grouped as much as possible into the same categories used for the girls. The first difference between these and the girls' responses is the over-all lower frequency. The girls sometimes set down in great detail just what is required to get in the leading crowd—but the matter seems somewhat less salient to the boys.

For the boys, a somewhat different set of attributes is important for membership in the leading crowd. The responses below give some idea of the things mentioned.

A good athlete, pretty good looking, common sense, sense of humor.
Money, cars and the right connections and a good personality.

Be a good athlete. Have a good person-
ality. Be in everything you can. Don't
drink or smoke. Don't go with bad
girls.
Athletic ability sure helps.
Prove you rebel the police officers.
Dress sharply. Go out with sharp
Freshman girls. Ignore Senior girls.
Good in athletics; "wheel" type; not too
intelligent.

By categories of response, Figure 33.1
shows that "a good personality" is important for the boys, but less strikingly so than
it is for the girls. Being "good-looking," having good clothes, and having a good reputation are similarly of decreased importance.
Good clothes, in particular, are less important for the boys than for the girls. Similarly,
the items associated with parents' social
position—having money, coming from the
right neighborhood, and the like—are less
frequently mentioned by boys.

What, then, are the criteria that are more
important for boys than girls? The most obvious is athletics. Of the things that a boy can
do, of the things he can *achieve,* athletic success seems the clearest and most direct path
to membership in the leading crowd.

Academic success appears to be a less
certain path to the leading crowd than athletics—and sometimes it is a path away, as
the final quotation listed above suggests. It
does, however, sometimes constitute a path,
according to these responses. The path is apparently stronger for boys, where scholarly
achievement is fifth in frequency, than for
the girls, where it is eighth in frequency. This
result is somewhat puzzling, for it is well
known that girls work harder in school and
get better grades than boys do. The ambivalence of the culture concerning high achievement among girls will be examined in some
detail later. At this point, it is sufficient to
note that academic achievement is apparently less useful for a girl as a stepping stone

to social success in high school than it is for
a boy.

An item of considerable importance for
the boys, as indicated on the bar graph, is a
car—just having a car, according to some
boys, or having a *nice* car, according to others.
Whichever it is, a car appears to be of considerable importance in being part of the "inner
circle" in these schools. In four of the five
small-town schools—but in none of the
larger schools—a car was mentioned more
often than academic achievement. When this
is coupled with the fact that these responses
include not only juniors and seniors but also
freshmen and sophomores, who are too
young to drive, the place of cars in these adolescent cultures looms even larger.

As a whole, how do the boys' membership criteria for the leading crowd differ
from the criteria for girls? Several sharp differences are evident. Family background
seems to matter less for boys—it is apparently considerably easier for a boy than for a
girl from the wrong side of the tracks to
break into the crowd. Clothes, money, and
being from the right neighborhood hold a
considerably higher place for the girls. Similarly with personal attributes, such as personality, reputation, good looks—all of
which define what a person *is.* In contrast,
the criteria for boys include a much larger
component of what a person *does,* whether in
athletics or in academic matters. Such a distinction can be overdrawn, for a girl's reputation and her personality are certainly determined by what she does. However, these
are not clear-cut dimensions of achievement,
they are far less tangible. Furthermore, they
are pliable in the hands of the leading crowd
itself, who can define what constitutes a
good reputation or a good personality, but
who cannot ignore football touchdowns or
scholastic honors. Numerous examples of
the way the leading crowd can shape reputations were evident in these schools. For example, a girl reported:

It is rumored that if you are in with either ——— or ——— that you've got it made. But they are both my friends. You've got to be popular, considerate, have a good reputation. One girl came this year with a rumor started about her. She was ruined in no time, by ——— especially.

The girl who had been "ruined" was a top student and a leader in school activities, but neither of these things was enough to give her a place in the leading crowd. At the end of the school year she was just as far out of things as she was at the beginning, despite her achievements in school.

The matter is different for boys. There are fewer solid barriers, such as family background, and fewer criteria that can be twisted at the whim of the in-group than there are for girls. To be sure, achievement must be in the right area—chiefly athletics—but achievement *can* in most of these schools bring a boy into the leading crowd, which is more than it can do in many instances for girls.

There is the suggestion that the girls' culture derives in some fashion from the boys: the girl's role is to sit there and look pretty, waiting for the athletic star to come pick her. She must cultivate her looks, be vivacious and attractive, wear the right clothes, but then wait—until the football player, whose status is determined by his specific achievements, comes along to choose her. This is, of course, only part of the matter, for in a community where the leading crowd largely reflects the "right families" in town (as in Maple Grove, whose leading crowd was described in the earlier quotation from an interview), the girls have more independent power. Furthermore, the fact that girls give the parties and determine who's invited gives them a social lever that the boys don't have.

It is as if the adolescent culture is a Coney Island mirror, which throws back a reflecting adult society in a distorted but recognizable image. And, just as the adult society varies from place to place, so, too, the adolescent society varies from school to school. . . .

. . .

Boy–Girl Relations and Their Impact on the Culture

What are the implications of these results? Let us suppose that the girls in a school valued good grades more than did the boys. One might expect that the presence of these girls would be an influence on the boys toward a higher evaluation of studies. Yet these data say *not*; they say that a boy's popularity with girls is based less on doing well in school, more on such attributes as a car, than is his popularity with other boys. Similarly for girls—scholastic success is much less valuable for their popularity with boys than for their popularity with other girls.

We have always known that the standards men and women use to judge each other include a large component of physical attractiveness, and a smaller component of the more austere criteria they use in judging members of their own sex. Yet we seem to ignore that this is true in high schools just as it is in business offices, and that its cumulative effect may be to de-emphasize education in schools far more than we realize.[4] In the normal activities of a high school, the relations between boys and girls tend to increase the importance of physical attractiveness, cars, and clothes, and to decrease the importance of achievement in school activities. Whether this *must* be true is another question; it might be that schools themselves could so shape these relations to have a *posi-*

tive effect, rather than a negative one, on the school's goals.

The general research question is this: what kinds of interactions among boys and girls lead them to evaluate the opposite sex less on grounds of physical attraction, more on grounds that are not so superficial? It seems likely, for example, that in some private schools (e.g., the Putney School) where adolescents engage in common work activities, bases develop for evaluating the opposite sex that are quite different from those generated by the usual activities surrounding a public high school. The question of practical policy, once such a research question has been answered, is even more difficult: what can a school do to foster the kinds of interactions that lead boys and girls to judge the opposite sex on grounds that implement the school's goals?

It is commonly assumed, both by educators and by laymen, that it is "better" for boys and girls to be in school together during adolescence, if not better for their academic performance, then at least better for their social development and adjustment. But this may not be so; it may depend wholly upon the kinds of activities within which their association takes place. Coeducation in some high schools may be inimical to *both* academic achievement *and* social adjustment. The dichotomy often forced between "life-adjustment" and "academic emphasis" is a false one, for it forgets that most of the teen-ager's energy is not directed toward either of these goals. Instead, the relevant dichotomy is cars and the cruel jungle of rating and dating versus school activities, whether of the academic or life-adjustment variety.

But perhaps, at least for girls, this is where the emphasis *should* be: on making themselves into desirable objects for boys. Perhaps physical beauty, nice clothes, and an enticing manner are the attributes that should be most important among adolescent girls. No one can say whether girls should be trained to be wives, citizens, mothers, or career women. Yet in none of these areas of adult life are physical beauty, an enticing manner, and nice clothes as important for performing successfully as they are in high school. Even receptionists and secretaries, for whom personal attractiveness is a valuable attribute, must carry out their jobs well, or they will not be able to keep them. Comparable performance is far less important in the status system of the high school, with its close tie to the rating and dating system. There, a girl can survive much longer on personal attractiveness, an enticing manner, and nice clothes.

The adult women in which such attributes *are* most important are of a different order from wives, citizens, mothers, career women, secretaries: they are chorus girls, models, movie and television actresses, and call girls. In all these activities, women serve as *objects of attention* for men and, even more, objects to *attract* men's attention. These are quite different from the attributes of a good wife, which involve less superficial qualities. If the adult society wants high schools to inculcate the attributes that make girls objects to attract men's attention, then these values of good looks and nice clothes, discussed above, are just right. If not, then the values are quite inappropriate.

A second answer to what's wrong with these values is this: nothing, so long as they do not completely pervade the atmosphere, so long as there are *other* ways a girl can become popular and successful in the eyes of her peers. And there are other ways, as indicated by the emphasis on "a nice personality" in the questions discussed above. Yet the over-all responses to these questions suggest that in adolescent cultures these superficial, external attributes of clothes and good looks do pervade the atmosphere to the extent that girls come to feel that this is the only basis or the *most important* basis on which to excel.

Effects on Girls of the Emphasis on Attractiveness

There are several sets of responses in the questionnaire indicating that girls do feel these attributes of attractiveness are most important. One is the responses to question 68 . . . , in which more girls checked "model" as the occupation they would like than any of the other three—"nurse," or "schoolteacher," or "actress or artist." As suggested above, a model is one of the occupations that most embodies these attributes of beauty and superficial attractiveness to men.

Further consequences of this emphasis on being attractive to boys are indicated by responses to a set of sentence-completion questions. Comparing the boys' responses and the girls' gives some indication of the degree to which the high school culture impresses these matters upon girls. The questions are listed in Table 33.2, together with the proportions responding in terms of popularity with the opposite sex or relations with the opposite sex.

To each one of these sentence-completion questions, girls gave far more responses involving popularity and relations with others than did boys. These responses suggest that the emphasis on popularity with boys has powerful consequences for these girls' attitudes toward life and themselves. A further indication that success with boys is tied to rather superficial external qualities is shown by the great proportion of girls who say that they worry most about some personal characteristic—most often an external attribute such as weight or figure or hair or skin, but also including such attributes as "shyness."

One might suggest, however, that the girls' concern with popularity and with the physical attributes that help make them popular would be just as strong in the absence of the adolescent culture. A simple comparison of these four sentence-completion questions suggests that this is not so. The question in which girls *most* often give responses involving relations with the opposite sex is the one referring directly to the school life: "The best thing that could happen to me this year at school would be. . . ." When the question refers to life in general ("The most important thing in life is. . . ."), then the boy–girl differential is sharply reduced. This suggests that it is within the adolescent social system itself that relations with boys and physical attractiveness are so important to girls.

The emphasis on popularity with the opposite sex has other effects on the girls, of which we have only the barest knowledge. One of the effects is on her feelings about herself. We may suppose that if a girl found herself in a situation where she was not successful in "the things that count," she would be less happy with herself, and would want to change, to be someone different. On the other hand, the more successful she was in the things that counted, the more she would be satisfied with herself as she was.

We have no measure of the objective beauty of girls, and we are not able to separate out those who are particularly unattractive in dress or beauty, to see the impact that these values have upon their conceptions of themselves. However, we can pick out those girls who are, in the eyes of their classmates, the best-dressed girls. This will allow an indirect test of the effect of the emphasis on clothes. On the questionnaire, we asked every girl: (I.40b.i.) "Of all the girls in your grade, who is the best dressed?" The girls named most often by their classmates are at one end of the continuum. Thus, if this is an important attribute to have, these girls should feel considerably better about themselves than do their classmates. Table 33.3

TABLE 33.2 Boys' and Girls' Sentence-Completion Responses Related to Popularity—Totals for Nine Schools*

		Boys	Girls
s.11.	More than anything else, I'd like to . . .		
	Responses involving popularity with opposite sex	5.4%	10.8%
	Responses involving popularity, unspecified	5.3	11.4
	Total codable responses	(2,343)	(2,776)
s.12.	The best thing that could happen to me this year at school would be . . .		
	Responses involving relations with opposite sex	4.5	20.7
	Responses involving relations with others, unspecified	3.2	9.0
	Total codable responses	(2,222)	(2,702)
s.13.	The most important thing in life is . . .		
	Responses involving popularity with opposite sex	6.3	7.4
	Responses involving popularity, unspecified	4.6	7.9
	Total codable responses	(2,151)	(2,737)
s.14.	I worry most about . . .		
	Responses involving popularity with opposite sex	9.2	13.9
	Responses involving personal attributes related to popularity (weight, hair, figure, etc.)	2.7	8.6
	Total codable responses	(2,201)	(2,803)

* These questions were asked in a supplementary questionnaire, filled out in the nine schools by the 6,289 students who completed the basic fall questionnaire early.

TABLE 33.3 If I Could Trade, I Would Be Someone Different from Myself

	Percent who agree	Number
All girls	21.2	(3,782)
Girls named 2–6 times as best dressed	17.0	(282)
Girls named 7 or more times as best dressed	11.2	(98)

shows that they do, and that those named most often felt best about themselves.

The effect of being thought of as "best dressed" by her classmates is quite striking, reducing by nearly half the likelihood of her wanting to be someone different. Or, to put it differently, the effect of *not* being thought of as "best dressed" by her classmates nearly doubles a girl's likelihood of wanting to be someone different.

To see the strength of this effect, relative to the effect of competing values, it is possible to compare these responses with those of girls who were highly regarded by their classmates, but in other ways. The following questions were asked along with the "best-dressed" question: (I.40b.) "Of all the girls in your grade, who . . . is the best student? . . . do boys go for most?"

The girls who were named most often by their classmates on these two questions and the previous one can be thought of as "successful" in each of these areas—dress, studies, and relations with boys. Insofar as these things "count," they should make the girls feel happier about themselves—and

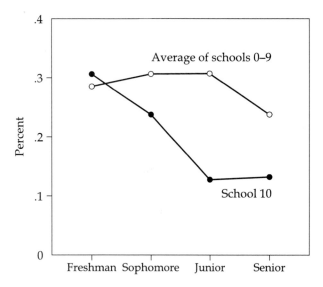

FIGURE 33.2   Proportion of Girls Mentioning Popularity or Good Looks as Important for Membership in the Leading Crowd. In All Schools and in a University Laboratory School (#10).

conversely, make the girls who are not successful less happy about themselves.

. . .

Altogether, then, it appears that the role of girls as objects of attention for boys is emphasized by the adolescent values in these schools. Its consequences are multifarious, and we have only touched upon them, but one point is clear: just "putting together" boys and girls in the same school is not necessarily the "normal, healthy" thing to do. It does not necessarily promote adjustment to life; it may promote, as is indicated by these data, adjustment to the life of a model or chorus girl or movie actress or call girl. It may, in other words, promote *mal*adjustment to the kind of life that these girls will lead after school.

Common sense is not enough in these matters. It is not enough to put boys and girls in a school and expect that they will be a "healthy influence" on one another. Serious research is necessary in order to discover the kinds of activities and the kinds of situations that will allow them to be such, rather than emphasizing the superficial values of a hedonistic culture.

The way in which such interactions can affect the value system pervading a school is shown clearly by a comparison with one of the two supplementary schools in the study, school 10. This is a private school, with students of upper-middle-class backgrounds similar to those of the students in Executive Heights, but in a very scholastic university setting. Figure 33.2 shows the importance over the four years of "good looks" as an attribute for membership in its leading crowd, together with the over-all average for the nine schools of the study. The contrast is striking. They start out at almost the same point in the freshman year. But in school 10, the importance of good looks goes *down* sharply over the four years; in nine schools of the study, the average even *rises* slightly, as dating begins in earnest in the sophomore and junior years, before dropping off somewhat in the senior year. This graph gives only the faintest hint of the different experiences these two school situations would present for a girl.[5]

This is not to suggest that all the schools of the nine in the study showed this same pattern; some did not. In particular, Marketville showed a continual decline similar to that of school 10, while several others showed a sharp rise in the sophomore and junior years, before decreasing among the seniors.

NOTES

1. This is graphically illustrated by A. B. Hollingshead, *Elmtown's Youth* (New York: Wiley, 1949), a study showing the various mechanisms by which the school reinforced the class structure. Because the present study includes "Elmtown" as one of its ten schools, it will be possible to show the greater cross-cutting of social-class lines that occurs in Elmtown today as compared to 1941.

2. A teen-age girl comments: This greater activity among boys is the reason that "being accepted" or being in the "right clique" means more to the girls, who have less to occupy their leisure time. Boys engaged in many activities have many different kinds of friends. They have different interests in common with different friends. Although they are friends they may have only one interest in common with a certain other boy and therefore could not be in a successful clique with all their friends. Because girls have fewer interests they form small cliques according to these interests.

3. To be sure, she sometimes has a hard time changing her looks or her personality; yet these are her own personal attributes, which she can do something about, except in extreme situations.

4. One cannot infer from the above considerations that single-sex high schools would produce more attention to academic matters. One other matter, evident in later chapters at St. John's, is the tendency of some adolescents in a single-sex school to have few interests in school. The opposite sex in a school pulls interests toward the school, and then partly diverts it to non-scholastic matters.

5. One author who studied a group of adolescents says this: "In the adolescent culture itself girls encounter many changes in the conception as to what constitutes desirable behavior, changes and even reversals in the value system and in the relative ranking of traits which are important for popularity and prestige. Perhaps the principal single change which we have found in our California group is that at the beginning of adolescence the group standards for conduct among girls emphasize a quiet, demure, rather lady-like demeanor. By the age of fifteen this has altered, and we find that the girls who are now most popular in their set are active, talkative, and marked by a kind of 'aggressive good fellowship.' These traits, which may in part be adaptations to the hesitant and immature social approaches of boys, must again undergo considerable change in the later years of adolescence, if a girl is to maintain her status in the group."

Harold E. Jones. 1953. "Adolescence in Our Society." P. 60 in *The Adolescent*, edited by Jerome Seidman. New York: Dryden Press.

Jones's results show changes which are in part due to maturation. It may be that the rise in importance of "good looks" among our sophomore girls, and the decline among seniors, are a result of this maturation. The example of school 10, however, shows that far more than maturation shapes the character of the culture from grade to grade.

34

CLASSROOM INTERACTION
Principled Conflict

Mary Metz

Classroom order is fragile. One child intent upon his own purposes can easily destroy the concentration of thirty-six others. One might expect that classes would be in a constant turmoil as a result of someone's intervention. But in fact most classes in Canton were conducted with civility and some semblance of concentration. Upper track classes even proceeded with decorum.

This relative peace is created by the students as well as the teachers. Classrooms have the peculiar quality of being intimate yet compulsory settings. Everyone must exist and interact in physical and social proximity for forty minutes a day, five days a week, for a whole school year. Everyone is motivated to reach an acceptable modus vivendi. The accommodation of teachers to students described in the last chapter is part of this adjustment. But beyond this, both teacher and students have reason to keep their conflicts with one another within bounds which will be tolerable during their long mutual association.

Nonetheless, conflicts do occur and they are occasionally sharp and in some classes frequent. Some of these conflicts arise over students' inclinations to engage in various pleasant activities which distract themselves or others from their schoolwork. The teacher intervenes to restore concentration upon the task at hand. Other conflicts occur when the students are motivated to disregard or to resist the teacher over a matter of principled disagreement about the character of the activity or the relationship they are mutually involved in.

The first group of conflicts is by far the more common. Virtually every teacher in every class must cope with at least one incident such as students whispering with their neighbors, sailing paper airplanes, drumming rhythms on their desks, or reading a novel in math class. The students recognize freely that such activities are illegitimate and will not be angered when told to stop. The amount of such activity varies noticeably from day to day with a given teacher and class. According to teachers, it varies with factors such as the weather, the day of the week, and outside activities ranging from domestic quarrels in someone's home to lunchtime ball games.

A few of the teachers observed handled this kind of disallowed behavior in ways which brought to the fore principled disagreements with the students. But in general, though a teacher's success in keeping this kind of distraction to a minimum required that his style of authority be accepted, it depended more directly upon his skill in classroom management, arrangement of the situation. To avoid these problems, a teacher needed to be adept at such devices as creating smooth routines for classroom chores, having alternative calming activities ready for days when the students came in excited from some previous event, or planning activities which were more interesting for sleepy Monday mornings or less taxing for energetic Friday afternoons. He also needed adroit use of personal influence in handling the hyperactivity or dreamy-eyed distance of particular students who were reacting to something other than the central activity of the class.

In Canton these conflicts occupied a good deal of time in class and a good deal of a teacher's attention, especially so if he were inexperienced or lacking in skill. But little more will be said about them here. Distracting though they might be, they did not stem from the core of the teacher–student relationship.

The occasional conflicts which arose from students' refusal to accept a teacher's definition of their relationship were far more bitter and lasting than conflict over a simple matter of distracting activity. However, these conflicts were not a direct result of students and faculty entering the room with different conceptions of classroom authority. . . . A certain mutual tolerance and respect smoothed relationships when students perceived teachers to be making a consistent effort in good faith to engage in *some* normatively defined form of authority. The sharp conflicts arose when students perceived the teacher to be defaulting on his obligation to establish a relationship of *any* kind of authority.

Nonetheless, some combinations bred more of these perceptions than others. In general, the better matched the students and the faculty member, the less conflict they had. The smoothest relations of all were between incorporative teachers and those few classes with even the dominant students also inclined to an incorporative pattern. These classes sometimes ran their whole course without challenge or conflict. High level classes with developmentally inclined students and developmental teachers also often passed without serious conflict, but there was likely to be at least debate or exchange, if only of an appropriate and allowed kind, over some point in the material. The least smooth congruent pairing was that of teachers who took a position of proto-authority and low track children. These classes often also passed without direct challenge or conflict, though usually not without some negative sanctions or at least warnings from the teacher. But here there was always a feeling of an underlying restiveness and often pantomiming between students, muttered editorial comments, and the drumming of fingers to express it.

The lower level groups engaged in relatively more restlessness and conflict than the top ones for any given amount of agreement with the teacher; so it is not clear that the pattern of proto-authority was a poorer match with these students than were other adult patterns with their corresponding students. The expectations of the students may have been equally well matched, but their willingness to cooperate still considerably lower than that of other groups.

Since teachers favoring proto-authority were generally as much interested in obedience as in academic progress, it is also open to question how much academic material was learned in their classes, despite the relatively good order. One of the most striking examples of the orderly consequences of matching teacher's and students' expectations occurred in a Level Four class in which the teacher succeeded in keeping the class operating as a group listening to him talk for forty minutes while they remained almost completely quiet. It was a nearly unique occurrence in classes of this track. The exercise at hand was the reading of answers to math problems, their correction, and the answering of questions, but it was clear that at least half the class were not even looking at their papers after the first few minutes of the period. The teacher carried on as though they had been following, and the class did not interrupt him.

The most harmonious combinations next to matched ones seemed to be ones of classes whose predominant approach was incorporative with either developmental teachers or ones using proto-authority. There was some restlessness in both cases. In the first, the students were partly testing limits and trying new patterns; in the second they were sometimes resentful in response to heavy-handed treatment of minor misdemeanors.

Classes combining lower level students and developmental teachers were. . . slightly more peaceful and more industrious than other lower level classes. They were more noisy and active than those with teachers using proto-authority and they included considerably more challenge to the teachers, but they also seemed to include more genuine attention to the academic task assigned.

The teachers whom students most vehemently opposed were *some* of the incorporative teachers with both top and bottom tracks and most of those devoted to proto-authority with the top tracks. However, these conflicts did not come simply from disagreement over the character of the relationship, but from other qualities which were correlated with the pedagogical positions of the teachers. The incorporative teachers who got into difficulties were ones who believed very strongly in the importance of teaching conventional behavior and academic content. They also believed strongly in their right to roles like that of parent or bureaucrat which should bring automatic deference and obedience. The resistance of children in the top and bottom tracks to both their teaching and their right to deferent treatment made them extremely angry and they responded with open hostility. Unlike the generalized disapproval of the proponents of proto-authority, this hostility was direct and personal in tone. The strong feelings behind the students' response grew out of their receiving that hostility.

Some of these teachers and many of those espousing proto-authority were shaky in their academic competence when facing the knowledge and the style of questioning of the top tracks. These students perceived this lack of competence as a lack of the quality on which a teacher's claim to authoritative status is based. They therefore were not ready to accept these teachers' orders without question. But the teachers exercising proto-authority considered unquestioning obedience a necessity. Conflict ensued.

When students were asked directly in interviews whom they liked most and least, their responses seemed to be based primarily on teachers' friendliness or hostility to students. There were a few teachers in each school who were outstanding either in their positive attitude to the children and faith in their capacity to learn or in their vehement hostility to any student who did not conform instantly to academic and behavioral expectations. These teachers were named as most or least liked, respectively, by nearly every child interviewed who had them in a class or even a study hall, and occasionally by students who encountered them only in extracurricular activities or the hall.

Often the same teachers were named also as those most and least learned from, but a surprising number of students even in low tracks made judgments about learning on the basis of some form of competence. Those in the low tracks would choose teachers who had ceased to try as those least learned from. Those in the top ones would name teachers who could not meet their academic challenges or those who refused to answer their questions or to let them speak in class.

Students systematically tested and assessed every element of the relationship of authority claimed by a teacher. They devised trials to find out if he could play the superordinate's role in a competent fashion. They discovered and assessed his conception of their own role. And they made judgments about whether his actions as a superordinate actually served to promote the educational goals which justified his claim on their obedience.

Rejection of the Teacher's Capacity to Play the Superordinate Role

All classes of children challenged teachers to find out if they were personally in control of the skills which qualified them to act as agents of the goals of the school. If they lacked the capacity genuinely to represent these goals, then they lost their claim to the right of command over students.

As indicated . . . children in the top tracks chose academic ground upon which to challenge the teachers. The teacher who made mistakes or displayed a lack of confidence in the face of such a challenge would, in these students' eyes, lose his claim to act as a legitimate agent of academic learning. He would be barraged with niggling questions and corrections as a demonstration of the students' lack of faith in his claim to authoritative status. However, if a teacher passed this test decisively he would be trusted to be capable of imparting knowledge and leading analysis, trusted to be a legitimate superordinate appropriately claiming authority.

One of the academically best prepared English teachers, who was teaching at Darwin, described this process. After some experience he had developed a quick recognition of such challenges and a strategy for unanswerably demonstrating his capacities.

The Honors kids instinctively test each teacher they get to see whether or not they're smart enough to teach them. For instance Dick Stein. The first day in class we were talking about what literature was, what our purposes were to be, and he talked about *Tristram Shandy*. Well, so I just gave him some of his talk back again, exchanged some rapid conversation about how this book related to that, how this concept related to the other. And piled it up over his head and buried him in verbiage.

That was the end of any problems with Dick. Dick and I get along beautifully. And he has a lot of troubles with his other teachers. Because he can put them down. He really knows a lot about some areas. But he's only fourteen years old.

Students in the lower levels had difficulty judging teachers' academic competence, unless they made blatant mistakes or failed to try to teach. These students did mention repeatedly in interviews that some teachers explained well or badly or were especially willing or unwilling to explain and to help a student if he were having difficulty. Faithful performance of academic duties and the capacity to meet the child's mode of comprehension was the test of competence here.

Lower level students made their most direct challenges of a teacher in matters of regulation of distracting physical activity. For these students part of the necessary qualification for occupation of legitimate superordinate status was the capacity to insist that students engage in official classroom activity. They would be boisterous, clearly watching a teacher to see if he could stop them, and they would make fantastic fibbing excuses . . . to see if the teacher were capable of directing their activity or could be fooled, distracted, or defeated by their energetic nonconformity. A teacher who could not successfully stop them was not considered competent to hold the office and would meet teasing and boisterous play all year.

Just as lower level students did some testing for academic competence, upper level students would also test to see if a teacher could keep them working, though much of the play they would try to get away with was verbal, including long digressions by the class as a whole from the subject officially at hand.

These tests of a teacher's competence to claim superordinate status were serious, and a teacher who failed them could have a great deal of difficulty in controlling a class. The students could often be cruel in their teasing and persistent misbehavior in such situations, but the cruelty was not purposeful, but a by-product of a childish joy in getting away with something. While such a teacher would not be respected and would be willfully disobeyed, he would not necessarily be resented or disliked. In fact students might even find him personally pleasant and congenial, especially if he lacked competence because he was an inexperienced teacher or was teaching outside his field of expertise.

I observed a clear demonstration of this attitude in following a first year teacher at Chauncey through her day. At the beginning of the year she did not know when and how to be firm. When she began belated and not very forceful attempts to take a stronger hand, her classes had long since learned to take advantage of their opportunity for recreation. However, she was a pleasant young woman with a sense of humor and clear good will toward the students. They took advantage of her but did not express any resentment toward her. Their actual good will became clear in a class during which the principal sat in to observe for the teacher's evaluation. During the period a window rattled loudly in the wind and a wall decoration fell from its place. The principal got up and fixed each, making clatters and bangs as he did so. This over, two workmen strolled in and spent most of the rest of the period hammering on some cabinets. Such noisy events would normally seize the attention and comment of much better controlled classes. But the children saw the principal and apparently understood his mission. Throughout the class they were deaf to the din, giving rapt attention and appropriate answers to the teacher. Though they would tease her for fun, they would help her when it counted.

However, though classes bore no enmity to teachers who lacked academic competence or the knack of controlling restless play, they quickly became bitter if the teacher attempted to compensate for his weakness as a superordinate in authority by controlling their actions through coercive methods. These teachers lost their right to control in not representing the values of the school. It is illegitimate for them to use coercive resources—which are granted as a supplement to authoritative control—as a substitute for effective moral claims.

. . .

Rejection of the Teacher's Definition of the Student Role

The students would engage in conflict with teachers who seemed to picture their own character or their school role in a way they found insulting. The lower track students' vehement rejection of teachers who made no serious effort to teach is an example of this attitude. The students took the teacher's reluctance as a sign of his belief that they were incapable of learning and responded with hurt and hostility to such teachers. Because these students liked and were accustomed to structured written lessons, even some of the teachers who attempted nondirective guidance in good faith seemed to these students not to take them seriously. They responded with anger. A student in Track Four at Chauncey describes the teaching of a man who attempted this pattern with only modest skill in a class in family living. Since he was not attempting to teach as she understood it, she held that he had no right to interfere with the students' activities in class.

I: Which of your teachers do you think you like the least?

R: Mr. Mundt.

I: And what's he like?

R: He don't never do anything in his class but talk and pick at people and things like that.

I: Umhum. Well, when he picks at people, do you mean he tries to get them to talk or he picks on—

R: He bothers them. Like if you were minding your own business—See he don't never do anything in there, but he talks and he never give any written assignments or anything. And once in a while he'll show a movie. And if he's not talking, nobody's talking, and then if you turn and ask somebody something, he gets mad and tell you to be quiet.

The students in the top tracks were most likely to reject teachers for their picture of the student role when they treated students as consistently frivolous or as younger than they were. They wanted, like the lower level students, to be taken seriously, and their demands were higher. An example of a teacher rejected on these grounds was Miss Bock, who had taught in the primary grades for most of her career and maintained much of the style and even the language which she used in that context. She was disliked by students at all track levels. An upper track student describes her classroom manner:

> She treats the kids like kindergarteners. And when she's angry, it's just like the old schoolhouse. See she goes (he claps his hands), "Let's come to order now." . . . She addresses the class as "children" all the time and these are kids that are thirteen and fourteen years

old and it sort of bothers them to be, you know—I mean they won't say this is why I don't like it, but it's just the atmosphere of the classroom. And I don't know. I think she'd probably be a good elementary school teacher.

This teacher was the only one in the study to speak of problems of classroom disorder as "naughtiness."

Rejection of a Teacher's Claim to Serve His Proclaimed Educational Goals

The strongest classroom conflicts occurred when the students perceived the teachers to be claiming the right to demand obedience while they clearly failed to serve educational goals. An incompetent teacher was *unable* to serve them, and so less strongly condemned than a teacher who willfully betrayed or neglected them. Such teachers seemed to be asking students to be personally subordinate to them, to obey their whims rather than the needs of the educational process. When students of any level perceived a teacher making such a claim, they rose in angry rebellion.[1] Students judged a teacher's good faith in serving educational goals according to their own definition of those goals. Thus disagreement over educational goals could appear to the students as the teacher's bad faith in their service. Similarly, in cases of disagreement over the relationship of the superordinate's role to the justifying goals, students often perceived teachers to be acting arbitrarily when the teachers perceived themselves to be defending their status as agents of the school's educational mission.

This kind of conflict often arose between high track classes and teachers who took an incorporative stance and a parental role, especially when they were teaching in the poorly defined subjects of English and social studies. (Similar teachers who took a bureaucratic role, followed proto-authority, or taught in more structured subjects such as mathematics, stayed close to texts which provided justification for most of their directions.) But these teachers lacked a clear textual referent and when asked by the students to justify a command referred to the teacher's right to personal discretion. In the students' definition of the relationship, the teacher's right to command rested upon demonstrating that his directions served educational goals. His status was questionable if he could not make such a demonstration.

Consequently confrontations occurred in which students said, "Why should we do it?" and the teacher in essence replied, "Because I say so!" To the student this reply looked like an attempt to impose simple personal subordination in the name of authority and he would grow angrier. "What does it have to do with what we're supposed to be learning?" he would ask, in effect. And the teacher would reply, in effect, "If your teacher says it has something to do with learning that is all you need to know. Now stop this impudent questioning." For the teacher, to give an explanation would be to weaken his claim to complex personal wisdom as the basis of his superordinate status. For the student, _not_ to give an explanation was to undermine almost completely the teacher's claim to be an interpreter of educational goals as the basis of his superordinate status. But because their definitions of the elements of authority were different the insistence of each upon his own definition destroyed his standing in the other's eyes as a person responsibly participating in a relationship of authority.[2]

· · ·

In lower track classes students most often perceived a teacher to be failing to act in

the service of educational goals either when he clearly did not make any effort to teach or when he gave a child a punishment but refused to name the crime or refused to believe the student's protestations of innocence.

A classic case is the following incident observed early in the study at Darwin. The boy in question was later interviewed and turned out to be a quiet and wary boy recently come from the South. Though the incident was never mentioned, the boy spoke angrily in general of teachers who punish you but won't tell you what you did.

[The students were working at their desks.] Miss Brown looked up and said to Stillman, "All right, go in the back corner without your books." There had only been a very quiet murmur in the room. I don't know whether Stillman was the source of it or not.

Stillman asked very quietly, almost in a mumble, what he had done. Miss Brown simply told him to go on, without his books. Stillman asked, this time clearly audibly, what he had done. Miss Brown said, "Don't talk back, Stillman. Go on back in the corner." Stillman said he was not talking back, he was simply asking what he had done. Why should he have to go back there?

Miss Brown said, "Because I'm telling you to." She looked down to her work again. Stillman just sat there. She looked up again and he mumbled that he wanted to know what he had done. Miss Brown said, "We'll discuss it later." Stillman still insisted that he must know what he did. Miss Brown picked up the pad of referral notices and told him warningly to go on back. He kept his ground silently and she said, "All right," and put down the pad. She told him to go out in the hall without his books and wait until she brought him the referral notice. "Go on, hurry up." Slowly and reluctantly but without pausing, he went.

In a quiet way Stillman was offering Miss Brown ferocious resistance. He stoically accepts a much larger punishment than his original one rather than yield to her in this matter of principle. It is not clear whether or not he was guilty of making the noise that caused her to look up, but the issue quickly became one of his right to have a justification for punishment versus her right to unquestioning obedience.

In the intimacy of the classroom, even the tone of voice in which a teacher gives a reprimand or punishment is important in a student's acceptance of its legitimacy. If the teacher's tone implies personal dislike or an attempt to humiliate, his action will be taken as a personal attack rather than an action in the service of legitimate classroom order and education. The students in the lower tracks have a finely tuned sensitivity in these matters.

. . .

Finally, the black children in all tracks check very carefully to see if their teachers seem to treat all students alike. This is particularly the case when the class is racially integrated. It is far more important to a teacher's claim to be acting in authority rather than out of a desire to be personally superordinate that he treat everyone similarly than that he be either lenient or kindly. One boy explained this is an interview. He was very angry at his French teacher who treated different people committing the same offence in very different ways. Asked what the relationship between strictness and fairness is, he explained it this way:

> Like my French teacher . . . she gives me a bad time *and* she's unfair, you know. But other teachers they give

everybody a bad time, you know, then that's fair. Like they give white, colored, Chinese, everybody gets a bad time, just mean teachers.

Conclusion

The chapter [has] documented the diversity of ideas and practices which both teachers and students in a single school bring into its classrooms. Not only the teachers but the students consider the classroom and the student–teacher relationship to be governed by norms growing out of the educational process and out of general principles of fairness and respect. The most fundamental of these have to do with the goals, roles, and relationships which constitute authority. Definitions of these norms use similar broad language to cover quite different specific ideas. Unless both parties are sensitive to these differences conflict can result.

In the long run the teachers adjust to the students as a body as much as the students adjust to them. Adjustments in the activity and style of interaction which take up the class hour are the most striking. Some teachers make these adjustments out of conscious analysis of the students and their needs and behavior. Others make them more gradually as they are pushed by events.

It is especially notable that in the lower two tracks essentially all teachers emphasized written work individually performed, and all used much of their resources for control more to keep noise levels down and tempers calm than to press for academic accomplishment. While there were still significant differences among the teachers as they dealt with a single track, the differences in a single teacher's behavior with different tracks were at least as important. One sees here the necessity of order as a precondition to learning in a school setting, and the relationship of students' willingness to embrace learning as a goal or moral order which supports authority to their willingness to be voluntarily orderly.

Where there was disagreement over the definition of authority, over the character of roles, relationships, or the moral order of school learning, some teachers adjusted to the students' definitions out of an analysis of their claims and arguments, while others did so out of an unarticulated sensitivity. Others never realized that students might have a serious normative model of authority different from their own and found themselves in chronic conflict with their students without ever comprehending its source.

The variety of students in each of Canton's schools and their challenging character made it difficult for teachers to develop smooth adjustments to them. The students were difficult to teach and they were difficult in varied ways. Perhaps the only classes which did not present a "problem" of some kind were top track classes with developmental teachers and those with only what I have called quiet students with incorporative (or developmental) teachers. The other matched pair, low track classes with teachers endorsing proto-authority, may have followed an uneventful course satisfactory to the participants, but it was one in which both concentrated on order and ignored learning.

Where students and teachers were not matched, one or both had to adapt or put up with persistent conflict. The top tracks could make life very hard for a teacher, and they might feel themselves put upon and fail to learn as much as they were able to. But it was the bottom track classes which presented the most serious problems for both teachers and students.

In these classes the pressures on teachers to stress order alone, or nearly so, were very strong. Even the developmental teachers who were energetically dedicated to induc-

ing these students to learn were less than spectacularly successful in their efforts. Their attempts to lure the students to their own pattern of authority by finding substance which would match their intrinsic interest were helpful but by no means sufficient. More striking were their efforts to gather other sources for control by using personal influence and by generating obligations for exchange through ignoring minor school rules and changing the classroom routine. All of these efforts helped, but they did not transform the classes into anything like a resemblance to upper track classes. Further, these practices complicated the maintenance of order in the school at large. . . .

The pressure on teachers to adjust to their students is important not just in the understanding of the character of a school but also in understanding teaching and teachers themselves. As teachers adjust to the particular students they encounter, they will develop distinctive outlooks which make them importantly different from teachers from different contexts who may use the same rhetoric.

　　　　　． ． ．

For the incorporatively inclined teachers the resistance not only of the poorest but of the best students could not but be discouraging and disheartening. Many teachers responded with a rigidity in pronouncement and practice which they probably would not have displayed in a context where students were more amenable to their efforts. Further, some of the developmental teachers in Canton were persons who had started with an incorporative philosophy and had gradually changed to a developmental one as they experienced the difficulties of applying an incorporative approach to Canton's students. These teachers tended to be above average in intellect and energy, thus adding to the relative luster of the developmental group. But in a context where students accepted an incorporative approach these teachers would have been likely to continue in an incorporative style.

. . .

NOTES

1. Their perceptions need not be correct from an observer's point of view, and they certainly

were not right from most of the teachers' point of view.

2. It is informative to compare the issues which arise in such clashes over authority to those in the moral dilemmas Kohlberg uses to delineate stages of moral reasoning. (See, for example, Kohlberg and Turiel, "Moral Development and Moral Education.")

35

SCHOOLS OR "SCHOOLS"?
Competing Discourses on Violence

John Devine

Two teenagers were shot to death at point-blank range in the hallway of a Brooklyn high school yesterday morning, little more than an hour before Mayor David N. Dinkins was to visit the troubled school to tell students they had the power to break free of the world of violence and drugs.
—New York Times, Feb. 27, 1992

Tuesday we were arriving at the school. The beginning of the day couldn't have been worse. We saw one of our students hand-cuffed and escorted by two police officers. . . . Her face was all scratched. I talked to K, another one of our students and the other girl who was in the fight. She was on

her way to the police car so I couldn't find out what happened. It's the fourth time I have seen a student leaving the school hand-cuffed. The image is truly painful. What can be so wrong in the school, or outside the school, that makes these things happen?
—Excerpt from daily journal of Hispanic male tutor

Two Conflicting Discourses

Both of the violent events recounted above took place in large New York City high schools. Accidental or intended, perpetrated with handguns, knives, or boxcutters, such episodes are no longer even front-page news in American newspapers. To begin to understand why such tragic incidents keep happening, one has to be willing to defer judgment on a range of presuppositions by which we explain American culture and schooling to ourselves. One extreme conservative view portrays the public schools as sites of total anarchy. In response, one liberal view chides us for manifesting any concern about school violence and unearths examples of how bad the schools were at the beginning of this century. Thus, a set of preliminary questions arises. Before we can inquire into ways of curing school violence, we must question why we are engaged in that inquiry. Are today's schools really violent? Are they that much worse than they were fifty years ago? Is not the phenomenon of violence confined to a few tough inner-city schools? Or is that view racist? Does not our focus on the negative just detract from all the good things that are happening in schools?

In the forefront of those who avow the existence of an ethos of violence in schools, one finds the right-wing politicians and journalists. To the questions above, the most conventional American response is represented by people such as Pat Robertson and William Bennett; this response discerns a moral and behavioral deterioration over the course of the twentieth century in all of American life—most especially in the public schools. Horace long ago taught us to beware of this *laudator temporis acti* mentality,[1] the attitude of the man who extols the past as he imagines it was when he was a boy. To these traditionalists, anyone holding out hopes for reforming the corrupt and chaotic urban school systems of today is a naive liberal. Vouchers, choice, and the creation of "proprietary" (i.e., business-run) or parochial schools are seen as our only hope for the future.

In reaction to the reactionaries, some authors deny that any problem exists, at least any that should be of serious interest. This opposing argument has the appeal of the counterintuitive. To the annoyance of many older Americans with fond memories of their school days, these authors assert that schools are not much more violent now than

they were fifty or seventy-five years ago and that there never was a golden age in American public education (Graham 1992). To prove their point, high turn-of-the-century dropout rates are resurrected, and lists of current school crimes (assaults, rapes, robberies) are downplayed as mere jeremiads concocted by fundamentalists and moralists (see, e.g., O'Neill 1994). We are told that we should be concentrating on school reform and on positive—and often-cited—models such as Theodore Sizer's Coalition of Essential Schools or James Comer's New Haven Plan rather than on merely dissecting failures. Even the mention of the word "violence" in connection with inner-city schools —especially when the topic is raised by a white male writer—is apt to bring cries of racism. In brief, many liberal academicians and intellectuals, for a variety of reasons, shy away from this painful topic of school violence. They are able to enforce this silence by accusing all those who want to raise the issue of being ideologically committed conservatives or worried hand-wringers who are unwilling to appreciate the many successes of our public educational system. Another variation of this thesis would claim that, however imbued with violence tough inner-city schools may be, the vast majority of them remain untainted. Hence, school violence is thought to be, at most, an issue limited to "tough" urban schools, like those of New York.

This discourse of avoidance crops up under many guises. Traditional educational writing races quickly over the word "violence," similar to the way a teacher tries to get on with the lesson after a disruptive incident. One way of doing this in any text is to combine the word with its less jarring quasi-equivalents: "vandalism"; "poor achievement"; "student malaise." Standard sociological doctrine, for example, holds violence to be a by-product of student alienation and suggests that creative methods must be found to reduce that alienation. This brand of social science focuses on discovering ways of increasing class participation, on getting students involved in school governance, on arranging smaller school and classroom settings, on developing trusting relationships, and on reframing the school culture to accommodate that of the student (see, for example, Newmann 1981). How could anyone quarrel with such fundamentally sound and demonstrably effective pedagogical tactics?

Pointing out the philosophical buttresses for a position, however, is not the same thing as totally rejecting it. Another large strand of mainstream analysis of the educational process is predicated on the Deweyan notion that all discipline should emanate from a student's intrinsic interest and involvement in the exciting business of learning. Classroom teachers who define themselves even partially as disciplinarians are seen as authoritarian ambassadors from the dominant culture, incorrigible taskmasters, and control freaks. It is believed that if the student becomes absorbed in the matter at hand—painting, writing, mastering a math problem—behavioral problems will simply disappear. If this is not happening—as in the case of highly troubled schools—efforts to reduce student alienation and increase motivation should be renewed. Or so the argument goes.

Thus, two diametrically opposed commentaries on school violence emerge: right-wing discourse, which magnifies it as chaotic; mainstream-liberal discourse, which minimizes it and psychologizes it as alienation. The first view says, "close the system down"; the second says, "reform its learning processes." Which side is right? Is violence everywhere, or is it nowhere? Is it just a product of the frenzied 1960s, or has it been there all along in one form or another? Is it only in the worst schools, or is it through-

out the system? Most important, can it be "fixed," and if so, how?

It is only by looking at the hierarchical nature of a particular system that one begins to understand how it is possible that both horns of the dilemma can be answered in the affirmative, how both sets of answers, seemingly mutually exclusive, could be true, and how the guises of both normality and frenzy can be present. The most accurate view of any hierarchical system is from the bottom, and one way to grasp that view is through long-term ethnographic fieldwork.

A Worm's-Eye View of the Structure

"Lower-tier school" is not an official designation of the New York City Board of Education, but everyone in the educational system appreciates its meaning. The large, overcrowded inner-city schools in which our tutoring program operates . . . all think of themselves as lower tier, and this worm's-eye view of the New York City high school organizational set-up is the best place to begin. The 126 regular public high schools in the city may be thought of as composing a pyramid divided into three strata. At the pinnacle are the four prestigious schools known as the specialized high schools.[2] Admission to these leading schools is limited to those students who are able to pass a competitive entrance examination. They are the pride of the New York City system, typically producing a bevy of Westinghouse Science winners and few dropouts. These are seen as highly desirable schools; 98 percent of the student body passes the stringent State Regents' exams, and flocks of graduates go off annually to attend Ivy League colleges.

Most high schools, however, fall into the middle stratum. These are neither the best nor the worst; here one finds many of the academic-comprehensive high schools located in fairly well-integrated neighborhoods. Board of education jargon for these middle-tier schools is "ed op" or "educational option" schools. The ed op schools offer a curriculum designed to prepare students for jobs in specific career areas (e.g., health, computer science, communications, business) and for college. Some of these are "total ed op schools," but most are just regular high schools offering a few ed op programs. Although not elite, the ed op schools are also viewed as highly desirable schools and, so, attract students from other neighborhoods who are serious about getting an education. "Ed op," therefore, means "magnet." In fact, one can conceptualize the top and middle strata together as a gigantic magnet drawing the best students to the top, as far away as possible from the worst students at the bottom. It is crucial to understand this most fundamental feature of the system. It is not only the private schools of Manhattan and the Catholic schools of the archdiocese that siphon the best and the brightest—and the wealthiest—away from the public system, as is often stated; rather, the system itself does the most thorough job of drawing "the best" to the top.

Defining "Lower Tier"

Occupying the bottom stratum of the pyramid are the lower-tier schools. Since no one has a precise definition of "lower tier," it is impossible to pin down the number of schools that can be so classified. But people well acquainted with the system have their own private listings of which schools fit into this most undesirable category: "lower tier" means more than just low test scores and poor attendance. By 1992, the board had installed weapons-scanning metal detector systems in the forty-one high schools with the highest number of violent incidents, partly to forestall potential lawsuits by

teachers, students, and parents who might, after a weapons incident, claim that the board had not done all it could to protect them. In the 1991–92 school year, the teachers' union counted 129 gun incidents, most of them in these schools.[3] By 1994, the number of "metal detector" high schools had grown to forty-seven; many were predicting that it was only a question of time until all high schools would have the "security package," which includes the full array of very expensive technological hardware. Most of these forty-seven are the very large, overcrowded neighborhood schools located in the most highly segregated, most deteriorated, and most violent neighborhoods. They either have no ed op programs or very mediocre ones and therefore have trouble drawing students from other parts of the city. In these neighborhoods, one finds most of the schools that are staffed with the greatest numbers of security guards.[4]

These schools are seen by teachers, students, and parents as the least attractive from every perspective. Inevitably, they are referred to as the worst in the city—even by their own teaching staffs. All the "objective" measurements support these "subjective" impressions: they have the highest dropout rates, the lowest graduation rates, the worst scores on standardized tests, the poorest attendance patterns, and the worst statistics on assaults and possession of weapons. Each of these schools is saddled with the burden of its reputation in the community. A fifteen-year-old Puerto Rican student who had dropped out of one of the specialized high schools and whose father—in full view of his wife and family—was killed on his way home from work by a local drug dealer told me that, in contemplating returning to school, he had ruled out going to the local (lower tier) high school because "it has a bad reputation" and because he knew too many kids there with whom it would be too easy to hang out and to cut classes. He was looking for a good ed op school, the euphemism for "safe" in the board's vocabulary of violence. This reluctance to call fear of violence by its proper name also infects the ethnographer. From my fieldnotes: "Once past 6–8 guards at the front desk, I began thinking how placid, how 'traditional' the school appeared today. Then one woman tutor told me about the very bright boy who was coming down to see them who wants desperately to leave because a gang in the school is threatening him, but that he cannot get a transfer until January."

Within the school reform movement, "magnet school" is an unproblematic concept. In enthusiastic press releases and in news stories, the concept of magnetism has retained its physical, almost magical, meaning: the power to attract. Magnet schools—strongly promoted by the U.S. Department of Education—have come to be thought of as ideal institutions of choice, irresistible places to which ambitious students are drawn. Other schools are admonished to imitate these models, which is precisely what they try to do.

There is, however, a darker side to this magic of the magnet. A magnet school draws students to it, but it also draws them away from other schools. A tenth-grade girl once announced exuberantly in our tutoring room that she had just gotten word she had been accepted at one of the ed op schools. Congratulations were extended, and we held a party for her accomplishment. But to our lower-tier school, which she was leaving, this move represented one more defeat: she was not only moving up the pyramid, she was also fleeing the bottom. What we were really celebrating was her move to a safer school, her escape from the possibility of violence. In our small festivity, we discovered ourselves dramatizing Gramscian hegemony, in the sense that we had unwittingly reenacted the values of the dominant society, had suddenly become aware that this small transfer was emblematic of the entire hierarchical structure. "Magnet school," therefore, has become a phrase whose most important subtextual connotation is that rarity, the much sought-after nonviolent school.

. . .

Freshman Orientation

What does the entering ninth grader encounter on the first day of class in one of these lower-tier high schools? Almost all of these schools, as already indicated, are situated in marginalized—and sometimes deadly—neighborhoods through which the students and their teachers must travel each morning and afternoon. In some of them, students pass lots filled with ten-foot high mounds of garbage that has spilled onto the sidewalks and into the street. Crack houses may be sighted within a block of the school; certain corners near the school are permanently inhabited by drug dealers. Graffiti is ubiquitous.

Entering the building, students will normally be diverted away from the main lobby and shunted to a side entrance (for better crowd control), where they will wait (outside, even in the most inclement weather), hundreds at a time, to meet the security guards who introduce them to the first *rites de passage* of a New York City high school in the 1990s: the wizardry of identity card machines, metal detectors, X-ray machines (for inspecting knapsacks), walkie-talkies, magnetic door locks, and a host of other forms of "security" technology. Students sometimes arrive at their first class half an hour late because they are waiting to be scanned.[5] Less obvious are the verbal exchanges and demeanors that introduce students to police culture and introduce the language of the street into the school environment. No one adverts to this subtle daily introduction of the criminal justice system lexicon onto the educational scene: "scanning," "holding areas," "corridor sweeps," and, as we shall see, the street vernacular that guards and teachers sometimes use in addressing students.

It is inaccurate to maintain, as some authors do (e.g., Alves 1993, citing Coon 1971), that American youth are not guided through initiation rites by adults. . . . I will suggest that, although teachers have progressively withdrawn from any meaningful role in this regard by detaching themselves from close emotional and social involvement with youth, these rituals have not become exclusively peer centered. The performance of these initiation rites, at least in the context of the schools, has been abdicated by the teachers and delegated to the low-status guards, who are ill equipped for the task of socializing youth into productive roles in Western society.

The students—even the ones who carry weapons—share the same hopes as the authorities, that all these devices will keep the school safe. But these jointly held hopes are obscured by the basic semiotics of the handheld scanner as it traces the contours of the student's clothing. The scanner is more than a technological marker of radical suspicion, inimical in every way to the school's historic and humanistic aim of fostering mutual trust, respect, and courtesy; it represents the first radical and direct reorganization of the student's body space, now no longer sheltered within a cloistered pedagogical universe, by the technological power of the state. One African American girl who had participated in our program told me that she transferred out of the school to the safety of an ed op school because one of the guards had made suggestive remarks as he moved the scanner in the vicinity of her legs. This police-power intrusion is happening within school space, which was previously conceived as a sanctuary. But it is important not to conceptualize the lobby as a space for

the reproduction of violence independent of other sites in contemporary America. The dominant society's demand for immediate results and success stories, its obsession with test scores, "back to basics," and Japanese competition, and its retrenchment on funding for all poverty programs reminiscent of the days of the Great Society have all contributed to this deterioration of public space.

In June 1995, this convergence of school space and state-sponsored containment of street terror moved from esoteric theory to explicit news release when Mayor Giuliani moved to place disciplinary control of the school system under the direct supervision of the police (Newman 1995). One tenth grader, commenting on the mayor's proposal, remarked that the mayor was apparently unaware that the police were already in his school, striding daily down the corridors, two by two, with weapons visible!

The formative and performative aspects of these first school lessons, then, pertain to the body, not to the mind. The ritual performance of daily scanning takes on a totally different aura in school lobbies than it does in airport entrances. Guard and student perform a duet of mutual mistrust while the students' peers stand or sit, watching this first lesson of the day: frisking. Reconstruction of the student body has begun.

A Place to Avoid

But even before they walk through the front door, these students have absorbed the rumors—from siblings, junior high school friends, and influential adults—about the school's reputation. Their junior high school guidance counselors have repeatedly reminded them that the local high school is a place to be avoided at all costs because of its history of violence. Their pastors have preached sermons exhorting their parents not to send them there. Groups of local ministers and priests have set up organizations opposed to the very existence of these schools. Some of their classmates go off to the more prestigious specialized schools and specialized programs. Not being accepted into these highly selective schools at the end of junior high school and being forced, as a result, to enter the local lower-tier school is widely interpreted as failure.

The students who are not accepted into the ed op high schools or who cannot afford a private or parochial school therefore have no choice but to attend these neighborhood schools. High school officials take it as a given that these "list notice students" (board jargon for students coming directly from neighborhood junior high schools) come to their first day of high school with chips on their shoulders, because they know they have been assigned to this lower-tier school rather than having freely chosen it. They represent the bottom quartile of their class— the students who were "passed along" just to get them out of the junior high school building—and they know it. The core of a typical incoming freshman class, then, is drawn from this "list notice" group of poor academic performers from the "feeder" schools. In one school, for example, a full 66 percent of the entering ninth-grade class was reading below grade level; 63 percent had scored below 50 on a basic math test whose scale was 0–100.

To this basic group are added the "over the counters" (OTCs) or "walk-ins" (board jargon for students who arrive from overseas after the start of the academic year), recent immigrants who may be provided with ESL and bilingual courses if they are from China, Haiti, or Spanish-language countries. Walk-ins account for as many as 800 students annually in one of our schools with a total population of 4000. Finally, there might be as many as 300 to 400 students who have been held back to repeat ninth grade; up to a third of a typical ninth-grade class may consist of these "holdovers" or "retreads." One principal stated the situation quite plainly: "The desirable students get siphoned off before they ever reach the [lower-tier] neighborhood high schools."

. . .

Put bluntly, the lower-tier schools do not have the luxury that the more prestigious or more powerful schools have of turning away students. Put even more bluntly, the issue of choice cannot be divorced from the issue of violence. The first serious result of all these factors for schools at the very bottom of the pyramid is overcrowding. The schools in which we operate are sometimes filled to 125 to 150 percent of capacity, and this overcrowding is alleviated only by low attendance patterns: on a typical day, up to a third of the students may be absent. These schools would not know what to do if all the students showed up on a given day. One of our schools currently has an enrollment of 2600, but only about 1800 attend on a given day; the principal admits quite openly that he is not unhappy about the low attendance pattern, since it alleviates overcrowding. In the next breath, however, he talks of the need for a more aggressive outreach program to attract the long-term absentees. Add to this picture the continuous movement of students in and out of the school: students coming and going due to family moves, disciplinary actions and suspensions, visits back and forth to the Caribbean, and absences due to fear of retaliation after a violent incident. Coming to school does not mean coming to class; cutting classes and walking the halls are two of the chief features of this novel school culture I will attempt to define. And all of these schools have high rates of teacher absenteeism.

. . .

Those who stay, and who set the tone of the school for new arrivals from overseas, are more than just "disgruntled." Realizing they have no alternative but to attend, they often enter with more than belligerent attitudes. They may enter with weapons in their pockets, armed to protect themselves, fearful of all they have heard about the school. Others, most of them recent immigrants, enter slightly dazed by all this and just seek a friendly face. It is for this reason that principals routinely ask us to work with the incoming ninth graders: they are indeed the most in need of academical, social, and emotional support. School officials feel that if students can make it to the eleventh grade, the last two years will most likely be more or less unproblematical. There is a good deal of evidence to justify their sentiments.

. . .

Inside the Lower-Tier Principal's Office

Let us eavesdrop at a not-so-imaginary staff meeting inside a principal's office in one of these lower-tier schools. He has brought together his key staff and union representatives. He tells them the school must move quickly to avoid further deterioration; the Vision schools will be proliferating soon, with several brand new schools opening in the next two or three years. He presents this recent move as a clear threat: "Our better students are going to be skimmed off to go to those new schools; that has been the history of the board of education." But he also gives them a model for attracting students to the school. He reminds them that the school is getting only the bottom group from the local junior high schools and that the overwhelming majority of them—close to 75 percent—do not graduate from high school. He proposes to inaugurate a program (usually some variant of an English-as-a-second-language or a bilingual program) that will

result in admitting more recent immigrants into the school.

If this plan takes hold, he explains to them, the number of list-notice students will be greatly decreased, perhaps even cut in half. And he reminds them of what they are all aware of: "most of our discipline problems are incoming ninth graders from the junior high schools," whereas in the case of most of the immigrant students coming in from other countries, "I'm not gonna say they're angels . . . but generally speaking, they do fine, in comparison." The blame is not put on the list-notice students themselves, but on the training they have received in junior high school: "Not that they're bad kids, but they just have the junior high school mentality." The junior high schools that feed these lower-tier high schools *also* have bad reputations. They are said to allow the students to "do nothing except play." As stated above, many students do not actually graduate from these schools but are passed on, because they "aged out" and are not permitted to remain in junior high school past age fifteen. Some students, it is said, know in September of their eighth-grade year that they have already aged out and that they will be passed on to a senior high school, so they do nothing but play around, if they bother to come to school at all. These students are not portrayed explicitly as "bad" but simply as arriving at the senior high school lacking the necessary qualifications. But the implications of the proposed policy that the system forces the industrious principal to make are clear: decrease the numbers of list-notice students (most of them African American), and increase the numbers of over-the-counter students (most of whom are West Indian).

The school's strategy for survival, he explains, consists of trying to attract the more academically able students from around the city. He would happily settle for even 10 percent to 20 percent of students whose scores were at grade level or above. "The main problem," he continues, "is that 88 percent of the youngsters coming in to the ninth grade this year were remedial in math." That means that the math department has to spend the entire first year, and sometimes two whole years, teaching junior high school math, and then, by eleventh grade, the students are just up to the eighth-grade level. They cannot begin algebra until their junior year. "The same thing is true in reading. We're not talking about bad kids, we're talking about kids who can't read." In concluding, our principal sums up his concept and his hope: by bringing in a new group, the school will have the opportunity to improve the discipline as well as the scholarship and to become a "viable high school where teachers can teach, principals can principal."

If this strategy is adopted, the school solves its problem by increasing its reputation throughout the system and by excluding many African American students (and even the lower-achieving Caribbean students), who, in turn, will have to be assigned to other lower-tier schools. Proposals of this nature are considered to be common-sensical; many African American teachers and Caribbean teachers assent to it as outlined. The relative success and preferred behavior of one ethnic group in comparison to native-born African Americans are accepted as a matter of course. These black students are not seen as excluded because of their race or ethnicity, and their futures are left in the hands of the board's processes. The hierarchy of the system thus stands the conventional positivistic research on its head and renders irrelevant questions such as whether black, white, or Hispanic students create the most violent incidents. These strategies for importing and exporting populations and the consequences they entail force us to ask the question of whether ethnicity constructs violence or is constructed by it. If the ejected

students end up on the streets, that is not considered to be the problem of this particular school, which feels it cannot take on the whole world's problems.

This scenario may never get beyond the planning stage; the only point in portraying it here is to illustrate the effect that the creation of ed op or Vision schools has on the ideology of those in the lower tier and to portray the way the system's constant skimming processes tend to worsen and segregate the schools at the bottom of the pyramid. Because these processes of creating "effective schools" or magnet schools or ed op programs under the guise of reform have been taking place since the mid-1970s (usually in well-integrated neighborhoods), the effect on lower-tier high schools in ghetto areas has been devastating. One junior high school principal whose school feeds one of our high schools told me that the high school "could reform itself til it's blue in the face," but parents still would not want to send their children to it because of the dangerous neighborhood surrounding it and because of the school's historical reputation in the community.

. . .

"It's a War Zone"

[U]nrecognized rites of passage, buried in the everyday routines of school life, are the means by which students are socialized into a world in which violence is considered part of the normal order of things. These rites involve more than the enactment of violent episodes; they also involve students' narratives—revealed in their dialogues with one another or with trusted adults—of their own experiences as well as their commentaries about the experiences of others. One of our students told me that "kids bring in a lot of pen knives that no one could detect . . .

razor blades . . . they have knives in their lockers in the gym; there are cracks in the walls where they can hide them." I asked one Haitian boy, a recent graduate, how he survived. "I gave them the impression I was somewhat dumb. . . . I set my own trend. . . . Some people would mock me and I would ignore them. Then they would look at me funny. . . . I would act eccentric."

The anthropology of the body draws our attention to how the body functions both as a transmitter and as a receiver of information (Lock 1993: 136). To interrogate current understandings of school violence, which harbor an unexamined mind-body duality, to understand how student knowledge is constructed, one must shift from the purely cerebral world of language and focus instead on materiality: the exchange of looks between peers, the slow strides in hall walking, the "hanging" in the halls, the rumpled cuffs down near the shoes, a group leaning silently against the wall, the sudden explosion on energy when something really starts to "go down." The space of the student's body is not discontinuous from the physical body of the school edifice or the surrounding neighborhood.

CLAUDE: You live in [the area]—it's like a war zone, right?
COREEN: Yeah.
FARLEY: It *is* a war zone.
CLAUDE: I told you I know every area.

Disorder unremittingly breaks through the routine, becomes part of it, and keeps the newcomer confused and off guard. One hears crashing glass falling from upper windows, but school staff proceed as if nothing has happened. Ear-piercing fire alarms go off and no one responds. Tutors doubt whether they should leave the tutoring room to go search for a student because there are gangs roaming a particular corridor or stairwell. From my fieldnotes: "Yesterday, K, a student,[6] was apprehended with an Uzi sub-

machine gun and several rounds of ammunition in the students' cafeteria. He was trying to hide the weapon in his girlfriend's knapsack when the guard arrived. He said he was going to 'waste' two students who had insulted him the day before. Word of this incident spread quickly throughout the teachers' cafeteria today. A disaster was averted."

The violence is camouflaged by a discourse of denial, since surfacing these issues to the level of consciousness of the entire school community—with no hope of changing the underlying conditions—would only make apparent the painful and ineradicable admixture of street culture and policing technology that had permeated the terrain of the school. I once suggested to a recently retired teacher that it might prove beneficial for teachers to get together and reflect on why and how some of the disturbing events were occurring so habitually in the school. She reacted: "As a teacher I didn't hear half of what was going on. . . . I would hear about it two weeks later. I would hear only about kids who got knifed on my floor. . . . When you are there, you get used to it. Why should we disabuse people and tell them what a culture of violence they are living in? What would you gain by pointing out to them how disastrous the place is? If they are adapted to it, why make them miserable? Why give them awareness, if they will have to stay there and work?"

These incidents, more disorderly than normally acceptable, now recognized, now shrouded by silence, spark the suggestion that one is dealing with a homogeneous culture of school violence, a suggestion that further implies that the public areas of the school, prior to the advent of these disorders, were privileged spaces, historically devoid of any implication of violence. It is tempting to posit a culture of school violence hermetically sealed off from the larger society and to forget about what is happening in the larger community: the inadequate public assistance for families in need, the almost complete marginalization of these populations, the reality of the gun lobby in Washington, and the television industry.

. . .

The problem with . . . ethnographer-generated observations about school violence is not that they are not "true" but that they force subsequent analysis into positing a suddenly intrusive and inert culture of violence that never strays far from the school perimeter or relates to contemporary political events outside that perimeter. A (male Hispanic) tutor's reflections on a (Hispanic) high school student's dream begins to nudge our analyses beyond the narrow confines of the school-seen-as-cloistered-sanctuary, albeit a violated one:

> The other day I also worked with Y. He is a bright student who has been with us since the beginning of his [high school] experience. Y was telling me of a dream he had the other night about the school. He dreamed that a school teacher and a security guard were shot in the hallway. He remembered seeing the teacher dead and the security guard bleeding. Violence is everywhere and the students see it as part of their everyday lives. What scares me most is that we have come to accept violence as part of our everyday lives instead of trying to solve the root of the problem. We try to leave the guns outside the school instead of taking them out of the streets.

In our attempts to understand how this sad state of affairs has come about, neither explanation—that violence evolved slowly and gradually became the norm or that it intruded suddenly from nowhere—seems adequate. We are left with a tension between these two polarities. One can neither affirm a homogeneity of violence within the school

perimeter nor infer that the school has a monopoly on the reproduction of violence in the community. The school walls are porous, violence flowing in and out, between community and school.

On the temporal plane, only a naive historicist reading of history can trace an undisturbed line of development from a supposedly pristine nonviolent past (i.e., up to the 1950s) to a supposedly chaotic present. The contrary thesis, a more sophisticated revisionist history of New York, insinuates a violent past doomed to endlessly reproduce itself (Sante 1991). The emotionality of the service provider, faced each morning with the expectant faces of children, forces one to reject this defeatist and hopeless position.

If we allow ourselves, however, to remain momentarily locked into an ethnography of the present, one is required to explain these sudden intrusions of the violent into the everyday. "It happens in bursts," said one teacher, referring to those few weeks out of a "normal" semester when the whole place erupts: the blood on the floor, kids beaten to a pulp, kids getting knifed, ethnic groups fighting, the Haitians versus the Panamanians, kids shaken down for guns in the hall, security guards luring them out of the classrooms in order to search them. Where does normality leave off and "abnormality" begin? Are "acceptable levels" of violence in inner-city schools now considered normal throughout American society? That youth carry weapons "in ghetto schools" seems to have become a generally accepted fact of life among the American populace today (DeWitt 1993).

Once again, emphasizing how the abnormal blots out the normal and modifies it easily slips into right-wing talk of totally chaotic schools. Yet the violent and the normal are reconciled and coexist in the everyday. On the same day in which a teacher talks quietly to a visitor about a curriculum project and students work productively in the context of a busy tutoring room, I write the following fieldnotes:

A meeting in the principal's office broke up fast when word arrived that a "female teacher had just been beaten up by a female student." The police had to come into the building. The teacher had to be taken to the health clinic and then to the hospital. The fight got so vicious that the male security guards would not break it up: "We're not touchin' females . . . unless they are starting to kill us; the lawyers would have a field day." The fight raged on until a woman security guard could be summoned over the walkie-talkies. When classes begin to change, outside the cafeteria, the hall deans and guards enlist some paras and teachers to form a human wall to make sure that students do not congregate around the principal's office. The girl who started the fight is still in the principal's office and they are afraid of retaliation. Police and deans have entered the hallways and put up wooden horses as barricades. Parents and students are waiting in the principal's office for suspension hearings, the outcomes of previous incidents. The principal is running around trying to take care of all this at once. The previous day a bulletin board was burned. Meanwhile, in the cafeteria, a huge fight erupts even while two policemen are there—all the kids standing on the tables cheering the fight. The principal, making his rounds, bursts into classrooms just to make his presence known. He orders kids to take off their hats, and teachers apologize to him for allowing the hats to remain on. There are a full 20 staff members (10 guards and 10 deans or paras) in the auditorium facilitating the scanning process. About 300 students sit in the audito-

rium watching their peers get scanned on the stage or mill about in the lobby; they are forced to wait in these areas (an improvement over a few years ago when they had to wait outside in the cold) until it is time to change classes. Ten additional guards and paras are working the lobby, so, all in all, 30 people are engaged in the process of getting the kids into the building. Three security guards are absent because they had to go downtown for a hearing about an earlier incident. This causes problems for the logistics of the guards, the chief topic of a late-in-the-day conversation behind the closed doors of the principal's office. Interrupting this conversation, the principal makes a phone call to another principal to try to convince him to allow a troublemaker to transfer to his school. (Before the call, the chief security guard advises the principal to downplay this student's problems and to stress the student's athletic abilities in making the case for the transfer.)

A "normal" school somehow keeps going on in the midst of all this, with our own students coming in and out of the tutoring room and attending their classes. How are teachers able to tolerate all this and sustain these two contradictory discourses? One stratagem is to relocate the abnormal to another space: one long-time teacher (now retired) related to me how frightened she was when her superintendent insisted that she visit a neighboring school with a very bad reputation, one in which three students had been killed the previous year:

It's funny, about a year or so before I left, they had some kind of program where they wanted social studies APs [assistant principals] to visit their counterparts and the superintendent sent me to [another lower-tier school]. I was very unhappy, I didn't want to go. I called the AP, I said you want to pick me up? You want to take me to work? You want to take me home? I'm not coming by myself. I was very unhappy; once I got in the school, it wasn't bad but I really didn't want to go. . . . It wasn't my turf.

To most outside observers, there was not a great deal of difference between the two schools. The veteran teacher was "never afraid in her own building," on her "own turf," despite her frank acknowledgement of the daily presence of weapons, but was terrified at the thought of going to the neighboring school.

Schools or "Schools"?

What do these coexisting contradictory discourses suggest about contemporary schooling in the lower-tier high schools of New York's inner cities? What does it mean when the terms "normal" and "wild" can both be predicated of a school with equal veracity? The suggestion I am making here is that, in order to make a first approach at the phenomenon with which we are dealing, we might provisionally make a distinction between the traditional institutions everyone calls schools and the institutions we are discussing here, which might be thought of as "schools." It is equally important to understand that, in denying these lower-tier establishments the appellation "school," we are not lapsing into the right-wing camp, which advocates nothing more than closing down the public system. The point of the quotation marks is not to indicate a totally chaotic situation but rather to stress the coexistence of these two prevailing discourses, the serpentine ways in which the discourse of "normal schooling" has learned to live more or less comfortably, more or less anxiously, along-

side the "discourse of violence," which also serves as a "normal" communicative strategy. The corollary of this cognitive shift is significant: even though the word *school* appears over the front door, and even though all the players (administration, teachers, and students) speak as if they are dealing with that familiar institution, such is not the case. The second corollary is that most of the educational literature—journal articles and school management manuals, even the most recent works on reform, written with the traditional school in mind—will not be of much help in dealing with this new entity, the "school." Contrary to the belief that a dedicated principal can turn such situations around, a hierarchical system, intent on fostering excellence at the top, can create a series of "schools" at the bottom of the pyramid. Part of my message, then, is a plea to debunk this "great man theory" of education, which always assumes that a "dynamic principal" can turn a bad school around, since all of these principals are essentially operating in truly unmanageable situations, as are their superintendents. The existence of "schools" is historically structured, and it will not yield to quick fixes.

· · ·

NOTES

1. Literally, "a praiser of bygone times," *Ars Poetica*, 1, p. 173.
2. The informal division described here is not to be confused with the board's official classification of school types: (a) academic-comprehensive; (b) vocational-technical; (c) specialized high schools; and (d) alternative high schools (schools for those who have dropped out or have been "pushed out" of the other regular schools).
3. The previous year (1990–91), the number of incidents was forty-five; the year before that (1989–90), the figure was twenty. (Ed Muir, Vice President for Security, United Federation of Teachers, interviewed by author.)
4. A few of these schools, due primarily to politically powerful principals, have been able to

keep the metal detectors out where the school leadership deems them counterproductive; how long they will be able to hold out, given the legal and insurance risks involved, is at present highly questionable. Given the possibility of a weapons incident and its dire consequences, the pressures on these principals from the central board and the union to accept this "security package" are enormous.

5. See Travis, Lynch, and Schall 1993.

6. Throughout this study, all student names (sometimes expressed as initials only, sometimes as given names) are pseudonyms.

REFERENCES

ALVES, JULIO. 1993. "Transgressions and Transformations: Initiation Rites among Urban Portuguese Boys." *American Anthropologist* 95:894–928.

COON, CARLETON. 1971. *The Hunting Peoples.* Boston: Atlantic-Little Brown.

DEWITT, KAREN. 1993. "Teachers Ask for Help with School Violence." *New York Times,* January 15, p. A14.

GRAHAM, PATRICIA ALBERG. 1992. *SOS: Sustain Our Schools.* New York: Hill and Wang.

LOCK, MARGARET. 1993. "Cultivating the Body: Anthropology and Epistemologies of Bodily Practice and Knowledge." *Annual Review of Anthropology* 22:133–55.

NEWMAN, MARIA. 1995. "School Safety Chief Resigns, Urging Job Be Done by Police." *New York Times,* May 31, p. A1.

NEWMANN, FRED M. 1981. "Reducing Student Alienation in High Schools: Implications of Theory." *Harvard Educational Review* 51:546–64.

O'NEILL BARRY. 1994. "The History of a Hoax." *New York Times Magazine,* March 6, pp. 46–50.

SANTE, LUC. 1991. *Low Life: Lures and Snares of Old New York.* New York: Farrar, Straus, Giroux.

TRAVIS, JEREMY, GERALD W. LYNCH, AND ELLEN SCHALL. 1993. *Rethinking School Safety: The Report of the Chancellor's Advisory Panel on School Safety.* New York City Board of Education. Unpublished manuscript.

PART V
Education and Life-Course Outcomes

The readings in the previous section demonstrated the role of schools in the formation of adolescent subcultures and the proliferation of student misbehavior. Schools also structure individual life outcomes after students leave school grounds. How do experiences in high school affect subsequent educational attainment? What types of coursework lead to the most profitable jobs? Do school experiences make someone more or less likely to commit crime? These and other questions are addressed by the readings in Part V, which explicate the relationship between education and life-course outcomes.

Criminologists who have looked at the role of education in predicting crime have demonstrated that schools are critical institutions in an individual's life course. The first reading in this section by noted criminologists James Q. Wilson and Richard J. Herrnstein summarizes research examining the links between schools, delinquency, and crime. In subsequent work, criminologists Sampson and Laub (1993) demonstrated that experience in schools can serve as a turning point in an individual's life. They argue that individual attachment to school, measured by grades and self-reported attitudes, affects a student's likelihood of delinquent behavior after leaving school. In recent related work, we show that young men who enroll in secondary vocational coursework, attend high schools with greater resources, and are exposed to peer settings conducive to learning are less likely to become incarcerated later in life (Arum and Beattie 1999).

In the following reading, James E. Rosenbaum and Amy Binder examine the actions employers take in their attempts to hire workers with specific skills. Through interviews with employers, the authors find that employers screen people for entry-level jobs through linkages with schools. Employers seek workers with mathematical and English skills, and some go to great lengths fostering links with school personnel to attract well-skilled employees. Once an employee holds an entry-level job, supervisors employ further screening measures to determine the person's readiness for employment in more advanced occupations. This reading demonstrates not only which skills are valued by employers but also how a school's institutional linkages to community businesses have important implications for student outcomes.

The next reading by Robert Reich, former secretary of labor under Clinton, suggests that professional and managerial jobs in the future will increasingly rely on critical thinking skills, problem-solving ability, and networking. Currently, only "the best" high schools and colleges in the United States teach these skills to their students. Reich argues that a decline in domestic manufacturing and the globalization of the economy has served to make skills of "symbolic analysis" more vital for individual job attainment. Thus, Reich has been a strong advocate of increasing government resources directed toward the training and education of a new generation of workers.

The final reading on life-course outcomes is Richard Arum and Michael Hout's contribution to a cross-national study of school-to-work transitions organized by Yossi Shavit and Walter Muller. (Shavit's related work, a collaboration with Blossfeld, appears in Part III of this reader.) In this reading, Arum and Hout explore labor market returns to different levels of educational attainment in the United States. They suggest that greater educational attainment receives corresponding financial rewards in the labor market. For example, a person holding a degree from a two-year college is able to earn an income roughly halfway between the income of a four-year college graduate and that of a person with a high school diploma. In a challenge to the work of researchers who have questioned the worth of vocational education, the authors identify positive labor market outcomes associated with specialized vocational education.

REFERENCES

ARUM, RICHARD AND IRENEE R. BEATTIE. Forthcoming "High School Experience and the Risk of Adult Incarceration." *Criminology.*

HERRNSTEIN, RICHARD AND CHARLES MURRAY. 1994. *The Bell Curve: Intelligence and Class Structure in American Life.* New York: Free Press.

SAMPSON, ROBERT AND JOHN LAUB. 1993. "The Role of Schools, Peers and Siblings." Pp. 99–122 in *Crime in the Making.* Cambridge, MA: Harvard University Press.

36

SCHOOLS

James Q. Wilson • Richard J. Herrnstein

When a child enters school, he or she becomes part of one of the few state-supervised institutions in our society that attempt to alter, by plan, individual differences in behavior. As a result, the schools become for many of us the locus of our fondest dreams and greatest disappointments. We hope that within their walls dull children will become brighter and gifted ones brighter yet, unruly children will settle down and quiet ones will assert themselves. Sometimes this happens, but just as often whatever differences existed among children upon entering school seem to become, if anything, greater by the time they leave.

Both as parents and scholars, we are aware that children begin school with differing intellectual abilities; though we expect all children to benefit from their experiences there, we are not surprised when children who seemed brightest in the early grades turn out to be among the brightest in the later grades and when the slower children remain slower than the others during all of the grades. We naturally become distressed when bright children do less well than expected and not-so-bright children seem to fall farther behind; in these cases, we often speak to the teachers or complain to the school authorities. But when a child's experiences in school seem to conform to the

child's natural aptitudes, we are usually contented, or at worst resigned.

We often have much different expectations, however, about the child's conduct in school. As parents, we want all children to comport themselves well in the classrooms. If a child begins the first grade displaying restless and impulsive behavior, we expect him to "settle down"; if a child starts off by being shy and withdrawn, we hope he will "open up." If the restless child becomes unruly and even violent, we often believe that it is because the teachers do not understand him, or even "pick on" him; if the withdrawn child never blossoms, we are inclined to think that it is because the teachers are "insensitive" to him. Sometimes we are right, but sometimes we are entertaining exaggerated expectations about the ability of schools to alter behavior. That exaggeration is often much greater among scholars than parents. Many students of child behavior and juvenile delinquency suppose that, though children may enter school with important constitutional differences in intellectual abilities, the only differences in behavior among children have been socially learned and hence can be socially unlearned. Children come equipped with a set of values and attitudes and labeled with a socioeconomic status; the attitudes and values can be modified and the socioeconomic status can be ignored, discounted, or (possibly) changed.

To the extent that one assumes that behavior is primarily determined by some continuing interaction between attitudes and social setting, the schools must bear a heavy responsibility for whatever behavior is displayed. There are at least two views about how schools ought to deal with a child who, on entering school, seems surly, rude, or impulsive. Persons who think the schools are "too soft" believe that teachers fail to discipline unruly children and thereby fail to inculcate proper standards of conduct in them. Whatever the child may have learned in the home, the school can, within broad limits, produce proper behavior in the classroom, and this in turn will help produce proper behavior later on in the child's life.

People who find the schools too harsh or restrictive, on the other hand, believe that teachers who confront an unruly or indifferent child will label him a "troublemaker" in ways that reinforce his tendency to make trouble. If the child seems uninterested in his studies or prefers some studies, such as manual arts, to others, the school's failure to adapt to these predispositions may frustrate his capacity to attain legitimate goals. If the child falls in with a group of disorderly youth during recess, he may well learn values that are at odds with what the school professes, and thus the school should worry about these peer relations.

Because schools exist chiefly to teach things that can be learned from books, because such teaching requires orderly classrooms and motivated pupils, and because the school system is embedded in the value system of the larger society, it would seem obvious that the schools are likely to satisfy neither kind of critics. In the view of both, the role of the schools in accounting for misconduct is likely to be a negative one—to the extent they make a difference at all, schools will tend to make matters worse. They will either fail to obtain the necessary level of conformity or require too much conformity, and thus they will harm difficult students by either rewarding their misconduct or stigmatizing, frustrating, or alienating their personalities.

That would, indeed, appear to be the lesson one could infer from the great majority of studies of the relationship between schooling and crime. Virtually every inquiry has concluded that young persons who have difficulty in school—low achievement levels, poor behavior—are much more likely than other children to be delinquents and become criminals. "A long series of studies—from 1936 to the present—have found negative associations between school performance (grades, educational tests, or liking for school) and delinquency."[1] Moreover, students who misbehave in school (by skipping classes, hitting teachers, or damaging school property) are much more likely than other students to drop out of school and to be delinquent.[2]

These findings, however, are consistent with several inconsistent theories. One is that children predisposed, by familial or constitutional factors, to misbehave will misbehave during and after school without regard to what happens there. Another is that predisposing factors are exacerbated by schooling so that individual differences in criminal tendencies existing independently of schooling are increased by school experiences. A third is that there are few, if any, important predisposing factors; rather, schools by means of either inadequate or excessive efforts to induce conformity produce delinquent behaviors in some children. In short, both the direction and the mechanism of the causal link between schooling and crime are unclear.

Alternative Explanations

Whatever else may be wrong with schools, they cannot be the sole cause of individual differences in criminality. For much of our early history, children did not go to school at all, yet some became criminals. Today, when most children are in school, some become involved in crime and others do not. Obviously, there must be some predisposing factors that, perhaps by interacting with school processes, determine which children are more likely to become delinquent. We already have a clue as to who the offenders are likely to be. Even after allowing for the defects of both official police statistics and self-report studies, it is clear that delinquent children are disproportionately males drawn from lower socioeconomic groups.[3]

The two most important theories of the school-crime linkage are the "common cause" and the "intervening variable" models. The first suggests that both difficulty in school and delinquency are the result of preexisting personal traits (the "common cause"); the second suggests that schooling is an important intervening variable that converts some preexisting (and possibly quite benign) personal traits into a disposition to commit crimes. If the first model is correct, schooling has little effect on criminality; if the second is correct, it has a great (though not exclusive) effect.

Common Causes

There are at least three sets of personal traits that might lead to both difficulty in school and to committing delinquent acts. First, children of low intelligence, especially the verbal component of intelligence, will have difficulty with schoolwork, particularly in those aspects that emphasize verbal skills. And if they do poorly at schoolwork, it stands to reason that they might express a dislike for it and drop out of school at the first opportunity. As we have seen, persons of low intelligence are also more likely than others to commit common predatory crimes. This may be because they do not understand the likely consequences of their actions, especially consequences deferred into the future, or because they find it difficult to manage

their relations with other people by verbal communication, or for some other reason. Second, children who are temperamentally impulsive, extroverted, and aggressive are likely to find school—which demands sitting still, being attentive, and acting cooperatively—boring, confining, and unrewarding. They will not do as well as others in their schoolwork and will find it more exciting to skip classes, act up, and drop out. Though impulsive, aggressive personalities may not differ in intelligence from more passive individuals; the former are overrepresented among delinquents and criminals. . . . Third, children who have been conditioned by their parents to ignore or discount the connection between actions and consequences (by, for example, being subject to inconsistent disciplinary practices) or who have been denied the opportunity to form a strong and affectionate bond with one or both parents may, whether they are constitutionally aggressive or not, find little connection between schoolwork and personal gratification, distrust or feel cold toward any source of adult authority, and not take seriously any claimed relationship between rules and conduct. Such persons will be troublesome in and out of school. Obviously, all of these factors may operate together in varying degrees.

. . .

Schools as Intervening Variables

The same personal traits that in the common-cause model create both school problems and delinquency are among those attributes that may lead the school to create or heighten delinquent activity. In this view, a boy (or, occasionally, a girl) with below-average intelligence, an impulsive or restless temperament, or a hostile or suspicious attitude toward schooling and adults may become delinquent as a consequence of being victimized by one or both of two processes.

First, he may suffer from being labeled (or "stigmatized") by the school as a misfit, so that he engages in misconduct he would not otherwise commit, as a result of a loss of self-esteem, receiving poor instruction from teachers who have decided in advance that he is a "failure," or being thrown into the company of similarly labeled youth who become unruly after being rejected by their teachers. Indeed, some proponents of this view doubt that there are any significant individual differences that determine school success—what appears to be a low IQ may in fact be the result of being tested unfairly, what seems to be low academic achievement may be the result of a "self-fulfilling prophecy" that leads teachers to give low marks to pupils they wrongly believe are dull, and what seems to be an unruly temperament may simply be the biased perception of teachers who judge all conduct by inappropriate "middle-class" standards.

Second, individual differences in aptitude and temperament may be real enough and teachers may avoid stigmatizing or rejecting such youth, but the school may offer a curriculum that the below-average or impulsive youth cannot master and finds irrelevant to his ambitions and life prospects. Misconduct and delinquency arise in this case out of frustration: Unable to do well in schoolwork that emphasizes verbal skills, some students will rely more heavily on their physical skills (including skills at fighting); unable to see any payoff from attending classes in history or mathematics, some students will act up in these classes or skip them entirely; convinced that students who do well in their schoolwork are no more deserving of the honors and opportunities that come their way than are students with less inclination to please the teacher, some of the latter will set right their own equity equations by taking things they want or by making life miserable for the "good" students.

. . .

Evaluating the Models

It is not possible to evaluate conclusively these competing explanations of the connection between having problems in school and committing crimes. The necessary research—carefully measuring individual differences among children in early life and then closely observing their experiences and misconduct during and after school—has never been done. And some of the research that has been done is woefully inadequate. . . .

. . .

With this in mind, we can turn to a closer examination of the mechanisms by which schools may have some effect on individual differences in criminality. The first of these is, loosely, the process of stigmatization. The argument has been made by several authors; perhaps the best known are Kenneth Polk and Walter E. Schafer, who have written two major accounts criticizing the schools for creating delinquency,[4] the first of which was published as part of the report of a United States government task force on juvenile delinquency. Though they claim that schools cause delinquency in many ways, an important part of their argument—and almost the only part for which they supply original data—has to do with the schools' tendency to label some children as lacking in ability or interest and thereby instilling in the students a lowered self-esteem and in the teachers an indifference (or even hostility) to the stigmatized pupils' educational needs.

The principal study by Polk and Schafer that provides support for the stigmatization argument was based on school data they gathered during the 1960s on nearly thirteen hundred students three years after they had entered one of two Midwestern high schools and, thus, at about the time they were either seniors or had dropped out.[5] The authors were especially interested in the effect on students of tracking, and so they examined separately the academic achievement, dropout rate, and extent of school misconduct and officially recorded delinquency of pupils in the college-preparatory and the noncollege tracks. The authors concluded that the rates of school misconduct and officially recorded delinquency were higher for students in the noncollege tracks than for the students in the college-preparatory tracks, and explained this by a combination of the mechanisms already described—the stigmatizing effect of being labeled "noncollege," poor teaching, arbitrary grading policies, exposure to an antischool student subculture, and the apparent lack of any connection between schooling and future employment prospects. The difficulty with drawing any of these conclusions is that the statistical tables apparently showing a relationship between tracking and misconduct do not control for those factors—intelligence and socioeconomic status—that are also associated with crime and that may explain all the relationship without reference to tracking. The way in which Polk and Schafer analyzed their data was so primitive as to render almost any conclusions for or against the stigmatizing theory (or any other theory) unwarranted.

. . .

The second mechanism by which schools might affect crime rates is the frustration hypothesis. Even if schooling does not stigmatize some boys in ways that lead them into crime, it may frustrate their ability to gain some legitimate goal. It may do this if pupils with poor verbal aptitude find themselves increasingly unable to master class material that requires verbal skill and, as a consequence, come to dislike school and rebel against it and its rules. Schooling may even produce this frustration-bred aggression, despite sincere efforts by teachers to help vulnerable students, if the students believe that none of the rewards of adult life to which they can reasonably aspire are contingent on doing well in schoolwork. Arthur Stinchcombe argued, on the basis of his study of students in a logging town in California, that boys from working-class families became rebellious (though not necessarily delinquent) as they realized that the schooling they were receiving had no payoff for them—they would end up with unskilled or semiskilled jobs regardless of what they did in school.[6]

The most complete and careful statement of this hypothesis is that supplied by Travis Hirschi.[7] His important research, alluded to in many other parts of this book . . . was based on questionnaires completed by over five thousand students attending public junior and senior high schools in Contra Costa County (near San Francisco), California. He analyzed the relationship between delinquency, both self-reported and officially reported, and a wide variety of familial and school factors. Here and elsewhere[8] he finds that delinquents have lower intelligence than nondelinquents, though in this study his measure of intellectual ability is not an IQ test but the Differential Aptitude Test (DAT) verbal scores, which are highly correlated with the verbal components of IQ.

Hirschi explicitly rejects the possibility that intelligence affects delinquency directly—for example, by reducing the ability of a person to foresee the consequences of his actions or to underestimate the risk of detection. Rather, the link between intelligence and delinquency is mediated by school experiences that have weakened his commitment to the conventional order. [T]he value attached to not committing crime (a good reputation, a quiet conscience) has been reduced for the less gifted person who has been frustrated by his inability to do well at schoolwork. A difficulty with this explanation, acknowledged by Hirschi, is that the correlation between aptitude scores and statements about whether the students like or dislike school, though in the predicted direction, is quite small: +.11.[9] If students who have difficulty with school turn to delinquency because of the dislike of schooling engendered by that difficulty, one would expect the correlation to be higher. On the other hand, Hirschi's multivariate analysis of the data suggests that when the effects of aptitude, grades, and attitudes toward school are simultaneously taken into account, each makes some independent contribution toward explaining the number of self-reported delinquent acts.[10]

. . .

But there are some important difficulties with the theory that low aptitude leads to poor schoolwork, which in turn causes frustration, a dislike of school, a rejection of its authority and, thus, delinquency. One is that, at least in the few studies that have been done on this topic, the association between low IQ and antisocial behavior is found in children well before they are of school age.[11] Of course, later on schools may intensify misconduct because of the frustration low-IQ pupils experience there, but so far as we can tell children with low IQs are more likely to have behavior problems even when they are four or five years old.

Another difficulty with the frustration theory arises from the fact, suggested by some studies, that students may do poorly in school for reasons having nothing to do with low intelligence, without becoming delinquent. . . . If children who do poorly in school because of low intelligence become delinquent, then why not children who do poorly because of other handicaps?

. . .

Changing Delinquency by Changing Schools

Perhaps the best way to find out whether schools contribute to crime independently of the personal attributes of their pupils is to see whether different kinds of schools lead to different rates of delinquency, controlling for the characteristics of the students. It is remarkable and a bit dismaying, given the great attention devoted to schools as influences on delinquency, that so little effort has been made to find out if different kinds of schools lead to different behavioral outcomes. . . .

. . .

One of the few systematic efforts—and without much doubt, the best of these efforts—to see what difference schools make was undertaken by Michael Rutter, a British professor of child psychiatry, on the effect of secondary schools in London on the children who entered them.[12] The research began in 1970 with a survey of all the ten-year-old children living in one part of London. It found that the behavioral problems of these children were strongly linked with "family adversity"—discord, mental disorder, parental criminality, and low occupational status. The children were then followed through 1974, after they had turned fourteen and been in secondary school for about three years. The schools served an inner-city, largely working-class area with a substantial immigrant population; over a quarter of the fathers of the children had been convicted of some offense, and 8 percent had been in prison. On tests of mental aptitude, the children were, on the average, well below the national norm. The twelve schools that were studied had many things in common (e.g., all required their pupils to wear some kind of uniform and all maintained a rather formal relationship between teachers and students). But there were also important differences: Some schools were all-boy, some all-girl, and some coeducational; some were small and some quite large; some were entirely financed by the government and some were dependent on church organizations.

Police records were combed for information on all delinquent acts committed by the students through age seventeen. As one would expect based on other research, the lower the verbal intelligence score of the youth and the lower the occupational status of the parents, the higher the probability of being delinquent.[13] These individual differences accounted for most of the differences in delinquency rates among schools, but not all. Comparing boys (girls had too few delinquencies to be included in the analysis) of similar verbal intelligence and socioeconomic status revealed that which school they attended made a significant difference in the probability of being a delinquent. For example, for similar boys, the proportion delinquent was three times greater at the "worst" school than at the "best" school.[14] . . . Within a given school, the relationship between intelligence and social class on the one hand and delinquency on the other was more or less stable. Schools, in short, did not eliminate the effect of these individual differences on crime, but they did seem to alter the magnitude of that effect.

On the whole, the schools that did the best job of reducing the expected level of delinquency were also the ones that did the best job of improving educational achievement, maintaining good attendance, and reducing misbehavior in school. This finding is interesting enough, but the great contribution of the Rutter study is that it also sheds light on why some schools do a better job than others. The physical and administrative arrangements of the schools made no difference: Size, floor space per pupil, age of buildings, pupil–teacher ratios, the source of financial support, and the socioeconomic makeup of the student body were unimportant. What was important was the "intellectual balance" of the student body and the "ethos" of the school organization. The schools that did the best job in reducing delinquency were those with the highest pro-portion of the most able students; the schools that did the poorest were those that had the highest proportion of low-IQ students.[15] Bear in mind that none of the schools had a large proportion of gifted children, who had mostly gone to highly selective British schools. But given the students they had, the schools that did the best—not only in reducing delinquency but also in improving attendance and enhancing educational attainment—were those with a "reasonable balance" of academically gifted children who, the authors speculate, found school rewarding, identified with its aims and rules, and set the tone for the rest of the students. When the proportion of low-IQ students became too high, they then set the tone for the school as a whole, a tone expressive of frustration and restlessness.[16] Whether the student body was balanced in socioeconomic terms was not important.

By "ethos" Rutter and his colleagues refer to the social organization of the school and the classroom. A desirable ethos—one that contributes to lessened delinquency and higher achievement—involves a teaching style that emphasizes the value of schoolwork, rewards good performance, and utilizes fair but firm disciplinary procedures. Good teachers are free with their praise while insistent on their rules. . . .

These two variables—intellectual balance and school ethos—contributed independently to reducing the expected level of delinquency, with the former being the more important.[17] We cannot say, of course, whether the decline in delinquency persisted after leaving school, whether Rutter's finding would hold true for American schools, whether he would have obtained different results if he had used delinquency rates (crimes per year per boy) rather than the percentage of boys ever delinquent, or whether any results would have changed if he had used self-reported rather than officially reported delinquency.[18] But as it now stands, this is the best research we have that shows how intelligence contributes both directly and indirectly, through school processes, to delinquency.

There is growing agreement among scholars as to the characteristics of those schools that seem able to enhance learning and maintain order. One recent review of several studies led to conclusions remarkably similar to those drawn by Rutter and his colleagues. Effective schools have an ethos based on clear goals, high expectations, and fair but firm discipline, and this ethos, in turn, seems chiefly to require parental involvement, strong leadership by the principal, and a stable and well-motivated staff that collaborates in planning a clear program.[19] For example, a large American survey sponsored by the National Institute of Education found that schools with low levels of crime were (not surprisingly) located in low-crime communities. But after allowing for that, the schools with little crime on campus were described by their students as having teachers who enforced the rules and who did so without displaying hostile or authoritarian attitudes.

A careful analysis of these data—drawn from over six hundred public schools and involving more than thirty thousand students—concluded that "when students report that rule enforcement is firm and clear, their schools experience less disruption." There was little evidence that "student participation in the generation of these rules is a necessary ingredient." What was essential was the "firm, clear, persistent, and even-handed application of rules."[20] Beginning in 1980, efforts have been under way in several schools across the country to implement this lesson, and a preliminary evaluation suggests that some may have been successful in reducing criminal victimization within schools and among specific groups of individuals within those schools.[21]

. . .

Efforts to use schools to produce more law-abidingness among children often focus on junior or senior high schools. This emphasis is understandable, given the fact that it is in these schools that the greatest problems of disorder and delinquency are likely to occur. But since we know that the high-rate, serious offender is likely to begin his career at an early age, we must wonder whether it might not be better to devise school programs to reduce the onset of delinquent inclinations among very young children than to organize such programs to cope with delinquent behavior among teen-age children.

. . .

Conclusions

The full story of the effects, if any, of schooling on crime cannot be told; the studies we have, informative as they are, leave many questions unanswered. But the evidence from the best of these studies is consistent with the view that individual differences affect crime rates both directly (the common-cause model) and indirectly (the intervening-variable model), the latter occurring as personal attributes interact with school processes. Boys with below-normal verbal intelligence will commit more crimes, on the average, than boys with higher verbal skills, whether or not they attend a good school, but if they attend a good one, their probability of committing a crime—and the probability of their brighter friends committing a crime—will drop. Perhaps the same relationship between schools and behavior exists with respect to other personal traits, such as temperament and attitudes. A "good school" seems to be one that, regardless of its socioeconomic composition, is not swamped with low-aptitude students and provides a firm but nurturant social environment in its classrooms. In the United States, such an environment appears to be more readily attained in private and Catholic schools than in public ones.

Boys who attend a poor or mediocre school are likely to find that the personal deficits with which they begin their schooling are unaffected or made worse. Success in schools comes to students with good verbal skills; boys without those skills are likely to seek other rewards, such as those that accrue to physical prowess. The benefits of schooling lie in the future; boys who are impulsive are likely to discount those future rewards heavily and allow their actions to be governed by more immediate consequences. Teachers expect their students to conform to rules and to defer to their authority; boys from cold families with inconsistent disciplinary practices are likely to attach little value to such teacher expectations and, if the teacher attempts to enforce those expectations in the same cold and inconsistent manner as the parents, the boys may well rebel even more. In this way, deficits that had a constitutional or familial origin accumulate and, possibly, worsen.

The accumulation of deficits can be moderated or reversed, but only with difficulty and then chiefly for the less serious offenders. The chronic, major offenders, as we have seen in study after study, begin their delinquent careers very early in life, well before schools make any very difficult demands. Special programs designed for the most troublesome youth. . . are not likely to have much effect, even though the boys themselves like them. There is some evidence—but as yet not much—that preschool programs aimed at preventing the emergence of high-rate offending may have some value.

Schools may also affect criminality in ways that are largely independent of what teachers do. A school, after all, brings together a large number of young persons. If the school is in a high-crime neighborhood, boys attending it will be more likely to meet high-rate offenders than if the school were in a low-crime area. Thus, the school may contribute to criminality because of the peer groups that form there. . . .

NOTES

1. Gottfredson, 1981, p. 436.
2. Bachman, Green, and Wirtanen, 1971; Gottfredson, 1981, pp. 441–42.
3. Elliott and Ageton, 1980; Hindelang, Hirschi, and Weis, 1979; Braithwaite, 1981; Gottfredson, 1981, p. 434.
4. Polk and Schafer, 1972; Schafer and Polk, 1967.
5. Polk and Schafer, 1972.
6. Stinchcombe, 1964.
7. Hirschi, 1969.
8. Hirschi and Hindelang, 1977.
9. Hirschi, 1969, p. 121.
10. Ibid., pp. 129–30.
11. McMichael, 1979; Richman, Stevenson, and Graham, 1982; Rutter and Giller, 1984, pp. 165–68.
12. Rutter, Maughan, Mortimore, and Ouston, 1979.
13. Ibid., pp. 77–78.
14. Ibid., p. 80.
15. Ibid., p. 156.
16. Ibid., pp. 159–60.
17. Ibid., pp. 173–75.
18. T. W. Nagel, 1982.
19. Purkey and Smith, 1983. Cf. also Rutter, 1983.
20. National Institute of Education, 1978; Gottfredson and Gottfredson, 1982.
21. Gottfredson, 1983.

REFERENCES

BACHMAN, J. G., S. GREEN, AND I. D. WIRTANEN. 1971. *Dropping Out—Problem or Symptom?* Vol. 3 of *Youth in Transition*. Ann Arbor, MI: University of Michigan Institute for Social Research

BRAITHWAITE, J. 1981. "The Myth of Social Class and Criminality Reconsidered." *American Sociological Review* 46:36–57.

ELLIOTT, D. S. AND S. S. AGETON. 1980. "Reconciling Race and Class Differences in Self-Reported and Official Estimates of Delinquency." *American Sociological Review* 45:95–110.

GOTTFREDSON, G. D. 1981. "Schooling and Delinquency." In *New Directions in the Rehabilitation of Criminal Offenders*, edited by S. E. Martin, L. B.

Sechrest, and R. Redner. Report of the Panel on Research on Rehabilitative Techniques. Washington, DC: National Academy Press.

———. 1983. "The School Action Effectiveness Study: Interim Summary of the Alternative Education Evaluation." Paper distributed by the Center for Social Organization of Schools, Johns Hopkins University, May.

GOTTFREDSON, G. D. AND D. C. GOTTFREDSON. 1982. *Victimization in Six Hundred Schools: An Analysis of the Roots of Disorder.* Baltimore, MD: Center for Social Organization of Schools of Johns Hopkins University.

HINDELANG, M. J., T. HIRSCHI, AND J. G. WEIS. 1979. "Correlates of Delinquency: The Illusion of Discrepancy between Self-Report and Official Measures." *American Sociological Review* 44: 995–1014.

HIRSCHI, T. 1969. *Causes of Delinquency.* Berkeley, CA: University of California Press.

HIRSCHI, T. AND M. J. HINDELANG. 1977. "Intelligence and Delinquency: A Revisionist View." *American Sociological Review* 42:571–87.

MCMICHAEL, P. 1979. "The Hen or the Egg? Which Comes First—Antisocial Emotional Disorders or Reading Disability?" *British Journal of Educational Psychology* 49:226–38.

NAGEL, T.W. 1982. "Do Schools Affect Delinquency?" Review of *Fifteen Thousand Hours. University of Chicago Law Review* 49:1118–36.

NATIONAL INSTITUTE OF EDUCATION. 1978. *Violent Schools, Safe Schools: The Safe School Study Report to Congress.* Washington, DC: U.S. Government Printing Office.

POLK, K. AND W. E. SCHAFER. 1972. *Schools and Delinquency.* Englewood Cliffs, NJ: Prentice-Hall.

PURKEY, S. C. AND M. S. SMITH. 1983. "Effective Schools: A Review." *Elementary School Journal* 83:427–52.

RICHMAN, N., J. STEVENSON, AND P. J. GRAHAM. 1982. *Pre-School to School: A Behavioral Study.* London: Academic Press.

RUTTER, M. 1983. "School Effects on Pupil Progress: Research Findings and Policy Implications." *Child Development* 54:1–29.

RUTTER, M. AND H. GILLER. 1984. *Juvenile Delinquency: Trends and Perspectives.* New York: Guilford Press.

RUTTER, M., B. MAUGHAN, P. MORTIMORE, AND J. OUSTON. 1979. *Fifteen Thousand Hours: Secondary Schools and Their Effects on Children.* Cambridge, MA: Harvard University Press.

SCHAFER, W. E. AND K. POLK. 1967. "Delinquency and the Schools." In *Juvenile Delinquency and Youth Crime.* Report of a task force to the President's Commission on Law Enforcement and Administration of Justice. Washington, DC: U.S. Government Printing Office.

STINCHCOMBE, A. 1964. "Institutions of Privacy in the Determination of Police Administrative Practice." *American Journal of Sociology* 69: 150–60.

37

DO EMPLOYERS REALLY NEED MORE EDUCATED YOUTH?

James E. Rosenbaum • Amy Binder

. . .

Although there is little doubt that many high school graduates lack strong academic skills

James Rosenbaum and Amy Binder, excerpts from "Do Employers Really Need More Educated Youth?" from *Sociology of Education* 70 (January 1997). Copyright © 1997 by the American Sociological Association. Reprinted with the permission of the authors and the American Sociological Association.

(NAEP 1990), sociologists have raised some doubts about whether employers really need better-educated workers. Berg (1971) contended that employers' reliance on education in making hiring decisions is not based on the actual skills needed for jobs. Rather, he argued, it fulfills an organizational desire for some kind of sorting criteria. Berg, Squires (1979), and Collins (1971) reviewed numerous studies that showed that educational attainments are unrelated to workers' productivity, turnover, or absenteeism.[1] Expanding on this argument, Collins (1971: 1018) concluded that "employers tend to have quite imprecise conceptions of the skill requirements of most jobs."

More recent multivariate studies, however, found relationships between academic achievement and productivity. Many studies in personnel psychology have demonstrated that cognitive ability is the strongest predictor of on-the-job performance in many occupations (Hunter and Hunter 1984). Similarly, econometric analyses have shown associations between test scores and performance (Barrett and Depinet 1991; Bishop 1993; National Research Council 1989) and between course work (and academic skills) and wages and employment (Cameron and Heckman 1993; Daymont and Rumberger 1982; Gamoran 1994; Kang and Bishop 1986). After an extensive review, Gamoran (1994) concluded that the preponderance of evidence suggests that there is a positive relationship between academic schoolwork and labor market outcomes.

Yet it is not clear whether employers act on these relationships. Research has found that employers fail to reward high school graduates for academic skills in terms of hiring, better jobs, or better pay (Bills 1988; Crain 1984; Griffin, Kalleberg, and Alexander 1981; Kang and Bishop 1986; Rosenbaum and Kariya 1991). Using data from the National Longitudinal Study of the High School Class of 1972 (NLS:72), Griffin et al. (1981) found that aptitude, class rank, and other school-performance measures have small and often insignificant effects on unemployment and job attainments of high school graduates who directly enter the workforce. Meyer and Wise (1982) showed that rank in the high school class of 1972 had insignificant effects on wage rates two years after graduation (1974), and Willis and Rosen (1979) observed that in-

creased mathematics and reading scores of high school graduates slightly lowered the wages of their first jobs. Despite their claims that they need workers with academic skills, employers do not offer immediate rewards to high school graduates with better academic performance. It is interest ing that although grades did not improve the wages of new high school graduates in the 1980s cohort of High School and Beyond, they had a strong payoff for these graduates' earnings 10 years later (Rosenbaum and Roy 1996).

Ray and Mickelson (1993) indicated that studies need to consider employers' actions, which sometimes convey messages that contradict executives' speeches. As if responding to this point, some recent research has looked at actions that employers take to get better workers. Studies of employers responses to school-work programs have found that employers have a limited commitment to such initiatives, offer few positions to students, and have low perseverance in these programs (Bailey 1994; Lynn and Wills 1994; Pauly, Kopp, and Haimson 1995). Bailey concluded that employers' behaviors raise some doubts about their commitment to skills. But these were studies of employers' responses to special programs, not the ordinary actions that employers routinely take to hire workers.

Nor do employers respond to their purported problems in obtaining workers with skills by providing academic-skills training. Zemsky (1994) noted that employers express highly negative views of the academic skills of high school graduates, but they do not use training programs to redress these deficiencies. In a survey of 2,800 employers, Boesel (1994, Table 2) discovered that 71 percent provided training to their employees, but less than 3 percent provided basic training in academic skills. Another survey of 3,000 employers found extensive complaints by employers about academic skills, but little indication of tuition benefits or remedial programs to address academic shortcomings (U.S. Bureau of the Census 1994). Commenting on these findings, Cappelli (1995:1) noted, "There has been a fair amount of noise in the business community about establishments having to provide remedial training. But it does not appear that they're doing it. It appears to be just noise." Cappelli raised the same issue as Berg (1971) did: Do employers really need academic skills, or are they complaining for other reasons?

Bowles and Gintis (1976) interpreted findings like those just mentioned to mean that employers do not really have a need for better academic skills and that employers' calls for academic skills are, at best, unwarranted and, at worst, a means of accomplishing some kind of social sorting, social control, or reduction in pay. Although empirical tests have not supported Bowles and Gintis's contention that employers need compliance, not academic skills (Cappelli 1992; Olneck and Bills 1980), these studies suffered from the same problems of measuring "needs" and "skills" noted earlier.

Methods

To discover whether employers actually value academic skills and act in accordance with their valuations, researchers must go to the right informants and use methods that are sensitive to the task. Rather than rely on the views of corporate executives (as blue-ribbon panels do), we interviewed the plant or office managers who actually hire entry-level workers. In the less frequent cases in which human resources departments handled the hiring of high school graduates, we interviewed managers in these departments.

To gain detailed information about the hiring process, we conducted one-hour interviews in employers' offices. Although observational methods would have yielded even better information, it is difficult to con-

duct observations in many organizations. Employers' detailed statements about their behaviors are a useful way to get at the intervening processes in a large number of organizations.

.   .   .

Since we were interested in how employers' attitudes limited youths' access to jobs in the primary labor market, we excluded businesses that are likely to offer only "youth jobs" without opportunities for advancement (such as restaurants and small stores). The sample cannot be considered a random sample of all employers, so statistical analyses would have been inappropriate. Yet it includes employers that have a wide variety of the kinds of entry-level jobs that are potentially available to high school graduates in graphics, manufacturing, skilled trades, financial services, office work, and so forth. These are mainly ordinary firms, not leading-edge, best-practice ones that are known for their high-skill demands (Murnane and Levy 1996), but they may offer the possibility of access to the primary labor market. They are appropriate for our purposes of discovering the range of academic skills that employers may need, the job conditions they may provide, and the range of costly actions they may take to obtain these skills.

Twenty-three of the 51 employers in this sample were located in the city of Chicago, and 28 were located in suburbs west of Chicago. The sample was composed mostly of small or medium-size firms, but it included a few large ones; the companies ranged in size from fewer than 10 to more than 80,000 employees.

Findings

This section probes the sociological contention that employers overstate their need for skilled workers. It investigates whether employers report a need for workers with specific academic skills and whether they indicate the relevance of specific academic skills to specific job requirements. It then examines if employers take any costly actions to realize their stated needs and, if so, what strategies they use and whether these actions are taken by those who report difficulty finding workers with academic skills.

Skills Needed for Entry-Level Jobs

Though one should be skeptical about the needs voiced by the top executives on American blue-ribbon panels, our first-line managers expressed similar concerns. Of the 51 urban and suburban managers who were interviewed, 35 stated that basic academic skills in mathematics and English are needed for the entry-level jobs they are seeking to fill, and many described specific job conditions or tasks that demand these skills. They were most certain about the requirements of their jobs after they had experience with workers with poor skills.

Mathematical Skills Thirteen of the 35 managers described the tasks that require mathematics skills in their entry-level jobs. Most reported that the jobs require workers who can do simple arithmetic and sometimes add fractions and that some jobs require algebra and trigonometry. The general manager of one Chicago steel manufacturing company said that the general-labor jobs in his plant require "the concept of adding or reading a ruler or tape measure." He added: "We would like to hire people who know eighth-grade math, such as knowing the difference between a fraction and a decimal, but kids aren't getting that from high school, and we generally don't see that level of knowledge." A manager at another Chicago manufacturer complained that many workers have fallen short in basic mathematics. When asked what experiences she has had with young employees, she recounted

the story of a young man she just hired to work full time in the shipping department:

> He came in my office and said, "You know, down in that shipping room you've got a lot of numbers out there." I said, "We've got a lot of numbers out there? Well yes, I guess we do." And he said, "I don't know a lot about numbers." I said, "Oh, do you want to learn?" He said, "Yeah, I think so." I said, "Have you noticed that there are periods between some of the numbers?" He said, "Yeah, what's that all about?" I said, "Where were you when they learned decimals in school?" He said, "I must have been absent."

English Skills Another 10 of the 35 managers reported that reading, writing, and communication skills are needed for their jobs and that their employees who are high school graduates do not even have simple skills. One office manager in a small suburban graphics company told of a secretary "who tried to spell *quick* with a 'w.' She didn't know that . . . all words that have 'q' need a 'u'!" Echoing an often-reported condition, a recruiter for a Chicago insurance company said that applicants for data-entry and claims-adjustment jobs "can't understand some of the questions on the job application" and that some men bring girlfriends to fill out the applications.

Another Chicago manager unhappily stated that many of his applicants for unskilled labor jobs "can't read and write beyond, I suspect, a fifth- or sixth-grade level, and when they can read, they certainly can't comprehend what they have read." This is often a serious shortcoming because many employers think that their jobs require better than eighth-grade reading and writing skills. A manager for a suburban manufacturer observed that "today's high school graduates don't comprehend as much. It takes them longer to catch on to instructions, and they can't read manuals for instructions as well as they used to, which are written at the 12th grade level." Another manager noted the needed to find workers who can "put together two or three sentences in a complete thought."

Both Mathematical and English Skills
Another 12 managers cited high school graduates' problems with both mathematics and English, saying that both types of skills are needed in today's entry-level jobs. A manager at a Chicago metal-parts manufacturer complained that even though his entry-level jobs require only seventh-grade reading and mathematics skills, he has a "terrible time getting even a 10 percent yield" for these skills in the applicants he interviews.

Of the 16 managers who stated that they had *no* need for employees with academic skills, 11 said that their entry-level jobs simply require no skills, and 3 more said that their jobs require occupational skills, but not academic skills.[2] A suburban production manager noted: "There aren't a lot of qualifications other than wanting to work." A suburban plant manager observed that academic skills are actually counterproductive; for such people, "within a year or so, they'll get bored and move on." A manager at a Chicago custom-gearing manufacturer reported that his company needs people with "technical ability . . . [for] grasping the skills needed for machine jobs."

Promotion to Higher-Level Jobs

Some managers noted that although academic skills are not needed in their entry-level jobs, these skills *are* needed for higher jobs in their companies that entry-level workers can move into. Even though these entry-level jobs are largely in the secondary labor market, in that they offer minimal pay, benefits, and job security, they can sometimes lead to the bottom rung of a career ladder to better jobs. Doeringer and Piore (1971:

167) referred to such jobs as "secondary jobs . . . attached to internal labor markets."

Employers note that upward movement is possible from such entry-level jobs only if workers possess adequate basic skills at the time of entry. Of the 35 managers who stated that they need workers with academic skills, 17 (48.6 percent) reported that although their entry-level jobs are undemanding, they allow some workers to move into higher-skilled jobs, and those jobs do require academic skills. Indeed, some employers prefer to recruit for their skilled jobs from entry-level workers who can learn the firm's procedures and techniques by observation.

. . .

On-the-Job Screening

Other employers used their entry-level jobs for what may be called on-the-job screening. A manager at a printing plant reported that his firm uses entry-level jobs as a way to discover if workers have the ability to advance in the future:

> Well, one of the questions I ask the pressman [the employee's supervisor] is, "Are they fast learners?" I ask, "How are they doing? Can they read and write? Are they picking up on the math and the instructions fine?" If that's true, there's no problem. I ask [their supervisors], "Hey, are these our future pressers?" They say, "Yeah." So that's the answer I'm looking for. That's what I'm looking for when we're hiring somebody: Are they going to be able to go up the ladder and become the feeder and the second man, then up to the first-man spot?

In entry-level jobs that offer on-the-job training or screening, if workers do only what is demanded by their simple daily tasks, they will not need academic skills. But if they can do only these daily tasks and lack academic skills, then they will not advance to more demanding jobs, which employers expect to fill from these positions.

Jobs that offer on-the-job screening may illustrate Berg's (1971) findings on the artificially high premium placed on academic skills, but they suggest a possible limitation of his study. That is, Berg may have found workers "overqualified" for the task demands of their present jobs because employers were preparing these workers to advance into higher jobs or were testing their capabilities. To the extent that employers use some jobs to train or screen workers for higher jobs, their job requirements will include skills needed for the higher jobs, but not for the entry-level jobs. . . .

. . .

Strategies to Increase Retention

When faced with workers who fall beneath a certain level of academic skills on the job, do companies undertake expensive actions that are designed to compensate for their workers' poor skills? If they do, we could infer that these companies have some commitment to their professed need for academic skills. We found that employers take three types of compensatory actions: increasing supervisors' responsibilities to assist and supervise less skilled workers, simplifying job tasks to match workers' poor skills, and accommodating good workers when they come along.

Increasing Supervisors' Responsibilities to Assist and Supervise Less Skilled Workers Many employers assign more experienced—and expensive—workers the task of assisting less skilled workers in performing their jobs, explaining the tasks in minute detail, and supervising their performance more closely. Often this is an additional task for a supervisor or manager. This kind of strategy occurred in 11 companies in our sample—in 9 of the 35 (25.7 percent) whose managers

stated that their companies needed workers with academic skills, but in only 2 of the 16 (12.5 percent) who stated that their companies did not. Apparently, those who said that their companies had jobs that required such academic skills were more likely to increase supervisors' responsibilities.

A manager at a Chicago manufacturer noted that her firm compensates for high school graduates' lack of basic reading and mathematics skills by repeatedly spelling out each task that must be done:

> We find if they can't understand the reading, they have to have an illustration, like we'll take a gauge and show them where it has to be. Instead of the workers being able to say to themselves, "This part has to be made within thousandths of an inch" and taking the part and measuring it to those thousandths, the foreman has to go over to the employee, pick up the part, pick up the gauge, set the gauge, and say, "If it does this, OK. And if it doesn't, not OK" and has to set up a scenario each and every time.

The plant manager of a small company succinctly summed up this strategy when he observed that he "basically just spend[s] time with them on the floor with a ruler and show[s] them the basic marks, and show[s] them how it works."

Simplifying Job Tasks to Match Workers' Poor Skills This strategy often requires additional costs. Of the 51 managers we interviewed, 23 (45.1 percent) reported that they must adapt job tasks to make up for the basic academic skills that their entry-level employees lack. Although 20 of the 35 (57.1 percent) managers who stated that the jobs at their companies need academic skills adapt job tasks to respond to entry-level workers' shortcomings in skills, only 3 of the 16 (18.8 percent) who did not mention such needs take such actions. Apparently, those who said that they need employees with academic skills are more likely to take these actions.

Many of those who were interviewed were matter-of-fact about the need to make jobs easier, as when one plant manager in a Chicago manufacturing firm said, "Yes, [simplifying] is a must. What I've done is gone all the way down to the grammar-school level to get them to understand simple, simple math." The plant manager at a suburban metal fabricator stated that his company has taken the ultimate step in bypassing workers' poor reading skills: "We have eliminated a need for math and reading skills altogether; every instruction we give workers is now verbal." A plant manager at a Chicago manufacturer agreed: "[We] only give people instructions for a certain amount of instructions at a time. Spoon-feed them a little bit." Both these managers thought that such "spoon-feeding" is an additional and costly burden that they would prefer to avoid, but they are struggling with problems of poor skills and find it is an unanticipated cost. There is much concern about the low-paid, low-skilled jobs in the work world and much criticism of employers for not offering better jobs. In these examples, however, we see employers who feel compelled to reduce the skill demands of entry-level jobs because of workers' limitations.

Altering Job Conditions or Rules to Accommodate Good Applicants or Workers

Such accommodations can occur either at the time of hiring (such as when an employer changes the hiring schedules to meet the needs of a valued applicant) or as a way to retain valued employees (such as when an employer allows an employee to work at home, rather than at the job site).

Of the 51 managers who were interviewed, 16 said that their companies try to accommodate valued employees in some way—13 of the 35 (37.1 percent) who reported the need for workers with academic skills, but only 3 of the 16 (18.8 percent) who did not. Again, those who stated the need for academic skills were more likely to take these actions.

. . .

Once a worker proves to be a valuable employee, supervisors are loath to lose them. To retain valued workers, some employers will accommodate their workers by allowing them to work flexible hours, at home, or in jobs they ordinarily would not hold. When the manager of a manufacturing firm in Chicago received a call from a valued former young worker who was moving back to the city, he enthusiastically asked, "How soon can you start?" Although it was a small firm and it did not have a job vacancy, he added that the company would "reorganize to have her back." The manager of a suburban metal shop explained: "When you see a guy or girl [is working] out well, has a good work ethic, you hate to let [him or her] go. I'll find a place for them. Because somewhere down the line I'm going to need that person again." This manager said that even in periods of slack demand, he will accommodate a skilled employee.

. . .

Recruitment Strategies

Employers participate in several different types of contacts with schools and other institutions to seek skilled high school graduates for their entry-level positions and use some of these linkages to provide information about prospective workers. Some activities, like apprenticeship programs, do not involve schools, but they are sometimes related to the need for workers with academic skills. School-related activities range from minimal involvement (job fairs) to high involvement (long-term links with teachers). Some of these linkage activities seem to be a form of investment in prescreening.

Apprenticeships Although apprenticeships have been praised as a type of training (Hamilton 1989), in Germany, apprenticeship programs also have a screening function (Faist 1992; Rosenbaum 1992). The managers of four of the companies use apprenticeships, and all four stressed that apprenticeship programs are a dependable way to screen their applicant pool for academic skills. Asked whether his company has trouble finding high school graduates with sufficient mathematics and reading skills, one manager of a Chicago manufacturing firm referred to his use of an apprenticeship program for hiring young, entry-level machinists-in-training: "They won't be in here if they don't have [academic skills]." Even before we asked about academic skills, this manager explained that the apprenticeship test of academic and job skills creates an "up-or-out" situation. For entry-level workers to become apprentices at his firm, they either have to pass the test that the apprenticeship program "administers and then they are enrolled in the apprenticeship program, or they [fail] the test and they are out of a job."

When asked if his company is willing to hire employees who have *not* passed the apprenticeship test, the manager at a suburban manufacturer responded, "Oh yeah, we'll put them out here and give them the work experience. But of course, it would be a lesser-degree job." Both these employers place a value on basic skills, and both have found a means of ensuring that their better entry-level positions are filled by high school graduates with these skills: They use apprenticeship linkages. Three of the four managers at manufacturing plants that use apprenticeship referrals were among those who said that their firms need workers with academic

skills. But while apprenticeships are a means of selecting applicants with academic skills, they are not common.

Close Links with Schools Employers' contacts with schools are far more common. Indeed, 42 of the 51 employers (82.4 percent) in our study have minimal contacts with schools—through job fairs at schools, talks to classes, or notices of openings for part-time jobs. But employers view these activities as community services to help students learn about work: they rarely regard them as leading to full-time jobs.

Some employers, however, have long-term, close linkages with school staff. Those who do frequently devote a substantial amount of time to these relationships; they serve on school advisory boards and try to hire recommended graduates of certain vocational programs. Unlike school-business partnerships, which are often short-lived (Lynn and Wills 1994), these contacts usually carry long-term obligations and last many years. When these employers have job openings, they ask school staff to nominate students. Employers see these long-term linkages as a way to get the straight scoop on young graduates' skills.

Of the 51 employers in our study, 13 have long-term contacts with teachers and counselors.[3] These linkages are much more common among employers who said they need academic skills; 12 of the 35 (34.3 percent) managers who said their firms need employees with academic skills used a close form of school linkage, compared to only 1 (6.3 percent) of the 16 who said his firm does not.

Despite the costs, several managers suggested that the investment of time involved in the closer form of contacts (trusted links with school staff) pays off in employees with better academic skills. One executive at a family-owned printing company in Chicago said that his company is still able to get workers with good academic skills from a local high school on the basis of the personal relationship his father established with a teacher from that school more than 10 years ago. Although this relationship is not without its costs (volunteered time on the school's advisory council), its benefits have been worth the sacrifices:

> I think we've had success because we have been able to reach inside the schools and talk specifically to certain teachers. . . . And the positive [aspect] of those contacts for us is that we're getting the straight scoop. And there [are] many times [when] we've called, and the teachers, the instructors, have told us, "Look, I've got a classroom full of kids, but there's no way I would send any of them to you." So, I don't know if the schools are doing a great job, but our success has been good because we've been handed, I think, a few of the better ones.

Asked to speculate why these links with schools work, one supervisor at a suburban metal company observed: "If someone is willing to put their name behind somebody and say, 'I think that this guy would work out good,' well, most people nowadays will not personally endorse anybody unless they're pretty confident they won't wind up with egg on their face." Because he expects the teachers he knows to care about their reputations, this supervisor trusts them to tell him the truth about applicants' skills. Through this link, he can efficiently and effectively prescreen applicants and hire only those who come highly recommended.

But employers' actions to recruit employees through selected networks has adverse implications for alternative channels, even from the same school. The managers of several companies that maintain long-term contacts with trusted teachers said that they are not willing to make an open channel of recruitment from the entire school, such as through co-op placement programs or the counseling office. When asked whether he would consider using other school programs to recommend potential workers, the manager at a Chicago printing plant with strong links to teachers reported:

> We bypass the typical channels. . . . I think the placement offices in . . . schools . . . they're out there, God bless them for it, but they're out there trying to get kids jobs, and I think they probably have less sensitivity to the workplace. I think the best of them probably have the idea that if they get the [kids] placed into [jobs], then they've done their job. And that's good [for their kids]. That probably is their role. But I don't know that it means that they fully understand what [my job requirements are] or whether they fully understand the students either. The teachers on the front line, I think they have their finger on the pulse a lot more.

Similarly, a manager at a suburban printing firm said that the principal of a local high school has done a laudable job in referring qualified applicants to him, but the counselors have disappointed him:

> You get a very strong distaste for working with high school counselors. I have very little use for high school counselors altogether because I don't know if their background is sociology with a specialty in psychology, or whatever it is, but the only applicants I've ever gotten from high school counselors have been absolutely worthless. . . . [They] have all just been really a waste of time.

In addition to distrusting conventional school channels for recommendations, employers who seek teachers' assistance in hiring students are also wary of putting too much stock in high school grades. Of the 13 employers with strong links to teachers or counselors, 8 reject the idea of using grades to measure employability. When asked if he thinks that school grades predict anything about work performance, the manager of a Chicago firm with such a link responded:

> Not in all cases. And that works both ways. There's a lot of people that come out of high school that have some great credentials and just never do anything, and then there are other young people who come out of high school with be-low-average grades that just have the will to succeed. For whatever reason, high school didn't grab them. So, actu-ally, at this point in time, I wouldn't put too much weight on grades. The [teacher's] comments I would put a lot of weight on if I know the teacher, but not typically the objective measures.

These comments help to clarify a puzzle in past research. Many employers (both in our sample and in the society at large, cf. Crain 1984; Griffin et al. 1981; Rosenbaum and Kariya 1991) choose not to use grades as a hiring criterion, even when they complain about not getting skilled workers. These findings suggest that the skills students learn in school are valued by some employ-ers, but the traditional ways of reporting those skills—grades—are perceived as un-trustworthy. Given this situation, employ-ers' investments in long-term linkages may be the one way of getting trusted informa-tion instead of using the grades they do not trust (cf. Miller and Rosenbaum 1997).

These findings also indicate that al-though employers pursue the productivity goals that economists assume, some employ-ers' means of obtaining trustworthy infor-mation about applicants' potential produc-tivity actually restrict access to those jobs to only students with the right contacts. Even students who have good grades but who lack access to these contacts will have their quali-fications mistrusted and may not be consid-ered by some employers. These links provide a good channel of access for students who have classes with linked teachers, and in inner-city schools, these students' best chance of getting a job is through their teach-ers. But only a small proportion of teachers have such contacts (Rosenbaum and Jones 1995), and these links represent structural barriers that prevent the labor market from operating in the unfettered way envisioned by economic theory, even though the links are created in pursuit of that theory's goal.

. . .

NOTES

1. Berg (1971:94) noted that measures of job per-formance are more dubious for white-collar jobs and that findings for professional and managerial work suffer even more from this problem.

2. Three managers did not directly answer the question, "Do you often find that high school graduates do not have the reading and math skills to work here?" One answered the question by discussing his applicants' poor vo-cational skills, one responded with informa-tion about his company's English-as-a-Second-Language program, and the other said that he had not noticed. All three of these ambiguous responses were coded as employers saying that basic academic skills are not lacking and were included in the subsample of 16 noncom-plainers.

3. This rate ($^{13}/_{51}$—25.4 percent) is likely to be higher than average. Holzer's (1995) four-city survey of employers indicated that 3–7 per-cent of firms' most recent hires came through school referrals, and analyses of the High School and Beyond data found that less than 10 percent of first jobs were found with help from schools (Rosenbaum and Roy 1996). Our exclusion of employers in the secondary labor market (such as restaurants and small stores) probably contributed to the higher rate here.

REFERENCES

BAILEY, THOMAS. 1994. "Barriers to Employer Par-ticipation in School-to-Work Programs." Presented at the seminar on Employer Participation in School-to-Work Transition Programs, Brookings Institution, May 4, Washington, DC.

BARRETT, G. V. AND R. L. DEPINET. 1991. "A Reconsideration of Testing for Competence Rather Than for Intelligence." *American Psychologist* 46:1012–24.

BERG, IVAR. 1971. *Education and Jobs.* Boston: Beacon Press.

BILLS, DAVID. 1988. "Employers and Overeducation." Paper presented at the annual meeting of the American Sociological Association, August 24, Atlanta, GA.

BISHOP, JOHN. 1993. "Improving Job Matches in the U.S. Labor Market." Pp. 335–400 in *Brookings Papers in Economic Activity: Microeconomics,* edited by Martin N. Bailey. Washington, DC: Brookings Institution.

BOESEL, DAVID. 1994. *BLS Survey of Employer-Provided Formal Training.* Washington, DC: U.S. Department of Labor, Bureau of Labor Statistics.

BOWLES, SAMUEL AND HERBERT GINTIS. 1976. *Schooling in Capitalist America.* New York: Basic Books.

CAMERON, STEPHEN AND JAMES HECKMAN. 1993. "The Nonequivalence of High School Equivalents." *Journal of Labor Economics* 11:1–47.

CAPPELLI, PETER. 1992. "Is the 'Skills Gap' Really about Attitudes?" Philadelphia: National Center on the Educational Quality of the Workforce, University of Pennsylvania. Working Paper.

———. 1995. "Employers Wary of School System." *New York Times,* February 20, p. 1.

COLLINS, RANDALL. 1971. "Functional and Conflict Theories of Educational Stratification." *American Sociological Review* 36:1002–19.

CRAIN, ROBERT. 1984. "The Quality of American High School Graduates: What Personnel Officers Say and Do." Center for the Study of Schools, Johns Hopkins University, Baltimore. Unpublished manuscript.

DAYMONT, THOMAS N. AND RUSSELL W. RUMBERGER, 1982. "Job Training in the Schools." Pp. 19–29 in *Job Training for Youth,* edited by R. Taylor, H. Rosen, and F. Pratzner. Columbus: National Center for Research in Vocational Education. Ohio State University.

DOERINGER, PETER AND MICHAEL PIORE. 1971. *Internal Labor Markets and Manpower Analysis.* Lexington, MA: Lexington Books.

FAIST, THOMAS. 1992. "Social Citizenship and the Transformation from School to Work among Immigrant Minorities." Unpublished PhD. dissertation, New School for Social Researh, New York.

GAMORAN, ADAM. 1994. "The Impact of Academic Course Work on Labor Market Outcomes for Youth Who Do Not Attend College: A Research Review." Unpublished manuscript prepared for the National Assessment of Vocational Education.

GRIFFIN, LARRY J., ARNE L. KALLEBERG, AND KARL L. ALEXANDER. 1981. "Determinants of Early Labor Market Entry and Attainment: A Study of Labor Market Segmentation." *Sociology of Education* 54:206–21.

HAMILTON STEPHEN F. 1989. *Apprenticeship for Adulthood.* New York: Free Press.

HOLZER, HARRY. 1995. *What Employers Want.* New York: Russell Sage Foundation.

HUNTER, J. E. AND R. F. HUNTER. 1984. "Validity and Utility of Alternative Predictors of Job Performance." *Psychological Bulletin* 96.

KANG, SUK AND JOHN BISHOP. 1986. "The Effects of Curriculum on Labor Market Success." *Journal of Industrial Teacher Education.* Spring:133–48.

LYNN, IRENE AND JOAN WILLS. 1994. *School–Work Transition: Lessons on Recruiting and Sustaining Employer Involvement.* Washington, DC: Institute for Educational Leadership.

MEYER, ROBERT H. AND DAVID A. WISE. 1982. "High School Preparation and Early Labor Force Experience." Pp. 277–347 in *The Youth Labor Market Problem,* edited by Richard B. Freeman and David A. Wise. Chicago: University of Chicago Press.

MILLER, SHAZIA R. AND JAMES E. ROSENBAUM. 1997. "Hiring in a Hobbesian World: Social Infrastructure and Employers' Use of Information." *Work and Occupations* 24:498–524.

MURNANE, RICHARD J. AND FRANK LEVY. 1996. *Teaching the New Basic Skills.* New York: Free Press.

MURNANE, RICHARD J., JOHN B. WILLETT, AND FRANK LEVY. 1995. "The Growing Importance of Cognitive Skills in Wage Determination." *Review of Economics and Statistics* 77:251–66.

NATIONAL ASSESSMENT OF EDUCATIONAL PROGRESS. 1990. *The Reading Report Card.* Princeton, NJ: Educational Testing Service.

NATIONAL RESEARCH COUNCIL. 1989. *Fairness in Employment Testing.* Washington, DC: Author.

OLNECK, MICHAEL R. AND DAVID BILLS. 1980. "What Makes Sammy Run?" *American Journal of Education* 89:27–61.

PAULY, EDWARD, HILARY KOPP, AND J. HAIMSON. 1995. *Homegrown Lessons: Innovative Programs*

Linking School and Work. San Francisco: Jossey-Bass.

RAY, CAROL AXTELL AND ROSLYN ARLIN MICKELSON. 1993. "Restructuring Students for Restructured Work." *Sociology of Education* 66:1–20.

ROSENBAUM, JAMES E. AND STEPHANIE JONES. "Creating Linkages in The High School-To-Work Transition." Pp. 235-58 in Restructuring Schools, edited by Maureen Hallinan. New York: Plenum.

ROSENBAUM, JAMES E. AND TAKEHIKO KARIYO. 1991. "Do School Achievements Affect the Early Jobs of High School Graduates in the United States and Japan?" *Sociology of Education* 64:78–95.

ROSENBAUM, JAMES E. AND KEVIN ROY. 1996.

"Long-Term Effects of High School Grades and Job Placements." Paper presented at the annual meeting of the American Sociological Association, New York.

SQUIRES, GARY D. 1979. *Education and Jobs.* New Brunswick, NJ: Transaction Books.

U.S. BUREAU OF THE CENSUS. 1994. *Educational Quality of the Workforce Issues Number 10.* Washington, DC: Author.

WILLIS, ROBERT AND SHERWIN ROSEN. 1979. "Education and Self-Selection." *Journal of Political Economy* 87:527–36.

ZEMSKY, ROBERT. 1994. "What Employers Want." Philadelphia: National Center on the Educational Quality of the Workforce, University of Pennsylvania. Working Paper.

38

THE EDUCATION OF THE SYMBOLIC ANALYST

Robert Reich

I have never seen anybody improve on the art and technique of inquiry by any means other than engaging in inquiry.
—JEROME BRUNER, *On Knowing* (1962)

As the value placed on new designs and concepts continues to grow relative to the value placed on standard products, the demand for symbolic analysis will continue to surge. This burgeoning demand should assure symbolic analysts ever higher incomes in the years ahead.

Of course, the worldwide supply of symbolic analysts is growing as well. Millions of people across the globe are trying to learn symbolic-analytic skills, and many are succeeding. Researchers and engineers in East Asia and Western Europe are gathering valuable insights into microelectronics, microbiotics, and new materials, and translating these insights into new products. Young people in many developing nations are swarming into universities to learn the symbolic and analytic secrets of design engineering, computer engineering, marketing, and management. By 1990, for example, more than one-third of all nineteen-year-old Argentines, Singaporeans, and South Koreans were pursuing college degrees.

But even with a larger supply, it is likely that Americans will continue to excel at symbolic analysis. For two reasons: First, no nation educates its most fortunate and talented children—its future symbolic analysts—as well as does America. Second, no nation possesses the same agglomerations of symbolic analysts already in place and able to learn continuously and informally from one another. While these two advantages may not last forever, American symbolic analysts will continue to enjoy a head start for the foreseeable future at least.

2

Americans love to get worked up over American education. Everyone has views on education because it is one of the few fields in which everyone can claim to have had some direct experience. Those with the strongest views tend to be those on whom the experience has had the least lasting effect. The truly educated person understands how multifaceted are the goals of education in a free society, and how complex are the means.

Recall that America's educational system at midcentury fit nicely into the prevailing structure of high-volume production within which its young products were to be employed. American schools mirrored the national economy, with a standard assembly-line curriculum divided neatly into subjects, taught in predictable units of time, arranged sequentially by grade, and controlled by standardized tests intended to weed out defective units and return them for reworking.

By the last decade of the twentieth century, although the economy had changed dramatically, the form and function of the American educational system remained roughly the same. But now a palpable sense of crisis surrounded the nation's schools, featuring daily lamentations in the media about how terrible they had become. The fact, however, was that most schools had not changed for the worse; they simply had not changed for the better. Early in his presidential campaign, George Bush bestowed upon himself the anticipatory title of "Education President." But, although he continued to so style himself after his election, the title's meaning remained elusive, since Bush

did not want to spend any more federal money on education and urged instead that the nation's schools fix themselves. Some people who called themselves educational "reformers" suggested that the standard curriculum should become even more uniform across the nation and that standardized tests should be still more determinative of what was poured into young heads as they moved along the school conveyor belt. (Of course, standardized tests remained, as before, a highly accurate method for measuring little more than the ability of children to take standardized tests.) Popular books contained lists of facts that every educated person should know. Remarkably often in American life, when the need for change is most urgent, the demands grow most insistent that we go "back to basics."

The truth is that while the vast majority of American children are still subjected to a standardized education designed for a standardized economy, a small fraction are not. By the 1990s, the *average* American child was ill equipped to compete in the high-value global economy, but within that average was a wide variation. American children as a whole are behind their counterparts in Canada, Japan, Sweden, and Britain in mathematical proficiency, science, and geography.[1] Fully 17 percent of American seventeen-year-olds are functionally illiterate.[2] Some American children receive almost no education, and many more get a poor one. But some American children—no more than 15 to 20 percent—are being perfectly prepared for a lifetime of symbolic-analytic work.

The formal education of the budding symbolic analyst follows a common pattern. Some of these young people attend elite private schools, followed by the most selective universities and prestigious graduate schools; a majority spend childhood within high-quality suburban public schools where they are tracked through advanced courses in the company of other similarly fortunate symbolic-analytic offspring,[3] and thence to good four-year colleges. But their experiences are similar: Their parents are interested and involved in their education. Their teachers and professors are attentive to their academic needs. They have access to state-of-the-art science laboratories, interactive computers and video systems in the classroom, language laboratories, and high-tech school libraries. Their classes are relatively small; their peers are intellectually stimulating. Their parents take them to museums and cultural events, expose them to foreign travel, and give them music lessons. At home are educational books, educational toys, educational videotapes, microscopes, telescopes, and personal computers replete with the latest educational software. Should the children fall behind in their studies, they are delivered to private tutors. Should they develop a physical ailment that impedes their learning, they immediately receive good medical care.

The argument here is not that America's formal system for training its future symbolic analysts is flawless. There is room for improvement. European and Japanese secondary students routinely outperform even top American students in mathematics and science. Overall, however, no other society prepares its most fortunate young people as well for lifetimes of creative problem-solving, -identifying, and brokering. America's best four-year colleges and universities are the best in the world (as evidenced by the number of foreign students who flock to them);[4] the college-track programs of the secondary schools that prepare students for them are equally exceptional. In Japan, it has been the other way around: The shortcomings of Japanese universities and the uninspiring fare offered by Japanese secondary schools have been widely noted. Japan's greatest educational success has been to ensure that even

its slowest learners achieve a relatively high level of proficiency.[5]

3

The underlying content of America's symbolic-analytic curriculum is not generally addressed openly in suburban PTA meetings, nor disclosed in college catalogues. Yet its characteristics and purposes are understood implicitly by teachers, professors, and symbolic-analytic parents.

Budding symbolic analysts learn to read, write, and do calculations, of course, but such basic skills are developed and focused in particular ways. They often accumulate a large number of facts along the way, yet these facts are not central to their education; they will live their adult lives in a world in which most facts learned years before (even including some historical ones) will have changed or have been reinterpreted. In any event, whatever data they need will be available to them at the touch of a computer key.

More important, these fortunate children learn how to conceptualize problems and solutions. The formal education of an incipient symbolic analyst thus entails refining four basic skills: *abstraction, system thinking, experimentation,* and *collaboration.*[6]

Consider, first, the capacity for abstraction. The real world is nothing but a vast jumble of noises, shapes, colors, smells, and textures—essentially meaningless until the human mind imposes some order upon them. The capacity for abstraction—for discovering patterns and meanings—is, of course, the very essence of symbolic analysis, in which reality must be simplified so that it can be understood and manipulated in new ways. The symbolic analyst wields equations, formulae, analogies, models, constructs, categories, and metaphors in order to create possibilities for reinterpreting, and then rearranging, the chaos of data that are already swirling around us. Huge gobs of disorganized information can thus be integrated and assimilated to reveal new solutions, problems, and choices. Every innovative scientist, lawyer, engineer, designer, management consultant, screenwriter, or advertiser is continuously searching for new ways to represent reality which will be more compelling or revealing than the old. Their tools may vary, but the abstract processes of shaping raw data into workable, often original patterns are much the same.

For most children in the United States and around the world, formal education entails just the opposite kind of learning. Rather than construct meanings for themselves, meanings are imposed upon them. What is to be learned is prepackaged into lesson plans, lectures, and textbooks. Reality has already been simplified; the obedient student has only to commit it to memory. An efficient educational process, it is assumed, imparts knowledge much as an efficient factory installs parts on an assembly line. Regardless of what is conveyed, the underlying lesson is that it is someone else's responsibility to reinterpret and give meaning to the swirl of data, events, and sensations that surround us. This lesson can only retard students' ability to thrive in a world brimming with possibilities for discovery.

America's most fortunate students escape spoon-feeding, however. On the advanced tracks of the nation's best primary and secondary schools, and in the seminar rooms and laboratories of America's best universities, the curriculum is fluid and interactive. Instead of emphasizing the transmission of information, the focus is on judgment and interpretation. The student is taught to get *behind* the data—to ask why certain facts have been selected, why they are assumed to be important, how they were deduced, and how they might be contradicted. The student learns to examine reality from many angles, in different lights, and thus to visualize new possibilities and choices. The symbolic-analytic mind is trained to be skeptical, curious, and creative.

4

System thinking carries abstraction a step further. Seeing reality as a system of causes and consequences comes naturally to a small baby who learns that a glass of milk hurled onto a hardwood floor will shatter, its contents splashing over anyone in the vicinity, and that such an event—though momentarily quite amusing—is sure to incur a strong reaction from the adult in charge. More refined forms of system thinking come less naturally. Our tendency in later life is often to view reality as a series of static snapshots—here a market, there a technology, here an environmental hazard, there a political movement. Relationships among such phenomena are left unprobed. Most formal education perpetuates this compartmental fallacy, offering up facts and figures in bite-sized units of "history," "geography," "mathematics," and "biology," as if each were distinct and unrelated to the others. This may be an efficient system for conveying bits of data, but not for instilling wisdom. What the student really learns is that the world is made up of discrete components, each capable of being substantially understood in isolation.

To discover new opportunities, however, one must be capable of seeing the whole, and of understanding the processes by which parts of reality are linked together. In the real world, issues rarely emerge predefined and neatly separable. The symbolic analyst must constantly try to discern larger causes, consequences, and relationships. What looks like a simple problem susceptible to a standard solution may turn out to be a symptom of a more fundamental problem, sure to pop up elsewhere in a different form. By solving the basic problem, the symbolic analyst can add substantial value. The invention of a quickly biodegradable plastic eliminates many of the problems of designing safe landfills; a computerized workstation for the home solves the myriad problems of rush-hour traffic.

The education of the symbolic analyst emphasizes system thinking. Rather than teach students how to solve a problem that is presented to them, they are taught to examine why the problem arises and how it is connected to other problems. Learning how to travel from one place to another by following a prescribed route is one thing; learning the entire terrain so that you can find shortcuts to wherever you may want to go is quite another. Instead of assuming that problems and their solutions are generated by others (as they were under high-volume, standardized production), students are taught that problems can usually be redefined according to where you look in a broad system of forces, variables, and outcomes, and that unexpected relationships and potential solutions can be discovered by examining this larger terrain.

5

In order to learn the higher forms of abstraction and system thinking, one must learn to experiment. Small children spend most of their waking hours experimenting. Their tests are random and repetitive, but through trial and error they increase their capacity to create order out of a bewildering collage of sensations and to comprehend causes and consequences. More advanced forms of experimentation also entail many false starts, often resulting in frustration, disappointment, and even fear. Exploring a city on your own rather than following a prescribed tour may take you far afield—you may even get lost, for a time. But there is no better way

to learn the layout or to see the city from many different points of view. Thus are symbolic analysts continuously experimenting. The cinematographer tries out a new technique for shooting scenes; the design engineer tries out a new material for fabricating engine parts. The habits and methods of experimentation are critical in the new economy, where technologies, tastes, and markets are in constant flux.

But most formal schooling (both in the United States and elsewhere) has little to do with experimentation. The tour through history or geography or science typically has a fixed route, beginning at the start of the textbook or the series of lectures and ending at its conclusion. Students have almost no opportunity to explore the terrain for themselves. Self-guided exploration is, after all, an inefficient means of covering ground that "must" be covered.

And yet in the best classes of the nation's best schools and universities, the emphasis is quite different. Rather than being led along a prescribed path, students are equipped with a set of tools for finding their own way. The focus is on experimental techniques: holding certain parts of reality constant while varying others in order to better understand causes and consequences; systematically exploring a range of possibilities and outcomes and noting relevant similarities and differences; making thoughtful guesses and intuitive leaps and then testing them against previous assumptions. Most important, students are taught to accept responsibility for their own continuing learning. (Japan's schools, it should be noted, are weakest in this dimension.)

6

Finally, there is the capacity to collaborate. As has been noted, symbolic analysts typically work in teams—sharing problems and solutions in a somewhat more sophisticated version of a child's play group. The play of symbolic analysts may appear undirected, but it is often the only way to discover problems and solutions that are not known to be discoverable in advance. Symbolic analysts also spend much of their time communicating concepts—through oral presentations, reports, designs, memoranda, layouts, scripts, and projections—and then seeking a consensus to go forward with the plan.

Learning to collaborate, communicate abstract concepts, and achieve a consensus are not usually emphasized within formal education, however. To the contrary, within most classrooms in the United States and in other nations, the overriding objective is to achieve quiet and solitary performance of specialized tasks. No talking! No passing of notes! No giving one another help! Here again, the rationale is efficiency and the presumed importance of evaluating individual performance. Group tasks are not as easily monitored or controlled as is individual work. It is thus harder to determine whether a particular student has mastered the specified material.

Yet in America's best classrooms, again, the emphasis has shifted. Instead of individual achievement and competition, the focus is on group learning. Students learn to articulate, clarify, and then restate for one another how they identify and find answers. They learn how to seek and accept criticism from peers, solicit help, and give credit to others. They also learn to negotiate—to explain their own needs, to discern what others need and view things from others' perspectives, and to discover mutually beneficial resolutions. This is an ideal preparation for lifetimes of symbolic-analytic teamwork.

Again, the claim here is not that America's schools and colleges are doing their jobs adequately. The argument is narrower: That our best schools and universities are providing a small subset of America's young with excellent basic training in the techniques essential to symbolic analysis. When supplemented by interested and engaged parents, good health care, visits to museums and symphonies, occasional foreign travel, home computers, books, and all the other cultural and educational paraphernalia that symbolic-analytic parents are delighted to shower on their progeny, the education of this fortunate minority is an exceptionally good preparation for the world that awaits.

NOTES

1. A dismally large number of surveys have charted the relative backwardness of the average American student. For a sample, see "U.S. Students Near the Foot of the Class," *Science*, March 1988, p. 1237.
2. *National Assessment of Educational Progress*, various issues.
3. On the tracking system, see Jeanne Oakes, *Keeping Track: How Schools Structure Inequality* (New Haven: Yale University Press, 1985).
4. In fact, university education is one of the few remaining industries in which the United States retains a consistently positive trade balance. As a university teacher, I continuously "export" my lectures and seminars to the rest of the world by virtue of the fact that over a third of my graduate students are foreign nationals.
5. See Merry White, *The Japanese Educational Challenge* (New York: Free Press, 1987); Thomas Rohlen, *Japan's High Schools* (Berkeley: University of California Press, 1983); W. Jacobson et al., *Analyses and Comparisons of Science Curricula in Japan and the United States* (New York: Teachers College of Columbia University, International Association for the Evaluation of Educational Achievement, 1986).
6. Suggestions for further reading about these skills, and how formal education can enhance them, can be found at the end of this book in "A Note on Additional Sources."

39

THE EARLY RETURNS
The Transition from School to Work in the United States

Richard Arum • Michael Hout

Human-capital theory approaches educational stratification from the point of view of investments and returns: young people invest in themselves and their futures by enrolling in school, and reap the returns on those investments in the labor market (Becker 1972). While the key issue for theorists is the return to this investment over the individual's whole lifetime, many young people have a much shorter planning horizon. They want to know about the immediate returns to their education. In particular, they want to know if staying in school will "pay off" with a good job right after leaving. Theory has begun to catch up with this reality. Manski (1993) proposes a model that explicitly addresses the "stay in school or go to work now" choice that young people make. In particular, he notes that students assess their prospects and choose according to what they know about those prospects, their sense of their academic ability, and how much they enjoy school.

The contributions of the human-capital investment perspective to understanding educational stratification cannot be denied. Nor should they be exaggerated. In particular, the human-capital investment perspective encourages us to look at education as a fungible linear accumulation, much like a financial investment. This is not the case. Students who opt for "school" enroll not only in a particular school, but also in a curriculum within that school. The actual course of study depends on the choices that students make and institutional constraints such as admission standards and enrollment limits imposed by the capacities of teaching staffs, classroom size, and budgets for supplies and equipment. This differentiation in educational systems complicates the human-capital account of educational stratification and challenges other kinds of theorizing as well.

In the United States the differentiation comes in the form of academic and vocational tracking in secondary schools and the proliferation of non-traditional programs in two-year community and junior colleges. These institutional arrangements offer an array of choices and constraints that defy the simple linear formulations found in most theoretical models. To attend to the differentiation of the educational system it is necessary to include track or higher educational sector in the measurement of educational investment and to look for links between each educational sector and particular occupational and wage outcomes.

Differentiation in the U.S. educational system is modest in comparison with those of many other post-industrial societies (Müller and Karle 1993). Thus comparative research must attend to cross-national differences in the extent of curricular and institutional differentiation. And because the transition from school to work can be much more closely regulated in some of these institutional arrangements, we must also develop theories and models of special school-to-work channels (see, e.g., Rosenbaum et al. 1990).

As long as it does not obscure the realities of educational differentiation, an investment-centered approach to educational decisions can resolve a problem that has vexed researchers who have focused on that differentiation. Most sociologists of education approach differentiation from an institutional perspective that asks about the "effectiveness" of various departures from a standard academic curriculum. Conclusions about the effectiveness frequently turn on the way the contrasts are drawn in a way that could be framed as a "compared to what?" dilemma. The effectiveness of vocational high-school programs is usually judged relative to secondary school general curriculum programs (Meyer and Wise 1982; Grasso and Shea 1979), but critics often compare them to academic tracks (see, e.g., Gamoran and Mare 1989). Scholars have recently reached a consensus on the implications of differentiating academic and non-academic tracks (Gamoran 1996), but recent work has highlighted how vocational programs are more effective than general track programs in facilitating employment in desirous occupations, particularly for women (Arum and Shavit 1995; also see Rumberger and Daymont 1984; Kang and Bishop 1989). Research on postsecondary education replicates the "compared to what?" dilemma. Young people who complete degree programs at two-year colleges do better in the labor market than those who stop after high school but not as well as those who earn degrees at four-year colleges (Monk-Turner 1983; Dougherty 1987; Brint and Karabel 1989).

An investment approach provides researchers with objective criteria for choosing a basis for their comparisons. From an investment perspective, the question of whether the pay off to a two-year post-secondary degree is "appropriate" depends on whether it is proportionate to the investment it requires (greater than a high-school diploma and less than that required for a four-year post-secondary degree). In addition to the obvious time difference between a two- and four-year degree, each year at a four-year institution costs more money than a year at a two-year community or junior college. The NLSY data-set we use does not contain tuition information, so we cannot fully implement the investment approach, but we address the returns to two-year degrees with both the time and money differentials in mind. If we find that the rewards to two-year degrees are midway between those of an academic secondary diploma and a four-year college degree, we will conclude that the investment is worthwhile. Those with the two-year degree break even on time and are ahead on money. We will draw a less sanguine conclusion if it turns out that the rewards to a two-year degree are closer to those of an academic secondary diploma than to a four-year degree.

The investment perspective makes more sense in the United States than it might elsewhere. In the United States education is undertaken by individuals; employers and unions have few institutional ties to schools. Like the investor who pays now in the hope of uncertain future gain, the American student spends time and money on skills that may or may not "pay off" in higher lifetime occupational success or earnings. In Japan, Germany, and elsewhere, schools cooperate with employers. They attempt to match the skills that they teach to the employers' needs; they also establish stronger institutional linkages that match graduates to jobs through work-experience programs and informal networks (Rosenbaum et al. 1990; Hamilton and

Hurrelmann 1994; Kerckhoff 1995). The institutional ties give employers a stake in the students' training and reduce students' risks.[1] With few exceptions, the United States lacks this kind of institutionalized cooperation between schools and employers. In the absence of these stable institutional linkages, students take courses that lack real-world content, train on outmoded equipment, and graduate with little knowledge of their prospective employers' needs. That makes the initial labor-market experiences of young adults unstable—marked by high rates of job turnover in nonunionized employment situations.[2]

Research Design

As our contribution to the international project designed to go beyond simple linear formulations, we employ a version of the CASMIN educational scheme (Ishida, Müller, and Ridge 1995) to model the links between class destinations and educational niches defined in terms of educational level and academic content. We supplement these analyses with a refined set of educational contrasts that take advantage of special features of the U.S. data. Given the weak institutional linkages between schools and employers in the United States (with some exceptions that are notable but not observed in our data), we expect the association between Müller's differentiated educational measure and first job to be weaker than it is in societies with strong institutional linkages. On the other hand, we expect the association between Müller's measure and first class to be stronger than the association between a more conventional measure of education and first class. Our supplementary analyses show that the returns to vocational preparation depend on the substantive content. Broad vocational programs yield almost

no return on the time invested in them, while trade, technical, business, and commercial programs have positive returns.

We analyze data from the cross-sectional representative sample of the National Longitudinal Study of Youth (NLSY). The cross-sectional sample consists of data on 6,111 individuals aged 14 to 22 years in 1979. They were re-interviewed annually throughout the 1990s, so they were 26 to 34 years old at the last contact. We use data up until 1991, the last year for which data is currently publicly available.

. . .

Educational Attainment . . . is measured at the time of school-to-work transition and coded to Müller's specifications. In the United States that amounts to:

- 1—left school prior to receiving a high-school diploma;
- 2a—high-school diploma, but no subsequent college degree, and self-reported enrollment in a vocational high-school program;
- 2b—high-school diploma, no college degree and self-reported enrollment in high-school general curriculum programs;
- 2c—high-school diploma, no college degree and self-reported enrollment in an academic (college-preparatory) high-school program;
- 3a—at least one year of college and attained an Associate of Arts degree;
- 3b—at least three years of college and a Bachelor of Arts or higher graduate school degree.

This schema, by concatenating track and niche within the measure itself, affords the opportunity for comparative work among countries with diverse institutional settings and employment climates. Requiring reports of successful attainment of a high-school diploma for educational categories 2a–2c, an Associate of Arts degree for educational category 3a, and a Bachelor of Arts degree for category 3b provides a strict constraint on entry into the advanced educational categories. Thus students who left school and later by their own initiative obtain a Graduate Equivalency Degree (GED) remain in the 1 category. In much the same way, high-school graduates who attend college but leave with only some type of educational or occupational certificate and not at least an AA remain at the CASMIN educational 2 level.

. . .

Findings

Descriptive Results

Men's and women's educational experiences differ slightly but significantly. . . . While men dropped out of high school before obtaining a diploma more often than women (21 percent compared to 18 percent), women attained junior college Associate of Arts degrees without continuing on to successfully gain more advanced post-secondary degrees (7 percent compared to 5 percent for men). Among high-school graduates with a vocational background, specialties are sex-typed; men enrolled in trade and technical programs (7 percent), while women enrolled in business and commercial programs (7 percent).

Despite their high levels of education, men and women in this cohort started out with humble occupations. More than half of the men started their work lives in blue-collar occupations (41 percent in Classes VIIab and 19 percent Classes V–VI); the women started out in clerical and sales positions (51 percent in Classes IIIab). Very few of these young people had the resources to set themselves up in business; witness

the negligible self-employment rate. Women held a slight edge in professional and managerial occupations (22 percent for women, 19 percent for men in Classes I–II).

Race and ethnicity play a part in educational and early occupational success. . . . Over 30 percent of high-school drop-outs are either African-American or Latino (32 percent for men, 33 percent for women, compared to their overall representation in the sample of 19 percent of men and 20 percent of women). Interestingly, African-Americans are less prevalent among both the male and female vocational track high-school graduates (category 2a). African-American and Hispanic men are more likely to end up in educational category 2c (high-school graduates from academic college preparatory tracks who have not gone on to attain further post-secondary school degrees) than either white men or female non-whites. While female non-whites are equitably represented in the junior college 3a category, they are significantly under-represented in the four-year college degree 3b category (Hauser 1993). Non-white men are disproportionately absent from both post-secondary educational categories; they make up only 10 percent of 3a graduates and only 8 percent of 3b graduates (Hauser 1993).

While the expansion of American higher education has spurred a significant amount of educational "structural mobility" (Hout 1996), parental education remains a prime contingency in a young person's own educational attainment. We see evidence for this in the social composition of the six CASMIN educational categories. . . . For persons who failed to attain a high-school diploma (1), one-half have parents with similarly low education backgrounds (compared to one-fourth of the sample as a whole). For men and women who attained a four-year college degree, two-thirds are from similar backgrounds (compared to one-third in the sample as a whole).

Men and women earn higher wages at higher levels of education, as expected. Men earn about 50 cents more than women with the same level of education.[3] This gender gap of 50 cents is less than the widely cited "sixty-nine cents on the dollar" women's wage, which would imply $3.45 per hour if men earned $5 per hour. However, recent data show that the gender gap is closing in the workforce as a whole, especially among younger cohorts (Spain and Bianchi 1996), so these data are not out of line with other recent statistics. The median hourly wage of women with incomplete secondary education is slightly less than $4; for men it is $4.50. College graduates earn $2 more per hour (on average) than high-school dropouts of the same sex. Wages vary more within levels of education than between them, however, indicating a high degree of uncertainty in the early returns to education. The interquartile range of wages within each level of education exceeds $2 and the range from the 10th to the 90th percentile spans $7 at the lowest level of education and $12 among college graduates. The lower tails of the college-educated categories' (3a and 3b) distributions are not much higher than those of the high-school educational categories (particularly for men). These long tails indicate low initial monetary pay offs for a small subset of the highly educated.

Women's first jobs have slightly higher status than the men's jobs, despite women's lower wages. The interquartile half of women (indicated by the boxes) have higher Duncan SEI scores than do men for all educational categories. Among secondary school graduates, the prevailing occupations for women are in the routine non-manual class (III) which has always traded off clean working conditions and the freedom from shift work for lower wages. The blue-collar jobs that male high-school graduates take pay more but offer less prestige and more varied

schedules. Among college graduates, men and women are matched at the 75th percentile; the difference comes in the long lower tails to the men's distributions (and long upper tail for men with four or more years of college and a degree). Women have more discretion over whether or not to participate in the labor force. They can use that freedom of choice to hold out for an "appropriate" job longer than their male counterparts. College-educated men accept first occupations with Duncan SEI scores that are lower than the jobs taken by half of the high-school educated men, as is shown in the lower edge of the college men's boxes and the long whiskers that show how the 10th–25th percentiles of college-educated men reach below the median status of high-school graduates' first jobs. For those men who attain a four-year college degree, the long upper whisker (spanning from the 75th to the 90th percentile), highlights that the relatively rare first jobs with the highest status (over 60 on the Duncan scale) go to men.

The fluid boundaries of the U.S. educational system allow individuals to move easily in and out of school throughout at least their first decade of labor-market experience. One young person in five takes advantage of this institutional laxity: 19 percent of the men and 21 percent of the women had more than one school-to-work transition before age 26, that is, approximately one-fifth of the respondents moved from school into the labor force, back into school and back into the labor force between 1979 and 1991. Another 8 percent of the men and 11 percent of the women reported being enrolled in school in either 1990 or 1991, when they were between 25 and 33 years old. Of the people in school in 1990–1991, 27 percent of the men and 38 percent of the women had already made a school-to-work transition a decade earlier. The 11-point gender gap suggests that child-rearing responsibilities add special contingencies to women's school-to-work transitions.

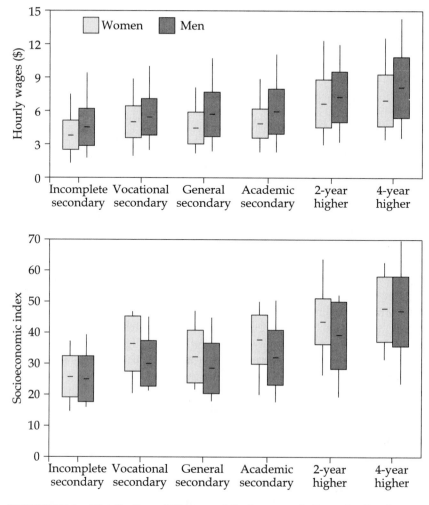

FIGURE 39.1 Distribution of Wages and Socioeconomic Status by Gender, for Those Aged 26–34, 1991. *Note:* Hourly wages are calculated in 1991 US$ (adjusted for change in annual average rate of pay); socioeconomic status is measured on the Duncan scale.

The low-cost junior and community colleges promote fluidity: 44 percent of women and 45 percent of the men with two-year college experience as their highest level of achievement have made more than one school-to-work transition. This finding suggests that the "cooling out" function attributed to two-year colleges (Karabel 1972) is not the product of a progressing, creeping educational chill, but rather often involves a period of students testing the waters both in the labor market and in post-secondary institutions. Many young people who left high school for work came back: 24 percent of women and 23 percent of men with academic secondary education made two or three school-to-work transitions and 18 percent and 19 percent of women and men with complete vocational education did so. . . . Relatively few of the people who go back to school fail to complete their high-school education; 86 percent of men and 91 percent of women with incomplete secondary education have not been back to school (that is, have made just one school-to-work transition).[4]

• • •

Determinants of Occupational Status and Wages

• • •

[The results indicate] that young people attain first jobs with higher Duncan SEI scores when they have obtained a four-year college degree than when they have earned only a two-year college degree. Similarly, high-school graduates obtain more desirable first jobs than high-school drop-outs, and first jobs that are significantly less desirable than those of persons who enter the job market with two-year college degrees. Among high-school graduates, the graduates of the general curriculum track do not do as well as male vocational trade and technical graduates and female business track students. While graduates of the college preparatory high-school track do better than general track students (reaping the expected positive return to their academic education even if they do not earn a junior college or higher degree), differentiating types of vocational programs demonstrates that there are no significant differences in effects between academic curriculum and either male trade and technical programs or female business and commercial ones.

The inter-generational transmission of advantage and disadvantage appears here in the positive effect of father's occupational status on the Duncan SEI score of the young man's first job. . . . Most of the effect of father's SEI is mediated by education; 55 percent of the total effect on men is indirect via educa-

tion and 65 percent of the total effect on women is indirect.

Young men who are African-American, in rural or non-Southern locations, and in areas of high unemployment are further disadvantaged. Young women in these categories do not obtain first jobs that are significantly worse than those of other women with the same social origins and education.

• • •

Obtaining a university degree pays off. . . . Persons who attained a two-year or four-year college degree earn higher wages than high-school graduates who in turn earn higher wages than high-school drop-outs. For men, surprisingly, little else matters; there are no statistically significant differences among high-school graduates from different curricular tracks nor between young men with two- or four-year college degrees. Women who attended a general curriculum track in high school, however, receive significantly lower wages than those who had attended business and commercial vocational programs. In fact, they do no better than women who dropped out of high school. More surprisingly, women enrolled in business and commercial programs also earn significantly higher wages than young women who completed their education in an academically oriented secondary program (but did not go on to college). Thus the differentiation in the American educational system gives an unexpected boost to the initial wages of those educated in the non-traditional tracks. The supposed monetary advantages of academic education are not realized in the initial phase of labor-market activity unless it is followed by further education.

Neither parental education nor father's occupational status affect the initial wages of women and men from this cohort that left school in the 1980s. That does not mean that origins more broadly conceived are unimportant. Parental income has strong indirect and direct effects on young people's experience with being in poverty (Fischer et al. 1996). By extension it presumably also affects their initial wages.[5]

Racial differences in earnings, thought to be declining, continue to contribute to stratification in the United States. African-American men received 15 cents less per hour than white men; the racial difference is smaller for women (a race–gender interaction that holds throughout the career, e.g., Farley and Allen 1987). This level of racial difference confirms both the persistence of race and its diminished quantitative importance. . . .

Men living outside metropolitan labor markets received 11 cents less per hour than young men who made the school-to-work transition while living in a suburban location (that is, in an SMSA, but not in a central city). Other geographical contrasts are not significant. A high unemployment rate in the local economy also depresses wage rates of first jobs slightly (more for men than for women). The range from the tightest to the most depressed labor markets in the United States in 1990 was about 6 percentage points; the expected difference in wages between those two places then would be about 15 cents per hour for men (about $312 in a year of working 40 hours per week) and half that much for women.

· · ·

Conclusion

American educational institutions have differentiated what they have to offer since the 1950s. Programs of secondary and post-secondary education have increasingly come to mark themselves as vocational or academic. The rationale is to tailor the education of students to the needs and opportunities of the labor market. This differentiation has affected the early careers of women and men in this cohort that left school and started work in the 1980s. In particular, vocational offerings of substance—business and commercial high-school programs for women and some trade and technical programs for men—have brought about a clear and consistent pattern of positive outcomes. Graduates of these programs had higher initial wages than their counterparts in both the general and academic curricula. They also had first jobs with higher Duncan SEI scores and better odds of being in [professional, managerial, or routine non-manual classes] than their general curricular track counterparts.[6]

A two-year post-secondary degree rewards its holder with employment prospects, occupational status, and pay that are intermediate between the rewards of an academic secondary diploma and a four-year bachelor's degree. This is strong confirmation of the "investment" perspective we have taken and human-capital theories of educational stratification in general. It calls into question those theories based on the "diverted dream" metaphor (Brint and Karabel 1989). On the other hand, the two-year degree may not be an orderly transition point. Both men and women with two-year college degrees had lower odds of reporting leaving school because they had received a degree, suggesting that they attempted to go on but failed in the attempt. Surprisingly, two-year degree holders and four-year degree holders do not differ significantly in initial hourly wages.

We emphasize at this point that we are analyzing "early returns." The early labor-market outcomes highlighted in this analysis are significant for understand the beginnings of careers. They take on added significance in the light of previous research which has demonstrated that an individual's first job has long-term effects on their occupational trajectory (Blau and Duncan 1967; Sewell, Hauser, and Wolf 1980; Hauser and Carter 1995). Nonetheless, we remain cautious in assessing these findings because the human capital associated with an individual's educational attainment also has effects later in the individual's occupational career. In particular, the educational advantages of university graduates (and those with advanced degrees) tend to come later in the career when promotions to positions of higher authority differentiate men and women within the same initial occupational group (Wright, Baxter, and Birkelund 1995; Althauser 1989).

The promising results of two-year colleges indicate that the tension between "channel of opportunity" and "cooling-out function" has tipped in favor of opportunity just at a point when the two-year colleges are about to be swamped by demographic changes (Hout 1996). In particular, the "echo" of the post-war baby boom will drive up the number of students seeking post-secondary education by 30 percent at a time when public resources to support two- and four-year colleges and universities are shrinking. The data show clearly that education mediates entry into white-collar positions, especially the professional and managerial ranks. . . . In that sorting, academic education is more important than other types. A differentiated vocational high-school curriculum, however, affects occupational outcomes for those that have not been singled out as the most likely candidates for the mental labors of the upper white-collar stratum. They earn higher wages when they are employed. To the extent that this curriculum specializes in areas that are valued by employers, these programs provide an alternative route to higher wages.

The weak to non-existent links between schools and employers make the transition to work uncertain for U.S. school-leavers. Those who first leave school before completing high school or immediately upon leaving high school seldom receive any institutional support in their job search. Many are disappointed by the outcome of that search and return to school. Younger people leaving the post-secondary system—on their first or second foray into the world of work—have more desirable credentials in hand, but little in the way of institutional support. Only those with post-graduate professional education can count on a circumscribed labor market to translate their credentials into an appropriate occupation. Even that narrowing of job tracks does not remove all of the uncertainties. The widest spread of earnings in first jobs is among the college graduates.

Does that produce more or less stratification in the United States than we would see if the structure were tighter? Comparing the United States to Germany suggests that looseness inhibits reproduction and stratification. The two-step chain of reproduction in Germany—the close association between origins and type of education and between type of education and first occupation—leads to a closer association between socio-economic origins and destinations in Germany than in the United States. Both links are weaker in the United States.

The "diverted dream" approach to educational stratification in the United States has suggested, though, that the United States is more stratified than it might otherwise be if the educational system was less internally differentiated—in particular if there were no vocational tracks in secondary schools and no two-year colleges. Our results question that point of view. First of all, it is not clear that vocational track students would finish secondary school if they had to take more academic courses (Arum and Shavit 1995). Second, employers value the skills acquired in vocational tracks by paying higher wages to vocational graduates than to general graduates. Third, the occupational status and earnings of persons with diplomas from two-year colleges fall between those with no post-secondary credentials and those with bachelor's degrees. This indicates that the returns to two-year degree programs are proportional to the time invested (and, given the low cost of these programs, the financial return may exceed that of a bachelor's degree). The students in vocational programs and two-year colleges are disproportionately from disadvantaged origins. By enhancing their graduates' chances for employment and their wages once they are employed, vocational programs in secondary schools and two-year colleges probably reduce the intergenerational transmission of inequality. They may also reduce the amount of inequality in outcomes by creating a valuable pool of nonacademic human capital, as Labor Secretary Robert Reich (1991) argues, but that conclusion does not necessarily follow from our evidence of positive returns for these kinds of educational pursuits.[7]

NOTES

1. There are some notable exceptions in the United States, where local schools and businesses have entered into partnership agreements (see, e.g., Stern, Raby, and Dayton 1992). The Federal government has recently provided limited funding to support, sponsor, and develop such linkages (Smith and Scoll 1995).
2. Individuals in the NLSY report an average of eight different jobs in their first eight years after school. Unionization rates by 1990 had also fallen to low post-war levels. The percentage of unionized workers in 1990 in the NLSY sample by educational category were:

	Female	Male
1	7	9
2a	9	17
2b	8	17
2c	7	16
3a	9	11
3b	9	6

3. Figure 39.1 presents box and whisker graphs of the percentile distribution of hourly wages (panel A), and socio-economic status of first job (panel B). Box and whisker plots show the 10th, 25th, 50th, 75th and 90th percentiles of a distribution. The bottom of the box marks the 25th percentile. The top of the box marks the 75th percentile. The line inside the box marks the median. The tip of the line up from the bottom of the box marks the 10th percentile. The tip of the line up from the top of the box marks the 90th percentile. The lines are called "whiskers." The advantage of a box and whisker plot over a simple line graph of means or medians is the ability of the box and whisker plot to communicate data on dispersion as well as data on central tendency in one image.

4. Recall that we did not "give educational credit" for the GED, so some of these persons at the lowest level may have obtained a credential without actually returning to school, and some of those who did return may have obtained a credential through the examination process.

5. Most sociologists prefer SEI and other indicators based on parental occupations to direct measures of parental income, in part because we think of occupation as a more reliable measure of "permanent income" than high schoolers' (or older peoples') reports of their parents' incomes while they were growing up. The results reported by C. Fischer et al. (1996) belie that conjecture. Despite the inaccuracies that undoubtedly infect the young people's reports of their parents' incomes, parental income is significant where neither SEI nor education are. The lesson is that we ought to be measuring parental income.

6. These results are particularly strong considering the methodology employed in this study. To remain consistent with the cross-national project, students from the general track who attended several years of college but did not attain a post-secondary degree were assigned back into 2b. The additional years of schooling many of them attained and their higher social origins may be responsible for their better outcomes. Finally, vocational curriculum was coded on the basis of self-reports; course transcripts provide more reliable information and are thus more strongly associated with occupational outcomes (Arum and Shavit 1995).

7. The large variance in wages within categories of educational attainment frustrates any attempt to derive the level of inequality implied by any pattern of returns to education.

REFERENCES

ALTHAUSER, ROBERT. 1989. "Internal Labor Markets." *Annual Review of Sociology* 15:143–61.

ARUM, RICHARD AND YOSSI SHAVIT. 1995. "Secondary Vocational Education and the Transition from School to Work." *Sociology of Education* 68:187–204.

BECKER, GARY. 1972. *Human Capital: A Theoretical and Empirical Analysis with Special Reference to Education.* New York: National Bureau of Economic Research.

BLAU, PETER M. AND OTIS D. DUNCAN. 1967. *The American Occupational Structure.* New York: Wiley.

BRINT, STEVEN AND JEROME KARABEL. 1989. *The Diverted Dream: Community Colleges and the Promise of Educational Opportunity in America, 1900–1985.* New York: Oxford University Press.

DOUGHERTY, KEVIN. 1987. "The Effects of Community Colleges: Aid or Hinderance to Socio-Economic Attainment?" *Sociology of Education* 60:86–103.

FARLEY, REYNOLDS AND WALTER R. ALLEN. 1987. *Beyond the Color Line.* New York: Russell Sage.

FISCHER, CLAUDE, MICHAEL HOUT, MARTIN SANCHEZ JANKOWSKI, SAMUEL R. LUCAS, ANN SWIDLER, AND KIM VOSS. 1996. *Inequality by Design: Cracking the Bell Curve Myth.* Princeton, NJ: Princeton University Press.

GAMORAN, ADAM. 1996. "Educational Stratification and Individual Careers." Pp. 59–74 in *Generating Social Stratification,* edited by Alan C. Kerckhoff. Boulder, CO: Westview Press.

GAMORAN, ADAM AND ROBERT MARE. 1989. "Secondary School Tracking and Educational Inequality: Compensation, Reinforcement or Neutrality." *American Journal of Sociology* 54:1146–83.

GRASSO, JOHN AND JOHN SHEA. 1979. *Vocational Education and Training: Impact on Youth.* Berkeley, CA: Carnegie Foundation for the Advancement of Teaching.

HAMILTON, STEPHEN AND KLAUS HURRELMANN. 1994. "The School to Career Transition in Germany and the United States." *Teachers' College Record* 96:329–44.

HAUSER, ROBERT. 1993. "Trends in College Entry among Whites, Blacks and Hispanics." Pp.61–104 in *Studies in Supply and Demand in Higher Education,* edited by Charles Clotfelter and Michael Rothschild. Chicago, IL: University of Chicago Press.

HAUSER, ROBERT AND WENDY CARTER. 1995. "The Bell Curve as a Study of Social Stratification." Paper presented at the American Sociological Association Annual Meeting, Washington, DC.

HOUT, MICHAEL. 1996. "The Politics of Mobility." Pp. 293–316 in *Generating Social Stratification,* edited by Alan Kerckhoff. Boulder, CO: Westview Press.

ISHIDA, HIROSHI, WALTER MÜLLER, AND JOHN M. RIDGE. 1995. "Class Origin, Class Destination, and Education: A Cross-National Study of Ten Industrial Nations." *American Journal of Sociology* 101:145–93.

KANG, SUK AND JOHN BISHOP. 1989. "Vocational or Academic Coursework in High School: Complements or Substitutes?" *Economics of Education Review* 8:133–48.

KARABEL, JEROME. 1972. "Community Colleges and Social Stratification." *Harvard Educational Review* 42:521–62.

KERCKHOFF, ALAN C. 1995. "Institutional Arrangements and Stratification Processes in Industrial Societies." *Annual Review of Sociology* 15:323–47.

MANSKI, CHARLES. 1993. "Adolescent Econometricians: How Do Youth Infer the Return to Schooling?" Pp. 43–60 in *Studies of Supply and Demand in Higher Education,* edited by Charles Clotfelter and M. Rothschild. Chicago, IL: University of Chicago Press.

MEYER, ROBERT AND DAVID WISE. 1982. "High-School Preparation and Early Labor Force Experience." Pp. 277–339 in *The Youth Labor Market Problem: Its Nature, Causes and Consequences,* edited by R. Freedman and D. Wise. Chicago, IL: University of Chicago Press.

MONK-TURNER, E. 1983. "Sex, Educational Differentiation and Occupational Status." *Sociological Quarterly* 24:393–404.

MÜLLER, WALTER AND WOLFGANG KARLE. 1993. "Social Selection and Educational System in Europe." *European Sociological Review* 9:1–23.

REICH, ROBERT. 1991. *The Work of Nations.* New York: Vintage Books.

ROSENBAUM, JAMES E., TAKEHIKO KARIYA, RICK SETTERSTEN, AND TONY MAIER. 1990. "Market and Network Theories of the Transition from High School to Work: Their Application to Industrialized Societies." *Annual Review of Sociology* 16:263–99.

RUMBERGER, RUSSELL AND THOMAS DAYMONT. 1984. "The Economic Value of Academic and Vocational Training Acquired in High School." Pp. 157–91 in *Youth and the Labor Market: Analysis of the National Longitudinal Study,* edited by M. E. Borus. Kalamazoo, MI: W. E. Upjohn Institute for Employment Research.

SEWELL, WILLIAM H., ROBERT M. HAUSER, AND WENDY C. WOLF. 1980. "Sex, Schooling and Occupational Status." *American Journal of Sociology* 86:551–83.

SMITH, NARSHALL AND BRETT SCOLL. 1995. "The Clinton Human Capital Agenda." *Teachers College Record* 96:389–403.

SPAIN, DAPHNE AND SUZANNE BIANCHI. 1996. *Balancing Act: Motherhood, Marriage and Employment among American Women.* New York: Russell Sage Foundation.

STERN, DAVID, MARILYN RABY, AND CHARLES DAYTON. 1992. *Career Academies: Partnerships for Reconstructing American High Schools.* San Francisco: Jossey-Bass.

WRIGHT, ERIK OLIN, JANEEN BAXTER, AND GUNN BIRKELUND. 1995. "The Gender Gap in Workplace Authority: A Cross-National Study." *American Sociological Review* 60:407–35.

PART VI
The Organizational Environment

In recent years, sociologists have refocused attention on the relationship between schools and communities. These efforts have identified the cultural, economic, political, demographic, and institutional forces that produce variation in the structure of schooling (Walters, James, and McCammon 1997; Arum 1996). Although such efforts are not new (see, e.g., Durkheim 1977, Waller Reading 9), scholars increasingly have focused on institutional factors responsible for this variation. Part VI consists of two sections: first, we present readings highlighting cultural and institutional factors underlying school variation; then we conclude the book with two readings providing sociological perspective on the recent politics of school reform.

The selection from Tobin, Wu, and Davidson presents results from a comparative investigation of preschools in three settings: Japan, China, and Hawaii. The authors' descriptive account identifies both commonalities and striking differences in the organization of early education in these three locations. From an anthropological perspective, the authors attribute differences in school practices to variation in national cultures associated with these three settings.

The second reading presents work from John Meyer, Richard Scott, David Strang, and Andrew Creighton. Meyer was instrumental as an early sociological proponent of a neo-institutionalist perspective. Meyer and Rowan (1977), for example, argued that schools developed common organizational practices because of institutional isomorphic pressures. School actions were based on taken-for-granted assumptions, and then justified and legitimated by reference to sets of institutional myths. In the reading presented here, Meyer and his colleagues offer data identifying historic changes in school structure. Authority for educational decision-making has increasingly shifted away from teachers and local communities and has become the responsibility of educational administrators organized at the state level.

Stephen Brint and Jerome Karabel in the third reading present a neo-institutionalist account of the growth and vocationalization of community colleges. Brint and Karabel argue that these changes in community college practices were due neither to internal student demand nor to external labor market needs. Rather, community college administrators defined a market niche for their organizations to satisfy their own institutional self-interest. Although the Brint and Karabel account is compelling, recent research by Dougherty (1994) suggests that their analysis did not properly appreciate the role of state and local political forces.

The fourth reading by political scientists John Chubb and Terry Moe is a highly influential work that provides an intellectual justification for the adoption of school voucher policies. Chubb and Moe contend that public schools, regardless of efforts at reform, will always be inefficient because of their organizational environment. Public schools face pressures from a range of democratic institutions in their environment (e.g., local school boards, state legislators, and courts). Chubb and Moe argue that organizational environments characterized by democratic control are inherently more inefficient than those subject to free market forces; efficient production of educational outcomes thus requires privatization. Empirical research on private sector competition, however, does not support Chubb and Moe's position (Arum 1996).

The second section of readings begins with an excerpt from Peter Cookson's book *School Choice: The Struggle for the Soul of American Education.* Whereas the earlier reading by Chubb and Moe provides intellectual groundcover for the school privatization movement, Cookson's work identifies the political actors responsible for promoting this educational policy. Cookson is highly critical of school voucher proponents' simplistic belief that the invisible hand of free market forces will serve as a panacea for all educational ills.

Our reader closes with an excerpt from David Berliner and Bruce Biddle's book *The Manufactured Crisis: Myths, Fraud, and the Attack on America's Public Schools.* In their study, Berliner and Biddle provide systematic evidence of U.S. public school success in providing increasing educational opportunities for more Americans. Berliner and Biddle maintain that public schools are under attack today for reasons other than organizational inadequacies and inefficiencies. Rather, conservative political forces have mobilized and organized attacks on public education as part of a larger reactionary social movement.

REFERENCES

ARUM, RICHARD. 1996. "Do Private Schools Force Public Schools to Compete?" *American Sociological Review* 61:29–46.

DOUGHERTY, KEVIN. 1994. *The Contradictory College: The Conflicting Origins, Impacts, and Futures of the Community College.* New York: State University of New York Press.

DURKHEIM, EMILE. 1977. "On Education and Society." In *Power and Ideology in Education,* edited by Jerome Karabel and A. H. Halsey. New York: Oxford University Press.

MEYER, JOHN AND BRIAN ROWAN. 1977. "Institutional Organizations: Formal Structure as Myth and Ceremony." *American Journal of Sociology* 83:340–63.

WALTERS, PAMELA, DAVID JAMES, AND HOLLY MCCAMMON. 1997. "Citizenship and Racial Inequality in Southern Schools." *American Sociological Review* 62:34–52.

The Cultural and Institutional Environment

40

A COMPARATIVE PERSPECTIVE

Joseph Tobin • *David Wu* • *Dana Davidson*

. . .

In this chapter we . . . offer an outsider's explicitly comparative perspective on the most significant differences and similarities in Japanese, Chinese, and American views of the function of preschool. We take the discussion outside the walls of the preschool, as we explore the question of how institutional child care affects and reflects change in the structure of the family.

We use questionnaire results as a departure point for our discussion. In addition to showing preschool teachers, administrators, parents, and child-development specialists our videotapes of preschools, we also asked them to fill out questionnaires. Three hundred Japanese, 240 Chinese, and 210 Americans answered questions including "What are the three most important reasons for a society to have preschools?" "What are the most important things for children to learn in preschool?" and "What are the most important characteristics of a good preschool teacher?" We use responses to these questions not to test hypotheses or to demonstrate statistical correlations but to facilitate

intercultural comparison of how three cultures prioritize the function of preschool.

Language

In China and Japan as well as in the United States, helping children develop language skills is believed to be central to the mission of the preschool. But although the three cultures share a concern for children's language, they have very different notions of the power and purpose of words.

In China, the emphasis in language development is on enunciation, diction, memorization, and self-confidence in speaking and performing. Chinese children learn in preschool to recite stories and inspirational moral tales and to sing and dance both alone and in groups. American and Japanese visitors to Chinese preschools are invariably impressed by the self-possession and command of language of Chinese children who flawlessly deliver long, rehearsed speeches and belt out multiversed songs.

Language in Japan, both in and out of preschools, is divided into formal and informal systems of discourse. Children in preschools are allowed to speak freely, loudly, even vulgarly to each other during much of the day. But this unrestrained use of language alternates with periods of polite, formal, teacher-directed group recitation of expressions of greeting, thanks, blessing, and farewell. Language in Japan—at least the kind of language teachers teach children—is viewed less as a tool for self-expression than as a medium for expressing group solidarity and shared social purpose. Americans, in contrast, view words as the key to promoting individuality, autonomy, problem solving, friendship, and cognitive development in children. In American preschools children are taught the rules and conventions of self-expression and free speech (Cazden 1988; Newkirk 1989).

Our questionnaire results demonstrate these differences. Japanese respondents gave less emphasis than Americans and Chinese to the importance of children learning to express themselves verbally: 38 percent of Americans and 27 percent of Chinese made "communication skills" one of their top three priorities for children to learn in preschool, as compared to only 5 percent of Japanese. . . . In contrast, Japanese emphasize skills in listening over speaking: the top Japanese answer to the question, "What are the most important things for children to learn in preschool?" was "sympathy, empathy, concern for others." Thirty-one percent of Japanese respondents made this their first choice compared to just 5 percent of Americans and 4 percent of Chinese. In China and the United States, where successful communication is believed to depend largely on the clarity of expression of the speaker, the emphasis is on teaching children to express themselves clearly, whereas in Japan, where successful communication is believed to depend largely on the empathic and intuitive abilities of the listener (Lebra 1976), children are taught less to express themselves than to be sensitive to others' spoken and unspoken forms of self-expression.

Language teaching in Japan, as in China, is centered on encouraging children to express that which is socially shared rather than, as in the United States, on that which is individual and personal. Preschool teachers in China and Japan use the techniques of choral recitation and memorization of stories much more than in the United States, where teachers spend a larger proportion of their time working with children individually, coaching them in how to express their personal thoughts and beliefs. In Japan, where language is viewed as a poor medium for expressing feelings but a useful medium for expressing social cohesion, preschool teachers frequently lead formal group recitation but rarely take an active role in modeling, correcting, or soliciting children's informal speech. In Chinese preschools oral skills are approached as an academic subject: Chinese teachers frequently correct children's mispronunciation and misusage and encourage them to learn public speaking as well as reading, writing, and arithmetic.

Preschool as School

In the midst of a self-proclaimed crisis of low academic achievement, many Americans are turning for answers to Japan, a country of high academic achievement and enviable economic success. The answers provided by Japanese preschools, however, are not the ones Americans expect to hear. In most Japanese preschools there is surprisingly little emphasis on academic instruction. Only 2 percent of our Japanese respondents listed "to give children a good start academically" as one of their top three reasons for a society to have preschools. In contrast, over half of our American respondents chose this as one of their top choices. . . .

While Americans are beefing up preschool and kindergarten curricula in an attempt to close the educational and economic gap with Japan, the Japanese are spending little time reading, writing, and counting in their preschools. But the Japanese de-emphasis on narrowly defined academic subjects in preschool does not reflect a lack of interest in academic readiness; instead it is part of a long-range strategy for promoting children's educational success. In a society worried about kyōiku mamas driving their children to succeed academically, preschools are seen as havens from academic pressure and competition.

Japanese preschool teachers do not need to teach reading since the majority of children in their charge learn to read at home. The relative ease of reading the Japanese phonetic syllabary (kana) as compared to reading English or Chinese ideographs makes learning to read relatively unproblematic in Japan (Stevenson, Azuma, and Hakuta 1986). But this alone cannot account for the Japanese preschool's lack of emphasis on academic instruction, since arithmetic, which presumably is equally difficult to master in any language, is also given little attention in most Japanese preschools. To prepare children for successful careers in first grade and beyond, Japanese preschools teach not reading, writing, and mathematics but more fundamental preacademic skills, including perseverance, concentration, and the ability to function as a member of a group.

As compared to only 5 percent of our American respondents, 16 percent of the Japanese and 20 percent of the Chinese who filled out our questionnaires listed perseverance (*nintai* in Japanese, *rennai* in Chinese) as one of the three most important things for children to learn in preschool. As Merry White (1987) and John Singleton (1989) point out, Japanese view learning perseverance as the key to character development. Lois Peak (1987) describes how Japanese preschool teachers cultivate perseverance in children by urging and cajoling their charges into dressing and undressing themselves and by steadfastly refusing to assist them with the task. Peak argues that the pedagogical pur-pose is less teaching how to dress oneself than cultivating the ability and willingness to persevere. Japanese parents and educators clearly are very concerned with children's educational achievement, but this concern leads not to an academic curriculum in the preschool, which most Japanese believe would be inappropriate and counterproductive, but instead to fostering a positive attitude to school and cultivating skills in thinking, studying, and getting along with others that will promote educational success later in life (Peak 1986).

Although Americans give great emphasis to the importance of academics in preschool compared to the Japanese, compared to the Chinese, Americans are laggards: only 22 percent of Americans compared to 37 percent of Chinese respondents chose "to give children a good start academically" as the top reason for a society to have preschools. Sixty-seven percent of the Chinese who filled out our questionnaires listed academics as one of the three top choices. The reasons for the Chinese emphasis on academics are multiple, including a Confucian cultural tradition of highly valuing early and strenuous study and a Cultural Revolution legacy that though it is anti-intellectual is even more profoundly antifrivolity. To the degree that the legacy of the Cultural Revolution continues to hold sway in China, the effect on preschools is largely to discourage nonideological, frivolous play and to encourage the learning of skills needed to be a productive member of society—reading, writing, computation, memorization, and clear speaking. Another effect of the Cultural Revolution is the "compensation mentality" it has produced in urban parents whose education or careers were disrupted when they were sent to labor in the countryside. Many of these parents look to preschools to provide their children with the educational opportunities they missed. Frustrated in their own careers, they tend to be very serious about those of their children.

Although two-thirds of our Chinese respondents emphasized the importance of academic learning, another third did *not* list "to give children a good start academically" as one of their top three reasons for a society to have preschools. Our interviews in Beijing and Shanghai suggest that especially in urban centers, particularly among child-development specialists and intellectuals, a less academically oriented, more balanced social-skills-and-play preschool curriculum is gaining favor. Ministry of Education authorities and normal school professors of preschool education, looking to the West, are working to rebuild and reform a preschool system left in tatters by the Cultural Revolution. In Chinese normal universities, a new generation of preschool education students is being exposed to the Western educational model of balancing academic learning with social and emotional development. Following graduation, these students are dispersing to preschools throughout China. New educational and play materials are also being developed and widely distributed. Papers calling for more classroom freedom and for a less narrowly academic approach to the preschool curriculum are appearing in academic and popular journals.

. . .

In the United States a similar battle is being waged in early child education circles—in this case between those who believe that "play is children's work" and those who believe that "work [academics] is a form of children's play" (Kagan and Zigler, 1988). The "play" advocates see the function of preschools as promoting emotional growth, interpersonal and social skills, and cognitive development (Robison 1983; Feeney, Christensen, and Moravcik 1987). The "work" advocates see young children as avid, able learners, ready to read, count, and learn about science, computers, foreign languages, and fine arts if only adults would raise their expectations and stop holding children back (Montessori 1912). American parents, often ambivalent, confused, or naive about the implications of choosing a preschool program that emphasizes academics, play, or a mixture of the two, find themselves torn between wanting to give their children an academic head start and worrying about the dangers of hurrying them (Elkind 1981).

The egalitarian thrust of the Communist Revolution in China, the postoccupation, democratic educational reform movement in Japan, and, in the United States, the twentieth-century diffusion of the middle-class dream of upward social mobility through education have meant that a majority, rather than, as in the recent past, only an elite minority of families in all three cultures, has come to view education—beginning with preschool—as the most sensible of parental investments. Realizing that there will not be room at the top (or even in the middle) of the economy for every family's children, parents in China, the United States, and Japan are anxious to give their offspring a fast educational start in preschool if not earlier. Yet this temptation to hurry children is tempered, especially in Japan, by the fear that children pushed too hard too early, as, for example, in high-pressured academic preschool, will suffer from educational burnout before reaching the end of the educational race. In general, academic instruction is stressed more in China, play is stressed more in Japan, and the picture is mixed in the United States. But in all three cultures preschool staff feel a similar and increasing pressure from parents to prepare children for academic and economic success.

Spoiling

Chinese parents, preschool educators, and child-development experts are very worried about the problem they call the "4-2-1 syndrome": four grandparents and two parents lavishing attention on one child. Chinese respondents (at 12 percent) were more than five times as likely as their American and Japanese counterparts to list "to reduce spoiling and make up for deficiencies of parents" as one of their top three reasons for a society to have preschools. But spoiling is not only a Chinese concern. In all three countries there is a strong feeling that contemporary home-reared children are at risk of growing up lacking the self-reliance they will need to make it in society.

In all three cultures preschools have a mandate to correct the excesses of parental overindulgence and to make children more independent and self-reliant: 80 percent of Japanese respondents, 67 percent of Chinese, and 66 percent of Americans chose "to make young children more independent and self-reliant" as one of their top three reasons for sending children to preschool. To Americans accustomed to thinking of Japan and perhaps China too as cultures of dependence these figures may be surprising. But the independence expected of children in preschools in all three cultures is less related to individualism, which is clearly an American and not a Japanese or Chinese cultural value, than to the ability to dress, feed, and control oneself, which is required in all cultures.

The term *spoiling* in the United States and Japan has meanings that include but go beyond the Chinese notion of spoiling (*ni-ai*) as parental and grandparental overindulgence and failure to discipline a child. Assistant Principal Higashino told us that Hiroki, the bad boy of Komatsudani, was spoiled (*amayakasu*) as a result of receiving too little rather than, as the Chinese hypothesized, too much love and attention at home as an infant and toddler. Japanese child development experts associate the problem of spoiling less with parental overindulgence than with the kind of narcissistic, overinvolved maternal investment in children common in areas,

such as new housing developments in commuting towns, where mothers are isolated and emotionally needy and look to their children for gratification otherwise lacking in their lives (Lebra 1984; Imamura 1987). In the United States, spoiling is often blamed on parents who are too busy with work or too preoccupied with their own problems to pay appropriate attention to their children, but who instead buy the children off with material goods, sweets, and television. The divorced father who once a week takes his young child out for ice cream, toys, and a movie is the figure in contemporary American popular culture most clearly associated with spoiling.

Although spoiling covers a somewhat different range of meanings and is blamed on different parental flaws in China, Japan, and the United States, all three cultures view it as a major hazard of modern parenting and see preschool as a proper venue for corrective action.

. . .

Working Mothers

In the United States increasing numbers of single-parent families, like China's single-child families, present children with a narrowed world. Single parents (usually single mothers) need child care at a minimum for the hours they are at work. Many single working parents use group-care homes instead of preschools, since home care is generally cheaper and allows them greater flexibility in drop-off and pick-up times as well as providing evening, weekend, and sick-day care unavailable at most preschools. In Japan, where single parents are much rarer than in the United States, their problems may be even worse. Thousands of Japanese mothers who work evenings and nights in the "water trade" (bars, brothels, and the like) place their children in unlicensed, unregulated "baby hotels" whose existence has been barely acknowledged by Japanese child-care authorities (Fuse 1984).

The percentage of working mothers of young children is over 90 percent in the People's Republic of China, 60 percent in the United States, and 40 percent in Japan. With aunts and grandmothers as well as mothers of young children employed, paid child care is a growing need. Yet only 8 percent of Japanese and 25 percent of Americans chose to "free parents for work and other pursuits" as one of their top three responses to the question, "Why should a society have preschools?" The figure was 48 percent in China, but this is still low for a society where virtually all women work outside the home and child-care alternatives are limited. Why didn't more respondents view freeing parents for work as a legitimate and important reason for a society to have preschools?

Perhaps, especially in China, where everyone works and thus every family with a young child needs some form of child-care assistance, freeing parents for work may strike respondents as so intrinsically bound up with the meaning of preschool—"a place where children go while parents work"—that they see no need to list this as a distinct function.

In Japan and the United States, where mothers are often erroneously and unfairly thought of as *choosing* to work (and thereby neglecting their children), this aura of choice brings with it the problems of defensiveness, shame, self-doubt, and guilt. Perhaps parents in the United States and Japan who feel guilty about having to place their children in child care longer or from an earlier age than they would ideally like may defend themselves from this guilt by rationalizing that the most important reason for placing the child in preschool has to do with the child's developmental interests rather than with

their own financial need or professional ambitions and desires. Other respondents, for reasons having nothing to do with guilt, may agree that preschools do free parents for work and see this as worthwhile, but not as important as preschool's other functions.[1] Alternative forms of child care, including paid home care and leaving children in the charge of relatives, also free parents for work, but there are other functions preschools alone can provide that better justify their value to society.

The relationship between women's work and child care has been affected significantly by the dramatic drop in the birthrate experienced in a single generation in all three cultures. Preschools can thrive and even flourish in times of falling birthrates if, as cohorts of children shrink, the percentage of young children enrolled in preschool rises. This is just what is happening, or has happened already, in China, Japan, and the United States. Although it may seem counterintuitive, as women have fewer children, preschool becomes more rather than less likely.

In eras when women had four or more children, pregnancy and child rearing consumed a great deal of their energy for a significant portion of their adult lives. Where large numbers of children are the rule, women work hard, but rarely in jobs that preclude their ability to care for, or supervise the care of, their young children. As the number of children women expect to bear drops to only one or two, the equation changes dramatically: for example, an American woman planning to have only one child is unlikely to decide that her child will need full-time attention and care long enough to justify sacrificing the lifetime emotional satisfaction and earning potential of a career. Or the cause and effect of this reasoning can be reversed: a woman who highly values her career may decide to have only one or two children on the basis of a calculation of how much time and energy she can afford to divert from her job to parenting without jeopardizing her future employment. A woman with a four-year-old child and a baby is likely to conclude that, as long as she is home anyway, she might as well keep her four-year-old home with her and save on preschool tuition. For a woman with a four-year-old and no baby it would make better economic sense to enroll the child in preschool in order to return to work.

For American women with low-paid, unsatisfying jobs, the equation is even more brutal. At the minimum-wage level in the United States, the cost of even inexpensive full-time preschool care for one child will eat up more than a third of her annual earnings. With two or more preschool-aged children the cost ratio makes working for minimum wage and putting children in preschool an unattractive option. Salaries have to rise dramatically above minimum wage before putting two children in child care makes much economic sense. But there is a further complication, as women earning considerably more than minimum wage will rarely be satisfied with or qualify for the least expensive preschool programs. Some American women who stay home with their own children supplement their families' earnings with a paid home job, which often means caring for a working neighbor's child. But for women who want or need to work full-time, having two or more children can be an overwhelming financial hardship. The story is much the same in China, where, as Tao and Chiu write, "Two children make a mother a slave to the household" (1985:155).

Some women (and men) place children in preschools to free their time for pursuits other than work. In the United States, nonworking women who can afford to do so often put their children in preschool for their own emotional well-being as well as for their

children's. For example, an American mother we spoke with told us "I'm a better mother if I don't have to mother all day." Another said "I need some time of my own each day to avoid going crazy." In the United States it is not uncommon for parents of preschoolers to themselves still be in school, finishing college or working toward an advanced degree. American women (and men) anticipating a career often choose to spend several thousand dollars a year on preschool as an investment in their future earning potential and life satisfaction. Again, this kind of investment becomes less likely with two or more children. When parents balance the cost of paid child care against the loss of earnings and jeopardy to a career, it is almost always the wife's and not the husband's earnings and career that are at stake, since full-time househusbanding remains an unpopular family option even in these supposedly liberated times.

What is the cost of children? In the United States the expense of preschool education at the beginning of parenting and college education at the end are parental concerns significant enough to affect parents' decisions about how many children they feel they can afford to have. To have a third child means to many parents not having enough money to care adequately for the first two. A third child might mean spending on preschool money that otherwise could be used toward a down payment on a first home or the beginning of a college savings fund. Just as the first two children are finally old enough to be in free, public, elementary school, having a third child might mean struggling for three more years on one income (the husband's) at a less than desired standard of living until the youngest child is old enough to begin preschool and free the mother for work.

In China it is society as a whole, facing staggering population pressures, and not just individual families that cannot afford more children. Chinese parents are urged by social pressures and economic disincentives to have only one child because if families had more, the nation as a whole could not prosper, and indeed, many might starve. As a society China makes a covenant with young parents: "You do the right thing by having just a single child, and we will make sure your child is healthy and well educated." Providing preschool education is one important way Chinese society keeps up its end of the bargain.

In Japan, where many women in urban and especially suburban neighborhoods are full-time, unemployed mothers, space and parental energy, as much as money, are important concerns affecting decisions about family planning. For parents living in apartment complexes, a third child would mean even more crowding. In his study of bank employees Thomas Rohlen (1974) points out that since young couples live in cramped company apartment buildings precisely during the years they are having their children, this acts as a powerful control on family size. In *The Value of Children: A Cross-National Study* (Arnold and Fawcett 1975) the problems of housing was found to be Japanese respondents' second most commonly chosen disincentive for having an additional child. Financial concerns were first. A third child might mean that a mother working part time to help save for a down payment on a home for the family would have to give up this work, sentencing them to several more years of cramped, inadequate government- or employer-provided housing. A third child might mean a dilution of the maternal energy needed to tutor, monitor, and encourage the first two children's educational careers (M. White 1987). Many, perhaps even most, Japanese parents are not committed wholeheartedly to pushing their children into and through "examination hell," but there are

many parents who commit virtually all of their spare time, energy, money, and even space in their home into directly or indirectly subsidizing their children's academic careers (Vogel 1971).

The nonworking mother of preschool-aged children, rare in China and a shrinking minority in the United States, is still common in Japan. But with only two children per family and housework becoming streamlined, how long will Japanese women continue to conceive of mothering and housewifery as careers? Historically, all but the richest of Japanese women have worked hard, mostly in agricultural work. It is only in the past thirty years or so, with the emergence of the new middle class, that the nonworking mother has become the norm (Steinhoff and Tanaka 1987). There are some indications that this is changing. Young women are becoming increasingly reluctant to give up their jobs when they marry, or even after their first child is born (Holden 1983; Carney and O'Kelly 1987). With housework rapidly becoming less time-consuming and the number of children per family shrinking, it is becoming harder for Japanese women to conceive of mothering as a full-time, lifetime job.

Currently, approximately two-thirds of Japanese children are enrolled in half-day nursery school and kindergarten programs (yōchien), one-third in full-time day-care programs (hoikuen), which serve working mothers. With the birthrate falling, some Japanese preschools will have to close, and a gradual shift in women's life-styles from full-time mothering toward a more job- or career-centered orientation seems to favor survival of hoikuen over yōchien in the long run. In all three cultures, a decline in birthrate will mean that for more and more women, mothering will cease to be a career, and full-day preschools will be more needed than ever before (O'Connor 1988).

Preschools and Parents

It is not only children who are served by preschools. Although parents are naturally reluctant to think of themselves as needing support, correction, and education, these are important functions of the preschool, albeit functions prioritized differently in China, Japan, and the United States.

In China, where preschools are expected to correct the mistakes and deficiencies of overindulgent parents, the role the preschool plays vis-à-vis the family is explicitly political and ideological: preschools, as society's representative, have the right and responsibility to socialize children away from a narrow identification with family toward citizenship, selflessness, and communal identity (LeVine and White 1986). In China preschool teachers do not work for parents; they work for society, and as public employees with a governmental mandate, they carry authority into their interactions with parents. This is expressed clearly on the walls of some boarding classrooms, where slogans state, "Teachers are even better than parents."

In the United States, the relationship between preschool teachers and parents is variable and often ambivalent. Some parents treat their children's preschool teachers as employees, as modern, institutionalized versions of the nannies and tutors parents in the West have retained and ordered about for centuries. In wealthy neighborhoods, where parents' income and social class is likely to be well beyond that of the poorly paid preschool teacher, the "upstairs, downstairs" feel of parent–teacher interaction is especially pronounced. For other American parents, their relationship to their children's teachers is more nearly equal but still adversarial, as they try subtly or not so subtly to get teachers to teach more (or less) reading, to move (or not move) their child into a special program,

or to use a stricter (or less strict) form of discipline to deal with their child's misbehavior. Believing that they know what is best for their child, optimistic about their chances of influencing teachers' approaches to instruction and classroom management, but aware that their influence and power over teachers are tenuous, many American parents engage in an ongoing dialogue with other parents, with teachers, and with preschool directors in school hallways, at parent–teacher conferences, and in other formal and informal gatherings. Most American preschool teachers and administrators seek parents' involvement in their school and want to hear their concerns, but feel, in most cases, that they know children's school needs best and that when differences of opinion arise they should listen, explain, compromise, but never just give in.

With some other parents, American preschool teachers play a role that is nurturant, supportive, even therapeutic rather than subservient or adversarial. Many American preschool teachers speak of the great neediness, loneliness, and desperation they sense in many parents' lives. American parents, overwhelmed by economic pressures, by separation and divorce, by the daunting demands of single parenting, by anxiety about their children's emotional, social, and academic well-being, and by their feelings of inadequacy as parents, turn to preschool teachers for friendship, advice, referral, crisis intervention, and emotional support. Teachers, generally sympathetic to these needs, but untrained in the skills required to respond adequately, do the best they can to be helpful and supportive in the few minutes they spend with parents in classroom doorways at the beginning and end of the school day. In a world many Americans find increasingly anomic and uncaring, a preschool can be an oasis of care and concern, a place children and parents turn to in hopes of finding advice, appreciation, and nurturance (Kagan et al. 1987).

Japanese nursery schools (yōchien) play a role vis-à-vis parents that though not as manifestly ideological as the role of preschools in China is nevertheless ideological and though not as manifestly therapeutic as the role of preschools in the United States is nevertheless therapeutic. Japanese nursery schools provide the prophylactic, community–mental health function of responding to the anomie, isolation, and confusion that confront many young Japanese mothers. Profound social and demographic shifts in postwar society have changed the shape of Japanese marriage and parenthood, creating a cohort of women in need of the camaraderie, support, contact, and counsel that in the past they would have received from relatives, friends, and community. Declining family size, the increasing nuclearization and isolation of families caused by the migration of young people from the countryside to the city and from center city to suburbs, and the reduced participation of women in work other than child rearing and housekeeping which have accompanied the rapid postwar rise of the middle-class life-style—these factors have combined in contemporary Japan to leave a vacuum of meaning and structure in many young mothers' lives, a vacuum that preschools help to fill.

Many young Japanese families live in sprawling apartment complexes in newly created communities an hour or more from the city center. Young wives spend their days in a world of women and children, where everyone is like them in age, income, and situation and yet no one is bound to others by blood, common history, or years of acquaintance or friendship (Imamura 1987). It is especially in commuting communities of this type that preschools can assume the therapeutic role of bringing isolated mothers together around child-centered tasks and activities, giving a young woman who feels very much alone in her child rearing a place to go each day and a sense of pace and structure to the weeks, months, and years (Higuchi 1975; Lebra 1984). Yōchien often offer activities for mothers including PTA meetings, talks on child rearing, and "mamas" volleyball teams. Many also offer late afternoon and Saturday *juku* (special classes) in art, music, and English conversation for preschool children, giving young mothers a chance to meet and socialize with other like-minded women while their children's lessons are in session (Imamura 1987).

Yōchien are ideological in the sense that they function to prescribe women's role behavior, to teach them their socially defined duty, their place in their separate sphere, and at times subtly to censure those who deviate too far from their appointed path. Preschool PTA officers in Japan are far more likely to attempt to bring into line a wayward mother than a wayward teacher or administrator. Yōchien mothers who fail to attend "optional" events at school or to send their children to school properly dressed and equipped are subjected to subtle and not so subtle pressure to come around. "Preschool mother" is a clearly defined role in Japan, an identity based on an easy-to-read script telling young women how to dress, act, speak, and rear their children.

What we are calling the therapeutic and political functions of preschools vis-à-vis parents are two sides of the same coin: Japanese nursery schools provide mothers with structure that is simultaneously supportive and restrictive, concerned and intrusive, reassuring and limiting. Compared to preschool in China and the United States, and even compared to Japanese hoikuen, yōchien both give more to and require more of mothers. But in all three cultures, in one way or another, preschools serve parents as well as children.

. . .

The Socioeconomics of Preschool

Preschools in China, Japan, and the United States reflect economic as well as social and cultural realities. In all three countries the quality and availability of preschool programs are a function of parents' and government's ability and willingness to pay for child care.

. . .

Preschools vary from program to program and city to city in all three countries, but this unevenness is most striking in China, where urban–rural differences in preschool education are enormous. For example, a 1985 comparison of urban and rural districts of greater Beijing reveals striking differences in preschool attendance (75 percent in the city, 34 percent in the countryside), in student-teacher ratios (22.7 students per class in urban districts compared to 35.2 students in rural areas), and in staff training (only 15 percent of preschool directors in the countryside had more than a junior high school education, whereas a majority of urban preschool directors had high school diplomas or better). Although China's eighteen normal universities have reopened and graduates are being placed throughout the country, in a nation with 170,000 preschools it will take many years to close the gap. Rural Chinese preschools today are often dirt-floored, poorly equipped baby-sitting services staffed by inadequately trained or even illiterate women too old for agricultural work.

In a country based on an ideology of equality, such elitism and urban–rural differences are serious problems for preschool education. Preschools serving children of party leaders, soldiers of the People's Liberation Army, city workers, university professors, hospital staff, and government bureaucrats on the average are much better funded, more professionally staffed, and better equipped than preschools run by neighborhood associations, factories, farm cooperatives, and rural villages. Thus despite the fact that officially there is no longer a class system in Chinese society, elitism is creeping back into child care. Although not officially sanctioned, nannies (*amah*) are again becoming common in Beijing, Shanghai, and other large cities where country girls come to live au pair with urban families and care for infants and toddlers. Where there are significant differences in wages and standards of living, as between urban and rural China, the care of young children tends to both reflect and contribute to these differences.

Compared to China, with its great differences between urban and rural preschools, and to the United States, with its great differences in child-care options available to the rich, the poor, and the middle class, there is more uniformity in child care in Japan. The government sets a national curriculum, licenses preschool teachers, and subsidizes preschools, contributing to a nationwide system of preschools similar in approach and quality.

Ninety-six percent of Japanese children have at least one year in preschool before entering elementary school. Tuition is much higher in Japan than in China, but Japanese preschools are inexpensive by American standards. Throughout Japan sliding-fee scales are available in public preschools, so that parents pay no more than they can afford.

Student/teacher ratios most Chinese and Americans would consider unacceptable help keep down the costs of preschool education in Japan. Yōchien operate with as many as forty children per teacher, hoikuen with as many as thirty per teacher. These classes are too large even by Japanese standards, and the extra ten children per class over the number most Japanese would consider ideal are a form of built-in tuition subsidy. Career paths of preschool teachers also work to keep Japanese preschools affordable. In Japan, where salaries in almost every field are linked quite closely to years of service, the short (four- to five-year) careers of most preschool teachers keep down personnel costs, which are the costliest line item in most preschool budgets.

The Japanese system of public and private preschools supported by a combination of government subsidy, parental tuition, high student/teacher ratios, and relatively low staff wages works, but not without problems. A decline in the birthrate and dramatic population shifts have meant that preschools in some areas of the country are being forced out of business while in other regions there is a shortage of preschool slots. The gap in quality and reputation between hoikuen, which traditionally have served the children of blue-collar, working mothers, and yōchien, which traditionally have served the children of wealthier, more gentrified, nonworking mothers, is narrowing, but still exists. Battles for control of preschool education between Mombushō (the Ministry of Education) and Koseishō (the Ministry of Health and Welfare) loom as the missions of the yōchien and the hoikuen grow more similar.

. . .

In the United States there is a striking lack of government support for preschool education (Hewlett 1986). Unlike culturally similar Western European democracies, the U.S. government has failed to provide more than token support for child care. An exception is Head Start, a federal- and state-supported program for children from disadvantaged homes. But at current funding levels Head Start has slots for less than 5 percent of the children it could potentially serve.

The absence of government support for child care, coupled with the great income and wealth differences that characterize American society, has led to a system of child care split along class lines. Sixty-seven percent of American families with yearly incomes over thirty-five thousand dollars have their young children in preschool as compared to 40 percent of middle-income families and less than 5 percent of families earning less than ten thousand dollars. The well-to-do can easily afford good preschools while the middle class struggles to pay tuition and the poor most often are left with second-rate proprietary child centers, family care homes, and inadequate makeshift arrangements.

Most American studies show that though there are no demonstrably negative effects on children who participate in good-quality preschool programs, mediocre or poor-quality group care can have negative short- and long-term effects on children's emotional, social, and cognitive development (Belsky, Lerner, and Spanier 1984). The absence of subsidized child care thus relegates children of the poor to a second-class start and works to replicate class distinctions from generation to generation.

. . .

NOTE

1. See Craig's discussion of schooling as consumption versus investment (1981).

REFERENCES

ARNOLD, F. AND J. T. FAWCETT. 1975. *The Value of Children: A Cross-National Study.* Honolulu, HI: East-West Center.

BELSKY, J., R. LERNER, AND G. SPANIER. 1984. *The Child in the Family.* Reading, MA: Addison Wesley.

CARNEY, L. AND C. O'KELLY. 1987. "Barriers and Constraints to the Recruitment and Mobility of Female Managers in the Japanese Labor Force." *Human Resource Management* 26:193–216.

CAZDEN, C. 1988. *Classroom Discourse.* Portsmouth, NH: Heinemann.

CRAIG, J. 1981. "The Expansion of Education." *Review of Research in Education* 9:151–210.

ELKIND, D. 1981. *The Hurried Child.* New York: Addison Wesley.

FEENEY, S., D. CHRISTENSEN, AND E. MORAVCIK. 1987. *Who Am I in The Lives of Children?* 3d ed. Columbus, OH: Charles E. Merrill.

FUSE, A. 1984. "The Japanese Family in Transition." *Japan Foundation Newsletter,* 12:1–11.

HEWLETT, S. 1986. *A Lesser Life: The Myth of Women's Liberation in America.* New York: Warner Books.

HIGUCHI, K. 1975. The PTA: A Channel for Political Activism. *Japan Interpreter,* 10(2), 133–140.

HOLDEN, K. (1983). "Changing Employment Patterns of Women." Pp. 34–46 *Work and Life Course in Japan,* edited by D. Plath. Albany: State University of New York Press.

IMAMURA, A. E. 1987. *Urban Japanese Housewives: At Home and in the Community.* Honolulu: University of Hawaii Press.

KAGAN, S. AND E. ZIGLER. 1988. *Early Schooling: The National Debate.* New Haven, CT: Yale University Press.

KAGAN, S., D. POWELL, B. WEISSBOURD, AND E. ZIGLER. 1987. *America's Family Support Programs.* New Haven: Yale University Press.

LEBRA, T. 1976. *Japanese Patterns of Behavior.* Honolulu: University of Hawaii Press.

———. 1984. *Japanese Women: Constraint and Fulfillment.* Honolulu: University of Hawaii Press.

LEVINE, R. AND M. WHITE. 1986. *Human Conditions: The Cultural Basis of Educational Development.* London: Routledge and Kegan Paul.

MONTESSORI, M. 1912. *The Montessori Method.* 3rd ed. New York: Frederick A. Stokes.

NEWKIRK, T. 1989. *More Than Stories: The Range of Children's writing.* Potsmouth, NH: Heinemann.

O'CONNOR, S. 1988. "Women's Labor Force Participation and Preschool Enrollment: A Cross-national Perspective, 1965–1980. Sociology of Education 61:15–28.

PEAK, L. 1986. "Training Learning Skills and Attitudes in Japanese Early Educational Settings." In *Early Experience and the Development of Competence,* edited by W. Fowler. San Francisco: Jossey-Bass.

———. 1987. *Learning to Go to School in Japan: The Transition from Home to Preschool Life.* Ph.D. dissertation, Harvard University.

ROBISON, H. 1983. *Exploring Teaching in Early Childhood Education.* Newton, MA: Allyn and Bacon.

ROHLEN, T. 1974. *For Harmony and Strength: Japanese White-Collar Organization in Anthropological Perspective.* Berkeley: University of California Press.

SINGLETON, J. 1989. "*Gambaru:* A Japanese Cultural Theory of Learning." In *Japanese Education: Patterns of Socialization, Equality, and Political Control,* edited by G. Shields. State College: Pennsylvania State University Press.

STEINHOFF, P. AND K. TANAKA. 1987. "Women Managers in Japan." *International Studies of Management and Organization* 16(3–4):108–132.

STEVENSON, H., H. AZUMA, AND K. HAKUTA, Eds. 1986. *Child Development and Education in Japan.* New York: Freeman.

TAO, K., AND J. CHIU. 1985. "Psychological Ramifications of the One-Child Family Policy." Pp. 153–65 in *Chinese Culture and Mental Health,* edited by W. Tseng and D. Wu. Orlando, FL: Academic Press.

VOGEL, E. 1971. *Japan's New Middle Class.* 2d ed. Berkeley: University of California Press.

WHITE, M. 1987. *The Japanese Educational Challenge: A Commitment to Children.* New York: Free Press.

41

BUREAUCRATIZATION WITHOUT CENTRALIZATION
Changes in the Organizational System of U.S. Public Education, 1940–1980

John W. Meyer • W. Richard Scott • David Strang • Andrew L. Creighton

Public school classrooms in the United States have changed greatly over their history. So has the organizational structure that holds these classrooms together in a national system. There have been great changes in the U.S. system of schools, districts, county offices, state departments, and national bureaus. One aim of this chapter is to describe some of these organizational changes over recent decades, using available data. Many important changes can be summarized with a very traditional word—*bureaucratization*. The framework of rules, pressures, and interests that hold a given classroom in place within the national educational system has become more explicit and formalized. The classrooms are connected by organizational rules and roles, by formulas and functionaries, by lawyers and accountants. Once held in place by the pressures in *society* that make much of U.S. life seem homogeneous, the classrooms are increasingly organized by the administration of the *state*.

Beyond tracing the bureaucratization of U.S. public education, a second main task of this chapter is to examine hypotheses about why this bureaucratization occurs. One common theme of most discussions is to see bu-

reaucratization as a consequence of the centralization of power, authority, and funding. Patriotic scholarship has often seen the decentralized and associational (rather than bureaucratic) character of U.S. public education as celebrating populist democracy. But accounts of the oppressive conformism and homogeneity within U.S. educational institutions raise questions about what the term *decentralization* might mean. In any event, we test below the hypothesis that the source of the bureaucratization of U.S. educational structure in recent decades reflects the expanded power of the federal government in the system.

Bureaucratization

In most countries, the rise of central educational bureaucracies precedes expanded mass public education. There is a national minister, compulsory attendance principle, curriculum, teacher certification system, and centralized structures of funding long before most children are enrolled (Ramirez and Boli 1987; Ramirez and Rubinson 1979). The U.S. experience has been quite different. A full century after this country developed the largest mass public education system in the world, a central educational bureaucracy of much substantive authority has yet to emerge. As of the last few years, there is a cabinet officer, but there is no national attendance rule, or curriculum, or teacher certification rule. And federal funding makes up less than 10% of public educational expenditures. The central body of functionaries has expanded but with fragmented authority over special programs rather than over the main structure itself (Meyer and Scott 1983).

We can move one level down from the national center and find earlier bureaucratic expansion. Education is, constitutionally, more a creature of the 50 states, and there has been some real bureaucratization at this level, which compels pupils to attend, defines teachers, specifies some features of curricula, and provides more than 40% of the funds. But historically, these developments at the state level postdate mass educational enrollment in the great northern and western bulk of the country. A system of mass education was already in place by the last third of the 19th century—the time during which most states developed rules of compulsory education, built up small state departments of education, elaborated curricula, and certified teachers.

To carry the point further, even the modern school district—a structure with a bureaucratic staff commonly controlling a number of schools in an area—postdates the creation of mass education (Kaestle and Vinovskis 1976; Tyack 1974). And so does the modern school—a large enterprise of many classrooms integrated by at least a small bureaucratic unit. Even in the cities, earlier 19th-century schools were small neighborhood structures.

The data we are about to review provide evidence of substantial organizational development. The average U.S. high school now has a larger administrative staff than that of the average state department of education in 1890 (Tyack 1974). Yet it would be a mistake to conclude from the history of bureaucratic elaboration that the term *centralization,*with all its connotations, applies. After all, the school was built up around universalistic rather than local rules and around general institutional beliefs rather than around formal

organizations. After independence, religious ideals became secular ones, and pressures for schooling were built into both national (the Northwest Ordinance) and state law. These were not bureaucratic forms—both national and local states were "states of courts and parties" (Skowronek 1982) rather than bureaucracies—but in both law and culture they embodied sweeping universalistic and national goals, not local ones (Meyer, Tyack, Nagel, and Gordon 1979). In education as in other areas, it is a mistake to infer from the weakness of the 19th-century national state as a bureaucracy to fragmentation as a purposive national society.

Dimensions of Bureaucratization

The discussion above raises the issue of different aspects of the general phenomenon called *bureaucratization*. In the literature, much of the discussion of different aspects or defining characteristics of bureaucratization—including Weber's (1946)—conceals in its typologies arguments that should be causal and explicit. For purposes of our discussion, the following distinctions should be made:

1. Most generally, bureaucracy involves *formalization* of rules and roles. Activities, rights, and obligations are removed from the web of interactions in society, located in an organization, and thus bounded off.

2. But not just any sort of formalization is involved. In most definitions, *rationalization* is another aspect of bureaucratization; that is, the formalized roles and rules must be integrated around unified sovereignty and purpose.

3. It is generally understood that bureaucratization in a domain is greater when the formalized rationalization involved extends over a wider domain; increased scale of units is another feature of bureaucratization.

4. Seen as the lateral extension of bureaucracy, this expansion clearly involves a measure of *homogenization* or standardization of subunits.

5. Seen as the vertical extension of integrative capability, it involves the expansion in number of *levels of authority.*

We provide below evidence on changes in all these aspects of bureaucratization in U.S. education and show that there is not much question but that great changes have taken place in recent decades.

The central question concerns the causal role of centralization in the whole process. In most usages, bureaucratization implies centralization or includes it as a dimension. It is assumed that bureaucracy reflects the expansion of the scale of administrative power. Such an assumption is involved not only in colloquial talk about bureaucracy but also in Weber's original discussions, which focused on Prussian models. In these models, and this historical experience, it was difficult not to see bureaucracy and centralization as intertwined and the latter as anything else but a cause of the former.

In our analyses below, we present evidence on this main question: Does the expansion of central power in U.S. education account for the increased formalization and scale and standardization in the system? The data suggest a negative answer to this question. In a concluding section we speculate on the meaning and implications of this point.

Bureaucratization in the Current Period

The research discussion of the history of bureaucratization in U.S. education is weakened by two common mistakes. One, alluded to above, is to mistake the rules or bureaucratic structure of the system as either similar to or a cause of public educational expansion. Thus histories focus on the educational reforms of a Horace Mann as if they *created* the schooling system. It then requires revisionists to note that these reforms may have played no role in the actual creation and expansion of the schools (Kaestle and Vinovskis 1976). So also with the state-after-state crusade for compulsory education after the Civil War: The revisionists' statistics have it that these great organizational reforms show no effects on enrollment expansion (Fishlow 1966; Solmon 1970). Similarly with the whole bureaucratization process of the turn of the century—there is no evidence of its association with expansion (Meyer, Tyack, Nagel, and Gordon 1979). Not only are educational expansion and bureaucratization distinct and decoupled processes, but one can argue that some negative relationships connect them (Boli, Ramirez, and Meyer 1985).

A second mistake is to assume that bureaucratization is all of a piece—that the creation of general rules, laws, or principles means enactment in organizational reality. The awareness in the modern literature on innovation that adopted policies are often not implemented (see Berman and McLaughlin 1975–1978; Hargrove et al. 1981; Weatherley 1979) is often underemphasized in more historical discussions. There is much decoupling here too.

Thus the literature on the creation of the large graded school and the modern district and superintendency focuses on the late 19th century. So does that on the bureaucratization of the state departments of education. And discussions of the general construction of the larger consolidated bureaucratic district and the standardized state educational system focus on the interwar period. Too much attention is directed to the period of legal and rhetorical excitement associated with a new phase of bureaucratization and too little on the longer organizational process.

Our own venture into historical description below considers post–World War II bureaucratization. We looked for organizational changes associated with the federalization of educational issues (and to a lesser extent funding) since the 1950s—such as the waves of federal reforms concerned with racial and other inequalities and with educational quality after 1957 and Sputnik and again in the late 1970s. What we found, however, looks more like the continuation of changes resulting from earlier reforms and longer trends. We found the construction of long-term bureaucratization rather than a shift in character or direction.

Data Sources

A main function of the national Office of Education since its creation in the 1860s was the reporting of data on education in the United States. This is a function now carried out by the National Center for Education Statistics, which surveys U.S. mass education every 2 years. NCES simply requests the states to provide summary data on basic educational matters; all the data presented in this chapter are thus state totals calculated by the states themselves. In itself, this process says much about the weakness of federal controls over education.

Although the surveys of state educational systems sometimes change in topic and method, there is enough continuity to make tentative inferences from comparisons plausible. We assembled reports from the period 1938 to 1980 to see what rough evidence we could get on changes in the bureaucratic shape of the national public education system during the period. Reports from 1940, 1946, 1950, 1956, 1960, 1966, 1970, 1974, and 1980 were used to approximate 5-year intervals (Statistics of State School Systems 1938–1980). Because statistics on Alaska and Hawaii were not collected for the first four periods, those cases are omitted

throughout to increase comparability. Other omissions of data for particular states are rare and commented on in the text. On the other hand, for many of the variables, data are missing for particular years. The tables simply leave those entries blank.

Formalization and Scale

The first two rows of Table 41.1 show the changing enrollment base of the system. Because elementary enrollment was practically universal through the period and the great bulk of it was in the public system throughout, the long enrollment increase and the more recent decline reflect demographic changes. Parallel changes affect the secondary enrollments, but to them must be added a strong secular increase in rates of secondary enrollment (and completion).

Numbers of teachers provide an alternative base figure to students, and in Table 41.1 we report mean numbers of teachers and student–teacher ratios during the period. Teacher data parallel student data but also reflect a long secular decline in the student–teacher ratio (Inkeles and Sirowy 1983). The results below are similar whether we use teacher or student data as their base, so we stay with the latter.

Our central interest is in the bureaucratization of schooling, and we turn now to address this question. The national data report the number of public schools of various types in each state. The size of schools is one indicator of bureaucratization: A system with many little schools is less organizationally developed than one with a few big ones.

Rows 5 and 6 in Table 41.1 report the mean numbers of schools and students per school, averaged across states. The latter is one crucial item for assessing bureaucratization. The curve for mean numbers of schools is graphed in Figure 41.1. The results show a striking change in mean school size during

TABLE 41.1 Selected Indicators of Bureaucratization and Funding, 1940–1980*

	Name	1940	1946	1950	1956	1960	1966	1970	1974	1980
1.	Enrollment	527,862	483,448	512,792	646,875	719,286	853,840	924,714	905,455	829,870
2.	Percentage enrolled of 5–17 cohort		.81	.80	.84	.83	.87	.90	.89	.89
3.	Teachers	18,175	17,246	18,965	23,530	28,009	35,340	41,784	44,506	45,046
4.	Students/teacher		27	26	27	26	25	23	21	19
5.	Schools		3,841	3,179	2,714	2,438	2,065	1,877	1,831	1,794
	Elementary		3,336	2,668	2,172	1,904	1,514	1,333	1,296	
	Secondary		505	510	541	534	550	496	487	440
6.	Students/school		142	176	254	309	402	471	469	
	Elementary		130	172	257		406	474	470	
	Secondary		229	233	277		429	527	579	
7.	Principals	765	696	910	1,104	1,313	1,595	1,868	2,073	2,186
8.	Students/principal		1,053	715	653	597	564	500	449	380
9.	Principals/school		.224	.332	.452	.549	.738	.943	1,048	1,160
10.	School districts	2,437	2,109	1,734	1,141	843	561	398	347	330
11.	Students/district		1,619	1,831	2,557	3,041	3,914	4,613	4,661	4,423
12.	Superintendents	260				277	284	270	267	
13.	Superintendents/district	.360			.598	.579	.688	.785	.844	
14.	Assistant superintendents				88	118	180	278	478	
15.	Assistant supts./district				.544	.750	1.027	1.783	1.950	
16.	School board members		7,405	5,850	4,646	3,551	2,621	2,115	1,987	
17.	Board members/district		4.349	4.365	5.186	4.779	6.375	5.657	5.865	
18.	Intermediate units (cases)				68(34)	66(31)	59(28)	55(25)	53(20)	
19.	SEA staff	74	114	161	187	208	318	400	448	
20.	Students/SEA staff		4,241	4,022	4,335	4,083	2,848	2,305	1,961	
21.	Revenue/student		207	281	353	433	595	786	868	892
	Percent federal		.6	2.7	5.79	6.40	10.13	10.13	10.42	9.30
	Percent state		35.0	38.1	38.27	39.89	39.85	41.60	42.67	46.69
	Percent local		64.4	59.2	55.69	53.70	50.01	48.25	46.89	43.99

*Entries are means of state values for 48 states.

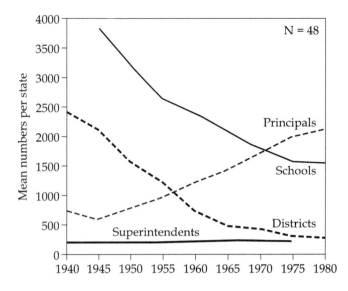

FIGURE 41.1 Mean Numbers of Schools, Districts, Principals, and Superintendents per State.

the whole modern period up to the middle 1960s. The mean school size increases from 142 to 440 pupils in the 1940 through 1980 period. An organizational change discussed in the literature as going on in the 1890s and 1920s is a main feature of the contemporary period.

These figures are divided between elementary and secondary schools in Table 41.1. This shows that the bulk of the decline in numbers of schools reflects the closing of elementary schools, while the numbers of secondary schools per state have stayed almost constant. However, the growth rates in mean numbers of pupils for elementary and secondary schools are quite comparable. Schools of either kind have expanded sharply between 1946 and 1980.

Note that these data describe state averages of the mean size of *schools* in the system. They do not describe the average experience of students. This is an important distinction: Although massive public attention has been focused on other issues, the educational system has been quietly continuing to clean out the hosts of little schools (often in rural areas) that were once its main organizational

feature. Thus the decline is most dramatic in the Midwest, where the educational systems are historically the most decentralized—although it is visible enough in every state. As schools become larger, they acquire other bureaucratic attributes such as specialized administrative functionaries. Our data contain state reports of numbers of school principals. In rows 7 through 9 of Table 41.1 we report state means of principals and also means of the ratios of principals to total students and schools. Mean number of principals per state is graphed in Figure 41.1. Although in 1940 less than a quarter of the schools have principals, in 1980 there are more principals than schools in the nation. This change from a situation in which few schools had specialized administrators to a situation in which almost all do involves a big step in formalization.

Now we consider the next organizational level. Schools are organized in school districts that have controlling authority over a wide range of issues from teacher employment to building ownership and maintenance. The great changes in education from 1890 to 1930 are commonly thought to have witnessed the consolidation of schools into modern rationalized district structures.

Rows 10 and 11 of Table 41.1 show the mean number of school districts per state and the mean number of students per district. The former is plotted in Figure 41.1. This curve indicates perhaps the most dramatic organizational change in the system. The number of school districts declines eightfold, from around 2,400 to 300 per state. Again, the long process of bureaucratization goes on at a very high rate long after it is assumed to have been accomplished.

. . .

At the school district level, the statistics give us rather detailed information on administrative structure. For instance, they report the number of school district superintendents in a state—a rather clear instance of a bureaucratic functionary. Rows 12 and 13 of Table 41.1 report, over time, the mean number of school district superintendents per state (see Figure 41.1 and also the ratio of school superintendents per district). Along with these data, Table 41.1 (rows 14 and 15) shows comparable figures for assistant

superintendents—another bureaucratic role recorded in the statistics. The results are striking: The average school district in the average state is *much* more likely to have a superintendent now than in earlier decades and is also much more likely to have assistant superintendents. The numbers of superintendents per pupil have not changed so much, but what has obviously changed is the proportion of districts that are large enough to be bureaucratized. By and large, the little districts have been eliminated and with them some of the prebureaucratic arrangements of U.S. education.

With the enlargement and bureaucratization of school districts, and the drastic decline in their number, there is a great decline in the amount of nonbureaucratic administration of the educational system. The classic U.S. structure of this sort is the local school board made up of laypersons assuming responsibility. Row 16 in Table 41.1, and Figure 41.2, shows that the mean number of school board members per state has declined sharply, from more than 7,000 per state to less than 2,000. The next row shows that, as for superintendents per student, the number

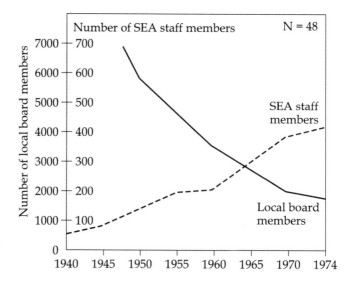

FIGURE 41.2 Mean Numbers of Local Board Members and State Education Agency Staff per State.

of board members per district is quite stable (in fact it increases slightly). Again, the change reflects the decline in numbers of districts. The modern cry for (and special programs to encourage) more community involvement accompanies a sharp decline in what was once the main mechanism for such involvement.

Above the organizational level of the school district, in many states, is an additional intermediate structure—most commonly, a county office of education. These offices handle a variety of special programs (such as vocational) or fundings (such as for various special handicaps) or both (such as for televised classes). The national data contain some information on the number of these units and the size of their administrative staffs.

The mean numbers of intermediate units per state are reported in row 18 of Table 41.1, with the number of states reporting intermediate units in parentheses. The means indicate a slow decline in the numbers of these units, implying that they have either expanded or been dissolved. The important datum, however, is the decline in the number of states reporting these units, from 34 to 20. Rather than expansion at this level, a more plausible account might be that a primary function of the intermediate units—to provide services to many small districts—has become unnecessary with the creation of larger, rationalized school districts. The intermediate unit may have been squeezed by expansion at other levels.

At the top of the chain of authority in the U.S. state-controlled system, and the nearest thing to a sovereign in it, is the state education agency (SEA). We have data on the size of the administrative staffs of these units, both absolutely and relative to enrollment. The data are reported in rows 19 and 20 of Table 41.1, and absolute staff size is graphed in Figure 41.2. The data show a steady and large increase in bureaucratic organization

of the state educational systems. The authority of these units, typically established in the last half of the 19th century but achieving symbolic sovereignty only in the 20th century, has become more extensive in the modern period.

At every level, then, our data show an enhanced scale and formalization in the educational system: Schools, districts, and states are all more bureaucratically organized in educational matters. Less is left to the informal political arrangements of the community, and more is managed by a highly developed formal organizational system.

Standardization

Bureaucratization involves the expansion in scale and formalization that we have shown above. The term also implies, in most usages, the notion of standardization or homogenization in the structure of roles and organizational subunits and a reduction in overall idiosyncrasy. Our national data on the organization of schooling in the various states provide some information on the issue of the standardization of educational organization during the modern period.

The basic question is the degree of variability in educational organizational structures across states. Had we more complete data, we could consider the same question across school districts or school organizations, but our present data set is at the state level. So we consider variability across state means in a series of simple analyses below.

. . .

Coefficients of variation for a number of our indices of bureaucratization are reported over time in Table 41.2. They show strikingly consistent increases in homogeneity among state educational systems in the modern period. The data show increased homogeneity among states in (a) the staff size of the state department of education,

TABLE 41.2 Coefficients of Variation, Educational Structure, 48 States
(Standard Deviation / Mean of State Values)

	1940	1946	1950	1956	1960	1966	1970	1974	1980
State education agency staffs	1.43	1.44	1.54	1.28	1.23	1.03	.92	.80	
Schools/school districts		1.50	1.56	1.35	1.28	1.15	1.07	1.03	1.03
Students/school districts		1.54	1.52	1.46	1.45	1.42	1.37	1.33	1.26
Students/school		.58	.54	.50	.46	.37	.35	.32	.30
Principals/school		.76	.64	.54	.48	.39	.30	.30	.30
Superintendents/ district	1.05			.83	.59	.41	.36	.29	

(b) the mean number of schools in a district, (c) the mean number of students in a school, (d) the mean number of students per school district, (e) the ratio of principals to schools, and (f) the ratio of superintendents to districts. The changes are quite consistent. Most of them are very large.

Clearly, the bureaucratization of U.S. education has involved a long-term movement, not just to greater scale and formalization but also toward a more homogeneous or standardized set of organizational structures in each of the states.

Centralization and Bureaucratization

Having established the strong trends in increased scale, formalization, and homogenization continuing in educational systems down to the present time, we move to our second concern. How are such changes to be explained? As already noted, a conventional explanation would link the growth of bureaucratization to increased centralization: the shift in power from lower to higher levels of government. Such shifts would be constituted, or at least indicated, by changes in the control of funds for public education. Certainly, contemporary images of educational change over the last two de-

cades stress the importance of the expanding federal educational budget in producing bureaucratization. Some older analyses call attention to the centralization of funding at the state level as having the same effect. (These latter are less likely to take a negative view of either the centralization or the bureaucratization involved. They are more likely to emphasize the process as involving efficiency, professionalism, and more recently equity.)

The data contain state reports of public school funding from local, intermediate, state, and federal sources. We report changes over time in state means in Table 41.1, row 21. The figures are graphed in Figure 41.3. First, we report mean state educational revenues per pupil in constant 1967 dollars. The means rise throughout the period. It is important to understand that in important ways the expenditure expansion involved *itself* indicates bureaucratization: the shift from amateur to professionally credentialed and paid teachers, administrators, and staff personnel; and the shift from local unpaid school board management to modern formalized structures all the way up to the state and federal levels.

Beyond this basic change in the nature of the educational system, the data show substantial changes over time in the locus of

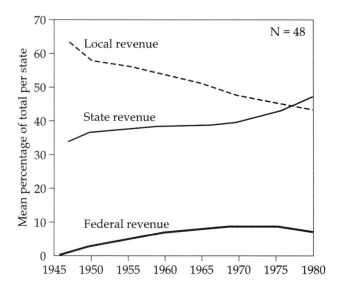

FIGURE 41.3 Mean Percentages of Total Education Revenue from Federal, State, and Local Revenue per State

schooling revenue. The proportions of federal and state revenues to total revenue both rise by about 10%, the federal from practically nothing to 10%, the state from 35% to 46%. The big change, then, is in local revenue, which declines from 64% to 43% (being finally topped by state revenue only in the late 1970s).

A caveat: The ultimate sources of revenue are not always the best guide to who controls the money. An original federal expenditure may be distributed by the state and come to be counted as, or have the organizational meaning of, state money. This may be an accounting problem, but it has substantive importance. The great increase in educational expenditures by higher levels of government in recent decades has in part gone to reinforce the power of the units already authorized to manage U.S. education—school districts operating under state authority. Just as, on other levels of analysis, the modern expansion in worldwide economic power has reinforced the authority of the nation-state, or the earlier construction of national stratification systems reinforced

the logic of individual citizenship, so the nationalization of U.S. education may be occurring through the funding and authorization of the expansion of state and local bureaucracy. It is a point to which we will return.

· · ·

Rethinking the Relation between Bureaucratization and Centralization

We have seen a strong trend toward expanded formalization and scale in U.S. public education, with schools, districts, and state organizations that are expanded in size and differentiated administratively. Clearly, a particular classroom and school is more *organizationally* connected to other classrooms and schools now than in the past. Funding is also more structured through state and federal governments now than in the past. There are several ways to think about this, the most common of which is to see it as the centralization of power and authority.

· · ·

There has indeed been a funding shift toward state and (to a lesser extent) federal revenue. And there are clearly shifts away from organizational localism and toward bureaucracy. Do these shifts constitute centralization? We consider the centralization of funding different from the centralization of substantive authority. The latter would involve the endowment of the state center with some right of power and purpose against society: the right to mobilize collective resources around the *center's* chosen collective goods. Increased centralization of educational funding in the 1960s, 1970s, and 1980s in the United States does not seem to have empowered the agents at the center. At the federal level, there is the ostentatious denial of any distinct federal purpose. There is only the assumption of responsibility for other prior goals of a highly decentralized kind: in the 1950s, areas impacted by federal activity; in the 1960s, minorities and the poor; in the 1970s, the handicapped. In all U.S. educational history, one finds only a shadowy reflection of the *organized nation-state's* autonomous purposes—a few military schools, an eviscerated vocational educational system, and the National Defense Education Act—as opposed to those seen as vested in society as a whole. The implication here is that one should not expect to find the expansion of federal educational funds, which are not allocated toward the reconstruction of education around nation-state aims, to produce bureaucratic centralization. In fact, in our related work (Scott and Meyer 1988; . . .), we had seen this "fragmented" character of the federal involvement in education as possibly generating laterally extended bureaucracy *because* it could not generate centralization. We will have occasion below to reconsider even this argument. At present, we simply note that the nature of federal involvement is not to be seen as centralist, given the absence either of legitimate sovereignty over education or distinctive purposes for it.

In the U.S. system, states do have sovereignty over education, and it makes a bit more sense to imagine that the expansion of their funding might lead to centralizing bureaucratization (see Doyle and Finn 1984). On the other hand, consider here the few distinct collective purposes or missions a U.S. state can have for its public educational system. Can Indiana mobilize its educational system, following the Prussian example, to help wage war—even Kulturkampf—against Illinois? The states play a role akin to that of service organizations as much as dynamic leaders and carry out a mission defined on a wider scale than their boundaries. They attempt, in funding, to equalize resources among communities, classes, and ethnic groups, following norms set by national courts and ideology or to upgrade education along nationally standard lines. One can see an impulse to bureaucratize standardization here but not to centralize around autonomous purposes.

. . .

Bureaucratization as Expanded Scale of Administration

Suppose we drop the fashionable social scientific language of power to talk about the process we observe and avoid the demonic image of increasingly centralized authorities using resources to dominate U.S. education. We are then left with the more traditional language of U.S. organizational thought, which talks about organization rather than bureaucracy and coordination rather than power. Perhaps such themes capture the reality of expanded scale that we observe better than do ideas that trace these developments to central nodes of power.

Once we see the changes as reflecting standardization, different causal imagery seems reasonable. Instead of thinking of the changes as reflecting nation-*state* power, other aspects of nation building seem more important; that is, society itself—not primarily the state—is being reconstructed along increasingly rationalized lines and on an enlarged scale. And the forces legitimately empowered by the changes, as well as those advocating them, arise in society more than in the state organization. Thus a whole series of changes in U.S. education reflect and emphasize standardization around highly professionalized models. They partly reflect, and most certainly enhance, the authority of the educational profession as part of national society. Similarly, there have been all sorts of pressures toward the involvement and equality of many different groups in national society, from classes to ethnic groups to regions and communities. There have been many different pressures toward general improvement (meaning, in part, conformity with standard national models) and the elimination of diversity and communal authority (backwardness) in various hinterlands. There have been many pressures for expanding educational services demanding larger scale of funding and control (such as vocational specializations, instruction in new subjects and for new groups, services in counseling and health). And there have been continuous pressures for the upgrading of the basic profession involved—teaching—that have led to more emphasis being placed on general certification controls.

. . .

Thus we see the expanded scale, formalization, and homogeneity of U.S. educational organization as reflecting the expansion of general national standards of education and the imposition of these on the particular subunit communities. In every area, general norms about education have expanded and become unified and national. Bureaucracies arise incorporating and reflecting them and maintaining their status in local jurisdictions. What we do not see is the emergence of a dominating organizational

center in the system, from which the other changes flow and by which they are integrated and regulated. There is much bureaucratization, but it is dispersed in the several states and their component districts.

. . .

Overall, then, there has certainly been centralization in the sense of the destruction of local and communal and particularistic control in U.S. education and its replacement by bureaucratic organization in districts and states (and the enlarged schools, too). We find a shift from the informal and political management of schooling to the bureaucratic form. From the local point of view, this is centralization. But at the other end of the scale, we do not find the emergence of a unified organizational center. There is rather the classic pattern of a profusion of professional standards, court decisions, special-purpose legislative interests, and a huge network of interest groups. It is the traditional liberal society, redrawn on a larger and more national scale. The local teachers no longer confront the local school board in quite the same way—both groups are now components of a much wider system of organized relationships, and teacher organizations make demands of taxpayers at district and state and national levels rather than local ones. Similarly, a whole network of organized interests affects the curriculum in much the same way as the past—but it is all done at a higher organizational level. We expect to find states much more involved in the curriculum in the future, reflecting these shifts—but we also expect to find the decisions made through the classic bargaining processes rather than by a single bureaucratic center.

From an organizational point of view, the educational map of U.S. *society* has been redrawn in a much larger scale but has retained something of its earlier form. The organizational changes occur at the bottom, where there is much more bureaucracy reflecting the national discourse about educational matters. This bureaucracy is a standardizing holding company for institutional rules and preferences built up externally. But these institutional rules continue to reflect the associational structure of liberal society—although now at the national level—rather than the organizationally integrated purposes of an emergent bureaucratic state center.

Conclusions

We find much evidence that recent decades have seen a rapid expansion of bureaucracy—formalization, expansion in scale, and standardization—in U.S. educational organization. The changes are national and nationwide and clearly reflect the expanded dominance of a national educational culture.

It is difficult, however, to see the process as driven by the rise of a dominating organizational center in the system and as thus reflecting a move toward centralization in this sense. Direct national funding is too small, and in our data too poorly correlated with organizational expansion at lower levels, to be a plausible candidate for an important causal role.

The modern changes, like earlier instances of U.S. bureaucratization (in education and elsewhere), reflect the expansion and imposition of standard models but not those of a central national organizational structure. It seems more reasonable to see the expanded national concern for (and even investment in) education as leading to a further expansion of the organizational units already endowed with sovereignty in the federal system. It would not be the first time in U.S. history where expanded national integration and coherence generated not an expanded and dominating center but empowered and homogeneous organizational subunits.

All these subunits reflect a complex institutional system that is made up of increasingly national elements (interest groups, professions, a correction system, court and administration rule, and so on). As education becomes a national business, local and state bureaucracy grows. It reflects a growing national institutional structure but not one controlled by the central bureaucratic state.

REFERENCES

BERMAN, P. AND M. W. MCLAUGHLIN. 1975–1978. *Federal Programs Supporting Educational Change.* Vols. 1–8. Santa Monica, CA: Rand Corporation.

BOLI, J., F. O. RAMIREZ, AND J. W. MEYER. 1985. "Explaining the Origins and Expansion of Mass Education. *Comparative Education Review* 29:145–70.

DOYLE, D. P. AND C. E. FINN, JR. 1984. "American Schools and the Future of Local Control." *Public Interest* 77 (Fall):77–95.

FISHLOW, A. 1966. "Levels of Nineteenth Century Investment in Education: Human Capital Formation or Structural Reinforcement? *Journal of Economic History* 26:418–36.

HARGROVE, E., G. SCARLETT, L. E. WARD, V. ABERNETHY, J. CUNNINGHAM, AND W. K. VAUGHN. 1981. "School Systems and Regulatory Mandates: A Case Study of the Implementation of the Education for All Handicapped Children Act. Pp. 97–123 in *Organizational Behavior in Schools and School Districts,* edited by S. B. Bacharach. New York: Praeger.

INKELES, A. AND L. SIRWOY. 1983. "Convergent and Divergent Trends in in National Educational Systems." *Social Forces* 62:303–334.

KAESTLE, C. AND M. VINOVSKIS. 1976. *Education and Social Change: Nineteenth Century Massachusetts: Quantitative Studies.* Final Research Report, Project No. 1-3-0825, Washington, DC: National Institute of Education.

MEYER, J. W. AND W. R. SCOTT. 1983. *Organizational Environments: Ritual and Rationality.* Beverly Hills, CA: Sage.

MEYER, J. W., D. TYACK, J. NAGEL, AND A. GORDON. 1979. "Public Education as Nation-Building in America." *American Journal of Sociology* 85:591–613.

RAMIREZ, F. O. AND J. BOLI. 1987. "Global Patterns of Educational Institutionalization." Pp. 150–72 in *Institutional Structure: Constituting State,*

Society, and the Individual, edited by G. M. Thomas, J. W. Meyer, F. O. Ramirez, and J. Boli. Newbury Park, CA: Sage.

RAMIREZ, F. O. AND R. RUBINSON. 1979. "Creating Members: The Political Incorporation and Expansion of Public Education." Pp. 128–60 in *National Development and the World System*, edited by J. W. Meyer and M. T. Hannan. Chicago: University of Chicago Press.

SCOTT, W. R. AND J. W. MEYER. 1988. "Environmental Linkages and Organizational Complexity: Public and Private Schools." Pp. 128–60 in *Comparing Public and Private Schools. Vol I: Institutions and Organizations*, edited by T. James and H. M. Levin. Philadelphia, PA: Falmer.

SKOWRONEK, S. 1982. *Building a New American State: The Expansion of National Administrative*

Capacities, 1877–1920. Cambridge, UK: Cambridge University Press.

SOLMON, L. 1970. "Estimates of the Costs of Schooling in 1800 and 1890." *Explorations in Economic History* 7 (supplement): 531–81.

STATISTICS OF STATE SCHOOL SYSTEMS. 1938–1980. From 1940 to 1956 published in the biennial survey of education in the United States.

TYACK, D. 1974. *The One Best System: A History of American Urban Education*. Cambridge, MA: Harvard University Press.

WEATHERLEY, R. A. 1979. *Reforming Special Education: Policy Implementation from State Level to Street Level*. Cambridge, MA: MIT Press.

WEBER, M. [1906–1924] 1946. *From Max Weber: Essays in Sociology*, edited by H. H. Gerth and C. W. Mills. New York: Oxford University Press.

42

COMMUNITY COLLEGES AND THE AMERICAN SOCIAL ORDER

Stephen Brint • *Jerome Karabel*

. . .

Today, the idea that the education system in general, and higher education in particular, should provide ladders of upward mobility is so familiar as to be taken for granted. Yet viewed from a comparative perspective, the emphasis in the United States on individual mobility through education is quite remarkable. To this day, no other society—

not Japan, not Canada, not Sweden—sends as many of its young people to colleges and universities as the United States does (Organization for Economic Cooperation and Development 1983). *The vast and expensive system of educational pathways to success that has been constructed in this country is both the institutional embodiment of this commitment to the ideology of equality of opportunity and a constant source of reinforcement of this ideology.* The shape of today's enormous system of colleges and universities—a system in which in recent years almost half the nation's young people have participated—is incomprehensible apart from this commitment.

Central to this distinctive system of higher education is an institution—the two-year junior college (or community college, as it came to be called)—that came into being just when the American educational system was being transformed so as to provide new ladders of ascent. The two-year college . . . has from its very origins at the turn of the century reflected both the egalitarian promise of the world's first modern democracy and the constraints of its dynamic capitalist economy. Enrolling fewer than ten thousand students in 1920, the American junior college had by 1980 grown to enroll well over four million students (Eells 1931: 70; U.S. Bureau of the Census 1987:138). The most successful institutional innovation in twentieth-century American higher education, the two-year college has in recent years spread beyond the United States and established roots in a growing number of foreign countries, among them Japan, Canada, and Yugoslavia.

Community Colleges and Democratic Ideology

With over one-half of all college freshmen now enrolled in two-year institutions (U.S. Department of Education 1986:111), the community college has come to be an integral feature of America's educational landscape. Yet as recently as 1900, the junior college was no more than a dream in the minds of a few administrators at a handful of America's leading universities. Enrolling under 2 percent of all college freshman in 1920 (U.S. Office of Education 1944:4, 6), the year in which the American Association of Junior Colleges (AAJC) was founded, the junior college came to play an increasingly pivotal role in the transformation of the nation's system of colleges and universities. Perhaps more than any other segment of postsecondary education, the community college was at the forefront of the postwar demographic expansion that changed the face of American higher education.

The transformation of American higher education was organizational as well as demographic. For the birth of the two-year college marked the arrival of an entirely new organizational form in the complex ecological structure of American postsecondary education. In terms of sheer numbers, no other twentieth-century organizational innovation in higher education even begins to approach the success of the two-year college, which grew from a single college in 1901 to over 1,200 institutions in 1980, representing almost 40 percent of America's 3,231 colleges. In 1984, over 4.5 million students were enrolled in two-year colleges nationwide (U.S. Bureau of the Census 1987:138).

When the junior college first appeared, the outlines of a hierarchical system of colleges and universities were already becoming visible. Nonetheless, the emergence of the junior college fundamentally altered the shape of American higher education, for it introduced a new tier into the existing hierarchy. Thus the two-year institution was not simply another of the many lower-status colleges that dotted America's educational landscape; it was a different type of institution altogether. Unlike even the humblest four-year institution, it failed to offer what had come to be considered the sine qua non of being an "authentic" college—the bachelor's degree.

What was behind the birth of this new institutional form with roots in both secondary and higher education? What explains the extraordinary growth of the two-year college during the twentieth century? And why has the provision of terminal vocational education—a function that, as we shall see, was for decades peripheral to the mission of the junior college—come to occupy an increasingly central place in the community college? The answers to these questions require an understanding of the peculiar political and ideological role that education has come to play in American life.

American Education and the Management of Ambition

All industrial societies face the problem of allocating qualified individuals into a division of labor characterized by structured inequalities of income, status, and power. Since occupying the superordinate positions in such systems provides a variety of material and psychological gratifications not available to those who occupy subordinate positions, the number of individuals who aspire to privileged places in the division of labor not surprisingly tends to surpass, often by a considerable margin, the number of such slots that are available. In advanced industrial societies, all of which have renounced to one or another degree the ideologies that have historically legitimated the hereditary transmission of positions, this problem of a discrepancy between ambition and the capacity of the opportunity structure to satisfy it is endemic. All such societies face, therefore, a problem in what might be called the *management of ambition.*[1]

In the United States, the management of ambition is a particularly serious dilemma, for success—as Robert Merton (1968:185–214) and others have pointed out—is supposed to be within the grasp of every individual, no matter how humble his (and, more recently, her) background.[2] Moreover, ambition and hard work have been held in more unambiguously high regard in America—a society that was bourgeois in its very origin—than in many European societies, with their aristocratic residues. From Benjamin Franklin to Norman Vincent Peale, the desire to succeed and the willingness to work hard to do so have been seen by Americans as among the highest moral virtues. One consequence of this belief that the "race of life" is both open and well worth winning is that more Americans from subordinate social groups harbor aspirations of making it to the top.

To be sure, not all Americans have joined the race to get ahead. Educational and occupational aspirations are systematically related to social class (Kerckhoff 1974; Spenner and Featherman 1978), and some segments of the population, especially in the racial ghettos of the nation's inner cities, have withdrawn from the competition all together (Ogbu 1978, 1983).[3] Even among those individuals who do harbor hopes of upward mobility, the depth of their commitment is highly variable and shifts in aspirations are common. Upward mobility has real social and psychological costs, and not everyone is willing—or able—to pay them. For many Americans, hopes of a "better life" crumble in the face of obstacles; consigned to low-status jobs, they nonetheless find fulfillment in the private sphere of family and friends. Moreover, aspirations to move ahead are often accompanied by a belief in the legitimacy of inequalities that are based on genuine differences in ability and effort[4]—*and* by doubts about whether one measures up.

The problem of managing ambition is particularly difficult in the United States. In 1980, for example, over half of high school seniors "planned" (not "aspired to") careers in professional/technical jobs. But in that same year, only 13 percent of the labor force was employed in such jobs (Wagenaar 1984). Even if one assumes that there will be a considerable increase in the number of such jobs in the future and that there is significant uncertainty in many of these "plans," it seems clear nonetheless that American society generates far more ambition than its structure of opportunity can satisfy.

. . .

In light of the extraordinary emphasis in the United States on individual economic success and on the role of education as a pathway to it, it is hardly surprising that there has been such a powerful demand from below to expand the educational system. What is perhaps more difficult to understand is the readiness of the state to provide the additional years of schooling demanded by the populace. After all, one can well imagine the state trying to control public expenditures by limiting the amount of education. Yet for the most part, governing elites have joined in a broad national consensus that favored the construction of an educational system of unparalleled dimensions.

There have been many sources of elite support for the expansion of education, among them adherence to the classic Jeffersonian view that a democratic citizenry must be an educated one, and a related commitment to the task of nation building (Meyer et al. 1979). But also critical, we wish to suggest, has been the implicit recognition that a society that promises its subordinate classes unique opportunities for individual advancement needs to offer well-developed channels of upward mobility.

No one could deny the inequalities of wealth and power in the United States. But what made these inequalities tolerable, perhaps, was that everyone—or so the national ideology claimed—had a chance to advance as far as his ability and ambition would take him. And once education became established as the principal vehicle of this advancement, it became politically difficult for any group to oppose its expansion.

The result of this interplay of popular demand and elite response was the creation of a huge but highly differentiated educational system, with unequaled numbers of students enrolled in it. America's commitment to the idea of equal opportunity guaranteed that there would be a tremendous amount of ambition for upward mobility among the masses; somehow the educational system would have a way to manage the aspirations that its own relative openness had helped arouse. The junior college was to play a critical role in this process, and it is to the complex pressures it has faced

both to extend and to limit opportunity that we now turn.

The Contradictory Pressures Facing the Junior College

From its very beginnings, the junior college has been subjected to contradictory pressures rooted in its strategic location in the educational system in a society that is both democratic and highly stratified. Its growth in substantial part a product of the responsiveness of a democratic state to demand from below for the extension of educational opportunity, the junior college's trajectory has also been shaped by the need to select and sort students destined to occupy different positions in the job structure of a capitalist economy. In the popular mind—and in the eyes of the many dedicated and idealistic men and women who have worked in the nation's two-year institutions—the fundamental task of the junior college has been to "democratize" American higher education, by offering to those formerly excluded an opportunity to attend college. But the junior college has also faced enormous pressure to limit this opportunity, for the number of students wishing to obtain a bachelor's degree—and the type of professional or managerial job to which it has customarily led—has generally been far greater than the capacity of the economy to absorb them. Poised between a burgeoning system of secondary education and a highly stratified structure of economic opportunity, the junior college was located at the very point where the aspirations generated by American democracy clashed head on with the realities of its class structure.

Like the American high school, the community college over the course of its history has attempted to perform a number of conflicting tasks: to extend opportunity and to serve as an agent of educational and social selection, to promote social equality and to increase economic efficiency, to provide students with a common cultural heritage and to sort them into a specialized curriculum, to respond to the demands of subordinate groups for equal education and to answer the pressures of employers and state planners for differentiated education, and to provide a general education for citizens in a democratic society and technical training for workers in an advanced industrial economy.[5]

Burton Clark, in a seminal article on "The 'Cooling-Out' Function in Higher Education," put the dilemma facing the junior college well: "a major problem of democratic society is inconsistency between encouragement to achieve and the realities of limited opportunity" (Clark 1961:513). By virtue of its position in the structure of educational and social stratification, the junior college has confronted the necessity of diverting the aspirations of students who wish to join the professional and managerial upper middle class, but who are typically destined by the structure of opportunity to occupy more modest positions. In such a situation, Clark notes bluntly, "for large numbers failure is inevitable and *structured*" (Clark 1961:515, emphasis his).

The junior college has thus been founded on a paradox: the immense popular support that it has enjoyed has been based on its link to four-year colleges and universities, but one of its primary tasks from the outset has been to restrict the number of its students who transfer to such institutions. Indeed, the administrators of elite universities who developed the idea of the junior college (and who later gave the fledgling organizational form crucial sponsorship) did so, . . . with the hope that it would enable them to divert from their own doors the growing number of students clamoring for access to higher education. These university administrators recognized that the democratic character of American culture and politics

demanded that access to higher education be broad; in the absence of alternative institutions, masses of ill-prepared students would, they feared, be clamoring at their gates.

The junior college thus focused in its early years on offering transfer courses. The reason was simple: Students who attended two-year institutions did so on the basis of their claim to be "real" colleges, and the only way to make this claim convincing was for them to offer liberal arts courses that would in fact receive academic credit in four-year institutions. For the first three decades of their existence, the junior colleges thus concentrated on constructing preparatory programs that, as the catalogues of the two-year institutions were fond of characterizing them, were of "strictly collegiate grade."

There was almost a missionary zeal among the predominantly small-town Protestant men who presided over the early junior college movement; their task as they saw it was to bring the blessings of expanded educational opportunity to the people. Proudly referring to their institutions as "democracy's colleges," they viewed the two-year institutions as giving thousands of worthy students who would otherwise have been excluded a chance to attend higher education. Yet they were also aware that the educational and occupational aspirations of their students outran their objective possibilities by a substantial margin; while some of their students had great academic promise, well under half of them, they knew, would ever enter a four-year college or university. Something other than college preparatory courses, therefore, would have to be provided for them if they were to receive an education appropriate for their future place in the division of labor.

The solution that the leaders of the junior college movement devised bore a striking resemblance to the one developed earlier by the administrators of secondary education at the point when the high school was transformed from an elite to a mass institution: the creation of a separate vocational education track. The underlying logic of the vocational solution is perhaps best captured in a speech given in 1908 by Dean James Russell of Teachers College, Columbia University, to a meeting of the National Education Association. Entitling his presentation "Democracy and Education: Equal Opportunity for All," Russell asked:

> How can a nation endure that deliberately seeks to raise ambitions and aspirations in the oncoming generations which in the nature of events cannot possibly be fulfilled? If the chief object of government be to promote civil order and social stability, how can we justify our practice in schooling the masses in precisely the same manner as we do those who are to be our leaders? (quoted in Nasaw 1979:131)

Russell's answer was unequivocal: The ideal of equal education would have to be forsaken, for only *differentiated education*—education that fit students for their different vocational futures—was truly democratic. Paradoxically, then, if mass education were to realize the promise of democracy, separate vocational tracks had to be created.

In a society that generated far more ambition for upward mobility than its structure of opportunity could possibly satisfy, the logic of vocationalism, whether at the level of secondary or higher education, was compelling. The United States was, after all, a class-stratified society, and there was something potentially threatening to the established order about organizing the educational system so as to arouse high hopes, only to shatter them later. At the same time, however, the political costs of turning back the popular demand for expanded schooling were prohibitive in a nation placing so much stress on equality of opportunity. What vocationalism promised to do was to resolve

this dilemma by, on the one hand, accepting the democratic pressure from below to provide access to new levels of education while, on the other hand, differentiating the curriculum to accommodate the realities of the economic division of labor. The aspirations of the masses for upward mobility through education would not, advocates of vocationalization claimed, thereby be dashed; instead, they would be rechanneled in more "realistic" directions.[6]

The leaders of the junior college movement enthusiastically embraced the logic of vocationalism and, by the 1930s, had come to define the decided lack of student enthusiasm for anything other than college-transfer programs as the principal problem facing the two-year institution. Their arguments in favor of expanding terminal vocational education in the junior college were essentially identical to those used by advocates of vocational education in the high school: Not everyone could be a member of the elite; vocational programs would reduce the high dropout rate; and occupational training would guarantee that students would leave the educational system with marketable skills.

. . .

Curricular Change in the Community College

Observers of the transformation of the community college from an institution oriented to college-preparatory transfer programs to one emphasizing terminal vocational training have tended to focus on one of two forces as the principal cause: either the changing preference of student "consumers" of community college education or, alternatively, the decisive influence of business elites. In the first, which might be called the *consumer-choice model*, institutions of higher education are regarded as responding exclusively to students' curricular preferences: what the consumers of higher education demand, they receive. In the second, which we shall refer to as the *business-domination model*, the curricular offerings of the community colleges are seen as reflecting the imprint of powerful business interests, which prefer programs that provide them with technically trained workers. Drawing, respectively, on classical liberal and Marxist approaches to the problem of institutional change, each of these models provides a theoretically plausible explanation for the trajectory of community college development, and, accordingly, commands our attention.

The Consumer-Choice and Business-Domination Models

· · ·

Both the consumer-choice and the business-domination perspectives capture something important, we believe, about the forces shaping community college development. Market forces have influenced student preferences, and the downturn in the labor market for college graduates in the early 1970s was indeed a major factor in the rapid community college vocationalization of the following years. And especially since the mid-1970s, business has influenced (occasionally directly, but more often indirectly) the shape and content of the curricula from which community college students select their programs.

Today student "consumers" eagerly enroll in community college occupational programs that they hope will lead them into relatively high-paying, secure jobs with opportunities for advancement. These choices, though based, we shall argue, on imperfect labor market information, are in part logical responses to the overcrowded market for college-trained persons and the difficulties of competing in such a market. The pro-

grams in which these occupational students enroll, in turn, are determined in part by industry's needs for particular types of "middle-level" manpower.

We believe that the indirect influence of business on community college curricula has always been great. The colleges have for some time sought to keep pace with manpower developments in the private economy. Indeed, the more enterprising two-year college administrators have studied regional and national labor projections almost as if they were sacred texts. Arthur Cohen, now director of the ERIC Clearinghouse for Junior Colleges at the University of California at Los Angeles, was hardly exaggerating when he wrote that "when corporate managers . . . announce a need for skilled workers . . . college administrators trip over each other in their haste to organize a new curriculum" (Cohen 1971:6).

Yet despite the consumer-choice and business-domination models' contributions to our understanding of recent developments in the community college, neither is an adequate guide to the past. Rather, they are most useful for the period since 1970, the year of the first signs of decline in the labor market for college graduates—and of little help for the period before that year. Since some of the most influential community college officials have been attempting . . . to vocationalize their institutions since at least 1930, that leaves forty years of history almost entirely unaccounted for by either model. Moreover, we shall argue, neither model captures some of the key dynamics of the process of vocationalization since 1970.

Before 1970, our study reveals, neither students nor businessmen were very interested in vocational programs. Most students (and their families) desired the prestige of a baccalaureate degree and resisted terminal vocational training. But despite the students' overwhelming preference for liberal arts programs, the leaders of the American Association of Junior Colleges and their allies pursued a policy of vocationalization for over four decades before there was any notable shift in the students' preferences. This policy decision cannot be explained by the consumer-choice model.

Similarly, most members of the business elite were indifferent to community colleges before the late 1960s. Indeed, for almost another decade after that, business interest in the community colleges remained modest and picked up only in the late 1970s, after the colleges had already become predominantly vocational institutions. The indifference of business people to programs ostensibly developed in their interests cannot be readily explained by the business-domination model. An adequate explanation of the community college's transformation thus requires a fundamental theoretical reformulation.

Toward an Institutional Approach

The framework that we propose to account for the transformation of American community colleges may be called, albeit with some oversimplification, an *institutional model*. Inspired in part by the classical sociological tradition in the study of organizations,[7] this approach can, we believe, illuminate processes of social change beyond the specific case of education. Perhaps the model's most fundamental feature is that it takes as its starting point organizations themselves, which are seen as pursuing their own distinct interests. Within this framework, special attention is focused upon "organizational fields" (e.g., education, medicine, journalism), which may be defined as being composed of "those organizations that in the aggregate, constitute a recognized area of institutional life: key suppliers, resource and product consumers, regulatory agencies, and other organizations that produce similar services or products" (DiMaggio and Powell 1983:148).[8]

Relations among organizations within the same field are often—but not always—competitive; accordingly, understanding the historical trajectory of a particular organization generally requires an analysis of its relationship to other organizations offering similar services. The dynamics of specific institutions, in turn, are rooted in their relationships to other major institutions. For example, the educational system must be analyzed in relation to the state and the economy. If the focus of the consumer-choice and the business-domination models is on the individual and the class respectively, the focus of this approach will be, accordingly, on the institution.

According to this perspective, neither the consumer-choice nor the business-domination model pays sufficient attention to the beliefs and activities of the administrators and professionals who typically have the power to define what is in the "interest" of the organizations over which they preside. Much of our analysis will focus, therefore, on explaining why these administrators chose to vocationalize despite what we shall document was the opposition of the student consumers (an opposition that casts doubt on the consumer-choice model) and the indifference of potential sponsors in the business corporations (which in turn undermines the business-domination model). Our analysis assesses the beliefs and organizational interests of those who pursued the vocationalization policy and the techniques they used to implement this policy over time. It also examines the forces, both external and internal to the community college movement, that facilitated or hindered implementation of the policy at different historical moments.

In skeletal form, our basic argument is that the *community colleges chose to vocationalize themselves, but they did so under conditions of powerful structural constraints*. Foremost among these constraints was the subordinate position of the community college in the larger structure of educational and social stratification. Put more concretely, junior colleges were hampered by their subordinate position in relation to that of the older and more prestigious four-year colleges and universities and, correspondingly, a subordinate position in the associated competition to place their graduates into desirable positions in the labor market.

Perhaps the best way to capture this dual structural subordination is to think of the structure of stratification faced by community colleges in terms of two parallel but distinct components—one a structure of labor market stratification and the other a structure of institutional stratification in higher education. From this perspective, educational institutions may be viewed as competing for training markets—the right to be the preferred pathway from which employers hire prospective employees. Access to the most desirable training markets—those leading to high-level professional and managerial jobs—is, and has been for decades, dominated by four-year colleges and, at the highest levels, by elite graduate and professional schools. Community colleges, by their very location in the structure of higher education, were badly situated to compete with better-established institutions for these training markets. Indeed, it is not an exaggeration to say that by the time that two-year colleges established a major presence in higher education, the best training markets were effectively monopolized by rival institutions.

Training markets are critical to the well-being of higher-education institutions. In general, those that have captured the best markets—for example, the top law, medical, and management schools—are the institutions with the most resources, the greatest prestige, and the most intense competition for entry. Viewed historically, community colleges had lost the most strategic sectors of this market before they could enter the competition. The best that the community colleges could hope to do, therefore, was to try to situate themselves favorably for the next available market niche. Therein resided the powerful organizational appeal of the two-year college's long-standing vocationalization project, a project that, as we shall show, had become widely accepted among community college administrators long before there was any decline in the demand for graduates of four-year colleges or any demand for vocational programs from the community college students themselves.

Because of their precarious position in the competition for training markets, community colleges tried desperately to fit themselves to the needs of business despite the absence of direct business interest in the colleges. Indeed, far from imposing on the community colleges a desire for a cheap docile labor force trained at public expense, as the business-domination model would have it, big business remained indifferent to the community colleges for the first sixty years of their existence. Yet because of the structural location of business in the larger political economy—and, in particular, its control of jobs—community colleges had little choice but to take into account the interests of their students' future employers. Thus business exerted a profound influence over the direction of community college affairs and pushed them in the direction of vocationalization without any direct action whatsoever. This capacity to exert influence in the absence of direct intervention reflects the *structural power* of business.[9]

Reduced to its essentials, then, our argument is that the community colleges found themselves in a situation of structured subordination with respect to both other higher-education institutions and business. Within the constraints of this dual subordination, the vocationalization project was a means of striking the best available bargain. We refer in the text to this deference to the perceived needs of more powerful institutions—even when such institutions made no conscious efforts to control their affairs—as *anticipatory subordination*.

This anticipatory subordination was rooted in the recognition by the community colleges that if they tried to compete with the existing better-endowed, higher-status institutions on their own terrain, they would face certain defeat. A far better strategy, it was determined after much internal debate with the junior college movement, was to try to capture an unexploited—albeit less glamorous—market in which they would not compete directly with institutions with superior resources. In return for accepting a subordination that was, in any case, inherent in their structural location, the community colleges would use vocationalization to bring a stable flow of resources linked to a distinctive function, a unique institutional identity, and above all, a secure—indeed, expanding—market niche. . . .

. . .

NOTES

1. The idea that all educational systems, capitalist and socialist alike, face a problem in the management of ambition is borrowed from Hopper (1971).
2. The belief that America remains a land of opportunity is a recurrent finding of sociological studies of American communities (see, for example, Warner and Lunt 1941, and Hollingshead 1949).
3. White youths, especially those from the most disadvantaged segments of the urban working class, may also withdraw from the competition to get ahead. For a powerful portrait of "leveled aspirations" in a low-income neighborhood, see MacLeod's ethnographic study of youths in a public housing project, *Ain't No Makin' It* (1987).
4. Kluegel and Smith (1986), for example, in a nationally representative survey of 2,212 Americans, find that economic differences among groups are often attributed to individual differences in such qualities as "hard work" and "talent." Moreover, many of the survey respondents view economic inequality as being legitimate in principle (Kluegel and Smith 1986:75–142).
5. The idea that education in the United States is pulled in contradictory directions by the logics of capitalism and democracy is discussed in Shapiro (1982; 1983) and developed at length in Carnoy and Levin's book, *Schooling and Work in the Democratic State* (1985). Katznelson and Weir (1985), in their historical study of education and the urban working class also develop this theme, focusing in particular on the conflicting pressures inherent in preparing students for life as both democratic citizens and workers in a highly inegalitarian division of labor.
6. The sources of the powerful impact that the ideology of vocationalism has had on American education are explored in Lazerson and Grubb (1974) and Kantor and Tyack (1982). On "career education", a form of Vocational education that exerted considerable influence during the 1970s, see Grubb and Lazerson (1975).
7. Among the key works on organizations that have informed our approach are Robert Michels' *Political Parties*, 1911, and Max Weber's *Economy and Society*, 79, especially the sections on "Domination and Legitimacy" and "Bureaucracy."
8. Our concept of "organizational field" is similar to Meyer and Scott's (1983:137–39) concept of a "societal sector" which, while building on the economists' concept of "industry," is broader in that it includes organizations that contribute to or regulate the activities of a focal industry group.
9. But we also emphasize, drawing on Bourdieu (1971, 1975, 1984), that fields are arenas of power relations, with some actors—generally those possessing superior material and/or symbolic resources—occupying more advantaged positions than others. The concept of "structural power" used here is indebted to the illuminating discussion of the relationship between power and participation in Alford and Friedland (1975). Our formulation differs somewhat from theirs, however, and is in fact closer to their concept of "systemic power."

REFERENCES

ALFORD, ROBERT R. AND ROGER FRIEDLAND. 1975. "Political Participation and Public Policy." *Annual Review of Sociology* 1:429–79.

BOURDIEU, PIERRE. 1971. "Intellectual Field and Creative Project." Pp. 161–88 in *Knowledge and Control: New Directions for the Sociology of Education,* edited by Michael F. D. Young. London: Collier-Macmillan.

———. 1975. "The Specificity of the Scientific Field and the Social Conditions of the Progress of Reason." *Social Science Information* 14:19–47.

———. 1984. *Distinction.* Cambridge, MA: Harvard University Press.

CARNOY, MARTIN AND HENRY LEVIN. 1985. *Schooling and Work in the Democratic State.* Stanford, CA: Stanford University Press.

CLARK, BURTON. 1960. *The Open Door College: A Case Study.* New York: McGraw-Hill.

———. 1961. "The 'Cooling-Out' Function in Higher Education." Pp. 513–21 in *Education, Economy, and Society,* edited by A. H. Halsey et al. New York: Free Press.

COHEN, ARTHUR M. 1971. "Stretching Pre-College Education." *Social Policy,* May–June 1971:5–9.

DIMAGGIO, PAUL AND WALTER W. POWELL. 1983. "The Iron Cage Revisited: Institutional Isomorphism and Collective Rationality in Organizational Fields." *American Sociological Review* 48:147–60.

EELLS, WALTER CROSBY. 1925. *The Junior-College Movement.* Boston: Ginn.

———. 1931. *The Junior College.* Boston: Houghton Mifflin.

HOLLINGSHEAD, AUGUST B. 1949. *Elmtown's Youth.* New York: Wiley.

HOPPER, EARL. 1971. "Educational Systems and Selected Consequences of Patterns of Mobility and Non-Mobility in Industrial Societies: A Theoretical Discussion." Pp. 292–336 in *Readings in the Theory of Educational Systems,* edited by Earl Hopper. London: Hutchinson.

KANTOR, HARVEY AND DAVID TYACK, eds. 1982. *Work, Youth, and Schooling: Historical Perspectives in American Education.* Stanford, CA: Stanford University Press.

KATZNELSON, IRA AND MARGRET WEIR. 1985. *Schooling for All.* New York: Basic Books.

KERCKHOFF, ALAN. 1974. *Ambition and Attainment.* Washington, DC: American Sociological Association.

KLUEGEL, JAMES R. AND ELIOT R. SMITH. 1986. *Beliefs about Inequality.* New York: Aldine De Gruyter.

LAZERSON, MARVIN AND W. NORTON GRUBB, eds. 1974. *American Education and Vocationalism: A Documentary History, 1870–1970.* New York: Teachers College Press, Columbia University.

LYND, ROBERT S. AND HELEN MERRELL LYND. 1937. *Middletown in Transition.* New York: Harcourt Brace Jovanovich.

MACLEOD, JAY. 1987. *Ain't No Makin' It.* Boulder, CO: Westview.

MERTON, ROBERT K. 1968. *Social Theory and Social Structure.* New York: Free Press.

MEYER, JOHN W. AND RICHARD W. SCOTT. 1983. *Organizational Environments: Ritual and Rationality.* Beverly Hills, CA: Sage Publications.

MEYER, JOHN W., ET AL. 1979. "Public Education As Nation-Building in America." *American Journal of Sociology* 85:978–86.

NASAW, DAVID. 1979. *Schooled to Order.* New York: Oxford University Press.

OGBU, JOHN U. 1978. *Minority Education and Caste.* New York: Academic Press.

———. 1983. "Minority Status and Schooling in Plural Societies." *Comparative Education Review* 27:168–90.

ORGANIZATION FOR ECONOMIC COOPERATION AND DEVELOPMENT. 1983. *Policies for Higher Education in the 1980s.* Paris: OECD.

SHAPIRO, HARVEY. 1982. "Education in Capitalist Society: Toward a Reconsideration of the State of Educational Policy." *Teachers' College Record* 83:515–27.

———. 1983. "Habermas, O'Connor, and Wolfe, and the Crisis of the Welfare-Capitalist State: Conservative Politics and the Roots of Educational Policy in the 1980s." *Educational Theory* 33(3–4):135–47.

SPENNER, KENNETH L. AND DAVID FEATHERMAN. 1978. "Achievement Ambitions." Pp. 373–420 in *Annual Review of Sociology,* vol. 4, edited by Ralph Turner, James Coleman, and Renee Fox. Palo Alto, CA: Annual Reviews.

UNITED STATES BUREAU OF THE CENSUS. 1987. *Statistical Abstract of the United States 1987.* Washington, DC: U.S. Government Printing Office.

UNITED STATES DEPARTMENT OF EDUCATION, CENTER FOR STATISTICS. 1986. *Digest of Education Statistics, 1985–1986.* Washington, DC: U.S. Government Printing Office.

UNITED STATES OFFICE OF EDUCATION. 1944. *Statistics of Higher Education 1939–1940 and 1941–1942,* vol. 2. Washington, DC: Department of Health, Education and Welfare.

WAGENAAR, THEODORE C. 1984. *Occupational Aspirations and Intended Field of Study in College.* Washington, DC: National Center for Education Statistics.

WARNER, W. LLOYD AND PAUL S. LUNT, 1941. *The Social Life of a Modern Community.* New Haven, CT: Yale University Press.

43

AN INSTITUTIONAL PERSPECTIVE ON SCHOOLS

John Chubb • Terry Moe

The American public school system is bureaucratic and political. This is a simple, accurate description that, in itself, carries no value judgment; for, despite the negative connotations so often attached to these characteristics, neither is intrinsically bad or undesirable. Virtually all organizations of any size are in some sense bureaucratic. They rely on hierarchy, division of labor, specialization, formal rules, and the like in order to coordinate and control their members toward common ends, and it is clear enough that some measure of bureaucracy is often quite necessary for effective social action.[1] Similarly, the public schools are no different from other government agencies in being political. All organizations in the public sector are shaped and surrounded by democratic politics, and, in some form at least, this is clearly necessary if democracy is to work.

The institutional perspective we develop in this chapter, however, will suggest that the public school system suffers from very serious problems along both these dimensions. We will argue that it has a bureaucracy problem and a politics problem, and that the two are closely related. Its bureaucracy problem is not that the system is bureaucratic at all, but that it is too heavily bureaucratic—too hierarchical, too rule-bound, too formalistic—to allow for the kind of autonomy and professionalism schools need if they are to

perform well. Its political problem is not that it is subject to any sort of democratic policies, but that the specific political institutions by which the schools are governed actively promote and protect this overbureaucratization.

The bureaucracy problem is the more immediate explanation for the schools' poor academic performance. The politics problem is the more fundamental: it explains the bureaucracy problem. Political institutions are the key to understanding why the public school system is not doing its job.

Politics and Markets

Any effort to develop an institutional perspective on schools runs immediately into a basic problem. In order to show that institutions have important consequences for schools, one needs to show that institutional variation leads to a variation in schools—yet American public schools are all governed through highly uniform institutions of direct democratic control. There is no significant variation in institutions on which to base an enlightening analysis.

Our solution to this problem is to look beyond the public school system and seek out alternative institutional arrangements to which it can be compared. This is why we find the private sector so useful. It helps us compare institutions—and thus, in the process, understand the public schools.

The private sector is not as homogeneous as the public sector, and this complicates matters a bit. About half of all private schools are Catholic, and the rest are a diverse lot of religious schools, college preparatory schools, military academies, schools for children with special problems or talents, and many other types of schools as well. All schools in the private sector, however, have two important institutional features in common: society does not control them directly through democratic politics, and society does control them—indirectly—through the marketplace. This is what makes the private sector distinctively different from the public sector as an institutional setting for schools.

Education is hardly unique in this respect, of course. Throughout American society, democratic control and markets are the two major institutions by which social decisions get made and social resources get allocated, and they rather consistently distinguish the public and private sectors. Governments rely on democratic control almost regardless of what they are attempting to accomplish, while in the private sector virtually all activities of a productive or commercial nature (as well as many other sorts of activities) are heavily structured by markets. Questions about which is more efficient, more just, or somehow better have long been the stuff of classic debates in political and economic theory. And less monumental variants—having to do, for instance, with the privatization of certain governmental services or the extension of democratic controls into new, previously private spheres—are practical issues that find their way into politics every day.[2]

In this chapter, we build our own perspective on schools around a comparison of these preeminent social institutions. As we do so, we will not try to represent all the variety and complexity we know to characterize schools in the public and private sectors. Our aim is to get beyond much of the detail of schooling in the two sectors and to focus attention on what is theoretically most important about them—their distinctive institutions. In this way, we hope to clarify the major differences that these institutions seem to make for the schools within them.

Authority and Decisionmaking

The place to begin in comparing democratic control and markets is with the distinctive ways in which they allocate authority and prescribe rules for exercising it. These properties set the foundation for educational decisionmaking, determining who has the right to make what kinds of educational decisions in what ways.

The public sector is built around public authority. Democratic institutions allocate decisionmaking rights by attaching public authority to elected and appointed positions of government—for example, school board seats and superintendencies—and by setting out rules that specify who can occupy these positions and how the authority attached to them must be exercised. The "winners" under these rules—including, implicitly, individuals and groups whose interests the officeholders represent—have the legal right to make public policies and to devise governmental structures that are binding on everyone in the polity. The "losers" have the obligation to accept and help finance these policies and structures, however much they may be opposed to them.

In this sense, democracy is essentially coercive. The winners get to use public authority to impose their policies on the losers. Teachers' unions, for example, might prevail over the opposition of administrators or parents on some issues. On others, business groups might succeed in imposing reforms fought by the unions. What makes this peculiar form of coercion broadly acceptable is that public authority does not belong to any individual or group. It is up for grabs. Anyone who plays by the rules and gains sufficient popular support has the same right as anyone else to take control of public authority and to specify the legitimate means and ends of public policy for everyone.

These properties supply the motive force behind democratic politics. Because public authority is enormously valuable and widely available, individuals and groups representing a diverse range of social interests have strong incentives to try to capture it, to exercise it toward ends they deem appropriate, and to prevent their opponents from doing the same. The result is a perpetual struggle for the control of public authority. During elections, the various interests struggle to place their partisans in public offices. Between elections, they struggle to influence how officials actually exercise their authority. Through it all, public authority remains a blank check on which everyone wants to write.

Public authority is also important for market institutions, but its role is far less central to decisionmaking. For markets to operate, governments must create a legal framework that specifies and enforces property rights. They must use their public authority, in other words, to impose a system of rules for determining who owns what property and for assigning to owners the authority to make certain choices about its disposition. Once such a framework is created, individuals are free to enter into exchanges with one another as they see fit, and markets take over.

Effective authority within market settings, then, is radically decentralized. In private sector education, the people who run each school decide what they will teach, how they will teach it, who will do the teaching, how much to charge for their services, and virtually everything else about how education will be organized and supplied.[3] Students and parents assess the offerings, reputations, and costs of the various schools and make their own choices about which to attend. No one makes decisions for society. All participants make decisions for themselves.

The kind of authority that market participants exercise, while public in origin, is extremely limited in scope. The owners of a school have the legal authority to create whatever kind of school they please, but they cannot require anyone to attend or finance it. They have authority over their own property, not over the property of others. Similarly, parents and students have the right to seek out whatever kinds of schools they like. But they cannot force schools to adopt specific courses, hire certain teachers, or pursue certain values. Nor can they force schools to grant them admission. They make decisions for themselves, not for the schools.

The key elements that supply the motivational foundation of democratic politics—the tremendous value, wide availability, and coercive power of public authority—are essentially absent from the marketplace. Individuals and groups do not struggle to capture something that is not there. In markets, their focus is much more myopic. They try to achieve their ends through voluntary exchange with others, and the benefits they receive arise from these transactions. The key to success—for schools, parents, and students alike—is having something to offer that other people want.

Constituents and Consumers

Almost everyone's first impulse is to think that the purpose of schools is to provide children with academic training, with essential information about society and the world, with an understanding of citizenship in a democracy, or something of the sort. On reflection, however, it should be apparent that schools have no immutable or transcendent purpose. What they are supposed to be doing depends on who controls them and what these controllers want them to do.

In the public sector, schools are controlled by whoever controls public authority. Popular myth, of course, lauds the role of local citizens and their elected school boards, but this is misleading. The public schools are not really "locally controlled" and are not supposed to be. The authority exercised by local governments is delegated to them by the states and can be modified or revoked at the states' pleasure. More generally, public authority over schools is legally vested in democratic institutions at all levels. State and federal governments—and thus their constituents—have legitimate roles to play in financing schools, setting standards, and otherwise making and imposing their own educational policies and organizational structures. This means that citizens everywhere, whether or not they have children in school and whether or not they live in the local school district or even the state, have a legitimate hand in governing each and every local school. They are all controllers.

The heterogeneous interests of all these constituents do not automatically find faithful reflection in the policies and structures of government. Democracy, like all other institutions, works imperfectly. Political resources are unequally distributed. The interest group system is biased in favor of some interests over others (the organized over the unorganized, especially). Politicians and administrators sometimes pursue their own interests at the expense of citizens' interests. And so on. As a result, who wins and who loses in politics is not necessarily representative of what ordinary citizens actually want.

These are well-known problems that plague all democracies in one way or an-

other, and they are the sorts of things that attract attention from many critics of American public education. They think the education system would be vastly improved if democracy's imperfections could somehow be overcome. Even if this were possible, however, the fact remains that democratic politics would still be a competitive struggle for the control of public authority. It would still be a game of winners and losers. On any given issue, the winners might include various combinations of interests: those of teachers' unions, associations of professionals, book publishers, ideological groups, or factions among the citizenry at large. But everyone cannot win, and the losers have to take what the winners dish out. This is the single most important thing to know about how interests get represented in a democracy. It is not an imperfection. It is what democratic control is all about.

Notice that we have said nothing so far about parents and students. The myth that parents and students are uniquely special in all this—that the schools are somehow supposed to be what parents and students want them to be—goes hand-in-hand with the myth of local control, and it is equally misleading. The proper constituency of even a single public school is a huge and heterogeneous one whose interests are variously represented by politicians, administrators, and groups at all levels of government. Parents and students are but a small part of this constituency.

A frequent complaint is that parents and students are not well enough organized to be very powerful. In the struggle to control public authority, they tend to be far outweighed by teachers' unions, professional organizations, and other entrenched interests that, in practice, have traditionally dominated the politics of education. This is true enough. But what it implies is that parents and students would get the kind of schools they wanted if they could somehow gain "appropriate" clout—if democracy, in other words, were less imperfect and did a better job of reflecting their interests. This is simply not the case.

The fundamental point to be made about parents and students is not that they are politically weak, but that, even in a perfectly functioning democratic system, the public schools are *not meant* to be theirs to control and are literally *not supposed* to provide them with the kind of education they might want. The schools are agencies of society as a whole, and everyone has a right to participate in their governance. Parents and students have a right to participate too. But they have no right to win. In the end, they have to take what society gives them.

In the private sector, the situation of parents and students would appear to be worse still. There they have no legal right to control the schools at all. The authority to control each private school is vested in the school's owner—which may be an individual, a partnership, a church, a corporation, a nonprofit agency, or some other form of organization—and the owner has the legal right to make all the decisions about policy and structure that, in the public sector, are matters for "the people" and their representatives to struggle over. Despite the formal dominance of owners, however, markets work to ensure that parents and students play a much more central and influential role in private sector education than they do when democracy gives them formal rights to govern. There are three basic reasons for this.

The first is that those who own and run the schools have a strong incentive to please a clientele of parents and students through the decisions they make.[4] This sort of responsiveness is perhaps the most obvious path by which markets promote a match between what parents and students want and the kind of education their schools provide.

It is not necessarily the most important, however.

The second arises from a basic prerequisite of market choice: people have the freedom to switch from one alternative to another when they think it would be beneficial to do so. If parents and students do not like the services they are being provided at any given school, they can exit and find another school whose offerings better meet their needs.[5] Even if schools were entirely unresponsive to their clienteles, then, this process of selection and sorting would tend to encourage a match between what parents and students want and the kind of education they receive.

The third arises from a basic property of markets that operates on the population of schools as a whole: natural selection.[6] Schools that fail to satisfy a sufficiently large clientele will go out of business (or, if subsidized, become an increasing burden to their patron organizations, generating pressures that work in the same direction). Of the schools that survive, those that do a better job of satisfying consumers will be more likely to prosper and proliferate. They may be joined or challenged at any time, moreover, by new schools that enter the marketplace to offer similar services in a better way, or perhaps to appeal to specialized segments of consumer demand that are not being met adequately. The dynamics of entry, success, and failure, driven by the requisites of parent-student support, all tend to promote the emergence of a population of schools that matches the population of parents and students.

A standard claim about public schools is that there are strong forces, including quasi-market forces, that tend to promote this kind of matching in them as well.[7] For instance, although the local public school is usually a monopoly, in the sense that all children living in a designated geographical area are typically assigned to a particular school, parents and students can still exercise exit and choice by taking account of school quality in deciding where to live. If they like the schools, they can move into the area. If they do not like them, they can move out.

It is true that residential mobility does tend to promote the kind of matching that occurs in markets; but it is a very rough and inadequate approximation to the real thing, even for those citizens affluent enough to move where they want when they want. In general, residential decisions involve many factors in addition to education—proximity to work, quality of housing, availability of public services—and, once they are made, the financial costs and personal adjustments entailed by moving are quite high. Low or declining educational quality need not keep parents from moving into an area, and it is even less likely to prompt existing residents to pick up and leave.

It might prompt them to consider a private school—another exit option that would help drain off the disgruntled and improve the average satisfaction of those who are left in the public sector. But here parents confront a major disincentive: public schools are free, private schools are not. Because of this cost differential, the perceived value of private schools must far outweigh that of public schools if they are to win students. To put it the other way around: public schools, because they are relatively inexpensive, can attract and hold students without being particularly good at educating them.

Lacking feasible exit options, then, whether through residential mobility or escape into the private sector, many parents and students will "choose" a public school despite dissatisfaction with its goals, methods, personnel, and performance. Having done so, they have a right to try to remedy the situation through the democratic control structure. But everyone else has the same right, and the determinants of political power are stacked against them. Democracy

cannot remedy the mismatch between what parents and students want and what the public schools provide. Conflict and disharmony are built into the system.

While this is an inherent feature of democratic control, we do not mean to imply that markets are somehow capable of perfectly satisfying parents and students. Obviously, they are not. Markets are inevitably subject to all sorts of real-world imperfections, just as democratic institutions are. Monopolizing, price-fixing, territorial agreements, and other restrictive practices by producers may limit the choices available to consumers. Consumers may be too poorly informed to make choices that are truly in their best interests. Transportation costs may eliminate many options. The unequal distribution of income in society may bias certain markets in favor of the rich and against the poor. To the extent that these and other imperfections are serious, markets are less likely to generate the diversity, quality, and levels of services that consumers want, and prices are likely to be higher than they otherwise would be.

These imperfections cannot be eliminated. They can be (and in fact are) substantially reduced by various means—antitrust laws, consumer information services, publicly assisted transportation, progressive taxation, and direct subsidies (for example, food stamps, housing vouchers), among others. These are governmental actions that, like the rules specifying and enforcing property rights, help create a framework more conducive to the beneficial operation of markets.[8]

It is a mistake, however, to place too much emphasis on these sorts of imperfections, just as it is a mistake to be obsessed with the imperfections of democratic control. Both systems are inherently imperfect. Both are easily criticized when compared with an ideal social state—the perfect market, the perfect democracy—that does not exist and never will. It is much more instructive to compare real-world institutions in terms of their basic, distinguishing properties and essential features. The crucial thing is not that they are imperfect, but that they are different.

When it comes to the basic issue of whose interests find reflection in society's schools, these two systems clearly function under real-world conditions to promote very different social outcomes. Under a system of democratic control, the public schools are governed by an enormous, far-flung constituency in which the interests of parents and students carry no special status or weight. When markets prevail, parents and students are thrust onto center stage, along with the owners and staff of schools; most of the rest of society plays a distinctly secondary role, limited for the most part to setting the framework within which educational choices get made. These differences are absolutely fundamental to the two systems, however imperfectly each may work in practice.

Bureaucracy and Autonomy

So far, we have discussed how democratic control and markets allocate authority and attach weight to social interests. These are rather abstract concerns that may seem to have very little to do with something so concrete as the organization of schools. But in fact they have a great deal to do with it. To see why, let's turn to what many educators view as the most fundamental organizational issue facing the schools today: the issue of bureaucracy versus autonomy.

Markets: Decentralization and Discretion

While markets decentralize effective decisionmaking authority to the suppliers and consumers of services, they do not automatically give rise to organizational structures that are themselves decentralized. The economic system obviously boasts all sorts of organizational forms, some of them highly centralized bureaucracies in which subordinate levels of organization have little discretion. Presumably, an educational market system might do the same if centralized organization were an efficient way to supply educational services that satisfy parents and students.

As a rule, however, this is unlikely to be so. One very basic reason has to do with the technical requirements of producing educational services. Because education is based on personal relationships and interactions, on continual feedback, and on the knowledge, skills, and experience of teachers, most of the necessary technology and resources are inherently present in the school itself, and thus are at the bottom of the organizational hierarchy (if there is one). Higher-level administrative units have little to contribute that is not already there.

It is no accident, for example, that so much attention in both the academic literature and the policymaking process has focused on teacher professionalism. True professionalism requires not simply that teachers be experts in their subject matters and the methodology of learning, but also that they have the autonomy to exercise discretion in applying it to the infinitely varying individuals and circumstances that make up their jobs. The widely accepted notion that education would be better if teachers were treated as professionals is but another way of saying that the schools already have (or should already have) what it takes to provide quality education—they just have to be allowed to use it.

A second basic reason has to do with the purely administrative requirements of controlling education from above. Effective bureaucracy is commonly built around rules that specify appropriate behavior, rewards

An Institutional Perspective on Schools

and sanctions that encourage such behavior, and monitoring to ascertain whether goals are being met, whether rules are being followed, when rewards and sanctions are called for, and whether rules and incentive systems need to be adjusted. All are rendered highly problematic in education, because good education and the behaviors conducive to it are inherently difficult to measure in an objective, quantifiable, formal manner. The measurement problem makes it difficult or impossible for education administrators to know what they are doing—and their controls, as a result, threaten to be ill suited to the ends they want to achieve.

While virtually everyone in a given school typically knows who the good teachers are, for instance, their assessments arise from actual experience and judgment, not from formal tests of teaching competence. As teachers are quick to point out, there are no formal tests that can adequately tap the intangible qualities that make someone good or bad at the job, it is impossible to hand down a set of rules from on high that will somehow transform bad teachers into good ones—and it is organizationally counterproductive to reward and sanction teachers on these grounds.[9] For the most part, the people at the bottom of the hierarchy do not have a serious measurement problem. They essentially solve it without really trying, just by taking part in the everyday life of the school. The people at the top are the ones with the measurement problem. The organization as a whole has a serious measurement problem only to the extent that there are people at the top who try to control the people at the bottom.

A third reason why centralized organization is unlikely to prove efficient arises from the market constraint that schools must, above all else, please their clients. The school staff members who interact with students and parents day in and day out are in a far better position than administrators to sense whether their clients are happy with the services they are getting. They are also better able to devise and implement whatever adjustments might be necessary to enhance the school's appeal. Again, they know what administrators cannot because it is a natural, integral part of their work in the schools.

A common demand on the part of parents and students is that students need to be treated and understood as individuals if they are to make the most of their educational experience. Given the variety of human personalities and family environments, this happens to make good scientific sense as well.[10] Principals and teachers can get to know their students, gain a sense for their special needs and talents, and respond accordingly. Administrators cannot. Administrators know students in terms of numbers, categories, rules, summary statistics, theories, and methods, all of which lead to precisely the kind of treatment that parents and students do not want: treatment that is insensitive to what is different or special or unique about them. Bureaucracy inherently requires equal treatment for people who are in fact very different. Schools can recognize and respond to those differences—as long as they are unconstrained by bureaucracy.

In a market setting, then, there are strong forces at work—arising from the technical, administrative, and consumer satisfaction requirements of organizational success—that promote school autonomy. Organizations that want to build and nurture successful schools will have incentives to decentralize authority to the school level. Similarly, schools that exist on their own, as well as individuals and groups that want to start schools from scratch, will tend to find that the requirements of success do not entail highly bureaucratic organization and indeed militate against it.

The advantages of autonomy are weakened when school leaders have agendas of their own that schools are intended to further, regardless of what parents and students might want. In some organizations—churches, for instance—those in charge may prefer "pure" schools to growing, prosperous ones, and the obvious way to see that their schools toe the line is through bureaucratic subordination. In private sector education, however, just as in other market settings, the hierarchical imposition of such an agenda on schools involves a painful trade-off: if schools are constrained in their efforts to please clients, dissatisfied clients can leave. Superiors seeking purity in their schools may consider this an acceptable price to pay, but it is still a price—one that threatens organizational well-being, can be fatal if unchecked, and can be countered by granting the schools a greater measure of autonomy. Thus, even if there are higher-order values to be pursued, market forces still discourage tight hierarchical control in favor of more autonomy. They also tend to weed out, through natural selection, organizations that ignore those market signals.

Politics: Bureaucracy and Hierarchical Control

In the public sector, the institutional forces work in the opposite direction. The raison d'être of democratic control is to impose higher-order values on schools, and thus to limit their autonomy. The schools are not in the business of pleasing parents and students, and they cannot be allowed to set their own agendas. Their agendas are set by politicians, administrators, and the various democratic constituencies that hold the keys to political power. The public system is built to see to it that the schools do what their governors want them to do—that they conform to the higher-order values their governors seek to impose.

Bureaucracy arises naturally and inevitably out of these efforts at democratic control. While most everyone seems to complain

that the public schools are overly bureaucratized, American political institutions give all the major players strong incentives to pressure for more bureaucracy, not less, when official decisions get made about what the schools ought to be doing, who should be doing it, and how. The same people who complain about bureaucracy find that it is their dominant political strategy.

. . .

Central Tendency and Variance

This comparison of politics and markets is an attempt to set out, as simply and clearly as possible, the logical foundations of behavior within each system and their consequences for the organization of schools. Along the way, we have tried to highlight institutional differences by emphasizing the general thrust of the various forces at work. Democratic control tends to promote bureaucracy, markets tend to promote autonomy, and the basic dimensions of school organization—personnel, goals, leadership, and practice—tend to differ in ways that reflect (and support) each sector's disposition toward bureaucracy or autonomy.

Obviously, we do not mean to say that all public schools look and perform alike or that all private schools do. While the most dramatic and theoretically instructive contrasts, in our view, are those that can be drawn across systems by comparing their central tendencies, we are able to draw these contrasts only after arriving at a basic understanding of school organization within each system. The same theory that allows us to understand why organization varies across systems, then, might also be employed to understand why organization varies within them.

The fact is that the central tendencies of each system can be expected to hide a fair measure of organizational variation. Markets tend to promote autonomy, but the population of private schools will not be entirely uniform. If we were to place these schools on a continuum ranging from highly bureaucratic to highly autonomous, we would expect their distribution to be skewed toward the autonomy end of the continuum—but there would still be a distribution, with some schools laboring under many of the bureaucratic constraints we have associated with democratic control. Similarly, were public schools placed along the same continuum, we would expect their distribution to be skewed toward the bureaucratic end—but, again, there would still be a distribution, and some public schools would prove to have many of the "effective school" characteristics we have associated with markets.

Some of the most interesting questions about within-sector variation have to do with these atypical schools, and thus with why some schools in one sector may turn out to look like those typical of the other. While we save most of our examination of these matters for our data analysis, we have already suggested perhaps the most fundamental reason for bureaucratization in the private sector: the imposition of higher-order values. When organizations have fixed values that they seek to pursue—values that are unresponsive to what parents and students want and may be quite inconsistent with the best professional judgment of teachers—they will tend to bureaucratize as a means of constraining behavior toward these ends. The most obvious candidates are churches. Even for churches, however, only some values—having to do with religion, morality, and perhaps discipline—are likely to be fixed; the rest, including those bearing on academics, are not, and thus are unlikely to be pursued through formal constraints.

It is no accident that the imposition of higher-order values should cause some private schools to look like public schools in their organization. The imposition of higher-order values is what democratic control in the public sector is all about, and this, in the final analysis, is why the public schools themselves are so heavily bureaucratic. There are strong forces at work, however, that prevent private schools from going too far in the bureaucratic direction. These are explained by the market and its incentives (backed by sanctions) to please clients and perform effectively. But they are also explained by the absence of bureaucracy-producing factors that are present in the public sector with a vengeance: the struggle to control public authority, the dangers of political uncertainty, the multiple levels of government.

Atypical private schools do not raise the most important questions about school organization, however. Given the crisis atmosphere that currently surrounds public education, the question of most obvious importance is why some public schools develop the kinds of organizations typical of markets. The answer is not that they are somehow able to escape the imposition of higher-order values. As long as public schools are governed by institutions of democratic control, everything about them is subject to the imposition of higher-order values through public authority. This is an institutional fact of life. The key to an answer rests with how public authority actually gets put to use— and why its impositions are different for some schools than for others.

While a comprehensive answer will occupy us, . . . it seems to us that two general conditions—which turn out, in fact, to be largely overlapping in American society— are especially important in this regard, and go a long way toward accounting for organizational variety within the public sector. The first is social homogeneity. The second, for lack of a better phrase, is the absence of serious problems.

Social homogeneity is important because of its relation to political uncertainty. When there are no serious conflicts of interests about important educational issues that set one faction off against another, the threats and costs of political uncertainty are low. This can happen when one group firmly dominates politics, but, more commonly, it should happen when there is simply broad agreement throughout the community about basic matters of educational policy (if not their details). In these settings, groups that succeed in gaining public authority for a time are not driven to formalize in order to protect their achievements from subversion by their enemies; there really are no enemies. Homogeneous politics should tend to have less bureaucratic schools.[11]

Bureaucracy is also inhibited by the absence of serious problems that schools appear incapable of solving on their own. When schools are plagued by problems—poor academic performance, drugs, violence, absenteeism, high drop-out rates—public officials come under intense pressure to take corrective action in the form of new policies. Much the same happens when the schools' problems are seen to be anchored in more fundamental problems that beset their student populations—economic hardship, broken families, poor nutrition, physical handicaps, language difficulties. Here there is pressure for governmental programs that address the educational symptoms of these problems, usually by requiring schools to provide certain kinds of services.

Part of the reason problem-infested environments promote bureaucracy is that they undermine whatever homogeneity may exist. When problems are numerous and truly serious, the political process is hardly a cooperative exercise in analytics. It is a fractious struggle to control public authority—a struggle to determine which problems get addressed, which of many proposed "solutions" will be adopted, how scarce public resources will be allocated, which constituencies will receive money and services, and

which constituencies will pay the bill. Interests are in conflict, the stakes are high—and so are political uncertainty and its corresponding incentives to formalize.

Even in the absence of substantial conflict and political uncertainty, however, those who exercise public authority would still be under strident demands from all sides to "do something" concrete, and they would still have strong incentives to formalize—to create new administrative rules and monitoring requirements—to ensure that schools behave in ways consistent with programmatic and budgetary intentions. This is especially true when state and federal governments are drawn into problem solving, since their at-a-distance control problems are especially severe and the threat of noncompliance especially great. But it is also true for those who exercise authority at the local level, since the predominant view in problem-infested environments is likely to be that the schools are failures that cannot be relied on or entrusted with substantial discretion. Why set them loose so they can fail again? Better to constrain them so they will behave differently—and then hold them formally accountable.

All this is compounded by the more specific effects that problem-plagued schools and environments have on the bureaucratization of personnel. Unions are likely to be stronger and more militant the worse the conditions in which teachers work. They are likely to seek more changes, more protections—and more formalization, since this is the means by which unions get what they want. In addition, the most problem-plagued schools are precisely the ones in the greatest danger of losing their best, most experienced teachers, who tend to use their formal rights within the public system to transfer to more desirable jobs at better schools in more problem-free environments. The consequences are felt throughout the school organization, as problem-plagued schools become more rule-bound in their practices, more difficult for principals to manage, more prone to internal conflict, increasingly drained of the talent they so desperately need—and thus even less capable of solving the severe problems that face them.

Clearly, then, we do not expect all public schools to have the same kinds of organizations. In the abstract, we might simply say that the extent to which individual public schools are bureaucratized depends on how public authority gets used to structure them, which in turn varies according to how homogeneous and problem free their environments are. Schools with homogeneous, problem-free environments should tend to be the least bureaucratic, while schools with highly heterogeneous, problem-filled environments should tend to be the most bureaucratic.

This abstract way of framing our expectations can usefully be restated in much more practical terms, reflecting familiar features of the American social landscape. The nation's large cities are teeming with diverse, conflicting interests of political salience—class, race, ethnicity, language, religion—and their schools are plagued by problems so severe, wide-ranging, and deeply rooted in the urban socioeconomic structure that the situation appears out of control and perhaps even beyond hope. Urban environments are heterogeneous and problem filled in the extreme.[12]

America's suburbs are not free from all this, of course. Suburban schools have also been faced by problems—drugs, especially—that are difficult to conquer. Nonetheless, the contrast between urban and suburban settings as environments for schools is striking. The contrast between urban and rural is perhaps less striking, since some rural areas are more burdened by problems (due to poverty, for instance) than suburban areas. But in general, rural areas should stand in clear contrast to the cities too.

A more concrete and illustrative way of saying how the organization of schools ought to vary within the public sector, then, is that urban schools should be far more bureaucratized than nonurban schools. It is among the latter, and especially among suburban schools, that we should expect to find instances of "effective school" organizations most similar to those associated with markets and private schools.

It is important to stress that the capacity of some public schools to develop reasonably healthy, effective organizations does not imply that all public schools can somehow do so. The fact is, suburban schools are lucky. They are more likely to be blessed with relatively homogeneous, problem-free environments, and, when they are, their organizations should tend to benefit in all sorts of ways as a result. Urban schools do not look like suburban schools because urban environments do not—and in the foreseeable future, obviously will not—look like suburban environments.

Moreover, the fundamental obstacle to effective organization among urban public schools is not their conflictual, problem-filled environments. It is the way democratic control tends to manage and respond to such environments. And this may well prove more troubling than we have indicated thus far. For democratic control threatens to generate a vicious circle of problems and ineffectiveness.[13] Precisely where the problems are the greatest—in poor urban areas—and thus where strong leadership, professionalism, clear missions, and other aspects of effective organization are most desperately needed, public authority will be exercised to ensure that schools are highly bureaucratized. There will be little discretion to allow for strong leadership. Teachers will be unable to participate as professionals. Talent will be drained off. Unions will insist on myriad formal protections. Principals will be hamstrung in their efforts to build a co-operative team. And so on.

The institutions of democratic control are thus likely to respond to serious educational problems by adding to the schools' already disabling bureaucracy—rendering them even less capable of solving the problems that face them. The more poorly the schools perform, the more the authorities are pressured to respond with new bureaucratic constraints, which in turn make the schools still less effective. Hence the vicious circle.

It is worth noting, finally, that even the lucky public schools, the ones with nice environments, do not escape entirely from the bureaucratizing tendencies of democratic control. They are still creatures of public authority, and, for this very fundamental reason, can never really be "like" private schools. Their relative autonomy is tenuous: it can be chipped away or simply destroyed should problems arise that propel the authorities to respond. And even as they enjoy autonomy, they tend to have less real discretion than a market setting would grant them—for their personnel, goals, leadership, and practices are all constrained by formal rules, protections, and requirements that, although less restrictive and troublesome than those for urban schools, are still likely to go beyond what the typical school must endure in a market setting.

This is why it is so important to understand the central tendencies of the two systems and their institutional foundations. The most basic causes of ineffective performance among the nation's public schools are only partially reflected in the differences between urban and nonurban schools, and it is a bit misleading, as a result, to think that we can learn what we need to know by restricting ourselves to an analysis of public schools. In our view, it is really what these public schools have in common—their sub-

ordination to public authority—that is at the root of the system's problems, and that inexorably skews the entire distribution of public schools toward the bureaucracy end of the continuum. Only when we take the public system as a whole and compare it with something else—to a market system, in our case—do these fundamentals and their wide-ranging consequences strikingly stand out.

Conclusion

The theoretical road we have traveled in this chapter has been rather long and complicated, taking us from the institutional foundations of politics and markets to their general implications for bureaucracy and autonomy to their more specific implications for personnel, goals, leadership, and practice. The purpose of all this, however, has been to say something quite simple and general about how schools can be better understood—and how, on that basis, they might be made more effective.

Schools, we believe, are products of their institutional settings. America's public schools are governed by institutions of direct democratic control, and their organizations should be expected to bear the indelible stamp of those institutions. They should tend to be highly bureaucratic and systematically lacking in the requisites of effective performance. Private schools, on the other hand, operate in a very different institutional setting distinguished by the basic features of markets—decentralization, competition, and choice—and their organizations should be expected to bear a very different stamp as a result. They should tend to possess the autonomy, clarity of mission, strong leadership, teacher professionalism, and team cooperation that public schools want but (except under very fortunate circumstances) are unlikely to have.

The primary lesson to be drawn from this comparison is not that private schools are inherently better than public schools. For . . . there is every reason to believe that, with the right governing institutions, the public schools could be disposed to develop these same effective school organizations. The differences between schools in the two sectors do not arise from immutable public-private differences. They arise from institutional differences. And this is the primary lesson. It is a lesson about the pervasive ways in which institutions shape the organization and performance of *all* schools, about the value of understanding schools from an institutional perspective—and about the crucial role that institutions and institutional reform ought to play in the thinking of those who want to improve America's schools.

· · ·

NOTES

1. Max Weber, *The Theory of Social and Economic Organization* (Free Press, 1947); and Charles Perrow, *Complex Organizations: A Critical Essay*, 3d ed. (Random House, 1986).
2. On the merits of politics and markets generally, see especially Charles E. Lindblom, *Politics and Markets: The World's Political Economic Systems* (Basic Books, 1977). On the government use of markets, see Charles L. Schultze, *The Public Use of Private Interest* (Brookings, 1977); and on privatization, see E. S. Savas, *Privatizing the Public Sector: How to Shrink Government* (Chatham, NJ: Chatham House Publishers, 1982).
3. Strictly speaking, the government establishes a legal framework in which private schools must operate, and this framework may include certain standards of operation such as graduation or teacher certification requirements. But the government must, according to a long-standing interpretation of the U.S. Constitution, permit private schools to operate. See *Pierce v. Society of Sisters*, 268 U.S. 510 (1925). Government, nonetheless, regulates private schools to some extent. See Neal E. Devins, ed., *Public Values, Private Schools* (Falmer Press, 1989).

4. This reason is emphasized most often by economists, for example, Milton and Rose Friedman, *Free to Choose: A Personal Statement* (Avon, 1981), pp. 140–78.
5. The concept of exit is developed generally in Albert O. Hirschman, *Exit, Voice, and Loyalty: Responses to Decline in Firms, Organizations, and States* (Harvard University Press, 1970).
6. The importance of natural selection in economic markets was first explicated in Armen A. Alchian, "Uncertainty, Evolution, and Economic Theory," *Journal of Political Economy*, vol. 58 (June 1950), pp. 211–21.
7. See Charles M. Tiebout, "A Pure Theory of Local Expenditures," *Journal of Political Economy*, vol. 64 (October 1956), pp. 416–24; and Paul E. Peterson, *City Limits* (University of Chicago Press, 1981).
8. Attempts to correct market imperfections require the use of public bureaucracy and are themselves subject to "political failures." Government remedies may therefore be less desirable than the imperfections they sought to correct. See, for example, George J. Stigler, "The Theory of Economic Regulation," *Bell Journal of Economics*, vol. 2 (Spring 1971), pp. 3–21.
9. The experiences of school districts with merit pay illustrate the difficulties of arriving at performance measures that are mutually agreeable to school authorities and teachers. See, for example, David K. Cohen and Richard J. Murnane, "The Merits of Merit Pay," *Public Interest*, no. 80 (Summer 1985), pp. 3–30; and Harry P. Hatry and John M. Greiner, *Issues and Case Studies in Teacher Incentive Plans* (Washington, DC: Urban Institute Press, 1985).
10. This is especially true where family circumstances deviate from the professional mainstream, such as in ghettos. See especially Comer, "Educating Poor Minority Children."
11. All may not be well in homogeneous communities either, for all local school systems are embedded in state and federal "communities" that are far more heterogeneous. As higher levels of government, especially the states, take on increasing authority for running local schools, governing weight will shift toward much more heterogeneous politics and increase the pressures for bureaucratization in even the most homogeneous communities. On the growing influence of higher levels of government, see Wirt and Kirst, *Schools in Conflict*, chaps. 9–11.

12. See, for example, Charles Murray, *Losing Ground: American Social Policy 1950–1980* (Basic Books, 1984); and Richard P. Nathan and Charles F. Adams, Jr., "Four Perspectives on Urban Hardship," *Political Science Quarterly*, vol. 104 (Fall 1989), pp. 483–508.

13. On this vicious circle, see John E. Chubb, "Why the Current Wave of School Reform Will Fail," *Public Interest*, no. 90 (Winter 1988), pp. 28–49.

The Politics of School Reform

44

REFORMERS AND REVOLUTIONARIES
The Drama of Deregulation

Peter Cookson

To understand the school choice movement requires a grasp of its political roots and a sensitivity to its philosophical origins; the choice controversy touches on issues that go to the very core of American life. The drama over school choice and public school deregulation has created a public theater where personalities have clashed and ideas have come into conflict. In this chapter, we examine the elements of this drama and create a context by which to place historically, philosophically, and politically the beliefs and passions that characterize the school choice movement.

Thunder on the Educational Right

By the time Ronald Reagan was elected President in 1980, school reform was in the air. Reagan's political agenda for education, however, was unfocused. In general, he supported conservative causes and argued strongly for such policy initiatives as tuition tax credits and private school vouchers. In his campaign, Reagan had suggested that the Department of Education be abolished, charging that it was little more than another example of big-government Democrats' eagerness for spending public monies to make government even bigger. Still, abolishing any department of the federal government is difficult at best. Vested interests become institutionalized, and once institutions take hold in a political environment, they are extremely hard to dislodge or disband. All in all, therefore, the conduct of American education during the first two years of the

Reagan presidency was pretty much business as usual—and the Department of Education survived.

In 1983, however, the National Commission on Excellence in Education, a blue-ribbon panel of educational leaders inside and outside of government, dropped a bombshell by way of its now-famous report *A Nation at Risk*. The picture the commission drew of American education was starkly pessimistic, even ominous: "Our Nation is at risk. Our once unchallenged preeminence in commerce, industry, science and technological innovation is being overtaken by competitors throughout the world. . . . The educational foundations of our society are presently being eroded by a rising tide of mediocrity that threatens our very future as a Nation and a people. . . . We must dedicate ourselves to the reform of our educational system for the benefit of all" (1983:1).

The report resonated with a general sense that, despite Reagan's cheerleading, something was wrong. The future was unclear; new challenges were threatening American smugness as number one. Significantly, the report began, "Our Nation is at risk," not "Our children are at risk." If we were failing, it was in good part because our schools were inadequate. Traditionally, Americans place a great deal of faith in education as a way of saving society from itself. Saviors, however, can easily become scapegoats in times of anxiety and doubt. In any case, the battle cry raised by the commission was echoed by other groups. . . .

In effect, the country in the 1980s and early 1990s engaged in what was possibly the greatest educational debate in its history. This debate can be divided roughly into three periods: 1983 to 1986, 1986 to 1989, and 1989 to the present. The first reform wave stressed the accountability of teachers and students. Forty-five states, for instance, raised their high-school graduation requirements. There was a greater emphasis on the

evaluation of teachers, and some states, like Arkansas, instituted competency tests for teachers (Hess 1992:7). The idea that simply raising standards would lead to greater student learning was, from a learning theory point of view, superficial at best. High jumpers do not break records simply because the level of the bar they are to jump over is raised. It is not surprising, therefore, that despite the attempts to legislate learning, standardized test scores continued to decline. Accountability alone could not transform schools.

The second wave of reform began in 1986, when the Carnegie Forum on Education and the Economy published *A Nation Prepared: Teachers for the Twenty-first Century*. The report called for restructuring schools through the professionalization of teaching and the empowerment of parents and students. Professionalization of teaching was institutionalized in school-based management innovations in such places as Dade County, Florida, and Rochester, New York. Parent and student empowerment resulted in two forms of policy options: radical decentralization and school choice. The most dramatic example of radical decentralization occurred in Chicago. The Chicago Reform Act, signed into law in December 1988, contained a number of elements, but by far its most dramatic component shifted centralized decision making to school-based management through local school councils at each of the city's 542 public schools. Each council is composed of six parents, two community representatives, two teachers, and the principal, elected by their own constituents (Hess 1992:13).

By the end of the decade, however, many educational reformers had come to believe that simply changing the internal organization of schools would not result in greater student learning because the very structure of the schools prohibited learning. What was needed was a transformation of the school systems themselves. The public school monopoly prohibited innovation because it was in the interest of professional educators to maintain the status quo. At this point some educators and policymakers began to suggest that in order to transform American schools, the so-called state monopoly of education would have to be broken. Thus, the reforms of the 1980s could be characterized as a movement from traditional notions of educational reform (such as improved teaching practices) to more radical notions (revamping the entire system). The conditions were ripe for a school choice coalition to emerge and challenge the educational establishment. The success of the new right in reshaping the American political, economic, and educational agenda made the idea of large-scale school choice credible. The philosophical foundations of choice, however, preceded the 1980s by over two hundred years. The concept of consumer sovereignty is embedded in American beliefs about what makes a good and just society.

The Origins of Choice

John E. Coons, law professor at the University of California at Berkeley, believes that school choice is the sword that will cut the Gordian knot of educational mediocrity. Coons has been a critic of the public school system for several decades. His reasons are moral and legal: for him, school choice is a matter of simple justice. "Our system of tax-supported education has for 150 years provided one of the primary embarrassments to America's image as a just society" (Coons 1992:15). Coons was one of the first proponents of a voucher system and has always been concerned with the ethical ends of school choice as well as with the means. In *Scholarships for Children* (1992), he and his colleague Stephen D. Sugarman essentially argue that school choice initiatives must include voucher components that favor the poor. For Coons, choice is an instrument of distributive justice and a medium of expression for the ordinary family; it serves the psychological welfare of the family; and it is the guarantor of a marketplace of ideas. In sum, school choice is synonymous with liberty. For him, the present system disregards family values because the child, in effect, is removed from the family's intellectual and moral beliefs by the government when he or she is placed in a public school. Coons believes that choice is a way of overcoming the divisions between family and state.

Coons, Sugarman, and the constitutional lawyer Stephen Arons have been at the forefront of the part of the educational reform movement that seeks to disestablish the public school system in the name of freedom. They are the latest embodiment of a fundamental belief in individual freedom that goes back to the time of the seventeenth-century social philosopher John Locke. Civil libertarians such as Arons maintain that compulsory education violates individual conscience and the First Amendment to the Constitution. When we force children to attend state-run schools, we are creating a tyranny of mind that hides behind the mask of supposed cultural neutrality. While private schools allow for some freedom, their costs prohibit those who are not wealthy from escaping the public school system. The core belief of libertarians is that every individual is responsible for his or her behavior and that the state has no business controlling the minds of its citizens, young or old. Over one hundred years ago, John Stuart Mill wrote about state-sponsored education as follows: "It is a mere contrivance for molding people to be exactly like one another; and as the mold in which it cast them is that which pleases the predominant power in government, whether this be a monarch, a priesthood, an aristocracy, or the majority of the existing generation, in proportion as it is efficient and successful, it establishes a despotism over the mind" (quoted in Arons 1983:195).

Similar convictions had been aired from the time of the American Revolution. Thomas Paine advocated a voucher system, and the struggle to create a public school system throughout the nineteenth century aroused deep political passions (Ravitch 1974). Arons, whose book *Compelling Belief* documents how public schools can threaten individual conscience, expresses this belief as follows: "The freedoms or powers guaranteed by the First Amendment would be meaningless if government had within its legal power to dictate the desires, values, aspirations, world view, or ethics of individuals seeking to exercise these freedoms or powers. The specifics of the Amendment in any period must, therefore, be interpreted as a right to individual consciousness" (1983:96).

The educational philosopher Jeffrey Kane (1992:50) has echoed Arons's sentiments: "Who is to determine what individual children will know, how they should view the world, how they shall govern their actions with others and understand themselves? Who has the right, through the schools, to guide the emerging intellect and spirit of individual children?" In effect, civil libertarians argue that a sacred core within each human being is debased when the child is forced to attend a school that he or she might not wish to attend. There is a purity and a moral absolutism to these arguments that are appealing. They are, however, slightly misleading because the U.S. Supreme Court in this century has consistently upheld the right of families to send their children to nonpublic schools. The landmark case concerning the autonomy of private schools was *Pierce v. The Society of Sisters* in 1925, which dealt with the issue of whether children in Oregon could be compelled to attend public schools. The state legislature had passed an essentially anti-

Catholic bill that was supported by the Ku Klux Klan. When the U.S. Supreme Court heard the case, it found that "[t]he child is not a mere creature of the State." According to Arons (1983:40), the "Court saw that schooling concerned socialization and development of the individual mind, and refused to make this influence the sole possession of the political majority."

Since the *Pierce* decision, public policy toward private schools has centered on two issues: regulation and funding. Because the American educational system is decentralized, each state has slightly different regulations concerning the operation of private schools, but almost all adopt a hands-off policy. Moreover, private schools do receive public dollars to maintain their programs (Cookson 1991). Another important Supreme Court decision that supports student and parental rights in terms of freedom of choice is *Wisconsin v. Yoder* (1971). Writing for the majority in that case, Chief Justice Warren Berger amplified the right of educational choice. "[The public] high schools tend to emphasize intellectual and scientific accomplishment, self-distinction, competitiveness, worldly success, and social life with other students. Amish society emphasizes informal learning through doing, a life of 'goodness' rather than a life of intellect, wisdom rather than technical knowledge, community welfare rather than competition, and separation from rather than integration with contemporary worldly society" (quoted in Kane 1992:49–50).

Clearly, in principle and to some extent in reality, Americans already have a great deal of educational choice. The problem is that the tuition of private schools, especially good private schools, prohibits those who are not affluent from exercising this right. Thus, it has been argued that unless we provide all families with the financial resources required to attend private schools, certain families are not treated equally under the

law, and this violates both our sense of social ethics and the Fourteenth Amendment to the Constitution. Civil libertarians argue that public education engages in monopolistic practices through compulsory education laws. Interestingly, both the right and the left have labeled the public educational system monopolistic, but for different reasons. To oversimplify slightly, the left tends to see public schools as controlled by the capitalist class. The socialist political economists Samuel Bowles and Herbert Gintis (1976) have argued that public education is little more than a mechanism for reproducing the class structure. Critics from the right accuse the public school system of being a bastion of fuzzy-thinking liberalism, secular humanism, and just plain mediocrity. One wonders, however, if American public education is in fact, as centralized, rationalized, and manipulative as its critics claim. To put the school choice controversy in perspective, it is extremely helpful to ground the discussion in the reality of how American public and private schools are governed and organized.

The Contours of American Education

One of the ironies of the 1980s was that the federal government became deeply involved in educational reform while at the same time arguing against federal involvement in social policy. This is doubly ironic because, in a legal sense, the federal government has very little authority over the public school system; it is the states that are responsible for public education. Moreover, the day-to-day administration of public schools is left to local authorities. Nonetheless, choice advocates inevitably argue that the public school system has historically precluded the right of choice (Everhart 1982). A former governor of Minnesota, Rudy Perpich (1989:A17), has described the public school system as

"autonomous and answerable to virtually no one. Large, hidebound bureaucracies administer school districts of many cities, and often are too removed from the reality of the schoolroom to address the basic problems."

Playing off the title of the historian David Tyack's book *The One Best System* (1974), critics of the public school system have argued that monopolistic practices have destroyed school-based autonomy. Is this true? Between 10 and 11 percent of American elementary and secondary students attend private schools, most of them religious in nature. Public education does not, in a strict sense, monopolize the educational marketplace, although obviously public schools do *dominate* the marketplace. Even within the public sector, however, there is more diversity than the critics of public schools acknowledge. The political scientist John Witte suggests we think of state control as falling on a continuum from "decentralized diversity to monopolistic uniformity" (1990:13). A decentralized and diverse system, he writes, would consist of schools ranging widely in terms of size, age groupings, pedagogy, curriculum, teacher-student interaction, and social affiliations. Schools would be run by local authorities and private groups, and regulations would be held to a minimum. At the other end of the spectrum would be a national system of schools that are standardized in terms of size, grade structure, curriculum, teaching methods, and evaluation. Student achievement and advancement would be uniformly judged, most likely through nationally administered examinations. The central government would be the locus of authority and schools would be financed by national funds. Curiously, in their zeal for criticizing the American system, many school choice advocates hold European and Japanese schools up as models to emulate, although these systems are virtual educational monopolies. Many European states have state-controlled curricula and a national testing policy that ruthlessly sorts and selects students regardless of what type of school they attend.

If we were to place American schools on the continuum suggested by Witte, we would see that the American system is far closer to the decentralized-diversity end of the spectrum than it is to the monopolistic-uniformity end. There are over fifteen thousand public school districts in the United States, comprised of approximately sixty thousand elementary schools and over twenty-three thousand secondary schools (Witte 1990:15). Some public school districts are extremely large, but most have fewer than six hundred students. It is true that in certain urban public school systems, such as New York's, there has been a tendency toward bureaucratic control. The city of New York educates approximately nine hundred thousand students a year, has more cafeterias than Howard Johnson has restaurants, and has a budget of over four billion dollars. New York, however, is not representative of the rest of the United States. Most school systems are much, much smaller and much more integrated into their communities. Research has shown me that, contrary to the image created by public school critics such as Chubb and Moe (1990), most public school administrators are extremely responsive to parents and to the electorate on whom they depend for funds.

Witte also goes on to point out that the "one best system" in fact is highly diverse in terms of the grade organization of schools. For example, 45.6 percent of American secondary schools are organized from grades nine through twelve. This means that the majority of secondary schools are *not* organized in this manner. Moreover, if we examine schools in terms of their student-body composition, we see that there is tremendous variation according to geographic region. For instance, schools in some states, such as Maine, Vermont, New Hampshire, and Iowa,

are almost completely white, while in other states, such as New Mexico, Mississippi, and Hawaii, white children are a minority, and student bodies in several large states, such as California and Texas, are extremely mixed racially. Inner-city schools have student populations that are nearly exclusively African-American, Hispanic, and Asian. Suburban schools tend to have few minorities, and rural schools fewer still. Schools also vary by the social-class composition of their student bodies, which directly reflects the socio-economic composition of their catchment areas.

In terms of curriculum and pedagogy, there are no monopolistic practices in the United States. As Powell, Farrar, and Cohen (1985) point out in *The Shopping Mall High School*, American education is a cacophony of curricula and teaching styles. In most American public schools, teachers have some latitude in determining how and sometimes what they will teach. I have worked in schools where teachers are encouraged to initiate new curricula and expected to adapt their pedagogical style to the needs of the students. It is true that not all public school teachers are highly motivated or imaginative, but the same could be said about private school teachers. In fact, from my research I would have to conclude that, by and large, pedagogical styles in private schools tend to be less imaginative and more "chalk-and-talk" than in public schools.

Furthermore, the authority structure in the American public school system is far from monopolistic. The federal government has no constitutional authority except in the area of enforcing civil rights. State departments of education are notoriously ineffective in ensuring that their regulations are enforced. Superintendents of school districts have little to do with what goes on within the classrooms in their districts, and building principals will tell you that while on paper their authority may look fairly impressive, in reality it is limited by the power of the teachers' unions and the informal norms of American education, according to which the classroom is the teacher's castle. Contrary to the image created by many public school critics, the delivery of educational products in American public schools is controlled not by a cabal of bureaucrats but by millions of teachers, all of whom consider themselves to be major authorities on educational practices. Compared to France, Germany, or Japan, the American public school system is radically decentralized, teacher-driven, and wondrously chaotic.

Notwithstanding the above, American public schools often resemble one another, not because of monopolistic practices, but because they represent the middle-class values that are enshrined in the public culture. Hard work, dependability, and respectability are the principles by which official school cultures are created. But those who have worked in schools also know that the official curriculum must compete with the student culture, which approaches learning with a certain indifference and holds respectability up as a kind of comic facade. American students do not accept authority lightly. The idea that they are victims of a state-monopolized curriculum and pedagogy is so out of keeping with reality that it borders on the ridiculous. Some of our students may be illiterate, and some may be subservient to their teachers, but a visit to any public school should quickly disabuse researchers of the notion that the state's monopoly of education is destroying students' spirits. What is keeping students from realizing their intellectual, artistic, and personal development are those cultural norms that elevate material acquisition over intellectual curiosity. The confusion between cultural uniformity and monopolistic practices has disoriented much of the discussion about school choice because much of the literature related to school choice does not sufficiently acknowl-

edge that most American schools, public and private, are expressions of the dominant American culture, for better or worse.

The Proximate Causes of the School Choice Movement

The well of disappointment about public education was far deeper in the early 1980s than most liberals imagined. Public education was pictured in the media as top-heavy, bureaucratic, and incompetent; moreover, the ideal of integration was threatened by continuing racial segregation. To understand school choice, it is important to return to *Brown v. Board of Education*. In 1954, the Supreme Court ruled that racial segregation could not be constitutionally supported on the basis of the "separate but equal" principle indicated in *Plessy v. Ferguson* (1896). In effect, the Court found that separate was not equal and that minority students in the United States were being deprived of their right of equal protection under the law. The *Brown* decision radically altered American public education. In fact, the first choice schools were "white flight" academies. In their panic to avoid sending their children to school with African-American students, white parents throughout the South withdrew from the public school system and established private academies that were often indirectly publicly funded. *Brown*, however, spoke to an even deeper American dilemma by mandating that public schools be racially integrated; it implicitly called for the redesign of American education. Despite the Court's decision, de facto segregation continued, north and south, because America's neighborhoods are segregated by race and class.

By the 1960s, it was becoming increasingly apparent that de facto segregation was, in the words of the Kerner Commission, creating two societies, one poor and minority, the other white and relatively affluent. Numerous studies called for the reform of public education in the inner cities, and several articulate critics testified to the damage public education was doing to minority students. Jonathan Kozol, in particular, mapped out the terrain of pain with startling clarity. Moreover, writers such as Michael Harrington (1962) showed Americans that poverty continued to exist throughout the country. When Lyndon Johnson became President, he sought to build the "Great Society" by creating an environment of equal opportunity, material abundance, and social justice. Along with Rev. Martin Luther King, Jr., Johnson and other liberals attempted to integrate the country through court decision and legislation. The passions aroused by the war in Vietnam effectively destroyed the political consensus required to make the Great Society a reality. Moreover, the black power movement challenged the integrationist ideal by arguing for separation of the races and for racial pride. The objective was to gain control of the schools in black communities so that they could teach African-American–centered curricula and the values of the local community. In the minds of black power advocates, public schools were little more than extensions of white power, white ideology, and white control. To make matters more confusing, a number of white educational reformers continued to criticize the public school system as morally and intellectually deadening. Many of these critics formed alternative schools in New York and other major cities. As we will see shortly, the alternative-school movement was one of the seeds from which the school choice movement grew.

In the meantime, the economist Milton Friedman (1962) was arguing that by its very nature public education was an affront to the ideals of freedom and marketplace accountability. In essence, Friedman laid the groundwork for an alternative model of school governance that emphasized parental choice and the belief that markets are better arbiters of personal and social good than are state-mandated regulations. During the 1960s, however, Friedman was a lone voice in the policy wilderness. The core consensus was frayed, but still intact. However, he played a critical role in establishing the ideological credibility of Adam Smith's notion of the invisible hand guiding public policy.

We should also keep in mind that public education in the 1970s was quite experimental. In particular, the open classroom was idealized and new curricula such as "Man: A Course of Study" were touted as helping students to grasp the structure of knowledge through "discovery" learning. Teachers' unions, particularly under the leadership of Albert Shanker, became increasingly powerful. Public education seemed to be entering an era of optimism and there was a deep belief in experimentation in those public schools that had the resources to innovate. This sense of relative well-being, however, stood in stark contrast to the continuing educational disaster within the inner city. In particular, forced busing in cities like Boston created racial confrontations that were often violent. Anthony Lukas, in *Common Ground* (1986), documents the trauma of forced busing in Boston. Public education was increasingly politicized and conservatives, in particular, began to question the viability and advisability of using a public school system as an instrument of court-mandated racial integration. In effect, a politics of resentment developed against the liberal core consensus. It was not until 1980, however, that this underground current of hostility broke through the surface of politics as usual; the conservative coalition led by Ronald Reagan challenged the core consensus by arguing against state power and for market power. The ideas of Milton Friedman emerged from the back offices of policy think tanks to take their place in the Oval Office.

Crystallization and Intensification: School Choice Comes of Age

We have already noted that the reform movements of the 1980s had little effect on the overall redesign of American education and that the public school system was battered politically, particularly from the right. With the election of Reagan, the right gained the political power and the platform to wage war against liberal reforms. The new-right conservatives were joined in this struggle by a wide variety of Protestant evangelicals, who characterized public schools as repositories of secular humanism. Highly motivated politically, most evangelicals supported Reagan with a fervor that was just this side of a holy war. They gained informal and formal power in national politics and found new allies in such places as the U.S. Department of Education. During the 1980s, the department shifted its emphasis away from public education and tilted distinctly toward private education and school choice. Virtually all Republican secretaries of education were conservative supporters of school choice, and the most recent one, Lamar Alexander, publicly championed choice without reservation.

The establishment of the Center for Choice in Education within the Department of Education represented the institutionalization of the evangelical impulse and the open acknowledgment of conservative educational causes. Many of the publications the center distributes originate in the Heritage Foundation and other conservative think tanks. One wonders why the federal government is distributing the *Phyllis Schlafly Report*, the personal newsletter of a woman known for her far-right views.

Through the Office of Research and Improvement, the department issued a booklet entitled *Getting Started—How Choice Can Renew Your Public Schools* (1992). The foreword to this document is by Diane Ravitch, a former assistant secretary of education. The center also distributes the work of Joe Nathan, a public school choice pioneer, and of Mary Anne Raywid, an educational philosopher and long-time choice advocate. Also available from the Center for Choice in Education is the literature issued by the Institute for Responsive Education, headed by Evans Clinchy, and several reports published by the Massachusetts Office of Educational Equity, directed by Charles Glenn. The above-mentioned names represent some of the guiding forces of school choice. Their "official" presence at the department demonstrates how intertwined the federal government has become with these special-interest advocates. "Civil Rights and Parental Choice," a report written by the libertarian lawyer Clint Bolick for the Department of Education, concluded that school choice was "every American's birthright—every American's *civil* right" (Bolick 1992:24).

The Department of Education is only one of many Washington-based public policy centers and institutes. Some of these centers have created what amounts to a conservative infrastructure which promotes market solutions to public problems. The Landmark Legal Foundation, a conservative public-interest law firm, for instance, has involved itself in several lawsuits concerning what its members believe to be state infringement on individual freedoms in the areas of public housing, economic liberties, and education. According to Debra Cruel, a former attorney with Landmark, "People long to be noble and nobility is self-governance." She believes that intrinsically American values are slipping away and that people want to be "free—without restraints." The Landmark

Legal Foundation also believes that the poor must lead a movement for individual liberation. An African-American, Cruel takes the position that traditional liberalism has failed to provide equal opportunity for minorities. A small but vocal number of African-Americans have come to question the efficacy of legislated equity. . . . Besides the Landmark Legal Foundation, other conservative advocacy groups such as the Heritage Foundation have showered the media with studies and policy papers creating the impression that choice is highly desired by the American people and is a superior method for reforming schools. As we will see . . . , much of this evidence is questionable.

The Washington lobbying infrastructure includes a variety of private school organizations that are strong advocates of school choice. Prominent among them are the National Association of Independent Schools (NAIS) and the Council for American Private Education. These groups have forged a collaboration with a number of religious and other private education groups, called the National Coalition for the Improvement and Reform of American Education. That most members of the coalition represent religious organizations tells us a great deal about the politics of private school choice. The members include Agudath Israel of America, the American Montessori Society, the Association of Military Colleges and Schools of the United States, Catholic Daughters of America, Catholic Golden Age, Christian Schools International, the Evangelical Lutheran Education Association, the Friends Council on Education, the Institute for Independent Education, the Jesuit Secondary Education Association, the Knights of Columbus, the National Association of Episcopal Schools, the National Association of Private Schools for Exceptional Children, the National Catholic Educational Association, the National Council on Catholic Women, the National Society of Hebrew Day Schools, the Seventh Day Adventist Office of Education, and the United States Catholic Conference (Walsh 1992:23).

Only very recently have private schools attempted to exert political power at the national level on behalf of some choice system. There are many reasons for this, but certainly the most significant is that many private schools are in a precarious financial situation and subsidized voucher programs would enable them to remain open. The viability of many Catholic schools in particular is questionable. In 1992 the Roman Catholic church undertook a mammoth publicity campaign, called "Discover Catholic School 1992." Nationwide, each of the church's 7,291 elementary schools and 1,296 high schools were asked to sell "an array of buttons, T shirts, pins, decals, posters, videos and banners that bear the logo of a proud galleon slicing through the waves, its sail emblazoned with a giant cross" (Allis 1991:48). Moreover, a variety of studies indicating that Catholic schools are superior to public schools in terms of student learning have been integrated into the policy literature and popular press. Nevertheless, Roman Catholic schools have suffered a dramatic enrollment decline—a 46 percent drop in students and a 29 percent drop in schools between the 1960s and the early 1980s (Erickson 1986:86). This trend has continued. At the same time that Catholic schools are suffering significant enrollment declines, other religious schools have been enjoying huge increases. For instance, the number of students in evangelical schools jumped by 627 percent, American Lutheran church schools grew 256 percent, and conservative Jewish schools grew 254 percent (Erickson 1986:87).

In the struggle to capture the minds, hearts, and votes of Americans, the school choice coalition also has been aided by think tanks, interest groups, and individuals who are not based in Washington and do not approach school choice from a religious or other private-school perspective. One of the most prominent and intellectually respected of these advocacy groups is the Manhattan Institute. It has released several studies about the benefits of school choice for poor, inner-city minority children. As we shall see, an examination of these data reveals that much of their evidence is unconvincing. Nonetheless, the Manhattan Institute continues to advocate school choice and is led by some of the country's most prominent banking and corporate executives, university professors, and Republican politicians, as well as a sprinkling of public school administrators and labor leaders. The institute's advisory board reads like a mini-*Who's Who* of the educational and business elite that constitutes the inner circle of the market-oriented school choice movement: Peter Flanigan (managing director, Dillon Read and Co.), Raymond Chambers (chairman, Wesray Capital Corp.), Linda Chavez (senior fellow, Manhattan Institute), John Chubb (founding member, Edison Project), James Coleman (professor of sociology, University of Chicago), A. Wright Elliott (executive vice president, Chase Manhattan Bank), Chester E. Finn, Jr. (founding member, Edison Project), Seymour Fliegel (former deputy superintendent, New York City Community School District 4), Colman Genn (superintendent, New York City Community School District 27), Richard Gilder, Jr. (partner, Gildner, Gagnon, and Co.), Nathan Glazer (professor of education, Harvard University), the Hon. Thomas Kean (president, Drew University), Joe Nathan (senior fellow, Humphrey Institute), Robert S. Peterkin (superintendent, Milwaukee Public Schools), Mary Anne Raywid (professor of education, Hofstra University), and Adam Urbanski (president, Rochester Teachers Association) (Domanico 1991).

However, support for school choice runs far deeper politically than the Washington and New York lobbying establishment. There is virtually no state in the Union in which grass-roots choice organizers have not made their impact on legislative and political processes. . . . Suffice it to say here that without the political pressure that has been brought to bear in each of these states, it is doubtful that these initiatives would have reached the floor of the legislatures. Choice initiatives have touched off ferocious political debates. In Pennsylvania, for instance, the battle for a choice bill was led by the Road to Educational Achievement through Choice (REACH), a coalition headed by the Pennsylvania Catholic Conference. Pitted against the 1991 choice bill was a coalition of twenty organizations led by the state teachers unions, the League of Women Voters, and the American Civil Liberties Union. Observers indicated that the school choice debate in Pennsylvania was even more vitriolic than the controversy that surrounded the legislature's passage of a restrictive abortion law. Threats and counterthreats were exchanged, and, according to one observer, "it was very hardball" (Diegmueller 1992).

Market-oriented reformers draw ideological support from a group of young conservative thinkers who are extremely well placed in the Republican party. These are the advocates of self-help, or the "New Paradigm"—actually a very old paradigm, whose origins can be traced to the market philosophy of Adam Smith. Essentially, the New Paradigm hypothesizes that state intervention to resolve social problems in fact creates more problems because it robs individuals of their freedom of choice, their integrity, and their capacity to influence markets as consumers. A representative of this New Paradigm is Chester E. Finn, Jr., who was called the Bush administration's "education philosopher—and the chief architect of Bush's master plan for fixing schools." Arguing that the "race is to the swift," Finn backs public funding for private schools and believes that competition with private schools will improve public schools. He goes so far as to imply that there is something unpatriotic about opposing private school vouchers: "It is un-American to force students to go to schools that they don't want to attend" (Toch 1991:46).

Choice made its first major national political breakthrough at the National Governors' Conference in 1986. In their report, *Time for Results*, the governors said, "If we first implement choice, true choice among public schools, we unlock the values of competition in the marketplace. Schools that compete for students, teachers, and dollars will, by virtue of the environment, make those changes that will allow them to succeed" (Paulu 1989:14). Three years later the White House held a workshop on school choice. President Bush spoke to the conference in near-reverential terms: "The evidence is striking and abundant. Almost without exception, wherever choice has been attempted—Minnesota, East Harlem, San Francisco, Los Angeles, and a hundred other places in between—choice has worked. . . . Bad schools get better. Good ones get better still, entire school systems have been restored to public confidence by the implementation of these choice plans. Disaffected families have been brought from private schools back into public education. Any school reform that can boast such success deserves our attention, our emphases, and our effort" (25–26). The future secretary of education, Lamar Alexander, also spoke about school choice: "The fact that so many people have come together . . . shows that this movement is kind of beyond all of us. It is bigger than all of us. It will keep going on after us, but perhaps we can do something to nurture it, and that is what we are all here for today" (25). Dennis Doyle, a senior research fellow at the Hudson Institute in Washington, D.C., and a workshop participant, summarized: "There is in the popular mind a vision of

cut-throat competition, of profit-taking buccaneers, swashbuckling across the State, people who are . . . merciless, kind of Atlas Shrugged/Ayn Rand types. Well, there certainly is that type of competition, but there is competition which is closer to home . . . and that is the competition which emphasizes the supremacy of the consumer, consumer sovereignty, and that, in fact, is what competition is all about" (14). Apparently, this deep faith in the marketplace was substantiated for those attending the workshop by fourteen-year-old André Lawrence, who testified, "I was very happy to decide which school I wanted to attend. It was like shopping, buying a pair of shoes, shopping around until you find something you like" (14).

The workshop participants concluded that there was virtually no educational problem that could not be solved by choice and that choice produces at least eight benefits (Paulu 1989:11–24):

1. Choice can bring basic structural change to our schools.
2. Schools of choice recognize individuality.
3. Choice fosters competition and accountability.
4. Choice can improve educational outcomes.
5. Schools of choice can keep potential dropouts in school and draw back those who have already left.
6. Schools of choice increase parents' freedom.
7. Choice plans increase parent satisfaction and involvement in the schools.
8. Schools of choice can enhance educational opportunities, particularly for disadvantaged parents.

President Bush included several provisions for school choice in his plan for reforming education called "America 2000." This proposal included a two-million-dollar education certificate support fund and a thirty-million-dollar fund for creating "National School Choice Demonstration Projects." If, however, one had to choose a single document that captured the imagination of the choice movement and legitimated the idea of school choice to the news media and, hence to the public at large, it would have to be *Politics, Markets, and American Schools* by the political scientists John E. Chubb and Terry M. Moe. . . . Essentially, Chubb and Moe believe that the natural operations of markets will drive out bad schools and reward good schools. They maintain that "markets offer an institutional alternative to direct democratic control," adding, "Without being too literal about it, we think that reformers would do well to entertain the notion that choice *is* a panacea. . . . Choice is a self-contained reform with its own rationale and justification. It has the capacity *all by itself* to bring about the kind of transformation that, for years, reformers have been seeking to engineer in myriad other ways. Indeed, if choice is to work to greatest advantage, it must be adopted *without* these other reforms, since the latter are predicted on democratic control and are implemented by bureaucratic means (1990:167, 217). Chubb and Moe address the question, Why are markets so effective? "A market system is not built to enable the imposition of higher-order values on the schools, nor is it driven by a democratic struggle to exercise public authority. Instead, the authority to make educational choices is radically decentralized to those most immediately involved. Schools compete for the support of parents and students, and parents and students are free to choose among schools. The system is built around decentralization, competition, and choice" (189).

By 1990, choice had won the moral and research high ground. A significant national movement had emerged beyond the Washington Beltway. Choice had caught the imagination of educational reporters; it was and is front-page news. Politicians saw choice as a way of reforming education without spending much money; choice also seemed to resonate with a cultural milieu that placed consumership at the center of the good life.

Voice, Exit, and Reform

We have examined how the school choice movement arose and entertained some speculations about why it did so in the 1980s. I have suggested that school choice is similar to a social issue. The 1980s were a time when markets seemed to triumph and individuals did not have to feel guilty about feathering their own nests. Privatization was and is a social policy and a cultural movement. The middle class, in particular, increasingly withdrew their support from public institutions, choosing "exit" over "voice" as a way of maximizing their interests (Hirschman 1970). By abandoning public institutions, the middle class could no longer influence public policy or participate in shaping the public agenda. The emphasis on the marketplace fed into a belief system in which a commodification of life seemed compatible with the good life. At the same time massive immigration from South America, Eastern Europe, and the Caribbean pressured the middle class to create their own educational enclaves. The fundamentalists were repelled by secular humanism and by a public school system that seemed to have lost faith with basic values. The melting-pot ideal that had animated belief in public education slipped from public consciousness, so that collective responsibilities were easy to deny. A large number of school choice lobbying groups arose throughout the country and placed the issue on the policy agenda. This is the stage upon which the school choice drama was set.

REFERENCES

ALLIS, SAM. 1991. "Can Catholic Schools Do It Better?" *Time,* May 27, pp. 48–49.

ARONS, STEPHEN. 1983. *Compelling Belief: The Culture of American Schooling.* New York: McGraw-Hill.

BOLICK, CLINT. 1992. "Civil Rights and Parental Choice." Unpublished paper.

BOWLES, SAMUEL AND HERBERT GINTIS. 1976. *Schooling in Capitalist America.* New York: Basic Books.

CHUBB, JOHN E. AND TERRY M. MOE. 1990. *Politics, Markets, and America's Schools.* Washington, DC: Brookings Institution.

COOKSON, PETER W., JR. 1991. "Private Schooling and Equity: Dilemmas of Choice." *Education and Urban Society* 23(2):185–99.

COONS, JOHN E. 1992. "School Choice as Simple Justice." *First Things,* pp. 15–22.

COONS, JOHN E., AND STEPHEN D. SUGARMAN. 1992. *Scholarships for Children.* Berkeley, CA: Institute of Governmental Studies Press.

DIEGMUELLER, KAREN. 1992. "Despite Defeat, Choice Bill Likely to Resurface in PA." *Education Week,* January 8, p. 31.

DOMANICO, RAYMOND. 1989. *Model for Choice: A Report on Manhattan's District 4.* New York: Manhattan Institute Center for Educational Innovation.

———. 1991. *A Model Public School Choice Plan for New York City School Districts.* New York: Manhattan Institute Center for Educational Innovation.

ERICKSON, DONALD A. 1986. "Choice and Private Schools: Dynamics of Supply and Demand." Pp. 82–109 in *Private Education: Studies in Choice and Public Policy,* edited by Daniel C. Levy. New York: Oxford University Press.

EVERHART, ROBERT B. 1982. *The Public School Monopoly: A Critical Analysis of Education and State in American Society.* San Francisco, CA: Pacific Institute.

FRIEDMAN, MILTON. 1962. *Capitalism and Freedom.* Chicago, IL: University of Chicago Press.

HARRINGTON, MICHAEL. 1962. *The Other America.* New York: Macmillan.

HESS, G. ALFRED, JR. 1992. "Too Much Democracy or Too Little?" Unpublished manuscript.

HIRSCHMAN, A. O. 1970. *Exit, Voice and Loyalty: Responses to Decline in Firms, Organizations and States.* Cambridge, MA: Harvard University Press.

KANE, JEFFREY. 1992. "Choice: The Fundamentals Revisited." Pp. 46–64 in *The Choice Controversy,* edited by Peter W. Cookson, Jr. Newbury Park, CA: Corwin.

LUKAS, ANTHONY J. 1986. *Common Ground.* New York: Vintage.

NATIONAL COMMISSION ON EXCELLENCE IN EDUCATION. 1983. *A Nation at Risk: The Imperative for Educational Reform.* Washington, DC: U.S. Government Printing Office.

PAULU, NANCY. 1989. *Improving Schools and Empowering Parents: Choice in American Education.* Washington, DC: U.S. Government Printing Office.

PERPICH, RUDY. 1989. "Choose Your School." *New York Times,* March 6, p. A17.

POWELL, ARTHUR G., ELEANOR FARRAR, AND DAVID K. COHEN. 1985. *The Shopping Mall High School.* Boston, MA: Houghton Mifflin.

RAVITCH, DIANE. 1974. *The Great School Wars.* New York: Basic Books.

TOCH, THOMAS. 1991. "The Wizard of Education." *U.S. News and World Report,* July 15, p. 46.

TYACK, DAVID B. 1974. *The One Best System: A History of American Urban Education.* Cambridge, MA: Harvard University Press.

WALSH, MARK. 1992. "Private-School, Religious Groups Join to Back President's Choice Proposal." *Education Week,* January 29, p. 23.

WITTE, JOHN F. 1990. "Choice and Control in American Education: An Analytical Overview." Pp. 11–46 in *Choice and Control in American Education,* vol. 1, *The Theory of Choice and Control in Education,* edited by William F. Clune and John F. Witte. New York: Falmer.

45

THE MANUFACTURED CRISIS
Myths, Fraud, and the Attack on America's Public Schools

David Berliner • Bruce Biddle

. . .

Mounting Problems

The popularization of American schools and colleges since the end of World War II has been nothing short of phenomenal, involving an unprecedented broadening of access, an unprecedented diversification of curricula, and an unprecedented extension of public control. In 1950, 34 percent of the American population twenty-five years of age or older had completed at least four years of high school, while 6 percent of that population had completed at least four years of college. By 1985, 74 percent of the American population twenty-five years of age or older had completed at least four years of high school, while 19 percent had completed at least four years of college. . . . It was in many ways a remarkable achievement, of which Americans could be justifiably proud. Yet it seemed to bring with it a pervasive sense of failure.

—Lawrence Cremin (*Popular Education and Its Discontents*, 1990, pp. 1–2)

The twenty-five years following World War II were unique in American history. These years generated not only a booming economy but also a huge expansion of public

education. During this period enrollment in America's high schools increased by 50 percent or more, and American colleges and universities more than doubled their capacities. At the end of this period, the United States had an educational system that was the envy of the world for the opportunities it offered to a much-expanded range of Americans.

Unfortunately, the same decades also generated problems for education that Americans found difficult to solve or, in some cases, even to think about clearly. These problems increased sharply during the 1970s, and by the end of the decade, American education was facing a number of dilemmas that called for careful analysis and remedial action. Unfortunately, neither was to be provided. Most of these dilemmas have yet to be resolved, and many have become worse.

For one thing, by the 1970s Americans were beginning to suspect that public schools could not fulfill the many expectations that had been expressed for them in the 1950s and 1960s. Those earlier years were a period of great optimism in America. The expansion of education that took place then was often justified by claims about the ability of public schools to accomplish a huge range of tasks. In those years schools were seen not only as providers of knowledge and cultural uplift but also as centers for hobby and recreational interest, objects of ethnic or community pride, solvers of social problems, purveyors of services for individuals and their families, and engines of economic growth. In retrospect, many of these expectations were unrealistic, but this was not understood at the time. And when the economy soured and social problems soared in the 1970s, these expectations became standards against which schools were judged and found wanting.

This dilemma was compounded because American schools were not provided funds with which to finance their expanded programs. As a rule, expansions in the 1950s and 1960s were matched by increased funding, but as the economy turned sour in the 1970s, Americans became less willing to fund the expansions in education that they still wanted. As a result, funding for education became strained, per-capita expenditures for primary and secondary education began to fall, and eventually they came to lag behind those in other Western nations. American educators were not unaware of this problem, of course, and by the mid-1970s, they were issuing anguished calls for additional tax dollars to match the expanded programs they were still being asked to provide.

Unfortunately, those calls were not answered. Instead, the 1970s brought not only economic stagnation but also increases in other demands for tax dollars, particularly those associated with medical care, entitlement programs, public aid, and debt servicing. And if this were not enough, by the late 1970s, America was in the grip of a serious inflation, which meant that each year the public schools had to plead for increased tax support merely to keep abreast of their mounting costs. (Like the Red Queen in *Through the Looking Glass,* the schools had to run as hard as they could merely to stand still.) By the end of the decade, then, public education in America was facing not only a loss of confidence but also the annual need to beg for additional funds from an increasingly strained public purse.

The expansion of American education had also generated dilemmas concerning curricula and educational standards. Prior to World War II, about 50 percent of all students in the country dropped out of high school be-

fore graduation, and only 20 percent actually entered higher education. This meant that in those years it was thought appropriate that public high schools conducted tracking programs in which a quarter of their students were selected for "college preparation" and were required to take a tough, focused curriculum; "vocational" curricula were provided for another quarter; and "general education" was offered to the remainder (who would shortly leave school). Contrast this with today's high school, where any student who withdraws from school before graduation is stigmatized as a "dropout," *all* students are encouraged to consider at least some form of post-secondary education, and tracking programs are widely questioned.

As time passed, American high schools also made curricular adjustments to accommodate the wider range of students they were now to serve. Some schools began to offer a broader range of courses, many focused on "soft" subjects (such as civics, health, personal development, or recreation), and some changed the contents of core courses so as to make them more "interesting." Many also began to relax their requirements and academic standards to encourage students to remain in school as long as possible. Thus, in many schools students with potential interests in college were no longer required to take foreign courses, four years of English, or three years of science and mathematics—which had been the norm for college-bound students in earlier years—and grading procedures were modified to make academic failure less likely.

These adjustments were controversial, of course. Parents with degrees in higher education could remember the tough, focused requirements and standards they had had to meet when preparing for college, and they became alarmed by new policies that were apparently "shortchanging" their children. Debates concerning curricula and standards had become common in school boards and state legislatures by the late 1970s. Moreover, some people began to reason that the "declining academic standards" of American high schools would inevitably generate a matching decline in academic achievement. (Such reasoning made untenable assumptions, of course. It ignored the fact that the earlier tough curricula had *never* been applied to the majority of students and assumed that high school students will only achieve if *forced* to do so by tough requirements. Repeated studies have shown that students are more likely to achieve when they are offered materials that are interesting and relevant to their needs than when they are coerced.)

As schools expanded their programs, they also came under pressure to provide better opportunities for blacks, Hispanics, women, students with disabilities, and other "minorities" who had been underrepresented among college-bound elites in earlier years. This was, of course, a threat to older people who had been members of those elites, since "social groups possessing a relatively rare and highly valued commodity that establishes their superiority over other groups are reluctant to see that commodity more widely distributed."[1] And if this weren't bad enough, in the late 1970s these pressures were often generated by court decisions and the federal government, which had the effect of reducing the powers of local school boards or of challenging the prejudices of powerful groups in local communities. (Court decisions and federal programs designed to promote racial desegregation, for example, were often resented by prejudiced white school boards.) By the late 1970s, then, some traditional power-holders were being threatened by changes in the public schools that they felt they could no longer control.

Finally, for years America has suffered from serious social problems that place pressures on public schools. Several of these problems escalated significantly in the 1970s. Violence and drug use increased, the urban centers of American cities were decaying, and poverty among America's children was growing. As a result, educators forced to cope with these problems were coming under increased pressure, and since they were not provided with extra resources to help them cope, their schools and programs often deteriorated.

By the end of the 1970s, then, American education was suffering from many dilemmas—dilemmas perceived somewhat differently by educators, school boards, suburbanites and urban dwellers, legislators, minorities, elite groups, bigots, ideologues, and other sets of concerned citizens. Most would have agreed, however, that public schools were then suffering from problems that needed attention. Thus, many Americans were becoming worried about education, and this worry set the stage for the critics and their actions.

The Entitlement of Reactionary Voices

If the 1960s go down in history as the decade of liberal educational reform, the 1980s will most likely be known as the decade of conservative restoration. Although many reforms were eroding by the late 1970s, they came under direct assault in the 1980s, especially after the election of Ronald Reagan.
   —FRED L. PINCUS ("The Rebirth of Educational Conservatism," 1984, p. 152)

Surely a major reason for increased criticism of schools in the 1980s was that reactionary voices were given more credence in America during that decade. When Americans elected Ronald Reagan, and afterwards George Bush, to the presidency, they made the expression of right-wing ideologies fashionable. Ideologues on the right had long been critical of the public schools, and once avowed conservatives were in the White House, those criticisms were granted legitimacy and given prominence by the press. This was, indeed, a break with recent history.

It's useful to look at the events that encouraged these reactionary ideas. America has always supported conservative notions; indeed, for years political thought in the United States has generally been to the right of political thought in other advanced countries. Early in the 1970s, however, a number of wealthy people with sharply reactionary ideas began to work together to promote a right-wing agenda in America. Their major tools for this were a set of well-funded family foundations such as the Adolph Coors Foundation and the John M. Olin Foundation among others. For the past two decades, these foundations have undertaken various activities to "sell" reactionary views: funding right-wing student newspapers, internships, and endowed chairs for right-wing spokespersons on American campuses; supporting authors who write books hostile to American higher education; attempting to discredit social programs and other products of "liberal" thought; supporting conservative religious causes; lobbying for reactionary programs and ideologies in the federal Congress; and so forth.[2]

From the beginning, these same foundations have also invested heavily in think tanks or institutes that can be counted on to express ideas—organizations such as the Heritage Foundation, the Hudson Institute, the American Enterprise Institute, the Hoover Institution, the Manhattan Institute, and the Madison Center for Educational Affairs. Over the past twenty years, these organizations have had a remarkable impact in America—in part, because they are well funded; in part, because they are able to make use of the press; and in part, because they have provided an alternative public

forum for prominent people who had also served, or would later serve, in key federal posts. The rhetoric they produced certainly helped to propel Ronald Reagan into the presidency, and even today the propaganda they generate commands significant press attention.

Despite its successes, this reactionary movement is not a monolith but actually represents a variety of ideological strands. These include, for example: classical conservatism a la Edmund Burke; "economic rationalism"; defense of the rich; religious fundamentalism; suspicion of the federal government; hostility to public education and the academy (in general) and to social research (in particular); and racial, sexist, and ethnic bigotry. Most analysts have identified several groups within this movement, and we distinguish here among three of them that have expressed somewhat different views about education: the *Far Right,* the *Religious Right,* and *Neoconservatives.*

The Far Right

A faction that had great influence during the early Reagan years is the Far Right (sometimes called the New Right, the Radical Right, or the Reactionary Right). One of the Far Right's major voices is the Heritage Foundation, and at earlier points we've quoted some of that Foundation's questionable opinions about education. Far Righters such as Edwin Meese and David Stockman were prominent within the early Reagan White House, Orrin Hatch and Jesse Helms can still be counted on to express Far Right ideas in the United States Senate, and some Far Right tenets have appeared in Rep. Newt Gingrich's "Contract with America."

In general, the Far Right blames the federal government for most of the problems facing American schools today. Fred Pincus, for example, quotes the following from the Heritage Foundation:

The most damaging blows to science and mathematics education have come from Washington. For the past 20 years, federal mandates have favored "disadvantaged" pupils at the expense of those who have the highest potential to contribute positively to society. . . . By catering to the demands of special-interest groups—racial minorities, the handicapped, women, and non-English-speaking students—America's public schools have successfully competed for government funds, but have done so at the expense of education as a whole.[3]

Such views reveal hostility both to the public sector and to the interests of minorities in American society.

Given such beliefs, a major goal of the Far Right has been to decentralize education so that all federal involvement in education is abolished or "returned" to the states or local communities. At a minimum, this means abolishing the Department of Education, closing down federal support for educational research, eliminating funds for categorical grants in education that support minorities, and reducing the influence of federal courts.

In addition, some from the Far Right seem to believe that *all* public expenditures are inherently feckless or pernicious (pick one) and advocate reducing the entire public sector as a matter of policy. This has led to all sorts of proposals for privatization—e.g., of the post office, of the TVA, of state prisons, of welfare services, and the like—proposals that have become more strident since the demise of communist governments in the former Soviet Union, where central planning had been excessive. And if other citizen services are to be privatized, why exempt the schools, which consume such a large portion of public funds? In particular, economists of the Far Right (such as Milton Friedman) have

argued that public-school districts should be replaced by a "free market" of competing private schools that are supported through tax credits or vouchers.[4]

Regarding the interests of "minorities," the Far Right argues that increased federal control has allowed powerful "vested interests" to have excessive influence in schools and that balance will not be restored until control over schools is "returned" to the states or local communities. (The vested interests they have cited include, for example, teachers' unions, educational associations, and federal bureaucrats; racial, religious, and ethnic minorities; women, the disabled, and homosexuals—indeed, presumably, anyone who is not WASP, male, and straight.)

To see how these ideas were expressed at the beginning of the Reagan years, we turn to a document designed to affect the president's early policies. In the second half of 1980, shortly before his election as president, Ronald Reagan appointed an Education Policy Advisory Committee that was to prepare a private set of recommendations for the new administration. This group was chaired by W. Glenn Campbell, director of the Hoover Institution, and we have been given a document dated October 22, 1980, that is labeled a "tentative draft" of the committee's report. We have been unable to locate a copy of the submitted report, but Glenn Campbell has assured us that it followed the "tentative draft" closely.[5] This "tentative draft" offers good insights into how the Far Right viewed education during this crucial period.

As one reads the "tentative draft," one is struck by how many of the myths and themes of the Manufactured Crisis it expresses. Educational achievement is reported to have declined sharply in America, and SAT and NAEP data are said to confirm this decline. Constant-dollar educational expenditures are said to have tripled in recent years. Discipline is said to have broken down in the schools. And these problems are seen as the product of federal interference that favors unruly minorities, bilingualism, and persons with disabilities; encourages mediocrity; and slights talented students. Public schools are called weak because they enjoy monopoly status, while private schools are stronger because they must compete in the marketplace. Educational research is "largely propaganda." Standards are falling and costs are rising in higher education because of federal harassment and because of the imposition of racial and ethnic quotas. And to solve these problems, the "tentative draft" suggests abolishing the Department of Education, restricting categorical grants in education, reining in the courts, and funding voucher plans to encourage private schools.

Members of the Education Policy Advisory Committee presumably had reason to expect good things from these recommendations. Candidate Ronald Reagan had already proposed to abolish the Department of Education and was known to favor school vouchers. As it turned out, however, the committee had less initial effect on administration policy than the Far Right had hoped. President Reagan's first secretary of education was Terrel Bell, former U.S. commissioner for education; and Terrel Bell did *not* favor abolishing the Department of Education. In addition, educational issues were not high on the president's early list of concerns. As a result, Bell was able to block some of the Far Right agenda.[6] Nevertheless, advocates for the Far Right remained prominent in the early Reagan White House, and they influenced education policy in various ways both during the Terrel Bell years and afterwards. Even today, some claims and beliefs of Far Right rhetoric may be detected in documents released by the Department of Education.

The Religious Right

A second reactionary faction, the Religious Right, also became prominent in the early Reagan years. The core of this movement seems to be represented by the Religious Roundtable, a network of leaders who help to coordinate its activities. Prominent figures associated with it include Jerry Falwell, Tim LeHay, Mel and Norma Gabler, and former presidential candidate Pat Robertson. Although the Religious Right did not secure "insider" positions in either the Reagan or Bush administrations, both administrations were beholden to it for political support and paid lip service to some of its ideas. The Religious Right also remains active today and wielded considerable influence at the 1992 Republican National Convention.

In general, the Religious Right argues that federal controls have been used to deny students the "right" to pray in schools; to restrict unfairly the teaching of "scientific creationism"; to encourage the appearance of "dirty," "anti-family," "pro-homosexual," and "anti-American" books in school curricula; and to enforce "cultural relativity" in courses on values and sex education. In the typical rhetoric of religious fundamentalists, these "evils" are bundled together as "secular humanism," a catch-all phrase that refers to educational philosophies that are "human-centered rather than God-centered."[7] Such "evils," they believe, can be countered only by doing away with federal controls in education or, paradoxically, by promoting federal laws or constitutional amendments that prohibit the government from imposing "secular humanism" on public schools.

In addition, advocates among the Religious Right argue that because public schools are *inevitably* used to promote "secular humanism," they are iniquitous and should be abolished completely! You might think that we're exaggerating this argument to make a point, but we aren't. According to one Religious Right advocate, Robert Thoburn,

> I imagine every Christian would agree that we need to remove the humanism from the public schools. There is only one way to accomplish this: to abolish the public schools. We need to get the government out of the education business. According to the Bible, education is a parental responsibility. It is not the place of the government to be running a school system.[8]

And how should "Christians" proceed to dismantle public education? They are urged to take all legitimate actions to hamper and discourage public schools, such as arguing against them in public debates and voting No in all school-bond elections. Moreover, "subversive" actions are also encouraged:

> Christians should run for the school board. This may sound like strange advice. After all, I have said that Christians should have nothing to do with the public schools. What I meant was that Christians should not allow their children to have anything to do with public schools. This does *not* mean that we should have nothing to do with them. . . . Our goal is not to make the schools better. . . . The goal is to hamper them, so they cannot grow. . . . Our goal as God-fearing, uncompromised . . . Christians is to *shut down the public schools,* not in some revolutionary way, but step to step, school by school, district by district.[9]

So, apparently, running for the school board under false colors would also be an acceptable means, given that the end is "pure."

Recommendations of the latter type held little charm for Ronald Reagan or George Bush, but both tried to accommodate Religious Right educational interests in their policies. Both made speeches favoring school prayer and "family values." Moreover, both argued that federal funds should be used to support religious schools through vouchers or other means. And the ideology of the Religious Right has clearly promoted dissatisfaction with public education over the years, thus also helping set the stage for the Manufactured Crisis.

The Neoconservatives

By the mid-1980s, a third faction had begun to emerge that claimed to represent "centrist" conservative thought, the Neoconservatives. Many people associated with the Neoconservative movement have had ties to the American Enterprise Institute, another conservative think tank, and their ideas often appear in *Public Interest, Commentary,* or (more recently) *The New Republic.* In addition, a set of influential Neoconservatives—William Bennett, Chester Finn, Lamar Alexander, and Diane Ravitch—came to dominate federal education policy during the late Reagan years and the Bush administration.

In general, Neoconservatives argue that American schools have suffered from two serious problems: a history of social experiments concerned with peripheral issues that made too many demands on schools and diverted them from their basic missions, and excessive federal intervention to promote educational equity. As a result, they argue, academic standards and discipline have eroded, and basic achievements in American schools have fallen and now lag behind those of other countries. This threatens both the moral integration of the nation and its ability to compete with other industrialized countries.

Neoconservatives also prescribe various steps that should be taken to meet these problems: schools should recommit themselves to academic excellence and require a larger number of basic-skills courses; higher academic standards should be encouraged through tougher grading procedures and national tests of student achievement; schools should maintain discipline and reassert their rights to discharge students who cannot meet reasonable standards for behavior; stress should be given to competitiveness and other values thought to be "traditional" in America; and greater effort on the part of teachers should be encouraged through merit pay, competency testing, and stronger requirements for teacher certification. Above all, schools and educators should be made "accountable"; they should be required to provide objective evidence of their accomplishments.

Neoconservatives also generally oppose the concepts of educational or hiring quotas for minorities as "reverse discrimination" and argue that the federal government has already "taken care of" most problems of educational equity. (This may come as surprising news to the many thousands of educators who today serve the needs of minority students in desperately underfunded schools in urban ghettos and isolated rural areas.) In contrast with the Far Right, however, Neoconservatives favor a strong educational role for the federal government to ensure that schools carry out their mission. In addition, Neoconservatives have been ambivalent about private schools, some (James Coleman, for example) urging that the federal government provide increased support for the private sector, others (such as the Twentieth Century Fund Task Force) arguing that "provision of free public education must continue to be a public responsibility of high priority, while support of nonpublic education should remain a private obligation."[10]

Neoconservative ideas were not new in the 1980s, but they emerged influentially during the later Reagan years and the Bush administration. A good deal of recent criticism of the schools reflects Neoconservative tenets.

Common Ideas

Despite their obvious differences, the three conservative ideologies we have reviewed share basic ideas about American education. All three are offended by recent changes in public schools and would like to return to mythic "golden years," when schools were more to their liking. All believe that public education has recently "deteriorated." All tend to be intolerant of the interests of minorities in education. All share a profound mistrust of both educators and students. (The former are never portrayed as trustworthy professionals; the latter are never thought to be capable of self-motivated learning.) And all blame "defects" in the public schools for problems in the larger society and propose changes in federal policy that will presumably cure those problems.

Moreover, spokespersons for both Far Right and Neoconservative positions argue that academic achievement has declined in recent years in American schools, and, given the dominance of these ideologies within the Reagan and Bush administrations, it is small wonder that those administrations promoted the myths that we tackle.... Ideologues committed to these beliefs had little reason to challenge simplistic "evidence" that public education was in trouble, and in the Reagan and Bush years they were provided marvelous opportunities to sell these beliefs from the bully pulpit of the White House.

Since the defeat of George Bush in 1992, reactionary rhetorics about education have been given less attention. Nevertheless, many Americans (including leaders in the Clinton administration) have embraced some ideas from these rhetorics, and the congressional elections of 1994 resurrected many conservative tenets. So educators may have to contend with the debris of reactionary educational thought for some time to come. Thus, it is worthwhile pointing out that, since they reflect prejudices against minorities and tend to ignore or misunderstand the *real* problems of American schools, rightwing educational agenda are usually misguided and are often dangerous. To quote Fred Pincus:

> Like the more humane liberal policies of the 1960s and 1970s, [conservative] educational policies have their own contradictions. In a society characterized by racism, class conflict, and economic stagnation, there is little that the schools can do to help create a better society. Liberal policies can make things less bad and create limited avenues of upward mobility for a few individuals. Conservative policies will simply lead to the reproduction of a blatantly inequitable social system.[11]

"A Nation at Risk," The Human Capital Ideology, and CRISIS Rhetorics

> *Since 1983 the United States has been besieged by a series of reports that severely criticize the nation's public school system. In prose befitting a public relations firm preparing the nation for war, the reports discover massive problems in the schools and recommend hundreds of solutions that, taken together, would cost about as much money as a major war.*
> —RON HASKINS, MARK LANIER, AND DUNCAN MACRAE, JR. (The Commission Reports and Strategies of Reform, 1988, p. 1)

As far as the public was concerned, the Manufactured Crisis began on April 26, 1983—the date when, amidst much fanfare,

the Reagan White House released its critical report on the status of American schools, *A Nation at Risk.* In many ways this report was the "mother of all critiques" of American education. The bashing of public education has long been a popular indoor sport in America, but never before had criticism of education appeared that

- was sponsored by a secretary of education in our national government;
- was prepared by such a prestigious committee;
- was endorsed by a president of the United States;
- made such explicit charges about a supposed recent, tragic decline of American education—charges said to be confirmed by both longitudinal and comparative studies;
- asserted that because of this putative decline of education the nation was losing its leadership in industry, science, and innovation;
- assigned blame for said decline to inadequacies in teaching programs and inept educators; and
- packaged its messages in such flamboyant prose.

To illustrate merely the last of these wonders, on its first page the report asserted:

> Our Nation is at risk. Our once unchallenged preeminence in commerce, industry, science and technological innovation is being overtaken by competitors throughout the world. . . . The educational foundations of our society are presently being eroded by a rising tide of mediocrity that threatens our very future as a nation and a people. . . . If an unfriendly foreign power had attempted to impose on America the mediocre educational performance that exists today, we might well have viewed

it as an act of war. As it stands, we have allowed this to happen to ourselves. . . . We have, in effect, been committing an act of unthinking, unilateral educational disarmament.[12]

This was heady stuff. *Never* before had such trenchant rhetoric about education appeared from the White House. As a result, the press had a field day, tens of thousands of copies of *A Nation at Risk* were distributed, and many Americans thereafter read or heard, for the first time, that our public schools were "truly" failing.

Terrel Bell was then secretary of education. Bell had previously helped to prevent Reaganaughts from dismantling the federal Department of Education. Why, then, did he sponsor the committee that prepared this alarming report? At an individual level, it appears that Bell sincerely believed in the simple idea that "declining academic standards" in American high schools inevitably meant that achievement had also declined, and he felt he had to do "something" to awaken concern for education within the White House.[13] At a deeper level, however, *A Nation at Risk* merely gave public voice to charges about education that right-wing ideologues had already been telling one another. Thus, it served to publicize tenets of conservative educational thought and was, as a result, embraced with enthusiasm by right-wing troops in the Reagan White House. (Actually, their enthusiasm was tempered. *A Nation at Risk* also called for raising the salaries of teachers and for increased federal funding of education, but these recommendations were conveniently ignored by the White House.)

The White House was not alone, however, in sponsoring critiques of public schools in the early 1980s. The same years also produced an explosion of independently generated books and commission reports about American education, some well meaning and scholarly, some not, *all critical.* Consider just the titles of some of these documents:

- *High School: A Report on Secondary Education in America*
- *A Place Called School: Prospects for the Future*
- *America's Competitive Challenge: The Need for a National Response*
- *Action for Excellence: A Comprehensive Plan to Improve Our Nation's Schools*
- *Making the Grade*
- *Business and Education: Partners for the Future*
- *Horace's Compromise: The Dilemma of the American High School*
- *Investing in Our Children: Business and the Public Schools*[14,15]

Why did so many highly critical reports about American education suddenly appear in the early 1980s? In part, these works expressed legitimate concerns. But they also reflected the blossoming of conservative ideologies then underway. In addition, many of these works revealed concerns about an economic crisis thought to be pending for American business, coupled with a belief that this crisis was linked to changes needed in education.[16]

In the early 1980s, concern began to be expressed by business leaders that the American economy was not keeping pace. Analysts began to refer to the "deindustrialization of America" and to observe that the United States had lost its once-competitive advantage in labor-intensive industries.[17] This suggested that America needed to develop a new industrial policy in order to "transfer labor-intensive, low-skill production to Third World developing countries, at the same time maintaining control over the entire world production process in ways that ensure the future competitive supremacy of the United States."[18] Such a need, in turn, implied that American schools should be training their students for somewhat different jobs—but what might those jobs be?

Answers to this question involved assumptions about the likely effects of automation, computers, robotics, lasers, telecommunications, and other new technologies on the labor market. Conventional wisdom had it that these technological innovations would gradually make manual labor obsolete but that America could enjoy a new burst of technological growth and development—with associated increases in productivity and standard of living—if only its labor system generated skilled workers able to plan and implement that kind of growth.[19] Thus, our educational system should stress skills appropriate to the new technologies— technological visualization; abstract reasoning; mathematical, scientific, and computer expertise; knowledge of specific technologies and production techniques; individual initiative; and so forth—because the evolving job market will need more workers with these skills.

This argument was actually an offshoot of yet another ideology that had evolved in the nineteenth century but that flowered in the late 1950s concerning "Human Capital."[20] Human Capital theorists argued that education should be thought of as "investing" in human resources and that appropriate investments in education can benefit industry and fuel the national economy. In early years this argument had been seized by canny industrialists, who realized they could reduce costs if the public schools could only be persuaded to provide the specialized training their firms would otherwise have to fund in apprenticeship programs. In addition, Human Capital arguments became a strong catalyst for the growth of educational systems in underdeveloped countries.

Although it remains popular today, Human Capital theory has never been sup-

ported by much evidence. In addition, analysts have raised questions about whether the new technologies will actually create or destroy more jobs.[21] They have pointed out that "unlike other technologies which increase the productivity of the worker, the robot actually replaces the worker. That indeed is one of the prime tasks for which robots are built"[22] and that it takes only a small number of highly trained people to design the robots, computers, and machinery that will replace large numbers of dangerous and boring jobs. Such arguments suggest that conventional industrial thinking about education was flawed, that the proposals it advocated would not have worked in any case. Indeed, recent employment statistics suggest that job growth is appearing not in "high tech" industries, but rather in *service* occupations and in the skilled crafts.

Nevertheless, conventional wisdom largely held sway. And as the business community came to think that deindustrialization was indeed a looming problem, and that this problem required changes in American schools, it began to sponsor reform reports that sought to remold education in "appropriate" ways. These reports argued that schools should:

- Revise their curricula to give more stress to information-age subjects and to science and mathematics;
- "Intensify" their programs by lengthening the school day or year, by raising academic standards, and by increasing core curricular requirements;
- Assist students with school-to-work transition problems;
- Stock classrooms with "the latest" instructional materials and computers;
- Stress achievement, individual initiative, free enterprise, and other values thought to help students become information-age leaders;

- Require upgraded levels of technical competency among teachers and provide programs to increase teachers' skills;
- Identify talented students at an early age and provide them with "enriched" educational experiences (and thus adopt or strengthen ability-grouping programs).

Some of these proposals would have generated changes that could benefit *any* student in the school. Others, however, such as the last we listed above, would have turned back the clock and recommitted America to an elitist model for education. In fairness, concern for the elitist implications of some of their recommendations often appeared in the reform reports, and most of the reports paid at least lip service to both "excellence" and "equity." Despite such protestations, however, most of the reports did not make clear how the twin goals of excellence and equity could be achieved while adjusting school programs to meet "the problem of deindustrialization." In addition, many of the recommendations made in the reports would have required additional funds for schools, and enthusiasm for providing these funds has not been great in recent years.

Although most of their recommendations were not funded, the reform reports certainly have had an effect on education. First, some of their proposals are still being debated as ways of "improving" American schools. Proposals for "intensifying" school programs, for example, by increasing hours in the school day or days in the school year, by assigning more homework, by covering more subject matter during lessons, and so forth, have proved popular among politicians—possibly because they appear to offer more bang for the same educational bucks. And some of the proposals the reports made to "strengthen" curricula in the sciences and mathematics eventually found their way into George Bush's America 2000 agenda and Bill Clinton's recent Goals 2000 legislation.

Second, the reports led to calls for greater contact between educators and industrial leaders. Such contact was needed, the argument went, to make education relevant to industrial needs, to increase the employability of graduates, and to improve productivity—thus enhancing America's ability to compete successfully in the global economy.[23] In response to these calls, many school districts set up "Adopt a School" programs or other arrangements that allowed members of the business community to exert more influence on their local schools.

Unfortunately, such programs also bring problems. For one thing, they can lead to overemphasizing the needs of business or industry when making decisions about education. They may lead, for example, to overstressing technological curricula rather than curricula concerned with moral, social, or aesthetic concerns. The latter, we would argue, are not only necessary for a well-rounded education but also may do more, finally, to preserve our democracy than a curriculum that focuses largely on business needs. In addition, when industrial leaders are given unique leadership roles in education, it is assumed, in effect, that they are peculiarly able to estimate the future educational needs of American society. This seems a dubious assumption; industrialists are often very bright people, but we know of no evidence to suggest that they are more prescient than other thoughtful leaders in the community.

Above all, the reform reports reinforced the belief, first announced in *A Nation at Risk,* that American education is in deep CRISIS. Moreover, the education crisis message has since been repeated endlessly by leaders in both government and industry and has been embraced by a host of journalists, legislators, educators, and other concerned Americans.

Thus, in a September 1991 address by President Bush: "The ringing school bell sounds an alarm, a warning to all of us who care about the state of American education. . . . Every day brings new evidence of crisis." And from a September 1991 article in *Time* magazine entitled "Can this man [Lamar Alexander, the newly appointed secretary of education] save our schools?":

> By almost every measure, the nation's schools are mired in mediocrity—and most Americans know it. Whether it is an inner-city high school with as many security checkpoints as a Third World airport, or a suburban middle school where only the "geeks" bother to do their homework, the school too often has become a place in which to serve time rather than to learn. The results are grimly apparent: clerks at fast-food restaurants who need computerized cash registers to show them how to make change; Americans who can drive but cannot read the road signs; a democracy in which an informed voter is a statistical oddity.[24]

The trouble with such messages is that they can lead to quick-fix or damaging "solutions" for minor distresses and to ignoring the truly serious problems of education and American society that need long-term effort. People can become blasé when critics cry educational "wolf" too often.

Americans need to keep two ideas about education clearly separated. The first is the notion that American schools are *generally* "mediocre." As we have shown repeatedly, the evidence simply does *not* support this claim. The second is that *some* American schools are terrible places. This is certainly true, but it is largely true because those schools lack resources and must contend with some of society's worst social problems. Thus, hysterical utterances about a broad, fictive crisis in American education are not

only lies; when they are believed, *they are likely to confuse and derail efforts that are badly needed to help our neediest schools. The Sandia Report* expressed it thus:

> Although we have shown that there are indeed some serious problems at all levels of education, we believe that much of the current rhetoric goes well beyond assisting reform, and actually hinders it. Much of the "crisis" commentary today professes total system-wide failure in education. Our research shows that this is simply not true. Many claim that the purpose of the rhetoric is to garner funding for reform; but, if these funds are used to alleviate a non-existing "crisis," education and educators will suffer in the long run.[25]

· · ·

NOTES

1. Cremin (1990, pp. 10–11).
2. Recent right-wing political activities in America are discussed, for example, in Crawford (1980); Diamond (1989); and Bellant (1991).
3. Quoted in Pincus (1984, pp. 152–53).
4. Friedman (1962, p. 89).
5. Campbell (1994).
6. See Bell (1988).
7. Diamond (1989, p. 85).
8. Thoburn (1986, pp. 152–53).
9. Thoburn (1986, p. 159).
10. Again, as quoted in Pincus (1984, p. 155).
11. Pincus (1984, p. 56).
12. National Commission on Excellence in Education (1983, p. 5).
13. See Bell (1988, Chapter 10).
14. Adler (1982); Boyer (1983); Goodlad (1983); Task Force of the Business–Higher Education Forum (1983); Task Force on Education for Economic Growth (1983); Twentieth Century Fund Task Force on Federal Elementary and Secondary Education Policy (1983); Martin (1984); Sizer (1984); Committee for Economic Development (1985).
15. We distinguish here between these early critical reports and a second group of reform proposals that appeared toward the end of the 1980s including *A Nation Prepared: Teachers for the 21st Century* (Carnegie Forum on Edu-

cation and the Economy, 1986); *Tomorrow's Teachers* (The Holmes Group, 1986); and *Time for Results* (National Governors' Association, 1986). By comparison, the latter were less critical and focused more on the teaching profession. We discuss their recommendations in Chapter 7.

16. See Spring (1985); or Martin (1984).
17. See, for example, Thurow (1982); Reich (1983); Committee for Economic Development (1983, 1984).
18. Shea (1989, p. 5).
19. See, for example, National Academy of Sciences (1983, 1984); National Science Board Commission on Precollegiate Education in Mathematics, Science, and Technology (1983); College Entrance Examination Board (1983); Lund and Hansen (1986); Servan-Schreiber and Crecine (1985).
20. See Schultz (1960); Denison (1962); Friedman (1962); Becker (1964); or Blaug (1970).
21. See Shaiken (1984); or Draper (1985).
22. Shaiken (1984, p. 157) and Draper (1985).
23. Timpane (1984).
24. Shapiro (1991).
25. Carson, Huelskamp, and Woodall (1991, p. 172).

REFERENCES

ADLER, MORTIMORE J. 1982. *The Paideia Proposal.* New York: Macmillan.

BECKER, GARY. 1964. *Human Capital: A Theoretical and Empirical Analysis with Special Reference to Education.* New York: Columbia University Press.

BELL, TERREL. 1988. *The Thirteenth Man: A Reagan Cabinet Memoir.* New York: Free Press.

BELLANT, RUSS. 1991. *The Coors Connection.* Boston, MA: South End Press.

BLAUG, MARK. 1970. *An Introduction to the Economics of Education.* London: Allen Lane.

BOYER, ERNEST. 1983. *High School: A Report on Secondary Education in America.* Princeton, NJ: Carnegie Foundation for the Advancement of Teaching.

CAMPBELL, W. GLENN. 1994. Personal communication.

CARNEGIE FORUM ON EDUCATION AND THE ECONOMY. 1986. *A Nation Prepared: Teachers for the 21st Century—The Report of the Task Force on Teaching as a Profession.* New York: Author.

CARSON, C. C., R. M. HUELSKAMP, AND T. D. WOODALL. 1991. *Perspectives on Education in America: Annotated Briefing—Third Draft.* Albuquerque, NM: Sandia National Laboratories, Systems Analysis Department.

COLLEGE ENTRANCE EXAMINATION BOARD, THE. 1983. *Academic Preparation for the World of Work.* New York: Author.

COMMITTEE FOR ECONOMIC DEVELOPMENT. 1983. *Productivity Policy: Key to the Nation's Economic Future.* New York: Author.

———. 1984. *Strategy for U.S. Industrial Competitiveness.* New York: Author.

———. 1985. *Investing in Our Children: Business and the Public Schools.* New York: Author.

CRAWFORD, ALAN. 1980. *Thunder on the Right.* New York: Pantheon.

CREMIN, LAWRENCE A. 1990. *Popular Education and Its Discontents.* New York: HarperCollins.

DENISON, EDWARD FULTON. 1962. *The Sources of Economic Growth in the United States and the Alternatives before Us.* New York: Committee for Economic Development.

DIAMOND, SARA. 1989. *Spiritual Warfare: The Politics of the Christian Right.* Boston, MA: South End Press.

DRAPER, ROGER. 1985. "The Golden Ram." *New York Review of Books* 32 (October 24), 46–49.

FRIEDMAN, MILTON. 1962. *Capitalism and Freedom.* Chicago, IL: University of Chicago Press.

GOODLAD, JOHN I. 1983. *A Place Called School: Prospects for the Future.* New York: McGraw-Hill.

HASKINS, RON, MARK W. LANIER, AND DUNCAN MACRAE, JR. 1988. "Reforming the Public Schools: The Commission Reports and Strategies of Reform. Pp. 1–22 in *Policies for America's Public Schools: Teachers, Equity, and Indicators,* edited by Don Haskins and Duncan MacRae. Norwood, NJ: Ablex.

HOLMES GROUP, THE. 1986. *Tomorrow's Teachers.* Lansing, MI: Author.

LUND, ROBERT T. AND JOHN A. HANSEN. 1986. *Keeping America at Work: Strategies for Employing the New Technologies.* New York: Wiley.

MARTIN, ROBERT L. 1984. *Business and Education: Partners for the Future.* Washington, DC: National Chamber Foundation.

NATIONAL ACADEMY OF SCIENCES. 1983. *Education for Tomorrow's Jobs.* Washington, DC: National Academy Press.

———. 1984. *High Schools and the Changing Workplace: Employers' View.* Washington, DC: National Academy Press.

NATIONAL COMMISSION ON EXCELLENCE IN EDUCATION. 1983. *A Nation at Risk: The Imperatives for Educational Reform.* Washington, DC: U.S. Department of Education.

NATIONAL GOVERNORS' ASSOCIATION. 1986. *Time for Results: The Governors' 1991 Report on Education.* Washington, DC: Author.

NATIONAL SCIENCE BOARD COMMISSION ON PRE-COLLEGIATE EDUCATION IN MATHEMATICS, SCIENCE AND TECHNOLOGY. 1983. *Educating Americans for the 21st Century.* Washington, DC: National Science Foundation.

PINCUS, FRED L. 1984. "From Equity to Excellence: The Rebirth of Educational Conservatism." *Social Policy* (Winter):50–56.

REICH, ROBERT B. 1983. *The Next American Frontier.* New York: Times Books.

SCHULTZ, THEODORE W. 1960. "Capital Formation by Education." *Journal of Political Economy* 68: 571–83.

SERVAN-SCHREIBER, J. J. AND BARBARA CRECINE. 1985. *The Knowledge Revolution.* Pittsburgh, PA: Carnegie Mellon Press.

SHAIKEN, HARLEY. 1984. *Work Transformed: Automation and Labor in the Computer Age.* New York: Holt, Rinehart, and Winston.

SHAPIRO, WALTER. 1991. "Can This Man Save Our Schools?" *Time,* September 16, pp. 54–60.

SHEA, CHRISTINE M. 1989. "Pentagon vs. Multinational Capitalism: The Political Economy of the 1980s School Reform Movement." In *The New Servants of Power: A Critique of the 1980s School Reform Movement,* edited by Christine M.

Shea, Ernest Kahane, and Peter Sola. New York: Praeger.

SIZER, THEODORE R. 1984. *Horace's Compromise: The Dilemma of the American High School.* Boston, MA: Houghton Mifflin.

SPRING, JOEL. 1985. *American Education.* New York: Longman.

TASK FORCE OF THE BUSINESS–HIGHER EDUCATION FORUM. 1983. *America's Competitive Challenge: The Need for a National Response.* Washington, DC: Business–Higher Education Forum.

TASK FORCE ON EDUCATION FOR ECONOMIC GROWTH. 1983. *Action for Excellence: A Comprehensive Plan to Improve Our Nation's Schools.* Denver, CO: Education Commission of the States.

THOBURN, ROBERT. 1986. *The Children Trap.* Fort Worth, TX: Dominion Press.

THUROW, LESTER. 1982. *The Zero Sum Society: Distribution and the Possibilities for Economic Change.* New York: Basic Books.

TIMPANE, MICHAEL. 1984. "Business Has Rediscovered the Schools." *Phi Delta Kappan,* 65: 389–92.

TWENTIETH CENTURY FUND TASK FORCE ON FEDERAL ELEMENTARY AND SECONDARY EDUCATION POLICY. 1983. *Making the Grade.* New York: Twentieth Century Fund.